One Hundred Years of Sea Power

GEORGE W. BAER

ONE HUNDRED YEARS OF SEA POWER

The U.S. Navy, 1890-1990

STANFORD UNIVERSITY PRESS
STANFORD, CALIFORNIA

Stanford University Press
Stanford, California

Printed in the United States of America

CIP data appear at the end of the book

Stanford University Press publications are
distributed exclusively by Stanford
University Press within the United States,
Canada, and Mexico; they are distributed
exclusively by Cambridge University
Press throughout the rest of the world.

Original printing 1994
Last figure below indicates year of this printing:
03 02 01 00 99 98 97 96 95 94

To E.K.B.

Acknowledgments

My thanks go to friends who helped, to Peter Kenez, Jack Talbott, Frank Uhlig, Bill Fuller, Julie Keesling, Ed Rhodes, and to all my colleagues in the Strategy and Policy Department of the U.S. Naval War College. The Naval War College Foundation provided funds for indexing. The views expressed in this book are mine, and are not to be construed as those of the U.S. Naval War College or the Department of the Navy. Solely mine too is the responsibility for any error. Map reproduced from *The Wilson Era: Years of War and After, 1917–1923*, by Josephus Daniels. Copyright © 1946 by The University of North Carolina Press. Reprinted by permission of the publisher.

G.W.B.

Contents

One Hundred Years of Sea Power

Introduction

A NAVY is a state's main instrument of maritime force. What it should do, what doctrine it holds, what ships it deploys, and how it fights are determined by practical political and military choices in relation to national needs. Choices are made according to the state's goals, perceived threat, maritime opportunity, technological capabilities, practical experience, and, not the least, the way the sea service defines itself and its way of war. This book is a history of the modern U.S. Navy. It explains how the Navy, in the century after 1890, was formed and reformed in the interaction of purpose, experience, and doctrine.

Around 1890 the U.S. Navy transformed itself according to a role and a structure expressed by the protean concept of sea power as an offensive battle fleet employed by a competitive maritime nation, elaborated that year in *The Influence of Sea Power upon History, 1660–1783* by Captain Alfred Thayer Mahan.[1] Mahan sought to change the way Americans thought about their security. He declared that Americans must see themselves as inhabitants of a maritime state in a world of strong opposing navies. He proclaimed a new strategy for the U.S. Navy—offensive sea control. He also prescribed a new force structure—the battle fleet. He said that the United States must, contrary to earlier practice, ready such a fleet in peacetime. Mahan's writings put the Navy at the center of national policy and provided rationale that would be used in the service's appeal for broad public support.

The well-being of the United States, Mahan said, and the success of its naval service, depended on understanding certain elements of sea power and following certain fundamental naval practices. Foremost among these practices was the offensive deployment of a battle fleet. That constituted a call for radical change. Before 1890 the Navy was a force of cruisers that operated in detached squadrons throughout the world and monitors that were confined to harbor defense at home. That kind of navy, said Mahan, was no longer adequate. Enemy ships approaching in fleet strength could not be stopped by commerce raiders. Enemy blockades could not be broken by harbor defenses. Americans had to understand that they faced a national security crisis that had to be met offshore. Control of the sea could be established only by a concentrated battle fleet that was ready to meet an enemy fleet in a decisive engagement. Command of the sea would prevent an assault on the United States and was the precondition of further naval missions, the establishment or destruction of blockades, and the protection or destruction of shipping.

The same year Mahan published his book, Secretary of the Navy Benjamin Tracy published an *Annual Report* calling for an offensive battle fleet, and Congress passed a Naval Act authorizing three first-line battleships of the *Indiana* class.[2] Sea-power ideas and the creation of an offensive fleet changed the way the Navy thought about itself, and the way Americans thought about their Navy. For a hundred years the broad political and social appeal of sea-power concepts gave the offensive-fleet Navy a central national standing. The doctrine of offensive sea control by battle fleets gave the service a sense of strategic initiative, operational independence, and corporate autonomy.

Navy leaders from Mahan onward knew—or should have known (many did not)—that, to secure the Navy's standing, they had to win public support. Military officers must at all times look in two directions. On the one hand, they must look toward their sources of policy guidance and backing—that is, toward the nation, the administration, and Congress, toward the definers of interests and dispensers of funds. On the other hand, they must look inward, toward the service itself, toward its particular corporate needs as a specialized combat force with its own requirements and methods of operation, needs that are expressed in service doctrine. Mahan, and the navalist writers who followed him, had found a way to merge these two perspectives through their concept of sea power, which identified the Navy with the nation and made the service integral to national policy. If the public accepted the proposition that the United States was a maritime nation under threat, one requiring a battle-fleet response, then the Navy could deduce an offensive strategy, even in time of peace, in the confidence that the required force would be provided. From the beginning, sea-power doctrine backed an acquisition program.

There were, however, many years in which there was no enemy at sea, when the country turned inward, or when the Navy's central position was challenged. Then the service's presumption of threat seemed inappropriate, and it could not count on support for a strategy of offensive sea control. In the 1920s and for several decades after World War II, it was hard for the Navy to make a case for a battle fleet. Sea-power doctrine was shown to have limits. Naval principles were seen as not a priori. The presumption that the service could declare why it would fight, how, with what, and where, no longer seemed to hold. During those years the Navy was returned to an instrumental status. After 1945 especially, the strategic environment and the position of naval force in national security were vastly different from what they had been during the previous 50 years, when the Navy was the self-confident shield of the Republic.

After 1945 the Army and the Air Force claimed they could deliver the strategic offensive. Air-power advocates co-opted the classic phrases of offensive sea control. They declared to a public fascinated by expanding technology that air and space, not the sea, were now the wide commons, the great highways of the world. Decisive victory was to be won by fleets of bombers in command of the air. Strategic readiness was vested in the Strategic Air Command and in Army divisions deployed overseas against a continental foe. The Air Force could win a general war against the Soviet Union quickly, cheaply, and at a distance. This claim perpetuated the offensive tradition of taking the war to the enemy as far from U.S. shores as possible, a tradition that formed the basis of American strategy for a century after Mahan.[3]

For an air-power enthusiast or an Army general, the United States was not an island nation but a continental state facing a continental foe. The Navy was no longer the country's first line of defense. The fleet of battleships and aircraft carriers had no strategic function. A maritime war of attrition had become irrelevant. The enemy was deep inside the world's largest landmass, beyond the reach of naval influence. The Air Force and the Army suggested that weapons could be defined by their natural element. The Air Force laid claim to the Navy's planes and missiles and the Army to the amphibious capability of the Marine Corps.

The prospect of being reduced to a transport and escort force, or becoming a support service without an independent strategic mission, haunted Navy officers. For 50 years the Navy had followed Mahan's dictum that the job of the Navy was to fight navies in fleet combat. Without a sea foe, did offensive sea control have any purpose? Was the Navy no longer central to America's destiny?

To reclaim a major combat position after World War II, the Navy argued along two lines—sea control and power projection. In the Cold War, in which the United States faced a continental power, access to the enemy's rimland was the key to containment. The Navy's job was to assure that access. But such assurance was easy because there was no threat to control of the seas. Therefore an offensive battle fleet was not required. So the Navy argued it could do something else as well. In a general war with the Soviet Union, or as part of a limited war of containment, the Navy could attack the land. That argument was supported by the tremendously successful naval campaigns in the Pacific during World War II, when aircraft carriers and the Marine Corps time after time attacked land targets and brought many other kinds of naval support to the land from the sea.

In World War II the Navy had reconciled offensive sea power with the air age. Reconstituting this experience in a postwar naval strategy was not easy. In the postwar decades, U.S. administrations favored the assumption that the Air Force could win a general war with the Soviet Union, or that the decisive battle would be between armies on the European continent. Naval utility lay elsewhere—in support and in serving the American and allied policy of peripheral containment. The Navy ably performed its role in wars of limited territorial objective (to use Julian Corbett's designation[4]), transporting, provisioning, and supporting troops in Korea and Vietnam and executing a host of other interventionist operations in which the United States wanted to press display and force along the world's coasts. These necessary and appropriate forms of sea power were fitted to practical needs, and the Navy adapted to them.

Institutionally, the Cold War Navy contended with an increasingly integrated national military establishment. Bureaucratic centralization reduced the independence that officers felt was essential to naval operations, and independence that met service needs at sea and to which classic sea-power doctrine had accustomed them. The Navy successfully resisted the unification of the armed services. But in 1958 Congress removed the operational control of the fleet from the chief of naval operations. Disposers of naval forces no longer wore "blues." Naval officers found themselves devoting more and more time to battles over budgets and disputes over roles, missions, and the ownership of weapons, without the internal confidence or external validation of a grand sea-power theory such as Mahan had bequeathed them.

Nevertheless, the Navy found a place within the national offensive strategy for a general war. It received permission to prepare to use seaborne bombers armed with nuclear weapons against land targets, thereby keeping the capital-ship carrier at the center of the battle fleet. With the development of a ballistic-missile-launching submarine force, the Navy reclaimed a central strategic mission. Later, under its "maritime strategy" of the 1980s, the Navy renewed its sea-control mission, pitting its attack submarines against the Soviet Union's strategic submarine-launched ballistic-missile reserve.

The growth of the Soviet sea force in the 1970s and 1980s revived the moribund sea-power doctrine. The U.S. Navy's maritime strategy declared, for perhaps the first time, the primacy of an offensive-fleet engagement. Even more ambitiously, the Navy sought to redefine the nature of a general war with the Soviet Union. The maritime strategy argued that a short, localized, but potentially disastrous nuclear war could—and should—be avoided by fighting instead a global, protracted, conventional conflict, a war of sea control and attrition that suited the maritime position of the United States and its allies. That approach would give the country control of the duration and shape of the war and hence the means of determining its conclusion.

Service declaration was not enough, however. The offensive maritime strategy of the 1980s was never institutionalized within the national strategy. Although the other services developed an offensive battle plan for Europe, neither the Army nor the Air Force, neither America's policy-making apparatus nor its strategic culture, saw anything to gain by associating itself with this renewed expression of offensive sea power. Opposing the development of plans for fighting a general war, the United States and its allies sought to avoid war altogether, or at least to localize any necessary conflict. Few planners were willing to move from the peculiar comfort of the bipolar stalemate to the consideration of a global war of movement with no guarantee of avoiding escalation to nuclear exchange. Deterrence doctrine, based on the huge airborne nuclear arsenal, was accepted as the way to avoid war. Mutual assured destruction, on which deterrence rested, was a theory of how war might be prevented. It was not a war plan because there could be no political purpose to a massive exchange of nuclear weapons.

With its maritime strategy, however, the Navy had reopened the possibility of using war as a political instrument. And it would be a different kind of war, one that called for fortitude and strategic sophistication, a long war demanding extensive social mobilization, sacrifice, and government interference in the economy—unpopular aspects of war that deterrence had been able to finesse.[5] For a people conditioned to the apparent stability of the mature Cold War, the Navy's way of warfare turned out to be too radical and too unreliable. Because any war with the Soviet Union risked escalation to nuclear conflict, the government concluded it was better to avoid war altogether. The Navy's maritime strategy, the product of an intensified arms race, did give the service a burst of new construction and filled many lockers, but it remained an isolated Navy vision.

At the end of the 1980s, the Soviet naval threat receded and with it the need for an opposing U.S. fleet. Events overtook the Navy's bid for strategic leadership. As the Cold War wound down, reconstitution of the American military establishment chipped away at the autonomy of all the services. The Navy, still the most versatile, responded by reaffirming its value in support missions and expeditionary warfare. A Navy White Paper in 1992 described the new turn of sea power as a "fundamental shift away from the open-ocean warfighting *on* the sea toward joint operations conducted *from* the sea. . . . Naval Forces will concentrate on littoral warfare and maneuver from the sea."[6] After one hundred years, the Navy retired Mahan's doctrine that defeat of the enemy battle fleet was the Navy's primary objective. Sea-power theory, and Navy practice, had again taken a new form.

PART ONE

ON THE SEA

1

Sea Power and the Fleet Navy 1890-1910

OFFENSIVE SEA CONTROL

Before 1890 few Americans thought that the United States was a maritime nation dependent for its security and its prosperity on control of its sea approaches or that the country needed an offensive battleship fleet. Since the Civil War, Americans had assumed that the United States was safe in its isolation, blessed by the good fortune that had placed one ocean to its east, another to its west, and weak states to the north and south. Geography was important to America's advantageous position, but equally important, if less acknowledged, was politics. A balance of power in Europe and the disinterest of its states sheltered the western hemisphere from incursions, and it was British free-trade policy, enforced by the Royal Navy, that kept the seas open to American commerce. With these benefits, which were largely beyond its control, the United States required only a modest navy to serve modest needs. In a favorable international environment the United States Navy ran on the cheap. The country enjoyed what has been called free security. In 1889 eleven nations had larger navies than that of the United States.

The paramount maritime interest of the United States was commerce, not security or prestige. Prestige rested upon prosperity. The Navy served maritime trade. In time of war, the Navy was to raid the merchant ships of the enemy, at least for the first few weeks, until the enemy reflagged them under neutral colors. Such a *guerre de course* did not require a big navy, a fleet, or even a home port. For instance, in the Civil War the Confederate sloop *Alabama* captured 69 vessels without even entering a Confederate port. In 1874 the Navy's premier officer, Admiral David D. Porter, wrote, "One vessel like the *Alabama* roaming the ocean, sinking and destroying, would do more to bring about peace than a dozen unwieldy iron-clads cruising in search of an enemy of like character."[1]

Neither the country at large nor naval officers thought these missions in support of American prosperity required command of the seas. Although U.S. cruiser squadrons were stationed around the globe, they were unconnected by strategy. In the age of sail, they needed few provisions. Wind was free and stores could be picked up almost anywhere. Ships could put into friendly ports, and thus the United States avoided the burdens and costs of colonies.[2]

Navy functions were limited. For coastal defense, a static strategy was enough. Monitors and mines, together with the Army's coastal artillery, defended home ports against invasion. Coastal warships of shallow draft were built to break close blockades of inshore traffic, for most water transport was near land. Warships were not expected to venture forth to break a distant blockade of oceanic trade. Such trade was not that essential to the country. All this defense was on a small scale. The country did not need much of a navy.

In the 1880s changes in naval engineering and international affairs forced a thorough rethinking of the Navy's purpose. The advent of the steamship meant the need for coaling stations, and the German and British navies were seeking them throughout the world. Warships were equipped with steel armor, heavier guns, and extended ranges, outclassing the American cruiser force. The balance of power among the states of Europe, on which the long peace of the nineteenth century had rested, gave way to imperial competition, much of which was played out upon the sea. For the first time in decades, U.S. naval officers faced the prospect of American territory being approached by powerful foreign ships. Lightly defended California was open to South American navies. The Caribbean was exposed to European penetration. And from Caribbean bases, a European power could dominate any trade that might pass through the prospective isthmian canal and, by sending warships through the canal, endanger the American west coast. An argument with Germany and Britain over Samoa, on which stood an American coaling station, revealed that the United States could become entangled in European policies even in the far Pacific. Every island and coastline in the world seemed up for grabs. In the fever of imperialism, isolation was no longer possible, invulnerability no longer taken for granted. The United States and its territorial interests could come under threat by sea. So the Navy rethought its strategy, its force structure and doctrine of operations, and the nature of its service to the nation.

Its purpose shifted from commerce protection to national security. Expectations after the Civil War that the United States would base an enormous trade on a great mercantile fleet—shepherded by the Navy—had proved false. America's overseas trade was small, and only around 14 percent of it was conducted on United States ships. The American merchant fleet in 1900 was no bigger than it had been in 1807.[3] A hundred years ago, as today, the government did nothing to encourage the general cargo fleet's growth. As a result, naval officers began to lose their sense of mission. The assumption that by protecting shipping the Navy served national greatness faded, or, rather, was transformed. Before the 1880s the Navy had identified its welfare with that of the country's economy.[4] From the 1880s onward, it increasingly equated its well-being with military power. On the first page of *The Influence of Sea Power*, Mahan wrote, "The history of sea power, while embracing in its broad sweep all that tends to make a people great upon the sea or by the sea, is largely a military history."[5] When Mahan wrote these words, the United States ranked twelfth among the world's naval powers. When he died in December 1914, it was third. Within two years after his death, the country was committed to a navy second to none.

The transformation of the Navy from a force of cruisers to one of battleships, from a defensive force to an offensive one, was based on arguments put forward by a group of navalists who sought no less than to change the country's strategic culture. Mahan was the group's most articulate spokesman. Mahanians included Rear Admirals Stephen B. Luce and Henry Taylor at the Naval War College, Professor James R. Soley at the Naval Academy, Secretaries of the Navy Benjamin Tracy (1889–93) and Hilary Herbert (1893–97), the administrations and congressmen who supported them, and particularly Theodore Roosevelt, first as assistant secretary of the Navy and then as president. The Mahanians wanted to turn the Navy into an offensive force, to establish a fleet of battleships at full strength *in peacetime*, to turn the United States into a world-class naval power. For this they had to build a popular and professional consensus on a new naval strategy.

First, they had to show there was a danger. The United States, Mahan wrote, was on the eve of a period of intense competition whose resolution might come only through war at sea. The benign circumstances of the past were over.

> The necessity of a navy, in the restricted sense of the word, springs . . . from the existence of a peaceful shipping, and disappears with it, except in the case of a nation which has aggressive tendencies, and keeps a navy merely as a branch of the military establishment. As the United States has at present no aggressive purposes, and its merchant shipping has disappeared, the dwindling of the armed fleet and the general lack of interest in it are strictly logical consequences. . . . In the present day friendly, though foreign, ports are to be found all over the world; and their shelter is enough while peace prevails.[6]

Now, however, it was precisely that peace that was at risk. Large nations were becoming globally competitive. Foreign navies sought world influence. This expansion would be turned against the United States. There was thus an imminent threat to the Monroe Doctrine. America's sphere of influence might become part of these countries' imperial spoil.

In 1890, the same year that he published *The Influence of Sea Power*, Mahan wrote an article entitled "The United States Looking Outward." He argued that it would not be long before a canal passed through the Central American isthmus. Once that canal opened, European attention would turn to the Caribbean, through which would lie a direct avenue to the Far East. A canal would not only bring foreign warships to the east coast of the United States and encourage them to seek bases in the American preserve of the Caribbean, but it would also expose the west coast to naval intrusion. Germany, say, or Great Britain, might establish fueling stations in the Caribbean to sustain their fleets on either side of the isthmus, and perhaps to dominate the canal. "Militarily speaking, and having reference to European complications only, the piercing of the Isthmus is nothing but a disaster to the United States, in the present state of her military and naval preparation."[7]

Central to the theory of sea power was the expectation of conflict. When a nation's prosperity depends on shipborne commerce, and the amount of trade available is limited, then competition follows, and that leads to a naval contest to protect the trade. Some state soon would challenge the United States in its own backyard. For its long-term economic and geopolitical welfare, and for its immediate hemispheric security, the United States was *and must see itself as* an insular nation. According to the new naval doctrine, it was no longer possible to rely on static shore defense or local commerce protection. The only certain way of stopping the threat of a massed enemy who was approaching by sea with intent to impose a distant blockade or insult the shore was by concentrating the Navy's firepower to meet the attacker offshore.

Mahan illustrated the doctrine of concentration in his study of the War of 1812. This war was the determining event for sea-power navalists. Neither the U.S. Army nor the U.S. Navy had then been able to protect the capital from seaborne attackers. Because the country did not want a large standing Army, it was the Navy that must be reordered for the national defense. In 1812, Mahan thought, even a weak force, as the American Navy then was, could have, if it had stayed concentrated and been willing to act offensively, compelled the British to keep their own approaching force united. That at least would have limited the range of a blockade.[8] Mahan was no proponent of the deterrent value of a fleet-in-being, but in 1812 so long as the British were unwilling to risk a costly battle at sea, an American naval threat might have also have kept them from putting troops ashore. On the other hand, a weak fleet, however concentrated, was not the answer to the question of national defense. A fleet-in-being might have to engage. Because battle was the ultimate purpose of a navy, what was required was a U.S. Navy of superior strength, concentrated for offensive operations, that would prevent an enemy from imposing any blockade or invasion threat at all. That was command of the sea. Anything less than superior fleet strength offensively employed would risk defeat in detail, permit at least a partial blockade, and expose parts of the coast and strategic strongpoints to enemy assault, as had happened in 1812.

Thanks to its isolation across an ocean over which an enemy would have to pass, the United States was in a good position for naval defense, as long as it had the proper force, bases in the Caribbean and along the east coast (from which fresh forces could be launched against an overextended foe), and an offensive sea-control strategy.

The importance of sea control, Mahan said, was as old as war at sea. Mahan had been first struck by the idea when he was serving off the west coast of South America—on a detached cruiser patrol—and read a history of the Second Punic War, which Rome won by its control of the western Mediterranean. From that point onward, Mahan combed history to illustrate his belief that the principles of sea power and naval warfare were constant. History for Mahan, as Donald Schurman noted, was "a military exercise that yielded some scholarly insights; not a scholarly search that yielded some military results."[9] History, however, was a major transmitter of ideas in the nineteenth century, and Mahan's thick historical descriptions, in which he set his vision of sea power, earned him international renown. Mahan was decorated with honorary degrees from major universities and elected president of the American Historical Association. His broad perspective and his insistence on a naval science led him to advance sweeping claims of historical relevance. Lacking evidence on the use of steamships in warfare, for instance, Mahan felt confident in deducing a doctrine of operations from the experiences of sailing ships. "I do not believe in certainties in war," he wrote, acknowledging tactical fog and operational friction. But he believed that fundamental principles of warfare were eternal, regardless of the types of ships involved, regardless of historical period, regardless even of whether battles were fought by navies at sea or by armies on land.[10]

Mahan took these principles of warfare from Swiss general A.-H. Jomini's studies of Napoleon's army campaigns. According to Jomini, all strategy is controlled by invariable scientific principles. These principles prescribe offensive action by massed forces against weaker enemy forces at some decisive point.[11]

Here was the basis of a strategy of sea control. Naval defense would take place offshore, away from the coastal guns and monitors, according to a strategy of forward deployment, concentration, and offense. Concentration, Mahan wrote, was "a word which may be said to include the whole of military art as far as a single word can."[12] For Mahan, concentration meant massed naval fire, and that meant a fleet. *Fleet concentration* was the byword; *never divide the fleet* its corollary. Of the offense, Mahan wrote: "The offensive element in warfare is the superstructure, the end and aim for which the defensive exists, and apart from which it is to all purposes of war worse than useless. When war has been accepted as necessary, success means nothing short of victory; and victory must be sought by offensive measures, and by them only can be insured."[13]

Issuing from fortified bases in key locations and dominating the strategically most important lines of sea communication, the Navy was to become a distant shield. "Every danger of a military character to which the United States is exposed can be met outside her own territory—at sea," Mahan wrote.[14] The nature of naval warfare, competition for world trade, and the threat to America's hemispheric position would, he wrote, "compel the revival of a war fleet."[15]

Ideas must be made flesh, and the navalists had the necessary supporters in the administration and in Congress. Secretary of the Navy Benjamin Tracy, in his *Annual Report* for 1889, spelled out Mahan's ideas of offensive sea control and a battle fleet:

> The defense of the United States absolutely requires the creation of a fighting force. . . . We must have a fleet of battle-ships that will beat off the enemy's fleet on its approach, for it is not to be tolerated that the United States, with its population, its revenue, and its trade, is to submit to attack upon the threshold

of its harbors. Finally, we must be able to divert an enemy's force from our coast by threatening his own, for a war, though defensive in principle, may be conducted most effectively by being offensive in its operations.[16]

Around 1890, then, the United States Navy gave itself a new mission and a way to explain it. The matter of explanation is important, for as Mahan knew, a strategy, to be sound, must command public assent.[17] That is why Mahan wrote to instruct public opinion, why he defined sea power in the broadest possible way. Mahan's list of conditions affecting sea power included human and natural geography, manpower, material resources, institutions of government, and national character. He made sea power a historical force, connected to a theory of inevitable struggle. He gave directions for the use of capital ships and the degree to which battles were planned according to eternal principles of war.

Mahan's concept of sea power, in short, joined purpose and means, as well as past and present, and explained the Navy to the public and the sailors. By its light, naval officers could deduce the Navy's function and the service's role in the national interest, and declare what kinds of ships were needed, in a popularly understood strategic context.

DOCTRINE

Mahan's was the most famous voice calling for an expanded role for the Navy in 1890, for a maritime destiny for the United States, and for a fleet configuration. But he was not alone. Within the Navy the strategic challenges posed by the times and by the operational opportunities of steamships had been widely discussed in the 1870s and 1880s. Peter Karsten described Mahan as a "quite conventional member of his generation of the naval aristocracy," whose prominence came when he was "officially selected by his seniors to perform the formal acts of synthesizing the new navalist philosophy of his colleagues and his age."[18]

That function was what Rear Admiral Stephen Luce had in mind for Mahan when, in 1886, he brought him to Newport, Rhode Island, to become the resident theorist at the recently founded Naval War College. A month before Mahan's arrival in Newport, Luce told the second Naval War College class: "Knowing ourselves to be on the road that leads to the establishment of a science of naval warfare under steam, let us confidently look for that master mind who will lay the foundations of that science, and do for it what Jomini has done for the military science."[19] That is what Mahan did, and more. He joined a doctrine of operations to a national commitment, a synthesis that was fundamental to the Navy's reconstitution and renewal.[20]

Critics said this put Mahan beyond the limits of his profession. Such a synthesis blurred a necessary distinction between policy and strategy by proposing an intrinsic connection between a certain kind of naval force and naval strategy, and national policy.[21] Today we say that the connections are arbitrary and contingent. One consequence of the blurring was that it simplified naval planning. If Navy officers could presume the national policy and the correct strategy, they could concentrate on operations. At first that appeared to be an advantage, for it permitted the Navy to focus on building a modern fleet. Later, it led to a reification of naval force, which confused those officers who, when policies shifted, had forgotten some of the requirements of the subordinate instrumentality that is fundamental to America's armed services.

Strategy is the bridge between national purpose and military operations. It is also a discrete undertaking. When the Navy thought it could simply deduce political direction, then the service, intent above all on its fighting mission, naturally put its emphasis where officers were most comfortable, on the Navy's ships and their operation, on means instead of ends. But strength is not strategy. Purpose originates with political guidance. If purpose was or could be accurately deduced from navalist doctrine, so much the better. Mahan aligned operations with culture, geography, and economics to embed the Navy in a political and social context and make strategy presumptive. Thereafter, when deduction was not possible, or when political guidance went contrary to the Navy's view of war (as, for instance, in many of the years of peace), too often the Navy simply kept its attention on its force structure, and great confusion ensued.

The tendency to focus on force and operations was made easier by Mahan's proposition of similarity, according to which the principles of naval warfare would force maritime states to think alike. An enemy's strategy, concept of operations, and force structure would be governed by the objective of fleet concentration for decisive battle and thus would be a mirror image of one's own. Success or failure of operations turned on the relative advantage of firepower and seamanship.[22]

It became easy, thus, to shift from political purpose to warfare pure and simple. Mahan's colleague Stephen Luce spotted this tendency to put the cart before the horse. In 1898 he wrote of Mahan's third book, *The Interest of America in Sea Power, Present and Future*: "Mahan has allowed the views of a naval strategist to dominate those of the political economist. . . . Sea power, in its military sense, is the offspring, not the parent of commerce."[23]

Still, the house of sea power had many rooms, and each served a different purpose. In combination they won a wide public acceptance. Mahan was forming a new strategic awareness. The United States could not ignore an era of struggle between sea powers. Essentially, sea power was an optimistic doctrine for the United States in the 1890s, however much it was expressed in terms of threat and cost. It suggested victory, prestige, safety, and prosperity. It was precisely the integrative capacity of Mahan's ideas that won them their popularity and gave the Navy its central position as a national institution.

And it brought ships to the Navy. As we saw in Secretary Tracy's report, sea-power doctrine from the beginning backed an acquisition program. Key congressmen and industrial leaders saw at once that an American construction program meant jobs and profits. Leaders of the armor, shipbuilding, and powder trusts rallied to the new navalism. The historian of this emerging military-industrial connection, Benjamin Franklin Cooling, described Tracy's battleship plan as "really a vast public works project designed to further stimulate the business community."[24]

Congress appropriates according to forecasts. It is best if a strategic consensus can be established long before forces are authorized, as well as before force is used. For this to occur, goals must be accepted as valid and realizable. With a goal, with a threat, with a doctrine, one can envision the characteristics of a war and forecast the forces needed. That is what Mahan and the navalists did through their new naval policy. They proposed a particular type of navy and a particular type of naval war. Other types of ships, war, and strategy, such as vessels less powerful than a battleship, or the *guerre de course* or static shore defense, were condemned as irrelevant or secondary. All navies would adhere to these conclusions. And like must be met by like. The job of navies was to fight navies. Sea-power doctrine explained what a fleet navy could do, how it could do it, why it should do it, and where.[25]

An experience of the remarkable Bradley Fiske illustrates that officers had much to learn. Fiske had entered the Naval Academy in 1870. In 1903, after 33 years of service, including action with Commodore George Dewey at Manila Bay, the then Commander Fiske was sent to a class at the Naval War College in Newport. Fiske recalled:

> One forenoon during the course Admiral Luce made an informal address that gave me the first clear idea I had ever had about war and the way it is carried on. Before hearing Luce that bright summer morning, I had a vague idea that a war was merely a situation in which great numbers of men or of ships fought one another. I had no clear idea connected with war except that of fighting.
>
> After the brief, but vividly illuminating, talk of Luce, I realized that a war is a

contest, and that fighting is merely a means of deciding the contest. I realized that, in every war, there is a conflict not only of purposes, but also of ideas, and that this conflict of ideas is not only in the causes of the war, but also in the way in which the contestants on each side wage the contest. I saw that in every war each side tries to effect some purpose, and that it merely uses fighting to effect the purpose. I saw that the side which understands its purpose the most clearly, which selects the best way of accomplishing its purpose, and which has the best machine ready when war breaks out, must win.[26]

The end and the means connected, for Mahanians, through sea power.

OPERATIONS

The Navy in which Fiske served in 1903 had only recently become like a machine. Officers in 1886 had argued the necessity of concentration to take advantage of the offensive opportunities of steam power, but nothing had been resolved.[27] The only modern fleet action in which a battleship was sunk was the battle of Lissa in 1866. There the *Re d'Italia* was sunk by ramming. Ramming was the preferred tactic because of the difficulty of loading, aiming, and firing the naval cannons of the time, when at least twelve minutes elapsed between shots. Until gunnery improved with the rifled breech-loading cannon, ramming and holing was the best tactic for a decisive engagement, and it put the *Re d'Italia* on the bottom.[28]

Until the introduction of the rifled breech-loading cannon, a tactical question remained. In 1890, the year Mahan published *The Influence of Sea Power*, Lieutenant Richard Wainwright was still puzzling over the question of what to do with a concentrated force. "What shall be the order of battle," Wainwright wondered, "and will the fleets stand off and use the guns, or will they close for a ramming encounter?"[29]

Ship modernization had started in the 1880s, when the cruiser force was brought up to date. Before that time, in the words of Admiral George Dewey, the American force was "the laughing stock of nations."[30] Advances in naval engineering led to a new class of larger, faster, and more heavily armed vessels—battleships. Foreign navies adopted the first ships of this type. The first two United States battleships were funded in 1886 and commissioned in 1895. They were the *Texas*, which displaced 6,315 tons, and the *Maine*, which weighed 6,650 tons. These ships were built to meet a shift in naval power in the western hemisphere as Chile, Argentina, and Brazil acquired modern warships. The battleship combined seaworthiness, range, and speed with heavy arms and armor, balancing "the greatest offensive power with an equivalent defensive power." The gun was almost at once accepted as the dominant offensive weapon, less risky than the close encounter required by the ram and more accurate than the torpedo. The battleship, more heavily armed and armored than a cruiser and, unlike a monitor, able to sail the ocean, could destroy anything else afloat except another battleship.[31]

Secretary Tracy, in his path-breaking *Annual Reports* for 1889 and 1890, declared that the United States needed twenty of these giants, swifter than any afloat, distributed in two fleets, with twelve ships in the Atlantic and Gulf of Mexico and eight in the Pacific. The battleships, Tracy said, must be ready for "concentration on any threatened point within their own field," to meet the enemy before it was upon American shores. Here was the beginning of the official doctrine of fleet force and offensive sea control, which henceforth underlay naval strategy.

Critics maintained then, and for a century thereafter, that emphasis on a capital-ship fleet made the Navy top-heavy. Secretary Tracy, and Mahan too, wanted the battle force to be balanced and interactive, Tracy calling for a cruiser-battleship ratio of 3:1, the cruisers sailing in support of the fleet and ready to control the seas—and hence commerce—once the enemy's capital-ship fleet had been sunk. Tracy also said that fleet size could not be declared a priori. Size should be determined by the threat, by the size of other navies.[32]

In 1889 the Navy's Policy Board went further in arguing for increased naval strength. It proposed a force of two fleets, one for long range and long endurance, able to threaten a potential foe in its own waters, and a second for action off the United States, able to prevent a blockade and keep an enemy from establishing a Caribbean base within striking distance of American shores.[33] Both Navy Secretary Tracy and Congress rejected this idea. Congressional isolationists feared that the acquisition of long-range ships would lead to overseas expansion. Imperialism was not the job of the United States Navy.

Yet Congress, insistent on defense, agreed to the strategy of using offensive action to deny European states bases in the western hemisphere. Even defensive results, as Mahan argued, must be sought by operations that were offensive in character. Naval strategy now began with that assumption. Passive coastal defense, main ships returned to safety in protected harbors in time of war, would not prevail against an enemy but instead give it command of the sea. Defeat came to France in the eighteenth century and to Russia in its war with Japan in 1904–5 because France and Russia tried to turn naval combat into what Mahan called a war of posts, in which offensive fleet action was subordinated to relief and protection of position. Those were insupportable uses of maritime assets. In each case, they compromised the essentially autonomous function of a major naval force. Fleets should be used for sea combat, not to protect a harbor or a fortress. The national shore should not be the main combat zone or the first line of defense. There was, however, a strategic function for shore bastions. It was to shelter the fleet until it was ready for an offensive sortie. That gave the U.S. Army a strategic mission. Passive Army ports were to support the Navy's mobile force.

In the 1890s the Army cast its ongoing harbor protection program in Mahanian terms. Lieutenant General John Schofield, former Commanding General, United States Army, wrote in 1897:

> In a country having the situation of the United States, the navy is the *aggressive* arm of the national military power. . . . For this purpose entire freedom of action is essential. . . . Hence arises one of the most important functions of land defense: to give the aggressive arm secure bases of operation at all the great seaports where navy-yards or depots are located. . . . Foreign conquest and permanent occupation are not part of the policy of this country.[34]

The popularity of offensive sea control, then, rested on its rationality. Mahan supported the position by stating that it was also based on historical fact. Past and present experience permitted reliable forecasting. The proposition of engagement with a hostile fleet of a single power, a force that was the mirror image of one's own—that was the agent of maritime goals identical, if opposed, to one's own—simplified the concept of naval warfare. The idea of an absolute command of the sea was easily grasped and was encouraged by the unquestioned but arbitrary assumption that the United States would face only one foe at a time. In a war of two battleship fleets for decisive sea control, there would be an obvious winner. Victory depended on concentrating superior force, a well-established principle of warfare. The concept of a decisive battle was attractive because such a battle was to be limited in duration, confined in scope, and cheaper in lives lost and treasure spent than any comparable engagement on land. The public appreciated the suggestion that this battle would be mercifully distant from the national threshold. Russell Weigley noted the value: the sound of gunfire and cries of pain would remain at sea. Sea-power doctrine promised a "relatively anesthetic victory in war."[35] More generally, sea power's popularity came from the fact that it answered questions of security, prosperity, patriotism, and history in terms of fundamental principles of warfare applied to naval strategy and operations.

The idea of forward deployment did not say how far out to sea the Navy was to meet the foe. It contained the notion of *over there.* But where, exactly, was the outer line of defense? "The enemy must be kept not only out of our ports, but far away from our coasts," Mahan had written.[36] But how far away? Sea-control doctrine held that battle with an approaching fleet should be joined where the American force was at the point of maximum advantage and the enemy at his point of maximum weakness. That meant where the enemy was at the limit of his extension of fuel and supply and where the Americans were still fully forced. Too far out, or in enemy waters, the United States force would be overextended, and the enemy would enjoy shorter lines of communication and nearby support. On the other hand, should the enemy get too close (as coast-defense doctrine allowed), he regained an advantage because the defending American ships (if they were not already concentrated as a battle fleet) would not have time to gather, to maneuver, or to avoid a close blockade.

It was illusory, said Mahanians, to rely on close-in offensive or defensive operations, such as blockading, blockade-running, or punching a hole through an encircling force, without first establishing command of the sea. Blockade, the final act, followed battle. And when one's own forces were facing an enemy blockade, hostile cruisers, well protected by battleships standing out to sea, could pick off one's fugitives and ignore the temporary setback of a broken ring. To avoid a blockade, Mahan wrote, a state must have "a military force afloat that will at all times so endanger a blockading fleet that it can by no means keep its place."[37] And a similar advantage was needed when one's own side was prosecuting a punitive blockade against enemy shores.

A long-range steam navy needed coaling stations. The farther from home U.S. warships were deployed, the greater the need for secure overseas bases. Thus, implicit in the need to exclude European states from the Caribbean and to protect the west coast, was the need for forward bases. Congressional isolationists were correct. Building a long-range naval force would open up the prospect of colonial expansion.

In 1890, when Congress authorized the first three first-line battleships—of the *Indiana* class (the *Indiana, Oregon,* and *Massachusetts*)—it limited the normal supply of fuel they could hold and hence their range. Congress designated them "coastline battleships" to make clear to the Navy that the vessels must never stray into competitive imperialism. The ships were meant to meet the enemy offshore. These ships each carried four 13-inch cannons and, in a heavy secondary battery, eight 8-inch guns and four 6-inch guns. Their main-battery turrets were on the centerline, distinguishing them from their two heavy-gun predecessors, the *Texas* and the *Maine*, whose gun turrets were off center and which were classified as second-class battleships. As mobile gun platforms, the battleships would be brought together for concentration. The area the Navy proposed they cover stretched from the mouth of the St. Lawrence River down to the Windward Islands and over to Panama, to prevent the establishment of any enemy coaling station in the Caribbean. Two years later Congress approved the *Iowa*, a prototype of the long-endurance first-line battleship. Congress designated the *Iowa* as a "seagoing coastline battleship" permitting it increased coal capacity, slightly faster speed, more seaworthiness, and more effective, faster-loading, easier-handling 12-inch guns. The ships of the *Indiana* class "were the first installment of a rational fleet plan."[38] The Navy had committed itself to an offensive strategy and to a peacetime fleet.

For Tracy, Luce, Mahan, and the other proponents of an expanded and reconceived Navy, the Naval Act of 1890, which authorized the *Indiana*, the *Oregon*, and the *Massachusetts*, was, as Robert Seager called it, both "a culmination and a beginning."[39] In 1892, welcoming a class of officers at the Naval War College, Mahan said: "All the world knows, gentlemen, that we are building a new navy. . . . Well, when we get our navy, what are we going to do with it?" That, as Philip Crowl commented, "was—and is—the question."[40]

The rethinking of naval operations for the battle fleet took place over the next decade when the battleships came on line.[41] As with any major new weapon system, there were important decisions to make. How big should a battleship be? To what extent should protection be sacrificed to speed and firepower to mobility? Should the ship carry guns of many different calibers, for use at many ranges against all sizes of vessels, or should it carry only big guns, exclusively for long-range use against other battleships? And early on, should the battleship sail alone or in a fleet?[42]

How ships are used is decided in part on the basis of strategic and operational factors, not just on the ships' design. Navy ships can be used either offensively or defensively, singly or together. The battleship permitted a different means of defense than that allowed by the monitor or by coast artillery. Withering gunfire from coastal fortresses guarding harbors, or from monitors within the harbors, could sink attacking or close-in blockaders. Such static force, however, could not prevent an offshore blockade. The value of a battleship, placed in fleet formation, was that it could meet a force beyond artillery range, destroy it at sea, and thereby prevent a distant blockade. It could do even more. It could remove all threat from the ocean approaches to the United States. From absolute sea denial, all else followed: safety, commercial freedom, and retaliation. An enemy rendered defenseless would find its own homeland open to blockade or assault.

From this perspective, commerce raiding was pointless as long as a superior enemy fleet remained at sea. For imposing an economic stranglehold, or preventing one, could come only after the defeat of the enemy's offshore battle fleet. Such a defeat required concentration. Those cruisers on distant stations, Mahan said scornfully, were, like policemen on single beats, unable to overcome a massed opponent.[43] Everything depended on destroying the enemy fleet. Once the opposing fleet was sunk, the wide commons would lie open, commerce could be conducted or interdicted, and the Navy could move at will.

The question was how to disable a battleship? Mahan believed in close encounters. He echoed Horatio Nelson: close fighting was good for morale. Mahan argued for ships that had guns of various calibers, ships that could push the offensive with close-in fire from their varied secondary batteries. Short-range shelling of topside control centers and of flammable wood fittings was more certain to disable the foe than a chance hit of long-range shot.[44] Recent events supported Mahan's view. In 1894 the Japanese beat the Chinese in the battle of the Yalu River using their 6- and 8-inch guns at short range to batter—not to pierce—the Chinese battleships. At the battle of Santiago de Cuba in 1898, the Spanish squadron was defeated not by the big guns of the Americans, but by their 8-inch ones (the Americans' 13-inch guns made no hits and the 8-inch ones made thirteen, out of 319 rounds fired in all).[45] There were tactical arguments for the superior effectiveness of faster-firing, smaller weapons, which could disrupt the enemy's command.

Against Mahan's position, officers H. C. Poundstone, William S. Sims, and Richard Wainwright argued that the new men-of-war could be sunk by guns of large caliber. These men insisted that big guns were accurate even at long range, and therefore could be more damaging than smaller weapons. Sims, a lieutenant commander and the Navy's inspector of target practice, took on Mahan in an article entitled "The Inherent Tactical Qualities of All-Big-Gun, One-Caliber Battleships of High Speed, Large Displacement and Gunpower." Sims's volume of weight stood against Mahan's volume of fire. Decisive action could, and should, according to Sims, take place in duels at long range. That led to the doctrine of all-big-gun ships.[46]

Opponents of Mahan used this debate to say Mahan could not extrapolate tactics for a modern battle from the age of sail, that he was a technological ostrich with his head stuck in a history book. Mahan admitted that his knowledge of what he called "the new naval monsters" slipped behind the times as the battleship evolved.[47] But Sims's use of evidence was itself shaky, and at the time, the issue remained sufficiently open that Mahan, had he cared to, could have continued the argument to his advantage.[48] But regarding the decision on what to build, Mahan was not part of the Navy's inner ring. The shots were called by the all-big-gun men in power. Admiral George Dewey, head of the Navy's General Board, was convinced of the merits of the big-gun design, its continually improving accuracy, its increasing rate of fire, better penetration of its shot, and its undoubted superior lethality. In 1906 Congress authorized a battleship to carry "as heavy armor and as powerful armament as any known vessel of its class, to have the highest practicable speed and the greatest practicable radius of action." The ship funded, the USS *Delaware*, was authorized to match the just completed British giant HMS *Dreadnought*. The *Delaware* (completed in 1910) was the first United States battleship to combine an all-big-gun battery with high-speed turbine propulsion engines.[49] "As for Captain Mahan," wrote a supporter of Sims's, "it would be an excellent thing for the service if he should confine his undoubtedly great literary ability to historical and literary questions."[50]

Yet there had really been no dispute on fundamentals. Mahan, it is true, held that history was a better guide to strategy and operations than unpredictable, always-changing technology was. History yielded principles of war. The full title of Mahan's book on naval strategy is *Naval Strategy Compared and Contrasted with the Principles and Practice of Military Operations on Land*. The premier principle, on sea as on land, was offensive concentration of firepower at the decisive point. That was all Mahan was after, and he conceded the case to the big gun when it was shown to be accurate and effective. Building the decisive weapon for the decisive battle was merely a functional matter. Destructiveness was all.

The more firepower that could be massed, the more powerful would be the destructive blows. That was the principle of concentration, of fleet organization. That was the way foreign navies were operating and the way they would have to be met. When the General Board of the Navy first convened in 1900, with Admiral Dewey presiding, it took as the basis of its strategic planning the need for the concentration of force.[51] Although a formal fleet would not be established until 1907, when President Theodore Roosevelt designated the Atlantic Fleet, there was by 1900 a widespread naval opinion, later confirmed by the Japanese victory over the Russian Baltic Fleet at Tsushima in 1905, that fleet formation was necessary. Maneuvers were conducted accordingly.

But who was the enemy? The U.S. government had declared none. The Navy could not declare one on its own, although it did the next best thing, which was to give a clear theoretical description.[52] Everything had to be inferred. Threats in the 1890s, for instance, might come from Germany, Britain, or Spain, or, after 1898 and U.S. acquisition of the Philippines, from Japan. These states were far away: the Europeans had to cross 3,000 miles of sea, the Japanese many more. Still, who knew what might happen? In the potential case of opponents' being on both oceans at the same time, two fleets would be needed. That was why Secretary Tracy had called for a two-ocean navy, one fleet for each coast.

Concentration of forces for defense of the homeland meant keeping the battleships close to home. Along the coasts were secure bases and reliable fuel supplies. The strategic advantage the United States held over Europe was the defensive space provided by the ocean. That was why the Navy had to enforce the Monroe Doctrine. Everyone thought that the construction of an isthmian canal would make the Caribbean one of the world's main commercial and strategic arteries. The worst that could happen was for a European power to establish a naval base in the Caribbean, or—an always haunting specter—for a hostile navy to receive friendly aid from Canada or a Latin American country.

The lesson Mahan drew from Russia's movement of its Baltic Fleet all the way to the Far East was that a European power, with a coaling station in the Caribbean, could attack the Pacific coast. Defense of the Caribbean was therefore all-important, as vital to the United States as the defense of the English Channel was to Britain. The Caribbean was the third seaboard of the United States. "One thing is sure," Mahan wrote, "in the Caribbean Sea is the strategic key to the two great oceans, the Atlantic and the Pacific, our own chief maritime frontiers."[53]

When, after the turn of the century, Pacific islands became part of the national interest, it was impossible to meet, from home ports, the demands of force concentration. Coal gave mobility, but it also limited movement. The replacement of the free and universal propellant of wind by steam, Mahan said, "while it has given increased certainty and quickness of movement to fleets, has also imposed upon them such fetters, by the need of renewing their fuel, that naval enterprises can no longer have the daring, far-reaching sweep that they once had, but must submit to rules and conditions that armies have long borne."[54] For the mission of overseas protection, an expanded force was called for, a force to be deployed from secure advance bases.

Expansion was therewith added to sea power. Forward-basing became part of offensive sea control. Sea control, in turn, was necessary for the protection of such a base, however heavily garrisoned it might be. As Mahan predicted, and the Pacific War of 1941–45 would prove, defense of a maritime empire was not accomplished by means of barrier outposts but by the offensive concentration of mobile naval force and by command of the sea.

From the growing body of concerned naval officers and sea-power advocates, then, the Navy around the turn of the century received a concept of operations, a definition of victory, a way to express its own political function, and a doctrine that gave order and direction to the men and ships of the service. Mahan and his colleagues assigned the Navy the dominant place in the protection of the country and in the advancement of its fortunes. They fitted new maritime means to new maritime ends. All in all, their interpretation of sea power imbued the Navy with confidence in its ability to understand and explain its purpose in a new maritime world.

2

The New Navy 1898-1913

FOOTLOOSE

The war with Spain in 1898 confirmed the new navalism. The Navy's operations in the war fulfilled the political objective, which was support of Cuban independence. But appetites grow with eating. At the end of a war of liberation in the Caribbean the United States was an imperial power in the Far East. A maritime war had transformed America's position in the world. As Mahan wrote, "What means less violent than war would in a half-year have solved the Caribbean problems, shattered national ideas deep rooted in the prepossessions of a century, and planted the United States in Asia, face to face with the great world problem of the immediate future."[1]

The Navy had followed a global strategy. It sought to control the waters of the major Spanish island colonies to wring concessions from the Spanish government. Offensively committed U.S. warships won two decisive battles on opposite sides of the globe. Four battleships of the North Atlantic Squadron beat a Spanish squadron off Santiago de Cuba. That battle gave the United States command of the sea in the main theater and decided the war. Victory in the Caribbean enabled the United States to support the Cuban revolution and opened the Atlantic so that the United States could threaten the Spanish homeland itself.

That deterred the Spanish government from reinforcing the Philippines. There, ten thousand miles away, Commodore George Dewey's victory in Manila Bay distracted the Spanish government and weakened its capacity to prosecute the war in the Caribbean.[2]

In the peace agreement, the United States took control of Cuba (which it then occupied until 1902), Puerto Rico, the Philippines, and Guam. In separate arrangements in 1899, the government annexed the Hawaiian Islands, took control of Eastern Samoa, and occupied Wake Island. These holdings became part of the U.S. claim to maritime greatness. They vastly extended the country's security perimeter. To defend them the United States relied on the Navy and the doctrine of offensive sea control. After 1898 the Navy indisputably served world power and was served accordingly.

The strategy of the campaign off Cuba was for the Navy to isolate the combat theater through local sea control. A blockade was put in place around the western part of the island and Havana Harbor to weaken the Spanish force. Perhaps then the rebellion could succeed even without American troops. If not, American soldiers could be safely transported to the island. If the Spanish tried to force the blockade with a relief expedition, its ships, wearied at the end of a 3,000-mile sail, would be engaged by the concentrated American fleet.[3]

The Spanish government did indeed send a relief squadron, headed by Admiral Pascual Cervera y Topete. Its purpose was to break the blockade, relieve Spain's beleaguered troops, and put down the rebellion. The Spanish government, however, had to protect the Philippines as well and so was forced to split its naval forces. Only part of the Spanish navy—four armored cruisers and three destroyers—went with Cervera to the Caribbean. Another squadron was readied in Spain to go out to relieve the Philippines. The remainder of the navy was held at Cádiz to defend the Spanish coast. Had Spain sent a larger force to Cuba and successfully contested control of the sea, the U.S. Navy would have had to raise its blockade and lift its cover of the U.S. Army's line of passage to Cuba.[4]

The Navy faced a decision. Should it keep its force on station so that the approaching enemy fleet would have to choose either to stay away from western Cuba or to enter into action in the area of American operations? Or should it dispatch its warships eastward in Mahanian fashion to meet the Spaniards on their approach? The American ships were in a good defensive position, concentrated, and near provisions in Key West. They would have prevailed in battle. The decision, however, was to take the offensive. The main ships of the North Atlantic Squadron, which was under Rear Admiral William T. Sampson, were sent on a search-and-destroy mission a thousand miles away in Puerto Rico to catch the approaching Spanish squadron when it replenished at San Juan. Thus the American blockade force was dispersed.

The interception failed. Cervera's squadron eluded the hunters, going south to refuel at Curaçao. Navy did not meet navy. There was no decisive engagement, no defeat of the oncoming force. Mahan's critic Julian Corbett, defining sea action in terms of a land result, wrote acidly of this failed interception and the Mahanian thinking that inspired it.

> It is a clear case of the letter killing the spirit, of an attractive maxim being permitted to shut the door upon judgment. Strategical offence in this case was not the best defence. "Seeking out the enemy's fleet" was almost bound to end in a blow in the air, which not only would fail to gain any offensive result, but would sacrifice the main defensive plank in the American war plan upon which their offensive relied for success.[5]

Cervera's squadron got through unseen and made it to Santiago de Cuba. But once in the harbor, the admiral discouraged and short of coal, the Spanish ships stayed put. Even though the North Atlantic Squadron had not prevented the Spanish force from reaching Cuba, it could seal the Spaniards in the harbor and send the Army in to root them out for battle at sea. From the beginning, the war with Spain was a joint operation, with each service supporting the other. At Cuba and the Philippines, the Navy's control of the sea isolated the enemy and enabled the Army to assault his land and dislodge his ships.

Bottled up, Cervera thought he was doomed. His only hope had been an early escape to Puerto Rico, where coal was stored, but at the risk of meeting the interception squadron. Without that coal, Cervera could never get back to Spain. Trapped by the American blockade, he did not try. The American Fifth Corps was landed to attack his ships from Cuban soil. Army victories at two controlling points—El Caney and San Juan—exposed the Spanish ships. Army artillery put them under fire. Cervera was ordered to take his chances at sea. After six weeks of virtual imprisonment, the Spanish squadron broke out of the harbor at Santiago de Cuba.[6]

From the harbor, the Spaniards sailed into the guns of Sampson's blockading fleet. A pursuit extending 75 miles along the coast near Santiago de Cuba ended in complete victory for the United States. Navy gunfire destroyed Cervera's squadron and recaptured uncontested command of the sea in the major theater of the war. The Army thereafter had unimpeded access to Cuba.

It was a victory for a maritime strategy. A European naval power had approached—indeed reached—the western hemisphere and was defeated at sea. That defeat decided the war. Furthermore, Spain's defeat was worldwide. Dewey's victory had created a power vacuum in the Philippines, Spain's main eastern colony. Imperialism abhors a vacuum, and Dewey soon shared Manila Bay with ships of five other naval powers—France, Austria-Hungary, Great Britain, Japan, and Germany—in addition to those of Spain. Fortunately for Dewey, the other ships stood aside. Upon Spain's defeat, and with the passive acceptance of the other states, the U.S. Army took over administration of the Philippines.

Sea control also permitted the Navy to threaten the Spanish coast. The Navy met a challenge to Dewey in Asia with a deterrent counterthreat in the Atlantic. To relieve the Philippines, the Spanish government had sent eastward through the Suez Canal a squadron more powerful than Dewey's, in the face of which Dewey planned to give up Manila Bay.[7] To prevent that, the Navy concentrated its fleet to threaten the ports of Spain itself. The destruction of Cervera's force had left the Atlantic open and put Spain at risk. Faced with this danger, the Spanish government recalled the reinforcement squadron, which was already outbound from Suez. The United States won the war with a global offensive strategy that was based on command of the Caribbean.

The destruction of the Spanish squadron off Santiago de Cuba validated the battleship as a gun platform. Public attention was caught by the *Oregon*, one of the *Indiana*-class coast-defense battleships authorized by the Naval Act of 1890 and the only heavy ship the Navy had in the Pacific. The *Oregon* made a dramatic run of 14,700 miles from Puget Sound through the Strait of Magellan to Key West (at a high average speed of 11.6 knots) to join first the blockade and then the battle. The *Oregon*'s voyage took 68 days, which showed the importance of building an isthmian canal to cut the time needed to move from ocean to ocean. The *Oregon*'s firepower, which consisted of the mixed batteries favored by Mahan and thus not wholly of big guns, by itself exceeded that of the entire Spanish squadron. And in the fighting, all of its guns were used. Gunfire from the major American batteries was inaccurate. Not a single shot from the 13-inch cannons hit, and only 4 percent of those from the 8-inch guns did so. Of the 9,500 rounds fired in combat, only 123 hit enemy targets. But that was enough in a one-sided contest. Relative advantage counts. The lack of heavy Spanish fire permitted Sampson to close from 6,000 to 1,000 yards and bring his lesser guns to bear en masse.[8] All in all, the naval battle of Santiago de Cuba proved the value of replacing a strategy of passive defense based on artillery, mines, and monitors with one based on offensive sea control.

Monitors had been retained for their political value as readily visible symbols of harbor protection. Their presence was comforting to citizens of coastal towns and to politicians of the eastern seaboard.[9] Monitors were part of the static-defense strategy the Mahanians were trying to change. These vessels were useful only for what Mahanians wanted to prevent—local bombardment. In addition, monitors were scattered and few. Unable to maneuver or to concentrate in heavy seas, they did not fit a strategy of defense through offensive sea control. For that, another type of gun platform was needed—the seaworthy, mobile, and heavily armed battleship.

The war with Spain, however, revived interest in harbor guards. When the Spanish squadron under Admiral Cervera left the Cape Verde Islands for the western hemisphere, citizens panicked in ports on the American east coast. The public demanded that the Navy distribute its men-of-war up and down the seaboard, a demand to which the service initially conceded by forming a flying squadron along the east coast. The squadron remained thus deployed until it was called south to reinforce Sampson. The dispersal of the men-of-war along the coast violated the principle of concentration, and shoreline protection violated the principle of forward deployment. As Mahan had written, "The enemy must be kept not only out of our ports, but far away from our coasts."[10]

Mahan recognized the popular fear even as he deplored it. The panic in 1898 showed how fragile the popular appreciation of the new naval strategy was. So he opened his *Lessons of the War with Spain* (1899) with a discussion of the problem of coastal protection. Mahan praised static defense as "the complementary factor in the scheme of national sea power." Its agent, however, should not be the monitor but the permanent, impregnable emplacements that held the Army's long-range coast artillery. Such forts and guns had long existed, and the Army was building new ones (and paying for them, which was no doubt sweet to Navy ears). Those guns should reassure the citizenry. But, Mahan said, the job of coast artillery should be redefined as well. The big guns were not just to protect harbors against raids. They were now to be part of the offense. Their job was to free the battleships for action and victory at sea. Out there, not on the coast, was where the first line of defense lay. The combination of a sheltering harbor fortress and an aggressive mobile fleet made this line possible.[11]

The Army had already accepted this proposition. In the 1890s it recast its mission of harbor protection in those terms. There was a fortuitous conjunction of the Army's fortification-renewal plan, which involved establishing a system of 500 heavy guns and 1,000 mortars in harbors and bays, with the Navy's call for the offensive use of battleships.

As President Theodore Roosevelt said in 1908 after he made the battleship fleet the Navy's central formation, the Navy must be "foot-loose":

> Let the port be protected by the [Army's] fortifications; the fleet must be foot-loose to search out and destroy the enemy's fleet; that is the function of the fleet; that is the only function that can justify the fleet's existence . . . For the protection of our coasts we need fortifications; not merely to protect the salient points of our possessions, but we need them so that the Navy can be foot-loose.[12]

In 1898, however, the Navy found itself stretched thin. It was short of the colliers, scouts, and supply vessels needed to maintain the blockade and prepare the Cuban expedition, and it had to scratch up whatever it could find.[13] The only warships the Navy Department sent to reinforce Dewey in Manila Bay were two monitors. Dewey had arrived in the Philippines in an unarmored cruiser. His magazines were only 60 percent full. European states had closed their Far Eastern ports, and Dewey was operating 7,000 miles from the nearest American navy yard. Dewey could not have sustained a prolonged engagement. He won in Manila Bay against an inept foe, but Spanish relief was expected, and within two weeks Dewey shared Manila Bay with ships of every great power except Russia. The German squadron was stronger than Dewey's and ready to fish in troubled waters. After the *Oregon* was transferred to the Caribbean, no battleship remained on the United States' west coast to assist Dewey.

With the experience of the Spanish-American War in mind, Congress in 1899 lifted its range restrictions on battleships. Defense of the nation would take place at sea. And because means ever interact with ends, naval engineers built more powerful, better-armored ships and equipped them with more effective long-range cannons. The secretary of the Navy, Charles J. Bonaparte, nailed the lid on the monitors' coffin in his *Annual Report* for 1905, saying that they represented an "outgrown" idea of defense, an "old heresy" exposed as useless as far back as the war of 1812 and now conclusively outmoded by "the lessons of recent warfare."[14] A year later, in 1906, Congress lifted tonnage limitations and passed a dreadnought bill, calling for construction of the most heavily armored, most powerfully armed, and longest-range battleship afloat.

The love affair with the battleship was in full flower. The *Oregon,* which had been authorized in 1890 as a coastline vessel, displaced 10,288 tons and had mixed batteries, the largest of which consisted of four 13-inch guns. By 1913 the country had 39 battleships that were either commissioned or authorized, including, since 1906, ships of the all-big-gun type. The *Pennsylvania,* authorized in 1913, weighed about three times as much as the *Oregon,* displacing 31,400 tons and carrying twelve 14-inch guns.

After 1900 the United States had an empire to maintain and a growing international naval competition to contend with. For a country in such circumstances, what better symbol of national pride and naval strength could there be than that sea-power marvel, the puissant battleship?

THE ATLANTIC

Mahan, at the conclusion of his book *Naval Strategy* (1911), had moved the notion of sea power further in the direction of naval strength. He wrote:

> It seems reasonable to say that, where merchant shipping exists, it tends logically to develop the form of protection which is called naval; but it has become perfectly evident, by concrete example, that a navy may be necessary where there is no shipping. Russia and the United States to-day are such instances in point. More and more it becomes clear, that the functions of navies is distinctly military and international, whatever their historical origin in particular cases. The navy of the United States, for example, took its rise from purely commercial considerations. External interests cannot be confined to those of commerce. They may be political as well as commercial; may be political because commercial, like the claim to the "open door" in China; may be political because military, essential to the national defense, like the Panama Canal and Hawaii; may be political because of national prepossession and sympathies, race sympathies, such as exist in Europe, or traditions like the Monroe Doctrine. . . . The United States, with no aggressive purposes, but merely to sustain avowed policies, for which her people are ready to fight, needs a navy both numerous and efficient, even if no merchant vessel ever again flies the United States flag.[15]

This view was contested by noninterventionists and small-Navy advocates who wanted to return to coast defense. They argued in Congress that a small fleet of limited-sized vessels could protect the United States. A large Navy meant large expense and imperialism. But they found it difficult to hold their position in the face of the changes going on around them.

The Navy's triumph and the island spoils transformed the world position of the United States. The country became a nation of two-ocean responsibilities, though it still had only a one-ocean battle fleet. Because the Navy measured threat by capability, it felt that the flag bearers of the world's other great navies, the big ships being built by the British, the Germans, and the Japanese, demanded counterweights. To do its job, the Navy would have to expand to a two-ocean fleet, or the government would have to reduce its commitments.

It was hard to balance responsibilities and capacities. U.S. rule of the Philippines was now a moral obligation and could not be lightly dropped. But the Philippines were not easily defended. At the end of the war with Spain, the U.S. government had not taken other Spanish islands in the Pacific, such as the Marianas or the Carolines, the kind of advance bases that were necessary for western Pacific action. Instead, these islands were snapped up by the German government.[16] It was not pleasant to contemplate what power might step into a political vacuum in the Philippines if the United States left. In any case, they were a hostage to fortune, which was all the more a problem because security in the Atlantic, not in the Pacific, was America's primary concern.

So where should the Navy base its battleship fleet? Until a canal was built, it could not swing the fleet between oceans—a bad idea, in any case, if the country had two-ocean responsibilities. Concentrating the fleet in the Atlantic made the most sense, to counter its great European counterparts. On the other hand, unsettled conditions in the Far East, the need to protect the Philippines, a desire to maintain the Open Door in China, and concern about the conflict brewing between Japan and Russia all argued for a forceful presence in the Pacific. As Ronald Spector wrote, "In truth, the navy was caught between two of its own dogmas: its commitment to the strategic 'truths' of Mahan, which demanded concentration at the point of greatest danger [the Atlantic], and its belief that economic rivalry was the all-important issue in international relations [the basis of its concern about the Pacific]."[17]

The Navy equivocated. Part of the battleship force was assigned to the Pacific and the rest to the Atlantic. Proponents of concentration deplored the division of the fleet. In 1903 the Navy's General Board recommended a force of 48 battleships, enough for a concentration of force in both oceans. But numbers alone were not enough for the Pacific, unless the American force was only expected to meet the Japanese fleet as the latter descended upon the western hemisphere. To be effective the American fleet needed an advance base west of Hawaii.[18]

The administration decided to give priority to the defense of the West Indies, choosing to meet the naval threat in the Atlantic and not to support commerce in the Pacific. Accordingly, in 1906 the Navy Department ordered all battleships to the Atlantic. Pacific interests would lie at risk, relying for their safety on diplomacy and Japan's inattention.

The Atlantic washed the country's most important shore, where population was the most dense and commerce the most active. Convenient coal fueled the fleet at its Virginia base. From the Atlantic the Navy could sail into the Caribbean, America's Mediterranean. It was the Caribbean and the eastern entrance to the planned canal that the United States needed to control.

After 1900 the prospective enemy was Germany, the United States' competitor for second place among the world's navies. Britain, of course, held first place. Anti-British sentiment remained vigorous in the Department of the Navy until the 1930s, but U.S.-British relations had been improving since the settlement in the 1870s of Civil War claims. It was widely thought that a British man-of-war had given Dewey support in Manila Bay, and this added to the warming trend. Halford Mackinder, the British land-power geographer, had extolled this supposed show of goodwill as "a first step towards the reconciliation of British and American hearts."[19]

In London, realism supported sentiment. A few years before, in 1895, President Grover Cleveland had concluded that the British were using a Venezuelan boundary dispute as a pretext for expansion, and he declared the United States would meet territorial aggression with "any means in its power." The Royal Navy had no reinforcements to send to the western hemisphere to counter this hectoring. It became clear to most British statesmen and to British public opinion that, with the rise of a truculent Germany close to home and with the Boer War going on, there was no point in provoking the United States. The British agreed to arbitration, and the increasingly assertive Americans seemed rewarded for their declaration of hemispheric supremacy. "In a very real sense," David Healy wrote, "the incident seemed to validate United States intervention in Caribbean affairs."[20]

For naval supremacy, the United States needed a regional coaling station and the capacity to deny a similar station to any European power. These two requirements were met with the victory over Spain, and they were confirmed when Cuba in 1903 ceded to the Navy the right to maintain a base at Guantánamo. With a local fuel supply, offensive sea control was possible. The British, the State Department, and many in the Navy thought that the coaling stations in Cuba and Puerto Rico would enable the Navy to secure American interests without putting fortifications as well at the prospective isthmian canal. Politicians wanted to be able to use more than just the fleet to defend the canal. They insisted that the United States reverse a long-standing British-American agreement that the canal's neutrality be maintained. Navalists supported this idea. Theodore Roosevelt, then governor of New York, wrote:

> If the proposed canal had been in existence in '98, the Oregon could have come more quickly through to the Atlantic, but this fact would have been far outweighed by the fact that Cervera's fleet would have had open to it the chance of itself going through the canal, and thence sailing to attack Dewey [*sic*] or to menace our stripped Pacific coast. If that canal is open to the war ships of an enemy it is a menace to us in time of war; it is an added burden, an additional strategic point to be guarded by our fleet. If fortified by us, it becomes one of the most potent sources of our possible sea strength. Unless so fortified it strengthens against us every nation whose fleet is larger than ours. One prime reason for fortifying our great seaports is to unfetter our fleet, to release it for offensive purposes; and the proposed canal would fetter it again, for our fleet would have to watch it, and therefore do the work which a fort should do; and which it could do much better.[21]

Congress agreed: sea control must be combined with direct canal defense. In 1901 the second Hay-Pauncefote Treaty conceded fortification rights to the United States, abrogating the earlier agreement on neutrality. With that, Britain gave the United States a free hand on the isthmus.[22]

A year later the Navy conducted an ostentatious winter maneuver during a joint British-German-Italian blockade of Venezuela. That was enough for the British. They began a strategic withdrawal from the western hemisphere.[23] The United States could have the canal and supremacy in the Caribbean. When the European states lifted their blockade of Venezuela in February 1903, British prime minister Arthur J. Balfour declared: "The Monroe doctrine has no enemies in this country that I know of. We welcome any increase of the influence of the United States of America upon the great Western Hemisphere."[24] The Royal Navy called back its West Indies Squadron.

It was to meet Germany's world policy that the U.S. Navy divided its fleet between the Atlantic and the Pacific. We can believe that the German government did not seek a conflict with the United States at Manila Bay and still recognize that the Germans intended to take whatever territory they could in the Pacific. Who knew whether the German government might not have taken control of the Philippines if Dewey's squadron had been beaten or had withdrawn?

Germany, after all, held the Marshall Islands and, by agreement with Spain at the end of the war, took the Carolines and the Marianas in the western Pacific. This had created a serious strategic problem for the United States because those islands were the stepping-stones of the Royal Road to Manila. German control denied them to the Navy. In 1899 an amicable partition of the Samoan islands did not dispel the suspicion in Washington that "at every disputed strategic point in the Pacific, Germany contested the American wishes during 1898 and 1899 while England seemed invariably to favor the United States."[25]

The unsettled condition in the Caribbean aggravated the sense of Germany's hostility. In 1902 the United States declared that the British-German-Italian blockade of Venezuela violated the Monroe Doctrine, restrained free transit by U.S. ships, and, so it was construed, constituted a possible threat to U.S. territory as well. To some extent the flurries of anti-German opinion this incident provoked in the United States simply expressed Dewey's and Roosevelt's sentiments. Could the Germans really threaten the United States? There were all but insuperable obstacles to European military action in the western hemisphere. Any land-based operations against the United States, by any state except Britain (which could march from Canada), would be overseas expeditions. The enormity of undertaking troop transport and maintaining logistical lines of supply and communication made that almost unthinkable.[26] Still, it was clear that with a coaling station in the West Indies, a German fleet could engage the U.S. Navy on favorable terms. Without that, the German ships would have to bring their coal from Europe. The Navy estimated that 97 colliers would be required to serve the German battle fleet and that Germany would still need an advance base because refueling could not be done at sea.[27]

We may note the vulnerability of a German overseas expedition and the political extravagance of provoking the United States. Yet in Berlin there were such plans. The German emperor William II refused to recognize the Monroe Doctrine. Germany viewed the United States as a major obstacle to overseas expansion, an unfriendly competitor, and in 1903 Germany's most probable future opponent. Germans wanted to colonize in South America. An island or two in the West Indies would support a regional force and put Germany in a position to control the prospective canal. There was even a plan for attack on the United States. When the imperial fleet was up to 38 first-class battleships, said the head of the German navy, then a decision could be made about whether to confront the United States.[28]

The result was a naval arms race. The U.S. secretary of the Navy, William H. Moody, said that Germany, as the United States's competitor for the world's second naval position, had replaced Britain as the measure of naval expenditures.[29] President Theodore Roosevelt thought that only a very powerful force could hold the Germans at bay. That was what he intended to display through the assemblage of the Navy's battleships in Caribbean maneuvers at the time of the blockade of Venezuela. Dewey himself, Admiral of the Navy, the highest-ranking officer in the service, on lifetime active duty, was in charge of the Caribbean maneuvers. Dewey's wife recorded that Roosevelt told her husband that his command would "put pride in the people and arrest the attention of the Kaiser."[30] Fifty-four ships made up the armada. "Never before had a full American admiral commanded a fleet at sea; never before had such a powerful concentration of American naval force been assembled."[31] That force could have overwhelmed the fourteen blockading ships from Britain, Germany, and Italy had Roosevelt asserted the principle of hemispheric exclusion.[32]

Still, the Navy did not want war with Germany. Some naval officers feared that in a war the Germans might seize a base in Venezuela, take the Philippines, and perhaps use their Atlantic force to advance against the United States. The officers were also concerned that the Navy might not be able to stop a sustained attack.[33] Nonetheless, the display of ships from all the U.S. Atlantic stations operating as a fleet made the point that the United States had a deterrent force.

Once the fleet was underway, Roosevelt claimed later, he sent the German emperor an ultimatum: submit to arbitration of the Venezuelan dispute or face a naval war. This claim that the Navy frightened the Germans away, of which there is no archival evidence, did much to enhance the service's reputation.[34] There were, however, European and local reasons for the German draw-back, reasons ignored or unknown in Washington. The blockade ended after a concession from Venezuela gave the British an excuse to withdraw. The British already had decided not to contest U.S. control of the canal. Now Britain's prime minister, Balfour, took the occasion to applaud the Monroe Doctrine. As a result, Germany was isolated. The bitter lesson for Berlin was that its navy could not act alone. The Germans took no base, won no island, and withdrew their ships. Their government was forced to reconsider its new course of aspiring to world influence.

The end of the Venezuelan blockade marked the retreat of German ambitions in Latin America. The German government realized that the urgent dangers it faced in Europe were far more important than its generalized dream of world influence. After 1904 its navy faced a greatly reinforced British fleet and a gathering of continental opponents. German naval attention had to turn to the North Sea. But to

Americans the events in the Caribbean had suggested the prospect of war, and not even Germany's preoccupation with Europe allayed Roosevelt's anxiety or that of his successor, William Howard Taft. What if Germany defeated Britain? It would then be in a much stronger position to expand into the western hemisphere or to move in the Pacific.

This frame of mind fueled a race in capital ships. America's declared goal was to hold the rank of second-greatest naval power, after Great Britain. In 1903, in reaction to the German Fleet Law of 1900, which called for a seventeen-year building program of a high-seas fleet second only to that of Great Britain, and in the aftermath of the Venezuelan blockade, the General Board proposed a "General Naval Scheme," a long-term building program for a balanced, comprehensive force of 48 battleships supported by auxiliaries. For every two battleships there would be one armored cruiser, three lighter and faster deck-protected cruisers, four scout cruisers, three destroyers, and two colliers, along with various support and supply ships for each squadron. A force of some 370 ships and their support vessels was to be ready by 1920, when Germany was scheduled to have 41 battleships and 20 large cruisers. This program served as the basis of the General Board's advice on construction for the next ten years.

The board was responding to a request from Secretary of the Navy Moody that it recommend a building program to provide "such strength for the navy as seems to the Board essential to the interests of the country."[35] The secretary did not state what these interests were. It was up to the board to deduce them and then to declare the threat and the Navy's mission.

In 1904 Admiral Dewey wrote to Secretary Moody:

> There is one nation in particular [Germany] with whom we must be prepared to show that we have the ability to pursue this policy [defense of the Monroe Doctrine]. In laying down and pursuing a building program, the question will always be greatly simplified if we bear in mind the clear proposition to prepare for a struggle with this power. Such a struggle is inevitable unless we studiously direct our efforts to prepare for it.[36]

Here was the sea-power prescription. It was clear to Dewey and the General Board that, if not the German navy, then some other navy sooner or later would have to be met on the high seas.

The Navy knew where its professional duty lay. Its problem was in securing public support. "The fleet," said the General Board, "is the growth of an inadequately expressed public opinion; and that growth has been spasmodic and sporadic, and has followed the law of expediency and of the temporary passing passions of non-understanding political parties, with little or no relation to the true meaning of naval power, or to the nation's need therefore for the preservation of peace, and for the support and advancement of our policies." The Navy, it said, must not be swayed by transient influences but must base its development on fixed priorities.[37] These priorities were protection of the shores, maintenance of the Open Door in the Far East, exclusion of Asian immigrants as several west coast states had requested, and exclusive control of the Panama Canal and contiguous waters.

Those goals required a sea-power position that went far beyond making a stand against Germany. They implied a navy operating in two oceans. But there was no word as to the administration's policies toward Germany and Japan or even toward Britain. Nor was there any indication of its policies regarding the national priorities listed above, or of how well those priorities fit with the Navy's operational doctrine of concentration and position. The Navy did not know if the administration would approve its deduction of the national interests or if Congress would approve its proposals for naval construction. The General Board made its recommendation from the naval point of view alone, basing it on the capabilities of other naval powers. How its recommendation might fit with foreign policy, what program Congress might accept, and how an administration might put the force to use, the Navy could only guess.

The General Board's General Naval Scheme of 1903, which called for a battleship force of 48 ships, was rejected by both the president and Congress. While all parties shared the goal of making the U.S. Navy the second strongest in the world, Congress and the president were content to move at a slower pace. They estimated a need for fewer battleships by defining existing armored cruisers as capital ships. Although Congress withheld approval of the construction program and the balanced force recommended by the General Board, it did agree to the idea of a big-ship navy, and by 1906 (by a British reckoning) or by 1908 (by Congress's count) the United States stood second among naval powers in the index of capital ships.[38]

The doctrine of concentration required that those ships fight in coordination and under a single command. That meant the establishment of a permanent battle fleet. Such a reorganization was undertaken by President Roosevelt and his naval advisers. In 1906 the Navy called home its battleships from the European and South Atlantic stations, abolished those stations, and combined the ships with the North Atlantic Squadron. In 1907 the great assemblage, which included all sixteen of the country's battleships, was designated the Atlantic Fleet. In his *Annual Report* for 1907, Secretary of the Navy Victor H. Metcalf wrote, "These sixteen ships formed, in weight and numbers combined, the most powerful fleet of battle ships under one command in any navy." The fact that they were to act together in fleet organization was what gave them strategic force as well as operational unity. The secretary continued: "Further, in the composition of its divisions, the fleet is homogeneous. . . . We may say, therefore, that the long-desired homogeneity is at last secured and that for the acquirement of tactical experiences and development of a powerful mobile force the Atlantic Fleet is in a most favorable condition."[39]

The Pacific had to do without battleships until 1919, when the German menace in the Atlantic disappeared. But in the reorganization of 1907, the Asiatic Squadron was strengthened and given the name Asiatic Fleet. In addition, all American forces in the Pacific were brought under a single command and designated the Pacific Fleet, with a central battle force of eight armored cruisers and eight light cruisers.[40]

Critics contended that the Navy was top-heavy, that sea-control doctrine, with its emphasis on fleet engagement, paid excessive attention to battleships and downplayed the tactical potential of cruisers, destroyers, and gunboats. Critics said those lesser craft would better serve the kind of action the Navy was most likely to face. For instance, the type of ship needed in Central America was the gunboat, of which the American supply was antiquated and sparse. Between 1890 and 1917, U.S. forces, almost all arriving by sea, intervened 33 times in Latin-American countries. Most of these interventions were landings of small detachments sent for only a few days to protect lives and property in places of temporary turmoil. In other cases the forces stayed for more than a decade, establishing semiprotectorates. In many of these actions—the landing at Veracruz, Mexico, is a notable example—gunboat operations had to be carried out by battleships and cruisers in the absence of lighter craft.

This criticism that the fleet was imbalanced was valid, as far as it went. It is true that the General Naval Scheme of 1903 had envisioned a more complex force structure than Congress provided, one that would have been configured for a variety of uses. But given the expectation of a major battle as part of an offensive forward strategy, the emphasis on capital ships followed naturally. The Navy faced states whose naval strategy and concept of operations were virtually identical to its own—states that subscribed to offensive sea control and whose force centered on the battleship fleet. Like must be met with like.

President Roosevelt left office with pressure still strong from Congress to disperse the battleship force among various ports on the east and west coasts. On March 3, 1909, he gave his successor, William Howard Taft, a word of advice.

Dear Will:
One closing legacy. Under no circumstances divide the battleship fleet between the Atlantic and Pacific Oceans prior to the finishing of the Panama Canal. . . . I should obey no direction of Congress and pay heed to no popular sentiment, no matter how strong, if it went wrong in such a vital matter as this. . . . It is now nearly four years since the close of the Russian-Japanese war. There were various factors that brought about Russia's defeat; but most important by all odds was her having divided her fleet between the Baltic and the Pacific, and, furthermore, splitting up her Pacific fleet into three utterly unequal divisions. The entire Japanese force was always used to smash some fraction of the Russian force. The knaves and fools who advise the separation of our fleet nowadays and the honest, misguided creatures who think so little that they are misled by such advice, ought to take into account this striking lesson furnished by actual experience in a great war but four years ago. Keep the battle fleet either in one ocean or the other and have the armed cruisers always in trim, as they are now, so that they can be at once sent to join the battle fleet if the need should arise.

Roosevelt sent a copy of this letter to Mahan with the comment, "I am sure that the fleet will never be divided."[41]

THE PACIFIC

In the years after Venezuela, the Navy's ships helped define America's world position. Roosevelt and Taft frequently sent squadrons on display visits to ports of friendly European countries. Showing the flag became, as Seward Livermore has shown, almost a national habit. Suggestive naval movements substituted for deeper diplomatic engagements. They also played a role in moving the country, in Livermore's words, "further out of its isolation and into the arena of world power politics," though with what long-term diplomatic effect it is hard to say.[42]

The display function was most obvious in the Pacific, above all in the 1907–9 voyage of the Atlantic Fleet, when it sailed around South America, up the west coast, on to Japan, and thence around the world.

When Japan destroyed the Russian fleet at Tsushima in 1905, Japan became overnight a potential adversary of the United States, in much the same way that a few years previous the victory over Spain had introduced America to Japan as a rival for influence in the western

Pacific (although not until 1912 would Japan declare the United States its primary threat). For Americans, the stakes were the security of the new island possessions, the Open Door in China, and, always in the background, concern about the defense of the western shore of the nation itself.

The problem for the Navy was how to offset Japan's geographic advantage. Japan had a battle fleet in the western Pacific. The United States did not. For more than 40 years, this was the main concern of Navy strategists. How could the Navy achieve decisive power when all its battleships were permanently based in the Atlantic? Also, with no secure bases in the western Pacific, how could it fuel its ships if they were sent to the Far East, without depending on foreign colliers?

As part of its search for bases, the Navy sought a port on the Chinese mainland. Here it ran into political opposition from China and Japan, the reluctance of the State Department to compromise the Open Door, and the expense of outfitting such a site. The Navy gave up its hope of a China port in 1906. It then turned to Subic Bay in the Philippines.

Subic, with its port of Olongapo, lay north of Manila Bay, above the Bataan Peninsula. If it could be made impregnable, Subic would give the fleet a secure base from which to sortie in defense of Manila. Manila was the political and strategic key to the Philippines. "Had the Spanish been in Subig Bay," Dewey wrote in 1903, "and that bay been properly defended, my victory at Manila would have been much more difficult."[43]

The initial problem was that the U.S. army controlling Manila and the main islands did not share the doctrine that related fortifications to offensive sea control. The Army position, argued vehemently by General Leonard Wood, who commanded the Philippines Division, was that the Navy, based at Cavite, should stay inside Manila Bay and act as a strictly local defense force. In 1904 a confidant of Wood's reported: "The Gen. thinks the Subig Bay scheme of the Navy absurd. Used simile of a man whose house was being robbed running down the street and climbing into a tree saying 'I'm here.' The robbers would say, 'All right. Stay there. We will despoil the house.' Manila is the strategic point and everything should be centralized there."[44]

Dewey condemned this opinion, on Mahanian grounds. A static defense led to the possibility of entrapment. The fleet might be bottled up in Manila Bay, unable to move to the offense. Dewey wrote to President Roosevelt in 1904 that to put the Navy in that position was like "a boxer trying to defend himself by holding his fist against his breast."[45]

Then the Army announced that it could not guarantee Olongapo's safety, that it could not protect Subic Bay against a Japanese attack from the land. By 1905 it was obvious that the threat to the Philippines was no longer from a European power that could attack Manila only by sea. That fact undercut the Navy's claim to the importance of Subic Bay. Japan could establish a military force on the islands, move overland, and render Olongapo useless. Olongapo was surrounded by hills, from which guns could rain devastating artillery fire on the ships at anchor, just as the Americans had threatened to do to Spanish ships at Santiago de Cuba and as the Japanese had done to Russian ships at Port Arthur. General Wood estimated it would take more than 80,000 men to hold the hills around Subic Bay. "The whole project is a foolish one," he wrote.[46]

Army opposition ended the Navy's hope of developing Olongapo. The services carried on a heated debate over the question of Subic Bay for several years but came to no resolution. Richard Challener wrote of the dispute: "The gravest threat to the Navy's strategy was not the navy of Imperial Japan but the Army of the United States."[47] The inability to make what appeared to be a strictly military decision on where and how to site and protect a base discredited the Joint Army-Navy Board. That board had been set up in 1903 to advise the military secretaries on interservice cooperation. Now its influence disappeared within the administration. Roosevelt became fed up with the interservice dispute over whether to establish the Subic base. It was in this mood that he wrote to the then secretary of war, William Howard Taft, on August 21, 1907: "The Philippine Islands form our heel of Achilles. They are all that makes the present situation with Japan dangerous."[48] Roosevelt resolved the interservice impasse by an executive decision in 1908. He gave up the idea of making Subic America's primary base in Asia and established the main base for repair and replenishment at Pearl Harbor in the Hawaiian Islands, a pullback of 4,767 nautical miles.

That decision, which abdicated naval defense of the Philippines, was taken in line with War Plan Orange, an emerging strategy for a Pacific war against Japan. War Plan Orange called for leaving the battle fleet concentrated in the Atlantic. Until the naval threat from Germany disappeared, or until the Navy had enough ships for a two-ocean battle force (as the General Naval Scheme had proposed in 1903), the Navy could stand on the defensive in the Pacific. The Army would hold Corregidor Island, at the entrance to Manila Bay, for at least 90 days while the Atlantic Fleet reassembled at the new anchorage in Hawaii (which itself was 2,091 nautical miles from San Francisco). The fleet would then launch an offensive across the ocean to relieve the garrison and open Manila Bay, from which it could then sail to subdue Japan.

For the moment, a squadron of eight armored cruisers was to stay in the Pacific. At the start of a war, these were to withdraw eastward out of harm's way. The American commitments west of Hawaii would be left at risk for the three months or so it was expected to take to swing the battle fleet around South America. During this interval, Japan would be free to sail as it pleased in the western Pacific.

Concentration in the Atlantic followed the injunction *never divide the fleet*. Mahan had called concentration "the A, B, C, of strategy," and of course it was.[49] Naval victory had always been based on having dominant power at the point of engagement. To separate battleships was to run the risk of their being defeated one by one. The Navy's General Board was emphatic on this point. It held firm to a single-fleet, Atlantic-first policy even when in 1907 there was a popular panic that war with Japan was on its way. The General Board declared in April 1907, "We have not nor shall we have in the near future, a sufficient number of battleships to hold both places [the western hemisphere and the Philippines] at the same time against the attacks of a European and a Japanese force, or either of them."[50]

Yet from these discussions arose in 1907 the proposal that if war with Japan were truly imminent, "not less than sixteen" battleships from the Atlantic Fleet (that is, all U.S. battleships then existing) should be sent to the Pacific as a precaution. Such a shift would not be a permanent repositioning. It would last only as long as war was at hand. This recommendation accorded with the general strategy of the emerging War Plan Orange and was based on the assumption that the United States would meet but a single fleet at a time.

To President Roosevelt the proposal was full of political potential. He had wanted something that would overcome congressional opposition to naval expansion. It was he who called, in addition to the repositioning plan, for a onetime global cruise of the Atlantic Fleet. The naval concentration during the British-German-Italian blockade of Venezuela had bolstered Roosevelt's opinion that no diplomatic act gained greater respect than a show of force.[51] The armada was to be Roosevelt's big stick in the Pacific. As he told Secretary of State Elihu Root on July 13, 1907:

> I am more concerned over this Japanese situation than almost any other. Thank Heaven we have the navy in good shape. It is high time, however, that it should go on a cruise around the world. In the first place I think it will have a pacific effect to show that it can be done; and in the next place, after talking thoroly over the situation which the navy board I became convinced that it was absolutely

necessary for us to try in time of peace to see just what we could do in the way of putting a big battle fleet in the Pacific, and not make the experiment in time of war.[52]

The Navy would test and display the strategic mobility of its battleships, its capacity to move a great fleet readily from one ocean to the other. The Russian Baltic Fleet only recently had sailed halfway around the world into Japanese waters. The Japanese met this fleet and beat it in a decisive battle. The American cruise would show a reach similar to that of the Russian fleet, but with a clearly superior force.

The great white ships of the Atlantic Fleet sailed from Hampton Roads, Virginia, in December 1907. Some observers feared that the fleet's move would provoke a conflict with Japan or tempt the Germans into action in the deserted Atlantic. Naval intelligence assured Roosevelt that there was no likelihood of a Japanese attack. Tokyo had no war plan. Its naval attaché in Washington, D.C., reported the obvious, that the cruise was designed to impress the Japanese. Statesmen in Tokyo resisted drawing a connection between this display of naval power and a dispute over the rights of Japanese immigrants to the United States that was arousing much bitterness on both sides of the ocean. The Japanese treated the cruise as a routine maneuver, and Japanese leaders took the occasion to show their desire for peace. As Roosevelt said, "Every particle of trouble with the Japanese government and the Japanese press stopped like magic." That, for Roosevelt, was the value of American sea power.[53]

Toward the Germans, Roosevelt held out a peculiar blandishment by appearing receptive to their overtures about a possible entente in the Far East. The Germans, eager to score against the British, wildly imagined that the cruise might expose a weakness in Britain's imperial position and that Australia might even fall away from the British Empire.[54] To show off their own fleet, the Germans sailed sixteen battleships to the Azores, displaying a newly extended range of maneuver. But in spite of the concern in Washington, the Germans did not try to make a gain in the western hemisphere.

The U.S. cruise went well. The administration was happy with its political effect. The Navy declared it an operational success, and there were agreeable surprises. Strategists found they had overestimated by more than a month the time it took to swing the fleet from one ocean to the other, and of course that time would be reduced further when the Panama Canal was completed. The cruise, and a subsequent voyage from Hawaii to Auckland, New Zealand, without refueling (a run of

3,850 miles), showed that the great ships had longer ranges than expected. The impressive radii did not solve the supply and refueling problems that would occur if the fleet operated on a war footing in Far Eastern waters, but they seemed to make less urgent an immediate need for a forward base such as the one the Navy had proposed for Olongapo. If governments were unreceptive (as in the case of the China base), if Congress was parsimonious (as in the case of its refusal to fund a two-ocean navy), and if the Army was reluctant (as in the case of Olongapo), then the fleet could base itself closer to home, at Pearl Harbor.

It was also shown, however, that without bases and colliers, the United States was dependent on British goodwill for supplies of coal and for port facilities. On the cruise, the fleet had consumed 430,000 tons of coal, which was delivered entirely (and sometimes erratically) by foreign vessels.[55] The extent of the logistical problem is indicated by the fact that the Navy had no modern colliers and only two under construction at the time of the cruise. In 1909 it added five more. These seven comprised the Navy's entire modern collier force before World War I.[56] Also, a dangerous design flaw in the battleships' turrets had to be repaired. The guns stood directly above the unprotected magazines, exposing the turrets to explosion if an enemy shell should ignite the powder. On the other hand, shipboard skills and what the General Board called the "power of self-maintenance" were greater than expected. The fleet was far from ready for battle, but on its return in February 1909, the Navy changed the color of the battleships' hulls and funnels from their customary white and ocher, respectively, to a forbidding wartime haze gray.

None of this changed the country's overall naval strategy. The primacy of the Atlantic and the fleet's concentration there was confirmed in 1909 when the Navy announced that Germany had displaced the United States as the world's second greatest naval power. The year before, after a decade of concern about how to make America's presence felt in the Far East, the government had decided to give up direct naval defense of the Philippines and not to maintain a strong regional force west of Hawaii. To protect its interests the country would rely on diplomacy and, for national security, mainly on its geographic isolation.

In his inaugural address in 1909, President William Howard Taft spoke vaguely of the need for "a suitable Army and a suitable Navy" that could command respect in any controversy "growing out of the Open Door and other issues." But Taft never developed a powerful force in the Far East. For Roosevelt, naval force on display had been enough because he had centered his Asian policy on good relations with Japan. Taft tilted toward China and hoped to achieve his Asian goals by diplomacy. But Taft found himself without allies. His wish for concerted action in support of the Open Door and against Japanese expansion in Manchuria came to nothing, save to make it all the harder for the administration to determine when, if, and how American force (though at present absent) might be used.[57] All Taft was left with was the growing enmity of Japan.[58]

Taft did strive to continue the naval buildup begun by Roosevelt. At least, he said he wanted to keep up the schedule of building two battleships a year. Taft declared that "there should not be the slightest question" about such an authorization. But he did not control Congress, and the building program tapered off to one dreadnought in 1912 and one in 1913. Roosevelt, now a private citizen, declared of the 1913 authorization that congressmen who refused to vote for two ships a year were "men unfit to represent the American people"—but of course they did represent them, and he did not.[59] The mood in Congress was not that the Navy had lost importance. It was that, for the purpose of defending the country, for the Atlantic war envisioned, and for the strategy of decisive battle (as opposed to pursuing complex and internationalized policies in distant Asia), the service, with the 39 battleships that had been either authorized or commissioned, had enough capital ships.

Indeed, the U.S. Navy in 1913 was reasonably strong. It was top-heavy with battleships, it is true. It could have used more cruisers and more destroyers. Submarine, aircraft, and mine programs needed boosting, but the American Navy was no worse than other navies at predicting the future. The service was undermanned, for it had made compromises with Congress to get the capital ships. It was less than ready, for Taft had pursued a foreign policy that was largely indifferent to the use of naval force. But according to its own evaluation, if brought up to readiness, it could meet what it thought would be the most likely threat to national security—an enemy battle fleet approaching the American shore.

3

Neutrality or Readiness? 1913-1917

WAR PLANS

In 1913 the Navy continued to regard Germany as its probable foe and naval preparedness as the main deterrent to Germany's sending a fleet to the western hemisphere.

The Navy's War Plan Black of 1913, which chartered a future war with Germany, iterated sea-power doctrine almost sublimely. It assumed that commercial competition was the main cause of conflict, that sea power obtained and protected commercial advantage, and that the state with the strongest navy would get what it wanted. German foreign policy, War Plan Black declared, was driven by population pressure and the demand for secure markets. When "conditions at home are no longer considered bearable, and Germany is strong enough, Germany will insist upon occupation of western hemisphere territory."[1] Against that threat the United States stood alone. Despite Britain's recent acknowledgment of U.S. preeminence in the hemisphere, War Plan Black warned that Britain might give comfort if not aid to Germany, covering its rear while the Germans engaged in the Caribbean. The British would rejoice to see their main rivals in conflict and the exclusionary Monroe Doctrine under attack.

War Plan Black set out to assure the United States of strategic independence and regional hegemony. It followed the regnant doctrine of naval operations: the American battle line would concentrate and then move out for the decisive engagement. Overextended and encumbered by its train, the German fleet would be defeated when it entered the Caribbean. There was no reason for American ships to stay behind to cover ports. The Army was close to completing an elaborate program, begun in 1886, to protect the major harbors of the United States. In 1914 the chief of coast artillery reported that almost all the coastal fortifications on the continent were in place.[2] And in any case, no one thought the Germans would be foolish enough to attempt to land on U.S. territory.

War Plan Black was as ignorant of the nature of the war to come as were the war plans of European states. Even more remarkable was its misreading of the existing international scene. For that, it has been described as "surrealistic."[3] Germany was tied to Europe. It is almost incredible that in 1913 Navy planners imagined the German government could, or would, dispatch thousands of men and the major part of its fleet on a transatlantic voyage to seize an island in the West Indies, where, overextended, the Germans risked confronting the massed battle fleet of the United States. The planners' fears might have been more plausible had the setting been 1903, around the time of the Venezuelan blockade, if at that time the British had been inclined to support such German advance, or in 1943, had Hitler gained control of the European landmass. But a German advance was not likely in 1913 with Germany encircled. In fact, the German government had concluded before 1913 that its big navy was a luxury and that its policy of world influence was a mirage. It accepted the consequences of the choke-hold imposed by its Austrian alliance, which bound Germany's fate to the continent and to its army.

That the Navy's war planning in 1913 reflected contemporary reality so slightly shows the dangers of presuming governments' policies. Naval planning was detached from the political world. Sea-power theorists gave little thought to the possibility that governments may try to avoid war, may have allies—or other enemies—that constrain them, or may pursue commercial ends by means other than command of the sea. Naval planners weighed enemies and opportunities by naval capacities alone. One did not require political guidance to see who was a potential enemy or what to do about it. Navies of other states would, by the logic of operations, be mirror images of one's own in force structure and purpose. Planners could count the capital ships of potential rivals, look at their bases, and conclude who posed what threat to America's use of the sea. Formulated more or less automatically, naval strategy and operations were self-evident.[4] Such isolated thinking was not unique to the Navy Department. In the same year of 1913, with equal aplomb, the German General Staff was honing its ill-fated plan to conquer France, and the U.S. Army filed a plan to invade Canada as part of a war against Britain.

It is not entirely appropriate, nonetheless, to dismiss War Plan Black as preposterous. Armed forces must plan for problematic futures. The goal was to assure America's strategic independence. After all, what if Germany won a European war? It might then move unconstrained across the Atlantic. War Plan Black need not be precise about when it would be called upon to meet an enemy fleet. What the plan did for the first time was to give commanders an overall guide to a strategy of offensive sea control, a guide by which they could roughly frame their operations in the Caribbean and off the Atlantic coast.

War Plan Orange, the plan for a war against Japan, was updated in 1914. That year and for 30 years thereafter, the Navy's biggest operational dilemma was how to deliver a superior force swiftly to the western Pacific and sustain it there. Orange did not solve the problem. Under the plan, in a war across the Pacific, the fleet was to sail to a designated advance base, Guam, and prepare to meet the main Japanese force, which would be encountered as the Americans steamed to the Philippines. Unfortunately, Guam was not ready. Nowhere in the theater were there support stations or dockyard facilities. War Plan Orange ran the danger of putting the U.S. fleet in the position of the Germans in War Plan Black, of moving it far beyond its supportable range, to a place where, far from home, it would meet a fresh enemy fleet operating in its own waters. In the Pacific, the United States had conceded to Japan the same advantage of position the United States itself held in the Atlantic. The only way around this concession was to give up a long-range thrust to the Philippines in favor of a graduated, island-hopping advance in which the fleet's entire course could be covered from bases along the way. Such a plan, however, was not worked out, and for twenty years war planners were divided between those who wanted to send the fleet straight through to Manila and those who wanted a measured advance along the mid-ocean islands.

In any case, the Pacific remained a distant second in strategic priority. The battle fleet was in the Atlantic, watching the fleets of Europe. At the very least, War Plan Orange depended on the absence of a threat in the Atlantic and on full operation of the Panama Canal. In 1914, neither of those conditions existed. Assuming that the canal was open for transit (the first ship passed through in 1914, but landslides and difficulties with the locks restricted passage for some time after that), it would still take many weeks for the Atlantic Fleet to swing west and get to the Philippines. During this time—two to three months or longer—the Japanese would command the western Pacific. Could the Army hold the Corregidor fortress at the entrance to Manila Bay for 60 days? For 100 days?

The problem with both war plans, of course, was that they were not tied to government policy. The Navy could make presumptive guesses, but it could not give answers to the essential questions of against whom, and when, war would be made. That was the province of the civil authorities. In 1914 the administration was not preparing for war with either Japan or Germany.

President Woodrow Wilson and the secretary of the Navy, Josephus Daniels, while deferring to the General Board on many aspects of the strategic and operational overview, would not concede political decisions. Foreign policy lay with the president. No one argued with that. What was absent, however, was an effective coordination between civil and military authorities. As a result, misunderstandings ran in both directions.

The office of the secretary of the Navy connected the administration to the fleet. In 1913 there was a strong body of opinion that Secretary Daniels was incompetent to guide the service. Daniels's critics included Rear Admiral Bradley Fiske, the secretary's aide for operations and principal service assistant; Franklin D. Roosevelt, Daniels's assistant secretary and ambitious subordinate; and Theodore Roosevelt and Henry Cabot Lodge, pugnacious elders in the opposition Republican party. Daniels and Wilson returned the criticism. They thought the Navy was beset by an entrenched, snobbish officer corps that was trying to usurp civilian prerogatives basic to the American system of government.

In 1913 the Army and the Navy went beyond the bounds of the politically acceptable in their reaction to the matter of Japanese exclusion. The Japanese government had protested discriminatory laws passed by the California legislature. The administration defused the tension with calm diplomacy. To officers, however, aware of the Philippines' vulnerability, the Japanese protests portended war. Rear Admiral Fiske and the Army's chief of staff, General Leonard Wood, called for reinforcement of the Philippines and for more ships for Pacific ports. They took their case to the press. The Joint Army-Navy Board, the Navy's General Board, and the war gamers at the Naval War College joined the call.

The administration considered these initiatives egregiously provocative to Japan and a serious breach of civil authority. President Wilson laid it on the line to Daniels: "When a policy has been settled by this Administration [the policy of no provocative naval movements in the Pacific] and when it is communicated to the Joint Board, they have no right to be trying to force a different course and I wish you would say to them that if this should occur again, there will be no General or Joint Boards. They will be abolished."[5] So outraged was Wilson at the leaks to the press that he halted the Joint Board's work and the body was not called together again until October 1915, when preparedness became part of government policy.[6]

So War Plan Orange received no support from the administration. Nor did War Plan Black, even though a powerful U.S. offensive force in the Atlantic fit the president's other needs. Wilson was determined to maintain the country's strategic independence. Such independence depended in part on preventing European intrusion into the western hemisphere. Wilson gave little attention to how this was to be done. Figuring that out was the Navy's job and would remain so as long as Navy operations concurred with the line laid down by civilian authority. It was quite appropriate for the Navy to plan for offensive operations and decisive battle in defense of the Monroe Doctrine.

Any officer on the General Board, and President Wilson and Secretary Daniels as well, would have been incredulous had they been told in 1913 that in four years' time the United States would be at war as part of a coalition force, that in the war the commanders of the battleships of the Atlantic Fleet would not even see the German High Seas Fleet, and that the U.S. Navy would operate almost exclusively in transport, in convoy, and in antisubmarine warfare. They would have been astonished had it been suggested that an invasion fleet would cross the ocean from west to east, not the other way around, that it would not be met by a hostile battle fleet, that the German force that did approach the American coast would be submersible, and that the U.S. Navy's main mission would be to carry safely hundreds of thousands of soldiers to fight on the distant soil of France. Such a vertiginous prospect was envisioned by no one in Washington in 1913, nor by anyone in Berlin or in London.

War Plan Black was right, therefore, in 1913 to concentrate on regional defense. Such defense transcended the question of whether there was an immediate German threat. Some state would soon enough challenge the U.S. position in the western hemisphere. If there was a war in Europe, a loser might seek compensation, or a winner might seek further victories with its superior force. It was thought simply to be in the nature of international affairs for a state to expand when it had the opportunity.

Within a year every great power except the United States was at war, and every power still had its capital-ship fleet intact.[7] Despite the absence of fleet actions at the start of the war, the doctrine of decisive battle lost none of its force. In the Atlantic there was no telling whose fleet the United States might face. The British were violating the doctrine of neutral rights. Who knew what a victorious Germany might do? If there was an unmet incursion into the hemisphere, Mexico might turn hostile. Japan, although it did not have the means for a conclusive naval war, acted with increasing freedom in the western Pacific, taking islands, gaining confidence, and making demands upon China. If, in a reversal of alliances, a victorious Germany joined with Japan, might they make a coordinated, two-ocean assault? The U.S. Navy had to be ready for any eventuality.

NEUTRALITY OR READINESS?

Readiness means a state in which existing warships are activated for immediate use. *Preparation* refers to longer-term development of the force structure, to the planning and building of the fleet. One must be aware of this distinction to understand the period between August 1914, when World War I broke out, and April 1917, when the United States entered the war. President Wilson's insistence on strict neutrality limited the readiness of the Navy. At the same time, with the Naval Act of 1916, the president began a buildup to prepare the country for the postwar world. The debate over neutrality and readiness did not change Navy fundamentals. For purposes of both combat and influence, the doctrine of offensive sea control by capital ships reigned.

The war in Europe took the United States by surprise. Because no national interests seemed immediately involved, Wilson told Congress in August 1914 that Americans must be "neutral in fact as well as in name . . . in thought as well as in action." That meant no talk about war. Wilson promptly muzzled the military. When Mahan said that Austria-Hungary was responsible for provoking the conflict and that Britain ought to impose a blockade on Germany, Wilson ordered all officers, active and retired, to refrain from "public comment on any kind upon the military or political situation on the other side of the water."[8]

No one argued that the United States should intervene. For one thing, the trend of the conflict was not clear. Top naval officers, including Rear

Admiral Fiske and Rear Admiral William Benson, who took up the new post of chief of naval operations (CNO) in 1915, thought that the Western powers could not hold out and that victory would go to Germany. That is why they wanted expansion of the force but saw no need for strategic innovation. Readiness was necessary for defense, not for intervention. Sooner or later Germany—or Britain—might sail against the United States. In the meantime, the United States should remain uninvolved and prepare.

For two and a half years, Wilson kept the country neutral. He expected a military stalemate that would enable him to avoid a military commitment and thus permit him to mediate a peace based on liberal values. The administration realized that its definition of strict neutrality retarded the fleet's readiness for immediate combat. But as long as the United States was not imperiled, readying the fleet for war might be construed as provocation and disturb the policy of neutrality. For that reason, Wilson forbade such activities.

When war broke out in Europe in August 1914, Rear Admiral Fiske asked Secretary Daniels to bring back to U.S. waters the scattered battleships of the Atlantic Fleet, except those needed in the Caribbean, and to put them on a war footing. The fleet had been dispersed. Battleships were on a punitive mission off Veracruz, Mexico, doing the work of gunboats in support of American troops landed there. Other battleships were on cruise. Atlantic units had gone for two years without operating as a fleet. Target practice and training had fallen woefully behind, and the morale of seamen was low. "The fleet is deteriorating like an eagle in a cage," wrote the aide for inspection.[9]

Out of position, divided, doing jobs suited to lesser vessels, the capital ships of the U.S. Navy in 1914 were not ready to meet the emergency Fiske thought was coming. "I could see the German machine smashing its way across the mineral-bearing part of France, crushing the comparatively improvised machines of England and France, and threatening the very existence of the United States—and we watching the spectacle as a child watches a fire spreading."[10] Fiske, Assistant Secretary Franklin D. Roosevelt, and the General Board expostulated with Secretary Daniels, but to no avail.

A conspicuous program of war readiness went against strict neutrality, and Daniels did not see a clear and present danger. The administration brushed aside the General Board's November 1914 warning that the naval force was inadequate to meet either a violation of neutral rights or a Japanese seizure of Germany's Pacific islands. Nothing must suggest engagement in the European conflict or a provocation of Japan.

When the Mexican expedition wound down in the autumn of 1914, Daniels did assemble the fleet in Cuban waters. By then, however, the main deterrent to any German action in the western hemisphere was not the U.S. Navy but the bog of war on the western front and the self-imprisonment of the German fleet.

Fiske and other reformers related the question of readiness to the issue of operational command. Their position, expressed throughout 1915 and 1916, was that readiness required plans and operations to be under the control of uniformed officers, not of civilian appointees. Not even neutrality should prevent the Navy from being trained, manned, and ready for combat. Readiness was the Navy's responsibility and should be kept in Navy hands regardless of any administration's policies. International law permitted even neutral armed forces to get ready to fight. Fiske and his supporters claimed that Wilson's definition of strict neutrality inhibited readiness to an excessive, even dangerous, degree.

The reformers wanted a general staff for the Navy. That demand went well beyond the ideas of central direction adumbrated by Mahan, Luce, and Taylor at the Naval War College at the turn of the century. Those modest ideas of administrative centralization had led to the creation of the advisory and impermanent General Board in 1900 and to the moderate recommendations of the Moody Commission of 1909. Those recommendations, written by a commission including Luce and Mahan, called for greater central supervision of the semiautonomous bureaus and boards that ran the Navy's shore establishment, the virtually independent fiefdoms concerned with personnel, ship construction, administration, and inspection. The commission also called for the creation of a more clearly operations-directed advisory body for the secretary.

In 1915, the more determined reformers called for something further, a virtually independent office of chief of naval operations that would be responsible for plans and operations and free from the vagaries of political control. Fretful over the politicians' shilly-shallying, over public apathy and ignorance, over a policy of neutrality that prevented naval readiness, and over the Navy secretary's inaction, they wanted a general staff to command what would be in effect an apolitical national fleet. Only so, they argued, could ship efficiency, personnel, and morale be kept in fighting trim and war plans be immediately translatable into action.

Wilson and Daniels were outraged by the idea of to any degree separating from political supervision the main fighting arm of U.S.

foreign policy. The idea struck at the heart of the principle of civilian control. They reviled the concept of an independent chief of naval operations as a brazen and un-American attempt to prussianize the Navy. Daniels and Wilson had not stood for any challenge to the authority of elected officials in 1913, and they would not stand for it in 1915.

To base training on contingency plans was one thing. To presume a political prerogative was another. There were certain decisions no service could take no matter how grand its opinion of itself. The Navy could not determine foreign policy. It could not declare the national enemy, contact possible allies, declare mobilization, or call up the reserves. With a chief of naval operations so enabled, the Navy would be loosed from its constitutional moorings. If the administration withheld action on readiness, even if that withholding hurt the fighting efficiency of the service, that was the way it would have to be. The responsibility of elected officials to determine policy could not be compromised.[11]

Argument went on in Congress and within the Navy Department throughout 1915 and 1916. In the latter year, hearings before the House Committee on Naval Affairs on the value of a chief of naval operations included favorable testimony from Rear Admiral Fiske, from the commanders in chief of the Atlantic and Pacific fleets, from a member of the General Board, from the president of the Naval War College, from the redoubtable Captain William S. Sims, and, circumspectly, from Franklin D. Roosevelt, assistant secretary of the Navy.[12]

Certainly the Navy in 1914 and 1915 was deficient in manpower and remiss in training. Naval officers could have done more about readiness on their own. Ship and fleet readiness in terms of repair, training, tactical exercise, gunnery competence, and fuel and stores was the Navy's responsibility, regardless of the administration's policy.

Yet adherence to the neutrality policy did constrain the Navy. Consider, for example, Rear Admiral William Benson, the officer closest to Navy Secretary Daniels, and the man installed as the first, suitably watered-down chief of naval operations in May 1915. Benson failed to urge the degree of readiness his professional judgment called for, precisely so he could follow both Wilson's definition of neutrality and the noninterventionist national mood. Explaining his position to Congress, Benson reflected:

> As a naval officer I would have had the fleet mobilized and I would have had many more vessels and would have had everything ready for anything we were called upon to do, if I had known that it was the intention of the people to go to war; but under the general conditions that existed, of our strict neutrality and the necessity for maintaining that attitude which had been made so evident by

the people of the country, I felt then, and I still feel, that the fleet as it was distributed, under the circumstances, and taking those things into consideration, was about as well as we could do.[13]

Elting Morison suggested Benson could have resigned to force the issue of readiness into broader public debate.[14] It is hard to see what his resignation would have accomplished, however. Benson did not feel strongly about the issue. He was a loyal servant of the administration. In addition, the issue of readiness was entangled with the emotion-charged arguments about intervention in the war and about the value of a general staff, and it is not clear which way public opinion would have gone on those issues.

Communication between civil and military authorities might well have been smoother, but the administration saw no need to revamp the Navy Department for that reason. Daniels ran the Navy to President Wilson's satisfaction.[15] In 1914, moreover, the public was unlikely to support the readiness the Navy wanted. Outside the service there was not the same sense of urgency. Fiske yearned for a Navy secretary like his hero Theodore Roosevelt. Absent that, he would have liked a general staff with a free hand, with himself as chief of naval operations, and a Congress with a deep and open purse. But that was too much to ask. Woodrow Wilson was not Theodore Roosevelt. Most of the Navy's officers put up with the existing situation. Only a few were as passionate on the issues of reform and a general staff as were Fiske and his ally William Sims. Most officers thought the Navy would be ready to do its job when the time came. For the moment, the United States was not at war.

And viewed fairly, Daniels and the president were not idle. Daniels moved slowly, but he did move. He appropriated the idea of a chief of naval operations and established the office in 1915. The post was given responsibility for plans and preparations, as Fiske had hoped, but it was also made subordinate to the civilian secretary. The CNO was not given direct control of the powerful Navy bureaus, the fiefdoms of the Navy's shore establishment. Still, creation of the office was a big step in enhancing professional authority. The position was linked to command of the fleets until 1940. As William Braisted wrote: "The chief of naval operations was the most important institutional innovation in the Navy Department since the creation of the new bureaus in 1842 as well as the outstanding achievement of the preparedness movement during the winter of 1914–1915."[16]

Fiske wanted to be appointed to the new post, which was the institutional successor to his position as aide for operations. But Daniels had had enough commotion. Benson was given the job, and the arguments about administrative authority ended. Then in 1915, in a move of much importance, Wilson took charge of long-term naval preparation. The following year, the great Naval Act of 1916 authorized a Navy second to none. These events showed that the administration and Congress took the Navy's role in foreign policy very seriously indeed. Criticism within the service abated. Restraints resulting from the policy of neutrality disappeared when the United States entered the war.

A final note on the readiness debate: The dispute over Daniels' stewardship and the argument over a general staff related only to the internal organization of the department, to how the service should be run. No one questioned that the purpose of a war would be defense of the western hemisphere. No one questioned that the war should be fought along Mahanian lines. There were no plans made to send warships to Europe, none to send Army troops overseas. Planners did not think that U.S. intervention would be central to Germany's defeat.[17] The British appeared to be containing the High Seas Fleet without assistance. U.S. planners looked instead to the postwar future.

THE NAVAL BILL OF 1916

In July 1915, after the Germans sank the *Lusitania* with loss of American lives, Wilson took up the cause of naval expansion.[18] He did this to give the United States strategic freedom for whatever moves the government cared to make in the years ahead. He asked the General Board for "professional advice" on how to establish a Navy second to none.[19]

Regardless of how the war ended, a self-confident challenger might emerge, be it Germany or Britain, or Japan in conjunction with either of those two. That was a sufficient reason to prepare a strong Navy. How else was freedom of the seas to be assured? How else was the United States to ensure its freedom of action in world affairs? Already relations with Britain were strained over questions of neutral rights. Wilson expressed his position to Edward House: "Let us build a Navy bigger than hers and do what we please."[20]

The General Board laid out its reasons why the United States must have a navy "equal to the most powerful" by 1925:

> Defense from invasion is not the only function of a Navy. It must protect our seaborne commerce and drive that of the enemy from the sea. The best way to accomplish all these objects is to find and defeat the hostile fleet or any of its detachments at a distance from our coast sufficiently great to prevent interrup-

tion of our normal course of national life. The current war has shown that a navy of the size recommended by this board in previous years can no longer be considered as adequate to the defensive needs of the United States. Our present Navy is not sufficient to give due weight to the diplomatic remonstrances of the United States in peace or to enforce its policies in war.[21]

This was sea power in the interest of American unilateralism. The General Board proposed as the first installment a vast five-year building program to provide 10 dreadnoughts, 6 battle cruisers (of which the United States then had none), 10 scout cruisers to screen the battle fleet's flanks, 50 destroyers, and 67 submarines (9 for the fleet and 58 for the coast). The battleships of this armada were to carry the biggest guns possible. The first four were to displace 32,000 tons and have eight 16-inch guns in the main battery. The other six of the group were to displace 42,000 tons and have twelve 16-inch guns. Wilson incorporated the board's proposal into the naval authorization bill that he submitted to Congress. The bill received widespread popular support. The battle of Jutland between a British and a German fleet took place on the eve of the vote on the naval building program, confirming, or so it seemed, the continuing importance of big ships and great battles. At Jutland fleets really had met and engaged. Spurred by this example, Congress passed the Naval Act of 1916.

The legislation gave the president and the Navy what they had asked for. Congress agreed to the construction, without interruption, of 156 ships. The preparedness campaign was won. The Navy for the first time had a continuous, comprehensive schedule for the construction of warships. One hundred and fifty-six vessels of all classes were to be begun by July 1919, with construction to be finished by 1922 or 1923. With this program the "United States entered a new chapter in its naval history."[22]

Was the emphasis on the battleship excessive? Critics noted that once the United States entered the war in April 1917, work on the battleships and cruisers was stopped so that destroyers and transport ships could be built for antisubmarine warfare and for carrying troops, aspects of sea power whose strategic importance the Navy had signally failed to envision. Therefore, according to the critics, the Naval Act of 1916 "was peculiarly ill-suited to the needs of 1917."[23]

True enough, but not quite to the point. The buildup of 1916 was not to prepare for intervention in the war that was being fought. Its purpose was to assure freedom of action for the United States, to assure the country's strategic independence in the war's aftermath. Who could say who would win or how long the war would last? Perhaps the

United States would face a coalition attacking from both oceans. Influential officers such as Fiske and Benson thought it likely that Germany would win the war. But whatever happened, the United States would be left to face the future alone, and that was the point of the Naval Act of 1916.[24] The United States had to be ready to face a battle of Jutland in the Caribbean, in the Pacific, or in both.

Still, the fact remains that the 1916 program left the fleet unbalanced. There were too few destroyers even for fleet duty, let alone for other tasking. The landings in Mexico had shown the need for small vessels. The submarine menace, the war in progress in the Atlantic and the Mediterranean, and the possible needs of the country should it choose to intervene might have suggested a different mix of men-of-war and a different naval strategy.[25]

Doctrine had blinkered naval planning, blinding it to dimensions of sea warfare other than fleet engagement. A look at the Mediterranean and North Atlantic would have suggested other forms of sea control. War Plan Black, whatever its long-term prospects, was becoming less and less appropriate. The Navy, accustomed to lots of lead time in planning and a long period over which to build, overlooked contemporary experience. Nor did Wilson's policy of neutrality help the service. David Trask referred to the period that ended with U.S. entry into the war as "lost years of miscalculation."[26]

For whatever reasons, before 1917 no one in Washington thought of redefining control of the sea, so the old formulas held. The General Board's position was expressed in its report of October 1916, in which it commented on the war in Europe: "Nothing apparently has occurred to modify in the essentials the broad principles laid down and the conclusions reached by the board in former years . . . the battleship remains, as heretofore, the principal reliance—the backbone—of the sea power of the nation."[27]

Josephus Daniels said that no one told him in 1916 that instead of battleships the country should have been building 300 destroyers.[28] And that was certainly true. The General Board in 1916 thought ten battleships were more important.

The Navy also had discounted, by doctrine and experience, the importance of building, or even emphasizing, submarines. In a report to Daniels in 1915, the General Board stated:

> The deeds of the submarines have been so spectacular that in default of engagements between the main fleets undue weight has been attached to them. . . . To hastily formed public opinion, it seemed that the submarines were accomplishing great military results because little else of importance occurred in the

maritime war to attract public attention. Yet at the present time, when the allies have learned in great measure to protect their commerce, as they learned a few months earlier to protect their cruisers from the submarine menace, it is apparent that the submarine is not an instrument fitted to dominate naval warfare. . . . The submarine is a most useful auxiliary whose importance will no doubt increase, but at present there is no evidence that it will become supreme.[29]

Was this a valid assessment or a grave strategic error? Again, the situation must be considered. In 1915 and 1916, U-boats did not menace the United States. Submarines were not the self-contained masters of the deep we know today. They traveled alone and on the surface, submerging only for brief periods to escape detection. No one in Washington thought that the submarine constituted a decisive offensive force.

In 1917 the U.S. Navy was still primarily a regional force. It based its operational planning and its mission of defense on the expectation that a single surface fleet would be met as it approached the western hemisphere. The Navy did not look far beyond that horizon and was left with a "general lack of accurate information about the true nature and extent of the submarine emergency and the measures required to cope with it."[30] Here was a major flaw in sea-power doctrine, which discounted, on principle, raiding and the *guerre de course*. No doubt the General Board should have shown greater foresight and prepared to counter a submarine threat to American mobility. But routine thinking, if not theory, stood in its way. It was the administration that added some 30 submarines to the Navy's request in the 1916 building program—and it did so for coastal defense.

And of course a critical consideration was that the United States was not in the war and did not expect to enter it. Physical isolation and political neutrality distanced Americans from the changing face of war at sea. Neutrality seemed to be working. The Germans had raised a storm with their early use of unrestricted submarine warfare, but they had twice backed off from this practice when confronted with stiff American protests. Until 1917 it was precisely to avoid provoking the United States that the German government forbade U-boats to attack American ships.

A decision to prepare for antisubmarine warfare, a decision to build destroyers instead of battleships, would have been a good strategic judgment in 1916 if the United States by that time had decided to enter the war on the side of Britain and France and if the government foresaw a benign, cooperative postwar world. Then, as part of a coalition strategy, U.S. destroyers, when they were ready, could have joined the war against the submarine.[31] But the decision to prepare for submarine warfare was not taken until 1917. In 1916, a policy of intervention, a strategy of limited operations for partial control of the sea, was not part of the administration's or the Navy's plan.

Clausewitz commented that "no one starts a war—or, rather, no one in his senses ought to do so—without first being clear in his mind what he intends to achieve by that war and how he intends to conduct it." Navy men in the United States in 1915 and 1916 would have replied: "Yes, we understand. Defense comes through the capacity to destroy the enemy's battle fleet. That is our strategy, and for this we have a plan of war and are building the ships." To them it was just a matter of the doing.

Within months the United States entered the war with new goals, with a new strategy, and with a new plan of operations. The prewar doctrine was put on hold, and the Navy fought a war without Mahan.

4

War Without Mahan
1917-1918

REVERSALS

In February 1917 the prospect of mediation disappeared with Germany's announcement of unrestricted submarine warfare against all vessels in the war zone around Europe, including those under the U.S. flag. This prompted Wilson to act. The president decided on war sometime in late March, but not because U.S. security was threatened or because he sought to preserve freedom of use of the North Atlantic sealanes (although the submarine challenge provided the proximate excuse).[1] Rather, with the prospect of mediation gone, Wilson decided he must bring the United States into the conflict to prevent Germany from dominating Europe and to assure the United States a place of influence at the peace table.[2]

The Naval Act of 1916 had authorized a strong Navy for the postwar era. Now, in entering the war, the United States had to secure control of the seas at once and send soldiers to fight on the soil of Europe. Only through intervention by force (with troops on the ground and ships on the sea) and only through a unilateral intervention (as an associated instead of as an allied power), would the United States gain sufficient authority to establish a new international order.

When the United States entered the war in April 1917, the fighting had already been going on for two and a half years. The only plan the Navy had ready was War Plan Black, which called for an offensive battle-line action against an advancing battle fleet. This was clearly inappropriate to the conflict at hand, unsuited both to the transport and supply needs of Wilson's continental policy and to the nature of the real threat at sea. The expected decisive fleet battle would not happen. The German High Seas Fleet was held in port and would have to defeat the British Royal Navy before it could arrive in the Atlantic, let alone in American waters, toward which, in any case, it no longer had any reason to go. The problem at sea in 1917 was the submarine. And sea control was to be won by the prosaic measures of patrol, mines, and convoy. Sea power as shipping, not as battleships, would win or lose the war.

Even as this reality was recognized, responsible naval officers were reluctant to give up their prewar position. The Navy's job was to assure the strategic independence of the United States not only in the war but also thereafter. Who knew how the war would end, who might win, and what force would remain at the country's disposal? It was not inconceivable that Britain would be forced into a separate peace with Germany, or winning, infringe on the U.S. preserve.

Such thoughts had jostled in the mind of the CNO, Admiral William Benson, in February and March 1917, in that difficult twilight of armed neutrality when Wilson still hoped to avoid war and permitted no major moves toward readiness, but when the Navy had to imagine what a war would be like. The Navy had to protect the sea-lanes of trade and transit and also "secure guarantees for the future." Protecting cargo ships and transport meant a defensive strategy, an antisubmarine campaign to ensure free passage of means of support, of goods to Britain and France, of Argentine grain, of Venezuelan oil, and of U.S. troops. Guarantees for the future meant maintaining the battle fleet to deprive any European state of a foothold in the western hemisphere and to ensure strategic independence. It was imperative, Benson wrote, to realize that "we have not only to act quickly but to act with a full realization that we may eventually have to act alone."[3]

As the United States moved from neutrality toward intervention in February and March 1917, naval strategists, on the changing tide of Wilson's reversal of American policy, moved from offensive to defensive sea control. Admiral Benson recalled the Atlantic Fleet from Cuban waters and concentrated it in Chesapeake Bay. At the same time he ordered construction of patrol craft. The national interest demanded a mobilization "that entailed the least possible degree of entanglement" because meeting a friend's need today might weaken the nation's position tomorrow.[4]

No serious thought had been given to how much the United States would cooperate with Britain and France, to how many warships would be deployed outside U.S. waters, to how the Navy would change its major focus from sea battle to transport and supply, or to how the inevitable demand of cooperation with the U.S. Army would be met for these tasks. Much time had been lost for planning, for consultation with the coalition, for discussion of service cooperation, for measures of mobilization, and for the development of new strategies. The time was lost because of Wilson's insistence on neutrality and because the Navy, the Army, and the State Department did not envision intervention in the war as becoming their top priority.

It is hard to imagine Navy leaders seeing the future differently, hard to imagine the government establishing closer connections earlier with the Allies, hard to imagine the Army and Navy sitting down and planning a campaign in Europe. Before 1917, to what end would they do so? Neutrality forbade consultation overseas. Until Jutland the Navy thought of defense of the western hemisphere in terms of surface control. Who had suggested it think otherwise? What policy would have led the Navy to think differently? After Jutland, of course, the prospect of decisive battle faded—although it never disappeared. That the German fleet was bottled up was tantamount to its destruction. What took planners on both sides of the Atlantic by surprise was the new campaign for control of the sea begun by the unexpected German submarine offensive and followed by the military consequences of the U.S. declaration of war.

America's isolation from the front and its self-conscious distancing from European politics had encouraged complacency. Space and time had been America's luxuries. Admiral Henry Mayo reflected that by the time the United States entered the war, "the enemy fleet [had been] contained by an allied navy and the enemy fully engaged with allied armies." As for the submarine menace, hostile German submarines did not appear in U.S. waters until nearly fourteen months after the American declaration of war.[5]

Still, from April 1917 the country was at war, and the submarine and the creation of the American Expeditionary Forces completely changed the strategic environment. It was not so much a matter of lost time as of the fact that "the armed forces had to adjust to a truly remarkable political reversal, something they could not do overnight. . . . It was not simply a matter of making the great technical transition from peace to war, it was a case of ideology."[6]

AGAINST THE HORNETS

It was going to be hard to maintain its strategic independence, for the United States had joined a coalition war. And the country was ignorant of the condition of its new associates in Wilson's League of Honor. The navies had developed no plan for cooperation. To protect neutrality, Wilson had forbidden the Navy to send observers to Britain or to the continent to watch the war's course.[7] Naval attachés reported only technical details. Said Chief of Naval Operations Benson, "I did not know, nor did anyone else on this side know, the details of any plans or policies that the Allies were carrying out."[8] Only on the very eve of U.S. entry did the Navy send Rear Admiral William S. Sims to London to establish the rudiments of naval cooperation.

Thus it came as a shock when Sims reported the gravity of the U-boat threat. In April 1917 it looked as though the 40 German submarines on station in the western approaches to the British Isles would starve the British into submission. Germany had wrested use of the sea from Britain with little submarines, not with great battleships.

Under regnant battle-fleet doctrine of command of the sea, capital ships would protect merchant shipping by first destroying the battleships that covered the raids of enemy cruisers. After a victorious battle of fleets, the lesser enemy cruisers could be picked off at will by one's superior forces. Protection of commerce was thus indirect, the product of destroying the cover that the enemy needed to maraud. Direct protection—patrol and convoy—were only secondarily important. But the Germans discovered a way around the battle-fleet doctrine. Submarines were not cruisers. They were raiders that could not be found. Their success did not depend on friendly control of the surface of the sea. Vessels of stealth had revived the *guerre de course*.

During the first ten days of April, as Sims made his way across the ocean and the United States went to war, German submarines sank 200,000 tons of British and neutral cargo ships. On April 13, Admiral John Jellicoe, Britain's First Sea Lord, handed Sims the most recent figures: 536,000 tons had been lost to the submarine in February and 603,000 tons in March. The projection for April was 900,000 tons. These were tremendous losses. The collapse of merchant shipping was imminent. A total of 1,149 ships entered British ports in February and March of 1916. A year later, during the same two months, fewer than 300 arrived. Herbert Hoover, an expert on food supplies and in touch with Sims in London, estimated that in the period before the summer harvest, Britain, France, and Italy each had only three to four weeks of wheat left in their reserve stock. "It is impossible for us to go on with the war if losses like this continue," Jellicoe told Sims. "'It looks as though the Germans were winning the war,' [Sims] remarked. 'They will win, unless we can stop these losses—and stop them soon,' [Jellicoe] replied. 'Is there no solution for the problem?' [Sims] asked. 'Absolutely none that we can see now,' Jellicoe announced."[9]

For the German high command, the war at sea had become a war of attrition off the British Isles. The German High Seas Fleet lay in harbor, intact but inactive, unwilling after Jutland to challenge the British Grand Fleet, which waited for it to come out. For the British the strategic stalemate in the North Sea was victory enough. The German surface fleet did not threaten the home islands, the sea-lanes, or the movement of troops and supplies across the English Channel. But in 1917 the submarine was tightening its death grip on the merchant shipping upon which the British war effort depended. The Royal Navy had failed to counter the U-boats by mining German ports, by using patrols and nets, or by arming merchantmen. That was why Jellicoe despaired. If Britain had to submit to terms before U.S. troops arrived on the western front, a final German military offensive might win the war.

The German hold was tightest around the western approaches to the British Isles, where the shipping lanes converged. In that area was a feast of targets, and U-boats could hunt within range of their own bases. To deal with this concentration of shipping, the Royal Navy adopted a strategy of sector patrols. Individual ships were not escorted—there were not enough naval vessels for that. Instead, in the tradition of offensive action, the foe was sought out and, if found, visually engaged and destroyed.

Hunting the hunters, however, did not solve the problem. As Mahan had said, patrol was like looking for a needle in a haystack. It was difficult enough to spot the U-boats on the surface. But it was even harder for lookouts to see a slender periscope or a narrow trail of bubbles or to discern an engine sound beneath the waves. In one week in September 1916, "three U-boats operated in the Channel between Beachy Head and the Eddystone Light, an area patrolled by forty-nine destroyers, forty-eight torpedo boats, seven Q-ships, and 468 auxiliaries—some 572 anti-submarine vessels in all, not counting aircraft." Those three submarines escaped the massive dragnet untouched and managed in that week to sink 30 ships and disrupt channel traffic.[10]

There was a further limit on Britain's ability to sustain the effort of war. Sea power in the form of shipping extends onto the docks. Britain needed more than the safe arrival of ships with essential supplies. It also had to get the ships unloaded swiftly and their goods distributed. This was a matter of domestic organization. Organization meant ordering the right goods and making the most efficient use of overloaded port and dock facilities. Every stage of the importing process required strong direction. This the British did not have in the first three years of the war.

In 1915 and 1916, port congestion was the most important limitation on the merchant fleet's carrying capacity. Martin Doughty concluded: "It is certainly clear that, in these years, losses of imports due to port difficulties considerably exceeded those due to enemy action in sinking British merchant ships. Even during the climax of the unrestricted submarine campaign in the early months of 1917, the Shipping Controller estimated that losses due to port delays closely approached those due to enemy action."[11] The important lesson here for maritime states is that maintenance of trade and transport across an ocean depends on more than sea control and keeping ships safe at sea.

In April 1917 the Germans thought they saw victory. General Erich Ludendorff, dominating the German war effort, predicted that if the U-boats maintained the April 1917 level of sinkings, Britain would sue for peace in five or six months. The highest echelon of the British government shared this assessment. Britain would be on its knees by August and unable to continue the war past October.[12] As Herbert Hoover said, "The situation was dangerous almost beyond description, and the anxiety in the whole of that period was terrific."[13]

To defeat the German strategy and to protect shipping, a better counterstrategy was needed. This was found in the venerable practice of convoy, a form of direct and strictly defensive sea control.[14]

Britain's Royal Navy had only a small number of destroyers available for this task. Half its destroyer force was screening the Grand Fleet. To lower this guard would imperil the main line of defense. The entry of the United States into the war promised assistance both with escorting and with maintaining the screen. U.S. assistance made it easier for the Admiralty to decide on April 30, 1917, to adopt the convoy strategy. U.S. warships filled the escort gap, and cobelligerency resolved the organizational problem of where to collect ships for transatlantic passage. The use of American ports made it possible to set specific schedules and assign places of assembly for the merchantmen. Their masters would then have a week's training in formation across the western Atlantic before they entered the danger zone.[15]

Convoying meant redefining sea control, giving up the assumption that the sea could be swept by battle or patrol. Convoy escorts sought to defend, not to destroy. "The two systems were alternatives, and no patrols were needed in areas through which the convoys sailed."[16] The object of escorts was to get the convoy through, not to sink U-boats. Escorts had to control only that part of the ocean over which the convoy was passing, and only for the time the cargo ships were using it. Escorts were concerned about the enemy only when U-boats immediately threatened their group of ships.

The transition between patrol and escort strategies, and the need of additional ships, is poignantly recorded in a British appeal to the United States made in early July 1917:

> The expectation is entertained that the convoy system, when in working order and provided that sufficient destroyers are available to form an effective screen, will serve to minimize losses. . . . But the method at present in use, viz., the employment of armed small craft in an attempt to prevent the submarines from using their periscopes for fear of an attack by ram or bomb, offers the only remedy for the next few months. The success of this method obviously depends on small craft being available in very large numbers and the critical character of the present situation is due to the fact that the forces of this nature at the disposal of the British Admiralty are not at present adequate for the work of protecting shipping in the danger zone. It is therefore of the utmost urgency that additional armed small craft should be made available for use in the area near the British and French coasts where the commercial routes converge.[17]

Sims spoke to Washington in the same terms. His message was simple, urgent, and anti-Mahanian. In the circumstance of the war *as it existed*, and for the purpose of the protection of shipping, the United States should send destroyers and submarine chasers to help the British in the North Atlantic. The ships were to be used first for patrol and then for escort. They were to be dispersed, not concentrated. The warships were to interact with shipping in treacherous waters, not simply wave shipping on over a victorious field. In the outcome of the struggle for shipping in the approaches to Great Britain, Sims declared, lay victory or defeat.

In Sims's view, if cooperation meant placing U.S. ships under British operational command to benefit from the experience and readiness of the Royal Navy, that was acceptable as the most effective way to fight the naval war. Nationalist pride should not stand in the way. As to the future, naval cooperation would lay the foundation for postwar collaboration. Then, said Sims, the United States would not have to worry so much about its strategic independence, for the country would not be alone in an anarchic postwar world.

Washington received Sims's views coolly. The administration and the

Department of the Navy rejected all contentions that "America's primary role was to provide unqualified assistance to the Royal Navy."[18] There were real differences between British and American naval policies. Before making an extended commitment, the very least that the Navy Department needed was a much clearer idea of the Admiralty's strategic and tactical plans. Of these it knew nothing.[19] On the other hand, officials were impressed with the seriousness of the British plight. Despite the United States's initial wariness about detaching destroyers for distant service, despite its reluctance to strip the Atlantic Fleet of protection it would need if the country found itself alone in the war (should Britain fold), the circumstances demanded some action. In the first week of belligerency, the U.S. Navy dispatched a flotilla of six destroyers to Ireland to be put under Admiralty command. Two dozen more soon followed. By July 1, 1917, 35 of the Navy's 52 modern destroyers were in or approaching European waters.

These ships were important in the Allied war at sea. Still, the Navy's *Return of the Mayflower*, as a popular painting of the first six destroyers steaming into British waters was titled, did not promise the same magnitude of support as did the Army's cry, "Lafayette, we are here!" and the subsequent arrival of 2 million U.S. soldiers in France. When Secretary of the Navy Daniels established a policy of "heartiest cooperation" with the Allies, he qualified it with the condition of maintaining "an adequate defense of our own home waters" and with a determination to keep the fleet undivided for postwar use. In July 1917, Daniels declared as naval policy the following requirement for the U.S. war effort: "While a successful termination of the present war must always be the first Allied aim and will probably result in diminished tension throughout the world, the *future* position of the United States *must in no way* be jeopardized by any disintegration of our main fighting fleets."[20] On unilateralism Daniels would not give an inch. The U.S. government was determined to fight an American war for American purposes, and to do so as it saw fit.

First, the battle fleet must be protected, and to that end a number of destroyers were kept on hand. Sims and the British Admiralty dismissed the possibility that U-boats would threaten the fleet off the east coast of the United States. Upon entering the war, however, CNO Benson could not ignore that possibility. As he said later, "My first thought at the beginning, during and always, was to see that first our coasts and our vessels and our own interests were safeguarded."[21] Benson did not know it, but an extension of the war zone westward to America was constantly under consideration in Berlin.[22]

Beyond that, who could say when the United States might need its fleet, and against whom? If the situation was as dire as Sims said, Britain might soon face defeat. All the destroyers in the U.S. arsenal might not be able to prevent that. Also, the British were vague about how many destroyers they wanted. Britain's record in antisubmarine warfare did not inspire confidence. Wilson thought the British lacked offensive spirit and were prone to making bad judgments. The president wrote to Sims on July 4, 1917: "In the presence of the present submarine emergency they are helpless to the point of panic. . . . In my view this is not a time for prudence but for boldness even at the cost of great losses. . . . The trouble is that their [the Admiralty's] plans do not seem to us to be very effective."[23] To Daniels the president wrote, "As you and I agreed the other day, the British Admiralty had done absolutely nothing constructive in the use of their navy and I think it is time we were making and insisting upon plans of our own even if we render some of the more conservative of our own naval advisors uncomfortable."[24] Instead of a patrol, or even a convoy system, Wilson thought the British should attack U-boat bases directly, or bottle the submarines up with mines. "We are hunting hornets all over the farm," Wilson told naval officers a month later, "and letting the nest alone."[25]

The analogy was weak. The president knew nothing of the difficulties of attacking German ports. Such attacks, with existing aircraft, were to prove unsuccessful when tried the following year. Sims pointed out the difficulties to him: "A sea attack alone upon German ports or any heavily fortified ports could not succeed against the concealed guns of modern defense."[26] But Wilson's complaint showed a concern that simply sending ships to Britain might not be enough. Behind it was the worry that if Britain went under, the United States would be left alone. In the Navy Department there was the specter of a renewed German threat, perhaps in conjunction with Japan. The Navy's insurance was its concentration of capital ships. Naval aid to the Allies came down to minor warships, those most useful in the war against the submarines. For the future, battleship power would be the guarantor of security and freedom of action, and nothing was done to diminish this or jeopardize the fighting capacity of the battle fleet.

With its insistence on independence and its sense of prospective as well as present naval danger, the United States placed little weight on the suggestion that the British should command American warships. Wilson and Benson did not share Sims's confidence that there would be a common interest once the war was over. Wilson said, "*England and France have not the same views with regard to peace that we have* by any means." The United States thus had to reserve its power for its own political goals.[27]

Daniels and Benson, as well as Benson's senior assistant Captain William V. Pratt and Admiral Henry Mayo, commander of the Atlantic Fleet, all had anticipated a British defeat. That led them in 1916 to reaffirm the battle-fleet doctrine as the basis of national defense. They continued to adhere to that doctrine when the United States entered the war the next year. The nature of the war, and Wilson's political purpose, however, gave the Navy missions of another kind for which it was not prepared: antisubmarine warfare, antisubmarine escort (convoy duty), coalition cooperation, and above all, the safe transport of American soldiers to France.

No use was found for the battle fleet. The battleship was no good against a submarine. The enemy fleet would not engage. No U.S. battleship fired a shot at an enemy battleship in this war. Force was dispersed in local patrol and escort duty. Defense of the Americas gave way to support of a land war in Europe. The Navy, traditionally proud of its position as the main agent of foreign policy, now took on the adjunctive mission of support of the Western Allies and of the American Army. Sea-power strategy became maritime strategy.

The lack of U.S. escorts, transports, and submarine hunters was felt as soon as the United States entered the war. "O for more destroyers! I wish we could trade the money in dreadnaughts for destroyers already built," Daniels wrote in April 1917.[28] To meet the need for troopships and destroyers, Pratt proposed that the Navy give up its 1916 building program.[29] It was not lost on the British that Wilson's concomitant buildup of a merchant marine fleet was part of his effort to improve America's standing as a trading nation and that an increase in transport vessels and cargo ships would shift comparative advantage in postwar merchant shipping to the United States.[30]

Pratt's recommendation was supported by Benson, Mayo, and Navy Secretary Daniels. On July 20, 1917, Daniels put the Naval Act of 1916 on hold. He ordered new battleship construction halted, and Congress agreed that some 200 more destroyers would be built beyond the 50 already authorized.[31] Because only a tiny fraction of these destroyers were completed during the war, the Navy, for escort and patrol in 1917 and 1918, relied on units from its existing force, on vessels from Allied navies, and on lesser craft such as converted yachts.

What the Navy needed was balance. Everyone agreed that more destroyers had to be built. The General Board counseled caution, however, warning against "disintegration" of the battle fleet. It wrote to

Daniels in August: "The battleship remains as heretofore the principal reliance of the sea power of a nation. . . . A new alignment of the powers after the present war must not find our fleet in all the types of vessels composing it, unprepared to meet possible enemies in the Atlantic and Pacific at liberty to act singly or jointly with all their naval powers against us." More of everything was needed—merchantmen and men-of-war, and battleships to lead them.[32] For most of the senior officers of the service, the needs of the present war, different though they were, had not rendered obsolete the doctrine of offensive war at sea.

MINES AND CONVOYS

The Navy proposed laying a minefield across the north end of the North Sea. The Americans were frustrated by what seemed to them an absence of British drive in antisubmarine warfare. In April 1917 the convoy system was still untried, its worth unknown. The idea of a mine barrier had immediate appeal. It would block U-boats' access to the Atlantic.

Germany was in a bad geographic position for a war at sea. If it was impossible for the Allies to catch the hornets or to destroy their nest, it might still be possible to seal them in the North Sea by stretching barriers across its exits. The principle also could be applied to the Mediterranean. Closing the Strait of Otranto would seal the Austro-Hungarian navy in the Adriatic Sea, and transit across the Mediterranean would be made safe too.

The mine project was popular for the same reason decisive battle was. Both promised a single and a simple solution. Both were methods of sea control based on metal instead of men. Both kept the war far from homeland waters. A North Sea mining operation could be kept largely in American hands. Daniels called the idea of the North Sea barrier "the most daring and original naval conception of the World War."[33] Until the convoy system got going, and convoy was primarily a British operation in any case, the mine barrier was a good hand to play.

The British did not share the American enthusiasm for the North Sea mine field. From the first proposal in April 1917 until its acceptance in principle in September, British officers, echoed by Sims, raised many objections. Laying the field was an enormous, perhaps insuperable, technical challenge. The gate would be 230 miles long—from the Orkney Islands to the territorial waters of neutral Norway—in deep and turbulent sea. Only a few mines were available, and those were of inferior quality. The new U.S. antenna mine was unproven. Ships for policing the barrier could not be spared from patrol elsewhere. The waters of neutral Norway constituted a gap. But the critics in the Admiralty were overruled on political grounds. When British Admiral David Beatty complained that the U.S. mines were unreliable and that unreliability characterized the barrier idea as a whole, the First Sea Lord, Admiral Rosslyn Wemyss, replied that acceptance of the plan was a quid pro quo. If Britain was to get support in its antisubmarine campaign, it had to go along with the Americans—with their enthusiasm, their mines, and their barriers.[34]

In March 1918, the British began laying mines in the portion of the North Sea field assigned to them. The Americans did not begin mining their section until June. Daniels wrote that "not laying the barrage earlier . . . was in my opinion the greatest naval error of the war."[35] In all, 70,263 mines were put down, 56,449 of them by the American squadron. To what effect? Four to six U-boats were sunk and several more damaged, "an insignificant return for the vast expenditure of materiel."[36] The barrier may have had some deterrent effect, but the evidence is impressionistic. Too far from German ports to be swept by German ships, the mine field was a permanent, but permeable, barrier. It did increase the risk of putting submarines to sea. It did not, however, as Daniels claimed, shatter the German crews' morale. The Germans could, for instance, in the absence of hostile patrols, skirt the barrier along the Norwegian coast. The barrier did not stop U-boat transit, but it did slow the traffic down. The Germans had to take the risk into account, monitor the field, and find the gaps, and Germany had no ships to spare. The mine field's deterrent effect would have been greater had the war lasted longer because there would then have been more time to improve the field. The barrier, however, was never completed, its gaps were never adequately patrolled, and many of the mines were defective. In this respect, as in others, the armistice in November 1918 stopped the momentum of the U.S. war effort just as it hit its stride.[37]

It was not the mine field that defeated the German submarine strategy, nor the destroyers on patrol. It was the convoys under escort that gave back to the Allies their use of the sea and permitted the replenishment of Britain and the American Expeditionary Forces in France. The convoy system beat the German U-boats, in both the Mediterranean and the Atlantic. And in this the U.S. Navy played an important, if secondary, role.

Cooperation with Britain in Atlantic and Mediterranean patrols and in escort duty with the convoys certainly assisted an ally in great distress. At the end of the war, 79 of the U.S. Navy's 107 destroyers were in European waters, with the detachments in Ireland and Gibraltar aiding a British destroyer force of around 400 ships. In an unprecedented division of the Atlantic Fleet, the Navy sent a squadron of five of the best U.S. coal-burning battleships to join the British Grand Fleet in the North Sea, and then moved them to Ireland. These ships were older than the oil burners, but they could draw on Britain's coal resources when oil was scarce. The canon of concentration was discarded to free some British warships from fleet duty and to encourage a more aggressive antisubmarine campaign. The worldwide dimension of the war was indirectly expressed in this dispatch of the U.S. battleship squadron to British waters. Division of the fleet was possible only because improved relations with Japan had reduced concern about the Pacific.[38]

The convoy system involved a tremendous amount of organization, conceived and administered by British shipping commands under the strategic direction of the Admiralty. Merchantmen were assembled in key ports abroad, kept together as they steamed across the Atlantic (or through the Mediterranean and up from Gibraltar, or off Scandinavia), kept away from U-boats known to British intelligence, brought to rendezvous with their escorts in the danger zone, moved into port, unloaded, and turned around. By the end of 1917, nearly 50 percent of the total British overseas trade was in convoy, and the proportion rose to 90 percent by the war's end. Of the 95,000 ships convoyed in the war, only 393 were lost.[39]

Despite early talk of using the convoy offensively, to attract U-boats so the destroyers could make a kill, a position favored by Jellicoe and Sims, the convoy acted more as a deterrent than as a magnet. Submarines avoided the concentration of escorts and instead sought out single targets so that they would have time to surface, fire, and reload in safety. The principle was this: In a convoy system, as Arthur Marder wrote, "*sinking submarines is a bonus, not a necessity.*"[40]

It helped, of course, when submarines were sunk. And as it turned out, convoy escorts sank as many of them as did destroyers on patrol. Also, when the U-boats, finding the oceans emptied of individual ships, went after inshore traffic, it was easier for patrols to get at them. In September 1917, ten U-boats were sunk. That month, loss exceeded German construction for the first time. Down with the boats went experienced commanders. The transfer of many seasoned officers from idle capital ships to submarine duty had already weakened the High Seas Fleet. Now, the deaths of the transferred commanders simultaneously undercut the German undersea campaign and the battle fleet's capacity to act.[41]

In engagement with submarines, the U.S. role was minor. The British were credited with 90 percent of the U-boats sunk, the Americans with only 5 percent.

The main purpose of the convoy was to establish safe use of the ocean. This it did, defeating the German strategy of exhausting the Allies within six months (the German target had been August 1917). German destruction of Allied tonnage in April 1917 was never matched after the convoys started in May. High losses did continue: sinkings during the last six months of 1917 averaged 392,000 gross tons of Allied merchant shipping (including 250,000 gross tons of British shipping) per month.[42] But the figures also showed a steady long-term decline that was attributable to the convoys.

Through a periscope, a convoy of fifteen cargo ships was not much more visible than a single freighter. For a hunter moving alone (the wolf pack did not appear until World War II), the convoy in an empty ocean was hard to find. Short of quarry, discouraged, and reluctant to attack a protected cargo fleet, the U-boats moved to inshore waters. There, against ships sailing alone, they sank 85 percent of the tonnage lost between November 1917 and October 1918. There, however, they also were exposed to patrols and mines, and to Allied submarines, which became, by late in the war, their most deadly antagonists.

By the end of 1917, it was evident that the German strategy of offensive unrestricted submarine warfare had failed. Germany had lost its gamble for a quick victory. Even so, the Germans kept it up. The U-boat campaign continued throughout the war months of 1918 and was extended to U.S. waters in May. The Germans added bigger boats, but they never found a way to overcome the convoy defense. More and more effort and cost were required to sink fewer and fewer ships. Neutrals were not frightened away from the shipping lanes. Most important, the German strategy provoked the greatest neutral to enter the war.

And the Western powers began to recover their losses. Replacements for sunk merchantmen were on the way. Civil administration in Britain orchestrated smooth movement through British ports. Germany had not forced a decision at sea and had not wholeheartedly tried to. Had Germany pushed its initial advantage harder, had it deployed a larger U-boat force, perhaps the outcome would have been different. There are too many variables for this speculation to lead to a conclusion. Nevertheless, Arthur Hezlet reminds us of the value of thinking flexibly about maritime strategies: "The defeat of the U-boat was not because the *guerre de course* could not by its nature be decisive: it was because the

Allies were able to be strong everywhere and make a gigantic effort."[43] It *was* a gigantic effort, and it paid off, although it was not the war that Mahan, or the German emperor, had foreseen.

TRANSPORT AND SUPPLY

In the war the main job of the U.S. Navy was to transport a national army across the ocean to the western front in France, get it there safely, and keep it supplied. On the land in Europe, not on the sea, lay Germany's center of gravity, and it was on the land, not on the sea, that the United States had to establish its position.

Wilson's purpose was to win the peace. For this he had to win the war. Independent and substantial participation would give him authority at the peace conference. Action on the western front was Wilson's continental imperative.[44] And the instrument of his policy, the U.S. Army, was to be self-sustained. Its commander, General John J. Pershing, said, "For all practical purposes the American Expeditionary Forces were based on the American Continent."[45] Conveying those troops safely was the Navy's top priority and keeping them supplied its second. It was "an undertaking of a magnitude without parallel in all history."[46]

In 1917, the Navy had been entirely unprepared for this mission. A battle force was asked to become the ferry to France. The service whose doctrine declared that navies exist only to fight other navies built and ran a reinforcement line for the Army. The Navy exchanged Mahan for logistics. Instead of deploying for decisive engagement, the U.S. Navy carried 6 million tons of cargo, a further 1.5 million tons of coal, and 0.7 million tons of fuel oil and gasoline. And with British help, it ferried 2 million American soldiers across the ocean and back again. "Our total effort in the war," said Pratt, "consisted less in the operations of forces at the front than in a logistic effort on the rear, in which the greatest problems we had to contend with originated and had to be solved here at home."[47]

It was a joint Army-Navy effort. "The Army organized and developed an efficient system for loading and unloading the ships at the terminal points. The Navy transported the troops and safeguarded them en route."[48] The semiofficial historians of this enterprise, Benedict Crowell and Robert Wilson, entitled their work on the transport of troops and supplies *The Road to France* and divided it into three parts: "The Land," "The Port," and "The Sea."[49] Each section of the transport operation demanded a separate and complete organization as well as coordination with the other sections. According to Crowell and Wilson, the operation was "a vast and perfectly ordered machine! . . . There was never a malfunction of crucial importance; never a grave slip-up. Its capacity for handling men seemed to have no limit."[50]

The transportation story is indeed a wonderful success. Yet it took a while for Britain to organize its shipping, and the same was true for the United States. There were shortfalls and lessons to be learned. The Army never matched its plans for troop transport with a plan to supply the requisite matériel. Concentration on the moving of soldiers led to a shortfall of some 35 percent in the supplies needed by the men in France at the time of the armistice. The existing organization at port facilities could not have handled the tripling of required daily output if the war had gone on an additional year or two and U.S. Army forces in Europe had reached 4 or 4.5 million men. Nor was there ocean shipping enough for the logistical support of the 2 million men already there. In 1918, "to serve a 100-per cent troop fleet, we had a 60-per cent cargo fleet."[51]

When the United States entered the war, no one had decided how big the expeditionary army was to grow, whether animal and mechanical freight should accompany the troops or be shipped separately on cargo vessels, how to balance ships between transporting men and supplies, how to organize port and inland facilities for moving troops, beasts, and equipment at both ends of the voyage, and so on. Lessons come from experience. The wonder is how well the Army and the Navy did so much in so short a time.

Until more ships were built, the Navy took whatever hulls it could find. Cargo ships were commandeered, some German liners in U.S. ports were impounded, and then, to reverse the German spring offensive in 1918—an action itself undertaken to end the war before the U.S. troops arrived en masse—British passenger liners arrived to help carry the men. By the end of the war, the Navy's Cruiser and Transport Force consisted of 24 cruisers and 42 transports, and the Naval Overseas Transport Service ran a cargo fleet of 453 ships. In its mission of troop transport, the U.S. Navy carried to Europe 46 percent of the 2,079,880 American soldiers who were in France in November 1918. It transported over half of these in converted German liners.

In response to the German thrust westward in March 1918, the stream of men from the United States became a flood. U.S. tonnage was not sufficient to carry them. Only the British had the additional capacity needed, and British ships doubled the carrying load. A million and a half soldiers were rushed to Europe during the six months of the spring and summer of 1918. The figure for July was 306,350, an average of

10,000 men per day. Overall, 49 percent of all the soldiers transported during the war sailed in British ships, mainly to British ports, as did a large percentage of the supplies. Without British assistance the U.S. force in France would have been only half as large as it was. Conversely, if the United States had not marshaled its own Army-Navy operation so successfully, its strategic mission might well have failed, with "fatal effect upon the war."[52]

Moving the American Expeditionary Forces across the ocean was an Allied triumph. Germany's worst fear was realized: it had not won the war before the Americans arrived. Nor could Germany continue the war afterward. So German leaders sued for peace. Pershing wrote, "When the Armistice was signed all projects for construction had been completed and supplies were on hand to meet the needs of 2,000,000 men, while further plans for necessary construction and for the supply of an additional 2,000,000 were under way."[53] U.S. troops had made the difference. Getting them there and keeping them supplied was the Navy's main contribution to victory.

And it got them there safely. Of the 1,720,360 soldiers transported in ships that were escorted by U.S. men-of-war, not one was lost to enemy attack or to mishap at sea. (Several hundred men were lost in eastward transit in ships not under American escort, and a few unladen ships were sunk on the westward return.) Imagine, Pratt reflected, what would have been the effect on national morale and on the war effort if the Germans had sunk a vessel like the *Leviathan* (formerly the German liner *Vaterland*), with a loss of 14,000 American lives.[54] The insistence on safety saved lives. It also maintained public confidence in the Navy and in the national cause.

Protection means escorts, and these were in short supply. The new destroyers were not ready, their construction having been authorized only in July 1917, the month the first troop convoy arrived in France. Ships gradually came in, however, from the 1915 and 1916 programs. By November 1918, 33 new destroyers had gone on duty in the war zone. Meanwhile, most of the Navy's cruisers were given escort work. Toward the end of the war, a few older battleships were added, a largely symbolic gesture because they were effective only against surface raiders (which were no longer a threat) and were of no use against U-boats (to which they might become tempting targets). To pick up convoys off France, 85 assorted ships were based at Brest, forming the largest group of American combatant ships overseas. To fill the need for transport protection, ships from the destroyer force in Queenstown (now Cobh), Ireland, on patrol with the Royal Navy, were called into escort duty. As

Daniels told Sims: "The paramount duty of the destroyers in European waters is principally the proper protection of transports with American troops. Be certain to detail an adequate convoy of destroyers and in making the detail bear in mind that everything is secondary to having a sufficient number to insure protection to American troops."[55]

Admiral Sims thought Washington's emphasis on troopship protection was misguided. British merchant shipping was what needed protection, and to that end he opposed the withdrawal of ships that were in waters around the islands. It made better strategic sense, Sims argued, to let troopships on their way to Brest simply outrun the submarines or get help from the French navy. The convoy artery of the U.S. troop transports was well below the channel's western approaches, where the U-boats lay. U-boats did not operate easily in the shallow waters south of Brest. They were far from home in that area. In strictly military terms, the German advantage lay in attacking cargo headed for Britain, not Americans en route to France.[56] An aide to Sims, John Leighton, bluntly stated the view of Sims's staff and of the Admiralty: "The slogan the 'Navy brought 'em over' is of minor importance. What the Navy did was to keep the Allies and their armies from starving."[57]

But in Washington's view, two nonnegotiable purposes were at stake: passage and safety. On these Wilson planned to base his postwar claims. In this regard, the United States had its own goal and its own strategy, and they differed from Britain's. Captain Pratt in Washington as the CNO's senior policy adviser pointed out to Sims in London that "the impelling reason of the British was protection to food and war supplies in transit. Our basic reason was protection to our own military forces in crossing the seas."[58]

In World War I, the United States used the Navy to maintain its strategic independence. As it turned out, that was easy. David Trask, in an important interpretation, showed that on the major issues, the Americans and the other Allied powers agreed: "During 1917–1918 the United States accepted the basic strategic decision of the European Allies—both on land and sea." The defeat of Germany—the precondition of Wilson's postwar political objectives—was to be achieved through "concentrating land power in France and by concentrating naval power against the enemy submarines in the Atlantic and the Mediterranean."[59] A shared strategy for victory did not threaten Wilson's postwar objectives. Defeat of Germany was a precondition of the settlement he wanted. Agreement on strategic views simply made wartime collaboration easier. In the future, Wilson would have a freer hand.

Differences of opinion regarding how much escort should be allotted to troop transports as opposed to cargo ships turned out to be differences of emphasis, not strategy. The Navy's long-standing concern over preparing for a fleet challenge from Japan, from Germany, or even from Great Britain was deferred until the war was over. The view of an isolated and beleaguered future, however, was not uniform. Sims and Pratt said that conflict with Britain was not necessary and that the postwar U.S. Navy might be configured for cooperation with the Royal Navy.

But neither the operational nor the political experiences of the short eighteen months of U.S. participation in the war caused the leaders of the Navy to alter their fundamental prewar position. By and large, the Navy treated its World War I missions as unusual and incomplete. Navy planners in 1918 doubted that the end of hostilities would usher in an era of peace. The Mahanian challenge lay ahead. In the postwar world, competition would continue, and in a world of powerful fleets, the battleship Navy and the strategy of offensive sea control would remain the nation's sword and buckler. Navies would still exist to fight other navies.

5

Parity and Proportion
1919-1922

AGAINST WHOM AND WITH WHAT?

At the end of 1918 the Navy's doctrine and its battleships remained intact and unused. The Navy did not reevaluate its battle doctrine in light of its wartime experience, and it reverted at once to prewar plans. The General Board in Washington and the Planning Section sitting in London recommended resumption of the deferred construction of capital ships. Of the eight authorized in 1916, only one keel had yet been laid. In the month before the armistice, in October 1918, the General Board proposed a second three-year building schedule, which would include construction of a mix of 28 additional battleships and battle cruisers to establish far and away the world's strongest sea force. Of these, the administration cut the battleships to 16, but this still doubled the number authorized in 1916 and aimed at the same goal: parity with, or even superiority over, Britain. With a strong navy, as President Wilson said, the country could do as it wished.

A big navy, then, was to serve the country's greatness. What mission it might take on, against whom it might sail, and in what sort of operation, were not known. There were, however, strong navies out there. That was what needed to be kept in mind.

To American naval officers, there seemed no reason, in the peace settlement after the war, for the United States to abjure its goal of parity with the world's largest navy. The nation was coming into its maritime destiny. The fleet must be commensurate with the country's great-power status. Naval strength gave the United States strategic independence. It also assured respectful attention to President Wilson's plans for peace.

For conceptually, as David Trask wrote, "The outcome of the war had vastly enlarged the horizons of naval expansionist thought among those in the London Planning Section."[1] In addition to deducing the usual national interests—security of the continent, free trade, the Monroe Doctrine, the Open Door in China—Navy thinking in the Planning Section reflected a Wilsonian sense of American exceptionalism and world mission:

> We have taken the lead in certain world policies. We have been able to do this through the known unselfishness of our motives and chiefly through the sudden rise in importance of our naval and military power. We are interested in seeing the growth everywhere of American ideals of international justice and fair dealing. There is no surer way of furthering this growth than in providing diplomacy with the sanction of a naval power that by reason of its greatness will be fearless.[2]

Fearlessness, and freedom to act, meant acquiring a naval force equal to that of the world's greatest navy. With a fleet the size of Britain's, other adversaries could be faced in turn. Sea power meant holding to the most demanding standard, and that was the Royal Navy. As Norman Friedman wrote, a fleet "nominally at parity with Britain could deal with Japan, whereas nominal parity with Japan would mean defeat in the Western Pacific."[3] The strong Navy could turn against either. Similarity of doctrine and of force structure among the major navies of the world meant that superiority could be defined as a function of naval construction.

Britain, however, was the proximate rival. After the war, said Sir William Wiseman, the British expert on American affairs, only two great powers would remain, and he posed a question: "Which is going to be the greater, politically and commercially?"[4]

The American claim to parity seemed to the British only an arithmetical camouflage for strategic advantage. The Royal Navy was stretched by worldwide commitments. Serious involvement in any quarter would drastically reduce its power in the others. Against this dispersed force, the United States could concentrate its fleet. "'Parity' between powers in such different circumstances was meaningless. Equality of fleets meant the granting of strategic superiority to the United States."[5]

No one held more firmly to the belief that maritime commerce and naval power were the interdependent pillars of American security and prosperity, and that only Britain could shake them, than Admiral William Benson, who remained chief of naval operations until September 1919. The country, he said in 1919, was "on the threshold of the keenest and most active commercial competition that the world has ever seen." A year later, as head of the U.S. Shipping Board, Benson saw his mission as one of leading, in the words of Secretary of War Newton Baker, a "fierce and final competition" with Britain for the world's trade.[6] Wilson agreed and wrote in 1920, "It is evident to me that we are on the eve of a commercial war of the severest sort, and I am afraid that Great Britain will prove capable of as great commercial savagery as Germany has displayed for so many years in her competitive methods."[7]

Such thoughts came easily to minds steeped in sea-power notions of struggle and rank. In the zero-sum world of mercantilist commerce and symmetrical naval doctrines, a state could rank number one or number two. And with maritime economic competition came the prospect of naval war. A naval staff memorandum forwarded to the president in April 1919 described the problem: "Every commercial rival of the British Empire has eventually found itself at war with Great Britain—and has been defeated. . . . We are setting out to be the greatest commercial rival of Great Britain on the sea."[8] A fleet report of January 1919 foretold the strategy: "The best way to destroy commerce is not to attack it directly, but first to destroy the forces that defend it. . . . The principal objective is the destruction of the enemy's main force."[9]

No one in the U.S. delegation to the Paris Peace Conference trusted in British goodwill. Outside the delegation, only Rear Admiral William Sims and Captain William Pratt, who, until January 1919, when he was ordered to sea duty, had been Benson's main assistant for policy, argued that wartime cooperation could continue. They approved of parity but thought that rivalry was not necessary. The two countries had compatible interests. The United States could be satisfied and safe, they said, with a Navy second to none.

Neither Benson, Secretary Daniels, nor President Wilson held this sanguine view. That is why they excluded Sims from the naval advisory staff they took to Paris.[10] A clash of national interests, they thought, would override the fraternity of shared victory. The British no longer had to concentrate their forces in home waters. And Britain had allies.

Who was Britain building against, except the United States? The same question was asked increasingly of Japan. Japan had been a British ally since 1902. It was moving outward in the Pacific, now holding the formerly German-controlled islands north of the equator—the Marianas, the Carolines, and the Marshalls. France and Italy were still allied with Britain. The numbers spelled trouble.

Military officers must think of a foreign state's capacity to do harm. The immense Royal Navy had to be taken seriously. Capacity, however, is not the same as political reality. Hence it is only part of strategy. In 1919 no one wanted war with the United States, certainly not Britain.

Still, it was naval capacity, the force of the fleet, that Wilson intended to put in his service. On that strength Wilson wanted to establish an international order that would lead to the limitation of arms. Whether one approved of the goal (as did Sims's friend and Benson's assistant Captain Pratt) or disapproved (as did Benson, for whom all was unbridled competition), the Navy was part of Wilson's semicoercive diplomacy, its ships stakes on the negotiating table.

So Wilson sought parity for political leverage and held to his construction program, threatening to build beyond parity to force Britain into compliance with his new international order. By the same token he gave Congress a stark alternative: either accept the League of Nations or the United States would have to go it alone. The only alternative to the League was an endless, expensive competition in naval arms.

Even if the League of Nations was established, the United States would need a great navy. The League must not be dominated by a single power. Without a countervailing force, the British, with the largest navy, could turn the League to their own interests. For instance, they might, under cover of enforcing some League resolution, violate the Monroe Doctrine. Therefore, for an effective League, for "the reign of law among nations," as the naval advisers grandly put it, British and U.S. naval power had to be balanced.[11] Hence the building proposals submitted by the administration in 1919 for ten more battleships and six more battle cruisers; hence the continued focus on Britain.

The British were at a loss to oppose the looming sea-power challenge. The U.S. battleship buildup—the program of 1916 and the more ambitious proposal submitted to Congress in 1919—was obviously directed against them. Conversely, of course, the Americans claimed that the British kept up their force level solely to oppose the U.S. Navy.

Daniels justified the U.S. claim to parity on the grounds of defensive responsibilities. American trade routes, he told Prime Minister David Lloyd George at the peace conference, were even more expansive than Britain's. As proof, Daniels displayed the maps reproduced overleaf.

"That is preposterous," Lloyd George retorted, according to Daniels. "You are a self-contained republic with no large empire. . . . Do you mean to say that your country dominates Mexico, Central America, and all South America?" Daniels denied that was his meaning, but that is what the maps showed and what he meant. Daniels was serious. To secure its regional position, League or no League, the United States intended to have parity and control the seas of the western hemisphere.[12]

The British were outraged. American overseas trade and responsibilities were not at all comparable to Britain's enormous empire, with its far more numerous, populous, and extensive territories, and its much more vital commercial connections. Lloyd George declared he would spend the government's last guinea to maintain the Royal Navy's superiority. Time after time he asked the Americans to acknowledge Britain's special position. Why this insistence on parity?, British statesmen asked. Britain was not the enemy. And if the Americans were so interested in arms limitation, why did they keep building? A naval race would ruin the League. Arms limitation must come first, then the League.

But for the United States it was the other way around. The League's viability depended on offsetting British power. Parity was a prior condition. So went the tug and pull over sea power in the spring of 1919 in Paris.

The messy situation got worse in early April 1919, when Lloyd George stipulated that an end to this naval rivalry was the condition for his agreement to include the Monroe Doctrine in the League's Covenant.[13] Britain would accept that limit to the League's universality only if the United States dropped its proposed naval construction and acknowledged Britain's position as the superior power at sea.

Gaining formal approval of the Monroe Doctrine as part of the Covenant was very important to Wilson. The goal of excluding European military force from the western hemisphere, so baldly portrayed in Daniels's maps, was a major feature of Wilson's assertive foreign policy. Sea power was the military instrument. So the administration insisted on recognition of both U.S. regional supremacy and U.S. naval strength.

Both sides realized it was foolish to push their argument too far. Britain did not threaten American security; the United States did not threaten the British empire.[14] The British could not afford an arms race that had no serious political purpose. Already they had stopped construction of capital ships. Nor was Wilson's position solid. In a Senate eager to return to normalcy and avoid involvement overseas, legislators

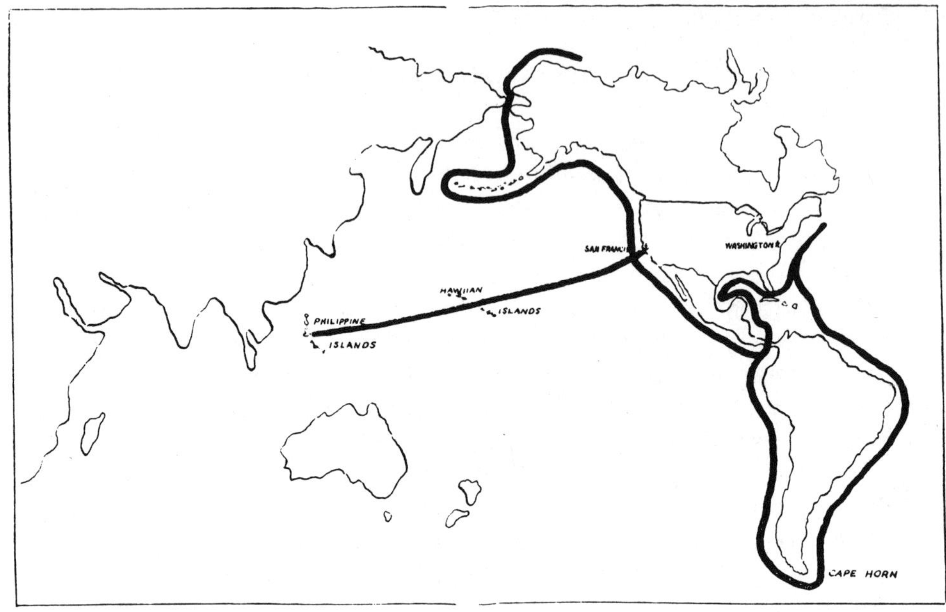

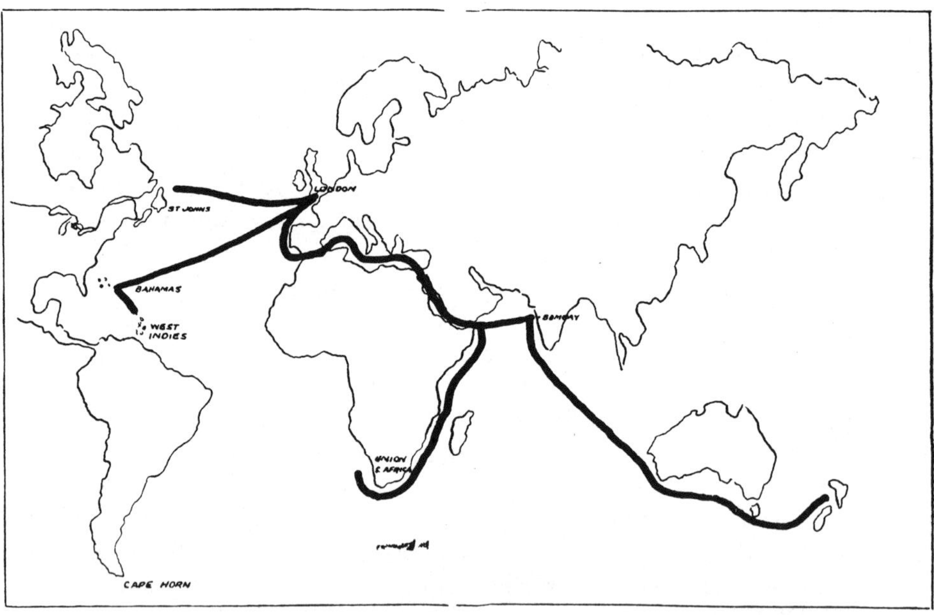

A comparison of U.S. and British naval defensive responsibilities. Reproduced from Josephus Daniels, *The Wilson Era: Years of War and After, 1917–1923* (Chapel Hill: University of North Carolina Press, 1946), p. 379.

had refused to approve the supplemental naval authorization for sixteen more battleships. The United States could still make good its claim to parity by fulfilling the deferred authorization of 1916, but it was time for a truce.

The British conceded Wilson the League and endorsed the Monroe Doctrine as part of it. Formally they received nothing in return. The administration refused their request to "abandon or modify" the supplementary building program proposed for 1919 and refused to change plans for the construction already authorized in the program of 1916. Still, Wilson and Daniels acknowledged the British concern. They withdrew their support for the 1919 program's sixteen new capital ships. Although the evidence is scant, both men no doubt wished to respond to the British concession. Wilson had what he wanted, the League incorporating the Monroe Doctrine. Also, the administration wished to avoid a struggle on Capitol Hill for the supplementary authorization, which it might lose. To this extent there was a certain phoniness about Wilson's position. The administration's 1919 program seemed unlikely to be passed by Congress. The 1916 program, in fact, was the real target of the British arms limitation effort. That, already authorized, was what they wanted the United States to "abandon or modify," and that program stood. Thus so did the American quest for parity. And therefore so did Anglo-American naval rivalry.

Some way around an arms race had to be found. The British government regarded the United States as a friend, not a potential enemy. There was no reason to continue this hostility over naval forces. Political will sought a political solution and found it in arms control.

A diplomatic solution was all the more appropriate because the U.S. Navy and the administration could not use commercial competition to justify further expansion of the fleet. Sea-power arguments, strong within the service, were not accepted outside it. Congress did not view economic competition with Britain, however serious or protracted, or some possible future trouble with Japan, as warranting a doubling of the capital-ship force. Hardly had the war ended, therefore, when the Navy's expansion plans died in the water. The administration was enfeebled by Wilson's incapacitation after a massive stroke in October 1919 and by defeats in Congress. Within the Navy Department there were still unresolved disputes about what constituted a balanced fleet. How were airplanes and submarines to be put to offensive use? How were the revived values of defensive sea control, the use of destroyers in direct ship protection, to be applied, given the battle-fleet doctrine? After the Paris Peace Conference, the Navy had not convinced the secretary, the president, Congress, the public, or itself that the country truly needed a massive enlargement of the capital-ship fleet.

ATLANTIC OR PACIFIC?

Captain Harry Yarnell, a key member of the CNO's Planning Division during this period, noted in April 1919 that "(a) We have no enemy in view. (b) We have no war plan to meet the enemy, even if we had one in view." War planning was, he said, like "trying to design a machine tool without knowing whether it is going to manufacture hairpins or locomotives."[15]

During the war Navy secretary Daniels had relied on two planning groups: his advisory General Board and the Planning Section on duty with Admiral Sims in London. At Paris he used the staff sent to the peace conference. The members of these groups all were Atlanticists by circumstance, tradition, and inclination. Each was concerned first with Britain, whether as friend or as foe.

War games at the Naval War College focused on the "vital factors of material superiority" of Britain. In these games, Britain was color-coded "Red." Recent experience, customary rivalry, and ample information made Red cases particularly accessible. Red games helped keep alive the idea that the Royal Navy posed a possible threat. Although these exercises at Newport reflected instructional convenience and not the prospect of use, they did reinforce the Navy's attention on the Atlantic.[16]

At the same time there was a shift in force and focus toward the Pacific. In 1919 the Navy Department consolidated planning in a Planning Division within the Office of Naval Operations. This division reported within the service, not to a political appointee. It was separate from the secretary's advisory General Board. It soon replaced the two Atlanticist planning groups—the London Planning Section and the peace conference staff—which were disbanded at the end of the war. Almost immediately the Operations planners presented the chief of naval operations, Admiral Robert E. Coontz, with two conclusions: (1) Japan was the United States's most probable foe, and (2) the development of a Pacific strategy should be the Navy's highest priority. For the next twenty years, the major problem of the U.S. Navy was what to do about Japan.

During the war, Japan's alliance with Britain as part of the anti-German coalition had muted concern about its expansion in the Pacific. The Navy Department put War Plan Orange on hold. Once the war was over, however, Navy attention turned again to Japan's proximity to the Philippines, to the possibility that Japan might establish an exclusionary position in China, and to the strategic meaning of Japan's new island holdings in the Pacific, the former German colonies. Japan was still in alliance with Great Britain. Together they might collude to exclude the United States from China, and a war resulting from U.S. military pressure against Japan might involve the British in some way as well.

Secretary Daniels's first move, in the spring of 1919, was to divide the Navy's main fighting force. Departing from the dictate of concentration, the Navy created two equal battle fleets, one in the Atlantic and one in the Pacific. The latter was based near Los Angeles to control the approach to the west coast. Daniels had various reasons for inaugurating what he called this "new epoch." One was to warn Japan not to move beyond the former German islands of Micronesia. Another was to satisfy calls for protection that were coming from residents of the west coast.

Proponents of concentration called the division strategically unsound, the result of domestic political pressure, not of military wisdom. Others said it was a bootless provocation of Japan. Rear Admiral Sims, for instance, held that Japan would be more impressed by a single, well-trained grand fleet, regardless of where it was located, and he thought the fleet should stay in the Atlantic. Daniels stuck to his decision. Two years later the Navy restructured the operational commands. If there was a threat of war, the fleets would go under a single commander. In 1921 the idea of two equal fleets was dropped. That year the Navy moved its ten most powerful battleships to the Pacific Fleet. With them, the balance of U.S. naval power moved to the Pacific, toward Japan.[17]

How the two fleets were to be used and for what purpose became the subject of a debate that lasted for twenty years. The ships had not been reassigned as part of national policy toward Japan. Nor did their movement constitute a strategy for the Pacific.

For the officers in the new Planning Division of the Office of Naval Operations, however, the 1919 division of the battle force between the Atlantic and the Pacific was a start. Next they proposed rounding out the fleet. They wanted more battleships to meet the Japanese surface fleet and more cruisers and a supplemental array of aircraft carriers, submarines, and support ships for the broadest range of naval action across the world's greatest ocean.

The Office of Naval Operations had developed a plan of campaign that went beyond the projection of an autonomous, long-legged battle fleet to the western Pacific. Its key was the establishment of a set of fortified island bases, strongpoints at Pearl Harbor, on Guam, and in the

Philippines. If these bases were impregnable, safe havens from which an offensive operation could be launched, they would deter any eastward aggression because a Japanese force could not pass them without exposing its flanks and rear. Should war come, the island bases would serve as mid-Pacific relay points for forces moving westward, forces whose job would be to seize Japanese islands as part of the offensive envisioned in War Plan Orange. At some point there would be a decisive naval engagement, followed by a close blockade to cut off imports to the vulnerable Japanese home islands.[18]

The Navy, however, found it hard to translate campaign ideas into strategy. The problem was summed up in 1919 when the Joint Army-Navy Board was reconstituted. The board, like the Operations planners, favored a Pacific emphasis. It reexamined War Plan Orange. But it needed political guidance. Captain Harry Yarnell, one of the naval members of the board's planning committee, said the board could not plan without a national policy. What were the country's interests in the Far East? If it came to war with Japan, did U.S. interests require complete defeat of the enemy, or a limited and perhaps only defensive war? Was it too costly to try to hold the Philippines? "These questions," Yarnell wrote, "are not for the War and Navy Departments to answer, but for the State Department."[19]

No help came from State, or from the president. Wilson was ill and removed from political leadership in the last months of 1919 and at the beginning of 1920. He was not interested in naval matters. The new chief of naval operations, Admiral Robert Coontz (CNO November 1919–July 1923), hoped to use his staff's plan to establish a "Navy point of view," so that officers could go before Congress "all of one decided opinion" and argue for an expansion of the fleet from a unified position.[20] Such unanimity probably would not have helped, even if it had been possible. Congress was not buying further commitment to the Pacific. A threat from Japan was too speculative to justify construction of expensive fortifications and additional ships. The war plan depended finally on support from American diplomats. But that was withheld as well. The State Department was not concerned about Japan's acquisitions in Micronesia. It was true that the Marianas, the Marshalls, and the Carolines lay athwart the route to the Philippines and that undefended Guam and the central telegraph exchange at Yap were in their midst. But the Japanese held the three island groups under League of Nations mandate, and under this arrangement the islands were to remain unfortified. As the diplomats saw it, that was enough. Freedom of the seas was not at risk.

Furthermore, when Secretary Daniels went to Congress for the appropriations hearings early in 1920 and presented a request based on the Operations staff's Pacific plan, he could not pretend, as head of the department, that the request represented a Navy consensus. For when Daniels spoke as Wilson's secretary, he slipped into the Atlanticist position, which was still based on the tired and hapless claim that the United States required a greatly expanded fleet if it stayed out of the League of Nations. That argument did not move Congress, which noted that the Navy spoke with several tongues. It was of no help to Daniels that during the very time of his testimony, in a separate hearing before a Senate panel, Rear Admiral Sims was accusing him of incompetence and irresponsibility in leaving the Navy unprepared for war in 1917.

Congress and the country were set on demobilization and economy. The idea of a strong naval force in the service of collective security died when the Senate rejected American membership in the League. Afterward no one supported the administration's position that independence from the League required an independent force. No one outside the Navy Department viewed Britain or Japan as threats sufficient to justify an enlarged building program. It seemed to Congress that all the Navy really wanted was more ships, even though the various voices within the Navy could not agree on why they were needed. So in 1920 Congress gave the Navy nothing for new bases, nothing for fortifications in the Pacific, nothing for more battleships, and nothing to round out the fleet. As far as Congress was concerned, the Navy neither had an acceptable strategic plan nor needed one.

THE WASHINGTON TREATIES

The question of what to do about the Navy was political, and through politics it was resolved. The new president, Warren Harding, took the lead, inspired by the plans of his Secretary of State, Charles Evans Hughes. The goal of Harding and Hughes was to reduce the threat of war, not to prepare to win one. In the preparation of the U.S. program, Secretary Hughes rejected the Navy's advice and the Navy's strategic assessment of the Pacific. At the Washington Conference of 1921–22, naval and military officers were excluded from every country's delegation except Japan's.

As we saw, the Navy had been making its own assessments. Right after Harding's inauguration, CNO Coontz asked Hughes to give the Navy "a general confidential statement of our national policies in the Pacific."[21] Hughes did not reply. So, naturally, the Navy continued to think in terms of the customary policies of the Open Door, the integrity of China, control of the Philippines and Guam, and the force that would be needed for a struggle for Pacific supremacy. It was for these goals that the Navy moved the bulk of its battle fleet to the west coast in 1921.

It was just at that point, in mid-1921, that Secretary of State Hughes deployed diplomacy instead of the battleships. At the Washington Conference he gave the Navy a radically changed national policy and a new framework for force planning. This was not at all what the General Board or the Planning Division had expected. Its officers by and large deplored the results. To Navy critics of the Washington Conference and of its successor, the London Naval Arms Limitation Conference of 1930, the decades of what became known as the "Washington system" and the "treaty Navy" were years of strategic drift and dangerous vulnerability in which a gutted force could not back declared national policy.

President Harding called the Washington Conference to avoid the expense and danger of a naval arms race. His administration took office in 1921 facing a Congress that was opposed to any resumption of naval competition, either with Britain or with Japan. Congress had tied an amendment to the naval appropriation for fiscal year 1921 that called on the administration to agree with Britain and Japan to cut naval building by half in the ensuing five years. The alternative to increasing strength was an agreement on proportional arms limitation. Congress's disapproval of the League and naval appropriations led Secretary of State Hughes later to write, "If Congress, as was practically certain, was not going to provide the appropriations necessary even to complete the existing [1916] program and we had no agreement for limitation, we were destined to fall behind the other great naval powers and thus get the worst of the competition our projects had started."[22] If Britain and Japan refused to cooperate in arms limitation, then the administration would have a conclusive argument to take to Congress to finish the 1916 program.

It was indeed time for a new tack. President Harding picked up the challenge and, in July 1921, sent out invitations to a conference on both arms limitation and establishing a stable order in the Far East. The invitation was original in that, reflecting the views of Harding and Hughes, it insisted that arms limitation and the Far East were connected and had to be dealt with at the same time. As it turned out, the Washington Conference was successful because the British and the Japanese were willing to cooperate. The package of treaties that resulted held considerable short-term benefits for all three governments. But their possible long-term consequences distressed the U.S. Navy.

Arms limitation caught popular attention. But which arms should be cut, which limited, and according to what criteria? It would not be a general disarmament, because land armaments were not considered. The United States had nothing to concede in that area, and France insisted on a security pledge of military intervention by the United States in return for dropping its guard against Germany. But the United States would not give such a pledge. A promise of an army intervention on the continent was out of the question for an isolationist, disarming America in 1921.[23]

That left naval arms. Secretary Hughes called for a yardstick. The General Board replied that it could not "define a 'naval unit' in such a way as to make it an accurate measure of strength of the navies of the world."[24] One weapon system stood out, however—one that held a similar place of rank and purpose in all the major navies. That was the capital ship. Battleships and battle cruisers were the most expensive weapons of the day. Navies themselves had made them the symbol of national power. They were the center of naval strategy. An agreement limiting capital ships was made possible by this comparability. Because all states held essentially the same doctrine of naval warfare, negotiators could count the tonnage and guns of capital ships to determine proportionality. Agreement was a matter of finding an acceptable ratio.

In preparing the U.S. program, however, the Navy and the administration thought along different lines. The General Board made a case for more, not fewer, ships. It paid no attention to the political fact that Congress had refused funds to build up the Pacific Fleet and to fortify the island bases. The board's advice was that so long as Britain was in alliance with Japan, or might ally with the Soviet Union or a revived Germany, security demanded a total force equal not just to that of the world's strongest navy but to the British and Japanese navies combined. To win command of the western Pacific, a strong battle fleet was necessary, and so were fortified bases in the Philippines, Guam, and Hawaii. The General Board recommended a "safe" capital ship ratio of 10:10:5, but only if the Japanese-British alliance was dissolved. That would give the United States battleship parity with Britain, twice as many battleships as Japan, and hold Japan beneath the 10:7 U.S.-Japanese ratio sought by Japanese officials.[25]

The ratios were all-important. They reflected a calculation of each country's naval requirements in light of its geographic position. A rule of thumb held that for every 1,000 miles a fleet steamed from its base, it lost 10 percent of its fighting efficiency. Lacking fortified bases west of Hawaii, the U.S. Pacific Fleet would have to sail 4,000 to 5,000 miles to reach the western Pacific. There Japan, operating on interior lines from closer ports, held the geographic advantage. To make up for that, to achieve equality, the United States must hold a capital-ship advantage of 10:5, or 10:6 at the least, and the latter ratio only if the United States reached a battle fleet of one million tons. A 10:7 ratio would give Japan decisive superiority at the point of contact.

Hughes rejected the General Board's recommendation of a 10:10:5 ratio. The United States would have to build up to meet such a ratio, and if the conference started talking about buildup and about each nation's potentially endless security needs, there would be no holding to an agenda of limitation or of anything else. Both Britain and Japan were poised between limitation and expansion. Congress was refusing more ships for the Pacific Fleet or funds to fortify island bases. Hughes declared that the board's ratio was too high.

The General Board returned with a warning that it would be disastrous to halt the building of the fifteen battleships and battle cruisers currently under construction. "These fifteen capital ships (building) brought Japan to the Conference. Scrap them and she will return home free to pursue untrammeled her aggressive program. . . . If these fifteen ships be stricken from the Navy list, our task may not be hopeless; but the temptation to Japan to take a chance becomes very great."[26]

This was no help to Hughes either, and he concluded that even aided by those sympathetic to his purpose, such as Assistant Navy Secretary Theodore Roosevelt, Jr., Chief of Naval Operations Admiral Robert Coontz, and William Pratt, (selected in June 1921 for rear admiral and assigned to the General Board), the Navy Department would not give Hughes what he wanted.[27]

Ending the deadlock required political intervention, a new international order for naval arms. Hughes provided the basis for such an order in the program he announced to an astounded conference on its opening day in November 1921, a program that he then carried out in negotiation. First, he called for an immediate halt to all capital-ship construction. A capital ship was defined as a warship displacing more than 10,000 tons or carrying a gun of over 8-inch caliber. Second, he called for the scrapping of certain existing ships. Third, Hughes established a British-U.S.-Japanese capital-ship tonnage ratio of 10:10:6. Last, he prescribed a similar ratio for auxiliary craft. On its part, the United States offered to give up most of the ships on which it had based its program of 1916 and to abandon the expansion program Wilson had proposed for achieving strategic independence. In return, the United States wanted the establishment of a ten-year naval holiday and recognition of its right to have a navy second to none.

The sacrifice of force was great indeed. As Hughes scuttled the Navy's construction program he proclaimed cooperation, not competition. One observer reflected, as he listened to Hughes read the names and numbers of the vessels that Hughes proposed be scrapped (70 capital ships, 30 of them American, 23 British, and 17 Japanese), "Mr. Secretary Hughes sank in thirty-five minutes more ships than all the admirals of the world have destroyed in a cycle of centuries." To mark the strategic significance of these proposals, Hughes concluded his speech with the words, "Preparation for offensive naval war will stop now."[28]

Elihu Root, former secretary of state and a member of the U.S. delegation, gave the astounding reasons that invalidated the Navy's strategic deductions about U.S. influence in the Far East. The U.S. delegation, Root said,

> started with the proposition that the United States would not be sufficiently interested in the open door or the preservation of Chinese integrity to go to war about them, and that Japan realized this probably better than the average American did, and that our naval program was very doubtful any way, because of the very strong opposition in this country to the immense expense involved. Therefore the first point in their minds was that we were not throwing away any weapon with which we could threaten Japan.[29]

To the officers of the Navy's planning staffs, the weapons Root and Hughes were talking about were those at the very core of U.S. naval force, those that formed the basis of the Navy's Pacific war plan and of its presumptive strategy, a strategy designed to ensure the declared U.S. interest of preserving the order in Asia. For that strategy a naval weapon should be forged, not abandoned, or policy should change to meet the loss of leverage. It seemed, instead, that the existing policy remained intact even though the government was conceding all leverage for its enforcement. Hughes's position prevailed because the leaders of the main naval states put their trust in diplomacy and arms limitation, not in sea-power doctrine.

Before the Washington Conference there had seemed little hope for arms limitation. Proposals had been made during the war and at the Paris Peace Conference, but the crippled end of Wilson's presidency could deliver neither on arms control nor on a Navy that could enforce collective security. In London the Treasury Ministry insisted on economy, and in 1920 the British government abandoned its one-power standard, opening the way for equality with the United States. But for the British, the enchantment of the concept of supremacy persisted, and just before Wilson's administration was replaced by Harding's, the British cabinet asked Parliament to resume building capital ships.

Beyond that was the British government's indecision over how to deal with its ally Japan. The alliance had become an embarrassment, poisoning relations with the United States. Americans looked on it as providing passive approval both of Japan's occupation of territory in China and of its possession of the former German colonies in the Pacific. The alliance, which alarmed the General Board, was up for renewal in 1921.

The British, then, came to Washington at a time when both their naval and their Far Eastern policies were under review. They had not found a way between the United States and Japan, a way to avoid what the chief British delegate to the conference, Arthur Balfour, described as the prospect of "eternal competition . . . with the U.S.A. and continued acquiescence in a policy [the suspension of Britain's ship construction] which would put us in third place among Naval Powers."[30]

In Japan, the government had not foreseen the repercussions of its expansion. Westerners had concluded that Japan's occupation of the Shandong Peninsula and of Germany's Pacific islands contributed to disorder in the Far East. That reaction surprised the Japanese. After all, their interest in large ships and sea power was only a reflection of the naval ambitions on grandiose display in Britain and the United States before the war. The Japanese were simply following Mahan. Their plans seemed a logical consequence of their regional and insular position. It seemed entirely appropriate to assume, by the standard measure of force comparison, that the United States was their primary hypothetical foe—and perhaps not such a hypothetical one, after all. Had not the United States in 1919 placed half its fleet, with more than half its naval firepower, in the Pacific? The only purpose of that shift was to coerce Japan.

Japan responded with a building program whose goal was a battle force 70 percent as large as that of the United States. In July 1920 the Diet approved the first installment of what is known as the "eight-eight" building program. This program was an effort to construct a fleet of 103 modern vessels at whose core would be 8 superdreadnoughts and 8 battle cruisers, each less than 8 years old.

Few in Tokyo understood how problematic the Japanese alliance with Britain was. Similarly, the Japanese were unaware of the extent to which Britain and the United States were looking for a way to limit their own building programs. What the government did know was that there was growing sentiment inside Japan itself for avoiding a naval arms race. The cost of the eight-eight program appeared to many to be more than their depressed economy could bear.

Harding's invitation offered a fresh start. But neither the British nor the Japanese had envisioned a conference to consider *both* arms control and a settlement of Far Eastern issues. The British had hoped to keep these matters separate; the Japanese saw the combination as a threat to their regional position. Japan was shocked that China, part of which it occupied and more of which it coveted, was invited. A Japanese elder statesman said, "Japan went to Versailles as a plaintiff; she will go to Washington as a defendant." The U.S. naval attaché in Tokyo reported that the Japanese looked upon the conference as "the greatest crisis since the Russian War and almost certain to ruin territorial aspirations and future as a great power."[31] Harding and Hughes were adamant. Arms control was the conference's priority, but the Far East must also be on the agenda.

Despite Britain's and Japan's reservations, in 1921 both countries were willing to agree to the American terms. A gathering of the British Empire's representatives had recently revealed strong opposition to continuing the alliance with Japan. To maintain it would doom a naval agreement with the United States. The British Foreign Office contended that Britain's long-term security depended on cooperation not with Japan but with the United States. Imperial interests would be protected if naval limitation were tied to a security arrangement that included the United States.[32] Nor did Hughes need to coerce his Japanese counterpart. Japan wanted good relations with the United States and was willing to cooperate to get them.[33]

In this cooperative political atmosphere were drawn up the three Washington treaties. By the terms of the Naval Arms Limitation Treaty signed in February 1922, the three main naval powers, the United States, Britain, and Japan, accepted a capital-ship ratio of 10:10:6.[34] The United States at last achieved in principle the long-sought numerical parity with the Royal Navy, at least in battleships. It was a prestige victory, for strategically, unless one were an unreconstructed Mahanian, it did not level the field. The Royal Navy would still have a larger navy of lesser ships and a global force. Britain did not give up its naval superiority.

The signatories proclaimed a ten-year holiday in capital-ship construction. They established a weight limit of 35,000 tons for any battleship. That was a U.S. victory over the British, who still dreamed of very large battle cruisers of 48,000 tons. Neither the United States nor Japan, with their regional bases, needed ships of such a size for their strategies of local control. On the other hand, the United States, when it looked beyond the western hemisphere, needed warships of sufficient size, say

35,000 tons, to have the long range and endurance to compensate for America's lack of advance bases, ships able to carry the heaviest of guns across the largest of oceans and arrive at the limit of their range of effectiveness, ready to engage a like force in decisive battle.

The United States agreed to scrap fifteen active battleships and cancel eleven of the fifteen capital ships then being built under the 1916 program. Only two battleships from that program were completed after the Washington Conference. One result of the downsizing of the capital ship force was the birth of a new generation of U.S. aircraft carriers when the hulls of two heavy cruisers were converted to the Navy's first fleet carriers, the *Lexington* and *Saratoga*, setting the pattern for the large, fast carriers of the future.

It was painful enough in Navy circles to scrap the battleships. What caused even more consternation was the U.S. agreement not to establish fortified advance bases west of Hawaii. That meant the Navy would have no secure harbors in the Philippines, at Guam, or in the Aleutians. It cut the heart out of the Navy's strategy of offensive sea control in the western Pacific.

The purpose of limitation, however, was equity. Japan would have enough strength to defend itself, but not enough for extended offensive operations. The United States would have enough to undertake a voyage to defend the Philippines, but not enough to arrive in the western Pacific with a force superior to Japan's. Yet without secure advance bases, a naval defense of the Philippines was at risk. If, as happened, the United States did not build up to its treaty limit and Japan did, the absence of forward bases might, by slowing the U.S. advance, give the Japanese navy an advantage of one-third in the theater of final combat. But Hughes held firm against Navy opposition. Base denial was a quid pro quo to Japan for accepting the 10:6 ratio.

Hughes conceded in part for diplomatic reasons, to strengthen the Japanese government against domestic charges of a sellout. It worked. With a 10:6 ratio, and with the United States devoid of any fortified base west of Hawaii, the Japanese government could claim regional superiority. The United States conceded naval control of the western Pacific to Japan. Even if the Americans built up, they faced the risk of overextension at the end of an unsupported transit. Confounding its critics and Japan's militant expansionists, the moderate Japanese government had shown the benefit of international cooperation. As Admiral Yamamoto Isoroku told his colleagues who complained that Japan had been humiliated by the treaty ratio, "The 5:5:3 ratio works just fine for us; it is a treaty that restricts the *other* parties." Vice Admiral Inoue Shigemi accused the Japanese navy's antitreaty faction of suffering from "ratio neurosis."[35]

The U.S. position likewise reflected domestic political realities. Congress wanted to reduce the likelihood of intervention in the Far East. It felt that diplomacy could take the place of force in protecting American interests. At Washington, and later at London in 1930, the United States put its faith in trust, in the continuation of moderate and cooperative governments, and in a world order of voluntary restraint.

What was the alternative? Both the administration and Congress in the 1920s and 1930s wanted to end the forward policy in the Pacific and prevent a naval arms race. That is what Hughes got by overriding dismay and teeth gnashing in the Navy and by ignoring, first, the potential fragility of a system based on the voluntary cooperation of Japan and, second, the danger of not backing declared interests with force.

The Four Power Treaty signed at the Washington Conference pledged the three main Pacific powers and France to accept the regional status quo, each party recognizing the island possessions of the others. This treaty was in effect a nonaggression pact, a corollary of naval arms limitation. Japan accepted U.S. possession of Guam and the Philippines. Also as part of this generalization of security, the treaty ended the alliance between Japan and Britain. That resolved a nettlesome political problem for the British and laid to rest the U.S. Navy's peculiar anxiety about a two-ocean war.

A good deal of U.S. resentment against the British remained, however. In Navy circles a widely held view was that at Washington, despite all the talk of parity, the British had come out ahead. Josephus Daniels called the parity agreement a fake. Watching the proceedings, he refused to join the jubilant applause. An acquaintance urged, "Get up, Josephus. This is the most notable day in our history. It connotes the end of war." Daniels stayed seated and replied, "You may cheer if you please at scuttling powerful ships of our Navy; others may do so, but I decline to applaud at my own funeral. I sweat blood to get the money to build these ships that are being destroyed. I decline to applaud the worst blow aimed at the Navy."[36]

Daniels had a right to lament. Most Navy officers shared his pessimism. "The Navy emerged from the Washington Conference psychologically bruised and physically curtailed," William Braisted wrote. "Never before in their memory had naval men found their views so overwhelmingly rejected by public opinion."[37]

The conclusion of Captain Dudley Knox, the most widely read critic of the treaties, was that "America resigned to Britain the predominance in Sea Power." Knox caught the Navy's mood in the title of his book about the conference, *The Eclipse of American Sea Power*. Knox's argument was that by giving up the building program and its potential of establishing U.S. capital-ship superiority, the United States had lost its chance of offsetting the broader maritime strength and overall weight of the Royal Navy. In fighting strength, for instance, no cruisers were given up, so in cruisers the British retained their commanding lead, and the United States continued to rank a poor third after Japan. Not a single U.S. Navy cruiser had been commissioned since 1908. And the sacrifice of the island bases, Knox repeated, without truly commensurate concessions by Japan, destroyed U.S. influence in the western Pacific.[38]

British critics at first arrived at a similar assessment of the treaties. Parity dealt a blow to the historical numerical predominance of the Royal Navy, but only in capital ships. Britain remained the preeminent sea power, with many bases worldwide to support cruisers, which in turn provided commercial protection and imperial maintenance.[39] Against this, American officers might rail (and competition was transferred from the building of battleships to the building of cruisers), but the treaties drew the sting from Anglo-American relations. They were a step toward settling naval-power balances without an arms race or pointless conflict. The logic of Hughes, not Mahan, won out, and improved relations were to pay great dividends in the first years of the next war.[40]

China had been excluded from the Four Power Treaty. A separate Nine-Power Treaty, which included China, recognized the principle of the Open Door. That was enough assurance for Hughes. America's China policy, like all the arrangements signed at Washington, was based on the goodwill of the states involved. The fundamental point of the Washington treaties was to create an atmosphere of trust in which the signatories would voluntarily conform to the treaties' terms. Maintaining the Open Door depended on the continuation of a moderate regime in Tokyo and political stability in China. For America was declaring, in effect, that its Open Door policy was not worth a war with Japan.

With these treaties Harding and Hughes dismantled the Pacific strategy on which the Navy and the Army had been working for two decades. Without a fortified base at Guam or in the Philippines, the country could not maintain a naval presence in the Far East. The British kept their bases, and so did the Japanese. Critics said that Japan, seen as the treaties' greatest beneficiary, was handed a regional dominance that was founded on a virtually impregnable defensive position. The Japanese government would no longer have to spend heavily on capital ships and could secure its defense with the navy it had simply by adding a few submarines. Before, to keep up its position, Japan had spent beyond its means. "Poverty," wrote Dudley Knox, "threatened to prevent successful naval competition with us."[41] The Washington agreements forfeited that U.S. advantage, and as a result, U.S. interests in the Far East became hostage to Japanese restraint.

In the face of criticism, the Navy hierarchy—Navy Secretary Edwin Denby, Assistant Secretary Theodore Roosevelt, Jr., CNO Admiral Robert Coontz, and Rear Admiral William Pratt, then on the General Board—argued back. Denby wrote in his *Annual Report* for 1922, "The Navy Department was entirely in sympathy with the purpose of this conference and lent its whole-hearted aid to the success of this endeavor."[42] Pratt defended the treaties from the position that a strictly naval view was too restrictive. According to him, the treaties brought more overall stability to the Far East than naval power could. Giving up the 1916 battleship program was a cost, but one worth paying to win trust among nations. And, Pratt asked, beyond that, what did the treaties really concede? Not the prospective bases or forts—they did not exist, and Congress had set its face against establishing them. Not a forward policy in Asia—that was never in the cards. Not an enlarged fleet—Congress would not support an arms race. If the concessions improved relations with Japan and Britain, that, after all, was national policy. Last, Pratt said, the capital-ship tonnage ratio permitted the Navy to state exactly what forces it expected other countries to have. The service could go to a now presumably respectful Congress with internationally validated requests and expect the legislature to give the Navy what it asked.[43] Sea power as naval strength was not given up at the Washington Conference. On the contrary, it was codified.

In November 1922, Secretary Denby framed the country's naval policy: "To create, maintain, and operate a Navy second to none and in conformity with the ratios for capital ships established by the treaty for the limitation of naval armaments."[44] With this formulation, and with policy in the Pacific clear at last, the Navy could plan strategy in a specified framework. Like it or not, the United States was in for a treaty Navy.

6

Treaty Navy
1922-1930

RED

"For the first time in the history of our country," Navy Secretary Denby wrote in his *Annual Report* for 1922, "the Navy and Congress have a definite naval policy and building and maintenance standard to work to, a standard which is proportionate to our position as a world power." By *definite naval policy*, he meant the calculation of sea power as capital-ship strength by the ratios and purpose of the Washington Conference. By *building and maintenance standard*, he meant the capital-ship parity with Britain that represented a prestige victory for the administration.

Denby stated the Navy Department's policy. One, that "the Navy of the United States should be maintained in sufficient strength to support its policies and its commerce, and to guard its continental and overseas possessions." Two, "to create, maintain, and operate a Navy second to none and in conformity with the ratios for capital ships established by the treaty for limitation of naval armaments."[1]

The spirits of an optimistic naval officer would have risen to hear Rear Admiral Pratt declare, "Instead of being opportunists from year to year, we now can point to a naval policy so closely linked to our national policies that not only may naval men know and more accurately forecast our naval needs, but our legislators better may understand and appropriate the funds necessary to maintain an adequate naval establishment, organized on a definite basis."[2] There was, after all, a lot to be said for having a definite framework such as that established by the Washington treaties in which to plan. Supposedly, from the perspective of all signatories, a fair balance had been drawn between the demands of national security and the maintenance of a stable international order. No state could pose an offensive threat to another. But a pessimist might have shared the view of Captain Luke McNamee, the director of naval intelligence, who wrote in February 1922, "The Conference has adjourned with general rejoicing and apparently Congress now thinks it is now free to abolish the Army and the Navy."[3]

Why did the country need a big navy in the 1920s? To support its policies, of course, but which policies, in what order, against what threat, and how? In a talk at the Naval Academy in 1922, Captain Frank Schofield of the General Board described the necessarily deductive dimension of the Navy's strategic thinking, even after the Washington Conference:

> There is not available any official statement of the national external policies of the United States. Even if there were such a statement it could not remain valid for a considerable length of time unless it were couched in the most general terms. It has therefore been necessary for the Navy to make its own estimate of national policies and to revise these as events justified. Such well-known policies as, Defense of Continental Territory, Defense of Outlying Possessions, Monroe Doctrine, Defense and extension of maritime commerce. No Entangling Alliances, The Open Door, Exclusion of Asiatics, and Limitation of Immigration. Protection of Our Nationals Abroad. furnish a general guide as to just what policies a navy must be ready to support.[4]

This process of estimating national policies did not reflect the close linkage that had been proclaimed by Denby and Pratt. Schofield's list was so broad, so globally demanding, and so full of potential for extending naval force far beyond treaty limits that it needed to be prioritized, and that had to be the job of U.S. statesmen.

In the view of many naval officers, it was a job that statesmen were not doing. The political arm of government seemed willfully ignorant of the military dimensions of the country's Asian commitments. To count on Japan's self-denial was to base policy on intentions instead of capabilities. If interests ever had to be protected by force rather than by trust, if Japan violated the treaty terms, if an expansionist government took power in Japan, then a Navy large enough to deter Japan or to defeat it in the western Pacific would be required. After the Washington Conference, however, Congress and the administration withheld authorization to build the Navy up to even treaty limits. To naval officers this seemed strategic folly. In December 1922, in the aftermath of the conference, the chief of naval operations, Admiral Coontz, created the United States Fleet and divided its main units between the Scouting Fleet based in the Atlantic, and the Battle Fleet based in the Pacific. The Navy's concern that trust was not enough was expressed in the unequal division of battleships: the twelve most modern went to the Pacific Battle Fleet; the other six went to the Atlantic Scouting Fleet.

The Navy's problems did not bother Presidents Warren Harding, Calvin Coolidge, or Herbert Hoover. Their optimism reflected the popular faith in disarmament, the belief that peace could be negotiated, that there was no need to prepare for war. It was this political atmosphere, not the terms of treaties, that in the last analysis determined the level of naval readiness and the Navy's force structure in the 1920s and 1930s. These attitudes, expressed in the treaties, encouraged antinavalist sentiment, led to a search for further force reduction, and by resulting in cuts in the Navy's missions and budgets, discouraged both innovation in naval technology and reform in doctrine. All this the political masters desired or accepted. A consequence was a limited naval force, and by the time the treaties came to an end in 1936 and Japan gave up its restraint, the leverage available to the United States had been severely reduced.[5]

In the 1920s, however, the presidents each shared the hope that military leverage would not be necessary, and they put their faith in treaties. The government was concerned with commerce, with maintaining a global open door. Business could not easily be translated into strategy. On the other hand, business meant competition. That fact had been a staple of U.S. sea-power doctrine from the beginning. The Navy stood behind merchants, supporting their interests in Latin America, holding ajar the door to the China trade, offsetting British influence in the Near East and the Far East, encouraging private economic development in the Philippines, and ensuring free passage over the sea-lanes. Further, the Navy had long held that economic rivalry could lead to war. The United States was an expansionary commercial power. This commercial expansion might run up against the powerful maritime empires and spheres of influence of Britain and Japan. In such a case, the outcome of the struggle for trade might be determined by naval force, a possibility to which the civil authorities turned only a half-opened eye.

Navy men remained angry about the Washington agreement on capital ships. Rear Admiral Pratt's endorsement was an exception. Pratt accepted the treaties, the limits, and the system of collective security as reasonable and valid national positions. His fellow officers did not. They said Pratt tacked too close to political winds and had lost the Navy perspective. The service felt robbed. There was no doubt the United States gave up a lot, more than any other state. Not only existing ships but also the bulk of its planned but yet unbuilt battleships were consigned to oblivion: fifteen predreadnoughts and the fifteen dreadnoughts from the 1916 authorization. The United States disarmed, built down. Other states simply agreed not to build up beyond the tonnage established for their forces. It was said that "they scrapped their blueprints, we scrapped our ships." After the Washington Conference the U.S. Navy was left with eighteen battleships of intermediate value.

The treaty restrictions applied only to what the Navy's General Board called "strength ships": battleships and battle cruisers of more than 10,000 tons or vessels carrying guns of more than 8-inch caliber. Aircraft carriers were not limited in number, though a maximum tonnage for the class was set. Carriers were restricted to batteries of guns no larger than 8-inch caliber. The big-gun battleship was still the essential ship of the battle line. No other weapon could deliver a decisive blow.

Airplanes still could not do so. In July 1921, in a much ballyhooed experiment, Army bombers sank the captured German battleship *Ostfriesland*. That did not convince surface-warfare officers that the day of the capital ship was over. They said it was a rigged test, a stunt. The *Ostfriesland* was a sitting duck, at anchor, unable to evade or to deliver a counterattack by antiaircraft fire. In another test two years later, against the battleship *Washington*, it took a combination of bombs, mines, and gunfire to put the vessel under. Of this test Rear Admiral Albert Niblack wrote that, though air, mine, and torpedo attacks were likely eventually to become the commonplace of naval warfare, still, for the present, "*the range and weight of gun projectiles remain the determining factors in war*, even if it shows me to be an 'ostrich' for daring to say so."[6] To officers in charge of naval planning in the mid-1920s, the land-based bomber, still a short-range aircraft, was a controllable threat. The value of naval air and the aircraft carrier was accepted, but only as auxiliary to the fleet. They were for scouting and for spotting the shots of the long-range cannons of capital ships.

Confidence in the battleship was reasserted by Chief of Naval Operations Admiral Edward Eberle (CNO July 1923–November 1927) in late 1924:

> The battleship of to-day, while not invulnerable to airplane attack, still possesses very efficient structural protection. . . . The battleship of the future can be so designed as to distribution of her armor on decks and sides, and as to interior subdivision, that she will not be subject to fatal damage from the air. . . . It can not be said therefore that air attack has rendered the battleship obsolete.[7]

To reduce the damage that bombs—and mines and torpedoes—might do, the Navy modernized. To the extent that Congress would provide the required funds, the great battleships were reconstructed to sustain heavier blows. Decks and hulls got more armor, and ships were recompartmentalized. Blisters (outer hulls) were added to deflect torpedo detonations. Antiaircraft batteries and improved fire-control systems were installed.

The concern about parity, however, was a recognition that there was more to war at sea than battleships and that the country was not keeping up with its rivals in the construction of the unrestricted classes of ships—namely, cruisers, destroyers, and submarines. In this regard Secretary Denby had predicted wrong. Congress did not fill out the fleet auxiliaries. Despite talk of a Navy second to none, despite the agreement on battleship parity with Britain and the favorable U.S.-Japan ratio, when one looked at the spread of naval forces and where they might be used, the U.S. Navy had slipped behind.

The particular object of concern was cruiser strength. Cruisers were the second most important warship class. They mounted a large array of weapons on a fast hull. They were more lightly armored than a battleship and therefore swifter. Heavy cruisers supported the battle line in combat, moving about to attack at will. The heavy cruiser could outgun all but a battleship itself, and it had the speed to outrun a battleship's cannons. Both heavy and light cruisers were the classic destroyers of commerce and the executors of blockade. Cruisers were to exercise sea control over shipping after the battle line, in victory over the enemy's main force, had established command.

Cruisers were particularly valuable to Britain and Japan, who operated them in support of their maritime positions. Britain's cruisers operated from the country's worldwide network of bases located at the major straits and along the major sea-lanes. Japan used its cruisers to support its powerful strategy of regional defense.

After the battleship limits were established at the Washington Conference, the focus of the naval race shifted to cruisers, for which limits on unit size, but no limits on total numbers, had been set. The world's three major navies turned the Washington ceilings of 10,000 tons and 8-inch guns into the standard for a generation of heavy (or treaty) cruisers, "a kind of junior capital ship."[8] In cruisers, the United States was far behind. Not a single cruiser had been commissioned in the U.S. Navy between 1908 and 1923. In 1926 the count of cruisers in existence or under construction, or which had been authorized or projected, was 63 in Britain, 43 in Japan, and 40 in the United States. The British total in the new 10,000-ton class was 12, double that of the United States.

Few outside the Navy were concerned by these facts. When big-Navy advocates in Congress introduced a bill to authorize ten more of the 10,000-ton cruisers, the prospect of passage—and of a naval arms race—was killed by Coolidge's policies of economy, reduced claims abroad, and international agreement. The president assumed that dollars and treaties, not warships, would maintain a liberal, capitalist world order and ocean access. In 1926 Congress's appropriations for the Navy were the lowest since the war. Then the administration declared that the alternative to cruiser competition was an international agreement on their limitation. President Coolidge called a conference for 1927 at Geneva to continue the work of the Washington Conference and extend the 10:10:6 ratio to auxiliary vessels, of which cruisers were the most important.

At the Geneva Conference, the dispute between the American and British delegations centered on the numbers of cruisers each country could have in prospective size categories. Both sides agreed that more light ships could be built than heavy ships within whatever overall tonnage limit a treaty might establish. But with their need for imperial defense, and sailing from worldwide bases, the British wanted more light cruisers than the Americans were willing to approve. The British declared an absolute overall need for 70 versatile, light cruisers that weighed 6,000 tons and carried 6-inch guns. (The British made this demand in spite of the fact that for commerce protection in time of war, they also could arm merchantmen with 6-inch guns, and British merchantmen outnumbered those of the United States five-to-one.) In addition, the British wanted strict limits on the numbers of heavy cruisers carrying 8-inch guns.

Within the overall tonnage limit, the Americans wanted fewer but larger ships, in particular a total of 30 or so heavy cruisers with 8-inch cannons—roughly five heavy cruisers for every three capital ships. These cruisers would be vessels of endurance, habitability, and firepower, fitted for establishing offensive sea control and for the needs of a distant Pacific war. But the British, concerned with being outfought regionally, would not approve such a large number of them.

No resolution was reached at the conference, which was attended by

Japan as well as Britain and the United States. The meeting lacked the leadership and insistence on a political framework that had brought success at Washington and that would result in a comprehensive agreement at London in 1930. President Coolidge envisioned that a conference on naval matters would be but a preliminary to the general disarmament conference then being prepared by the League of Nations. Thus at Geneva, he left it to the naval leaders to set the agenda, and, without political guidance, they were not willing to negotiate. The American naval delegate was Rear Admiral Hilary Jones of the General Board, a man said to view the world through a porthole. He and the U.S. delegation never strayed from the Navy's recommendations.[9]

The British, Rear Admiral Jones said, showed "a desire to standardize navies in types [of vessels] that were of small value to us [including submarines and light cruisers] and fix the main limitations in types that would be of value to us."[10] The British were equally exasperated. Lord Jellicoe wrote from Geneva: "The American programme has only one object in view, viz., Equality with Great Britain on the sea. We cannot help it if they build up to our required standard, but we can avoid lowering our standard to suit them."[11]

The argument against the British position was presented to the American public in the classic connection of cruisers to commerce. According to this argument, British maritime superiority, backed by many light cruisers and the smaller gun, offered the potential for interdiction on a vast scale.[12] Thus the British really were posing a concealed economic challenge. Because of this challenge, the U.S. Navy was demanding parity. This argument, grounded on the Navy's role in the protection of American trade, appealed to public opinion.

It is likely, however, that the U.S. delegation dissembled. If commerce protection was what it really wanted, there was an argument that the 6,000-ton, 6-inch gun ships could do the job. The Navy's real interest was in preparing for a war with Japan. It talked about defense of trade and the need to meet armed merchantmen when what it really wanted was to increase its Pacific force. The bottom line for most officers was parity with Britain in overall cruiser tonnage and a favorable ratio with Japan—namely, the 10:10:6 formula—and, with the exception of heavy cruisers with 8-inch guns, no limit on the number of ships that each state could build within the tonnage limit for each class. With such terms, in which the proportion of heavy cruisers to overall tonnage would favor the United States, the Navy could go to Congress and, if Denby and Pratt were right that Congress would build to the top, get support for the battle fleet in the Pacific and be able in wartime to cut the sea-lanes on which Japan's economy depended. It was to justify such a building program, without insulting Japan, that the Navy used traditional Anglophobia and the demands of trade as a cover.[13]

Rear Admiral Frank Schofield, promoted to that rank in 1924, came back from Geneva convinced that the United States might face a two-ocean war against a British-Japanese alliance. The Navy must be ready, he said, "for a strategic offensive in the Pacific and a strategic defensive in the Atlantic."[14] Admiral Charles F. Hughes, chief of naval operations from November 1927 to September 1930, shared this view. Staff work continued on the prospect of a global conflict, on War Plans Red, Orange, and Red-Orange.

It is hard to recapture the persistent Anglophobia that existed in Navy circles in the 1920s. It is exemplified in a report of the Joint Army-Navy Board from the spring of 1930, a report that is all the more expressive because it shows that the attitude continued even after the London Naval Conference established full U.S.-British parity:

> The most probable cause of war between RED [the British Empire] and BLUE [the United States] is the constantly increasing BLUE economic penetration and commercial expansion into regions formerly dominated by RED trade, to such extent as eventually to menace RED standards of living and to threaten economic ruin. . . . The foreign policy of BLUE . . . is primarily concerned with the advancement of the foreign trade of BLUE and demands equality of treatment in all political dependencies and backward countries, and unrestricted access to sources of raw materials. In this particular it comes in conflict with the foreign policies of RED.[15]

This prospect, however, was an a priori product of doctrine, not realism. There were no serious policy disagreements between the two states. War between them was politically unimaginable. What kept the idea alive in the Navy Department and Congress was the sense of commercial rivalry. There was also a festering resentment based on the idea that the United States had been duped at the Washington Conference, that its prestige victory of U.S.-British battleship parity had been because of a continued overall British naval and maritime superiority. The sense of inferiority was hard to shake, because for the Navy it rested on technical assessment. An after-action report on a war game held in 1925 read, "The BLUE Fleet as it exists today can not engage the RED Fleet in gun action with any prospect of victory."[16] The thought that the United States remained second-rate irritated Anglo-American relations until the mid-1930s.

Still, no matter how irritated the Navy and the Coolidge administration became with Britain after the abortive conference in 1927, there was no threat from that country, nor any from Japan. Japan was a passively cooperative participant at the Geneva Conference. It enjoyed the advantages of the Washington treaties. It did build in excess of treaty ship sizes by as much as 20 percent, a violation that went almost unnoticed because of the absence of verification processes. But its government was not bent on war, and the United States overlooked what news it had of Japanese evasion.[17] U.S. policy was to avoid provocation and thus to avoid a costly defensive commitment in the Philippines. Navy officers were more worried about the Far East than were their political masters.

The different assessments of the U.S. role in the western Pacific, of how to define interests there, and of how much to commit illustrate the gap that existed, during the 1920s and into the 1930s, between the civil authorities' policies and the military's war plans. The strategy mismatch resulted because certain questions were left unanswered. Was the Philippines a permanent possession to be defended, a transitional holding, or what? Was the protection of China's integrity something for which the government might someday have to use force? Navy strategists did not accept the administration's declared positions as final. Some of these positions were too ambiguous, others too conditional. Officers thought they had a clearer long-term idea of what the political authorities might have to fight for. Their worst-case deductions, however, received very little support.

In the aftermath of the Geneva Conference, the Navy declared that, instead of seeking further equality with Britain, it must, within the Washington framework, build to the particular needs of the United States, to whichever force size was required. No new battleships could be built because of the ten-year moratorium. Therefore, the General Board, vigorously supported by Navy Secretary Curtis Wilbur (March 1924 to March 1929), recommended the construction of 33 heavy cruisers to bring the American total to 43. The chairman of the House Committee on Naval Affairs recommended a building program of 71 ships, including 25 heavy cruisers, 32 submarines, and 5 aircraft carriers. Wilbur urged that the angle of elevation of the battleships' large guns be increased so that the guns' range would match that of their British counterparts.

Congress rejected the building proposals. Its attention was turned not to rearmament but to the astounding proposal of Frank B. Kellogg, secretary of state from 1925 to 1929, that states reach a general agreement to give up war altogether. It is enough to quote the first article of the 1928 "General Pact for the Renunciation of War" (sometimes called the Kellogg Pact) to show the pact's idealism and its explicit rejection of

Clausewitz's basic proposition that war is an instrument of policy. The article read, "The High Contracting Parties solemnly declare in the names of their respective peoples that they condemn recourse to war for the solution of international controversies, and renounce it as an instrument of national policy in their relations with one another." That trumped even Hughes's claim at the Washington Conference that the "preparation for offensive war would stop now." It certainly cooled interest in naval rearmament.

Yet Coolidge, in his last days in office, was irritated enough with the British to declare in favor of the building program. In December 1928 the Senate had simultaneously before it the largest naval construction bill since the great Naval Act of 1916 and the Kellogg Pact. The debates that session, George Davis observed, were worthy of Voltaire.[18] In the midst of all the Panglossary, however, there was enough realism in Congress, or at any rate annoyance with the ongoing (and ambitious) British cruiser-building program, to pass an authorization of fifteen heavy cruisers and one aircraft carrier. Congress added its usual hope that the president would, by calling another naval conference, find the construction unnecessary.

THE LONDON NAVAL TREATY OF 1930

That is what President Herbert Hoover did. Hoover was antimilitary and, like Secretary Hughes ten years before, hopeful of establishing a moral force of trust. He rejected the concept of a national mission of expansion and of a foreign policy backed by arms. The Navy existed only for self-defense. Early in his administration he indicated his opinion on the limited utility of military force. He asked, "Are our defenses strong enough to prevent a successful landing of foreign soldiers on the continental United States and ultimately on the Western Hemisphere?"[19] Beyond that, the Navy was not needed or used in his foreign policy. It was seen only as something to cut.

With the London Naval Conference of 1930, the United States completed the form of its treaty Navy. This conference would be the last international success in limiting naval arms. Agreement was reached between the United States, Britain, and Japan. France and Italy came and left without signing. The former insisted on a guarantee of continental security, which the United States refused to give.

Hoover and British prime minister Ramsay MacDonald were in firm control of the conference. They were determined to end the antagonism between their countries, and equality of naval arms was the way to do this. Hoover and MacDonald were not going to be thwarted by the objections of naval leaders. To avoid the muddle of Geneva, the statesmen had devoted seven months to preliminary diplomatic preparation.

The U.S. Navy took a hard line. Chief of Naval Operations Admiral Hughes and the General Board, which was represented by Rear Admiral Hilary Jones, demanded an absolute minimum of 21 heavy 10,000-ton, 8-inch-gun cruisers. This the British Admiralty opposed, seeing it as tilting the overall balance against them. As at Washington and Geneva, it seemed to the political authorities that the naval officers stayed locked into a parochial and shortsighted point of view. Secretary of State Henry Stimson, serving from 1929 to 1933, was a former Army colonel and from 1911 to 1913 had been secretary of war, and so he was no stranger to interservice rivalry. He described the Navy leadership as tied to "the peculiar psychology of the Navy Department, which frequently seemed to retire from the realm of logic into a dim religious world in which Neptune was God, Mahan his prophet, and the United States Navy the only true Church."[20]

Navy opinion was divided. In Rear Admiral William Pratt, commander of the U.S. Fleet, Hoover and Stimson found an expert to head the London delegation's technical advisory staff. A professional brought in by the administration to counterbalance the mainstream opinion of Hughes, Jones, and the General Board, Pratt was willing to accept a lower number of heavy cruisers to meet British objections. He considered the light ships with 6-inch guns to be suited to the new naval order.

Pratt accepted the position of the State Department because he thought agreement with Britain and international arms limitation made, in the largest sense, good strategy. In his defense of the Washington treaties, published in 1923, Pratt had declared that "the Navy is first, the statesman's tool, and second, the warrior's weapon."[21] Turning inside out the inevitablists' traditional view that competition would necessarily lead to conflict, Pratt presented naval cooperation as a basis for peace. Whereas Hughes, Jones, and the General Board worried about an imbalance in wartime and kept their focus on Japan, viewing the United States as standing alone with unilateral naval requirements and with capabilities inferior to those of the British, Pratt believed British intentions could be accepted as cooperative, put his trust in a best-case political alliance, shared Hoover's Anglophilia, and took hope.[22]

The London Naval Conference established, at last, quantitative equality in number and tonnage between all major classes of vessels in the U.S. and British navies. This was the formal acceptance of the mathematical parity the Navy had sought for more than a decade, hollow though it now seemed. Both states agreed to a total of fifteen battleships apiece and to an extension of the moratorium on capital-ship construction for another five years, through 1936. The British government, against the wishes of many of its admirals, modified its demand for expanded cruiser construction, dropping from 70 to 50 the number it would build. Most of those built would be light. The United States, to comply with the established cruiser tonnage limit of around 323,000 tons, reduced the number of heavy cruisers it planned to build to a maximum of eighteen, three of which (out of deference to Japan) it was to postpone building for some years, meanwhile making up the remaining tonnage with lighter cruisers.[23] The parity totals, it should be borne in mind, included ships yet unbuilt, and U.S. Navy officers wondered whether, even though the ships were allowed, they would ever be authorized, funded, and constructed.

But of course that was not Britain's problem. By 1932 the Royal Navy possessed 52 cruisers to the United States's 19, and it maintained a lead of the same proportion throughout the 1930s. The British had not given up sea-power superiority. With its extensive maritime system of communications and supply, its global system of naval bases and stations, its immense merchant marine, and its already existing large naval force, the British at the London Naval Conference, as Gregory Kennedy wrote, "lost little or nothing in the way of real naval power to the United States, and they kept it for the decade."[24]

Accommodation on the matter of heavy cruisers meant accepting fewer of them, only half the number most U.S. officers had wanted, and making up the remaining tonnage with lighter ships. For most officers this was surrender, giving up an independent determination of force needs and thereby endangering the U.S. position in the Pacific. Against them Pratt argued that agreement on parity in cruiser tonnage would end the arms race and Anglo-American ill will and would strategically be more effective in securing U.S. interests than would anything that could be done unilaterally through sea power. If it came to war with Japan, which Pratt did not expect, the United States would not have to worry about a war in the Atlantic as well. The statesmen at London were willing to "take risks for peace," as the expression went. So was Pratt. Most of the Navy was not. But officers were given no alternative, and they accepted the result.

Pratt's pragmatic support of the Naval Arms Limitation Treaty of 1922 and now of the administration's position in London left him distrusted within the service. He was accused of selling out to the politicians and internationalists, of taking an ideological or self-serving stand incompatible with naval needs. Rear Admiral Frank Schofield told Congress that 70 to 80 percent of the Navy's officers disagreed with Pratt's position at London.[25] The treaty Navy meant fewer ships and no new bases. After the London Conference, Pratt relieved Admiral Hughes as chief of naval operations. At the ceremony marking the change of command, Hughes refused to shake Pratt's hand, extended no congratulations, and left the ceremony precipitously, a display of curtness that illustrates the officers' anger and frustration.

Stimson's memoir declares:

> A more ridiculous goal [than parity] can hardly be imagined. On every ground, the United States should have been happy to see the British Navy just as big and strong as the British pocket-book would permit—excepting of course as this size might stimulate rival building. That America should have no other important object than a fleet as big as the British was utter nonsense. . . . [But] no treaty without parity would have received ten votes in the American Senate, so the American delegation brought back parity. What good it did his country, Stimson was never able to say.[26]

It did, however, result in a distinct improvement in Anglo-American relations that had enormous political and strategic importance in the years ahead. Hoover and MacDonald took advantage of a propitious moment to bury the old hatchet and pursue economy through disarmament. That was what the administration could claim for the London Conference.

The treaty gave the United States no control over the political future of Japan or China. The U.S. position toward Japan rested not on a systematic East Asian policy but on a complacent hope that the arms agreements would encourage moderate opinion in favor of the Pacific status quo and thereby enhance America's only remaining instrument of influence, economic diplomacy.[27] In the short term the gamble worked; but success was fragile. After a few years the Japanese government let the treaties lapse and turned to a policy of expansion and war, and the United States had no way to stop the Japanese.

The London agreement was a subject of great dispute in Tokyo. The moderate parliamentary government and conciliatory naval officers of the treaty faction were opposed at home by the same anti-internationalists who had fought the Washington terms a decade earlier and who in the mid-1930s were to set Japan's course toward autarchy and expansion. The dispute was particularly intense within the Japanese navy. To the supporters of the treaty, heirs to Admiral Katō Tomosaburō and the men in the Naval Ministry who had signed at Washington, an arms race with the United States would be ruinous, and peaceful coexistence and diplomatic adjustment were by far preferable to rivalry and conflict. According to these men, Japan should define its future as a great power—the greatest in Asia—not autonomously but within the international community and not through violent revisionism but through gradualism. The Imperial Navy, they argued, was defensive. As it stood, the navy could take full advantage of Japan's distance and stand off any American advance. The fleet's main job, argued the treaty faction, was to deter the United States from making such a move; and Japan's regional naval position, secured by the treaties and the cordial relations with America, provided that deterrence.[28]

Opposed to the London agreement were the fleet faction around the Naval General Staff and Admiral Katō Kanji. These men were bitter about the 60-percent capital-ship ratio accepted at Washington. They saw their navy and the world in Mahanian terms, with the United States as an inevitable economic, cultural, and probably military competitor against whom Japan must have a powerful fleet prepared for decisive battle. The Japanese had their own destiny. The Anglo-Saxons had denied them the equality they deserved, dooming them to an inferior status. As army officers demanded expansion in China and a breakaway from the restraints of the treaty system, so the fleet faction argued that the long-sought ratio of 10:7 was the minimum acceptable for national security. If it was not achievable in battleships for a conventional Mahanian main-force interception strategy, it might be found in cruisers, destroyers, and submarines for an interception-attrition strategy. This modified Mahanian strategy, if based on high levels of training, on innovative tactics such as night fighting, and on improved weapons such as a superior torpedo, might be able to take down an approaching U.S. fleet.[29]

Hoover's administration recognized this conflict within Japan and sought to bolster the moderate government by conceding it a 70 percent ratio in light cruisers and destroyers and equality in submarines. In heavy cruisers Japan took a formal ratio of 60 percent of the Anglo-American parity level, but in effect got 70 percent because the United States agreed not to build up to its limit during the life of the treaty. These concessions made possible Tokyo's acceptance of the three-power London Naval Treaty. The treaty was ratified after what a contemporary called "probably the most contested battle ever fought between the Privy Council and the Cabinet in the constitutional history of Japan," an observation indicative of impending trouble when one considers how close the Japanese government was to being overtaken by militarists.[30]

The London treaty was the high-water mark of the liberal hope to control the forces of war. The United States, Britain, and Japan each lived up sufficiently to its terms and to the terms of the Washington naval agreement as well. But all further efforts at disarmament and collective security failed. When the London treaty expired in 1936, the world environment had been transformed by depression and aggression. In every country it seemed that an arms race, if not war, was the only way to attain security in the midst of international anarchy. Peace is a consequence, not a cause, of international equilibrium. Arms limitation works only if there is political self-restraint. Such an equilibrium, and such restraint, existed between 1920 and 1930. They disappeared almost immediately thereafter.

7

Adapt and Innovate 1931-1938

THREE PRINCIPLES

Until the end of the 1930s the United States was sunk in economic depression and political isolation. In a passive foreign policy the Navy played a passive role. Constrained by treaty limits and antiwar sentiment, it maintained its cohesion as a fighting institution, its doctrine of offensive sea control, and its fleet. What it lacked was a strategy to guide it.

Waldo Heinrichs, Jr., wrote of the three interrelated concepts by which the Navy set its course in the 1930s: "The first of these was War Plan Orange, which provided the rationale for a big navy. The second was the concept of the 'balanced fleet,' which served as the best available compromise of competing perspectives and interests within the navy. The third was the concept of the 'treaty navy,' which provided public justification for naval growth."[1]

Taken together these concepts gave the Navy a threat, confirmed its sea-control strategy, and defined a force structure. The Navy modernized its battleships. It developed doctrines and designs for the aircraft carrier and the submarine. The Marine Corps founded an amphibious-assault doctrine, although it was not integrated into Navy battle plans.

There was a weakness in the Navy's position. Its view of sea power was presumptive, hermetic, and hence unreliable.

THE PROBLEMS WITH ORANGE

War Plan Orange was the Navy's primary war plan for twenty years. Its principle was sound: get the fleet out to the western Pacific, establish sea control, and defeat Japan through blockade. War Plan Orange remained a staff forecast. In the 1930s the Navy had no reason, and no way, to execute it.

Basic War Plan Orange originated in the Joint Army-Navy Board as a two-service plan for a war with Japan. Politically it had no meaning and was ignored by civil authorities. In the Navy's version, iterated at the operational level by the Battle Fleet command in the Pacific, it was the centerpiece of the doctrine of offensive sea control and was used for staff training, for budget requests, and for arguments with the Army. War Plan Orange kept the focus on the only theater where fleet action might take place.[2]

Operations received the main attention because, lacking an answer to the primary question of all strategic thinking—namely, What is the political goal of the military action?—that was all there was for the Navy to think about. Captain Harry Yarnell had posed the problem of absent policy to the Joint Army-Navy Board when it took up War Plan Orange after World War I. What were the interests of the United States in the Far East? Were they worth defending? Should the Army and the Navy plan a limited or an unlimited war against Japan? How much, if any at all, was the country willing to spend to hold the Philippines, to keep open the trade routes in the Orient, and to defend the Open Door in China?

To none of these questions did political leaders give the services an unambiguous answer. Communication with departments outside the services was almost nonexistent; it was similarly limited between the services. Not until the end of 1935 did the State Department detail a representative to the Joint Army-Navy Board, and then only after entreaties by the secretaries of War and Navy warning that if the country went to war with Japan it might lose. This connection, though late and loose, was nonetheless "one of the earliest efforts to co-ordinate national policy with military strategy."[3] In fact, little came of it. The State Department's representative was Stanley Hornbeck, longtime chief of the Far Eastern Affairs Division. He advocated a tough stand against Japan on the grounds that Japan, unable to overcome its deficiencies in resources, would back down to American demands rather than risk war.[4] The problem was that Hornbeck's opinions were his own. They did not represent State Department policy. Until around 1938 a gap yawned unbridged between what the Navy and the Army thought they should do in the Pacific and what their political masters would permit.

So the Navy forecast according to its own doctrine, according to its customary deduction of inherent national interests, and according to its staff estimates. From these estimates came its positions on War Plan Orange, and it held to these positions despite political disinterest, Army opposition, budgetary restrictions, and a foreign policy of high intentions and no teeth.

Two features kept War Plan Orange afloat. One was that the Navy's deduction of policy seemed as good a bet as the statesmen's gamble on retreat from the Far East and Japanese cooperation. There were interests in the western Pacific worth fighting for. First, the Philippines were a national responsibility. Any Japanese assertion of regional domination would challenge the economic and political order the United States wanted to maintain in Asia. Second, War Plan Orange fit the Navy's strategic disposition. It also fit the enemy's. Japan's naval strategy was more Mahanian than America's. In both countries the idea of inevitable challenge by a maritime competitor and a strategy of offensive sea control justified a high-seas battle fleet.

Yet War Plan Orange was not part of national strategy. Therefore, it lacked national justification. Congress would not authorize the ships or bases to make it work—nor would the Army cooperate—just on the basis of the Navy's predictions. Plan Orange operations were defined by doctrine alone. That rendered them unrealizable, but it did not mean the Navy gave them up.

Political leaders declined to make a commitment in the Far East to what the Navy planned to defend there. Presidents, first Hoover and then Franklin Roosevelt, held firm to the Washington and London treaties until the agreements expired at the end of 1936. The presidents forbade fortification of the naval bases in the Philippines and on Guam. Without such strongpoints the battle fleet could not sustain a campaign. Yet if the bases in the Philippines were lost and the capacity to reconquer them was not in hand, if the United States could not, in putting its Navy against Japan's, win and go on to isolate the home islands, then War Plan Orange was worthless and hence strategically pointless.

Japan's invasion of Manchuria in 1931, a deliberate violation of its agreement to maintain China's territorial integrity, did not shake Hoover's complacency. Manchuria was far from the portals of commerce to which the Open Door applied. In any case, Hoover, like presidents before and after him, was not going to enforce the Open Door. The Japanese foreign minister saw this and told his colleagues the United States would not go to war over China.[5]

What could the United States do about Manchuria or any violation of the Washington system? It might have brought three forms of pressure against Japan—military, economic, and diplomatic. But what military force could be used? Sending troops to Manchuria was out of the question. The government was neither prepared nor willing to consider naval action. Even had it been, the United States would have to act alone. Hoover's military advisers told him that a war with Japan meant the initial loss of the Philippines, five years of preparation, and four to six years of fighting.[6] That ruled out force.

The administration rejected economic boycott as provocative. There remained diplomacy. For most of the world the issue of Manchuria was the sanctity of agreements, not the defense of China. Secretary of State Stimson appealed to international morality. That was all the administration wanted to do, all it could do. Russell Weigley said that "the Manchurian crisis is an especially noteworthy illustration of the failure to formulate a coordinated diplomatic and military policy."[7] That failure was deliberate. A paper strategy fit a paper policy.

Hoover did not see the need for rearmament. He thought the job of the armed forces was to assure "that no foreign soldier will land on American soil."[8] For that, the services were strong enough. The members of the General Board, keepers of the Navy faith, pushed to build up to treaty ceilings, to a treaty fleet with treaty terms as the minimum, as the Japanese were doing. Those who proclaimed a long-term competition in the Pacific were a small minority, however, isolated from political and public opinion. For the administration Japan was not the enemy. Arms and expense were. The president wanted to balance the budget. Military spending meant debt, and that Hoover was determined to avoid.

His position, which kept the U.S. force below the treaty ceiling, was accepted by Secretary of the Navy Charles F. Adams, Chief of Naval Operations Admiral William Pratt, Secretary of War Patrick Hurley, and Army Chief of Staff General Douglas MacArthur. In September 1931, nine days after Japanese troops invaded Manchuria, the administration canceled all naval construction for fiscal year 1933 and halved the dozen destroyers already funded for 1932.

For Hoover, and for the nation at large, the Navy was afloat to deter or repel direct attack on the United States. Onshore coastal protection was the province of the Army's Coastal Artillery. During the 1930s air-power advocates in the Army challenged the Navy's responsibility for meeting the enemy offshore beyond the range of Army batteries. The Army Air Corps claimed that its land-based aircraft, above all the B-17 four-engine bomber introduced in 1937, could prevent enemy ships from nearing the coast. This was a claim for a strategic rather than only a support function for air power. It was not accepted by the high command of either service. Army planes were held to no more than 100 miles offshore. Nevertheless, the Army Air Corps did not give up its claim to long-range defense. The controversy over who had offshore authority smoldered through the 1930s.[9]

For their part in accepting Hoover's economizing and his hope of arms reduction, Adams and Pratt of the Navy's treaty faction were accused of betraying the Navy, of reneging on their promise to deliver a treaty force, of letting down the national defense. It is true that they were inspired by the hope that agreements could prevent an arms race. They were also pragmatists and must be credited with delivering to the Navy the most Hoover and Congress would give.[10]

Hoover's eyes in 1932 (when not on the domestic economy or his reelection campaign) were on Geneva, where a long-awaited general disarmament conference was under way. By proportional reduction, wars might be avoided or their destructiveness reduced. Hoover proposed to cut the world's armies and navies by about a third. Tanks and large land guns would be abolished, the number and tonnage of all major classes of warships slashed, and all military aircraft except scout planes eliminated.

There were no takers. The general disarmament conference, meant to culminate in arms-limitation agreements, came to nothing. When Hoover left office in 1933 there was no hope of further agreement.

Hoover had stated in his 1928 presidential campaign that he would build the Navy to treaty strength, to the point where it was "equal to the most powerful in the world." That did not happen. In 1931 the Navy's estimate of the situation concluded that War Plan Orange had little chance of success "due to failure to initiate and carry on a well-balanced program of new construction."[11] In 1932, at the end of Hoover's presidency, Japan was superior to the United States in cruisers, had a 4:1 advantage in modern destroyers, and was still within treaty limits. The U.S. decision to give battleship modernization priority over aircraft carrier development was made in this context. Pratt and Adams could not neglect the behemoths because battleships were the best means of taking maximum firepower across the Pacific against the main firepower source of the enemy. The two officers stretched available funds, but they were "caught in a circle of uncertainty, a circle in which the demands of military technology ran against treaty limitations, and where increasing appropriations were eaten up by more, and more expensive, weapons"—the carrier, the submarine, and naval air.[12] A balanced approach required nudging but not displacing the capital-ship doctrine.

The first formal war plan against Japan had been put forward by Rear Admiral R. P. Rodgers back in 1911, before Japan held the islands in Micronesia. Rodgers's plan assumed the Japanese would initially take the Philippines. In reaction, U.S. forces would sail from Hawaii to Okinawa, cut the central Pacific axis, seize the Marshalls and the Carolines (in those days from Germany), recapture Manila, and then strangle Japan by blockade. Rodgers's plan was prophetic in its acceptance of the initial loss of the Philippines and in its island-hopping forecast, going as far as to suggest sailing straight to Okinawa and Formosa rather than trying to mount extensive land operations to recapture the main Philippine island of Luzon. The plan is worth noting as a deviation from sea-control dogma. Rodgers, president of the Naval War College, did not make decisive battle his strategic goal, and he envisioned a long war.[13]

The Joint Army-Navy War Plan Orange of 1924 returned to the direct line of attack. Its authors reasoned that public opinion would not support a protracted campaign. It was therefore necessary to relieve the garrison in the Philippines with great speed. In the tradition of the Great White Fleet, the dash by the Navy would be made straight from Hawaii to Manila, a move that became known as the "through ticket." Fifty thousand reinforcements would be carried to the garrison in the Philippines while the battle fleet prepared for decisive engagement. With command of the sea the United States could starve Japan into submission. This plan was a committee confection full of hard-to-meet conditions. Crossing the ocean would take most of the country's tankers and a third of the ships of the U.S. merchant marine. The ships would arrive at Manila Bay to find base facilities inadequate for handling the volume of men and matériel that were required for an extended campaign. The plan was a mirage: no matter what the transportation problems, the troops to carry and support such an operation did not exist. The Army was not about to commit 50,000 men to the campaign.

So Navy thinking changed. If the Philippines could not be relieved and an offensive war could not be conducted from Hawaii, one alternative was a progressive advance across the central Pacific, capturing the Japanese-controlled islands in Micronesia—the Marshalls, the Carolines, and the Marianas—which lay athwart the route and thus were possible obstructions in the line of transit. Taking those islands would deny Japan protected bases for ships and aircraft. On these bases rested the Japanese plan of forward defense, which called for the attrition of the extended westbound U.S. fleet before the decisive battle.[14] Such an island-hopping campaign based on the Rodgers model would be costly and prolonged, and neither the Army nor the Navy prepared for the amphibious operations it entailed. It was lucky, when war came, that the Marine Corps had.

Another alternative was a bypass to the south. This was logistically difficult and would take a long time. Yet another possibility was to draw back to a defensive position at Hawaii. Because withdrawal or delay would expose the Philippines, Guam, and Samoa and leave all American trade in the far Pacific imperiled, the Joint Board in 1926 decided to stay with the idea of a strategic offensive in the central Pacific, but with a slower rate of advance. It would be a long war. Without reinforcements the Army could not hold the Philippines, and the Navy would have to fight its way there stage by stage.

The slow advance and the ban against improving naval fortifications made Army reinforcement of its Philippines garrison all-important. The Army had only a few men there: 4,000 Americans and 7,000 Filipinos. Against those a 1928 estimate had said that the Japanese, in control of the sea and most likely of the air, would land 300,000 men within 30 days after war began, 50,000 of them within the first week. In 1930 the entire U.S. Army stood at only 145,000 men. The Army could not assign even a third of these to the Philippines.[15] Operation in the Pacific was the Navy's major justification of its force level. For the Army it was a drain on meager peacetime resources and a distraction from its mission of continental defense. In Army eyes, War Plan Orange described a disaster.

And it remained a plan without political backing. The Manchurian crisis showed that the United States would not defend the Open Door or China. What, then, would it do? What in fact could it do? In 1932 the United States Fleet maneuvered in the Pacific and then collected at Hawaii. The exercise gratified the Navy. It did not intimidate Japan.[16] There was no political resolve behind the deployment. Strategy luffed.

In 1933 the Army commander of the Corregidor fortress at the entrance to Manila Bay (to which the Philippines garrison was gradually repairing) said that if Philippine defenses were not strengthened, the islands should be given up. He said, "To carry out the present ORANGE plan with its provisions for an early dispatch of our fleet to Philippine waters would be literally an act of madness." Holding a rocky strongpoint did not give the Navy a base. The Japanese could capture Manila from the land and deprive the United States use of the bay. The Army commanders in the Philippines argued that the government should remove American forces from China and the Philippine islands and take up a line running from Alaska through Hawaii to Panama as the "strategic peacetime frontier in the Pacific."[17]

The Joint Board refused to accept the conclusion that the Philippines could not be held with the forces on hand or that reinforcements could never arrive in time. The highest Army leaders also rejected talk of pulling out. Until otherwise instructed by civil authority, the job of the Army was to hold on as best it could. Strategy formulation was not seen as a two-way street. As a matter of service principle, the Army central staff in Washington refused to influence foreign policy by discussing the Army's capability, or lack thereof, to fight a war. Even had its leaders wanted to withdraw from the Philippines, they faced a Navy veto on the Joint Board. The Navy, wedded to forward deployment, insisted on an Army defensive action in the Philippines regardless of the outcome, to divert Japanese forces and so contribute to an eventual naval victory.[18]

In 1933 a war game at the Naval War College confirmed that direct transit to Manila was infeasible. In 1935, maneuvers showed that the fleet could not cross the ocean unless it denied central Pacific bases to the enemy. As if the maneuvers involved a rehearsal of Japanese strategy, the U.S. battle train was severely attrited by "enemy" submarines and then "destroyed" in a battle off Midway.[19] The conclusion was that the advance must take the Royal Road, seizing the Japanese-controlled islands in Micronesia. Sea power took on an assault function and connected its mission to the land.

Here was the basis of a complete Pacific campaign, but it received no support from Congress, which refused to fortify Guam or permit seaplane bases on Wake or Midway islands. The administration abided by the Washington nonfortification agreement until it expired at the end of December 1936. Whether the Japanese violated their agreement not to fortify the Marshalls, the Carolines, and the Marianas remains in dispute. There was no verification process for any of the naval arms-limitation treaties, which was one of their chief weaknesses, and the U.S. government and the League of Nations preferred ignorance to on-site inspection.[20]

The progressive island-hopping advance meant a certainly fatal delay in relieving the Army garrison in the Philippines. Relief plans were moot. The Army continued to refuse to provide the thousands of men needed to assault and capture the Japanese-held islands in the central Pacific, let alone the men needed to reinforce the defense of Manila Bay. In its advance across the Pacific, the Navy would be on its own. That makes more important the fact that the Navy failed to integrate into its operational planning the fine theoretical work done on amphibious assault during this period by the Marine Corps. Nor did it support the Marines' amphibious exercises by providing transports and matériel, even though the most recent iteration of War Plan Orange had been carried out as a stage-by-stage offensive through the islands to keep the advance under the cover of land-based air.[21]

It was at this point, in mid-decade, that the service secretaries informed Secretary of State Cordell Hull that their position in the Far East was so weak that the United States might lose a war with Japan. As German and Italian bellicosity restored the Atlantic's strategic importance, the concentration on the Philippines and the continuation of the vulnerable Army garrison there was, in Army eyes, the result of giving War Plan Orange "an undue and unsound influence upon national policy."[22] In November 1937 the Joint Board concluded that War Plan Orange was "unsound in general" and "wholly inapplicable." Germany might once more penetrate the western hemisphere. The Pacific war plan required revision in light of Atlantic needs.[23]

On such grounds it is conventional to conclude that Orange had become "even more unrealistic than before."[24] Ronald Spector characterized the Joint Board's persistence in holding on to Orange as a form of psychological and political denial.[25] But one may also conclude that War Plan Orange was based on the following Navy insights: first, that the Pacific strategy must be maritime; second, that to control Japan's home islands and eliminate its will to fight, maritime superiority had to be gained by destroying or taking command of Japan's capital ships and merchant marine; and third, that to achieve maritime superiority, conquest of the Japanese-held islands in Micronesia was essential. That any war plan in the 1930s was largely speculative is understandable. Invasions requiring thousands of men had to be unrealistic given U.S. political conditions. In the 1940s, however, such invasions materialized. The experience of World War II proved the fundamental features of War Plan Orange to be correct.[26]

What made the plan unworkable in the 1930s lay outside Navy control. The Navy did what it was supposed to. It planned for war and forecast the means needed to prosecute it. Continual war-gaming of Plan Orange was an "enforcer of strategic realism," and fleet maneuvers revealed many of the plan's weaknesses, such as an inadequate island-assault doctrine, just in time for rectification before American involvement in World War II.[27] Here is Edward Miller's conclusion:

> How, then, is War Plan Orange to be judged? It was one of the longest thought-out plans of the war and the most successful. . . . The "Through Ticket" may have been wishful thinking, but the strategies of counterattack and siege were sound and the central Pacific island-hopping route was excellent. War Plan Orange persevered for forty years and eventually won the war. What more can one ask of a great plan?[28]

Nonetheless, a war plan is not a strategy, and in the mid-1930s the United States did not have a strategy for the Pacific. Should the services plan for a defensive or an offensive war? No one decided. The question of what kind of war should be fought and for what purpose was still open. Navy staffers thought the country had interests worth defending and planned an offensive war accordingly, but political approval remained unclear.

The result was a compromise of interests and no time frame for action. In the Joint Board's 1938 version of War Plan Orange, the Army accepted naval operations west of Hawaii. But the Army left unclear what it would do about the defense of the Philippines, to which it assigned no reinforcements. The Navy dropped its call for an offensive war and for the destruction of Japan's naval forces. It kept its plan for a measured move to the west, to which the Army agreed eventually to commit men to assault Pacific islands, and the final defeat of Japan by blockade, but it established no timetable. Overall, the services conceded the initial loss of Guam and the Philippines. The Army gained Navy recognition of a defensive security line for the eastern Pacific, anchored on Alaska, Hawaii, and Panama, while the general strategy for the defeat of Japan was phrased vaguely as "military and economic pressure."[29]

By this time Japan had embarked on an aggressive foreign policy, was at war with China, and was linked with Germany and Italy in the Anti-Comintern Pact. That did not mean Japan sought war with the United States. The pastiche that was War Plan Orange, indicative of the uncertainties of American policy in the Far East, could be interpreted as a sign that the United States would offer no opposition to Japanese expansion.

PUSHING THE LIMITS

Preparedness was impossible until the government declared that a threat existed. Rearmament came only at the end of the decade, in response to the dramatic rise of Japanese and German armed aggression. Until then, the Navy built not according to the force requirements of its war plan but according to treaty numbers and to budget requests framed to create domestic jobs.

At the opening of the 1930s, a Navy second to none was a receding goal. Japan and Britain were building up to the quotas permitted by the treaties. The United States was not. The fleet had only about 65 percent of the major combat ships permitted, while Japan had almost 100 percent of its quota afloat, and Japan's ships were largely new vessels. The Navy had expected the administration and Congress to build to the levels authorized. They did not because of the absence of a maritime threat, because they expected further arms-limitation agreements, and because of the Great Depression. The United States had not established parity with Britain in the designated ship classes. Instead of the 10:6 ratio with Japan, by 1935 the proportion was 10:8, giving Japan regional superiority. It was obvious the Navy was slipping in manpower and training. Its aging fleet drifted toward obsolescence. Operational efficiency had eroded. In 1933, all but four of the hundred or so destroyers of World War I vintage, for instance, were overaged.

The Navy's revival in the 1930s began not because of its war plans or security forecasts, but because of the connection between arms and jobs, because of the effort to pull the country out of the Depression. Armament became part of recovery. Shipbuilding contracts equaled employment. Chief of Naval Operations Pratt and the General Board argued for an eight-year program that would include the building of 119 ships, both to replace existing vessels and to increase the total number of ships. Pratt's program would cost almost $1 billion, of which in fiscal year 1934, $253 million would go for 32 new ships and for aircraft.[30] The new president, Franklin Roosevelt, responded to this proposal in June 1933 by assigning $238 million from the new National Industrial Recovery Act to replacement construction, designating shipbuilding as a public work. Not a keel had been laid under Hoover, and so it appeared that the Navy had turned the corner.

Navy Secretary Claude Swanson (March 1933 to July 1939) opened his *Annual Report* for 1933 with these words:

> No such building program has been undertaken by this country since that of the year 1916 when President Wilson sought to bring the Navy of the United States to a position inferior to none.
>
> The recent program is in close accord with the purposes of the National Recovery Act, since it will substantially aid employment and the restoration of commercial, industrial, and agricultural activity. Approximately 85 percent of the moneys spent on this naval construction will go directly into the pockets

of labor; about half at the shipyards and the remainder scattered throughout the country among the producers and fabricators of raw materials. Every State will benefit.[31]

The Navy's fortunes brightened further with the passage of an important supplement to the 1934 appropriation bill. This supplement, sponsored by the service's great supporter Representative Carl Vinson (joined in the Senate by Park Trammell), authorized the Navy to build up to treaty limits and to replace ships as they became overaged. The supplemental bill permitted the Navy to determine the building program without getting specific congressional approval of each ship. It was, however, an authorization only, not an appropriation of money. Roosevelt's Bureau of the Budget stated that administration endorsement entailed no financial obligation. No figures were mentioned, save that the treaty limits should be met by 1942. The timing of construction was left up to the president, and the appropriation of money to make it happen remained at the pleasure of Congress.

The subvention from public works funds was not an unencumbered gift, nor was it repeated. Armament construction, which was geared to foreign policy, and economic recovery, which was entirely domestic, were programs cut from different cloths. The Navy wanted ships ready to fight, built in Navy yards under Navy control. The administrators of national recovery wanted depression relief and thus arranged for 85 percent of the construction to be carried out by private shipbuilders. The Navy and the Department of Labor each thought too much was taken out of its own hands. The marriage of naval construction and national recovery was successful in the long run—the Navy got money, ships got built, jobs were created—but it was full of honest disputes about purpose and jurisdiction. Roosevelt, when he intervened, came down on the side of the Labor Department.[32] Similarly, passage of the Vinson-Trammell bill did not guarantee an increase in congressional appropriations. The appropriation of $302 million for fiscal year 1935 was lower than that for fiscal year 1934, and although it was considerably enhanced by public works monies (another $113 million), the construction program for which the Navy hoped had only begun.[33]

These appropriations preserved the base of fleet construction—that is, the replacement of overaged vessels. Replacement, however, was not expansion. Preparedness would require more, and a war with Japan would require a new industrial structure that could mass produce naval weapons. That national mobilization would come only with hostilities and the demand for rapid victory. Before then, in the mid-1930s, when it replaced ships instead of expanding the fleet, the Navy was limited to maintaining existing construction capabilities.[34]

The government's objective was to avoid a war, not to prepare for one. On the horizon loomed another arms-limitation conference, set for London in 1935. Roosevelt wanted to reach an understanding with Japan. He proposed

> a new treaty for ten years on the present ratios but with say a general reduction of twenty percent; that if Japan should refuse that then we should offer to renew the Treaty just as it is for a period of five years; that if Japan then refused that she would be on the defensive and England and the United States and perhaps also France and Italy could proceed to sign a treaty . . . with a provision for parity between the British and ourselves, the level of which would go up or down depending upon what Japan might do.[35]

Until that was settled Roosevelt held the Navy to short rations and foreign policy on a short leash.

Roosevelt's proposal was not part of a larger strategy to support or replace the Washington system.[36] He was simply testing arms control, parity, and proportionality.

The Second London Naval Conference, which took place in 1935–36, came to nothing. After it, the treaty structure collapsed and a naval arms race began. Preparations for war in Japan and Germany demanded that the U.S. government respond with a strong foreign policy and its correlative, a great expansion of American naval (and ground and air) force. Recognition of this fact was slow in coming. The time lost could have been used for rearmament.

The Second London Naval Conference failed because in January 1936 the Japanese delegation walked out. The government of Japan had seesawed between confidence and pessimism. War Plan Orange suggested enemy encirclement. The Vinson-Trammell bill of 1934 foretold the loss of what was a de facto 10:8 ratio. That ratio had given them regional superiority and to maintain it the Japanese government agreed to let its navy exceed the treaty quotas. And at the end of 1935, on the eve of the Second London Naval Conference, Japan's Imperial Navy was under the control of the Mahanian fleet faction. It had an offensive sea-power strategy for the defense of the empire which its proponents thought was certain of success.

Japan's strategy was pure Mahan. Japanese naval forces would attack the U.S. fleet as it crossed the Pacific, whittling away its fighting effectiveness by 30 percent. To that end Japan established a perimeter of island bases and airfields, developed the fastest and most powerful long-range torpedo, built up a comfortable advantage in cruisers and destroyers, and acquired a modern submarine force and a solid line of aircraft. Attrition would bring the fleets into rough equivalence, which would give Japan the strategic advantage thanks to its proximity to the theater of combat. At the appropriate moment, when the Americans were overextended and worn down, the still untouched Japanese battle fleet would engage. The assumed location of this decisive battle, originally expected in home waters, moved steadily eastward as the Japanese deployed further forward and as land-based aircraft joined the interception campaign. In 1934 the place of the main fleet encounter was moved to a line between the Bonins and the Marianas. (In 1940 it would be set further out, in line with the Marshalls.) A U.S. defeat on the high seas and a U.S. inability to project force into the western Pacific would cause the United States to concede Japan's paramountcy in a maritime sphere of influence that took in all of East Asia, and the war would be over.

To prepare to carry out this strategy, the Japanese fleet faction insisted that the government abandon the arms-limitation treaties. The country could not be bound by an agreement that forbade the building of battleships and limited the size of those afloat to 35,000 tons and their cannons to a 14-inch caliber. The key to the country's war plan was the gigantic 64,000-ton *Yamato* class, superdreadnoughts, displacing almost 70,000 tons when carrying nine 18.1-inch guns elevated to 45°. These would be the most powerful fighting vessels ever launched, the heaviest and most heavily armed and armored. Their construction would end the ratio neurosis that had bedeviled Japan's navy for years and move the country's capital-ship strength beyond the 10:6 ratio, giving Japan superiority in a capital-ship battle. With a jump of perhaps five years on the United States, and the advantage of location, this force would guarantee victory.[37]

The cabinet in Tokyo was willing to give up international cooperation on naval arms and on China. It was not, however, motivated by an expectation of war with the United States. Toward the United States, the Japanese government was willfully complacent. It pulled out of the treaty system because it had decided Japan would henceforth go it alone, come what may.

Japan's new course broke the Washington Conference agreements. In December 1934 the government announced it would not renew the Washington naval arms-limitation treaty, which was due to expire two years later, and that in any further naval agreement, it would reject all ratios and accept no less than parity, with no ceiling on guns at 14 inches, a limit the United States wanted.

Parity was the position Japan took to the London Conference of 1935, a position the United States refused to concede. So the Japanese delegation walked out. The period of cooperation in an international system was over. Within the year the Imperial Japanese Navy won cabinet permission for a force "sufficient to maintain command of the sea in the western Pacific against the United States," for a policy "to advance into the South Seas while maintaining the empire's foothold on the continent," and for a force of 12 battleships, 12 aircraft carriers, 28 cruisers, 96 destroyers, 70 submarines, and 65 air groups. The navy also received cabinet approval to build more carriers, destroyers, and submarines as needed. Expansion southward was to be peaceful if possible; but the Japanese force would be strong enough to face a challenge by the United States if it came to that.[38]

For the next two years Roosevelt tried to continue a passive policy in the Pacific and to avoid an arms race. His instrument was diplomacy; he had neither the means nor the will for coercion. Peace plans were floated without effect. Roosevelt suggested neutralizing the Pacific islands, but to no avail. Secretary of State Hull's policy of moral suasion was predictably futile.

Meanwhile, Germany and Italy overthrew the postwar settlement. One need simply utter the names Ethiopia, the Rhineland, Spain, Austria, and Czechoslovakia to call up the characteristics of the period, the renewed aggression and the impotent response. Japan in the immediate aftermath of quitting the London Naval Conference had joined the Axis states in the Anti-Comintern Pact of 1936, reflecting the Japanese army's concern that its aggression in Manchuria might bring it into conflict with the Soviet Union. Japan's army was considering further action in Manchuria; the navy was considering expansion to the south. In either case, war with one or more European powers was likely.

In 1937 Japan invaded China and began an undeclared war. Japanese planes sank the USS *Panay*, a gunboat that was escorting three American oil tankers on the Yangtze River. Chief of Naval Operations Admiral William Leahy (January 1937 to August 1939) said that the United States should immediately blockade Japan as a warning against further expansion in China and against any more attacks on Americans. Roosevelt and Hull, however, thought that Congress and public opinion would not support such an action, which would be tantamount to war, and closed the incident after the Japanese government apologized and paid an indemnity.[39] From the U.S. perspective, the only bright spot in the Far East was that China had not fallen. China had become Japan's continental ulcer.

In 1938 Congress expanded the U.S. Navy for the first time since World War I. It at last appropriated money to fund the construction authorized by the 1934 Vinson-Trammell bill. Thus the Navy could build up to the number of ships allowed by the old treaties. That number was still the U.S. standard for construction even though the treaties themselves had lapsed. To this appropriation was added a second Vinson bill, that authorized—but did not fund—a 20-percent increase in the total tonnage of the Navy beyond the 1934 Vinson-Trammell authorization.

This was expansion, not just replacement—expansion beyond the treaty quotas but in proportion to the treaty ratios, to ensure but not upset the balance. The expansion was a defensive measure. As Vinson said, "Had the Washington and London treaties remained in effect it would have been unnecessary for us to come before Congress with this building program." Britain and Japan had gone beyond the treaty ratios, and the United States had to keep up.[40]

Two features of the second Vinson bill are very important. Not the size of the expansion it called for, which was proportional to that of the recent expansion of other navies, and which was modest if one envisioned a possible increase of foreign involvement to the point of a war such as that foreseen in War Plan Orange. What was important was, first, the way its supporters posed the security issues, and most notably, the way Roosevelt did so in his message to Congress on national defense in January 1938: "As Commander in Chief of the Army and Navy of the United States it is my constitutional duty to report to the Congress that our national defense is in the light of the increasing armaments of other nations, inadequate for purposes of national security and requires increase for that reason." Faced with darkening horizons in the east and west, rearmament was now justified not by its contribution to economic recovery but by its contribution to the national defense. Second, Roosevelt and Vinson proposed, for the first time, a two-ocean navy. Said Roosevelt: "We cannot assume that our defense would be limited to one ocean and one coast and that the other ocean and the other coast would with certainty be safe. We cannot be certain that the connecting link—the Panama Canal—would be safe. Adequate defense affects therefore the simultaneous defense of every part of the United States of America."[41]

It remained to be seen how the expanded Navy of the 1938 appropriation and Vinson's second bill would serve U.S. foreign policy. But the value of the legislation was evident following the outbreak in 1939 of war in Europe. Fighting for its life at home, Britain had nothing to spare for the Pacific. The United States, committed to a major Atlantic presence, faced Japan alone. In June 1940 Congress passed Vinson's third bill, the appropriation for the 20-percent increase that had been authorized in 1938. The 1940 bill also authorized a further 11-percent increase in the fleet. The next month Congress passed the most important act of all. Cognizant of the immense political responsibilities the United States was about to shoulder, Carl Vinson was determined to have an adequate force in place. His fourth bill, passed in July 1940 in the wake of the fall of France, authorized a 70-percent increase in the U.S. fleet. In the summer of 1940, with the British beleaguered and the French fleet out of operation, the United States could no longer count on Britain and France to contain German aggression in the Atlantic. The United States would have to look after its own defense. Rather than decrease the Battle Fleet, which was concentrated in the Pacific, it was necessary to create a second, independent battle fleet. This meant a massive increase in the Navy's size. Thus Vinson's bills of 1940 ended the era of the ratio-determined treaty Navy. In its place came a two-ocean Navy for a global war.

A BALANCED FLEET

With its appropriations in the 1920s and 1930s, the Navy had constructed a balanced fleet. More than a phrase chosen for political effect, *balanced fleet* expressed the Navy's needs. Developing its mixed force, the Navy tried to build up to treaty limits, integrate new designs, and satisfy the competing claims of its several internal communities.

Through 1936, force development was constrained by the naval treaties. With battleship construction forbidden and the building of carriers and submarines restricted, the Navy had to consider its mix of ships and their operations carefully. Money was always scarce. The Navy had to use it wisely.[42]

By and large it did. Studies by Thomas Hone and others show that the service learned from experience and improved armor, propulsion, gunnery, aircraft, and submarines.[43] Decisions were based largely on merit, not on prejudice, and the Navy designed "some of the best warships ever constructed."[44] But tight budgets meant less flexibility because, with less experimentation, care had to be taken to avoid costly failures. Small budgets also encouraged conservative conceptualization, limiting strategic innovation. That reaction to scarcity, and lack of broad public support for a strong Navy, helps explain some of the most criticized aspects of naval planning during this period, such as the failure to integrate amphibious doctrine into war plans.

The Pacific remained the chief subject of strategic planning. For battle in the Pacific, the center of the combat force remained the battleship. There was a reason for this other than slavish devotion to the battle line. There was sentiment for the great ships, of course. Most of the Navy's top admirals were former battleship commanders, and their "gun club" was a ticket to advancement. But the centrality of the battleship was based on the fact that it was the best way to transport firepower across the Pacific Ocean and to bring it to bear upon the Japanese fleet. Only the battleship had the endurance to sail across the ocean under attack from Japanese airplanes, submarines, and cruisers and, at the end, be ready to meet the enemy fleet in a second Jutland. A battleship's long-range heavy cannon could shoot farther than a torpedo, and its shot fell more accurately than a bomb. Only a battleship was likely to sink another battleship. That was why through the 1930s it remained the main weapon for a strategic war at sea, and that in turn gave it primary claim on construction funds and operating budgets. "As late as 1940," Ronald Spector wrote, "the Naval War College [in a pamphlet to students titled *The Employment of Aviation in Naval Warfare*] was pointing out that it takes 108 planes to carry as many large torpedoes as one squadron of destroyers and 1200 to carry as many large bombs or large projectiles as one battleship."[45]

The Japanese could defend against torpedoes by armoring their hulls or adding impact-absorbing blisters. Their cruisers and destroyers could attack U.S. torpedo-launching ships. Lack of bases meant that the Navy could not rely on the submarine as an offensive weapon until its range and numbers were increased. Horizontal bombers (as opposed to dive-bombers) had a hard time hitting ships under way and could be held off with antiaircraft fire. Before the mid-1930s the dive-bomber, though a fearsome weapon against the unprotected flight decks of carriers, could not carry enough heavy bombs to sink a battleship. Battleships led the Japanese fleet; U.S. battleships would have to meet them.

The Washington Treaty of 1922 had recognized the battleship's dominance. That is why it froze their numbers (eighteen for the U.S. Navy) and the weight of each ship (a maximum of 35,000 tons for all signatories). The United States abided by these terms—and observed the holiday that halted new construction—until the treaties expired at the end of 1936. No battleships were built between 1921 and 1937, when construction of the *North Carolina* began. In the interim, the Navy preserved and modernized. The most important change, the conversion of engines from coal to oil, began in the 1920s. Oil improved speed and lightened the fuel load. The fact that oil gave the fleet a longer range, made fueling more convenient, and was easier to get than coal in the Pacific partially offset the absence of support bases west of Hawaii.[46]

New designs in propulsion equipment meant that when battleship rearmament began again, the Navy could build the vessels ever larger and ever swifter.[47] Speed was important. In 1936, naval intelligence revealed that the speed of the battleship *Nagato* was above 26 knots. The *Yamato* was expected to do much better than that.[48] The maximum speed of the first ships of the *North Carolina* class, which were begun in 1937 and 1938 and finished in 1941 and 1942, was therefore raised to 27 knots; and that of the four ships of the *South Dakota* class, begun in 1939 and 1940, was put at 30 knots. The last of the U.S. battleships, the four of the *Iowa* class, begun in 1940 and 1941, could sail at 35 knots, faster than any Japanese battlewagon, and in firepower they were virtually the equivalent of the most heavily armed Japanese ship.

Battleships, then, remained at the core of the strategy of offensive sea control. Huge distances were involved; huge ships had to be faced. Vinson's two-ocean naval bill of 1940 envisioned fleets built around a *Montana* class, in which design emphasis returned to the tradition of heavy armor and heavy guns, at the expense of speed. These ships would weigh 60,000 tons and have twelve 16-inch cannons shooting 2,700-pound shells. Ships of this class were never built. While they were being designed, the aircraft carrier became the major ship of war and the carrier battle group replaced the big-gun battle line.

The fact that there were only a few battleships, however, meant that renewed attention was given to what cruisers, destroyers, carriers, and submarines could do. Strategists knew that war with Japan could take various forms. Emphasis was on fleet engagement, where Japan placed it too, but no one could predict what might happen before such a war, which elements of naval force might be important, or when or where they might be needed. It was essential to prepare broadly, to make adjustments in operations and doctrine as new weapon systems came on line, and to allow for innovation and mistakes. The design process was inherently inefficient and unpredictable. John Reilly compared the design track of a new class of ship to the action in a soccer match, as the design passed "from place to place and back again."[49] Rapid developments in one weapon could make another obsolete, as when the carrier-based airplane supplanted the seaplane.

Diversity was increased by modern technology, where innovation never stops. What is remarkable is what the Navy did within its limits, not what it did not do.[50] After the attack on Pearl Harbor, an offensive fleet was immediately put into action—without a battleship. Submarines received a new mission, to act independently in a war of attrition against all enemy vessels. When the war came, a new structure for rapid mass production of all kinds of naval weapons was at once created. All that, and the Navy's victory at sea, was made possible by the managerial and doctrinal accomplishments of the previous decade.

The Navy also neglected important areas, partly through shortsightedness and partly its straitened circumstances. Navy planning was poorly coordinated with American diplomacy, the two being connected only through the naval arms-limitation agreements. There was no planning for anything less than unlimited war against Japan. Without Army or State Department agreement on War Plan Orange, the Pacific campaign was the Navy's own. Defense of the Philippines was the Army's responsibility, but it would commit no men for subduing the islands that lay athwart the route to its garrison on Corregidor.

The Army's refusal to make such a commitment makes all the more notable the Navy's failure to integrate into its battle plans the Marine Corps's theoretical work on amphibious operations. Particularly egregious was the Navy's failure to work on air-ground-naval fire-support coordination, or assign transports and logistical support to the Marines' exercises.[51] There was no serious planning for an offensive submarine campaign of attrition of merchantmen, even though starving Japan's island empire was the final phase of Orange strategy.

Nor was there planning for the transport of Army troops. This was understandable with regard to the Atlantic. Who, before the end of the 1930s, even thought of the need for another ferry to France, for another landing on continental Europe? The experiences of 1917–18, overwhelmingly of transport and antisubmarine warfare, did not seem in the 1920s and early 1930s to forecast the operations of the future. No American intended an invasion of Europe, and even less of Japan.

Likewise, there were no serious preparations for convoy escort. Again, World War I did not seem to offer any guidance. Germany, denied battleships and submarines by the Treaty of Versailles, had no naval capability until Nazi rearmament in the late 1930s. For antisubmarine warfare the U.S. Navy held to the doctrine of patrol.

In the United States, torpedo manufacture was a cottage industry. Between 1923 and 1940, all torpedoes came from only one source, the Naval Torpedo Station at Newport. All other manufactories had been closed down in the aftermath of the Washington Conference. At Newport, torpedoes were made by a guild. Isolated and inward-looking, this group had no competition or sense of urgency and was detached from sea experience. The testing of the $10,000 copies was conservative and theoretical and not carried out under fleet conditions. In addition, technical defects that made the torpedoes unreliable to the point of uselessness were not revealed until World War II at immense cost in lives, time, and opportunity. Output was small. In no year before 1936 did production exceed 381 torpedoes. The output for 1937 was 591. For 1938 it was 765, and for 1939 still only 788. No one in the 1930s was thinking of another torpedo war.[52]

Destroyers and cruisers received attention as scouts and protectors of the battle line in a Pacific war.[53] Those ships, and soon aircraft carriers, were to offset Japan's attrition strategy. Destroyers, and then the carriers, were to screen the battle fleet from torpedo attack. Cruisers, used offensively, were to join in the fleet engagement as defenders of the battleships. In the final phase of the war, destroyers and cruisers would apply the blockade.

Perhaps ship size and guns were overemphasized. Until more battleships were available, heavy cruisers, as Thomas Hone wrote, were the "*expendable* major surface unit."[54] And yet, until fast battleships were built, the cruisers—both the heavy and the light—formed the shock brigade. They were vital defenders where speed and power were required, being used, for instance, to escort carriers that could steam at over 30 knots. In 1936, the United States had eighteen heavy cruisers and nineteen light ones.

It is often asserted that the Navy stinted the carrier in the 1930s, that it failed to see the potential of seaborne air power. In the distribution of funds, it was not a question of ignoring the carriers and the naval air force. It was a matter of allocating limited funds.[55] The eighteen treaty battleships, few but enough to form a fleet, needed first modernization and then replacement, and then to be increased in number. Treaty restrictions dictated design. They held the total weight of U.S. carriers to 135,000 tons. Carrier design also was slowed by the extensive deliberation deemed appropriate to the peacetime development of an entirely new system. Carrier design was not held back just by hostility to the idea of fleet air. It took experience to establish the value of carriers. The controlling question was, Did naval air have an offensive capacity?

That was what Rear Admiral William A. Moffett, the first chief of the Bureau of Aeronautics (which was established in 1921), set out to prove. Moffett was determined to keep naval air within the Navy. He fended off Army moves to absorb it as part of a unified air service. Naval aviation, said Moffett, must go to sea on the back of the fleet. The air arm was part of the sea arm, compatible, supportive, not independent or different. Pilots were naval officers first. It was to be naval air, fleet aviation. Its purpose was to aid the striking power of the great guns of the battleships and cruisers. Airplanes were the issue, not their carriers. Even battleships and cruisers launched their own airplanes. In 1927, of fourteen aircraft squadrons, only five were connected to aircraft carriers.[56]

In the beginning the carrier was a spotter auxiliary. With an unprotected flight deck that was very vulnerable to enemy guns, it stood out of range, away from the main fleet. From there it sent its pilots up to peer over the horizon. The aircraft essentially was a higher spotting platform. Far better than spotters in the masthead cages, pilots could see an approaching enemy and call for range corrections of the falling shot. Indeed, the indictment that the Bureau of Ordnance failed to adapt gunnery to new technology, that it "failed to maintain its supremacy because it neglected to seek out and apply the aggressive creativity that would have helped it to maintain its edge in spite of advances in alternative weapons," is supported by the fact that it was not the Bureau of Ordnance but the Bureau of Aeronautics that developed aircraft spotting, which in turn revolutionized gunnery in the 1920s and 1930s.[57] "Naval Aviation, an Evolution of Naval Gunfire" is the title of an article on the subject.[58]

Airborne platforms were so useful as scouts and screens of the battle line that planners envisioned a permanent patrol of dirigibles along an arc running from Hawaii through the Bonins to Alaska, covering the western approaches to the United States. The rigid airships' very long-range reconnaissance capacity and phenomenal endurance gave them strategic value. They had three times the speed of the fastest naval vessel and ten times the range of airplanes, which, incidentally, they could carry as well.[59]

Moffett never for a moment envisioned taking aviation out of the fleet, and it became increasingly apparent that aircraft and the carriers could do more than scout and spot. They could be part of the Navy's offensive strike force. Moffett set out to get as many carriers as he could, any way he could, and to get many specialized types of airplanes as well, scouts to be sure, but also bombers and fighters, so that Navy air could take on more ambitious offensive roles.[60] Until 1934, the United States had only three or four carriers, the experimental noncombatant *Langley*, whose flight deck was laid on the top of a converted collier, and the *Lexington* and *Saratoga*, which had been converted from unfinished heavy cruisers in the wake of the Washington Treaty build-down. The

Ranger, the first carrier designed to the purpose, was commissioned in 1934 at 14,500 tons. On these four ships, the Navy worked out the tactics of its carrier air. The General Board made this easier by not insisting on controlling aircraft designs in the same way it dominated ship design.[61]

Moffett received early support from many officers, including certain members of the battleship commanders "gun club," who appreciated the value of scouting and spotting and who carried aircraft aboard their own gunships. William Sims, for example, proponent of the big-gun battleships, became an early convert to naval airpower and after World War I ran simulations at the Naval War College that helped familiarize officers with the value of naval air. Moffett himself drew on support that went all the way back to a General Board conclusion of 1919:

> Aircraft have become an essential arm of the fleet. A naval air service must be established, capable of accompanying and operating with the fleet in all waters of the globe. . . . Fleet engagements of the future will probably be preceded by air engagements. The advantage will lie with the fleet which wins in the air . . . airplane carriers for the fleet [should] be provided in the proportion of one carrier to each squadron of capital ships.[62]

And Moffett, in his own right an organizational genius, won the congressional support that enabled the Bureau of Aeronautics to survive all the storms of gun-club opposition and the jealousy of the other matériel bureaus who resisted its decentralized autonomy. When Moffett ran into opposition to his emerging offensive doctrine, he was not shy in stating that the battleship was becoming obsolete. Perhaps he thought the opposition to Navy air was stronger than it really was. In 1933, a month before he died in the crash of the dirigible *Akron*, he wrote:

> My experience in the Navy justifies me in saying that any new weapon has been received with suspicion and antagonism by the Navy as a whole. Even the great Admiral Luce said that steam would always be auxiliary to sail. Steam had to fight its way for years. . . . Aviation is going through the same experience, although the situation has been improving steadily for years. This did not surprise me, and my former service and experience with steam and the attitude of the Navy toward it, has been of great assistance to me in being patient when endeavoring to do all that I could to assist in indoctrinating the Navy as a whole in regard to aviation and its importance.[63]

The carrier as a separate offensive striking force, as the center of a new tactical formation, was established in the famous Fleet Problem IX of 1929. In this exercise, the Blue fleet, with the new carrier *Lexington*, was to advance to the Pacific through the Panama Canal. The Black fleet, in the Pacific, with the carrier *Saratoga*, was to approach the Gulf of

Panama, where the two fleets would engage. Inventive naval aviators proposed running the *Saratoga* ahead of the battle line and launching its planes to hit the locks of the canal, thus denying the "enemy" transit to the Pacific and "winning" the battle before it took place.

The *Saratoga* made an all-night, 30-knot dash to a position 140 miles off the west coast of Panama, launched 70 planes before dawn in a surprise attack and 13 in a second strike. Without interference they "destroyed" the locks and airfields of the Pacific side of the canal. Almost all of the aircraft were recovered back on *Saratoga*'s deck at sea. One of the authors of the operation, Eugene Wilson, said that Admiral William Pratt, in charge of the Black force, called the strike "the most brilliantly conceived and most effectively executed naval operation in our history."[64] For air supporters it hardly mattered that the Blue fleet had already gotten through the canal. The exercise summed up a decade of thinking about and preparing for using the carrier as a separate striking force for the assertion of offensive sea control. In this instance, the assertion took the form of an attack on a land target.

In light of the usefulness of the exercise, it seems almost churlish to note that had it been war, the 78 planes that returned to the *Saratoga*'s deck would have found her underwater because she had been "sunk" several times that morning, twice by battleship fire, once by four "torpedoes" from a submarine, and once by her sister ship, the *Lexington*, which found the carrier undefended while the planes were still returning from the attack on the canal. This last "sinking" was somewhat anomalous because before it occurred, the *Lexington* herself had been put "out of action" by battleships and "destroyed" by friendly planes that mistook her for the *Saratoga*.[65] Yet the fact that the *Saratoga* was "sunk" is important. The vulnerability of the platform was the weak point in carrier doctrine.

The fleet exercise in 1930, Problem X, studied for the first time as complete tactical units carrier groups consisting of one carrier, four cruisers, and two destroyer squadrons. In this exercise, planes scored heavily against battleships, showing how quickly command of the air could be seized and how that command might affect a battle at sea. It was time to answer important questions. Should there be a few large carriers or many small ones? How did a carrier group relate to a fleet battle plan? Should the group be a defensive or an offensive formation? At bottom, what was to be a carrier's war use? Should it be a supportive or an autonomous instrument of sea control?

The argument for a smaller carrier arose when the Pacific campaign was reassessed in light of a possible war in the Atlantic. The large fleet carriers *Yorktown* and *Enterprise,* whose construction was begun in 1934 as a result of President Franklin Roosevelt's public works supplement, were of a size and range that fit the battle fleet in the Pacific. Because they were vulnerable to gunfire and air strikes, they were to operate miles from the battle line, protected by cruisers and destroyers. Proponents of the smaller carriers argued for a different plan of operation. The next war, they said, might call for dispersal, not concentration. In the Atlantic, carriers might have to spread out, attacking trade and securing routes, acting against isolated units, with command of the sea defined in terms of area control, not destruction of an enemy fleet. In the Pacific, too, critics of large carriers continued, the naval war might not be decided in a single fleet-on-fleet engagement. More and more, attrition strategists were thinking in terms of huge expanses of ocean, which might have to be covered for protracted periods. For that type of sea control, many small carriers acting autonomously at the center of a fast carrier task force would be better than a few all-too-valuable, all-too-vulnerable large ones tied to the battle fleet.[66] The Navy built and tested both types of carriers. Lighter ships, including the *Wasp* (begun in 1936), the *Hornet* (begun in 1939), and the ships of the *Essex* class (the first of which was begun in 1941), were of immense importance in the war to come.

In 1930 dive-bombers were slow and short-range and did not carry enough ordnance to sink a battleship. They could, however, with only one or two bombs, disable a carrier's unprotected flight deck. Within a few years, the dive-bomber gained the ability to threaten a battleship, as the plane's speed, range, and bomb load increased. By the second half of the decade, dive-bombers had become the carrier's major weapon, more accurate than the horizontal bomber, faster than the torpedo plane, and compact enough to be carried in substantial numbers aboard a carrier.

Moffett's prediction about naval aviation was borne out, although not in a sequence or in circumstances that he or anyone else imagined. Quick recognition of carriers' offensive value followed the entirely unpredicted decisive destruction of the battle line at Pearl Harbor by planes from six Japanese aircraft carriers in the largest carrier strike launched up to that time. The way to a carrier doctrine of sea control was opened in a day. In the study of biological evolution there is a notion called punctuated equilibrium. To its detractors it describes cumulative changes; to its proponents it describes an adaptive leap. In this instance there was a combination of both—a slow operational evolution that accelerated in a matter of hours into a huge strategic leap. On

December 7, 1941, the carrier became the main capital ship of the U.S. Navy. That month there were 8 carriers, with 521 planes aboard them. On V-J Day, only four years later, the Navy had afloat 28 larger and 71 smaller aircraft carriers, and naval aviation commanded 41,272 planes. There were fewer than a dozen battleships at the end of the war with Japan. So swiftly did the change occur that when the battleships at Pearl Harbor had been repaired, they were sent back to sea as part of a carrier battle group.

The planning, experimentation, and technological developments of two decades made possible rapid wartime adaptation and expansion. That was, and is, the rationale of a balanced fleet.

The submarine traced a similar path. Like carriers, submarines were given an unplanned independent offensive mission on December 7, 1941, when, with the battle line out of action at Pearl Harbor, the Navy released them for an unlimited war of attrition. This adaptation was made possible by years of discussion about the submarine's mission and size. In debates in the 1920s, some officers had wanted the boats stripped down and small, at around 800 tons, for coastal defense and mine laying. Others wanted them large, up to the 2,000 tons permitted by the London Treaty of 1930, for close support of the fleet. This larger type would be equipped with air conditioning, efficient vapor-compression distilling plants, and diesel-electric propulsion. It also would be swift enough to maintain the 17 knots prescribed for the battle fleet and be ready either to act as part of a concentrated force or to carry out reconnaissance or attacks. These large boats need not be of long range if there were bases near the battle zone from which they could operate, but the Washington treaties, while they set no limits on the number of submarines that could be built, had deprived the Navy of fortified bases in the western Pacific. Existing boats did not have the endurance to operate far west of Hawaii. Operational capability therefore did not match the strategic requirement of long range. For supporters of the smaller boats, the large, equipment-burdened submarines were too costly—not in money but in size, because with total national submarine tonnage limited by the London Treaty to 52,700 tons, it seemed more sensible to make more and smaller boats of shorter range, not fewer and larger ones for longer tours of duty.

A third position on the submarine, favored among submariners at the end of the 1920s but which made little doctrinal headway in the Navy at large until the end of the next decade, favored a medium-sized boat of around 1,450 tons whose mission would be to conduct an autonomous campaign of attrition against enemy warships. This submarine was to operate independently both of the fleet and of coastal patrol.[67]

The arguments about mission and design went on for years. In 1936 the General Board in a compromise created a boat of moderate size, at 1,450 tons, a high-performance vessel of oceanic cruising radius, designed for close fleet support and for attacking major surface combatants. Three dozen of these submarines were built in the late 1930s. They were of the *Sargo-Salmon* class. To them were added in 1940 the sturdy 2,000-ton boats of the *Gato* class, whose mission was described in a 1939 doctrine that read, "The primary task of the submarine is to attack enemy heavy ships. A heavy ship is defined as a battleship, a battle cruiser, or an aircraft carrier."[68] *Gato* boats had a cruising range of around 11,000 miles and a surface speed of 10 knots. The 77 *Gato* boats, together with the 119 of the almost identical but deeper-diving *Balao* class, were the submarines with which the Navy fought the war.[69] The boats of *Sargo-Salmon*, *Gato*, and *Balao* classes were called "fleet submarines."

Despite their title, these boats were not integrated into the fleet. The problem was the submarine's vulnerability in the fleet operations for which they were designed. Boats on or near the surface, or even in a shallow dive, were susceptible to attacks by aircraft or sonar-equipped destroyers. Their record in avoiding detection in exercises was so poor that they were detached from close operations with the battle fleet and assigned to scouting, mining, and launching independent attacks on capital ships. Since the 1920s this last mission was exactly what imaginative submariners had argued should be the submarine's primary role. In the fire of emotion after Pearl Harbor, it was but a small step of operational doctrine to redefine that mission as unrestricted submarine warfare—in this case against Japanese merchantmen in a comprehensive campaign of attrition, as well as against major Japanese warships.

8

Are We Ready?
1938-1940

A STRATEGY GAP

In the summer of 1939 war began in Europe. President Roosevelt and the armed services shared the popular hope that the country might stay out. Neutrality acts had been passed in 1935, 1936, and 1937, and in response to the start of the war, again in 1939. Sea power would protect the United States. No one, Roosevelt said in September 1939, "has ever suggested in any shape, manner or form the remotest possibility" that U.S. troops would be sent to fight in Europe. He repeated this position in the presidential campaign a year later and on into 1941. Roosevelt was elected to a third term in 1940 on his assurance that several recent measures—a destroyers-for-bases deal with Great Britain, the first federal military draft in peacetime, and a limited mobilization—were precautionary acts of self-defense. The defensive courses of action advocated in the campaign by both Roosevelt and his opponent Wendell Willkie had "a numbing effect on policy."[1]

The United States Fleet was home-ported in southern California without strategic direction. The Navy continued to hold to the concept of total naval war expressed in War Plan Orange, by which it could claim a fleet mission and a fleet budget. This remained an operational and not a strategic position in the absence of political approval. At the end of July 1939, on the eve of war in Europe, Admiral William Leahy, chief of naval operations from January 1937 to August 1939, expressed the familiar theme of forward offensive action in his *Annual Report*: "If peace cannot be preserved our broad naval strategy must be offensive and the U.S. Fleet should engage and defeat the enemy fleet wherever it can be brought to action." He recommended no limit on how far out the Navy might extend its power. During that same summer of 1939, a new book entitled *Sea Power and Today's War*, by the popular navalist Fletcher Pratt, concluded with a description of "tomorrow's great naval battle." There will be only one big battle, he wrote, and it will be between big-gunned battleships. "One [battle] will be enough."[2]

Hemisphere protection had been the rationale of the naval rearmament bills and was the top priority of the Rainbow War Plans of 1939. Under these plans, the Army was to protect bases from which the Navy would operate. The bases were placed as far forward as Congress would permit, forming a defensive arc from Alaska, through Hawaii (where the Army in the summer of 1939 had 21,475 men), through the Panama Canal (where there was an Army garrison of 13,451 men), and into the Caribbean. In addition, the Army stationed 10,920 men in its Philippine Department. Because Army airplanes could not fly far out to sea, the Navy would confront any hostile force, which could approach only by ship. Enemy airpower would be a problem only if hostile bases were established in the hemisphere. From such bases short-range land-based aircraft could support an enemy naval action. In 1939 the Army was gravely concerned that pro-Axis sympathies in Latin America might lead to the establishment of such air bases.[3]

Germany, victorious in its westward invasion in Europe in 1940, stood poised to defeat Britain and then, perhaps, to attack the western hemisphere. If a single expansionary and exclusionary power controlled the landmass of western Eurasia and its offshore islands, the United States would be exposed. Defense called for war readiness, for aggressive strategic thinking on how to influence the course of the war in Europe.

The British navy, long the shield of the western hemisphere, was after 1940 dedicated to national survival. In the Pacific, where until 1940 the United States had expected a measure of assistance from European naval powers, no serious aid was any longer possible. As they faced the Germans at home, the French, the Dutch, and the British began to lose control of their colonies. The Vichy government in France conceded Japanese occupation of the north of Indochina. The Dutch could not protect the East Indies. British naval strategy for the Far East was in disarray.

The immediate concern of Roosevelt and his strategists in May and June 1940 was that if Britain fell, Germany would take over the British fleet. In addition, they feared fifth columns of Axis sympathizers in Latin American governments who might offer Germany bases for strikes against the United States. In the summer of 1940 the administration withheld military aid to desperate Britain in order to keep force levels up in the United States.[4] In East Asia, meanwhile, Japan, despite being bogged down in its China quagmire, was set to pluck the colonies that the mother countries in Europe could not defend. It was essential that President Roosevelt clarify the position of the United States. Fundamental executive decisions were needed to guide naval strategy.

Roosevelt waited. The Germans had not crossed the English Channel. That meant there was still time. In August 1940 Roosevelt transferred to Britain some aged destroyers that Churchill had asked for three months earlier. The transfer showed the administration's confidence that Britain would survive, that its ships would not fall under German control. The destroyer deal was not meant as a promise of further support. In return for the destroyers, the United States received basing rights in Newfoundland, Bermuda, and Trinidad. That extended the U.S. sea frontier several hundred miles farther into the Atlantic. This was an act of hemisphere defense, not a commitment to intervene in Europe. In October 1940 Secretary of War Henry Stimson said, "Our Fleet was the only reserve we had for national defense . . . and, in consequence, it should not be committed to any theater unless or until it developed that our national existence was at stake in that theater."[5]

Roosevelt observed America's reaction to a speech by William Bullitt in August 1940 to judge the public mood. "The truth is," Bullitt said, "that the destruction of the British Navy would be the turning point of our Atlantic Maginot Line. . . . It is as clear as anything on this earth that the United States will not *go* to war, but it is equally clear that war is *coming* towards the Americas. . . . I am certain that if Great Britain is defeated, the attack will come." The speech received a mixed reception: it called forth contributions that enabled two million copies of it to be printed, but it was also denounced by isolationists, who claimed that the sentiments it expressed were "little short of treason."[6] With opinion divided, Roosevelt moved slowly.

We do not know Roosevelt's intentions. A variety of interpretations have been offered: He intended to drag the country into war—he sought to keep it out. He was ignorant of reality—he worked well with what he had. He showed statesmanlike foresight—he was negligent. He was rigid—he temporized. He was an interventionist—he was an appeaser.

He was arbitrary—he was merely rhetorical. He held the lamp of democracy—he almost let it go out. Perhaps it is best to agree with the conclusion of Robert Dallek:

> In the years 1939–41 Roosevelt had to balance the country's desire to stay out of war against its contradictory impulse to assure the defeat of Nazi power. Roosevelt's solution was not to intensify the conflict by choosing one goal over the other but rather to weave the two together: the surest road to peace, he repeatedly urged the nation to believe throughout this difficult period, was material aid to the Allies. And even when he concluded that the country would eventually have to join the fighting, as I believe he did in the spring of 1941, he refused to force an unpalatable choice upon the nation by announcing for war.[7]

Still, this did not add up to strategic planning. The steps taken in the summer and fall of 1940—the signing of Vinson's two-ocean Navy bill, staff talks with the British, the destroyers-for-bases deal, the draft, the beginnings of the arsenal of democracy, the positioning of the fleet at Hawaii, the embargo on the export of scrap iron and steel to Japan—bought time but did not provide direction. To be sure, time was needed. The General Board reported in July 1940, in its second "Are We Ready?" survey, that the Navy was not ready to fight a world war.[8]

The question of matching capabilities to political maneuvering was raised in May 1940 when, at the close of its annual exercises, Roosevelt ordered the United States Fleet to remain in Hawaii instead of returning to California. No one told the fleet's commander, Admiral J. O. Richardson, why the fleet should stay there or for how long. Richardson asked Chief of Naval Operations Admiral Harold Stark (CNO from August 1939 to March 1942) why the fleet was being forward-deployed. For war against Japan? If that was the case, it should return to California to prepare. There, not in Hawaii, sailors could train. There, not in Hawaii, were supply depots adequate for war. Further, Richardson asked, for what kind of war was the fleet being deployed? "I know of no flag officer who whole-heartedly endorses the present ORANGE Plan." The only approved Rainbow plan in his possession did not apply to his command. It was Rainbow 1, for the defense of the western hemisphere against an Atlantic threat. If the fleet's purpose in Hawaii was "to influence the actions of other nations by our presence," if it was held forward as a deterrent, it could not be a credible threat until the Hawaii base was built up to support it.[9]

Stark answered Richardson:

> Why are you in the Hawaiian area? Answer: You are there because of the deterrent effect which it is thought your presence may have on the Japs going

into the East Indies. . . . Along the same line as the first question presented you would naturally ask—suppose the Japs do go into the East Indies? What are we going to do about it? My answer to that is, I don't know and I think there is nobody on God's green earth who can tell you. . . . The above I think will answer the question "why you are there." It does not answer the question as to how long you will probably stay. . . . Nobody can answer it just now. Like you, I have asked the question, and also—like you—I have been unable to get the answer.[10]

That was not enough for Richardson, who wanted guidance to prepare his fleet. Richardson then extended his concern to a criticism of the administration's policy itself. The Asian interests of the United States were few and of minor importance, especially in view of the threat from Germany. In the face of that immediate peril, the United States should not be looking after the interests of other countries in Asia. Richardson wrote to Stark in May 1941, "It seems that, under present world conditions, the paramount thing for us is the security of the Western Hemisphere. This, in my opinion, transcends everything—anything certainly in the Far East, our own or other interests. South America is the greatest prize yet remaining. Until the outcome in Europe can be more clearly seen, security in the Western Hemisphere seems to be the most important consideration for us." In any plan to ensure that security, Hawaii was the wrong place for the fleet to be.

Richardson was right to say that an "inadequately manned *Fleet in being*" would not deter Japan. It was a dangerous illusion, he wrote in September 1940 to Secretary of the Navy Frank Knox (secretary from July 1940 to April 1944), to let the American people think that the Navy was a "mobile Maginot line" behind which the public was safe. Should the deterrent gambit fail, the United States faced "war or the inevitable loss of prestige" if it could not wage and win one. To be capable of winning a war, realism and sacrifice were needed, not false complacency.

Richardson wrote to Stark again in October 1940. As commander in chief of the United States Fleet he faced the prospect of war "without an applicable directive." While he could, he said, "in the absence of a clear picture of national policy, national commitments and national objectives, formulate his own plans other than for obvious measures of security and defense and for accelerated preparation for further eventualities . . . successful operations in war can rest only on sound plans, careful specific preparation and vigorous prosecution upon confidence in the success of the course being pursued."[11] Such plans and preparations did not exist in the autumn of 1940. In October 1940 an officer in the Army's War Plans Division wrote: "The military policy should conform to and be capable of supporting our foreign policy in that region [South East Asia]. At present the two are inconsistent; one or the other should be changed."[12]

Richardson took his criticisms directly to President Roosevelt. The fleet, he warned the president in October 1940, was not prepared for war and should be returned to California. Nor, he said, ignoring the services' customary deference to policy, would the fleet's presence in Hawaii restrain the Japanese government. It might "influence a civilian political government, but . . . Japan had a military government which knew that the fleet was undermanned, unprepared for war, and had no train of auxiliary ships without which it could not undertake active operations." Roosevelt disagreed, but how strongly is open to conjecture. He told Richardson, "I can be convinced of the desirability of returning the battleships to the west coast if I can be given a good statement which will convince the American people and the Japanese Government that in bringing the battleships to the west coast we are not stepping backward." Roosevelt's preoccupation with the psychological impact of gestures was dangerous, or at the least "embarrassing," Richardson told Congress. For Roosevelt, however, bluffing was something he could do. It might have some short-run effect when no other means of influence existed. One problem was that the services, planning on a total naval war, had offered him only the narrowest of force options. The years of economy and restricted strategic thinking, as well as the long-standing gap between diplomacy and military preparation, had reduced the nation's capacity for action. If Richardson's criticism of Roosevelt's deterrent posture had not already cooked his goose, he added an indictment he had prepared before leaving his flagship. "The senior officers of the Navy," the commander in chief of the United States Fleet said to the president of the United States, "do not have the trust and confidence in the civilian leadership of this country that is essential for a successful prosecution of a war in the Pacific."[13]

None of this swayed Roosevelt. Regardless of its unreadiness, the fleet would remain in Hawaii. Maybe its presence would restrain the Japanese. Maybe it would not. Who could tell? It was not inflammatory, nor would it be interpreted as appeasement. Roosevelt may have thought the Navy was stronger than Richardson allowed it was. He probably imagined his bluff would be more effective than it turned out to be. He did think the United States had to do something, or hand over Asia to Japan by default. The bulk of the battle line stayed in Hawaii, and there it lay at anchor on December 7, 1941.

There was a close connection between Hitler's conquests and the southward aggression of Japan. Germany and Japan were associates in the Anti-Comintern Pact of 1936. On that pact Japan placed its hope of containing the Soviet Union, with whom it now shared a 2,500-mile frontier in Manchuria. The Soviet army there was the biggest outside threat to Japan in the China war. The Anti-Comintern Pact was the keystone of Japanese policy until the Germans shocked the world in 1939 by reversing their position and signing a nonaggression pact with Moscow, without telling the Japanese. That shattered the anticommunist front and ballooned Japan's fear of the Soviet Union.

Tokyo responded by taking another tack. After the German victories in Europe in 1940, Japan renewed its ties with the Axis powers in the hope that a new connection, the Tripartite Pact, might lead to a rapprochement with the Soviet Union, Germany's new treaty partner. Soviet friendship would serve as well as the lost policy of constraint to secure the northern border of Manchuria and free Japan for southward expansion. The Japanese government saw such an agreement as a diplomatic prerequisite to the southern advance.[14]

The Tripartite Pact was also a warning to the United States. America would pay a high cost if it opposed Japanese expansion. An antidemocratic alliance could threaten the western hemisphere as well.[15] The Japanese foreign minister told the emperor that the Tripartite Pact was "a military alliance against the United States."[16]

The connection weighed on American planners. In its February 1938 revision of War Plan Orange, the Joint Army-Navy Board had already raised the possibility of a two-ocean war. In the summer of 1940 Congress passed two naval authorization bills, the first one increasing the combatant force by 11 percent and the second authorizing a two-ocean Navy. The Rainbow plans of 1939 sketched a range of five alternatives in case of war: limited unilateral hemispheric defense; concerted campaigns with Britain and France in the Pacific; independent action in the Pacific along the lines of War Plan Orange; extended unilateral hemispheric defense; and coalition action with Britain and France for the projection of "the armed forces of the United States to the Eastern Atlantic and to either or both of the African or European Continents, as rapidly as possible consistent with [hemispheric defense], in order to effect the decisive defeat of Germany, or Italy, or both."[17]

America's Pacific policy of 1940 emanated from "a government divided against itself. . . . The problem . . . was not the absence of a foreign policy, but too many policies within one administration."[18] Combative hard-liners pushed for harsh economic and petroleum sanctions and naval demonstrations against Japan. Other officials wanted to limit U.S. interests in Asia and turn toward Europe. The military was concerned that a war might come before it was ready. The General Board, in its first "Are We Ready?" report to the secretary of the Navy at the end of August 1939, had concluded that the Navy was not ready to meet a serious emergency, an opinion that it repeated in its second "Are We Ready?" report a year later. Meanwhile, fast-moving events in 1940 and 1941 winnowed the Rainbow plans down to the fifth of the alternatives listed above.

Conflicting counsels demanded political clarification. Roosevelt and Secretary of State Hull were on a tightrope, trying to keep the United States out of a war while trying to stop German and Japanese aggression.[19] These would become contradictory positions if the Axis powers ignored U.S. warnings. The United States could not stand by if its declared interests were imperiled, yet—and here was the problem—it was not ready to defend them. The country had adopted defensive positions in the Atlantic and the Pacific. At the same time, to help the British in the Atlantic, to help China, and to create a network against aggression in the Pacific, the government would have to go beyond strict defense. It would need ready force, which it did not have. The best that can be said for Roosevelt's temporizing is that he had to deal with a poor match of American goals, commitment, and force, but temporizing is a risky way of bridging a strategy gap.

ATLANTIC FIRST

And a gap remained. To close it, in November 1940 CNO Stark circulated a memorandum on strategic choices. Stark wanted to prevent the Navy from being "caught napping" without a strategy for war. He pushed his superiors, President Roosevelt and Secretary Knox, for a decision on where he should lead the Navy. The moment was opportune. The presidential campaign was over. British endurance gave the United States some breathing space, although Stark thought Britain could not hold on for long without more help. The destroyers-for-bases deal concluded in September 1940 brought the United States closer to the European conflict. Now the British were asking for aid—for more ships for the North Atlantic and for U.S. ships for Singapore. Stark had to reply.

The agents of foreign policy, he told Knox in a memorandum, the uniformed services and the diplomats, needed to know "the National Objective," needed an answer to two fundamental questions: "Where should we fight the war, and for what objective?" With an answer to these, Stark said:

I can make a more logical plan, a more appropriate distribution of the naval forces. . . . and can more usefully advise as to whether or not proposed diplomatic measures can adequately be supported by available naval strength. . . . That is to say, until the question concerning our final military objective is authoritatively answered, I cannot determine the scale or the nature of the effort which the Navy may be called upon to exert in the Far East, the Pacific, and the Atlantic.[20]

Stark's memorandum, submitted to Knox and the president in early November 1940, was a thorough review of strategic options. It showed the wisdom of Carl von Clausewitz's dictum, often cited but less often followed, that "no one starts a war—or rather, no one in his senses ought to do so—without first being clear in his mind what he intends to achieve by that war and how he intends to conduct it." Stark in effect demanded that the abstract and incomplete Rainbow plans be put in a policy context. That was the first step to making them into a strategy. He wanted Roosevelt to choose among four alternatives: Should the United States make the principal military effort in defense of the hemisphere? Should it take a full offensive against Japan with Dutch and British support and stay on the defensive in the Atlantic? Should it plan to give military assistance to the British in Europe and to the British, Dutch, and Chinese in the Far East? Or "shall we direct our efforts toward an eventual strong offensive in the Atlantic as an ally of the British, and a defensive in the Pacific?" This last alternative was known as Plan D, or "Plan Dog" in military parlance.

Roosevelt read Stark's list and made no choice. Faced with this indecision, the Army and the Navy followed the logic of Stark's analysis. That logic led to Plan Dog, which became the cornerstone of America's victorious strategy in the war. Admiral Stark's memorandum earned Louis Morton's praise as "perhaps the most important single document in the development of World War II strategy."[21]

Stark posed the question, "Where should we fight the war, and for what objective?" He answered: Europe first, for the defeat of Germany, and then "an eventual strong offensive in the Atlantic as an ally of the British." Thus did Stark turn attention from aid to war, from assistance to participation, from the Pacific to the Atlantic, and from hemisphere defense to an overseas offensive war that would be taken onto the European continent.

These were momentous conclusions. If followed they would reverse the Pacific orientation of the Army and the Navy and, in the midst of a climate of independence and neutrality, engage the United States in a coalition war. Roosevelt did not want to draw such an unambiguous conclusion. The president wanted to undertake no actions for which American force was inadequate. He probably also wanted to keep the United States out of war. After the summer of 1940 the threat to the western hemisphere lessened. For another year Roosevelt would not go beyond aid to Britain. Stark argued that was all well and good, but one had to think further ahead. To be secure and prosperous the United States must have free use of the Atlantic and access to European markets and to the colonial empires. For that, Germany had to be defeated.

Aid was only half the answer. Aid did not destroy the threat. Helping a neighbor defend himself, loaning him a garden hose when his house is on fire, as Roosevelt put it in the Lend-Lease discussion of December 1940, was not the same as going after the arsonist. Stark called for the country to think ahead to war aims and the way to achieve them. He declared that Germany's hold on continental Europe must be broken. No matter how much aid Britain received, it could not defeat Hitler alone. To be sure, Britain's survival was the immediate priority. Should Britain fall and its Commonwealth dissolve, the United States would be exposed, its vital trade routes shattered. Without trade and raw materials, the U.S. economy would falter. The country would not be able to produce the arms it needed. If Britain fell, the western hemisphere would be open to Axis penetration. If Britain fell, there would be no forward bases from which to take the fight to the enemy, no way to bomb or invade a German Europe. Stark had learned the great lesson of 1917. America's security demanded more than a maritime strategy. It demanded a continental commitment. The country would have to send an expeditionary force. It was not possible to secure American interests by sea power alone. The only certain way to defeat Germany was to defeat it on land. If it came to war it would be American boys, after all, over there. And for a war of that magnitude, the United States had to prepare for a total, modern, industrial war. That was part of the lesson of 1917.[22]

Mounting an all-out offensive across the Atlantic would mean leaving little force for the Pacific. To bring policy into line with resources, Stark said, the country should reduce its commitments in the Far East to avoid conflict with Japan. Offense in the Atlantic, defense in the Pacific: that was Stark's choice.

Unfortunately for strategists, while the general terms of an Atlantic offensive seemed clear, those of a Pacific defense were not. Policy, and Plan Dog, left major questions unanswered. Did defense mean preserving the status quo in Asia, more or less re-creating the Washington treaty system, with Japan compelled to leave European colonies and

China alone? In the circumstances of a European war, only the United States could enforce such a system. That went beyond defense in the traditional sense and imperiled the Atlantic. Or did defense mean a pullback to the Alaska–Hawaii–Panama Canal arc to support the Europe-first policy of Plan Dog? Such a pullback would give Japan freedom of action west of Hawaii and concede the Philippines, China, and all the possessions the British, Dutch, and French were too weak to hold, including Hong Kong, Singapore, Indochina, and Indonesia. Both of these definitions of defense were incompatible with existing resource commitments.[23]

Roosevelt, typically, simply accepted both. His policy was Europe first, though perhaps only for the short run, coupled with continuing assistance to China and opposition to Japanese expansion. To politicians then as today, the spectrum of choice seemed more elastic than it did to the military. Military officers wanted a reliable framework within which to plan. Politicians expected something to turn up.

On February 1, 1941, the Navy dropped the designation United States Fleet. In its place it created the Pacific Fleet under Admiral Husband Kimmel (Richardson was relieved of his command for crossing the president) and the Atlantic Fleet under Admiral Ernest King. The Asiatic Fleet remained, continuing under the command of Admiral Thomas Hart. Secretary Knox made it clear that the Asiatic Fleet would not be reinforced and that its ships would not go to Singapore to support the British. Admiral Hart said that his fleet "was of minor combat value, and had been so for a long time." All his ships, Hart used to say, "were old enough to vote."[24] Readying for war, Hart had already moved his ships from Shanghai to Manila. The Pacific Fleet remained at Hawaii with its unclear mandate. Some of its ships were to be reassigned to the Atlantic Fleet.

Although the Army was anxious for its garrison in the Philippines, in 1940 it accepted Stark's argument of Europe first. No one favored aid to Britain more than Secretary of War Stimson did. Plan Dog henceforth guided joint Army-Navy war planning. The British were of course delighted, despite their concern for their empire east of the Suez Canal. This was a big step toward what Prime Minister Winston Churchill knew was the only way to beat Germany. As he told his First Sea Lord, Admiral Sir Dudley Pound, in February 1941: "The first thing is to get the United States into the war. We can then settle how to fight it afterwards."[25]

With Roosevelt's quiet approval, talks began with British officers, leading to the American-British-Canadian staff agreement of March

1941 known as ABC-1. Germany's early defeat was the main war aim of both states. The principal U.S. military effort was to be exerted in the Atlantic and European area, which was defined as the decisive theater. In the Far East, the U.S. Pacific Fleet was to be employed "offensively in the manner best calculated to weaken Japanese economic power, and to support the defense of the Malay Barrier by directing Japanese strength away from Malaysia." In reality this meant first holding to a line of defense along the Alaska-Hawaii-Panama arc until sufficient force was collected to move westward. ABC-1 was approved by Admiral Stark and Army Chief of Staff General George Marshall, and the Joint Army-Navy Board was told to work up a war plan along its lines. This work was completed in May 1941 and embodied in Rainbow 5, which was now reworded in terms virtually identical to those of ABC-1, and both of these statements of objectives and missions (they were not operational plans) were sent on to the president for approval.

Roosevelt, however, did not give his approval. Nor did he disapprove. He held back, insisting that the international situation was so fluid that it was premature to make any war-planning decisions. Every week brought something new. Roosevelt had told his military leaders in January 1941 to "avoid a state of mind involving plans which could be carried out after the lapse of some months; we must be ready to act with what we [have] available." If war came, that was another thing—and he asked in that case, Rainbow 5 and ABC-1 be returned to him. But in the meantime, measures short of war would suffice.[26] On March 27, 1941, the same day that ABC-1 was completed, Congress appropriated $7 billion of Lend-Lease assistance, which Roosevelt soon began sending to Britain, and then to Russia, a tremendous victory for the proponents of aid. But it was money, not men. The vote was meant to keep the United States out of the war, not get it in.

Roosevelt, his eye on public acceptance, resisted Stark's conclusion that the defeat of Germany required a campaign on the continent. Accordingly, and because the Army was so undermanned, Rainbow 5 was deliberately vague on if, when, and how many men might be needed in Europe. It seems that during this period, when the service secretaries (Knox and Stimson) and the service chiefs (Stark and Marshall) accepted the idea of an expeditionary force, Roosevelt and Churchill were thinking of sea power and air strikes, not of millions of soldiers fighting their way toward Berlin, Rome, and Tokyo. Secretary of the Interior Harold Ickes reported that at a cabinet meeting in May 1941, the president, after commenting on the battles of Crete and the eastern Mediterranean, said "it looked as if we would have to go back and found our military policy on the sea-power theory of Admiral Mahan." As Roosevelt saw it, Ickes said, "the determining thing at present is control of the seas."[27] Robert Sherwood cited the opinion of Rear Admiral Harry Yarnell, as more representative of naval officers' than was Stark's. Yarnell wrote in January 1941: "We should never send an army of millions abroad in any future war. The navy and air force must be adequate to carry on offensive war in enemy waters. The frontier must be the enemy coast."[28]

Ever in search of alternatives, Roosevelt did not put the services on a prewar footing. In July 1941 Stark wrote of his talks with the president "To some of my very pointed questions, which all of us would like to have answered, I get a smile or a 'Betty [Stark's nickname], please don't ask me that!' Policy seems something never fixed, always fluid and changing."[29] So Stark failed in his first objective. Roosevelt would not make the policy decision on whom to fight and for what, the decision that Stark and Marshall badly needed. It appears Roosevelt thought, at least until the spring of 1941, that the country might avoid war.

For all that, the strategy gap was closing. Both Army-Navy and American-British planning staffs accepted the argument of Plan Dog, which was to put Europe first and fight a coalition war—and so did Roosevelt, at least as far as a Europe first position went.

Readiness was the problem. A two-ocean Navy would not be afloat for several years. In its third "Are We Ready?" review, delivered to the CNO in June 1941, the General Board said, "The issues in the Orient will largely be decided in Europe." To protect the western hemisphere, the report went on, "we should, without question, go to war to prevent the defeat of the British Commonwealth and the resultant practically certain extension in this hemisphere of European political and military power." However, the Navy was not ready for a two-ocean war. The General Board declared that the Navy had only 40 percent of the battleships it should have for war, 60 percent of the heavy cruisers, 30 percent of the light cruisers, and 40 percent of the destroyers. And virtually no thought had been given to transporting troops abroad, or to the logistical demands of conducting a war on the European continent, let alone in the Pacific or in both places simultaneously.[30]

In the Atlantic, the Navy needed more ships for patrol, for escort, and for possible landings to prevent German occupation of Atlantic islands. Until the ships were built, the Atlantic Fleet had to draw on those of the Pacific. Reinforcements were promised at the time of the fleet reorganization, but when Japan signed a neutrality pact with the Soviet Union in April 1941, freeing itself from the threat to Manchuria and opening the way to advances southward, the Navy postponed the draw-off, to keep a fleet-in-being at Hawaii. The Navy made this concession to support complicated negotiations that Hull and Roosevelt were conducting, in which a Department of State notion of deterrence loomed much larger than in the Department of the Navy. The service chiefs thought that the Japanese would be more impressed with a fleet-in-action in the Atlantic, or gathered for duty in the Caribbean, than with an unprepared fleet lying idle at Hawaii. But neither Hull nor Roosevelt was adept at integrating force and diplomacy in those days, nor were the service chiefs adept at making their arguments.

New destroyers were coming on line, and over 100 laid-up vessels from World War I were recommissioned, ships no longer capable of fleet action but able to do antisubmarine patrol. Fifty of the ships had been promised to the British in the bases deal that was concluded in September 1940. Waldo Heinrichs suggested that Stark's enthusiasm for aggressive convoy protection early in the spring of 1941 was motivated in part by a fear of losing more to Britain, by a belief that "the navy had to join the battle [of the Atlantic] to save its ships."[31]

Preparation for patrol, then convoy, and possibly war, meant in 1941 "Making the Best of What We Have," as Admiral Ernest King titled a message to his Atlantic Fleet in March 1941.[32] King had told Roosevelt that he saw his Atlantic responsibilities as "a big slice of bread with damn little butter." When in May 1941 Stark, in anticipation of the sending of some British heavy ships from the Atlantic to Singapore, gave the order to transfer a quarter of the Pacific Fleet to the Atlantic—three battleships, the carrier *Yorktown*, four light cruisers, and two squadrons of destroyers—Roosevelt asked King how he liked the butter he was getting. King replied, "The butter's fine, but you keep giving me more bread."[33]

Protection of the western hemisphere was always the top responsibility. Of 93 submarines on duty in December 1940, two-thirds were on defensive duty in the Atlantic. For patrol the Navy shared the offshore air reconnaissance mission with the Army Air Corps, in a dangerously muddled and ambiguous relationship. Unity of command over air patrol of the coastal frontier was never established so there was no locus of final responsibility. Surface ships and aircraft were spread out over the neutral zone. The Navy's neutrality patrol had gradually extended a safety belt eastward to 1,000 miles. The patrol's ships operated from Canadian and Caribbean bases established by the destroyer deal with Britain. The president might have sent Hitler the map of exclusionary claims that Josephus Daniels had flourished before an astonished Lloyd George twenty years before. Roosevelt said in May 1941 that the defensive outposts might have to include Iceland, Greenland, the Azores, and maybe even the French West African port of Dakar across from Brazil. The German threat might be direct, or it might take the form of local subversion. Throughout 1940 and 1941 Roosevelt used the imperative of hemisphere security and of a German threat to Latin America to argue against isolationists and, increasingly, for intervention.[34]

In July 1941 Roosevelt accepted Stark's proposal that U.S. forces relieve the British division garrisoning Iceland. The Marine brigade sent there had to be supplied, for which warships were dispatched for convoy escort. That was a major step because Iceland was within the German war zone, where U-boats were instructed to sink neutral shipping on sight. Iceland was also a mid-ocean refueling base for British and Canadian escort destroyers, and it stood opposite Greenland on the strait through which U-boats sortied out into the North Atlantic. Roosevelt, in relieving the British, sent U.S. ships into an area marked by the Germans for hostile action.

The United States moved close to cobelligerency. British merchant ships joined the U.S.-escorted convoys. What, after all, was the point of Lend-Lease and cash-and-carry of arms, the U.S. policy of assuring British survival by measures short of war, if goods could not be sent safely? If British merchantmen joined a protected, neutral U.S. ship en route to Iceland, that at least secured it for the western leg of its journey and relieved the Royal Navy of an extended duty.[35] To assist with these operations, the Coast Guard, familiar with the waters around Greenland from its iceberg patrols, was made part of the Navy in November 1941. For commanders aboard warships it all came down to rules of engagement. What if they actually encountered a German ship or airplane? "Were they to shoot first and let the Navy explain, or only fire if fired upon: Was it to be Concord Bridge or Lexington Green?"[36] That was the unanswered question of 1941. Was the United States at war or at peace in the Atlantic?

The answer was, something of both. It is as hard for us now to divine Roosevelt's purpose as it was for the Navy's leaders then. Was he, as Waldo Heinrichs has said, "determined to control the Atlantic and place the nation on a path risking war to ensure it?"[37] Did he think the Germans would not force war? Did he hope simply to safeguard the Americas while helping the British hang on? Or, most likely, was Roosevelt buying time while events unfolded at home and abroad? It cannot be ruled out that he thought America might stay out of the war. "No problem of World War II is more fascinating to the historian, none more difficult, than the question of President Roosevelt's leadership," and no time is harder to assess than that of his gradual involvement in the Atlantic in 1941.[38]

Perhaps there is a further dimension, a Russian connection. Having identified common aims in the Atlantic Charter with Prime Minister Churchill in August 1941, Roosevelt could build public and congressional support for a possible alliance with Britain. At the same time, the Soviet Union, displaying heroic resistance to the German invasion of June 1941, was on Roosevelt's mind as the key to Germany's defeat and to the minimization of American losses. He rightly related the German invasion of the Soviet Union to the future of the Atlantic and to a deterrence policy toward Japan. The survival and continued resistance of the Soviet Union were necessary for the defeat of Germany. To help, the United States could supply the Russians and prevent the Japanese from opening a second front against them in Siberia. For that, control of the Atlantic was required and pressure on Japan. Events on the Soviet western front were thus a possible reason for sending Marines to Iceland and for deciding to escort the convoys.[39] On the liberal principles of the Atlantic Charter, by which Churchill and Roosevelt had pledged to support self-government in Europe and free movement at sea, Roosevelt could base an anti-German policy in wartime, in peacetime, or in between. It is for good reason that Roosevelt's admirers and detractors, then and now, have been reminded of Woodrow Wilson and the sequence of declarations and events that led to war in 1917.

In August 1941, however, the United States was not in the war, and that is the point. The United States was neutral, and it seemed as though that might be enough. It was not clear how, if, or when it would enter, despite Stark's Plan Dog, despite Roosevelt's global strategy, despite the Atlantic Charter, and despite British expectations. Britain had survived the attempt to bomb and starve it into submission. The Red Army had stopped the German invasion of the Soviet Union, forcing a protracted war in eastern Europe. The battle of the Atlantic was turning against Germany. The coasts of the western hemisphere remained untouched. Maybe all measures short of war would suffice.

Churchill told his War Cabinet that the president had said "he would wage war, but not declare it, and that he would become more and more provocative." If the Germans "did not like it, they could attack American forces."[40] Perhaps. Churchill repeated this in other places, and the British staff received the same impression of Roosevelt's position at the Atlantic Conference. Churchill also may have exaggerated to bolster his government's morale. One can never be sure in assessing Roosevelt's intentions, no matter what he said. There is no evidence that he issued orders to the Navy to provoke an incident, and Roosevelt often said what visitors wanted to hear.[41] Maybe Roosevelt would have preferred keeping U.S. involvement at the level of an undeclared war if the German government had been willing not to increase hostilities and if war with Japan could have been avoided.[42] The German army was fully engaged in the east, and Hitler told his navy to avoid incidents with the United States at least until the middle of October, when he expected to defeat the Soviet Union.

Coalition strategy was not discussed at the Atlantic Conference. The United States turned down a British request to send ships to Singapore and the Middle East. It would not disperse its fleet to protect the British Empire. For their basic security the British were still alone. Despite Churchill's optimism, for all of Roosevelt's sweet words, the British delegation to the Atlantic Conference of August 1941 had to remember, as Arthur Marder wrote of the American-British staff agreement of March, that *"the United States neither accepted an obligation to go to war, nor stated the circumstances in which she was prepared to do so."*[43] William Langer and Everett Gleason wrote that at the Atlantic Conference "the breadth and depth of the differences dividing the two parties were so manifest as to preclude even tentative agreement on the strategy of victory."[44] Although no strategic planning took place, what Roosevelt did, and maybe all he could do, was declare liberal political stakes. National purpose, after all, leads to policy, and that is the first step toward a strategic plan.

And at the Atlantic Conference Roosevelt did promise to escort British ships to Iceland. This was direct involvement. In September 1941 the United States, though not at war with Germany, became a cobelligerent with Britain in the battle of the Atlantic.

Germany had not extended its war zone to the western Atlantic, but its submarines took several actions against U.S. ships. What is most notable about these incidents is that war did not follow. In September 1941 the destroyer USS *Greer*, on a mail run to Iceland, provoked an inconclusive engagement with a U-boat. In October the destroyer *Kearny*, returning from Iceland, was hit by torpedoes, and the *Reuben James*, on convoy escort some 700 miles east of Newfoundland, was sunk by a German submarine with the loss of over 100 American sailors. To these events Roosevelt responded with denunciations of Germany, a declaration of "active defense," and orders to the Navy to shoot on sight to protect the convoys. He asked Congress to rescind neutrality legislation prohibiting the arming of U.S. merchantmen and to permit them to enter the German war zone around the British Isles.

But that was not a call to war, however much Roosevelt might have been preparing the way for belligerency. The incidents had not packed the emotional power needed to carry a country into war, to marry emotion to intellect in the service of strategy. The losses were considered those of sailors on dangerous duty. The men were, as Admiral King wrote Stark, doing "the jobs they are trained to do." Stark declared, "Whether the country knows it or not, *we are at war*," but this opinion was not shared by the public or the Congress.[45] Perhaps many felt that "the astounding thing was not that there had been a few sinkings of American ships, but that there had not been many more."[46] Perhaps in October Roosevelt thought intervention was inescapable, as his Navy Day speech that month signaled. But revision of the neutrality legislation, permitting the arming of merchantmen and their transit to belligerent ports, passed in November 1941 with the smallest Senate majority (50 to 37) on a major foreign policy decision since the European war had begun. The House vote was also close (212 to 194). If nothing else, the vote showed that Congress was deeply divided, that it was split by partisanship as well as conviction. Isolationists considered the passage a victory.[47]

Nor was Hitler ready to expand his war. To the frustration of his navy, which in July had asked for a declaration of war against the United States, Hitler replied with an order to avoid engagements until his conquest of the Soviet Union was complete. By December 1941 this completion had not happened, and the German navy had lost the strategic initiative in the first phase of the battle of the Atlantic. Germany was unable to deny Britain use of the sea. Even limited surface and air escorts were enough to protect convoys. Convoys were routed according to British signals intelligence, which beginning in mid-1941 read the German naval code. Serious losses befell the German surface fleet with the sinking of the enormous battleship *Bismarck* and the pocket battleship *Admiral Graf Spee*. That led to a strategic withdrawal of German surface ships from the Atlantic.[48]

Men of reason might conclude that the policy of undeclared war was working. However much Stark, and perhaps Roosevelt, saw a long-term need for war, it would take something more than reason or exhortation to galvanize the country for fighting one. Within days, an event at sea did precisely that, brought policy and strategy into common harness and created a national will ready for sacrifice and for the use of violence to the utmost. That event took place not in the Atlantic, but on the opposite side of the globe.

PEARL HARBOR

The attack on Pearl Harbor was a genuine strategic surprise. Yet it is not a mystery why war came to the Pacific. War came because the Japanese government had committed itself to a policy of aggressive expansion and the domination of Asia, which the United States opposed.

The two states sought radically different political orders for Asia. Japan wanted imperial command of northern China and southeastern Asia. The United States wanted a pluralistic international order based, as Secretary of State Cordell Hull stated in April 1941, on four liberal principles: territorial integrity and sovereign independence, noninterference in the domestic affairs of other states, equality of commercial opportunity, and nondisturbance of the status quo in the Pacific by other than peaceful means. At the very least, Hull's principle of equality of commercial opportunity meant Japan must give up its exclusionary claims in China.

A hardening of positions took place in 1941. Roosevelt decided that the United States must play an active part in maintaining a stable Pacific system. He linked this stability to the security he sought in the Atlantic. The interests of the United States opposed forceful closure of markets at either end of the Axis. Roosevelt wrote in January 1941 to Joseph C. Grew, his ambassador in Tokyo, "I believe that the fundamental proposition is that we must recognize that the hostilities in Europe, in Africa, and in Asia are all parts of a single world conflict. . . . Our strategy of self-defense must be a global strategy."[49]

Roosevelt did not want war, but he would not drop assistance to China. Support for the independence of China, after protection of the Philippines, was the touchstone of his Asian policy. There was a military reason for this, so long as a Chinese army held on. Waldo Heinrichs described it: "An anti-Japanese coalition was inconceivable without China, which so absorbed Japanese manpower and resources, including one and a half million casualties in four years of war."[50] The second objective of Roosevelt's Asian policy was the maintenance of the European colonial holdings. As was true of the presidents before him, however, given the priority of the Atlantic and the naval situation there, he had little force to back this up. Roosevelt's instruments of influence on

Japan were diplomacy, economic pressure, and a loose alliance against aggression.

Already in the summer of 1940, a number of prohibitions had cut Japan off from the U.S. war materials market. Talks took place between the United States and British and Dutch East Indies authorities about mutual assistance because the British and Dutch colonies in that area were now virtually unprotected. The plan to shift a quarter of the Pacific Fleet to the Atlantic for patrol and convoy was made with the understanding that it would be balanced by the transfer of British warships to Singapore. China was made eligible for Lend-Lease aid. These moves, like Hull's declaration of the nonnegotiable four principles, were part of a tough stance that emerged in the spring of 1941 and was meant to compel Japan to choose between membership in an international order and acceptance of a potentially untenable isolation. Official opinion, encouraged by hard-liners Secretary of the Treasury Henry Morgenthau and Stanley Hornbeck, adviser on political relations in the State Department, was that Japan would back down if the pressure were kept up.[51]

The Japanese were surprised by this firmness. They thought that American involvement in the Atlantic would give them a free hand, that the United States would accept Japanese moves as faits accomplis. Now they found the Americans apparently determined to deprive them of their Asian destiny. Japan's failure to end its war with China, the formation of the entente of the ABCD countries (America, Britain, China, the Dutch East Indies), Japanese anxiety about the Soviet Union, and the support the United States was giving to China and Britain left Japanese leaders feeling isolated, and they decided against concession.

There was considerable disagreement in Japan on what to do. All the Japanese leaders accepted the need for expansion to ensure economic independence and political autonomy. The dispute was over direction and cost. Military planning in 1940 had been a tug and pull between the army's northern continental strategy, centered on the conquest of Manchuria, and the navy's southern maritime strategy, aimed at controlling the mineral resources of the Dutch East Indies in particular, and the wealth of Southeast Asia in general. Each strategy had accepted war and the risk of that war expanding.

In the north, the war against China had become Japan's continental ulcer. The army could neither win nor withdraw. To give up Manchuria would deny the rationale of expansion. If Japan was not a continental power, it would revert to minor status on its islands. Added to that was a fear of Soviet intervention in Manchuria. A border defeat in 1939, even though Japanese troops had outnumbered Soviet soldiers in the theater by two to one, gave the Japanese a healthy respect for the Soviet army. The continental commitment was enormously costly, but there was no way out. Its largest army overseas was there until 1945, over one million Japanese combatants that had to be sustained. During its campaigns to the south, Japan never ceased pouring men and equipment onto the continent, assets it might otherwise have used to defeat its maritime opponents.

In the south, war would come if the Dutch would not concede peaceably to Japanese demands. That could bring the United States and Britain into a Pacific war. In 1940 the Japanese had no strategy for a two-front war. Joint planning could not even establish which enemy to face first in the south, or what to expect. The navy planned an opening attack on the Philippines and prepared to meet a counteroffensive by the United States Fleet. The army planned to attack Indonesia and Malaya.[52]

Military planning is not the same as war, however, and before the middle of 1941, war with the United States was not, except in imperial naval circles, a foregone conclusion. Yet the structural dilemma was clear. Japan was being surrounded. Unless it could withstand this pressure and establish political security based on economic independence, it would have to give up its autonomy. The solution was to establish a resource-rich empire that was defensible in a war with the Soviet Union or with the West. And that would have to be done right away.[53]

This desire for action lay behind the occupation of southern Indochina in July 1941. The occupation was a preliminary not so much to a move on the Dutch East Indies—although that was the ultimate objective of the larger southern strategy—as it was to an offensive war against the Soviet Union. Such a war was being prepared for six weeks hence, to take advantage of an expected quick German success in Europe and of Germany's invasion of the Soviet Union that June.[54]

The consequences of that invasion weighed heavily on Roosevelt. On its outcome hinged the future of his Atlantic policy. He was convinced, argued Waldo Heinrichs, that "the survival of the Soviet Union was essential for the defeat of Germany and that the defeat of Germany was essential for American security. This more than any other concern, to his mind, required the immobilization of Japan." A Japanese attack to the north would imperil the Soviet Union's life-or-death struggle with Germany, whereas containing any move to the south would overstretch the strategic capability of the United States.[55]

Yet the United States could not ignore the obvious Japanese intention to look southward. Somehow Japan had to be kept from moving either north or south, and in the summer of 1941 there was precious little military force available for a containment policy. Diplomacy and trade restrictions would have to serve for the moment, and on the use of those the government was divided.

On July 1, 1941, the day before Japan's Imperial Council made its decision to move south, Roosevelt wrote to Interior Secretary Ickes,

> I think it will interest you to know that the Japs are having a real drag-down and knock-out fight among themselves and have been for the past week—trying to decide which way they are going to jump—attack Russia, attack the South Seas (thus throwing in their lot definitely with Germany), or whether they will sit on the fence and be more friendly with us. No one knows what the decision will be but, as you know, it is terribly important for the control of the Atlantic for us to help to keep peace in the Pacific. I simply have not got enough Navy to go round—and every little episode in the Pacific means fewer ships in the Atlantic.[56]

One thing is certain. The Japanese were shocked by the severity of the reaction to their move in Indochina in July 1941. Hull broke off conversations with the Japanese ambassador, and Japanese assets were frozen in the United States, Britain, the Philippines, New Zealand, and the Netherlands. The United States and the Dutch East Indies embargoed the export of oil to Japan. The Army organized a Far Eastern Command in the Philippines under Douglas MacArthur. American assistance to China surged.

The U.S. Navy was split on the oil embargo. But senior admirals, the War Plans Division, and CNO Stark opposed tight controls, claiming they might provoke Japan to attack in Malaya and the Dutch East Indies "and possibly would involve the United States in early war in the Pacific." The Navy was not ready for war, and Stark, his attention on the more dangerous enemy in the Atlantic, accepted the risk of letting Japan build up its petroleum reserves until the German threat was met.[57]

The State Department paid no heed to Navy concerns. It had adopted a rigid policy of pressure regardless of the state of readiness of American armed forces, on the assumption that Japan would back down. That policy, however, was not quite what Roosevelt had in mind. The president and the chiefs of the military services hoped to leave room for negotiation. Roosevelt's view of the embargo was that it should be partial, discretionary, and nonprovocative. Ickes noted that Roosevelt "was still unwilling to draw the noose tight. He thought that it might be better to slip the noose around Japan's neck and give it a jerk now and then."[58] But Roosevelt was about to leave for the Atlantic Conference, and the executors of the embargo in the Departments of State and Treasury made the ban on oil comprehensive—a development the president was not aware of until early September 1941, when he decided that a withdrawal to his more flexible position would be a show of weakness to a now more militant Tokyo and undermine his emerging alliance with Great Britain.[59]

Japanese leaders, with a petroleum stockpile of only two years, took the oil embargo as an act of belligerency.[60] To break the ring of encirclement, to defend Japan's position in Asia, to continue the war in China, to end the indecision and division within Japan's government and the disagreements within the armed forces, to gain the resource base necessary for regional control—in short, to assert Japan's autonomy, cultural unity, and national destiny—the Japanese government on September 6, 1941, decided that if a diplomatic settlement was not in hand by early October, Japan would go to war.

The prime minister Konoe Fumimaro, and Emperor Hirohito thought their terms could lead to negotiations, although the concessions demanded of Britain and the United States (ending aid to China, building no new military facilities in Asia, abetting Japanese economic expansion) were unlikely to be accepted. Japan's army and navy flatly rejected a diplomatic settlement. Diplomacy could not solve Japan's fundamental defense problems. For a serious, long-term settlement, Japan must expel the British, the Dutch, and the Americans from East Asia. Only war and a New Order would preserve Japan's independence.

On the day war began in Europe, September 1, 1939, Rear Admiral Nakahara Yoshimasa, a major architect of the Japanese navy's southern strategy wrote,

> Finally the time has come. This maritime nation, Japan, should today commence advance to the Bay of Bengal! Moss-covered tundras, vast barren deserts—what use are they? Today people should begin to follow the grand strategy of the navy, altering their old bad habits. Japan must be brought back to its maritime traditions placing the main emphasis on the development of the navy. (We should not hesitate even to fight the United States and Britain to attain that end).[61]

War took on mystical aspects of social and racial revolution. At the Imperial Conference on September 6, 1941, the chief of the Navy General Staff, Admiral Nagano Osami, Japan's oldest officer, concerned with the spiritual perpetuation of the national mission and perhaps worried about rebellion at home, argued for war as an intrinsic good, even if it ended in defeat: "If we are determined to be true to the spirit of defending the nation in a war, even if we might not win the war, this noble spirit of defending the fatherland will be perpetuated and our posterity will rise again and again." War for many Japanese, win or lose, had become an end in itself, as had the assertion of Japan's culture mission. For Nagano, according to this assessment, it hardly mattered whether war was directed against the United States or the Soviet Union.[62] But in reality it did, and Nagano himself was an architect of the southern strategy.

Two decisions set the stage for the showdown with the United States. First, in August 1941 the army postponed an invasion of Russia and adopted a defensive stance in the north. The war with China would continue—there was no way out of that. But the next move would be to the south. The second decision, in September, was to act against the United States as soon as the political leaders gave the go-ahead for war.

War preparations were well under way. On November 5 the new cabinet of General Tōjō Hideki, the former army minister, decided on war in December if no diplomatic satisfaction was received from Washington by then. Japan's only chance for victory would be to begin the war at once. The navy, long ambivalent about a war against the United States, conducted research that showed U.S. naval strength over the course of the next few years would increasingly overwhelm Japan's. The U.S. naval building appropriation in 1940 alone was greater than the funding of a decade of Japanese naval construction. At the end of 1941, Japan's naval strength was 70 percent that of the United States. But at that moment, the United States was building more surface combatants than it had in commission, and it had three times as many ships under construction as Japan did. If current trends continued, the Japanese force would be reduced to 65 percent that of the United States by the end of 1942, to 50 percent by the end of 1943, and to 30 percent by 1944.[63] Japan's relative position would never be better than it was in 1941.

Admiral Yamamoto Isoroku, commander in chief of the Combined Fleet, was charged with planning the naval combat. Yamamoto had earlier declared that war with the United States was "out of the question! To fight the United States is like fighting the whole world."[64] Once the decision was made in favor of war, Yamamoto thought the only chance was to act fast. Yamamoto did not plan to defeat the United States or Britain, but he thought an initial victory, if it were dramatic enough, combined with the two countries' preoccupation with Europe, might discourage them from an all-out campaign in the Pacific. Time thus won would enable Japan to secure itself within a well-defended imperium. It must be remembered that no matter how extensive Japan's goals seemed to the West, in Japanese eyes, they were limited.

It had to be a short war. "If you insist that we really do it," Yamamoto had told Prime Minister Konoe Fumimaro, "you may trust us for the perfect execution of a breath-taking show of naval victories for the first half-year or full year. But if the war should be prolonged into a second or third year, I am not confident at all."[65] There was no plan for a protracted war, no idea of how to bring a long war to an end.[66] Yamamoto was throwing the dice. It was all or nothing for Japan, and then or never.

The opening moves were clear enough: a simultaneous attack by the navy on Hawaii and the army on the Philippines and Singapore, to be followed by an army assault on the Dutch East Indies. When the bastions of the American, British, and Dutch opposition were destroyed, Japan would consolidate its defensive perimeter, cut the West's communications to Asia, pluck the West's remaining and exposed colonial dependencies, destroy the paths of support to China, and enjoy the benefits of German victories in Europe, which would force both the Soviet Union and the United States to face away from Japan.

The centerpiece of the Japanese navy's strategy was a surprise attack launched from aircraft carriers against the U.S. Pacific Fleet anchored in Hawaii. Operation Hawaii was a revolutionary shift in Japanese naval planning. When Yamamoto became head of the Combined Fleet in August 1939, he inherited a defensive strategy that was the spiritual legacy of Katō Kanji and Alfred Mahan. The naval high command saw itself in a mortal naval and imperial competition with the United States, although at the same time it hoped to avoid war. The Washington-London treaty system was no longer in place to control this competition. For defense, the Japanese navy at first planned a strategy of attrition and annihilation. The navy would deplete the U.S. battle force as the latter made its way across the ocean and past Japanese island bases, from which land-based air and submarines would attack it. Then, somewhere in the Bonins or the Marianas, the fleets would meet in a great battle for command of the sea.

Yamamoto disagreed with this plan, which failed to provide for the needs of the southern strategy and left the timing of operations to the enemy. For the advance south, the navy would have diverse tasks—transport, regional sea control, and support of the army—in widely separated areas. At the very least Yamamoto wanted to move the decisive battle eastward, as far as possible from the South Pacific. In a major reversal of existing doctrine, he proposed taking the offensive at once, and doing so outside Japan's defensive palisade.

The U.S. Pacific Fleet was at Hawaii, in mid-ocean. If Yamamoto could draw those ships out, or if they sortied to rescue the Philippines from a Japanese invasion, he might force them to a decisive engagement in the region of the Caroline and Marshall islands. This was not an unreasonable idea. In fact, it fit the American plan. Although Rainbow 5 gave Pacific forces a defensive role at the outbreak of war, that was an elastic designation, and the Pacific and Asiatic fleets were to take the tactical offensive. The Pacific Fleet was to support British operations in defense of the Malay Barrier by diverting Japan through attacks on the Marshall Islands and raids on Japanese sea communications and positions. The fleet was also to support British naval forces south of the equator and to prepare to capture the Marshalls and the Carolines.[67]

These plans suited Admiral Husband Kimmel, the master of the Hawaiian battleships, the commander of the Pacific Fleet, and a transpacific thruster. Kimmel believed in battleships. He had developed a plan to take his battle fleet far to the west in search of a Pacific Trafalgar, in which he hoped to lure the Japanese Combined Fleet into a central Pacific ambush for the climactic engagement for ocean mastery. Washington had limited the extent to which he could probe westward should war come, but sea power was ocean victory, and for Kimmel battleships were the decisive weapon for the expected battle of the Pacific. Carriers were only fleet auxiliaries.[68]

So Kimmel waited for war. Admiral Yamamoto thought on. If Japan acted by surprise, departing from its doctrine of defense, it could inflict more certain and more complete damage on the United States. Yamamoto had profound respect for the recently developed capabilities of air power. These capabilities raised the possibility that Japan might disable the Pacific Fleet in port by destroying with airplanes ships at anchor and picking off with submarines any that put to sea. Such a blow would at once change the strategic balance in the Pacific and, in the words of the Japanese Combined Fleet's chief of staff, Rear Admiral Ito Seiichi, "thereby confuse the enemy at the outset, and deprive him of his fighting spirit."[69] The Japanese fleet, unengaged, would return westward unscathed and ready for further battle at sea. Japan would gain time to establish its Pacific defenses and could turn safely to its vital interests—China and Southeast Asia. The American people might be so demoralized by the loss that they would be prepared to negotiate a Pacific settlement. The attack, Yamamoto wrote, should "decide the fate of the war on the very first day."[70]

Yamamoto's staff developed the plan for the attack on the Pacific Fleet at Hawaii in the course of 1940 and 1941, gearing it to improvements in shallow-water torpedoes, in bombing tactics, and in the coordination of a carrier task force. In November 1941 Japan's Naval General Staff gave final approval to Operation Hawaii. It was to be launched simultaneously with an attack on the Philippines and Singapore. There was always the chance that the carrier force might be spotted or that last-minute diplomatic negotiations might succeed. In either case Yamamoto could withdraw the fleet without harm, such flexibility being a primary virtue of naval force. The main operational worry of the naval officers was that on the day set for attack (December 7, Hawaii time), the Pacific Fleet might be out to sea and not lying at anchor in Pearl Harbor or Lahaina Roads. That risk would be taken. On November 25 a task force of 6 carriers, 355 airplanes, and an escort screen of destroyers, with radios shut down for total secrecy, headed out on a northward arc that was designed to avoid detection.

The next day, November 26, Secretary of State Hull ended a round of negotiations with the Japanese ambassador that had begun four months before. The wisdom of, and reasons for, this move have been much debated. Roosevelt genuinely wanted to avoid a Pacific war. Two weeks earlier he had told Hull not to let the talks "deteriorate and break up if you can possibly help it. Let us make no move of ill will. Let us do nothing to precipitate a crisis."[71] On the other hand, pressed by Churchill and Chiang Kai-shek, fearful of the charge of appeasement, and freighted with long-standing U.S. policy, the government would not give in to the Japanese demand that it cease assistance to China. In addition, intercepted diplomatic messages and reports of troop movements southward from Shanghai and onto the South China Sea made Roosevelt suspicious of Japanese sincerity. Hull rejected the Japanese negotiating position and countered with demands that ended the discussions.

The service chiefs did not want an early war. They wanted Hull to propose a 90-day truce, to buy time for a defensive buildup and to establish an offensive deterrent in the Philippines, where large-scale reinforcements and B-17 bombers were to be sent in December. Hull took a hard line without consultation. It is on this point that debate over Hull's decision to break off the talks centers. After all, Hull himself described the major objective in the four months of talks since the July occupation of southern Indochina as having been "to give ourselves more time to prepare our defenses."[72]

On November 5, 1941, three weeks before the negotiations ended, the

Joint Army-Navy Board had submitted to President Roosevelt a memorandum that stated the country's strategic position and the problem for the Navy of a forward policy against Japan. The board took the Navy's problem so seriously that it resubmitted the memorandum on November 27, the day after Hull ended negotiations. The document read:

At the present time the United States Fleet in the Pacific is inferior to the Japanese Fleet, and cannot undertake an unlimited offensive in the western Pacific. In order to be able to do so, it would have to be strengthened by withdrawing practically all naval vessels from the Atlantic except those assigned to local defense forces. An unlimited offensive by the Pacific Fleet would require tremendous merchant tonnage, which could only be withdrawn from services now considered essential. The result of withdrawals from the Atlantic of naval and merchant strength might well cause the United Kingdom to lose the Battle of the Atlantic in the near future.

The current plans for war against Japan in the Far East are to conduct defensive war, in coöperation with the British and Dutch, for the defense of the Philippines and the British and Dutch Indies. The Philippines are now being reinforced. The present combined naval, air, and ground forces will make attack on the islands a hazardous undertaking. By about the middle of December, 1941, United States air and submarine strength in the Philippines will have become a positive threat to any Japanese operations south of Formosa. The United States Army Air Forces in the Philippines will have reached the projected strength by February or March, 1942. The potency of this threat will have then increased to a point where it might well be a deciding factor in deterring Japan in operations in the area south and west of the Philippines. By this time, additional British naval and air reinforcements to Singapore will have arrived.

From this the Joint Board, emphasizing the concurrence of Admiral Stark and General Marshall, concluded:

a) . . . The primary objective of the two nations [the United States and Great Britain] is the defeat of Germany. If Japan be defeated and Germany remain undefeated, decision will still not have been reached. In any case, an unlimited offensive war should not be undertaken against Japan, since such a war would greatly weaken the combined effort in the Atlantic against Germany, the most dangerous enemy.

b) War between the United States and Japan should be avoided while building up the defensive forces in the Far East, until such time as Japan attacks or directly threatens territories whose security to the United States is of very great importance [basically, the Philippines, Malaya, and the Dutch East Indies, or Thailand west of 100 degrees East or south of 10 degrees North where a threat to these could be mounted].

c) If war with Japan cannot be avoided, it should follow the strategic lines of existing war plans; i.e., military operations should be primarily defensive, with the object of holding territory, and weakening Japan's economic position.

Specifically, Stark and Marshall recommended "that the dispatch of United States armed forces for intervention against Japan in China be disapproved.... That no ultimatum be delivered to Japan."[73]

The State Department argued that this position was tantamount to giving up on China. But the position of the service chiefs and the Joint Board was to avoid war, and their caution reflected the very weak deterrent potential of U.S. forces in the Pacific at that time.

The Navy's containment mission was a lost dream. It was not, as Hull asserted, the shotgun in the closet to back up his negotiations. The Japanese understood this full well. Neither the Pacific Fleet nor the Asiatic Fleet could stop convoys of Japanese invasion forces from Indochina, landings in Thailand or on the Malay Peninsula, or Japanese control of the resources of the Dutch East Indies. There was no opposition to Japanese movements in the South China Sea or the Gulf of Siam. As to British forces, Japan planned to attack them in its move south. The light U.S. Asiatic Fleet in theory was to help Britain defend the Malay Barrier, but it remained at Manila and was receiving only limited defensive reinforcements—some patrol planes and a dozen submarines (raising the total number of submarines to 29), but no surface ships. If confronted by the Japanese Combined Fleet, Admiral Hart had authority to retire the Asiatic Fleet to bases in the Indian Ocean.[74] The British Royal Navy was sending some heavy ships to Singapore, and the battleship *Prince of Wales* and the battle cruiser *Repulse* arrived there on December 2, on what was to be their final duty.

So sea power was no deterrent, and Yamamoto planned in any case to sink many of the major vessels in the first hours of the war. The deterrent role was claimed by the U.S. Army. After years of neglect and puzzlement, in which it saw its duty to defend the Philippines vitiated by confusion over the country's interest in the islands, the Army turned in 1940 and 1941 to rebuilding its Philippine defense force. Marshall realized that the Army's garrison in the Philippines would become more vulnerable as naval assets were diverted to the Atlantic. In July 1941 Lieutenant General Douglas MacArthur was recalled to active duty and given command of the newly established United States Army Forces in the Far East. The Philippine army was folded into the U.S. service. Fortunately, at this juncture resources were available to the Army, the result of enlarged appropriations, the draft, and a newly developed air force. Secretary of War Stimson insisted that Japan would respect only force. He thought he was putting that force in place. But the advantages of an offensively oriented containment strategy were not pressed by the Army or taken up by the State Department. Had there been better coordination, Hull may have found a reason for a three-month tactical delay—namely, to get a containment policy in order and enough force to back it.

Military and political hopes increasingly rested on the Army Air Corps, and in particular on a long-range heavy bomber, the B-17, which by flanking any southern movement by Japan, could control the South China Sea, hold convoy routes hostage, and contain Japan at home. In a few months the Army would be ready to carry out either a defensive or an offensive strategy in the Philippines. Air power could defeat a landing force attacking Luzon. In addition to that, said Major General Henry H. Arnold, chief of the Army Air Forces (created from the Army Air Corps in June 1941), it could protect Formosa and bomb Japan itself. Of 220 B-17s scheduled for production by February 1942, over half were earmarked for the Philippines. Stimson said the bombers permitted the United States to establish itself in the islands "in a way it hadn't been able to for twenty years." The Army secretary wrote to Roosevelt on October 21, "A strategic opportunity of the utmost importance has suddenly arisen in the southwestern Pacific. . . . From being impotent to influence events in that area, we suddenly find ourselves vested with the possibility of great effective power."[75]

Roosevelt's global vision of an offensive deterrent strategy in Asia would enhance security in the Atlantic. The threat of an offensive air attack against Japan would pose for it the problem of a second front. As a result, Japan would not be able to attack the Soviet Union, whose sustained battle with the German army Roosevelt considered the key to victory in Europe.

Army air-power enthusiasts claimed that Army air had defensive and deterrent power, and perhaps even enough offensive power to beat Japan by itself—on its own, without the Navy. As Waldo Heinrichs said, the Army "was coming to view the Pacific not as a strategic liability after all but as an asset."[76]

To put this strategy in place, more time and a closer connection to the nation's diplomacy were needed. MacArthur's ground troops required more months to prepare, and an adequate force of bombers was not expected in the Philippines until February or March 1942. An effective air force required a balance of bombers, interceptors, antiaircraft artillery, base support, and radar. At the end of November 1941 there were only 35 B-17s in the Philippines, 2 antiaircraft units, and 2 working radar sets.[77] The Army had not yet changed the strategic picture in Asia.

That was why in November the service chiefs, even though they expected Japanese aggression somewhere in the near future, recommended avoiding provocation, hasty action, or any ultimatum. It was also why Hull's decision of November 26 to break off negotiations and to give Japan a set of demands (interpreted as an ultimatum in Tokyo), the major item of which was to withdraw from China (an impossible condition for the Japanese army), was a shock to the U.S. military and has received so much criticism. As William Langer and Everett Gleason wrote, Hull's independent action was "both bad strategy and careless administrative procedure. . . . The argument that by this date no practical difference could have been anticipated does not alter the seriousness of this breach of fundamental rules for achieving sound decisions of national security policy."[78]

Why Hull did this we do not know. Jonathan Utley concluded he was suffering "burn-out."[79] Hull simply did not connect his diplomacy of high principle with the armed forces' state of readiness. Separating the two, as he had throughout the negotiation period, Hull concluded the time for diplomacy was over. Hull told Secretary of War Stimson, "I have washed my hands of it, and it is now in the hands of you and Knox, the Army and Navy."[80]

Even more important was a structural problem. The government did not make civil-military coordination routine from either direction. The State Department followed high-minded policies, expecting diplomacy, principle, or economic pressure to carry the day and ignored the importance of taking military readiness into consideration. The Navy, long the keeper of the flame in the Pacific, had made the pitch for preparedness. But because the possibility of a threat from Japan had not been taken seriously, the Navy had never received the bases or ships it sought, and by 1941 it had, as a result of a new and urgent national policy, turned to the Atlantic. Army leaders, who had resisted involvement in the Pacific, found that when they had a force on the way that might make a difference, their long-established habits of avoiding influence on policy and the absence of interactive strategic mechanisms left them without ways to translate the Army's potential into new policy directions. Fundamentally, the strategy gap was a failure of the system.[81]

Still, there is no reason to think that Hull could have prevented war. The military officers in Tokyo were determined to achieve autarky for Japan. The only way to settle the contest of two competing visions of the future of Asia was by war. Russell Weigley made an observation that probably corresponds to Roosevelt's thinking and to Tokyo's: national policy may sometimes have to ignore the state of military readiness and run the risk of war despite an imbalance between force and policy, in the interest of larger principles and broader political considerations.

This is acceptable, Weigley suggested, if the state is confident it can win a war.[82] It is also acceptable if the state is so desperate that no other way of protecting vital national interests seems possible.

Admiral Stark recalled telling the Japanese ambassador:

> If you attack us we will break your empire before we are through with you. While you may have initial success due to timing and surprise, the time will come when you too will have your losses but there will be this great difference. You not only will be unable to make up your losses but will grow weaker as time goes on; while on the other hand we not only will make up our losses but will grow stronger as time goes on. It is inevitable that we shall crush you before we are through with you.[83]

Even though this was true, and some major Japanese leaders knew it to be true, in the Pacific, where specific interests were at stake and the U.S. military unprepared, the risk of separating diplomacy and force was very great. Some opportunity was lost by not exploring the question of whether a more effective policy of deterrence could have been based on a buildup in the Philippines. Admiral Hart quotes Roosevelt as saying he thought, in light of information from Marshall and Stark, that the Army and Navy were ready. "If I'd known the situation, I could have babied the Japanese along quite a while longer."[84]

Wars begin when one state tries by force to change a power relation and another state opposes that attempt by force. In the Pacific, the United States and Japan sought mutually incompatible orders for Asia. Given the American position, Japan's national goals could not be met by negotiation. Japan therefore decided upon war as an instrument of policy. The United States was determined to oppose Japanese goals if aggression went too far. War would then become an instrument of policy for the United States, too. In this circumstance, with the cessation of negotiations, leaders in both countries turned to the imminence of war.

Where would it begin? In what circumstance? And for what immediate purpose? Americans thought the Japanese were certain to launch a surprise attack somewhere. No one thought that it would be against U.S. territory. The service chiefs, expecting the first aggression to be in Thailand, wanted American intervention to be conditional. On November 27, Marshall and Stark repeated their strategic assessment of November 5: the United States should offer armed resistance only if the Japanese expeditionary force then afloat in the South China Sea advanced beyond certain lines in Thailand and thus threatened Singapore or the Dutch East Indies; but given the U.S. force then available, opposition could only be weak.[85] It did not seem reasonable that, when the

Japanese were apparently committed to China and southward conquest, they would first attack the Philippines or Hawaii.

Hawaii especially was far from the line of advance. The Japanese war aim, after all, was limited. It was regional imperium, not the defeat of the United States. So why would Japan go out of its way to attack Hawaii, where almost all U.S. naval strength was concentrated, where Kimmel was waiting for a major engagement, and where with considerable effort the Army had established a formidable defense of the Pacific Fleet? If one thinks in terms of a Mahanian battle taking place when Japanese forces were moving southward, it is indeed very hard to envision a decisive engagement being opened in Hawaiian waters. The risk to Japan was simply too great.[86]

Still, with the United States knowing war was imminent, knowing the Japanese penchant for surprise, knowing from its own exercises that a carrier air attack on Hawaii was not out of the question, why was the country caught unaware when the waves of Japanese planes descended on the densely parked aircraft of the Army and the closely packed ships of the Navy battle line that were resting at Pearl Harbor on December 7, 1941?

Blame is often placed on intelligence. In that area, failure had many fathers. The United States lacked an apparatus for swiftly distributing potentially relevant intelligence data to local commanders. Separation of diplomatic and military decryptions was behind the failure to send to naval intelligence such signals intercepted from Tokyo. These signals asked the Japanese consul general in Honolulu to establish what was in effect a bombing grid over Pearl Harbor and to report on the disposition of the Pacific Fleet. Presumably naval intelligence would have seen the military significance of this bomb-plot message and dispersed the concentrated ships, which were America's main source of military power in the Pacific. Without that information, the local naval command, which assumed it was getting all significant data, did not know the extent of the danger.[87]

Further, the United States had not penetrated Japan's operational security. No American knew of Yamamoto's plan or of the approaching task force.

> Not one intercept, not one datum of intelligence ever said anything about an attack on Pearl Harbor or any other possession. . . . that information could only have been generated if the United States, years before, had insinuated spies into Japanese government offices, or flown regular aerial reconnaissance of the Imperial Japanese Navy, or put intercept units aboard ships sailing close to Japan to pick up naval messages that a greatly expanded codebreaking unit

might have cracked, or recruited a network of marine observers to report on ship movements. The intelligence failure at Pearl Harbor was not one of analysis, but of collection. . . . For these reasons, intelligence remained marginal to American decision making before Japan's surprise attack.[88]

That brings us to the question of local readiness. The Army was responsible for the protection of the fleet and naval base at Hawaii. Why were its planes not on long-range patrol? Why were its radar and its antiaircraft batteries unmanned? The Navy also had a responsibility for offshore scouting "to give timely warning of an attack."[89] Why were its units not in action off the islands? Why on December 7 was the Army's air fleet sitting wingtip-to-wingtip at Henderson Field, and the battleships anchored bow-to-stern in the harbor?

Again, the first short answer is that no one imagined a surprise attack. From seaman to commander in chief, the assumption was that war would begin with a Japanese action in the Far East. The local threat for which Lieutenant General Walter Short's Hawaiian Department was prepared was sabotage. That is why the airplanes were clustered wing-to-wing. Still, Short failed his mission.[90] Even though his air force and Kimmel's were far smaller than needed, they were not on alert at a time of imminent warfare in the Pacific. Short had 25,000 men on Hawaii. He had bombers ready to attack an enemy fleet. But not having sighted one, and being in a condition less than a state of war, he left his aircraft warning system and antiaircraft batteries undermanned and under-organized. The first radar sighting of the approaching Japanese air wave was dismissed as a flight of B-17s expected from the mainland. Above all, Short failed to imbue his men with a sense of urgency. Nor did his superiors in Washington insist otherwise.

There was almost no coordination between the services for long-range aerial reconnaissance. That was the consequence of a decade of neglect, when responsibilities for offshore patrols had not been clearly delineated. Only three weeks before the Japanese attack, the Joint Army-Navy Board had reconsidered the question of a unified defense arrangement for Hawaii. The Army argued that no unity of command was essential, and there the matter rested.[91] Both Short and his naval counterpart, Rear Admiral Claude Bloch, needed planes, but they never pooled what aircraft they had for a 360-degree patrol of the sea. Bloch did not ask Kimmel for use of Pacific Fleet planes for such a mission, and Kimmel did not volunteer them. There were patrols of submarines and aircraft, but they were limited in distance and sector. No one expected an air attack. The Navy watched for submarines, the Army for saboteurs.

On December 7 Kimmel had most of his ships in port, save a few out on various duties. The carrier *Lexington* was ferrying aircraft to Midway, and the carrier *Enterprise* was returning from a delivery of planes to Wake Island. An assortment of cruisers and destroyers and seven submarines were on maneuvers or patrol. Some of the Pacific Fleet's ships, including one battleship, the *Colorado*, and the carrier *Saratoga*, were on the west coast of the United States. The rest of the vessels of the battle fleet, including the other eight battleships, were massed in the anchorage without torpedo netting and without their antiaircraft guns manned or their men on alert. The main elements of American force in the Pacific were sitting ducks, and that is how the 360 planes of Vice Admiral Nagumo Chuichi's First Air Fleet found them.

9

Sea Control
1941-1942

HOLD AND BUILD

Pearl Harbor and the egregious declarations of war four days later by Hitler and Mussolini made war popular in the United States. Thereafter the government drew on an outpouring of hatred and revenge. President Franklin Roosevelt translated these passions into national idealism and mobilization for total war. A "crusade in Europe" is what General Dwight Eisenhower called the war against Germany. General Douglas MacArthur called the war against Japan a "holy mission."[1]

So intense was the shared passion that once the war began the government could leave war aims at the generalities expressed a few months earlier in the Atlantic Charter, notably opposition to aggression, self-determination of peoples, equal access to trade and resource opportunities, freedom of the seas, the final destruction of tyranny, and a "permanent system of general security." For most Americans the goal boiled down to unconditional surrender, a concept introduced in 1943 to secure Allied cohesion. Comprehensive but vague, the formula of unconditional surrender reduced the danger of any member of the alliance making a separate peace. It permitted the three chief Allies—the United States, Britain, and the Soviet Union—to hold very different visions of the postwar world order without having to decide between them. And it mandated for each state a total national effort for unlimited war.

Roosevelt took up the formula of unconditional surrender without consulting his military advisers.[2] It had no precise strategic content. It suggested that there was no limit to war except the availability of means, no restraint to action except immediate considerations of coalition warfare.

The United States, almost from the beginning, was able to launch simultaneous offensives in two oceans and seize the initiative in both theaters because of the unparalleled mobilization of its citizens, the implacable determination of their leaders, and the strategic vision of the Navy. The comprehensive war effort in the United States, Britain, and the Soviet Union was the reason for Allied success. Japan and Germany never mobilized their societies so thoroughly. That fact, even more than their limited resources, was the cause of their defeat.

The U.S. Navy entered the war, Edward Beach calculated, having logged only 56 hours of actual fighting in its history.[3] In less than four years, that Navy made itself mistress of the world's seas and expanded to become the greatest maritime force ever created. At the surrender of Japan it could point to an incomparable record of combat success, joint operations in every theater, and an astounding growth in its strength. The Navy, which on July 1, 1940, had 203,127 personnel on active duty, on August 31, 1945, mustered 3,408,455. On July 1, 1940, the Navy had 1,099 vessels on hand; on August 31, 1945, this number was 68,936, of which 1,166 were major combatant ships. In service when the war ended were 23 battleships, 99 carriers, 72 cruisers, around 380 destroyers and 360 destroyer escorts, and 235 submarines. Most were recently built, well-supplied modern ships, superior to those of the enemy and fitted with the most advanced technology of the time.

The Navy's prewar cultivation of a large number of shipyards resulted, under the well-managed wartime economy, in an explosive growth in ship production.[4] From July 1940 through August 1945 more than 110,000 naval vessels were built in 325 shipyards. Of these ships 1,286 were major combatants, including 10 battleships (4 of them of the 45,000-ton *Iowa* class), 18 large aircraft carriers (all but 1 of them of the 27,100-ton *Essex* class), 9 smaller aircraft carriers of the *Independence* class, 110 escort carriers, 2 large cruisers, 12 heavy cruisers, 33 light cruisers, 370 destroyers, 504 destroyer escorts, and 217 submarines. Of the grand total, 84,022 were landing craft, World War II creations on which depended the worldwide strategy of amphibious assault. Also in service at the war's end were some 41,000 naval airplanes, out of 74,032 delivered to the Navy during the previous five years. All 41,000 had been integrated into fleet duty.

The Navy in 1945 bought more fuel than any other agency in the world. It also used enormous amounts of ordnance. In the naval bombardment of Okinawa's shore defenses in the spring of 1945, the Navy shot 505,000 rounds. In August 1945 the Marine Corps had 485,000 men and deployed around 3,400 aircraft, 640 tanks, and 62,000 other vehicles. During the war the Coast Guard, under the operational control of the Navy, grew from 13,800 active-duty personnel to 171,200 and by the end commanded 3,174 vessels.

In the five years before August 1945, the U.S. Navy had expanded almost 20-fold in personnel, 6-fold in naval tonnage, 60-fold in numbers of vessels, and 24-fold in naval aircraft.[5] Its fighting force was deployed throughout the world and could conduct offensive operations in any sea it chose.

The Department of the Navy ordered, allocated, and commanded this prodigious maritime power. In all three activities it was extraordinarily successful. It was supported by a public that recognized the Navy's importance, by an unstinting Congress, and by a president and commander in chief whom the Army chief of staff once asked to stop referring to the Navy as "us" and to the Army as "them." Organizational tugging and pulling did occur within the department as a result of the Navy's institutional decentralization and its division of authority between civilian secretaries and naval commanders. The Navy has always been made up of various communities that sometimes find themselves at cross-purposes. During the war, for example, the autonomous bureau chiefs reported to the secretary and resisted efforts of the chief of naval operations to bring them under his control. As Robert Albion said, "No one, starting afresh, would have ever designed anything like the Navy Department."[6]

The secretary of the Navy had long since established the principle of civilian administrative control. The chief of naval operations reported to him. So did the heads of the bureaus of ships, aeronautics, naval personnel, ordnance, yards and docks, supplies and accounts, and medicine and surgery. Reformist officers wanted to put the CNO in charge, a military leader able to determine how the Navy used its force as well as what it should get and when. In their view a senior naval officer could define the national naval mission just as effectively as a politician or a businessman could—and had probably already done so. Following the mission with a professional eye, the officer should be empowered to make sure the Navy got what it needed. No secretary conceded such authority. The final say in policy determination, mission definition, and administration remained in civilian hands.

When war came operational control was recast. Administrative and policy direction remained with the secretary, Frank Knox, assisted by James Forrestal, his under secretary (Forrestal became secretary after Knox died in April 1944). They were assisted by skilled civilian executives brought in for the duration of the war, including Ralph Bard, Artemus Gates, Jr., and Struve Hensel. Naval command was vested in the chief of naval operations, Admiral Harold Stark, who was responsible to the secretary. Within days of U.S. entry into the war, Roosevelt reestablished in Washington the position of commander in chief of the United States Fleet and gave it to the aggressive commander of the Atlantic Fleet, Admiral Ernest King.

Coordination of the three U.S. fleets with one another and with coalition forces and the global scope of the Navy's war required a detached and central command. Only a single authority close to the policymakers could establish overall strategic direction, fit campaigns and operations to it, and distribute resources accordingly. King insisted that his position be called CominCh, which after Pearl Harbor was an obvious improvement on the ominous-sounding CinCUS (pronounced SINK *us*). The post was located in the capital and unencumbered by its former attachment to the Pacific Fleet commander. King was to report directly to the president, the final authority for policy and strategy. In removing CominCh from secretarial control, Roosevelt gave a naval officer "powers that had been denied to the Chief of Naval Operations ever since that office had been established in 1915."[7]

It was expected that King would direct strategy and run the ships under Roosevelt's eye, while CNO Stark, under Secretary Knox, administered the department, ship construction, and logistics. Secretary Knox said: "I am not trying to run the military end of the Navy Department. But I have insisted that the administration of the Navy Department was my job."[8] Such an administrative duumvirate within the Navy made no sense to Stark or to King, as confusing areas of responsibilities. In March 1942 Stark resigned, reasoning that King, in the superior position of CominCh, should also hold the senior post of CNO to avoid overlapping duties. Roosevelt agreed, and from March onward King reported as CominCh to the president on the conduct of the war and as CNO to the secretary of the Navy on the conduct of the shore establishment. Those two jobs made King "the most powerful naval officer in the history of the United States."[9]

The nation's military command was coordinated for strategic planning. King represented the Navy in the new grouping called the Joint

Chiefs of Staff (JCS), a body also responsible directly to Roosevelt. The JCS superseded the Joint Army-Navy Board, which itself had been taken into the Executive Office of the President a couple of years before. Four men made up the Joint Chiefs of Staff: King, Army Chief of Staff General George Marshall, Lieutenant General Henry H. Arnold of the Army Air Forces, and Admiral William Leahy, Roosevelt's personal chief of staff. Leahy, by seniority, was chairman. The Joint Chiefs dealt with the broadest formulation of national strategy and represented that strategy when they sat as part of the Combined Chiefs of Staff, the body that determined U.S.-British strategy. The independence with which King operated within the Department of the Navy stemmed from his responsibilities at this high level of strategy formulation that made him answerable only to Roosevelt.

Although King's titles perpetuated the distinction between civilian-administrative and military-operational authority, they also clouded the distinction somewhat. When King became CominCh, he asked for authority over the department's bureaus. Roosevelt refused. When King became CNO, however, Roosevelt gave him, "under the direction of the Secretary of the Navy," charge of "the preparation, readiness, and logistical support of the operating forces" and "the coordination and direction of effort to this end of the bureaus." This was a massive concession. As King's biographer stated, "The expediency of war and a stroke of the President's pen had eliminated four decades of political opposition to CNO control of the bureaus."[10]

Still, directing an effort was not the same as having final command authority, and King's attempt to make his position administratively more powerful brought him into conflict with his civilian superiors. King shared the reformist view that the Navy should be, and was, nonpolitical, that its only purpose was to fight. From that proposition, however, King concluded that the logistical tail behind the fighting tooth should be under the authority of a line officer. Everything should revolve around operations, so logically there should be no distinction between planning and distribution (a military function) on the one hand and procurement (traditionally a civilian function) on the other.[11]

To Knox and Forrestal, as it had been twenty years earlier to Secretary Josephus Daniels and his assistant secretary, Franklin D. Roosevelt, that was wrongheaded logic and pernicious thinking. Knox and Forrestal opposed putting naval officers in charge of administrative planning. They thought officers ignored the political dimensions of policy and mobilization, tended to have a capital-ship fixation, and were usually poor managers with little foresight.

That generalization was unfair. We have seen the innovations the

Navy made in the 1930s. But in fact, in 1942, King's operational training had not provided him with the best perspective for the broad management of wartime production. America's was not a military economy even during the war. Forrestal's civilian experts were able more skillfully to fit Navy procurement to the national agenda. They developed contract procedures, tended to labor relations, and connected military needs to a mobilized—but still civilian—economy. In January 1942 Forrestal removed procurement from military control, establishing a new Office of Procurement and Material, which was to be headed by an under secretary under himself. It turned out to be one of the most important features of the Navy Department during the war, and it brought in the materials King needed as cheaply and as rapidly as possible.

King, however, saw civilian control as part of an administrative power-grab. He tried to get logistics back under his supervision. King's own planning expert said that "it was almost a disease with him to be working on reorganization."[12] The attempt was misconceived. No one could understand how King's new arrangement would work. Its operational emphasis foretold a lack of overall coordination. The rest of the Navy would have suffered. Roosevelt, Knox, and Forrestal thought King's idea was bad government, bad management, and bad Navy. The president, supported by the anxious bureau chiefs, shot down King's plan. He wrote to Knox, "Tell Ernie *once more*: No reorganizing of the Navy Dept. set-up during the war. Let's win it first."[13]

In 1945, as the war wound down, Forrestal resolved the problem with a compromise. He strengthened the military side of the department, as King wanted. The functions of CominCh and CNO were combined in the position of the chief of naval operations, giving the incumbent a permanent, central professional authority, and when he sat with the Joint Chiefs, his combined functions put him on a par with the Army's chief of staff. As Forrestal himself wanted, civilian control was strengthened too. The operational commander was made responsible not just to the president but also to the secretary. The Office of Procurement and Material stayed in secretarial hands.

This pushing and pulling did not hurt the war effort. All those ships and all those men were, in the last analysis, the result of cooperation within the entire naval establishment. The secretaries, the top Navy brass, and the country's strategic planners agreed on two things that kept the officers happy: expansion and action. Yet King's unpleasant, irascible personality led him to be unduly slighting in his relations with his secretaries. He disliked Knox and loathed Forrestal. He thought

Knox was a security risk who could not keep a secret. The less the secretaries were told, the better.

So King cut the secretaries off from naval strategy and operations. That dismayed Knox and infuriated Forrestal, but in truth both grand strategy and major operations were being planned outside the department. Roosevelt consulted with the Joint Chiefs, not with the service secretaries or even with the secretary of state. That was King's excuse for ignoring his departmental superior. And as a naval commander he thought he had the right to keep the execution of strategy—the campaigns and operations—behind closed military doors. Neither the secretary of war nor the secretary of the Navy was on the regular distribution list of JCS papers.[14] Still, in the Army Department, Marshall and Stimson worked in adjoining offices, walking and talking back and forth, the general briefing the secretary. In the Navy Department it was as if the office floors of King and the Navy secretary were different worlds. King claimed that his offices in Washington were not part of the department at all. They belonged to the fleet and "might theoretically put out to sea at any time."[15]

King estimated that he spent no more than 2 percent of his time acting as CNO. His main job was to fight the war. He delegated CNO functions such as procurement to his capable vice chief, Vice Admiral Frederick Horne. Ninety-eight percent of King's time was devoted to being commander in chief of the United States Fleet. Two-thirds of that time he allocated to planning with the JCS and the remainder to fleet command, making and executing the strategy of the greatest navy in the greatest war in history.

The paramount question was how fast the country could launch offensives across both oceans. The United States, alone of the Allies, had the choice of turning east, west, or both—or in theory, with its coasts protected, neither. Never giving up the policy of putting the defeat of Germany first, military and political leaders, prodded by Admiral King, were determined to fight a global war from the beginning, and to fight it offensively. This all-important decision meant that the fight was to be taken to both major enemies *simultaneously*. Thomas Buell, King's biographer, states that King's insistence on simultaneous offensives was "the most important contribution to victory he would make in the Second World War."[16] To position a force strong enough to invade the homelands of both Germany and Japan meant gaining, and maintaining, control of both great oceans. And at first it would have to be done with the men and matériel on hand. Although there was the promise of an enormous increase to come, it is important to remember that the invasion of Morocco and the battles of the Coral Sea, Midway, and Guadalcanal were fought and won with the equipment, men, and doctrines of the prewar Navy.

The immediate objective of U.S. policy was to keep Germany and Japan tied to their exhausting continental wars while the Americans readied two second fronts, both from the sea. Each enemy state saw itself as a land power. The main effort of Germany was against the Soviet Union. It would worry about the West and the oceans when the continental war was won. Japan too was committed to continental expansion and defense. It was embroiled in China. Japan had turned to the sea because it needed a resource base and security in its rear to win on the Asian mainland.[17] It was the job of the Imperial Japanese Navy to gain these advantages and then to devise a protective barrier. The oil of the Dutch East Indies was necessary for the conquest of China and for the defense of Manchuria from the Soviet Union. On the continent the Japanese army had stationed over a million men.

The United States followed a classic strategy by which a maritime power engages a continental foe: support of one's allies already fighting on land and intervention in the land war at a time and place of one's own choosing. Essential to both elements was use of the sea. Only by sea could the United States support the resistance of Britain and the Soviet Union, and only by sea could it gain access to the enemy's shores.[18] Air power did not change the essentials of this maritime strategy. Airfields within range of the foes had to be established on land won by attack from the sea or on the soil of maritime allies. By sea, then, with a cumulative and sequential strategy, the United States would prolong the continental wars of Germany and Japan and, in due time, when America was ready, force those states into fighting in a theater of operations that was advantageous to the United States.[19]

Sea control was thus the first step in the Victory Program. In the war against Germany the immediate need was to bolster Soviet resistance and maintain Britain as an advanced staging area. The second step was to invade the European continent. In the Pacific, the first step was to aid China and maintain the line to Australia. The next step was to stage a limited offensive to prevent Japan from closing its Pacific ring. The final step was the advance toward the home islands. Britain and the Soviet Union could be reached by sea. China, on the other hand, was almost cut off by Japan's advances in Southeast Asia. Japanese control of the Philippines, Guam, Hong Kong, Singapore, the Dutch East Indies, Burma, and various island bases meant that routes to China, whether by land and air over the Himalayas or, until 1943, by landings planned for the Chinese coast, could be established only at enormous cost. The problem of access to China was never solved.

In both oceans the United States sought the initiative. That meant the Navy had to secure and extend sea control. To do this it fought two distinct naval wars simultaneously. In general, in the Atlantic the Navy sought local sea control—that is, safety for the convoys and support for invasion forces. Destruction of the U-boat force was a desirable goal but subsidiary to assuring sea control. In the Pacific, with the Marine Corps and the Army, the Navy faced Japan's powerful surface fleet, naval air force, and heavily defended island garrisons.

In the first months the Navy held its position and built. All the vessels it had in the Pacific after Pearl Harbor were some treaty cruisers substituting for the lost battleships, a couple of carriers, and the submarines. Hawaii, the American west coast, and northern Australia stood exposed to an aggressive and victorious enemy. Deployment of U.S. forces in the central Pacific west of Hawaii required island bases, which would have to be fought for foot by foot.

AGAINST THE SEA WOLVES

The Navy's primary missions in the Atlantic were to protect convoys supporting allies and to transport, cover, and supply American troops for their unprecedented amphibious assaults across the ocean. In the Atlantic there was never a battle between fleets during the war. The Navy's only battleship engagement was the shelling of the immobilized French battleship *Jean Bart,* which was undergoing repairs in port at Casablanca. Because Germany aimed at continental self-sufficiency there was no German shipping to attack.

The defeat of Germany was the primary war aim. Germany was the most dangerous enemy and the one against which massive force most readily and most effectively could be applied, first through aid to Britain and the Soviet Union, then through bombing raids from Britain, and finally to invasion and assault against the Siegfried Line. Shipping lanes to Europe were much shorter than those to the Far East. Most U.S. industrial production moved to Atlantic and Gulf ports. Goods could be put ashore in the large, established ports of Britain and the Soviet Union far more easily, and in far greater quantities, than they could anywhere in Asia. No place in the Far East compared to Britain as a base from which to launch an invasion force. Northwestern Europe was a better field of action for the huge forces of the U.S. Army than were Pacific islands.[20]

American strategy centered on a cross-channel invasion. Army Chief of Staff General George Marshall held on to that position through thick and thin. An invasion was planned because the War Department, and the Navy Department too (in Stark's Plan Dog memorandum), knew that only by defeating German ground forces would Germany be forced to give up. The invasion would be cross-channel because Army forces could concentrate in Britain, which was in effect both an unsinkable aircraft carrier and a close-in landing barge available for the continental assault. The War Department wanted to maintain a single main line of communication and to direct its primary effort at one main front. That meant Europe first.[21] Hitler's war against the Soviet Union left Germany exposed in the west. The sooner the Allies established a beachhead on the continent the better.

This was sound strategy. All Hitler's plans depended on the control of Eurasia. Then Germany would have, he told his naval chief in 1942, an "easily defendable, blockade-safe *Lebensraum*," where it could hold out against the futile efforts of the "Anglo-Saxon naval powers."[22] For that he did not need much of a navy. Hitler had learned from the previous war. He reversed Emperor William II's sequence for establishing German greatness. Hitler's plan was continental control first, then world policy.

The leaders of the German navy were left out of the prewar planning for continental expansion and were divided on what kind of naval war to fight. The minority, represented by Captain Karl Dönitz, argued for a submarine *guerre de course*. Dönitz said that with 300 submarines he could defeat Great Britain. The majority, led by the head of the navy, Grand Admiral Erich Raeder, argued for a large surface fleet. Part of this fleet would tie the British Home Fleet to the North Sea, and the rest would sweep the seas of enemy convoys, destroying in detail a frantic and dispersed Royal Navy.

Hitler chose the surface fleet. He gave Raeder to understand, however, that there would be no need for action before the mid-1940s. He could conquer Europe without sea control. Britain, Hitler thought, was not a major threat. Raeder therefore carried out construction at a leisurely pace. His Z Plan envisioned a balanced fleet of 23 battleships, 4 aircraft carriers, about 40 cruisers, 58 destroyers, and 241 submarines by 1948. Hitler stopped the construction called for by the Z Plan shortly after the war began. At that time Raeder's surface fleet existed only in skeleton form: one aircraft carrier, the *Graf Zeppelin*, which was still under construction; the great battleship *Bismarck*, which was on duty; and the *Bismarck*'s sister ship, the *Tirpitz*, still unfinished. The land and air war came years before the German navy was ready for surface war at sea. Nor was the submarine force built up. In September 1939, Dönitz had only 57 submarines in operation.

Hitler's disinterest in sea power left the coast of western Europe exposed. The United States based its strategy on this fact. The Soviet Union kept the bulk of the German army away from the sea. Britain would be the springboard for the western attack. For two years Hitler had tried to bring the British to terms, had failed, and had turned away. He had not drawn a defense perimeter through the Azores and the Cape Verdes. Gibraltar, controlling the ocean entrance to the Mediterranean, remained in British hands. Hitler's last-minute plan to fortify the Channel Islands was not enough to close the open ocean frontier. His concentration of naval force in Norway was not a bad idea. It impeded reinforcement of the Soviet Union and tied up important British naval units. But it was not a substitute for command of the sea, control of the English Channel, or isolation of the Mediterranean.

The capital ships of the Kriegsmarine hardly moved during the war. They had shown some value early on as surface raiders, mainly in distant seas. In the all-important North Atlantic, however, they suffered devastating losses and were pulled back. The day after Hitler declared war on the United States, he canceled all Atlantic surface sorties and ordered the battle cruisers at Brest, the *Scharnhorst* and the *Gneisenau*, to withdraw from the Atlantic ports. The surface fleet was sent to Norwegian seas in anticipation of an invasion there. At the end of 1942, after prolonged idleness, when a substantial German surface force failed to stop a convoy off Norway, Hitler threatened to scrap all the big ships, turn them into submarines or into tanks for the eastern front, and remount their cannons as shore batteries. A fleet-in-being strategy was not enough for Grand Admiral Raeder, who resigned in January 1943. The navy command went to submarine chief Karl Dönitz. Hitler's naval strategy became whatever the attack submarine could do.

Dönitz was a pioneer U-boat tactician. In the 1930s he had developed new ways of using the submarine as a commerce destroyer. One innovation was the use of short-range attacks to improve the chance of a kill when engaging a convoy, which might escape during the submarine's underwater reloading time if the U-boat was too distant. Another tactic was the nighttime surface attack. Submarines at this time traveled and attacked on the surface as much as possible, diving only to escape a counterattack or bad weather. The more they stayed on the surface, the more they held the initiative. Surface action, before airborne radar was introduced, also reduced the likelihood of sonar detection. A third tactic was the use of submarines in a pack. That brought together a group of six to twelve boats at a place where naval intelligence had determined a convoy would pass.[23] The attack was focused on a concentrated target. The target's concentration, plus the U-boats' stealth, gave the submarines their advantage at the decisive point of contact.

Dönitz's strategy followed the tonnage, or stock, doctrine, which is to sink more cargo vessels than the enemy can produce. Dönitz thus sent his boats wherever the killing field was most crowded. When the field thinned, or when defensive measures improved, he moved his U-boats elsewhere. Dönitz wrote: "The strategic task of the German Navy was to wage war on trade; its objective was therefore to sink as many enemy merchant ships as it could. The *sinking of ships* was the only thing that mattered." In principle it did not matter whether the ships were laden or empty, what they were carrying, or where they were. What was important was to send the enemy's hauling capacity to the bottom. "The enemy's shipping constitutes one single, great entity. It is therefore immaterial where a ship is sunk."[24] For this mission the submarine was the most effective weapon, more certain than any airplane, more efficient than any surface ship. Cheap and deadly and capable of approaching by stealth, killing in secret, and disappearing before counterattack, the submarine opened a new chapter in the history of the *guerre de course*.

To critics, Dönitz's decision to attack shipping tonnage instead of targets of immediate military value was a failure of strategic insight. His submarines paid no attention to conventional assessments of sea control. Even in a *guerre de course*, said Raeder and the German Naval Operations staff, a distinction must be made between quantity and quality. Empty ships, which represented carrying capacity, might be preferred on the grounds of opportunity, but they were not as important as freighters carrying weapons and men to the battlefront. Critics pointed to a serious oversight: Britain might not be able to make up shipping shortfalls, but it was likely to find an ally that could. Another criticism was that Dönitz made no effort to confront the warships of Britain's Royal Navy. His doctrine assumed that the use of submarines in commerce raiding would be decisive. Because of this, Dönitz opposed their use in other elements of strategy—for instance, in fleet support, reconnaissance, or attacks on large warships. It was a matter of choice because Dönitz did not have enough submarines for both missions. Only 26 U-boats were operational in April 1941, and these were not enough to stand up to improved British countermeasures.

Dönitz's best chance at success was in 1940 and 1941, when Britain was still on its own and U-boats held the noose. Then, and perhaps only then, if Dönitz had had the 300 boats he wanted and had not faced the increasingly effective countermeasures of the Royal Navy, his strategy might have worked.[25] As it was, despite the horrendous British losses, by the end of 1941 the convoy system, American support, and various practices of antisubmarine warfare had checked the sinkings.

Even in the first period of heavy sinkings between June 1940 and May 1941, Dönitz did not meet his goal, which was to destroy more cargo ships than the enemy could supply. British defenses were steadily improving, as central direction and close cooperation between intelligence, the British Admiralty, the Royal Canadian Navy, and the British Royal Air Force (RAF) outfoxed the U-boat command. Between May and August 1941 British intelligence progressively increased the speed with which it read the German naval code. By August it was reading the essential Home Waters settings of the German naval Enigma code machine the instant the machine sent a message. Although disguises often permitted the concealment of a U-boat's position, German policy of close central direction from shore permitted British radio directional finders to pick up transmissions and locate the boats. Fine coordination of intelligence and operations gave the British the combat edge. The Admiralty rerouted convoys to evade the U-boats and gave the convoys better cover. These advantages were to some extent offset by limited German access to British naval convoy ciphers, but the overall edge lay with the British until the beginning of 1942.[26]

Thus in the period before the United States entered the war, the U-boats began to find the North Atlantic pickings thinned as well as the danger increased. Following a strategy of opportunity, Dönitz went where ships were easiest to sink. He was ready to give up the North Atlantic if he could find a more fertile field for plunder. War with the United States came in December 1941, and Dönitz seized the opportunity to maraud the unprotected waters of the American coastline. If the tonnage strategy was based on correct assumptions, all enemy shipping was part of a single network. A strike against the Americans was a strike against Britain and the Soviet Union, for a ship sunk off Florida was just as valuable as one sunk off Ireland or Murmansk.

When in 1942 Dönitz was asked why he did not concentrate his operations near Europe, he reiterated that enemy shipping should be seen as a collective whole, that his own offensive strategy was global:

> It is therefore immaterial where any one ship is sunk, for it must ultimately be replaced by new construction. What counts in the long run is the preponderance

of sinkings over new construction. Shipbuilding and arms production are centered in the United States, while England is the European outpost and sally point. By attacking the supply traffic—particularly the oil—in the American zone, I am striking at the root of the evil, for here the sinking of each ship is not only a loss to the enemy, but deals a blow at the source of his shipbuilding and war production. Without shipping the sally point cannot be used for an attack on Europe. . . . I consider that we should continue to operate the U-boats where they can sink the greatest tonnage with the smallest losses, which at present is in American waters.[27]

In January 1942 Dönitz ordered five U-boats down from the Newfoundland Bank to the U.S. coast. His inshore offensive was Mahan's nightmare come true. A European power assaulted the main corridor of U.S. maritime commerce unopposed. The United States lost sea control directly off its shore. It was like a blockade. Conventional engagement doctrine did not apply. The United States was unprepared to defend its coastal trade or to smite the dispersed assailants conducting a guerrilla war on the country's threshold.[28]

In the first six months of 1942, the United States endured "the greatest maritime massacre in her history."[29] Some 2.34 million tons of shipping capacity was sunk in the western hemisphere, most of it along the eastern and Gulf coasts of the United States.[30] If Dönitz's goal was to down 700,000 tons of cargo capacity per month, he was well on his way. Historians have compared to Pearl Harbor the enormous losses of merchantmen along the eastern sea frontier and in the Caribbean, the lack of U.S. preparedness to meet the threat, and the length of time it took the United States to defeat the perpetrator.

The explanation for this state of affairs is that Admiral King and Admiral Royal Ingersoll, King's replacement as commander in chief of the Atlantic Fleet (CinClant), and their small staffs held too long to the inappropriate concept that a convoy must be strongly defended by potentially offensive escorts. King did understand that the answer to the threat to merchant shipping was the convoy, not the patrol or the antisubmarine sweeps that Woodrow Wilson had derided as a hunt for hornets all over the farm. King insisted, however, that the convoy's escort force have offensive capacities. He associated two different strategic purposes—the defense of ships and the destruction of U-boats. King imagined a convoy vicinity into which the predatory U-boats would be drawn and then destroyed. That was an attrition strategy, using the convoy as bait. King saw the convoy as a means as much as an end. Whatever its utility in antisubmarine warfare, King's strategy could not be executed because he had too few ships and he was not willing to pull the destroyers he did have from their equally vital convoy duty in the western Atlantic.

In King's thinking, until what he considered adequate numbers of warships became available for the escort mission, the United States would have to make it through the inshore U-boat campaign without convoys. No strategy can be carried out unless the means are available. The United States in the first year of the war had to hold and build.[31]

The British tried to convince King that he could convoy with fewer and weaker escorts if he used a strictly defensive strategy. The escorts' goal, after all, was not to kill submarines but to get cargo ships through. A year before, the Royal Navy had established this doctrine for British escort operators. Their job was not attrition but delivery, not to destroy but to discourage, to assure "the safe and timely arrival of the convoy."[32] Because submarines ran and fired on the surface, only a small number of escort vessels was needed, particularly if, as along the American coast, they were supplemented with land-based aircraft patrols.

Why did it take the U.S. command so long to realize this? There is no doubt that King rejected British advice. There is no doubt that his position bordered on the dogmatic, that his small and harried staff gave too little attention to strategic alternatives on the convoy issue. One reason for this was that the Navy tended to see readiness as a matter of force, not organization.[33] Ships were in short supply, it is true. More important, however, the organization to use those at hand did not exist. There was no central organization to draw together the assets and the information of the four commands that would have been needed to run a convoy defense of merchant shipping along the east coast, however one defined the mission of the convoys' escorts.[34] The four commands were King's CominCh; Ingersoll's CinClant; Rear Admiral Adolphus Andrews's Eastern Sea Frontier; and Rear Admiral Arthur Bristol, Jr.'s destroyer force, whose mission was to escort ocean convoys in the western Atlantic.

In the years before the war, officers had foreseen a need for smaller vessels, which could be used for the defense of convoys, but thought they would not be required before 1942. Preparation stalled when construction shifted to larger ships and to the dual-purpose fleet-or-escort destroyers, which could fight an ocean war. The Navy assumed that small craft could be built rapidly after a war began, but so long as dominant opinion held that the purpose of escort was to kill submarines, larger warships would be preferred to the smaller vessels that were suited only to convoy defense.

The Navy made up its patrol and escort debits in record time, but in the early months of 1942, the ships simply were not there. For instance the production of destroyer escorts, which were designed for the all-important North Atlantic convoy duty, was delayed even during these months, when priority was given to cargo ships and landing craft, which likewise had been unanticipated needs. The first destroyer escort did not sail until February 1943, and by the end of June 1943 only 25 of them had been commissioned.

Furthermore, recent direct American experience of both patrol and convoy was limited. The Support Force of the Atlantic Fleet, which for six months had been patrolling and conducting offshore convoys, had had almost no contact with submarines. Before the U.S. declaration of war, U-boats had avoided American ships on Hitler's direct command. The critical situation in the Mediterranean caused every available Atlantic U-boat to be shifted to the Gibraltar area. Their absence from the Atlantic kept Roosevelt's undeclared war from escalating. It also limited the experience of the Support Force of U.S. destroyers on ocean convoy escort.

The lack of an organizational unit to address the problem of coastal convoy was reflected in the difficulty of sending ships and information across the carefully tended boundaries between Rear Admiral Andrews's Eastern Sea Frontier and Admiral Ingersoll's Atlantic Fleet. Committed to oceanic convoy duty, Ingersoll never gave Andrews the inshore escort and patrol craft he needed. Andrews in turn refused to organize coastal convoys until he had the escort vessels, and King, the sole authority able to move forces between operating areas, refused to transfer destroyers from the Atlantic convoys to coastal convoys.

Consider the following correspondence. In January 1942 Ingersoll wrote, "Converted vessels will not yield much and until the new PC's [patrol craft] begin to get in service I think we are in for a beating from the subs." Two weeks later King wrote to Ingersoll proposing the release from the Atlantic of some 21 destroyers for coastal convoy escort. Ingersoll did not want to give up his destroyers, and King let him keep them. King then asked Rear Admiral Andrews for his suggestions. Like Ingersoll, Andrews thought the convoy system should wait for an adequate escort force. Thus the matter drifted. Michael Gannon is right that "when King thought of convoys he thought of destroyers," and King's dictum that "inadequately escorted convoys are worse than none" prevailed.[35] The Navy, with its strong tradition of regional responsibilities, continued to see the problem of the protection of shipping as one of capabilities and equipment, not organization.[36]

The core fact is that the British were correct in saying that convoys even lightly escorted would render shipping safer, especially against a submarine acting alone and mostly on the surface. Convoys reduce the area where targets are to be found, as experience in both world wars showed. The British offered to make the lessons of their experience available to the Navy, to show the Navy the benefits of standardization and organization. To British bewilderment, the Navy turned down the offer and the advice. King preferred having no escort to having one that could not do the job, which was defined as not just defending the escort's charges but killing the attacker as well. King wanted to keep up the delivery of goods for war production, and at the moment merchantmen sailing alone provided more shipping capacity and moved goods faster, even with their relatively greater losses, than could slow convoys whose escort, as he had defined it, he could not yet provide.[37]

Now we come to what may be the clue to how this story's parts—the Navy leaders' concern with adequacy of the escort, King's insistence on destroyers, and King's rejection of British advice—might be connected. In Navy eyes, the brief experience of joint American-Canadian North Atlantic convoys in the fall of 1941 had shown the failure of light cover.

Marc Milner established this connection, showing that poorly prepared Canadian deployments on the Newfoundland-to-Iceland route resulted in devastating losses when slow, lightly covered convoys were picked off by U-boat packs. The Navy derived from this experience a lesson that British expostulations could not shake. According to Milner, "The Americans saw in these ill-fated Canadian operations their worst fears about poorly escorted convoys and vowed to have none of it."[38] Until a stronger, more offensive escort force became available, coastal convoys would have to wait. In March 1942 the Navy's Board on the Organization of East Coast Convoys came out against "weakly escorted" convoys. As Milner has written, "No jury-rigged groups of motor launches, yachts, trawlers and clapped-out vessels for the USN: its coastal convoys were to have destroyer escorts or none at all."[39]

The Navy had not yet made the necessary distinctions between inshore and oceanic convoys, between antisubmarine warfare and antisubmarine escorts. There was a critical distinction between a convoy operating in the open ocean and one operating in the coastal traffic along the east and Gulf coasts. The open-ocean convoys faced wolf packs beyond the range of land-based air cover and so required a heavier escort force. Coastal convoys, however, could be defended by partial escorts if they were covered by land-based aircraft as well.[40]

Here we must note the pitiful organizational unreadiness of the coastal air patrol. With submarines so much on the surface and the sea-lanes running along the coast and near Caribbean islands, air was the best means of surveillance. With airborne radar, until the German submarines developed early-warning devices, aircraft were an exceptionally potent offensive force. This was proven in the RAF's sweeps of U-boats transiting between the ocean and their pens in the Bay of Biscay. Radar-equipped aircraft had been particularly effective against submarines operating far from home on coastal patrol. But the air forces of both U.S. services clung to their autonomy. Who controlled coastal air defense was still unresolved after twenty years of squabbling. The failure to resolve this issue had contributed to the disaster at Pearl Harbor and now bedeviled the creation of an integrated antisubmarine system along the east coast.

For the first four months the United States was in the war, the eight to fourteen U-boats on station and operating individually along the U.S. east coast and in Caribbean waters enjoyed, without centralized and effective opposition, a target-rich and undefended environment. Tactically, the German campaign was provisional and improvised.[41] The U-boats were refueled and retorpedoed by first commercial tankers from Europe and then, after April 1942, by submarine tankers. German sailors were astonished to see U.S. merchantmen sailing as if it were peacetime. Unrestricted radio chatter gave cargo ships' locations. U-boat captains nailed freighters and tankers as they stood outlined against the undimmed lights of coastal resorts or against buoy lights. In the first four months of 1942, these few U-boats sank 198 freighters and tankers, which had a total capacity of 1.2 million gross tons. None of the ships sunk was in convoy or under escort. Naval patrols, made with predictable regularity, were easily avoided. Shore beacons gave German commanders their bearings. They could not believe their good luck.

Faced with the slaughter and with stern Army disapproval of its conduct of the war to date, the Navy in April 1942 began a partial convoy system called the Bucket Brigades.[42] The system was for daylight use only. Ships moved in 120-mile hops, only in daylight, and were very lightly escorted. The measure was enough, however, to thin the waters of the east coast. Looking for more game, Dönitz moved south to the Caribbean. There he found oil tankers from Venezuela and ore freighters from the Gulf. In May 1942, U-boats sank 34 ships off the U.S. east coast, 26 in the Gulf, 29 in the Caribbean, and 19 in the Antilles—108 ships altogether, with a total capacity of 491,000 tons. In response, the Navy tightened up. Coastal cities were blacked out. The Navy created a coastal convoy system between Key West and Halifax, adding new escort vessels as they were commissioned. Convoy measures were extended to the Caribbean in June, expanded in July, and in August 1942 were combined in an interlocking system from Gulf ports to New York, where connection was made with the transatlantic convoys.

Air cooperation came only after foot-dragging at the highest levels. Admiral King's appeal for land-based patrol aircraft was turned down by the chief of the Army Air Forces, Major General Henry Arnold, on grounds of service autonomy. Declaring that the Navy's leadership was unimaginative and unaggressive, Secretary of War Henry Stimson took on the antisubmarine mission. He equipped Army planes with more efficient radar and told Army pilots to hunt and sink U-boats before they struck the newly formed convoys. Although the Air Force did not favor using its bombers for that purpose, no better alternative was yet available, and the War Department, free from convoy responsibilities, embraced offensive antisubmarine warfare.[43]

Cooperation came when the Army realized the extent of its own losses. In June 1942 the head of the Army, General Marshall, noted:

> Of the 74 ships allocated to the Army for July by the War Shipping Administration, 17 have already been sunk. 22 per cent of the Bauxite fleet [bauxite ore being the source of the all-important metal aluminum] has already been destroyed . . . Tanker sinkings have been 3.5% per month of tonnage in use. . . . I am fearful that another month or two of this will so cripple our means of transport that we will be unable to bring sufficient men and plans to bear against the enemy in critical theatres to exercise a determining influence on the war.[44]

King returned with his request for land-based patrol aircraft, and this time it was granted. Army air was at last allocated for Navy antisubmarine patrol in support of convoys.

The submarine threat was overcome by making the prey less vulnerable, not by killing the predator. In the summer of 1942 the Navy extended the convoys to the Gulf and the Caribbean, and air coverage arrived. In July Dönitz turned back to the North Atlantic for a new pack offensive on the ocean convoys to Britain.[45] In the first six months of 1942, in Atlantic and Arctic waters, U-boats had sunk 506 Allied and neutral merchant vessels and tankers with a total shipping capacity of 2.8 million gross tons. Dönitz, however, still had not won the tonnage battle.

The reason was that U.S. shipbuilding had made up the losses. Productivity won the battle of the Atlantic. The Ships-For-Victory program was in full swing. The first Liberty ship had been launched in September 1941. It was a prefabricated vessel of 7,176 gross tons (that is, cargo capacity by volume) and could sail at 11 knots when loaded. Production burgeoned, and in October 1942 the U.S. Maritime Commission, which was supervising construction, announced it had reached its goal of launching three ships a day. It was possible to build a Liberty ship in less than two months. Production in December 1942 exceeded that in all of 1941. In the first six months of 1943, 711 ships were produced. A total of 19 million tons of carrying capacity were produced that year. Altogether between 1939 and 1945, 2,708 Liberty ships and 2,893 vessels of other types were built in Maritime Commission shipyards. Another 176 ships were built under contract with civilian shipyards. Thus the Maritime Commission program created a total of 5,777 ships for use in the war, primarily to carry cargo and fuel.[46] It was the greatest shipbuilding program in history. The War Shipping Administration was created in February 1942 to operate the cargo fleets, and the U.S.-British Combined Shipping Adjustment Board coordinated resources and allocated tonnage for cargo and troop transport. During the war, the United States fully met Mahan's definition of a maritime nation.

Meanwhile, through 1942 and into 1943 the Atlantic campaign continued. The fear that the U-boats might yet cut off American deployment to Europe never left strategists' minds. There would be no victory without sea transport. To project power overseas, to sustain allies and invasions, ships had to get through. "The most unstable element in the logistical process," wrote Richard Leighton and Robert Coakley, "was not the capacity to produce, but the capacity to deliver fighting power to the firing line. . . . For a year and a half after Pearl Harbor, the most basic expectation upon which any plan of operations had to rest—the number of troops and the amount of armament that could be made available at the time and place needed—could never be much more than a wishful estimate."[47]

The construction under way did not meet all needs. And it remained hard to allocate what had been built. The winter of 1942–43, the height of the campaign of the Atlantic, was a period of frustration. Roosevelt was slow to set priorities, and when he finally did in 1942, he went against the advice of King and Marshall. Those two pushed for an early cross-channel invasion. This the British refused until the American buildup, code-named Bolero, was complete. To keep up civilian morale by offensive action, Roosevelt ordered participation in the British-inspired invasion of North Africa. This invasion was opposed by King and Marshall on military grounds because it necessarily drew escort and transport ships from the North Atlantic and from the Pacific, where their offensive strategies called for as much reinforcement as could be mustered. The shipyards could do only so much. The needs of an escalating world war had jumped ahead of resources.

Shortages had consequences. Leighton and Coakley wrote, "Failure to make provision in 1941 and 1942 for a large and versatile fleet of amphibious shipping, would, until late 1944, constitute the most persistent and restrictive single limitation on a war in which all the principal avenues of advance lay over water."[48] There were never enough ships. King had to shift what he had from one ocean to another and, in the European theater, between fronts. This shifting raised British suspicions that his heart was not in the desperate antisubmarine campaign in the North Atlantic.[49]

Ships there in the winter of 1942–43 sailed in the worst storms yet seen in the century. Against them the U-boats were having a tremendous success. Between July 1942 and May 1943, they sank 780 merchantmen of some 4.5 million gross tons. At last Dönitz had more U-boats. As a result of the building program going on in Germany, in May 1943 he could put 120 boats into the North Atlantic. And he knew where to send them. German intelligence read the British convoy code. Dönitz was also lucky. For a good deal of the time, the British did not know where the U-boats were. Between February and December 1942 the British lost their ability to read the signals between Dönitz and his commanders.

At the same time, Dönitz faced growing Allied strengths. The most important was the outpouring from U.S. shipyards. Beginning in July 1942 the United States built more ships than the Germans sank. Furthermore, all aspects of the convoy system were now in place, and at each end of the ocean, workers in ports were efficiently loading, unloading, and distributing goods. By the end of the winter of 1942–43, the new German submarine code had been broken, and with Ultra intelligence again available (although decodings were often irregular, delayed, or unclear) it was possible to renew direct offensive action against the U-boats or try to evade them. The two sides, it was said, watched each other through secret windows. "Between February and June 1943 the battle of the Atlantic hinged to no small extent on the changing fortunes of a continuing trial of cryptographic and cryptanalytic resourcefulness between the B-Dienst [German naval intelligence] and the Allies."[50]

Most convoys made the trip safely. The risks were high, but luck, the skill of Allied tracking rooms and routing departments, and the blessings of escorts, led most around the danger zones. In the year before May 1943, even during a period of impaired intelligence, about 60 percent of the 174 scheduled North Atlantic convoys were steered clear of wolf packs. The invasion force Britain sent to North Africa, a huge armada, "the most valuable convoys ever to leave these shores," the First Sea Lord, Admiral of the fleet Sir Dudley Pound, anxiously told

Churchill, was sent out during the intelligence blackout and, protected by air as much as possible, arrived at Gibraltar without incident. The 102-ship Western Naval Task Force sent from the United States to North Africa likewise arrived undetected, in part because radio direction finders helped the ships avoid U-boats. The invasion of North Africa caught the Germans by surprise. Dönitz rushed his U-boats down from the North Atlantic too late. No Allied ships were lost in transit.[51]

But throughout the winter of 1942–43, enlarged packs of German submarines sank ships in waters to the north. In January 1943 the British appealed for more American help. At Casablanca that month, the Combined Chiefs of Staff agreed that defeat of the U-boats was the primary security issue the military had to address. The British requested 65 additional escort vessels, 12 escort carriers, and as many very long-range aircraft (B-24 Liberator bombers) as could be delivered. Without these ships and planes, the British warned, the convoy system might default.

In March 1943 an Atlantic convoy conference was held in Washington. At that time the U.S. Navy was escorting only 4 percent of the northern transatlantic convoys. The navies of Britain (in the eastern Atlantic) and Canada (in the west) were sharing the main burden. The United States held escort responsibility for convoys in the Caribbean, for the tanker convoys to Britain, and for the central Atlantic convoys to Gibraltar and Casablanca. The moment was critical. That month, the British War Cabinet was told, "We are consuming ¾ m. tons more [of all goods] than we are importing. In *two months*, we would not meet our requirements if this continued." More U-boats were coming into service, more than the Allies were sinking, and the new submarines could cover greater areas. Rerouting the convoys was no longer a way to evade the submarine; the changing of routes just took the convoys into other packs. Convoys were regularly losing six or more ships in encounters with submarines. A report of the British Admiralty stated that the U-boats never came nearer their objective of cutting the connections between the Old World and the New than they did in the first twenty days of March 1943. And at that time, a convoy might have seven to nine escorts, a number that increased by a carrier and eighteen more ships when a support group joined the convoy.[52] The effectiveness of the convoy system was thrown in doubt. Yet there was no alternative for Britain or for Allied strategy. Convoys had to get through.

What was needed was air cover. The snorkel was not yet in use, and so the submarines still operated on the surface, exposed to air surveillance. British microwave radar was a decisive innovation. It could not be detected, and so U-boats had no diving time as planes approached. "Radar," wrote Dönitz, "and particularly radar location by aircraft, had to all practical purposes robbed the U-boats of their power to fight on the surface."[53] In the critical spring of 1943, however, an air gap 300 miles wide existed in the middle of the ocean, beyond the reach of land-based aircraft, and it was there that the U-boats congregated in safety. As a result of the convoy conference in Washington, 80 U.S. Army and 60 Navy long-range and very long-range planes were sent to North Atlantic convoy duty. That narrowed the air gap from the west while the British Coastal Command shaved it from the east. Soon U.S. hunter-killer groups, consisting of an escort carrier with radar-equipped planes and a number of destroyers or patrol boats that were designed to operate directly in the convoy routes, sailed in and closed the air gap altogether. In April 1943, when the campaign of the Atlantic was at its peak, aircraft flew 2,459 missions for convoy protection and patrol.

On May 24, 1943, Dönitz, now commander in chief of the German navy, withdrew his U-boats from the North Atlantic and ordered them to operate on the U.S.-Gibraltar route, southwest of the Azores. "We had lost the Battle of the Atlantic," Dönitz later wrote.[54] He thought the withdrawal would be only temporary, perhaps a year or so. German engineers were improving radar countermeasures and building an acoustic torpedo (which the Allies countered with a towed noise-maker). The addition of the snorkel ventilator gave the submarines greater underwater range. Above all, in Dönitz's mind and in Hitler's, was the imminent introduction of the huge diesel-electric wonder class of attack submarine, the Type XXI, which would be swifter underwater than a convoy escort.

In May 1943 Admiral King unified the U.S. antisubmarine command, named it the Tenth Fleet, and took charge of it himself. The Tenth Fleet brought under central direction all operations of patrol and convoy and of intelligence and planning. The Tenth Fleet did not have a ship. But with King in charge, it had the authority to direct all antisubmarine activity and detach ships and airplanes as needed from the various Atlantic commands. In September 1943 it took over from the Army Air Forces the antisubmarine use of shore-based air power. In a trade-off that summer, Army Air agreed to give its antisubmarine-equipped Liberators to the Navy in return for an equal number of unmodified bombers from the Navy's inventory.[55] That ended the dispute over the provenance of land-based air for antisubmarine duty, which had for so long hampered the antisubmarine campaign. By the summer of 1943, the Navy had in place an organization under the commander of the

Navy himself that concentrated all antisubmarine intelligence, the decisions of force allocation for escort and search, the control of convoys and routing, and the development of tactical doctrines for the continuing battle against the sea wolves.

Dönitz never regained the initiative. He sent his packs back to the North Atlantic in September 1943, telling them they were engaged in "the decisive struggle for the German race." Against the superior odds conferred by technological advantages, Dönitz, embracing Nazi ideology—he was Hitler's chosen successor—urged the triumph of the will. It was to no avail, and at an immense cost in German lives.[56] Allied intelligence made it possible to divert almost every convoy. Bombers picked off submarines that were transiting the Bay of Biscay on their way between the ocean and their bases on the French coast. Those bases, the Atlantic pens, had withstood an enormous Allied aerial bombardment—showing how difficult it could be to get the hornets in their nests if the nests were strong enough. These submarine bases were lost to Germany not by direct air or sea assault, but by the conquest of the land behind them, the result of the Normandy invasion of June 1944.[57] Aggressive groups of U.S. escort carriers, guided by Ultra intelligence, covered the mid-Atlantic, attacking supply submarines. In a three-month period in the summer of 1943, these hunter-killer groups sank sixteen submarines, half of which were tankers. In November Dönitz again withdrew defeated. His losses affected combat efficiency. In December 1943 the average time of operational command of 168 of his U-boat commanders was only 8.1 months, and 30 percent of them had been in command less than 3 months.[58]

On Navy Day, October 25, 1943, Admiral King declared, "Submarines have not been driven from the seas, but they have changed status from a menace to a problem." In one regard the United States remained exceptionally lucky. The Japanese never launched a comparable submarine offensive. Had they mounted a *guerre de course*, the American war effort in the Pacific would have been severely threatened. Because they did not, throughout the war the United States could devote its limited escort and patrol resources to the German threat in Atlantic.[59]

There the U.S. Navy did not let up. Dönitz, however, held to his hope of delivering a mortal wound. Germany produced an average of 24 new U-boats each month in 1943. If he did not yet have his miracle boat, Dönitz would make do with improved conventional craft. The snorkel worked. It made a submarine hard to spot from the air, and after June 1944 the longer range it gave the boats partly offset the loss of their

Atlantic bases. But the submarines never returned to their earlier level of success. With the tonnage strategy defeated, Dönitz shifted to support of the Wehrmacht's land operations. This too the Allies countered. At the time of the Normandy invasion, for instance, 350 Allied aircraft covered 20,000 square miles to protect the invasion flotilla. These planes sank 6 U-boats the first day of the operation. The whole area from southern Ireland to Brest was covered by air patrol at least once every 30 minutes, day and night. Ten escort groups stood by to block the western approaches to the channel. Of the 43 U-boats that had operated, or tried to operate, against the invasion force, 18 were sunk. In the last three months of 1944, only 14 merchantmen in convoy across the Atlantic were sunk. By contrast, 55 German submarines were sent to the bottom during the same period. In October 1944 the two convoys on the Murmansk run were protected by 3 carriers, 1 cruiser, and up to 32 escort vessels. In the last month of the European war, even when few U-boats operated in the Atlantic, Allied airplanes flew 6,314 antisubmarine missions.[60]

After the Normandy invasion Dönitz sent most of his submarines to Norwegian redoubts to wait for the miracle boats. Bombers hit the new boats' production facilities, and the Red Army overran the Baltic yards. But Allied naval leaders could never be sure that Dönitz would not pull some surprise. Submarines remained a potentially very serious threat. At the end of the war, operation of perhaps as many as 50 of the new Type XXI boats was imminent.[61] The submarine war was "the one campaign of the Second World War that lasted from the first day to the last."[62]

The number of ships sunk by German U-boats worldwide had been large indeed. The force sank 2,603 Allied and neutral merchant ships for a total of 13.5 million gross tons. It also sank 145 enemy warships and auxiliaries and damaged 45 others. Of the merchantmen, 757 went down flying the U.S. flag, and more than 6,000 U.S. merchant seamen were lost at sea. The submarine war was also costly to the Germans. Out of a total force of 1,170 commissioned U-boats, of which 863 became operational, 681 were lost to enemy action. About 70 percent of the U-boat sailors lost their lives—28,000 of 40,900 men.

In defeating the U-boat, the Allies established sea control. That saved Britain and made possible the invasion of Europe. Where and when to launch the invasion were the only big questions left unanswered. For Admiral King and General Marshall, a cross-channel assault could not come soon enough.

THE EARLY OFFENSIVE IN THE PACIFIC

In the Pacific at the beginning of 1942, the U.S. battle fleet was out of action, the air force at Hawaii devastated, and half the Army's B-17 bombers and fighters in shambles in the Philippines. With the destruction of that air power, "the Japanese had removed in one stroke the greatest single obstacle to the advance southward."[63] The U.S. Army's garrison in the Philippines had reeled under a Japanese invasion of Luzon three days after the Pearl Harbor attack. The only weapons remaining in the Pacific, greatly outnumbered by those of Japan, were some heavy cruisers, a few dozen submarines, and four carriers.

The submarines had been ordered to launch an unrestricted attrition campaign at the beginning of the war. Blockade of the Japanese home islands had always been the final phase of the Pacific strategy. An attrition campaign would follow the struggle for control of the surface of the sea. In both Japanese and American plans fleet engagement and interdiction were closely connected, although each reversed the order of the other. The concept of the war expressed in the Navy's Orange Plan of 1929, which called for "an offensive war of long duration, primarily naval throughout . . . directed toward the isolation and exhaustion of Orange [Japan] through control of her vital sea communications and through offensive operations against her armed forces and her economic life." The United States's national mission was defined as "to impose the will of the United States upon Orange by destroying Orange Armed Forces and by disrupting Orange economic life, while protecting American interests at home and abroad."[64]

To counter the threat of a blockade the Japanese too thought in Mahanian terms, although attrition—of the American fleet—was to precede a decisive battle. The Japanese view of war's duration, however, was radically different from the American. A short-war strategy and Yamamoto's carrier strikes had been imposed by the recognition that Japan could not outlast the United States in a long war.[65]

In a dramatic example of strategic misjudgment, Japanese leaders neglected to defend themselves against the threat of an offensively employed submarine force. They made no preparation to protect their vital merchant shipping. Their defensive strategy lulled them into ignoring antisubmarine warfare. The lack of preparation made some sense. The Americans would have to transit the world's largest ocean to reach Japanese waters. Also, the U.S. Navy shared with the Japanese an emphasis on fleet submarines for support of the battle line. But the

Japanese navy "vastly underestimated the capability of American submarines . . . [and wrongly assumed] that Americans were inherently unsuited to strenuous submarine duty." Japanese strategists thought the U.S. boats could operate no more than two weeks on an attack mission.[66] Why did Japan need to protect its shipping if it was never going to be reached by the enemy?

This position undertook an enormous risk by turning a blind eye to Japan's greatest vulnerability in time of war, its absolute dependence upon seaborne imports. In the mid-1930s Japan imported 79.1 percent of its oil and all of its wool and cotton. In 1935, almost 70 percent of its scrap iron came from the United States. The Japanese merchant fleet was the world's third largest, at 2,146 ships.[67] To protect these ships, the imperial navy relied on its battle fleet. That strategy proved to be devastatingly misguided. The failure to attend to antisubmarine measures, convoy protection, and mining—in short, to a balanced fleet and a backup strategy—resulted in a false view of the nature of the war.

With Japan so exposed, why then, in the 1930s, had not the United States Navy planned for a comprehensive, independent, offensive submarine attrition campaign against merchantmen as well as against warships? One reason was that Navy leaders did not want to detach submarines from fleet support. The sequence in their plan was first battle, then blockade. Further, cautious submarine commanders were not confident that their boats were ready for the demands of patrol off Japan. The absence of advance bases weighed heavily on their minds.

Also, unrestricted submarine warfare was prohibited by international agreement. The infamous German practice of silent and indiscriminate attack—what a submarine does best—had brought the United States into war with Germany in 1917 and had been vehemently denounced by the United States as contrary to the rules of war. Wilson wanted to abolish the submarine, and so did Coolidge. The Treaty of Versailles forbade the German navy from even possessing U-boats, as punishment for its *guerre de course* during World War I. Explicit rules for raiding merchant ships of belligerents had been established. At the Washington Conference in 1921, the United States proposed that "a merchant vessel must not be destroyed unless the crew and passengers have first been placed in safety" and that a violator of this rule "shall be deemed to have violated the laws of war"—that is to say, to have become a pirate. The London Naval Treaty of 1930 repeated these proscriptions and applied them to submarines. In 1937 the British editor of *Brassey's Naval Annual* wrote:

One tangible result has so far been achieved by fifteen years of naval treaty-making—an extension of the undertaking to refrain from "unrestricted submarine warfare" . . . If the naval conferences with which we have become so familiar have accomplished nothing else, they have at least induced the principal naval Powers of the world to abjure that use—by ships, at least—of methods which were stigmatized in the last war as barbaric.[68]

To many officers in the U.S. Navy, a code that insisted merchantmen be warned before attack and crews be saved was, from a war-fighting perspective, "entirely worthless."[69] It meant that a state would have to give up submarine raiding as a form of warfare. "Observing these rules," John Talbott wrote, "would have required a submarine to operate on the surface, surrendering the elements of stealth and surprise that made it such a formidable warship, giving away its position to merchantmen equipped with radios, exposing its fragile hull to gunfire and aerial bombardment, imposing on its captain the impossible burden of taking aboard his vessel passengers for whom there was no room."[70]

An international agreement it was, however, and the United States had accepted it. That explains why submarine doctrine in the 1930s was written for attacks on combatants and for fleet support missions, but not for a *guerre de course*. Recall the formulation of 1939: "The primary task of the submarine is to attack enemy heavy ships." Robert Kuenne concluded that "it is doubtful . . . this declaration can be taken wholly at face value." Officers must have seen the code as a political restraint on the natural use of the weapon. Revisionist ideas and exercises had accustomed them to thinking of independent offensive operations that would be launched against warships initially but could easily be taken beyond international agreement to attack merchantmen as well.[71]

In any event, the Navy cast international prohibitions aside after Pearl Harbor. On the afternoon of December 7, CNO Stark gave the order: "Execute unrestricted air and submarine warfare against Japan." In the words of Theodore Roscoe, "The polite little law book went overboard. Converted by a directive into commerce raiders, American submarines in the Pacific went to war to sink everything that floated a Japanese flag."[72]

The United States was on its own in the Pacific. The Soviet Union might have opened a second front in Manchuria, thereby doubling Japan's continental involvement. But the Soviets had nothing to spare for the Far East and in December 1941 declared their neutrality, deciding to treat the Pacific as a separate war. Both the Soviet Union and Japan held to their neutrality pact of April 1941. Not until August 8,

1945, three months after Germany's defeat and, notably, after Hiroshima, when U.S. forces were approaching the Japanese home islands, did the Soviet Union break its neutrality agreement and enter the war against Japan.

The British could not help. They, like the Soviets, were engaged in a life-and-death struggle in Europe. The cost of the German war had mortally weakened the British position in the Far East and bankrupted its naval plans. Its reluctant effort to play a part ended in disaster when three days after Pearl Harbor the *Prince of Wales* and *Repulse*, sent on American insistence to reinforce the British position in the Far East and sailing without air cover, were sunk by Japanese naval air. This was "the first case in the history of naval warfare when capital ships under way were sunk by an attack carried out exclusively by aircraft."[73] Hong Kong and Malaya fell to Japan. Britain's fortress-base at Singapore fell in February 1942, and Japan gained control of the waters around Ceylon by April. As a result, the Japanese could move freely in the Indian Ocean. Luckily for the Allies, the Japanese navy did not pursue the strategic opportunity this gave them.

It might have done so with crucial effect. The eastern Mediterranean was closed to the British. A Japanese advance through the Indian Ocean could have cut off the British supplies that were moving north through the Red Sea for the desert war against the German general Erwin Rommel. A Japanese advance also could have cut the Lend-Lease line that passed through the Persian Gulf and was supporting the front in the southern Soviet Union. With a relatively small effort at sea control, Japan might have opened the way to a German victory in both those theaters. The consequences would have been enormous. The Soviets would have reduced their pressure on the Manchurian border, where most of Japan's soldiers were stationed. The United States would have had to turn its attention fully to Europe, withdrawing its opposition to Japan's expansion in the southwest Pacific. Japan could have consolidated its barrier defense and its new maritime empire. Not to take full control of the Indian Ocean at this time was "one of the greatest strategic blunders of the war."[74] The Japanese failed to do this because they had a limited concept of the war and did not understand the indirect effects of sea power.

In the United States, Pearl Harbor raised the question, How safe is the west coast? Would the Japanese sail east of Hawaii? West coast cities were blacked out, shores patrolled, and harbors made alert against attack. In the most unwarranted action taken in the name of national defense, the Army, claiming military necessity, moved American citizens of Japanese ancestry to inland internment camps. Nothing is more indicative of the fear of the time than the expectation that Japanese-Americans would collaborate in an invasion. In Hawaii, where prewar fear of sabotage had distorted the islands' defense strategy, not a single disruptive incident occurred. East coast residents had their own fear of shelling and saboteurs as U-boats sailed brazenly off the seaboard and burning cargo ships were seen from shore. On the nation's ocean edges, the war came close to home.

The Navy's first job was to protect the coasts. That meant holding the central Pacific defensive position, the Alaska-Hawaii-Panama arc. Second, as part of an extended defense, the Navy had to maintain the supply line to Australia, America's main ally south of Japan, and get as many airplanes and troops there as possible.

The Navy's position might have been worse. The raid on Pearl Harbor, conceptually brilliant, flawlessly executed, and tactically successful, was a strategic disaster for Japan. It inspired a war of revenge and made it easy for the U.S. Navy to get approval for an early offensive. Furthermore, Vice Admiral Nagumo Chuichi's planes had not destroyed the Pacific Fleet. His pilots, following mission orders, concentrated on airfields and the battle line. Nagumo had rejected their advice to launch follow-up attacks against shore installations and other ships. The result was that cruisers and submarines remained intact, as did the carriers out at sea. So did America's mid-Pacific naval base. Its machine shops were ready for ship repair, and 4.5 million gallons of fuel oil and aviation gasoline in highly exposed fuel farms were left untouched by the Japanese invaders. The raid did not knock out the Navy or Hawaii.[75]

The Japanese advanced in the South Pacific, working southward from their huge staging base at Rabaul to cut Australia off from the United States. This was the advance King was determined to blunt. Prewar American plans had not envisioned major operations in the South Pacific and certainly did not envision action there without help. ABC-1 foresaw joint action with the British and Dutch to hold the Malay Barrier and, following the tradition of War Plan Orange, a U.S. advance across the central Pacific from Hawaii to the Philippines, through the Carolines and Marshalls.

Those plans no longer applied. Malaysia was lost, and so were the East Indies. The Philippines too had to be written off. General Douglas MacArthur's highly touted B-17s, which were supposed to deter Japanese expansion or be used in a campaign of preemption or reprisal, lay in ruins, destroyed along with the fighter force on the first day of the war, while still on the ground at Clark Field. Their destruction was a disaster like Pearl Harbor, and though MacArthur did not have to endure the amount of blame heaped upon Admiral Kimmel and General Short, he was subject to the same accusation of dereliction of duty. The B-17s had not stopped the invasion of the Philippines. Nor had the 29 fleet submarines on coast-defense duty. War correspondent Hanson Baldwin wrote, "We had the greatest concentration of submarines in the world there, but we didn't do a thing!"[76] MacArthur withdrew to the Bataan Peninsula. Although that sealed the fate of Manila, it was in accord with the mission assigned the Army in War Plan Orange—namely, to hold the entrance to Manila Bay. The defense of Bataan forced the Japanese into an unexpected four-month campaign.[77] But relief of Bataan and Corregidor was no longer in American war plans.

Such a defense was impossible. The Navy did not have the strength to break through to the Philippines, and it did not try. War Department planners told Marshall that to rescue the Army garrison and retake the Philippines required an expedition of at least 1,500 aircraft, 7 to 9 battleships, 5 to 7 carriers, 50 destroyers, 60 submarines, and auxiliaries. Such an expedition, from the Army—and one must say from the national—perspective, was "an entirely unjustifiable diversion of forces from the principal theater—the Atlantic."[78] In early March 1942 MacArthur left the Philippines to take command of the defense of Australia. Twelve thousand U.S. soldiers remained in the Philippines under Major General Jonathan Wainwright. Those on Bataan surrendered to the Japanese in April. In early May 1942, Wainwright gave up Corregidor, a tremendous defeat for the United States.

Where the Navy turned and where the Japanese were headed was to the south and southwest Pacific. Roosevelt talked of defending the vital flanks of the Japanese advance. One of these flanks was the line of islands to Australia. The other, a British responsibility, consisted of a movement by land toward Burma and India. If Australia was isolated or lost, the United States would face a much more costly and protracted war. To prevent Japan from sealing a defensive cordon in the South Pacific, the United States had to deny it the island strongpoints. Island bases under American control, on the other hand, would block the Japanese advance and permit limited U.S. offensives. From the beginning, King and his staff planners Rear Admirals Charles Cooke, Richmond Kelly Turner, and Forrest Sherman (who later joined Nimitz's staff) planned in terms of offensive sea control. The campaign would begin in the Solomons, its aim being first to stop the Japanese and then to turn them back so they could not consolidate a force on New Guinea for the invasion of Australia.

In March 1942 King summarized for President Roosevelt an American plan for the first stage of the Pacific war: "Hold Hawaii. Support Australasia. Drive northwestward from New Hebrides."[79] An early offensive from the south would relieve pressure on all other Pacific areas, including Hawaii and Alaska and "even India," King told Roosevelt. This was genuine strategic thinking. In March 1942 King "anticipated the entire course of the war in the South Pacific to the middle of 1944."[80] A limited U.S. offensive, and King's immediate strategy of hit-and-run carrier raids to keep the Japanese off balance, showed that after the shocks of Pearl Harbor and the Philippines, the country would take risks to regain its position in the Pacific.[81]

These plans for the South Pacific came when the country was still stunned by the disasters in the Pacific, when the U-boat threat was at its height, when there was talk in Washington of abandoning Australia and New Zealand, and when King's commander in the Pacific, Admiral Chester Nimitz, wanted to keep his force in the central Pacific for the protection of Hawaii, Alaska, and Samoa instead of sending it to the South Pacific. At such a time it took strong strategic vision to see how to capture the initiative and determine the first moves in an area of remote islands far from the central Pacific route that had been long considered the most direct line of counterattack against Japan.

It was not clear when this offensive could begin. One problem was in organizing the force. In the Pacific in March 1942 the Navy had three carriers—the *Enterprise* and the *Lexington,* fortuitously safely out to sea during the Pearl Harbor raid, and the *Yorktown,* recently arrived from the Atlantic. The *Saratoga* had been torpedoed in January and was out of operation for five months. The *Hornet* arrived in April. That was all that was available for taking on the main arm of the Japanese naval offensive, its victorious carrier air force. To King the best approach would be to make hit-and-run raids with the carriers. To Nimitz's staff in Honolulu it was not obvious that the carriers should be risked to save New Guinea. Their position as the capital ships around which operations had to be organized was, after all, the result not of combat performance or naval doctrine but of the need to fill the gap left by the chance disablement of the battleships.

Still that was the situation, and Admirals King, Nimitz, and William Halsey put their trust in the new configuration of the Pacific Fleet. They took the fleet's Battle Force and Scouting Force and reorganized them into several Task Forces, each with a carrier at its core. That ended the doctrine of the indivisibility of the battle fleet and the centrality of the battleship. In the battle of the Coral Sea in May 1942 and then at

Midway in June 1942, Nimitz used the mobility and long-range striking capacity of aircraft in place of the gunfire from battlewagons. "Thus the battle fleet, which had been the center of navy thinking and planning for over thirty years, quietly disappeared."[82]

Perhaps Nimitz would have preferred otherwise. Neither the Japanese nor the U.S. command fully realized that war at sea had entered a new phase. The carrier had yet to be proven. At the battle of Midway, Admiral Yamamoto Isoroku stood by in the superbattleship *Yamato*, the most powerful ship that had ever been built (it had fully loaded displacement of almost 70,000 tons, a top speed of 27 knots, and guns of 18.1-inch caliber), waiting to engage in the great Mahanian shootout. Nimitz, however, went for attrition at Midway, and his battle commander Rear Admiral Raymond A. Spruance declined main-force engagement because, as Nimitz said, "Common sense dictates that we cannot now afford to slug it out." Midway was a battle structured by U.S. weakness in surface firepower.[83]

During the battles of the Coral Sea and Midway, the U.S. battleships that had been refloated after Pearl Harbor were in San Francisco Bay because Nimitz could find no use for them in King's strategy of movement. Oilers and escort destroyers could not be spared for them, nor could air protection. As Nimitz wrote to King, "Offensive employment battleships does not fit in with hit-and-run operations, and their independent or supporting use precluded by lack of air coverage and antisubmarine protection."[84]

Nevertheless, battleships did serve in the Pacific war. The *Washington*, for example, fought an important engagement off Guadalcanal in November 1942. Battleships bombarded shore emplacements before invasions. Attached to carrier Task Forces battleships could engage Japanese battleships and cruisers and so protect the carriers, whose decks were extremely vulnerable to heavy surface gunfire.[85] But the idea of a fleet organized around a battleship, the concept that had ordered U.S. naval doctrine since Mahan, became obsolete without ever having been used in battle.

At first, in early 1942, King used the carriers as raiders to keep the Japanese from solidifying their defensive perimeter. Overriding Nimitz's warnings that his force was "markedly inferior in all types to enemy" and that hit-and-run raids would not relieve the pressure on the southwest Pacific, King insisted on action at once. In this decision, King was entirely correct. The cost of not acting, in lengthening the war, expanding the theater, and making it harder to assault a more self-sufficient enemy, was enormous, perhaps even prohibitive. King ordered Nimitz to attack Japanese ships and bases "continuously" with his carrier air.[86] In March 1942 King ordered Nimitz to station one carrier permanently in the South Pacific.

King also wanted the insurance of land-based air, which for both the United States and Japan was the basic cover of naval action. The Pacific war has been described as a set of campaigns for the control of airfields. King was laying the framework for an oceanwide naval strategy. He garrisoned Efate as a base for Army bombers. He established a naval base south of Samoa. His problem was that the Army had earmarked its troops and planes for Europe and did not want them drained away by what General Marshall called King's "suction pump." Brigadier General Dwight Eisenhower, chief of the War Plans Division, wrote in February 1942, "We are being drawn into a deployment in the Southwest Pacific that far exceeds original planning objectives and which in the absence of powerful air and naval forces . . . is not warranted."[87]

Eisenhower was expressing the irritation caused in the War Department by the fact that King was going beyond the defense of the hemisphere and the route to Australia. A Pacific offensive would slow Bolero, the concentration of force in Britain for an invasion across the channel. In January 1942 Eisenhower had written:

> The struggle to secure the adoption by all concerned of common strategical objectives is wearing me down. Everybody is too much engaged with small things of his own. We've got to go to Europe and fight—and we've got to quit wasting resources all over the world—and still worse—wasting time. If we're to keep Russia in, save the Middle East, India and Burma; we've got to begin slugging with air at West Europe; to be followed by a land attack as soon as possible.

The next month he added:

> The Navy wants to take all the islands in the Pacific—have them held by Army troops, to become bases for Army pursuit and bombers. Then! the Navy will have a safe place to sail its vessels. But they will not go farther forward than our air (Army) can assure superiority. The amount of air required for this slow, laborious and indecisive type of warfare is going to be something that will keep us from going to Russia's aid in time!![88]

These differences in focus and phase exacerbated the growing competition for resources. Eisenhower mentioned aircraft and troops. The Joint Chiefs in March 1942 approved King's request for Army garrisons at Efate and Tongatabo, but beyond that it held force levels for the South Pacific to "current commitments." Priority went to the buildup in Britain, which was "intended for offense at the earliest practical time." The only Army air that King got for Tongatabo was for defense—a pursuit squadron of 25 planes. Naval air would have to defend Efate.[89]

Competition was equally intense over shipping space and oceangoing landing craft. The lack of shipping was the major constraint on all strategic thinking throughout 1942, and in fact throughout the war. It was easier to send troops than to follow up with supplies and reinforcements, especially when new theaters were being established, as in North Africa, or where tremendous danger threatened, as in the south and southwest Pacific in the path of the main Japanese offensive. Cargo ships were scarcer than troop transports. Men could be sent to the South Pacific, Eisenhower wrote in January, "But I don't know when we can get all their equip. and supply to them. Ships! Ships! All we need is ships!"[90]

This was the refrain heard constantly, year after year. Whether troops and supplies went east or west, they went by water. Resources had to be carefully allocated. What, for instance, was the value of matériel and the cost of shipping on the north Soviet convoy in 1942? Policy called for helping Soviets kill Germans who might otherwise kill Americans. But by how much could the convoy be reduced? And for what alternative? In building programs, to take another example, should the development of cargo ships be given priority over the development of oceangoing landing craft, which were essential to offensive action? Crash construction was ordered for both cargo ships and landing craft, but choices still had to be made regarding scarce supplies. The Navy at first favored warships and cargo vessels. As a result, landing craft suffered, and therefore so did offensive plans in every theater.

Lack of means did not in early 1942 keep Marshall and Eisenhower from insisting on an early cross-channel invasion. Nor did it stop Admiral King from pressing a strategy of "hold and build" and of moving to the offensive "as rapidly as the accumulation of the necessary means rolls out."[91] "Important as the mounting of Bolero may be," King wrote in May 1942, "the Pacific problem is not less so, and is certainly the more urgent—it must be faced *now*." Forces necessary "to hold what we have" in the Pacific must not be diverted "to any proposed operation in any other theater."[92]

There had to be some resolution of these contending views. There was as yet no unified war plan, none that saw the Atlantic and Pacific strategies together. This problem was exacerbated because in the Pacific there were two commands and two strategies. In March 1942 Army General MacArthur, who was subordinate to Chief of Staff Marshall but treated almost like an Allied sovereign power, was made commander in chief of the southwest Pacific area, centered in Australia. Navy Admiral Nimitz, closely monitored by King, commanded the rest of the Pacific. MacArthur thus found a role that suited him and which the overall Pacific strategy could support, and the Navy was able to go about its advance across the central Pacific. The dual command worked without serious interference of one theater with the other because, ultimately, it turned out that there were resources and room enough for both in the war against Japan.

More widely, in the beginning, tension between Atlantic and Pacific requirements also remained strong. In May 1942 the Army and the Navy asked President Roosevelt for a decision on "Pacific Theatre *versus* Bolero." Roosevelt replied that Bolero must continue. The president was determined to put forces in action on the other side of the Atlantic in 1942. He did not know where or how, but action was needed to reduce the pressure on the Soviets and to bolster the war effort at home. King had not yet asked for an offensive capability in the Pacific. He had talked defense—Roosevelt's decision on Bolero came on the eve of the battle of the Coral Sea—but he had also returned continually to the position that Japanese action and American weakness demanded immediate and aggressive use of all theater assets, including Army air.[93]

Meanwhile, in the months after Pearl Harbor, the Japanese fleet stayed beyond reach, in the Indian Ocean and in the waters of the East Indies. It never went farther to cut British lines to the Middle East or to attack India. Nor did it move to the southwest Pacific to support the southern barrier against the Americans. Then, in April 1942, the Japanese navy turned to the central Pacific.

During this period, all the U.S. Navy could do was launch its hit-and-run carrier raids to upset Japan's invasion schedule in the south and southwest Pacific. These raids have been dismissed as of minor importance. Nimitz disliked them as distractions from preparing for the central Pacific advance. In reality, however, these early carrier raids greatly disturbed the Japanese naval command. Japan could not counter the U.S. strikes. The raids "forced the Japanese navy to recast their entire Pacific strategy"—to delay the advance toward New Guinea, to occupy certain islands to improve the palisade defense, and to search for a way to protect their flank. From this situation came the plan to lure the U.S. carriers into a trap where they could be destroyed.[94] That was the origin of Japan's Midway operation, an attack on American territory that the Pacific Fleet would have to contest, either to defend the territory or to recover it. Midway, however, was a decoy. The real prize was the Pacific Fleet, which Japan's Combined Fleet would ambush.

The sixth and most dramatic of the hit-and-run raids came in April 1942 and catalyzed Admiral Yamamoto's plans. A carrier task force, led by Admiral William Halsey in the *Enterprise*, joined the newly arrived *Hornet* and moved up to a position some 650 miles off Japan. There the *Hornet* launched sixteen long-range Army bombers commanded by Army Air Forces Lieutenant Colonel James Doolittle. The planes struck Tokyo—the imperial capital and the heart of the enemy empire. The attack, coming just after the fall of Bataan and as the Philippines fell, raised morale in the United States. Thirty seconds over Tokyo were revenge for Pearl Harbor.[95]

The air attack did little material damage, but it did a lot of harm to Japanese confidence. It destroyed the aura of invincibility. The army and the navy had not safeguarded the emperor and the Japanese people from direct attack. It showed that the United States had not accepted a limited war. It showed that the palisade was not enough. The enemy had pierced the empire's innermost defenses. Something new was needed. The raid on Tokyo ended opposition to Yamamoto's Midway plan.

During the Tokyo raid, King and Nimitz held their breath. Half their carrier force was off on a nonessential mission while they faced two major battles. Naval intelligence had predicted a Japanese advance by sea toward the eastern end of New Guinea to seize the Australian air base at Port Moresby on the Coral Sea (thereby reducing the threat to the strongpoints of Rabaul and Truk) and to establish another air base for Japan's southern defense perimeter. This operation was to be followed by a much bigger one in the central Pacific, involving most of the Combined Fleet. The target of the larger operation was not clear, although it was probably Midway, the westernmost fortified outpost of the United States.

Admiral Yamamoto's Midway strategy was as bold as his earlier plan for Pearl Harbor, and it was even more essential to Japan's victory. In a sense it was finishing the job. With the Pacific Fleet destroyed, Midway occupied, and perhaps Hawaii itself invaded and conquered, Japan would have no rival in the central Pacific. If Yamamoto took a strongpoint in the western Aleutians, Japan would control the North Pacific as well. Japan would then close its defense line, which would stretch from Attu through Midway, Wake, and the Marshalls and Gilberts. This would be followed by an invasion of New Caledonia, the Fijis, and Samoa and the isolation of Australia. Japan would be master of the western ocean. Defeat and the impregnable barrier would cause the Americans to negotiate peace. Yamamoto knew this was the last chance for Japan to limit the war. The U.S. Navy was still sailing prewar ships, fighting with prewar equipment. The fruits of the great Naval Act of 1940 were not yet on the sea, but they were coming. Japan had to win before U.S. war production made up, and surpassed, its losses and made possible a counteroffensive backed by unlimited means. The Japanese barrier strategy stressed control of space. Yamamoto now stressed control of time. He had to win quickly, or not at all.[96] He had to seek the foe, not wait until the foe came to him.

The Midway operation involved a great risk. Japan for the first time undertook offensive operations outside its defensive perimeter, beyond the range of its land-based air. Yamamoto was moving the Combined Fleet forward to engage on Japanese initiative. Previous (and subsequent) strategy kept the Combined Fleet in a protected defense zone, within which the decisive engagement would be fought against a worn-down and overextended American force. For that, the Japanese could no longer wait. The American fleet was as weak as it would ever get. Midway had to be the decisive battle.

Japan's defensive operations at this time in the southwest Pacific had nothing to do with its offensive operation in the central Pacific. Given Midway's importance and its strategic uniqueness, the only explanation why the Japanese navy went ahead with a campaign in support of an army attack on Port Moresby is bad coordination at the top levels of Japanese command. Given Japan's limited naval force, the two operations were contradictory. Mobile forces were tied up in the Coral Sea in support of a defensive structure of island garrisons when they were needed for the decisive battle off Midway.[97]

It is true that the Japanese did not expect to meet a major American force in the Coral Sea. That they did so was owing to U.S. naval radio intelligence. The code breakers and direction finders permitted Nimitz to choose the time and terms of the battle. Also important was the determination of Nimitz and King to take on the Japanese. King's offensive spirit and attention to the South Pacific in the hit-and-run raids had overcome Nimitz's reluctance to commit large forces a long way from Hawaii. Nimitz had become accustomed to moving his carriers in and out of the South Pacific.[98] Now the chance for a fleet engagement arrived, and King and Nimitz decided to go beyond raids, to confront the Japanese fleet—not in the central Pacific but in the Coral Sea.

Nimitz sent his two available carriers, the *Lexington* and the *Yorktown*, and readied whatever land-based air he could get from the Army's island airfields or from Australia. A victory over the Japanese carrier strike force, which had wandered free for many months, would fulfill King's directive to hold the South Pacific. On the other hand, Nimitz could not risk losses in defending New Guinea that would render the fleet helpless before the forthcoming central Pacific offensive.[99] Engaging in the Coral Sea was thus a departure from strategy and a strategic gamble.

What Nimitz and his subordinate commander Rear Admiral Frank Jack Fletcher had going for them was intelligence of the Japanese movements. Fletcher was waiting for the Japanese when they arrived. In the battle of the Coral Sea of early May 1942, his force of two carriers, three cruisers (two of them Australian), and a few destroyers turned the Japanese back. Coral Sea was a battle fought entirely by carrier aircraft. The Army B-17s from Australia were ineffective against the invading fleet. No surface ship on either side saw an opposition warship. It was, as King famously described it "the first major engagement in naval history in which surface ships did not exchange a single shot." It was also a victory for radio intelligence, confirming its value in time for its use at Midway. At the battle of the Coral Sea, King drew his own barrier in the South Pacific, barring Japanese naval forces from moving south of the Solomons and holding a vital flank of the Japanese advance.[100]

Among U.S. ships in the battle, the *Lexington* and a destroyer and an oiler were sunk, and the *Yorktown* was damaged. These were serious losses, leaving Nimitz with only two carriers in the Pacific—Halsey's *Enterprise* and *Hornet*, which were rushing southward after their Tokyo raid. The Americans, with the strategic initiative, could absorb the loss, heavy as it was, because they could always decline a future battle. The Japanese could not absorb theirs with Yamamoto's Midway operation imminent. They found themselves down by a carrier division needed for the next operation of the war.[101] The Japanese losses were therefore severe. Damage to two carriers and the loss of 80 aircraft reduced by a third Japan's carrier striking force for Midway. In the immediate aftermath of the battle of the Coral Sea, however, the Japanese knew only that they had been stopped and forced to postpone the attack on Moresby. By faulty intelligence Yamamoto was led to believe that both the U.S. carriers in the battle had been sunk. He was therefore all the more confident that he commanded a superior force and that he was operating according to a superior tactical doctrine. What he did not know was that Nimitz had the Japanese plans and positions.[102] As in the Coral Sea, that knowledge at Midway gave the Americans the incalculable advantage of surprise.

Midway was to be a Mahanian scenario, Japan's naval strategy foreshortened into one engagement. An invasion of Midway Island would force the Pacific Fleet into counterattack, whence it would be weakened by submarines and air strikes and then destroyed by the seven battleships of Yamamoto's Main Body battle line. Gunfire still mattered. Yamamoto's was indisputably superior, and he counted on night battle, in which the Japanese were skilled and the Americans were not. Despite subsequent criticism of Yamamoto's division of his force, part of which he sent to the Aleutians, part to invade Midway—and his further division of the Midway force into the strike force sent against the Pacific Fleet, and the covering, determining Main Body that he was holding back for the final engagement—his plan followed a classic line, which makes it all the more plausible that the Japanese command thought it held the advantages of both superior strength and complete surprise. American signals deception had convinced Yamamoto that Halsey's two carriers, the *Enterprise* and the *Hornet*, were still in the south, and his intelligence reported that the *Yorktown* had been sunk. He believed he would face no naval air and could put the Hawaii fleet under his guns. Midway was as good as Japanese, and the Pacific too.

The Japanese Combined Fleet comprised 162 warships and their auxiliaries, including 8 battleships, 8 heavy cruisers, 4 heavy carriers, 3 light carriers, 16 fleet submarines, and numerous destroyers and troop carriers. Nimitz had a total of 76 warships, all of prewar vintage, about a third of which were deployed with the North Pacific Force to protect the Aleutians. He had no battleships, and he could not "slug it out." Rather, Nimitz had to avoid meeting the enemy directly and win through attrition. His intelligence network gave him the benefit of surprise. He disposed off Midway his three carriers, which were concentrated and coordinated under Rear Admirals Fletcher and Raymond Spruance, the latter replacing the bedridden Halsey. The damage sustained by the *Yorktown* in the Coral Sea had been repaired in two days of heroic work at Pearl Harbor Navy Yard. Yamamoto was the one who sailed into a trap.

Yamamoto never saw the battle. His surface fleet never fired a shot at an enemy vessel. As at Coral Sea, it was a duel of carrier air. When he heard that all four of his carriers were lost to dive-bombers, Yamamoto knew his battle plan was in ruins. He did his best to close in on the Americans and bring his superior gunpower to bear, but Task Force 16 under Spruance declined battle and evaded him. Yamamoto ordered a general retirement.

In the battle of Midway, the Japanese lost 4 carriers, 1 heavy cruiser, 253 planes, their best pilots, and their offensive spirit. The loss of the pilots was serious. It shattered the Japanese naval air force, which had been the terror of the Pacific. The best pilots had not trained their successors. They had stayed in the cockpit instead of rotating as instructors through training schools, as was the American practice. Once lost, they could not be replaced.[103] The kamikaze strikes that came later resulted from this lack of skilled pilots. It does not take much flying skill to guide an airplane on a one-way suicide mission.

Yamamoto failed to win the ocean. The attacks on Midway and the Aleutians (in which Japan did take Kiska and Attu) were the last operations the Japanese initiated. While the surface fleet (except for the carriers) remained intact, its command gave up the offense. Yamamoto retreated behind the barriers to control space, not time. That was not a victory strategy. Still, most Japanese commanders remained highly confident of their fighting skills, their equipment, the advantage of interior lines, and the righteousness of their cause. They had plenty of success before Midway. More, they were sure, would come. But they dropped plans for the invasion of New Caledonia, the Fijis, Samoa, and Port Moresby and for attacks in the Bay of Bengal and against India. For American strategists, Midway unexpectedly solved their South Pacific problem. Japan no longer had the strength to force its way southward. The United States would never have to fight another defensive campaign.[104] With the battle of Midway in the first week of June 1942, the balance of sea power in the Pacific shifted in favor of the United States.

10

Strategic Offensives 1943-1944

ATLANTIC LIFT

The purpose of the Atlantic campaign was the safe transport of men and supplies for the assault of the European continent. The projection of power ashore was part of a maritime strategy. Troops could be collected on American soil easily enough. The mission was to lift them, their equipment, and their supplies safely overseas and then onto the enemy-held continent. This would not be like the ferry to France of the previous war. There were no friendly ports of debarkation on the continent. Access to the land had to be fought for. Huge numbers of supply ships and landing craft were required for the greatest amphibious operation in history. Through 1943 these vessels were in short supply.

Admiral King supported the policy of Germany First.[1] He insisted, however, on the importance of simultaneous action in the Pacific. Only once, in July 1942, did King—and Marshall—grow so exasperated at what they took to be British stalling over a cross-channel operation that they proposed a Pacific alternative, in which priority was to be given to an offensive in the Solomons. Until the end of 1942 there were, after all, more Army troops in the Pacific theater than in Europe. Roosevelt refused to countenance such a change of focus. Germany was the prime enemy, the more dangerous foe. The United States was committed to an alliance, denial of which would have disastrous postwar consequences. Defeat of Japan would not contribute to the defeat of Germany. Serious as Marshall and King were about a Pacific First alternative, they accepted Roosevelt's political wisdom.[2]

Roosevelt wanted to put American troops into action in Europe as soon as possible, even before the great cross-channel buildup was complete. Against the advice of Marshall and King, he accepted a British plan, called Torch, to invade French North Africa. U.S. military leaders opposed Roosevelt's move as political opportunism, a costly deviation from plan, and bad strategy. North Africa would divert resources from a concentration in western Europe. Its military purpose seemed only to be support of British imperial interests and the relief of a beleaguered British force. *Scatterization, theateritis, periphery-pecking complex,* and *localitis* were terms used by Army planners.

They had a point. Yet Marshall's hope for main-force European action was unrealizable before 1944. The Bolero buildup was a long way from completion. Torch was the only way the United States could mount an offensive on the other side of the Atlantic in its first year of war.

The president was right. Torch was good for morale. It accelerated mobilization. It broke the deadlock over strategy within the alliance. It was a decision suitable to the president's position as a war leader. Torch drew assets from Bolero and the battle of the Atlantic, but it solidified the coalition and heartened the public. Marshall said later that the great lesson he learned in the war was that in wartime the politicians have to do *something* important every year and that in Europe the year 1942 could not simply be one of hold and build.[3]

The United States took its main action on the Atlantic seaboard of Africa, not within the Mediterranean. The British wanted Americans to land in Algeria or Tunisia, to support the desert war against Major General Erwin Rommel's Africa Corps. The United States, though willing to lend troops to the Mediterranean, insisted on keeping its naval force outside the Strait of Gibraltar. The government did not want to risk being involved in a British loss in North Africa, appearing to fight for British interests in the Near East, or being trapped in the Mediterranean if the Germans seized Gibraltar. In November 1942 the United States landed on the Atlantic coast of Morocco while the British landed, with some American troops, in Algeria. The Vichy governments of Morocco and Algeria surrendered to superior force.

The American invasion of Morocco was completely amphibious. Rear Admiral Kent Hewitt's Task Force 34, with its Western Naval Task Force of 102 ships carried 35,000 American troops across the Atlantic in a single movement. Soldiers embarked in Virginia and went ashore in Africa.[4] Torch was launched while the submarine war in the Atlantic was at its height. November 1942 was the worst month of losses to the U-boat in the war, the only month when more than 600,000 gross tons of cargo-carrying capacity of shipping worldwide were sunk. It was not until six months later, in May 1943, that Dönitz conceded that he had lost the battle of the Atlantic. It was not until July 1943 that King thought he had enough of the new destroyer escorts to protect convoys, construction of destroyer escorts having been postponed since mid-1942 so landing craft could be built for Torch. It was thanks to good luck as well as good intelligence and planning that the ships of the Western Naval Task Force were not sighted by a U-boat on their transit to Africa and that another 340 ships of the British support and assault convoys made it safely into the Mediterranean from the British Isles for the attack on Algiers.[5]

Preparing for Torch absorbed the major part of naval planning and construction during 1942. No one had foreseen the need for such an array of amphibious equipment so soon, a need that was met by a crash production program. Procurement of amphibious equipment (except wheeled vehicles) was the Navy's responsibility. In the twelve months from May 1942 through April 1943, the Navy built, from a standing start, 8,719 landing craft.

This production came at the cost of other programs. Landing craft took precedence over Liberty ships, destroyer escorts, and light carriers.[6] Torch took place just as the Navy was straining to build up offensive power in the Pacific and while it was trying to protect shipping in the Atlantic. There was not enough steel, machinery, yard space, or skilled labor to meet all the nation's wartime needs at once. Changes in procurement were driven by changes in strategy. Switching from the Bolero buildup and from escort and antisubmarine missions to the assault of Africa—at the same time the nation was turning the tide in the Pacific—forced logisticians to produce new classes and types of equipment, make heroic improvisations in construction schedules, and continually reallocate resources. The result was a severely overstressed procurement system.[7]

The swift changes of the first two years of U.S. participation in the war did not permit much logistical predictability. Escort ships, mass-produced for wartime service, were needed for the battle of the Atlantic. Lack of them had imperiled Atlantic transit for a year. "All plans for offensive operations are hampered and limited because of the critical shortage of escort vessels," said Roosevelt in November 1942.[8] But just when the construction of destroyer escorts got under way, the North African invasion called for landing craft to be given highest priority. Work on the destroyer escorts was postponed. Each ship design required different materials, production schedules, and demands on shipyards' time. After Pearl Harbor, for instance, large carriers became the fleet leaders, so the program for building five superbattleships was postponed. Cruisers also took on more importance, and those lost in Pacific battles had to be replaced.

The high rate of landing craft construction achieved late in 1942, an official noted, was obtained "only by cutting across every single combatant shipbuilding program and giving the amphibious program overriding priority in every navy yard and every major shipbuilding company. The derangement . . . will not be corrected for about six months [from April 1943]."[9] Yet once the decision for Torch was made and a Pacific offensive was foreseen, no one could deny the need for landing craft. Much of war is catch-up, and everyone's wish for a solid strategy to which logistical planning could easily adhere was simply unrealizable while fast-moving global operations and the demands of coalition cohesion called for rapid adjustments. It is a credit to Navy Secretary Forrestal, the procurement officials, and the work force in the yards that so much was done so well in so little time. Every building program was an emergency.

Torch was an improvisation, and it is easy to sympathize with the frustration of military planners. It took a year and a half for the Allies to hammer out agreement on some of the major strategic lines of the war. Roosevelt, ever conscious of the swift movement of events, was reluctant to tie himself to specifics until the last possible moment. Everything was moving very fast. In November 1942, the battle of the Atlantic was fully engaged. The Western Naval Task Force launched the greatest invasion in American history, the first ever across an ocean, opening the Allied land offensive against the European Axis. At the same time in the southern Solomon Islands, in the South Pacific, where no American had expected to fight, 35,000 marines were holding on in Guadalcanal, having gone ashore in August undersupported and undersupplied in a limited counteroffensive. There marines constituted an invasion force the Navy had to protect against the advancing Combined Fleet of the Imperial Japanese Navy.

The fighting at Guadalcanal was desperate and prolonged. The Japanese had to seal the breach in their southern line of defense. They had to neutralize all-important Henderson Field, which in American hands denied them air superiority over the southern Solomons. A Japanese invasion force was put ashore, and unable to reach Guadalcanal by air from Rabaul, the Japanese sent a naval armada to put the field under battleships' guns. The U.S. Navy met these forces less than a week after Vice Admiral Hewitt's forces went ashore in Morocco, on the other side of the world. In the Solomons, planes from the *Enterprise* and land-based aircraft from beleaguered Henderson Field destroyed two-thirds of the Japanese invasion force of some 15,000 men and all their supplies. The U.S. force met the naval armada in one of the rare battleship contests of the war, a battle that occurred the same week the *Massachusetts* was shooting at the immobilized *Jean Bart* at Casablanca. Salvos from the battleships *Washington* and *South Dakota* sank the battleship *Kirishima*. Mainly, however, the fierce surface battles around Guadalcanal were fought with the 8-inch guns of the Navy's treaty cruisers and destroyers and with air power. Both sides suffered heavy losses; two dozen warships went down on each side. That was too many for Yamamoto. His naval air arm was crippled by the loss of half its aviators, and he ordered the Combined Fleet to retire. In addition, the sinking of many cargo and transport ships ended Japan's transport of reinforcements to Guadalcanal. In February 1942 the Japanese evacuated the island.

The tremendous endurance of the undersupplied marines at Guadalcanal prevailed in a horrendous six-month war of attrition, and the Navy's blockage of the Combined Fleet stopped the Japanese offensive to the south, keeping the line to Australia open. Victory at Guadalcanal turned the Pacific war around. Admiral William Halsey wrote: "We seized the offensive from the enemy. Until then he had been advancing at his will. From then on he retreated at ours."[10] That, in a nutshell, describes the Pacific war after 1942.

The grand strategy of the European war was decided at the summit meetings between Roosevelt and Churchill, who were backed by U.S. and British military leaders sitting as the Combined Chiefs of Staff. At Casablanca in January 1943, Roosevelt pronounced the draconian formula of unconditional surrender, which deferred questions of political settlement and thus made military decisions the first order of alliance business.

The central military problem was the allocation of resources between the war against Germany and the war against Japan. It was a problem debated, however, only in general terms. Vagueness bedeviled the logisticians, who had difficulty tailoring preparations to operations. The problem of allocation frustrated military leaders insofar as one theater was starved and its opportunities forgone because of the drainage of resources to the other. At the same time, the United States, as the main supplier, was able to keep allocation decisions in its own hands. This moved the balance of influence to the United States. From 1943 onward, U.S. productivity counterbalanced initial British domination of European strategy. The extent of U.S. mobilization turned the United States into the coalition's senior partner. Control of ships and men gave Roosevelt control of Allied strategy.

At the Casablanca conference the British argued for further action in the Mediterranean, invasions first of Tunis and then of Sicily. Roosevelt and King acceded because relocating the front to the channel was impossible in 1943, and the Bolero buildup could continue meanwhile. What the American high command did not want was to get bogged down in the Mediterranean. Torch had been different. Casablanca was on the Atlantic, with access to the high seas. The decision to clear up North Africa and recover control of the Mediterranean was made after intelligence predicted strong resistance to a channel landing in 1943 and reasonable odds for a successful Allied invasion of Sicily.[11] Beyond that, all American commanders resisted any further push toward the eastern Mediterranean. Even the Italian campaign worried military leaders as a potential dead end. They feared a dissipation of resources in a nonessential theater that would prolong the war and weaken American public support.

Roosevelt had scuttled a true Pacific First alternative in 1942, but the idea remained alive in the Navy Department through 1943. The service was ready for a Pacific war. Almost all of its combatants were stationed there. The Army too was there in force. At the end of 1942 there were 350,000 soldiers deployed in the Pacific theater. They had been sent to hold the Pacific defense and stayed to support the emergent offensive. The U.S. victory at Guadalcanal and the control of the ships on which Allied action depended gave Washington a powerful veto on just how far the Mediterranean strategy would proceed. What emerged was a "balancing of 'diversions,'" as Maurice Matloff called it, in which the Pacific became America's Mediterranean. There was "a lever by which the Americans could exert pressure on the British to bring them back to the cross-Channel assault."[12] That operation was cast in stone at Cairo and Teheran in November and December 1943, when Roosevelt and Churchill agreed that Operation Overlord, the cross-channel invasion, and an associated invasion in the south of France, called Anvil, would be "the supreme operations of 1944." Nothing was to be undertaken in any other part of the world that would jeopardize their success.

The Navy's role in the invasions of Europe, from the July 1943 invasion of Sicily to the June 1944 invasion of Normandy, was to provide safe transport of Army troops and equipment and to support amphibious assaults on hostile coasts. In 1943 and 1944, in Sicily, at Salerno, at Anzio, in Normandy, and in the south of France, American and British soldiers went ashore fighting for the beachhead under often withering air, artillery, and machine-gun attack. After the beachheads were established, Europe became the Army's war.

Safe passage and support of land operations required sea control. By mid-1943 the Allies had established control in the North Atlantic and in the Mediterranean. German and Italian surface combatants remained boxed up in their home ports. Dönitz withdrew his U-boats from the North Atlantic in May 1943 and waited for German naval engineering to give him back his advantage. Seeking better hunting, he moved to the central Atlantic convoy route, to the South Atlantic, and to the British-patrolled Indian Ocean.

In 1943 King had in place his antisubmarine staff in the administrative Tenth Fleet. They were increasingly experienced in managing convoys and commanding destroyer escorts and light escort carriers at the center of roving hunter-killer groups. In mid-1943 the Germans lost one submarine for every ship they sank. King knew though that he was in a race with time. He feared that when the 1,600-ton Type XXI U-boat became operational, Germany would launch a perhaps unstoppable U-boat offensive.[13]

Meanwhile, worldwide U-boat losses mounted: 237 were sunk in 1943 and 242 in 1944. Dönitz tried an offensive in the North Atlantic again in September 1943, but he was soundly defeated. He never received his miracle weapons and never regained the initiative. By April 1944 only 50 U-boats remained in the Atlantic. Proof of the Allied success was that the German navy could not oppose the all-important invasions of France in 1944. After mid-1943 the U.S. Navy could claim reasonable security in its use of the sea. Samuel Eliot Morison called the Allied defeat of the submarines "a task the magnitude of which was second only to defeating Japan."[14]

Protection of merchant shipping, a Navy responsibility, was far more important in the Atlantic than in the Pacific. The Japanese submarine threat was so weak that vessels ran independently from U.S. ports to a point about 750 miles southwest of Guam, where escorts picked them up for convoy. But in the North Atlantic, 1,134 principal convoys sailed under the protection of combined American-British-Canadian naval forces almost all the way across the ocean—a total of 47,997 merchant vessels with 8,233 escorts. The peak year of 1944 saw the sailing of more than 380 convoys, including 18,856 merchant ships and 3,070 escorts.

The central and southern Atlantic routes were the responsibility of the U.S. Navy. Between December 1942 and March 1945, the service escorted 24 troop convoys to the Mediterranean, transporting a total of 536,134 men. Not one troop ship was lost. Thirty fast tanker convoys, averaging seven tankers apiece, sailed from the Caribbean to the Mediterranean between February 1943 and June 1944. Not one tanker was lost. Between November 1942 and the end of the war in Europe on May 8, 1945, 11,119 cargo ships sailed in 189 United States–Gibraltar and Gibraltar–United States convoys, with the loss of only 9 of the ships escorted by the U.S. Navy.[15]

The prewar plan for transportation had envisioned the practice of the previous war: the Army would operate the ports of embarkation, and the Navy would provide the sea transportation, manning Army transports. But when war came, that plan was set aside, and the Army and the Navy ran separate transportation operations. That is not to say that each service necessarily operated its own vessels. The Army, for instance, operated only around 150 of its own ships. Most troop transports and cargo ships were controlled and operated by a wartime agency, the War Shipping Administration. Its job was to allocate ships, and that required the cooperation of the Army and Navy. Wanting a ship was not the same as getting one. Much negotiation about availability took place. Neither service was willing to surrender control to the other. As a result, no unified transportation system was ever established. But the wartime mood of cooperation meant that the procurement and employment of ships, the use of cargo space, and the control of port operations all came about with relative ease. That made possible the country's astounding projection of power overseas.

In the course of the four years of U.S. participation in the war, 7,639,491 troops were embarked at Army-controlled U.S. ports; 4,791,237 of them were transported to Atlantic areas and 2,848,254 to the Pacific. Merchant-shipping capacity available to the Allies doubled during the war, reaching a total of 88 million deadweight tons. "Sea transport, in all its varied forms, became the most important single element in logistics."[16] The record of U.S. security and mobility, of construction and transport, was an unparalleled expression of American sea power.

Getting troops and supplies ashore was the Navy's other mission. Until ports were seized and put into operation (on the eastern side of the Atlantic, that meant Casablanca, Palermo, Naples, Cherbourg, and Marseilles), landings had to be made from sea. The buildup of landing craft was under way. General Marshall said in 1943 that his military education and previous war experience had been based on roads, rivers, and railroads, but that since the beginning of this war, "I have been acquiring an education based on oceans and I've had to learn all over again. Prior to the present war I never heard of any landing-craft except a rubber boat. Now I think about little else."[17]

The Normandy invasion of June 6, 1944, took place from an armada of about 5,000 ships and craft (4,266 for the landing, and 702 gunnery and other support ships, including 6 battleships, 2 monitors with 15-inch guns, 2 cruisers, and 119 destroyers and destroyer escorts), and hundreds of other combatants, minesweepers, tugs, and auxiliaries. The landing craft first conveyed five assault divisions and then transported twelve more. Men-of-war provided neutralizing gunfire, shooting many miles inland to the complete surprise of the Germans. Field Marshal Rommel reported to Hitler that the Allied naval gunfire was such "that no operation of any kind is possible in the area commanded by this rapid-fire artillery, by either infantry or tanks."[18]

No larger fleet had ever been assembled, and it is unlikely that any greater ever will be. The main lesson learned in the earlier amphibious operations was that local air cover was essential to success. The Normandy invasion was supported by 3,500 heavy bombers, 2,300 medium and light bombers, 5,000 fighter planes, 1,400 airborne troop carriers, and 3,300 gliders. With land bases in Britain, no aircraft carriers were needed or used in the Normandy invasion. The American assault force was supported by 2,479 U.S. Navy ships and craft; about 124,000 Navy officers and men took part. Within twelve days after D-Day, 314,514 troops, 41,000 vehicles, and 116,000 tons of supplies had been landed on American-held beaches on the Normandy coast, and the British in the same period landed approximately the same numbers and amounts on beaches controlled by them. Within a month, despite a severe and disruptive storm, the combined buildup, with roughly equal contributions made by the United States and Britain, stood at 929,000 men, 586,000 tons of supplies, and 177,000 vehicles. The Allied armies stood poised for the push out from their lodgments and for the march toward Germany. On July 4, 1944, 28 days after D-Day, the millionth American soldier landed in France.

The bridge across the Atlantic had been built by the Allied navies. Pursuing a maritime strategy, they destroyed the German threat at sea so as to assault the German army on land. The landing of the invasion force in Normandy seems all the more remarkable when one realizes that it came just as the United States was launching the largest invasion force ever assembled in the Pacific for a tremendous assault on Saipan, the key to the defense of Japan. Conducting two such enormous offensives simultaneously on opposite sides of the globe, across the two greatest oceans, and against the inner defenses of two entirely separate and powerful enemies would have seemed impossible two years before. That it could be done was the result of the United States' global offensive strategy, its immense mobilization effort, and its command of the seas.

PACIFIC COMMAND

In the spring of 1942, after only five months of war, the Japanese could say that they had won what they sought to the south and that they had done so at an astonishingly low cost. None of the great imperial powers had protected its territory. On schedule, Japan had established a vast maritime empire, taking control of the seas between Pearl Harbor and Ceylon. Having achieved their limited goal, the Japanese planned a war of defense, in the hope that the United States would accept Japan's new sphere of influence.

The Americans did not act according to the plan. Japan faced not an enemy chastened to accommodation, but one thirsting for revenge and a punitive victory. At the beginning of 1943, Japan, its capital bombed, its advance stopped at the Coral Sea, its naval air force and offensive spirit beaten at Midway, its army and navy turned back at Guadalcanal, its line of defense incomplete, and its enemy on the offensive, faced the question of whether it could make the Americans give up before U.S. war production overwhelmed Japan's zone defense and put the Japanese homeland under direct assault.

The U.S. Navy had anticipated a long war and began preparing for it with the building program of 1940. The Japanese had expected a short war of annihilation and were not prepared to make up their heavy initial losses. Only a few Japanese leaders, notably Admiral Yamamoto, realized the advantage conferred by America's economic strength and the dangers faced by Japan in a war of attrition. Japanese ship construction continued to be based on the assumption that Japan would prevail by a decisive battle of annihilation. Accordingly, ships were built for combat within the defense zones. There was no systematic effort until too late to protect within these zones the sea lanes over which the vital cargo ships passed, to meet and match the American submarines, to mount a *guerre de course*, or, after Midway, to make another try for offensive sea control. Each of these omissions was an astonishing strategic lapse. H. P. Willmott wrote that Japan's and Germany's "inability to build upon their initial successes was arguably the most important single ingredient in their defeat."[19] Pinning all their hopes on the battles expected under their strategy of zone defense, Japan's leaders left exposed all other dimensions of the country's maritime position, failing in every other way to protect the empire's vital access to the sea or to make corresponding threats to American cargo, tanker, and transport shipping. The complete absence of a Japanese attrition campaign meant that the U.S. advance moved virtually unimpeded, except when faced with major battle, and that U.S. troops and supplies could sail eastward without escort up to the battle zone.

The offensive strategy of the United States exposed the weakness of Japan's perimeter defense. Static island fortresses, even with air bases, did not constitute an impenetrable palisade unless a navy held local command of the sea. That command Japan never attained. Its navy simply lacked the force and range to cover a line that stretched from Burma through Malaya, Sumatra, Java, Timor, and the Bismarcks, and then up through the Marshalls to the Kurils. At its furthest extent, this enormous ocean perimeter measured 14,200 miles, a stunning example of imperial overstretch.[20] Nor could the Japanese bring the Americans to decisive battle.

The United States, with its dual advance and very flexible naval strategy, kept the initiative. It dispersed its fleet into task forces that threw the enemy off balance. The Americans could assault, or simply bypass and isolate, the Japanese barrier's strongpoints, attacking as they chose and wearing the empire down. From the beginning, American strategy was to destroy Japanese war production, first by submarine, then by raid, and finally, closing in, by blockade and bombardment.

The Americans used time and space as the Japanese could not. H. P. Willmott has described the position of the American command:

> Victory was not going to be won by the side that spread its resources in an effort to be protected and secure at every point, but by the side that was able to concentrate massed fire power to destroy the enemy's similar capability. The war was about the projection of mobile fire power into waters that in orthodox terms would otherwise have been controlled by enemy surface forces. Islands in the Pacific were as relevant as a Jutland-type battle line would have been. Mobile resources were superior to static assets.[21]

Submarines were the first U.S. vessels to enter the Japanese defense zones. In December 1941, after Pearl Harbor, Admiral Nimitz took command of the Pacific Fleet on the deck of the submarine *Grayling*. Throughout the war the flagship of the Pacific Fleet was a submarine. Offensive operations were directed at every enemy ship. In support of naval operations, the U.S. submarines sank 201 warships, a third of all those sunk by the American forces during the war. The warships sunk by the submarines included 1 battleship; 4 fleet carriers, including the 68,000-ton *Shinano*, the largest carrier of its time; 4 escort carriers; 12 cruisers; 42 destroyers; and 23 submarines. In their campaign of attrition against the Japanese economy, U.S. submarines sank 1,113 ships of the Japanese merchant marine, over half of all such ships sunk by American forces. The Japanese war economy could never make up the loss of that merchant tonnage or of the cargoes that were sent to the ocean floor.[22]

U.S. submariners might have done more, and done it earlier, had they not gotten off to such a shaky start. Submarines were ordered to go out on attack patrol at the outbreak of war, to destroy Japanese ships wherever they were found. The large size and endurance of submarines built for Pacific fleet duty were well suited to extended patrol in the vast ocean. Still, the raiding mission was a new one, and submariners had to learn it in time of war. Not until the end of 1943 did they have the doctrine, experience, and weapons for an effective *guerre de course*.

Clay Blair, Jr., has indicted the Navy for being too slow in developing the attrition campaign. There was, Blair argues, "a failure of imagination on the highest levels . . . to set up a broad, unified strategy for Pacific submarines aimed at a single specific goal: interdicting Japanese shipping services in the most efficient and telling manner," and above all, stopping the bottlenecked traffic traveling north to Japan through the Luzon Strait. "Had it not been for these command weaknesses, misconceptions, and technical defects, the naval war in the Pacific . . . might have been shortened by many, many months."[23]

At first the submarine force needed more aggressive captains. Those trained in fleet-support tactics turned out to be too cautious on attack patrol. Captains who saw their boat as an independent weapon, not as an auxiliary, finally came on board during 1942 and 1943.[24] And by the beginning of 1944, at long last, skippers were getting torpedoes they could count on. During the previous two years, submarines had been sent out inadequately armed. Torpedoes were few, being produced slowly as works of mechanical art. They also were inadequately tested. As a result, they divided lower than their settings, and their fuses did not work. Bad "fish," as torpedoes were called, meant lost opportunities. The submariners' frustration is expressed in this attack log of the legendary Lieutenant Commander D. W. (Mush) Morton, who commanded the *Wahoo* in the Sea of Japan in the summer of 1943:

15 August. Fired one torpedo at a freighter. Miss.
Fired one torpedo at a freighter. Dud.
Fired two torpedoes at a freighter. Both missed.
Fired one torpedo at same freighter. Miss.
17 August. Fired one torpedo at a freighter. Miss.
Fired one torpedo at a freighter. Miss.
18 August. Fired one torpedo at a freighter. Miss.
Fired one torpedo at a freighter. Miss.
Fired one torpedo at same freighter. Broach.
"Damn the torpedoes."[25]

The Navy revamped the manufacturing process, and by 1944 the service finally had enough torpedoes—although submarines still wanted a larger warhead. In 520 patrols in 1944, U.S. submarines fired a total of 6,092 torpedoes, more than they had fired in 1942 and 1943 together.[26]

The submarine attrition strategy called for concentration on the heavy traffic of the Luzon Strait and the South China Sea. Patrols into the East China Sea and the Sea of Japan closed in on the home islands. Boats on hunt-and-kill missions were equipped with radar. They formed packs on the basis of communications intelligence, which broke Japanese water transport codes and directed the submarines to their targets. By August 1944 the U.S. Army had intercepted almost 750,000 water transport messages. The sailing orders among these messages were sent to Navy submarine commands. That intelligence "was the key to the undersea ambushes that ultimately destroyed the Japanese merchant marine."[27]

Merchant shipping was of immense importance to their war effort, and the Japanese made a disastrous strategic mistake in not taking steps to protect it. They were overconfident. Prewar opinion had held that submarines would not be a problem, and shipping losses were underestimated by a factor of three. Japanese officers expected American submarines to be attached to the fleet. They thought American sailors would not be willing to undertake prolonged, uncomfortable operations at great distances from their bases. The assumption that a decisive surface battle would clear the seas of threat supported the neglect of the sea-lanes that linked shipping and empire. For the first two years of the Pacific war, most Japanese merchantmen sailed unarmed and unescorted. In December 1941 the Japanese navy assigned only 12 old and poorly equipped destroyers, 100 torpedo boats, some subchaser and small air units, and 210 converted merchant vessels to protect all Japanese shipping throughout the vast empire. Radar went first to fleet combatants and came only late to escorts and merchantmen. Intelligence was poor. Detection devices, especially sonar, were good, but not until 1943 were destroyers armed with effective depth charges.

Above all, for more than a year and a half there was no central authority to set routes and specify escort procedures. Responsibility for directing merchant shipping between the homeland, the southern part of the empire, the China coast, and the island garrisons was split between four autonomous commands—the navy, the army, the Transportation and Communication Department, and the Munitions Department. Not until August 1943 did the government form an independent Combined Escort Command. By then the Japanese merchant fleet had been reduced to 80 percent of its prewar size. In August 1944, with minimum wartime requirements set at 4.5 million tons of imports, Japan received only 3.25 million tons. At that time, the Combined Escort Command was placed under the direction of the Combined Fleet. But by then it was too late.[28]

The Japanese began the war with an adequate merchant cargo capacity of 6.2 million tons. By the end of the war, U.S. submarines had sunk 1,113 cargo ships and tankers, totaling 4,779,000 tons of capacity, 60 percent of what American forces sent down, with a personnel loss to the Japanese merchant marine of 69,000 dead and injured. Japan could not make up its losses. At the end of the war, cargo tonnage was down to less than 2 million tons, despite 800,000 tons added by capture and 3.3 million tons of new construction during the war. Most of what remained was unusable. In August 1945 Japan had in service only 12 percent of its prewar merchant fleet, and because of fuel losses only half of that, some 312,000 tons, was in operation. By comparison, that the Allies at that time had 88 million deadweight tons of merchant shipping capacity, double what they had at the beginning of the war.

Merchant ships sunk meant cargoes lost. This attrition deprived Japan of the raw materials it had gone to war to gain. The ships contained war-sustaining cargoes that never reached Japanese factories, Japanese civilians, or Japanese soldiers in their fortresses and bases. The cargoes included machines, tin, oil, rubber, minerals, textiles, grains, munitions, cloth, chemicals, fertilizers, and merchant seamen, all very difficult to replace.[29] By the time the Japanese realized the need to increase their industrial war production, they had nothing to do it with. The year before Japan entered the war, steel production was 5.12 million tons. In 1945, it was 0.8 million. By August 1945 there were only 90,000 tons of oil left in Japan. Without energy independence or free use of the sea, Japan could not win the decade-long struggle for the domination of northeastern Asia, control the southern part of its empire, or hold off the Americans.

Under any circumstances, however, Japan's productivity could not have kept pace with America's, and that is the essential fact of the war. During the war, the U.S. produced 11 times as much coal as Japan, 222 times as much oil, over 13 times as much steel, almost 40 times as many artillery shells, and so on. The war's long-term outcome was never in doubt.[30] Had the Japanese protected themselves better against the American attrition strategy, however, their capacity to resist would have been much stronger, and it is fearsome to imagine what the consequence of an extended war might have been.

In the battles of the first year of the Pacific war, each side sustained heavy losses. The United States took a capital-ship loss of 40 percent, Japan 30 percent. The United States made up its losses and then added more and more ships to its force. Japan did not even make up its losses. America's 1940 building program made all the difference. By 1943 it contributed to Navy operations fast aircraft carriers; light, 6-inch-gun cruisers; destroyers; and aircraft. Appropriations for 1940 alone outweighed a decade of Japanese shipbuilding and began a pace of naval renewal the Japanese war economy could not match. After the first intense campaigns, the United States needed only a five-month breather to regroup its naval forces and replace its losses. The Japanese required a naval pause of fifteen months. In 1943 only 3 aircraft carriers were under construction in Japanese yards, while 22 were being built in the United States. In 1943 Japan's aircraft production was only 20 percent of America's.[31]

The Japanese prime minister, General Tōjō Hideki, said that the destruction of shipping by U.S. submarines was one of the three principal factors in Japan's defeat. The other two, Tōjō said, also elements of offensive sea control, were the strategy of bypassing island strongholds and the ability to self-supply fast-carrier forces so that protracted operations could be conducted without returning to base.[32]

As the Americans advanced, aircraft joined in destroying supplies and controlling the sea. Main ports in the home islands and ports that were key to imperial traffic, such as those at Saigon, Singapore, and Shanghai, were mined from the air. Reconquest of the Philippines by U.S. forces isolated Japan from its southern resource base and cut off shipping in the South China Sea. U.S. land-based air patrols from Iwo Jima, Okinawa, and bases in China brought the remaining routes under attack. Japan faced devastating shortages of bunker oil and aviation gas. It had to move its fleet far to the south to put it near a fuel source. Carrier-air attacks on the Hokkaido ferries reduced coal supplies to the factories on Honshu.

Theodore Roscoe wrote, "Japan lost the Pacific War on the date that her merchant fleet losses exceeded all possibility of replacement." That date, he concluded, came in the spring of 1944, with the closing down of the route from Singapore to Japan. After that, "the Empire went out of business." And so did Japan's war machine.[33] The campaign against Japanese cargo ships and tankers "remains perhaps the only example in modern history of the prosecution of a *guerre de course* to a strategically decisive result."[34]

FORMING THE DUAL ADVANCE

In 1943 the U.S. Navy's strategy of offensive sea control was in full swing. The Navy's approach was one of mobility and innovation. Naval campaigns were unbound by dogma. Flexibility was the watchword. The strategy was exemplified by the self-sustaining fast-carrier task force, which was always on the move, provisioned at sea, combining and recombining at will. Behind the naval effort was a country mobilized for war, the source of the men, the submarines, the *Essex*-class fast carriers, and everything else.

The Pacific war was run by a committee, the Joint Chiefs of Staff. Formally, they acted as agents of the Allied Combined Chiefs of Staff. In practice, the U.S. Chiefs set the goals, and they supported King's plan of early and constant pressure on Japan. They recommended an early offensive to the president, and they held to it in counsel with the British.[35]

Beneath this high command was an operational oddity: a dual command in the Pacific. The Joint Chiefs divided the Pacific into two sections. One was the Pacific Ocean Areas, which was placed under a commander in chief, Admiral Chester Nimitz. The other was the Southwest Pacific Area, placed under a supreme commander, as the incumbent General Douglas MacArthur called himself. Each commander was responsible directly to the Joint Chiefs, although instructions were handed down along service lines: Marshall instructed MacArthur; King instructed Nimitz. When and where coordination was required, between commands or between the services, the requirement would go up the double chains of authority for decision by the Joint Chiefs and then down again as service instruction. In practice the divided command was an alliance mediated by the Joint Chiefs. MacArthur charged that the absence of a single command and single strategy extended the war "with added casualties and cost."[36] It is hard to see an alternative, save giving sole command to Nimitz and his superior central Pacific sea-power strategy. MacArthur himself by seniority and national reputation had forced a dual command, and his obstinate insistence on a progressive advance toward the Philippines made the dual strategy necessary. Washington, which did not want to choose between the strategies, was able to afford both and so avoid decision.

It was King himself who had proposed the awkward compromise. There was no admiral senior to MacArthur, and few officials, civilian or military, wanted to bring MacArthur back to the United States. The military feared a congressional reform in which MacArthur might end up as the single head of the armed services. He was a potential political rival to Roosevelt. In 1942 there was a flurry of interest among his supporters in proposing MacArthur as a presidential candidate for 1944.[37] King had another concern. He wanted to be sure that the Pacific was the Navy's war no matter what MacArthur did. King would not allow an Army general whom he thought knew nothing of sea power to be put in command of the Navy's ships. King paid the price of duplication and negotiation to keep naval operations in Navy hands and MacArthur overseas.

Within the general mandate of "unremitting pressure," the key to Pacific strategy was its flexibility, based on the country's long-term confidence. Policy flexibility accommodated such uncertainties as how China and the Soviet Union might participate in a continental war against Japan and allowed for the eventual end of China as a major Allied theater of operations and the addition of the Soviet Union to the Allied side. Strategic flexibility permitted exploitation of rapidly changing circumstances. It even permitted a postponement of the decision on whether the area of main effort would be the central Pacific, the South Pacific, the southwest Pacific, China-Burma-India, or a combination of these.

Flexibility made possible the dual advance itself. It let the JCS exploit operational opportunities, such as bypassing the great Japanese bases of Rabaul and Truk, speeding up the pace by going for the Marianas, and deciding at the last moment whether to turn the advance toward China, Luzon, Formosa, or Japan's home islands. Flexibility encouraged the ready adaptation of weapons systems, notably submarines for attrition war, fast-carrier task forces, and very long-range bombers. Flexibility was a nightmare, however, to those charged with procurement and supply. Logistical planners despaired when the Combined Chiefs or the Joint Chiefs approved operations for different areas of the world at the same time regardless of whether there were resources to cover them all.[38]

The Guadalcanal campaign in August 1942 had exposed the outermost Japanese line of defense. MacArthur wanted a follow-on campaign that would move up through the Solomons toward Rabaul, New Guinea, and the Philippines. For King, that was peripheral. King wanted a true sea-control operation directed at the heart of the island empire, not a thrust lost among its extremities.[39] It would be better to open a new front to the north, in the central Pacific, and begin the amphibious conquests of Japan's main outer defenses, the steppingstones to the imperial homeland.

King wanted to carry out War Plan Orange, directing it at the Marianas. The Marianas, not the Philippines, were the strategic key. The Japanese could not let the Marianas fall. That meant the Japanese fleet would come out to battle, and the question of fleet control could be settled once and for all. In the open central Pacific, the carriers could operate with the maneuvering room unavailable to them in the narrow waters of the Solomons and New Guinea. By a thrust to the Marianas, the Navy would cut the enemy's lines to Truk, its great naval base in the Carolines. From the Marianas the Navy could support the recapture of the Philippines, and (at this stage of King's planning) renew the connection to China, further tying Japan to the continent. There was more to be gained by a swifter, less costly attack through the central Pacific than by MacArthur's slow if steady march from the south. At the Marianas the decisive naval battle would be joined and from there the United States could strike northward directly at Japan.

Roosevelt and Churchill approved the opening of a new front across the central Pacific at the Trident Conference in Washington in May 1943. There was some British resistance, owing to their considerable concern that the China-Burma-India theater was being slighted and their uncertainty about what role they would play in a central Pacific operation. But their tacit approval, drawn from the declaration that the Allies should "maintain and extend unremitting pressure . . . and [attain] positions from which [Japan's] ultimate surrender can be forced," gave King an open door.[40] Approval of a second front, however, was not the same as approval of two independent advances. For all King knew, the mission of the Navy in the central Pacific might continue to be, ultimately, the support of MacArthur's advance from the south. That was not, in his opinion, the best way to defeat Japan in the shortest possible time.

In August 1943 King received unexpected support from an Army quarter. The Army Air Forces planned to introduce in 1944 a new heavy bomber with a 1,500-mile range, the B-29. The Air Forces had not decided how to use the B-29 against Japan. At first it thought the planes would operate from China and be supplied through India, but no one could rely on there being secure bases in China, and the cost and trouble of supply across the Himalayas was enormous. To attendees of the Quebec Conference in August 1943, the central Pacific advance suggested the establishment of air bases in the Marianas—on Saipan and Tinian—that would be completely under American control. That created a hitherto absent Army interest in the central Pacific, at least among officers of the Air Forces.

Such was the fluid nature of the Pacific war that three years after it began, there was still no specific long-term plan for the defeat of Japan. The big change had been with regard to China. Its internal quarrels destroyed the hope that it would be a major continental ally, that it would be a part of a maritime strategy to hold Japanese forces on the mainland while the Navy attacked Japan's oceanic rear. At the Quebec Conference, the political leaders instructed military planners to draw up a plan for the defeat of Japan under which Japan could be defeated within a year after Germany's surrender. The Cairo and Teheran conferences in November and December 1943 endorsed the dual offensives under way in the Pacific and decided to reduce activity in the China-Burma-India theater. China was thereupon relegated to a secondary role. The war against Japan came to rely increasingly on naval strategy. At Teheran the Soviet Union promised to join the Pacific war three months after Germany's defeat. That made the idea of American bases in the Marianas all the more important, as oceanic counterweights against Soviet continental power, and so enhanced the central Pacific thrust. King did not want to have to rely on Soviet aid to beat Japan.

Once the dual advance met on the edge of the Philippines-Formosa-China triangle, put a choke-hold on Japan's lines of traffic, and secured air bases perhaps in China and certainly in the Marianas, and once the Japanese were forced back to their last ring of defense—the home islands, Korea, Manchuria, and Shantung—then the Joint Chiefs could choose how and where to mount the final assault. This assault could be by blockade, as the Navy thought would suffice; by bombing, as the Army Air Forces preferred; or by invasion, as the Army thought would be necessary.

The refusal at the beginning of 1944 to establish final goals in the Pacific or even priorities between the two lines of advance meant that operations took place in that year based on not much more than the idea of pushing forward, of "unremitting pressure." Operational flexibility turned this vagueness to a virtue. The two Pacific theaters expanded independently. Their commanders held onto the assets they had, asked for more, and went after targets of opportunity. The policy of unconditional surrender, and the absence of Allied constraints in the Pacific, meant that the Joint Chiefs had almost unfettered freedom in their military planning. There was no political goal save the surrender of the enemy, and the government seemed prepared to leave that to the force of arms. Thanks to the outpouring of war matériel from American factories, the United States could wage a total war without political limits. The shape of the dual advance would be determined by the answer to a simple question: Which of the two advances could more quickly, and with less cost, force the Japanese to give up?

MacArthur argued that his advance, though roundabout and slower, was safer and less costly. His air force chief, hoping to have the new B-29s sent to himself, dismissed the idea of seeking bases in the Marianas as "just a stunt."[41] Critics of the central Pacific advance had in mind the bloody invasion of Tarawa in November 1943. The U.S. capture of that strongly defended atoll in the Gilberts cost the Second Marine Division almost 1,000 dead and 2,000 wounded. Tarawa was the first major amphibious action in the Pacific. Taking the island was an important victory because it opened the way to the Marshalls. To military professionals, the cost was justified. They learned the lessons for which they paid—how to improve coordination between a beaching party and its fire support, how to achieve closer command and control in combat, and what equipment (above all, amphibious tractors) was needed for beach assaults.[42] But the losses had shocked public opinion, and MacArthur used them to turn the central Pacific campaign from an autonomous operation into a dependent one that supported his own advance.

He sent this message to Washington:

> I do not want command of the Navy, but must control their strategy, be able to call on what little of the Navy is needed for the trek to the Philippines. The Navy's turn will come after that. These frontal attacks by the Navy, as at Tarawa, are tragic and unnecessary massacres of American lives. . . . The Navy fails to understand the strategy of the Pacific, fails to recognize that the first phase is an Army phase to establish land-based air protection so the Navy can move in. . . . Don't let the Navy's pride of position and ignorance continue this great tragedy to our country.[43]

Nimitz too was distressed by the heavy losses at Tarawa. But he stood by the central Pacific strategy, and above all by the prospect of its forcing a decisive naval engagement for command of the seas. He wrote in mid-January 1944, "When conflicts in timing and allocation of means exist, due weight should be accorded to the fact that operations in the Central Pacific promise at this time a more rapid advance toward Japan and her vital lines of communication; the earlier acquisition of strategic air bases closer to the Japanese homeland; and, of greatest importance, are more likely to precipitate a decisive engagement with the Japanese Fleet."[44]

But to what extent should the goal of capturing the Marianas be sacrificed to the two-pronged convergence on the Philippines? Without a decision on how and where the final assault would be launched in the Pacific war, Nimitz felt obliged to use his great naval force to support MacArthur's advance. He would do so in part by taking the Marshalls to protect the Army, in its movement to the Philippines, from the much-feared Japanese force on Truk. Truk, in the Carolines, was the largest Japanese naval base outside the home islands. Capturing the Marshalls was the Joint Chiefs' order, a Navy mission. The Marshalls, notably Kwajalein, Roi-Namur, and Eniwetok, were needed as air bases to protect the Gilberts. But what of the larger, rugged islands of the southern Marianas? They were beyond the range of land-based American air support and within the range of Japanese bombers from Japan's inner defense ring. The harbors of the southern Marianas were not up to Navy demands. Nimitz discounted the value of the B-29s. The distance to Japan was so great the bombers would be without fighter protection, and for safety's sake they would have to bomb from such high altitudes that they would most likely miss their targets. At the end of January Nimitz recommended that rather than attack the Marianas, his central Pacific force go straight to the Palaus, which were about 600 miles due east of Mindanao, and then to the Philippines in support of MacArthur.[45]

The Marianas, however, were the key to King's central Pacific strategy, the key to sea power. They were the islands from which the Navy would dominate the western Pacific. Their capture would, just as readily as the capture of the Palaus, permit invasion of the Philippines and hence open up the sea routes to the bases in China, which at this point was still King's long-range objective. Submarines and aircraft from the Marianas could at once cut essential supply and reinforcement lines to Truk. Those were King's reasons for wanting to take the Marianas; he was not concerned about providing B-29 bases. "Of course," he wrote Nimitz, "[establishing bases for the B-29s] was never the object. That was merely one of the results that would ensue from this operation, which was to be taken to dry up the Carolines, facilitating the capture or neutralization of the Carolines, and to speed up the clearing of the line of communications to the northern Philippine area."[46] With the Japanese supply routes cut and Truk pinched off, the Japanese could not supply or reinforce bases farther south in the Marshalls, in the Bismarcks (where on New Britain the enormous holding base at Rabaul was defended by 100,000 well-supplied men), or in New Guinea. From the Marianas the United States could cover the sea communications of MacArthur's advance on Luzon. From the Marianas the American advance could turn, depending on the circumstances, toward the Philippines, Formosa, China, or Japan itself, once the script for the final act was written.

King thought that MacArthur's slow advance across New Guinea toward the southern Philippines was a sideshow. To make it a major strategy, he wrote Nimitz, "to the exclusion of clearing our Central Pacific line of communications to the Philippines is to me absurd. Further, it is not in accordance with the decisions of the Joint Chiefs of Staff."[47] King agreed that taking the Philippines was essential to cutting Japan's East Indies supply route and opening the sea-lanes to China. But an attack on the Philippines could be staged better and carried out more quickly from bases in the central Pacific than from New Guinea.

This is where the *Essex*-class fast carriers came in. These carriers were concentrated in task forces but decentralized in action. The self-sustaining fast-carrier task forces replaced the surface battle line. They eliminated dependency on land-based air and so made unnecessary a progressive advance from island to island. They were perfectly suited to the drive through the central Pacific, able to isolate the widely dispersed island garrisons and prepare the way for amphibious operations. They were also capable of making swift and daring moves and, in combination with the other warships, were ready for decisive battle. Here and nowhere else, the United States held the strategic advantage.

Such arguments did not shake General MacArthur's commitment to the New Guinea–Mindanao line. MacArthur had declared that a return to the Philippines was his personal destiny and a point of national honor, and in addition, a strategic necessity. The islands, and MacArthur, were fraught with political significance. The Filipinos were resisting Japanese occupation. If the United States did not come to their rescue, it would have no future on the islands. No American strategist denied the importance of the Philippines. King simply thought he had a better strategy, a faster way, to win the war. He would share the effort and support MacArthur in taking Luzon, but he also insisted on the value of establishing sea control in the central Pacific. King would not stop MacArthur's advance, but he could protect his own. He ordered Nimitz to continue toward the Marianas.

The JCS at last gave strategic endorsement to the dual advance in March 1944. They ordered that operations be continued in both areas, under separate commands. Now strategy was clear. Nimitz was given his own offensive. His mission was to win the war, not to support MacArthur. To speed the southern advance, the Joint Chiefs ordered MacArthur to bypass Rabaul and take the northwest coast of New Guinea. Nimitz was ordered to bypass and isolate Truk and to take the southern Marianas. Thereafter, not before, he was to seize the Palaus to provide a base for the support of MacArthur's attack on Mindanao.

This plan was a victory for King. In practice it gave strategic priority to the central Pacific.[48] In the campaign for the Marshalls, in January and February 1944, the Navy and the Marine Corps applied the lessons learned at Tarawa. These, in Ronald Spector's words, boiled down to "more of everything": more extensive preparatory naval gunfire against shore defenses and inland airfields; more and better armed landing craft and assault vehicles to bring the troops ashore; full-scale air support, including fighter planes to strafe the beaches; and better command and control for the assault.[49]

Operations in the Marshalls also showed the value of leapfrogging. Instead of attacking the eastern Marshalls, the islands for which his commanders argued on prudential grounds and which the Japanese had apparently reinforced, Nimitz jumped ahead 400 miles to the more lightly defended and strategically more central atoll, Kwajalein. This practice of island-hopping was a main reason Tōjō gave (along with submarine attrition and the self-sustained mobility of the fast-carrier task forces) for why the United States won the war.

The U.S. victory on Kwajalein in February 1944 came after "one of the most complicated amphibious campaigns in history."[50] The campaign involved days of preliminary shelling. The pilots of Vice Admiral Marc Mitscher's Task Force 58, part of Admiral Spruance's great Fifth Fleet, shot down 150 Japanese planes. Out of 41,000 American servicemen committed to the invasion force at Kwajalein, only 372 soldiers and marines died. On the Japanese side 7,870 of 8,675 men fell.

To protect the next operation, the invasion of Eniwetok, aircraft from Mitscher's carriers raided Truk to prevent interference from that much-feared base 700 miles to the east. Truk had been bypassed, not invaded, but it could be attacked. Spruance put a patrol around Truk to catch escaping ships, several of which he sank while strikes by fighters and dive-bombers from Mitscher's carriers destroyed some 30 Japanese merchant ships in Truk Lagoon and 275 planes. To the Americans' great surprise, Truk, long considered the most powerful outpost in the central Pacific defense chain, turned out to be poorly defended and empty of the major units of the Japanese fleet. The assumption that the Japanese had heavily fortified their mandated islands in the 1930s turned out to be false. The destruction of almost 80 percent of the air power at Truk, much of it on the ground, showed the growing weakness of the Japanese air force and the growing strength of American carrier air. For the first time, a major base had been disabled without the aid of land-based air power or amphibious invasion.[51] The weakness of the Combined Fleet was also exposed. Outgunned and outclassed by the augmented Pacific Fleet, alarmed by the fall of Kwajalein, the Japanese realized they could not stand up to the Navy in the Marshalls and had withdrawn their main units westward to the Palaus.

The campaign in the Marshalls and the raid on Truk showed that the U.S. Navy could move at will and could provide the air cover and sea control needed to jump from island to island without first establishing bases and air stations on land for ground-launched air support. The establishment of the vast U.S. Fifth Fleet and its fast-carrier air force, Task Force 58, led to the birth of a new type of independent, self-sustaining naval offensive, which made possible the sweeping strategy of the central Pacific. The United States did not need advance bases on land—it brought along its own at sea. Sustained mobility, the essence of the Navy's Pacific operations, was made possible by the 2,930 ships of the indefatigable service squadrons. These ships kept troops and warships supplied so that they, and above all the fast-carrier task forces, could conduct campaign after campaign without conventional base support.[52]

This was the greatest forward naval deployment possible. It was the third reason Tōjō gave for the American success. Japan could not match the ability of U.S. warships always to be on the offensive, concentrating and separating, without rest. After 1943, a powerful force could stay at almost any station for as long as the U.S. government wished.[53] It was with this instrument of naval power, able to move and concentrate at will—and with the immense courage and stamina of the sailors, the Army troops, and the marines—that the Americans seized, held, and pressed without cease the strategic initiative in the Pacific throughout 1944 and 1945.

The dual offensives caught the Japanese in a whipsaw. From what quarter would the next attack come? What was the next American objective? Where should Japanese forces concentrate? The Imperial General Headquarters accepted the loss of Rabaul, the Bismarcks, and Japan's holdings in the outer ring. It could give up no more, however. Its New Operational Policy brought it back to the Absolute National Defense Zone, established in September 1943, which included the Kurils, the Bonins, the Marianas, Truk, the Palaus, Dutch New Guinea and Biak, and Singapore. It was on this ring that the United States was closing. Already Japan had found that because of the pressure it faced in the central Pacific, it could not send reinforcements to stop MacArthur's movement along the New Guinea coast. Thus it did not follow up on a possible advantage when, in the operation against the island of Biak, MacArthur made his landings without naval support.

Considerable effort was expended by the United States to make the two theaters of the dual advance complementary. They could also be mutually supportive. Task Force 58, the fast carriers from the Fifth Fleet, went south in March 1944 to lure the Combined Fleet out from the Palaus and thus to draw away the threat to MacArthur's operations on the New Guinea coast. A month later the task force supported MacArthur's assault on Hollandia, enabling him to move beyond land-based fighter cover and commence his rapid advance toward New Guinea's northwest tip. Army access to the Japanese military codes enabled MacArthur both to achieve total surprise in his 1,000-mile leap toward the New Guinea tip and to cut off Japanese forces in the process. "Never has a commander gone into battle as did the Allied Commander Southwest Pacific, knowing so much about the enemy."[54] By July 1944 MacArthur stood poised for an invasion that November of the Philippine island of Mindanao.

The two advances were also competitive. The two theaters competed for ships and troops. The Bougainville campaign at the end of 1943, with its carrier-air attacks on the bases of Rabaul and Kavieng, and the invasion of the island of Biak off the New Guinea coast in May 1944 were made without the cover of naval superiority. These risky moves were made with partial forces at a time when the main body of ships and air power was massed in the central Pacific. When Admiral Halsey ordered Rear Admiral Frederick Sherman's carrier group to raid Rabaul, the odds were almost unacceptable. Halsey expected the virtually unprotected carriers to be heavily damaged or sunk. But the marines on Bougainville had to be protected from the Japanese forces at Rabaul. An observer recalled that Halsey looked 150 years old as he made the decision to go ahead—his son and namesake was serving on one of the carriers. In a subsequent strike against Kavieng, Sherman was ordered in with his carrier groups virtually "naked," to an area, as he said, "the farthest yet advanced into enemy waters with the weakest screen ever assigned to large aircraft carriers." These operations succeeded, but they showed that risks attended operations that did not have the advantage of a concentration of force.[55]

The dual advance gave the United States the incalculable advantage of choosing when and where it would strike. The Japanese never knew what to expect. The Japanese fleet under Vice Admiral Ozawa Jisaburo could not determine the best time and place for its operations. The range of American initiatives was too great. Just naming the whereabouts of Ozawa's enemies—MacArthur approaching the Philippines and Spruance heading toward the Marianas—shows Ozawa's problem, tied as his strategy was to concentration for a major battle. So strong was the victory fever, however, so persistent was the Mahanian tradition among Japan's high command into 1944, that Japanese officers still commonly thought a decisive victory at sea might be enough to win the war. The problem was how to force the battle.

11

Victory Drives 1944–1945

THE MARIANAS AND LEYTE GULF

The Japanese navy failed to stop MacArthur's advance in New Guinea or Nimitz's advance in the Marshalls. Vice Admiral Ozawa Jisaburo moved his fleet westward. For the decisive battle, whether it was to be fought against MacArthur or against Nimitz and Spruance, Ozawa needed more than a force at sea. He needed the support of land-based air.[1]

Ozawa's opportunity arose in the Marianas in June 1944. Spruance at first thought the Japanese fleet would not engage because it had declined an opportunity to attack MacArthur at the island of Biak. But Japan's inner defense ring had to be protected at sea or it would be lost. Japanese troops had dug into Saipan, Tinian, and Guam. Ozawa had one more chance when the Americans approached the Marianas.

Ozawa's plan was to envelop Spruance's Fifth Fleet between two air-power onslaughts, one based on land, the other from carriers at sea. First he would soften up the American invasion force with shuttle-bombing from island bases on Guam, Rota, and Yap, and then hit it with his carrier air. Japanese carrier planes outranged those of the Americans by 210 miles. That meant Ozawa could launch planes while keeping his carriers out of range. His aircraft could also refuel and rearm on island bases and then take off again. Ozawa's advantage was in this double-air position.

U.S. submarines spotted the Japanese force as it left the Philippines. That gave Spruance a chance to take the initiative. He sent the pilots of Vice Admiral Marc Mitscher's Task Force 58 to destroy the ground-based aircraft and airfields on the islands, on which Ozawa's envelopment strategy rested. The pilots carried out their mission. That eliminated the threat from land-based air. Ozawa could not close his vise.

Spruance and Mitscher then stopped Ozawa's sea-launched airplanes. On one day, June 19, American carrier pilots downed 297 planes from Japanese carriers and destroyed at least 100 land-based planes, for a total of close to 400 aircraft, the largest number of Japanese planes destroyed on any single day in the war. The United States lost only 25 airplanes that day. No U.S. carrier was hit, even though Spruance ordered Mitscher to stay on the defensive, insisting that the carriers absorb the raid rather than pursue the attackers. The day after this magnificent defense, Mitscher launched a bold counterattack. His pilots took off in the late afternoon at the last possible moment for a daylight strike, when the enemy targets were at the very limit of the Americans' range. The U.S pilots sank one carrier and damaged two. That was enough for Ozawa. He had lost 476 planes, 445 pilots, and 3 carriers (2 of them to U.S. submarines). Two other carriers, those hit by the U.S. pilots, had been damaged. Ozawa gave up the prospect of decisive battle and retired with his 6 remaining carriers and his 5 great battleships and 10 heavy cruisers intact.

That battle, the battle of the Philippine Sea, was a major defeat for Japan. Although the Japanese saved their fleet, they had not taken command of the sea around the invasion point. Further, the battle all but annihilated what remained of Japanese naval air and, with it, the offensive mobility of a strong carrier force. From this near destruction of its naval air, a process that had begun at Midway, the imperial navy never recovered. The loss of planes could be made up, but not the loss of pilots. Japan did not have the organization or the time to train more. The next major engagement, off Formosa in September 1944, destroyed what remained of Ozawa's skilled aviators.

The strategic punch of the Japanese carrier air force was gone for good. In the final great naval engagement of the war, an engagement connected with the invasion of Leyte, the only use Ozawa could find for his carriers was as decoys, sailing them without an effective complement of planes or pilots. To defend Okinawa against invasion in April 1945, the Japanese turned to suicide runs by the kamikazes.

In the battle of the Philippine Sea, the fact that the Japanese fleet got away when it might have been destroyed made Spruance's decision not to engage it one of the most controversial of the war. Should Spruance have realized that Ozawa was after his carriers and not after the American transports and amphibious force? Should Spruance therefore have been more aggressive and pursued the Japanese fleet as his aviators wanted, to eliminate naval opposition? Or was Spruance correct in deciding that his primary job was to protect the transports and amphibious forces of Vice Admiral Richmond Kelly Turner's Joint Expeditionary Force and the men under Marine Lieutenant General Holland M. Smith as they moved onto Saipan? Those soldiers and marines, spearheading the largest invasion force ever assembled in the Pacific, were fighting an entrenched and determined foe for an objective of major strategic importance. Should Spruance have jeopardized their position for the chance of a decisive naval victory?

Spruance thought not. He would not move his guard of the amphibious forces even for the chance of establishing full command of the seas. His battle plan was defensive. He had to protect his flanks. Spruance could not rule out the possibility that Ozawa was preparing for a super-Jutland, or that he was planning a deception. The Japanese might have split their forces as they had at Midway. Spruance thought Ozawa's target was the transports, not the carriers. Spruance had to be ready for a possible end run against the thousand and more U.S. troopships and their support craft. He was willing to risk his carriers but not Turner's transports and amphibious fleet. For the sake of the invasion, Spruance gave up a Pacific Trafalgar.[2] It is hard to argue that he was wrong.

Off Saipan, again in the battle for Leyte Gulf, and then at Iwo Jima and Okinawa, the mission of the U.S. Navy was to protect and assist the invasion of an island. One can debate the strategic value and cost of these operations—only the Marianas campaign has escaped criticism.[3] The point, however, is that Navy commanders, with the exception of Halsey at Leyte Gulf, supported forces assaulting the land. The U.S. Navy was turning from the autonomous naval strategy of Mahan to a maritime strategy of supporting land operations. Until the very end, when opinion split on what the nature of the final operation against the home islands should be, the naval war in the Pacific was less and less a search for fleet engagement and more and more a matter of attrition on the one hand and advance on the other. The advance was measured by the number of islands that were taken to support the anticipated blockade of Japan's home islands and to secure airfields for the bomber offensive the Army Air Forces had proposed.

In the battle of the Philippine Sea, the American objective was capturing Saipan, not destroying the enemy fleet. That meant support of the invasion of Saipan, not an autonomous naval action. Spruance did his job. The Navy met the enemy fleet at sea with Navy air, maintained sea control, and isolated the battlefield. Spruance also gave direct support to the invasion of Saipan. Navy planes mauled land-based enemy aircraft. Naval gunnery pounded defensive positions, although the result of battleship gunnery support was judged "disappointing."[4] The coordination of the Navy, the Army, and the Marine Corps was not. Philip Crowl wrote that "without doubt [this coordination was] the outstanding feature of the campaign." It confirmed "that current amphibious doctrine was sound and could be employed, with modifications, against any Japanese-held island or land mass."[5]

The invasion of Saipan in June 1944 was strategically comparable to the invasion of Normandy, which took place at the same time. Together, the two invasions served as a testament to the capacity of the United States to wage a war that breached the home walls of two major enemies simultaneously on opposite sides of the globe. After Saipan and Normandy, Japanese and German leaders knew the war had entered its final stage. The march on Germany had begun from the west, and Japan was now within bombing range.

The fall of Saipan in early July 1944 was a disaster for the imperial government. Tokyo had no plans for the next move. General Tōjō Hideki, who had led Japan into war, resigned as army chief of staff and prime minister. The government that replaced his, charged with reconsidering Japan's position, elected to continue the war. It decided that the political fabric of the country could not sustain the humiliation of surrender. The senior statesmen feared a revolution more than they feared a military defeat.

In August 1944 a newly constituted Supreme War Council took stock of the situation. The Absolute National Defense Zone had been broken. Reserves were exhausted. The civilian population had nothing more to give. Despite these realities, the Supreme War Council on August 19 decided the war must continue. It authorized a counterattack, a final total mobilization to defend the Philippines. Hope renewed that the Americans might give in after a major defeat. This hope was as old as the war itself. It had caused the war, and it was held in spite of all past experience.

Three years earlier, Japanese leaders had expected that the United States would be distracted by German successes. Now in mid-1944 they imagined that the United States would be embroiled with the Soviet

Union over the victors' spoils in Europe. Perhaps a stunning blow in the Philippines would discourage America from additional fighting in the Far East. Anyway, said General Umezu Yoshijrō, the army chief of staff, what was most important, win or lose, was a demonstration of Japan's resolve. The proponents of peace rationalized that, if after a supreme effort Japan's position continued to deteriorate, a peace cabinet would be formed.[6]

So the war went on. The Imperial General Headquarters prepared last-ditch operations in the innermost ring, which consisted of the Philippines, the Ryukyus, and Hokkaido. The Japanese, however, did not know where the next American blow would fall.

Nor did the Americans. "If the Japanese in the summer of 1944 had tried to base their defensive plans upon American intentions, they would have been without useful information."[7] In Washington in March 1944, the Joint Chiefs of Staff, balancing between the Army and the Navy, had approved the Marianas campaign without stating what was to follow. Both advances continued without prioritization and without guidance toward a specific goal. Instead, they were given the general assignment of applying "unremitting pressure." MacArthur controlled New Guinea by the end of July 1944. After capturing the Marianas, Nimitz took the Palaus to cover MacArthur's right flank for his move to the Philippines. The expectation was that in February 1945 MacArthur would begin an offensive against Luzon and Nimitz an offensive against Formosa, two points on the strategic triangle whose third point was the China coast. What would happen until then, or after, was not stated, and even the Luzon and Formosa objectives were tentative. Beyond New Guinea and the Marianas nothing had been decided.

Throughout the summer of 1944, the Joint Chiefs debated the matter of which island should be invaded first—Luzon or Formosa. They reached a decision only in October. The arguments that eventually settled the dispute in favor of Luzon were based on logistics and enemy actions. The manpower and supplies that would be needed to invade Formosa first could not be met in 1944. Marshall could not send Army reinforcements to the Pacific until the war in Europe was over. Troops and ships could not be shifted in the Pacific without jeopardizing the Leyte operation, which would have to be preliminary to the Luzon campaign and which the Army would not give up.[8]

There was a logistical bottleneck in the second half of 1944. The United States was launching major offensives in a two-front war. The European advance took enormous resources. In the Pacific, cargo handling was limited by a shortage of discharge facilities in the islands. Docks, service troops, and off-loading equipment were all in short supply. There were slowdowns, labor disputes, and crowding. The system was overloaded. In October 1944, for instance, as the Leyte task force was under way, 86 vessels clogged Hollandia harbor. Of these, 38 were cargo ships, and of those, only 9 had actually been routed through the appropriate regulating officer. The supplies of the other 29 "could just as well have remained in the United States, because they were no closer to being in the hands of troops while idly awaiting discharge in the Hollandia harbor than if they had been held in San Francisco."[9]

The final argument against a Formosa-first operation was the turn of military events. A Japanese offensive ran over most of the air bases in eastern China. That made access to the China coast more difficult, but at the same time, thanks to the Marianas campaign, bases in China had become less important. The Army Air Forces, on grounds of security and access, preferred to bomb Japan from the Marianas.[10]

These considerations led to the decision to invade Luzon instead of Formosa, with the understanding that the Navy would follow the invasion with a renewal and extension of the central-Pacific advance early in 1945. That advance would include the invasions of Iwo Jima in the Volcano Islands, 650 miles south of Tokyo, and of Okinawa in the Ryukyus, 850 miles southwest of Tokyo. In October 1944 the Joint Chiefs ordered MacArthur to occupy Luzon on December 20 and directed Nimitz to give him the support of the Pacific Fleet. After all the debate, it was, said Marshall, "not a difficult decision."[11]

Two U.S. fleets participated in the invasion of Leyte in October 1944. That invasion was the initial stage of the American return to the Philippines and, as it turned out, the death knell of the Japanese empire. The Central Philippine Attack Force was composed of the Seventh Fleet, which absorbed the loan of a large number of units from the Pacific Fleet. The Seventh Fleet was now the largest fleet in the Navy. It consisted of 738 ships commanded by Vice Admiral Thomas Kinkaid. Kinkaid's job was to transport, land, and establish on Leyte 174,000 troops of the Sixth Army (counting reserves, there were 202,500 ground troops in all). The covering force was the Third Fleet under Admiral Halsey. Halsey and Task Group 77.4, under Rear Admiral Thomas Sprague, were to support the operation by carrying out air strikes over Formosa and Luzon and by holding off Japanese naval attacks on the invasion force. If possible, Halsey and Sprague were to bring the Japanese fleet to decisive battle.

There was no overall commander for the operations. Kinkaid took orders from MacArthur, who took his from Washington. Halsey was directed from Pearl Harbor by Nimitz, who like MacArthur reported to the Joint Chiefs. Divided command meant "there was the obvious danger that the fleets might be operating at cross-purposes, with no officer at hand authorized to restore order."[12] The consequences of the division are in dispute. Postmortems of the four separate actions that are collectively called the battle for Leyte Gulf led to accusations of failure of mission. Halsey asserted that a single, united command would have made things clearer; Kinkaid said that division would not have been a problem if each commander had stuck to his job. Each thought the other "could—and should—have covered the San Bernardino Strait."[13]

The table of organization of the covering American naval force is staggering to review. Altogether, the Navy employed 17 fast carriers, 18 escort carriers, 18 battleships (including 5 of the 6 old battleships recovered from Pearl Harbor), 7 heavy cruisers, 16 light cruisers, 95 destroyers, 14 destroyer escorts, and 45 PT boats. The carriers of Task Force 38 were prepared to launch 1,000 planes. Submarines were on patrol off the straits.

Halsey's men and ships were battle seasoned, but they were tired. They were Spruance's Fifth Fleet under a different name, flushed with successes from the Marianas campaign, from a naval battle off Formosa, and from other fiery operations that had wiped out local Japanese land-based air before the invasion of Leyte began. Halsey held command because King rotated commanders with campaigns. That practice gave an admiral and his staff time to prepare for the next operation while a fresh replacement fought the one at hand. Accordingly, after the Marianas, in mid-August 1944, Spruance and Turner were sent to Pearl Harbor to ready the moves against Iwo Jima and Okinawa, while Halsey, and Turner's replacement as commander of the Fifth (which had been redesignated the Third) Amphibious Force, concentrated on the Philippines. Mitscher's fast carriers, designated Task Force 58 when part of Spruance's Fifth Fleet, became Task Force 38 in Halsey's Third Fleet, with Mitscher staying on for the Leyte invasion after which he was relieved by Vice Admiral John S. McCain. This double-echelon system was possible because of an abundance of skilled commanders—and because of the need to find a major command for Halsey after his South Pacific theater was turned by American advances into a basing area.[14] The system of rotation worked well, at least for the admirals. It exhausted sailors and pilots. The changing of their commanders gave them no rest. The arrival of a new commander meant that another major action would follow almost immediately upon the one just completed.

For Japan, defense of the Philippines had to be all-out. Japan faced bombardment and starvation. Although the B-29s did not start their runs over the home islands until November 1944, airfields being built in the Marianas warned of what was to come. Merchant shipping was in shambles. Fuel was almost gone. Japanese officials understood that defeat in the Philippines meant the end of their maritime empire.

The 432,000 men of the Japanese army in the Philippines prepared to meet the Americans wherever they landed—on Mindanao, on Leyte, or on Luzon. The Japanese were confident that they had the strength and position to turn the Americans back, so long as they had the support of the Japanese fleet. The Philippine defense was reinforced by army land and air units from China, a reinforcement that had been denied the navy for the defense of the Marianas. Over half the Japanese troops deployed outside the home islands were still in China and Manchuria, proof of Japan's continuing continental commitment.

For the Japanese navy it was do or die. After the battle of the Philippine Sea, the commander in chief of the Combined Fleet, Admiral Toyoda Soemu, had sent his heavy surface ships to an anchorage off Singapore, while Ozawa took his Mobile Fleet back to the home islands in a fruitless attempt to reconstitute his air squadrons. The navy should have been concentrated in the Inland Sea, where carriers could train with surface forces. The destruction of tankers by U.S. submarines, however, had created such a shortage of refined fuel oil in Japan that there was enough at home only for the carriers. The carriers had to go where their planes were produced, where safe airfields lay, and where pilots could train. The surface fleet was forced to move to the East Indian source of its fuel supply. This division of forces was disastrous to preparations for combined action. The two parts of the fleet planned to rendezvous in Singapore for training before heading for the Philippines. But they never did. The Americans landed before the Japanese were ready for them.

Toyoda later described the Navy's position to American interrogators:

> Our Task Force and our air squadron were not ready for operations at the time that your campaign began. We felt that to take the Task Force into Leyte was a big gamble; and while it would not be accurate to say that we were influenced by public opinion, questions were beginning to be asked at home as to what the Navy was doing after loss of one point after another down south, such as Marianas and Biak. So after having consulted headquarters in Tokyo and having obtained their consent, it was decided to take this gamble and to send the whole fleet into the Philippine operations. . . . Should we lose in the Philippines operations, even though the fleet should be left, the shipping lane to the south

would be completely cut off so that the fleet, if it should come back to Japanese waters, could not obtain its fuel supply. If it should remain in southern waters, it could not receive supplies of ammunition and arms. There would be no sense in saving the fleet at the expense of the loss of the Philippines.[15]

The policy drawn up by the naval high command in Tokyo was to hit the American invasion force at the beachhead to prevent a lodgment. If that was not possible, if landing operations had already begun, then the navy was to destroy the transports in their anchorage, to deny the invasion its support. Decisive naval battle was no longer an objective. The navy was to avoid the superior U.S. carrier task force. That was the lesson the high command had learned from the Marianas, where Ozawa never got near Saipan.

The Japanese officers in Singapore who were preparing the Philippine defense, however, opposed this plan of the high command. They argued that the circumstances demanded a decisive battle. "Our one big goal was to strike the United States fleet and destroy it," said Rear Admiral Koyanagi Tomiji, chief of staff to Vice Admiral Kurita Takeo, commander of the Japanese Second Fleet. That meant annihilating the U.S. carrier force. The convoys could be picked off later. To proceed according to the high command's policy, in light of the string of American victories, was in the officers' view to run the battle backward and to head toward disaster. For if the U.S. Third Fleet and Task Force 38 continued to exist, if sea and air control were not established by Japan, then the Philippines and the Japanese navy would remain under the gun, and further U.S. invasions would still be possible. The naval high command in Tokyo overruled the local critics. Permission was given to engage in fleet battle only if the American striking force came within range. The primary mission at Leyte was to attack and destroy the transports at anchorage in the gulf.[16]

It was a plan that went into operation too late. Time was lost in debate and rendezvous. The Americans landed on Leyte's beaches before the Japanese were ready and were entrenched on the island four days before the Japanese navy entered Philippine waters.

Kurita commanded what the Americans called the "Japanese center force." It consisted of five battleships, including the gargantuan new ships *Yamato* and *Musashi*; ten heavy cruisers; two light cruisers; and fifteen destroyers. Kurita's job was to approach Leyte from the north, by way of the San Bernardino Strait. Vice Admiral Nishimura Shoji's southern force, after it was joined by ships from home waters under Rear Admiral Shima Kiyohide, comprised two battleships, three heavy cruisers, and eleven destroyers. It was to approach Leyte from the south by the Surigao Strait. These two attack forces, assisted by naval and army airplanes from island bases, were to converge on Leyte Gulf—Nishimura's was to arrive first, Kurita's two hours later—and put the invaders under their heavy guns.

To provide a diversion, Ozawa's force of four carriers, two hybrid battleship / carriers (which were able to launch aircraft but not recover them), two light cruisers, and some destroyers was sent to act as a lure to the north. Ozawa could not defend himself or attack in force. His job was to draw Halsey's supporting task force north, tempting Halsey to take the chance of destroying the carrier fleet that Spruance had forsworn off the Marianas. Meanwhile, the heavy guns of Kurita and Nishimura could isolate the American troops on the beachhead.

Ozawa could not defeat Halsey's carriers, but he could entice them into the range of land-based aircraft flying from Luzon and Formosa. The Japanese could thus use land-based air in a way that had eluded them in the Marianas. This time, however, given the badly crippled state of Japanese naval air, the land-based jaw of the air-envelopment vise was the only one available. Ozawa's own position was, as he said, "all sacrifice. . . . I had not much confidence in being a lure, but there was no other way than to try." It was, if one accepts Ozawa's postwar testimony, a suicide mission.[17]

The early Allied landings made it impossible to interdict the invasion. The Japanese goal then became the destruction of the support craft—the transports and the ships in the convoys. Success demanded precision timing, the simultaneous arrival of the southern and central forces in Leyte Gulf. That never happened. The simultaneous arrival was thwarted by American naval actions.

The battle for Leyte Gulf of October 1944 was, in tonnage engaged and space covered, the greatest naval battle of all time. And it was the last great naval battle of the war. A total of 42,800 Japanese officers and sailors and 143,668 Americans and Australians took part. More Americans fought in this battle than were in the entire Navy and Marine Corps six years before.[18] Altogether, in the defense of the Philippines, Japan lost 68 warships, including 3 battleships, 4 carriers, 10 cruisers, and 9 destroyers. The Americans lost 1 light carrier, 2 escort carriers, 2 destroyers, and 1 destroyer escort. The fighting of October 25, 1944, off the island of Samar, in which the Japanese lost 4 carriers, 1 cruiser, and 2 destroyers, has been characterized as "the most destructive single day in modern naval history."[19] The Allied victory finally and thoroughly destroyed the offensive power of the Japanese navy and realized the sea-power goal of American naval planners of the previous 40 years.

The battle for Leyte Gulf consisted of simultaneous surface and air engagements. The first, in the center of the battle area, was the battle of the Sibuyan Sea. This was a carrier-air and submarine attack on Kurita's force as it approached the San Bernardino Strait. Kurita, short on fuel and without antisubmarine patrol, depended on air cover from land-based fighters, which he did not get. Preliminary American carrier attacks on bases on Formosa, Okinawa, the Palaus, and Luzon had destroyed the more than 600 planes (and over 150 vessels) and shot down the leader-pilots who were meant to support operations in the Philippines and to protect the advancing naval force. Thus Kurita was left without air defense, and American carrier air from Task Force 38 sank the superbattleship *Musashi*, hit four other battleships, and forced the heavy cruisers to retire. Kurita reversed course, delaying both his passage through the San Bernardino Strait and the critical junction planned in the south with Nishimura.

To the south, in the Surigao Strait, Nishimura had to break through into Leyte Gulf. He decided to do so at night, hoping that Japanese training for night battle would be to his advantage. He sailed his force straight into American radar and a well-set trap. Six prewar U.S. battleships (5 of which had been recovered from Pearl Harbor), 8 cruisers, and 29 destroyers waited in ambush at the strait's northern end. Nishimura's force was set upon by torpedo-shooting destroyers. Then, as it plowed forward through the destroyers' gauntlet, it was battered by the heavy units of the U.S. battle line, which were capping the strait's exit. Flight from the pursuit of radar-directed ships and gunfire was impossible. Nishimura's large ships could not operate freely in the confined waters. Of Nishimura's force, only one destroyer escaped unscathed. Compared to the thousands of Japanese sailors lost, only 39 Americans of Rear Admiral Jesse Oldendorf's force were killed and 114 wounded. The battle of Surigao Strait was entirely a battle of surface gunnery, and it showed the skill the Americans had achieved in night warfare and radar detection. "It was the last naval battle in which air power played no part, except in the pursuit. It was the last engagement of the battle line."[20] Nishimura had sailed through without waiting to be joined by Shima's supporting force. After entering the strait, Shima retired without engaging. The southern approach to Leyte Gulf was blocked, the southern claw of the Japanese pincer removed.

To the north, Ozawa's job was to pull Halsey's Third Fleet away from the San Bernardino Strait so Kurita's main striking force could get through to Leyte Gulf and join Nishimura in the attack on the transports. Ozawa's feint worked. Halsey followed the decoy, thus making one of the most criticized decisions of the war. Seeking movement and decisive battle with the Japanese carriers, he followed Ozawa northward instead of standing guard to prevent Kurita from entering the San Bernardino Strait.

In interrogation after the war, Admiral Ozawa said that his planners "always tried to adapt the operation plan according to the characteristics of the United States commander."[21] If so, they picked the right tactic to deal with Halsey, who prided himself on his aggressiveness and bold action. He had heard the criticism poured on Spruance after the battle of the Philippine Sea for allowing Ozawa's fleet to escape. Halsey did not want to let Ozawa get away again.

Halsey knew that Kurita was heading for the San Bernardino Strait and that Kurita's force would be under his guns. But instead of engaging, or even leaving the newly formed surface force called Task Force 34 on guard, he set out after Ozawa with Task Force 38, taking Task Force 34 along to assist in the kill. Halsey commanded 64 ships against Ozawa's 17. Halsey made the decision to pursue Ozawa partly on the assumption that the Seventh Fleet could handle Kurita and partly because he was spoiling for decisive battle against the carriers, whose force he overestimated. He considered the carriers the key to the mission overall because of the range of carrier air. If he could destroy them, Halsey wrote, "our future operations need fear no threat from the sea."[22]

It was a judgment call. Halsey operated under an order that read, "In case opportunity for destruction of the major portion of the enemy fleet is offered or can be created, such destruction becomes the primary task." Halsey decided that meant the carrier force. He had earlier written Nimitz, "My goal is the same as yours—to completely annihilate the Jap fleet if the opportunity offers." The order quoted above, however, did not cancel or supersede the preceding order to "cover" the invasion and protect the beachhead.[23] It has been argued that Halsey could have divided his fleet and that he had the information which would have allowed him to deduce that he could have safely done so. That he did not, Bernard Brodie suggests, and that he followed Ozawa, was Halsey's misapplication of the two oldest principles of sea power: concentration of force, and attack on the main enemy battle fleet. Halsey misapplied the second principle by erroneously assuming that Ozawa's carrier-led fleet was the principal Japanese force.[24]

Halsey's decision to follow Ozawa meant that he left open the strait toward which the Japanese center force was steaming, and he did not adequately inform the other commanders that the strait was no longer protected or even watched. It was a serious mistake. It cannot be justified by Halsey's success in the battle off Cape Engaño, in which his carrier air in 527 sorties sank all four of Ozawa's unprotected carriers. In this action, Halsey could not follow up his attack by bringing the ten ships of Ozawa's retiring force under the guns of his fast battleships. Meanwhile, the very emergency Halsey was supposed to prevent was occurring to the south. Kurita was coming through the strait unopposed and heading for Leyte Gulf. Halsey, having left the exit open, sent help in the form of the battleships of Task Force 34 and a cover task group of carriers.

Kurita, to his surprise, had sailed through unscathed. His order from Admiral Toyoda read, "All forces will dash to the attack, trusting in divine guidance."[25] Kurita anticipated meeting Halsey and expected to pound the American aircraft carriers to death with his battleships' 18.1-inch guns. What he found standing off the island of Samar instead was the small escort force of Rear Admiral Clifton Sprague—six slow escort carriers, three destroyers, and four destroyer escorts—on patrol. Sprague was astonished to see Kurita's massive force loom ahead. Against overwhelming odds and without substantial reinforcement (Halsey's force was 400 miles to the north) Sprague counterattacked. He sent three destroyers and the aircraft from his escort carriers against the huge Japanese battle fleet, while he covered the retreat of the rest of his force with smoke.

The shock tactic worked. Kurita did not know what he was facing. He thought it was a much stronger force, the southern group of Halsey's fast carriers. Kurita slowed down, unable to see what was going on, lacking reconnaissance, increasingly uncertain who had him under attack. He thought he was surrounded. Kurita did not know what had happened to Ozawa or the disposition of other American forces. He knew that if he continued without air cover, his surface ships would soon to be under ruinous air attack, and he preferred to face this attack in the open sea rather than in the narrow confines of Leyte Gulf. The U.S. air attacks prevented sustained and accurate gunnery against the mysterious force engaging him off Samar.

Already since leaving Borneo, Kurita had lost a superbattleship and six heavy cruisers. He had relied on the support of land-based air. That help was now gone. The handful of support submarines did nothing. Kurita's schedule was completely upset. He was beset by a force of undetermined size. He was not sure he could sustain his ships under murderous fire if he did get into Leyte Gulf. Kurita decided, only 40 miles from the gulf, to abort his mission. He withdrew to the north, back toward the San Bernardino Strait. Toyoda, who had ordered the all-or-nothing operation, might have pressed on had he been present at the head of his fleet, following his prescription of relying on divine guidance and historic precedents of sacrifice.[26] But Toyoda was in Japan.

Kurita's decision has been the subject of much debate. Had he been aware of the immediate tactical situation, he would have known that Halsey's move north had uncovered the beachhead. With Halsey gone and Oldendorf in pursuit of Shima's retreating force, Kurita had the advantage of surprise. Had he realized the weakness of the force opposing him, one school of thought holds, he might have destroyed Sprague's ships and steamed on toward Leyte Gulf, engaged the Seventh Fleet even at heavy cost, and shelled the exposed Americans on the beach. Had he done so, he might have won a major surface engagement, cut off MacArthur at least temporarily, and given time for Japanese reinforcements to arrive for the defense of Leyte. Russell Weigley leveled a harsh judgment of Halsey's action: "Whatever might have been done, it was wrong that the amphibious forces in Leyte Gulf should have been so dangerously exposed to the big guns of Kurita's battleships and cruisers."[27]

We should not, however, overdraw Kurita's position. His own formation had many serious weaknesses and would have been put under terrible pressure. He received no reinforcements. The ships he had counted on to help him were being destroyed in the other battles for Leyte Gulf. Kurita "did not abandon a sure thing." Even had he continued, he would have won a tactical victory at best, not the campaign.[28]

With Kurita's withdrawal, the second, northern as well as the southern arm of the Japanese pincer disappeared. The naval threat to the Americans' Leyte invasion was over. The great naval battles of October 1944 destroyed the Japanese navy as a fighting force. It would never again be used in fleet action. Sea control was in American hands. And so was the fate of Japan, for from the Philippines the United States could cut the maritime routes to and from Japan's all-important Southern Resource Area.

Japan's naval strategy had failed. The imperial navy never had the strength or the mobility to cover its defense perimeter, against and through which the Americans moved when and where they chose, avoiding the decisive battle of the prewar Japanese plan. After the Marianas, Japan could not even keep its battle fleet together. Ships extracted from the battle for Leyte Gulf had to be divided between Singapore, where there was fuel but no ammunition, and home waters, where there was ammunition but no fuel.[29] The only effective weapon left was the kamikaze. The navy had launched its first organized suicide attacks in the battle off Samar.

IWO JIMA AND OKINAWA

The U.S. Navy had supported MacArthur's invasion of the Philippines as part of the policy of "unremitting pressure" and as part of a compromise worked out by the Joint Chiefs of Staff. Strategically, the Navy's preference was always to renew the central-Pacific thrust, with a sea blockade and an air bombardment of war industries as the fastest and most economical way to put the noose around Japan and to pull it tight.

Admiral William Leahy made this point to the Joint Chiefs in September 1944. The Philippine reoccupation should go ahead, but "America's least expensive course of action is to continue and intensify the air and sea blockade, with an intensified air bombardment of Japan's war industry."[30] That meant a return to the central-Pacific strategy. As part of the endless round of compromise between the services, in October 1944 the JCS promised the Navy that, in return for the Pacific Fleet's support of the Army's invasion first of Leyte and then of Luzon, there would be a central-Pacific invasion of Iwo Jima followed by an assault on Okinawa. Iwo Jima, a midpoint on the bomber route between the Marianas and Japan, lay about 750 miles from Japan. Okinawa was 800 miles west of Iwo Jima and only 330 miles from Japan.

Plans for that campaign were brewing in the Pacific command even while Formosa was still King's goal. In September 1944 Fifth Fleet commander Admiral Raymond Spruance won the agreement of Nimitz and his planning officer, Rear Admiral Forrest Sherman, that Formosa was the wrong target. King concurred. The cost of invading Formosa would be too great, and the Army would not supply the force. But the Army would support an attack on Okinawa, and the Marine Corps could invade Iwo Jima. With the Marianas already under control, the advance would be part of a steady march along interior lines toward the final defenses of homeland Japan.

Taking Iwo Jima would benefit the Army Air Forces. It would eliminate an early-warning post for Japan, give land-based, tactical air cover to the fleet when it moved within range of home-based Japanese air, and provide an emergency landing field and refueling base for the bombers of XXI Bomber Command. Okinawa would anchor the blockade of Japan, preventing Japanese movement along the China coast and thus cutting an essential link to the mainland.

Spruance stated the Navy interest, reasserting a traditional service sentiment that became stronger as the final act approached. The goal, Spruance said, was to force Japan to "die on the vine." The benefits of using Iwo Jima as an emergency airfield helped sell the plan to the Joint Chiefs. Bombing would no doubt be valuable in the final attrition strategy. But the inspiration and ultimate goals of the island campaigns were sea power and winning the war by naval blockade.[31]

Taking Iwo Jima and Okinawa was also an attractive alternative to acquiring bases on the coast of China. As far as the Navy was concerned, China had become superfluous. In the last months of 1944 and in early 1945, the idea of establishing bases on the China coast disappeared. A Japanese offensive against Chiang Kai-shek confirmed the weakness of Chiang's cause and resulted in the occupation of the very bases the Americans had sought. Of more significance, Halsey's carrier force, sustaining itself in the South China Sea and moving at will, in January 1945 racked up the second most destructive month of the war against cargo tonnage and the most destructive month against Japanese tankers. An independent, self-sufficient U.S. Navy did not need bases on the continent to drive the enemy off the sea. Iwo Jima and Okinawa thus became the nodal points of the final act. In October 1944 the Joint Chiefs gave the order to take them, but to do so only after the Navy had rendered its support to MacArthur's invasions of Leyte and Luzon.

That decision was the Joint Chiefs' "last important strategic directive of the war."[32] It put the Navy's central-Pacific strategy back on track. It was not, however, a plan for the final defeat of Japan. That plan was still not written at the end of 1944. Whether victory would come by direct or indirect means, by way of China or through a direct move against Japan, by using or not using Soviet assistance, by siege or assault—all remained unresolved. The question of whether the strategy would be one of blockade and bombardment, as the Navy and Air Force wanted, or one of invasion, as the Army prescribed, remained undecided at the highest level.

The decision to invade Luzon after Leyte was made over King's objections. King wanted a steady push through the Ryukyus, progressively encircling Japan's southern lines of communication. He did not want to tie up the Navy in the fight for the rest of the Philippines. The protracted and costly Luzon operation diverted attention from King's strategic plan, and "he regretted the decision the rest of his life."[33]

The invasion of Luzon did not come until January 1945 and took six months to complete. The U.S. Army took almost 47,000 battle casualties, including 10,380 dead; the Navy took 2,000 casualties, mostly from kamikazes. With the operation moving much slower than expected, when would Halsey's Third Fleet return to the central Pacific? The timetable for fleet involvement in the great operations of 1945 was tight. The invasion of Iwo Jima was set for February and of Okinawa for April.

MacArthur, since December 1944 holding the five-star rank of General of the Army, wanted Halsey to stay around for invasion support, to provide local defense. Nimitz, since December 1944 holding the five-star rank of Fleet Admiral, thought the best way to deter Japanese interference in the Philippines was by pressing them at home, by forcing the central-ocean offensive. He thought the Japanese would then be unable to concentrate naval interference and that therefore only a few of his units—not the whole fleet—would be sufficient to cover the Philippines.

Nimitz's view prevailed. In its five-month tour, the Third Fleet had protected the invasions to liberate the Philippines. It had destroyed over 7,000 Japanese planes, sunk 90 warships, and laid waste more than 550 cargo ships. Carrier air had for the first time "met and defeated land-based air power as opposed to air power based on scattered island groups."[34] Thereafter, fleet power was needed in the central Pacific for the final thrust. Still going strong despite being savaged by a typhoon in December 1944, the fleet moved north in January 1945 to support the invasions of Iwo Jima and Okinawa. There was the usual switch of commanders and fleet designations. Halsey, returning to Hawaii, was relieved by Spruance, and the Third Fleet became the Fifth Fleet. This arrangement lasted through the invasion of Iwo Jima in February by marines, and through that of Okinawa in April by other marines and by Army forces.

It is hard to imagine, wrote the Marine Corps historians Jeter Isely and Philip Crowl, "a target more difficult for the amphibious assault than was Iwo Jima." Its capture by the largest body of marines committed to combat in one operation in the war "is the classical amphibious assault of recorded history." U.S. casualties were around 30,000. "In this operation the Japanese managed to take a toll of American casualties equal to their own dead, a feat not earlier accomplished nor later repeated."[35] Defensive entrenchments absorbed heavy naval gunfire and aerial bombardment. The marines were under Lieutenant General Holland M. Smith, the commanding general of the Fleet Marine Force, and Major General Harry Schmidt, the landing force commander. They wanted ten days, or at least four, of naval gunfire before they hit the beach. Spruance, in overall charge of the operation, gave them three.

The marines indeed could have used more prelanding gunfire. But Spruance wanted to suppress some of the approximately 5,000 aircraft the Japanese were hoarding on the home islands. The assault on these, he thought, had to be carried out simultaneously with the prelanding gunnery attack, otherwise the Japanese air would go after his invasion fleet and its transports, rendering the invasion nugatory. It was this use of carrier air to attack Japan, together with a limited supply of U.S. naval ammunition and a lack of assurance that one or two more days of pummeling would make a difference, that led Spruance to set the prelanding barrage at three days. In the event, there was no serious interference by Japanese air or surface forces, and the three days of bombardment were enough to get the marines onshore.[36]

Iwo Jima was captured foot by foot during vicious land fighting, a triumph of the marines' courage in combat and of meticulous planning. Close to 6,000 marines died. Marines know well the meaning of the photograph of the American flag being raised on Mount Suribachi. Iwo Jima's strategic value was the support it provided for the air offensive against Japan. The Americans now had an air base 600 miles closer to the home islands. If Japan could be subdued by air and by naval blockade, the United States would not have to invade the enemy's stronghold. That was the meaning of Iwo Jima and of Okinawa.

Okinawa was invaded on April 1, 1945, by an amphibious assault force of 183,000 troops, mainly from the Army. This force was under the command of Vice Admiral Richmond Kelly Turner for the amphibious phase, and under the expedition leader, Lieutenant General Simon B. Buckner, once ashore. The troops were carried to the shore and supported by a fleet of 1,213 ships and craft. That force in turn was protected by the warships of Spruance's Fifth Fleet, Spruance being also in command of the entire joint Army-Navy Task Force conducting the campaign. The Fifth Fleet comprised 40 carriers, 18 battleships, and about 200 destroyers. Four of the carriers and two of the battleships were contributed by a British fleet. The Iwo Jima argument about preassault bombardment did not recur. The Americans landed unopposed. The defenders had withdrawn to fortified, interlocking positions in the hills, from which they later subjected the approaching infantrymen to withering fire. Attempts to dislodge those defenders resulted in vicious land fighting. The Navy suffered losses standing up to kamikaze raids. The Okinawa campaign cost the United States more men than any other in the Pacific war. At Okinawa, American casualties on land and sea totaled 49,151 men, of whom 12,520 (soldiers and marines) were killed or missing.[37] The battle of Okinawa lasted longer and was much fiercer than expected. When the campaign ended early in July 1945, the United States had breached the inner ring of Japanese defenses, and the home islands stood exposed.

Army and Marine Corps losses resulted from the decision of the well-entrenched Japanese to fight, if not to the last man (7,400 surrendered), then at any rate with grim determination. The Japanese government, fearful that antiwar sentiment would rise within the country, threw its troops and the remnant of its offensive navy and air force at the Americans. About 110,000 Japanese soldiers were killed defending the island. Approximately 7,800 Japanese aircraft were shot down, sixteen warships were sunk, and four warships were damaged.

Okinawa was the hour of the kamikaze. The kamikaze corps had become part of a special attack-suicide concept that included not only airplane pilots but land and sea forces as well. Kamikaze tactics were costly, expending men and planes, but with few experienced pilots it was the most efficient way to use Japanese aircraft against the American fleet. In the first use of kamikazes, in the battle off Samar, the purpose had been, with 24 pilots and planes, to dive onto the vulnerable decks of American carriers to put them out of action long enough for Kurita to reach Leyte Gulf. The principle followed by the commander of the First Air Fleet was that Japan "can no longer win the war by adhering to conventional methods of warfare." Kamikazes were next used to great effect against ships approaching Luzon. By the start of the battle of Okinawa, kamikaze goals had been inflated to encompass the destruction of an entire enemy task force. The U.S. Navy had not expected kamikaze attacks on a scale as large as that experienced at Okinawa. During the battle, ten major assault waves, consisting altogether of 1,465 suicide planes, descended on the Fifth Fleet, often with fighter escort. In addition, there were 435 attacks by individual kamikazes. Kamikazes were the great surprise of the war. In addition to them, probably more than 4,000 conventional sorties were flown by Japanese torpedo planes and dive-bombers.[38]

The Navy had no effective defense against the suicide attacks. The Americans at Okinawa both on sea and on land were unusually exposed because Okinawa lay within range of Japanese land-based air and beyond the range of American land-based air cover. The sailors aboard the more than 2,000 U.S. ships took a severe pummeling. A total of 4,907 U.S. sailors were killed, the largest number in any operation of the war. The suicide planes sank 26 U.S. ships and damaged 164, out of a total of 36 U.S. ships sunk and 368 damaged in the battle.[39]

The U.S. carriers did what they could. Spruance, again in overall charge of the campaign, had sent Vice Admiral Marc Mitscher's Fast Carrier Force (now called Task Force 58), the British carriers, and the B-29s from Army Air Forces Major General Curtis LeMay's XXI Bomber

Command against as many Japanese airfields as they could find on the southernmost home island of Kyushu and on Formosa. But the fields were scattered and the planes hidden. Neither the Navy nor the Air Force could suppress the kamikaze threat, and the antiaircraft fire of U.S. picket ships and of the target ships themselves was only partially successful. The Navy never had a harder month in the war than that of April 1945, when the kamikaze attacks were more intense than at any other time.[40]

The Japanese suicide operations were part of a joint offensive plan of special attack. The opening kamikaze attacks of early April were combined with the last sortie of the Japanese surface navy. Five days after the invasion of Okinawa, the largest battleship in the world, the *Yamato*, accompanied by a light cruiser and eight destroyers, set out from Japan on a one-way cruise to the invaded island. The *Yamato* was given only a one-way supply of fuel and no air cover. The little fleet's purpose was twofold. First, it was to draw U.S. carrier aircraft away from the support they were giving soldiers and marines on the island, to enable the Japanese defenders to counterattack. Second, the fleet was, if at all possible, to plunge on to Okinawa and pump shells onto enemy positions. But the ships did not survive an attack at sea. Picked up at once by submarines and aircraft, the battleship, the cruiser, and four of the destroyers were sunk by Mitscher's bombs and torpedoes. The *Yamato*'s commander went down tied to his compass stand.[41] That was the end of the surface force of the Imperial Japanese Navy.

On July 2 the American command declared the Ryukyus campaign over. As it turned out, the battle of Okinawa, the most complex amphibious operation in the Pacific, was the last battle of World War II. That would not have been the case had Japan not surrendered six weeks later because the American plan was to conquer Japan by amphibious invasion.

TO TOKYO BAY

From the beginning of the war, the goal of American operations was to destroy the center of Japanese industrial and political strength, which lay between Tokyo and Shimonoseki, along the southern shores of the island of Honshu. For 40 years the Navy had said this could be done by sea control, by imposing a crippling blockade. Blockade, even more than attrition, was the Navy mission. For four years the Army Air Forces, or the AAF, on the same principle of deprivation and pain, had envisioned bombing the Japanese into submission. Navy and AAF strategies were now in parallel development. The conquest of islands had given the AAF air bases nearer and nearer Japan. Doctrinal assumptions in both the Navy and the AAF suggested that, with siege and blockade, air power and sea power, and wearing the enemy out, invasion would be unnecessary.

It also was unnecessary after Okinawa to divert Japan by seizing bases in eastern China. Although King and Spruance still toyed with the idea of taking some offshore islands for air bases, neither the Navy nor the AAF needed them after Okinawa. China moved to the periphery. Americans, intent on ending the war quickly, were not impressed by the argument of the British Chiefs of Staff that greater control of the war should be gained to recapture former British bases in Malaya and Southeast Asia. From the U.S. perspective, it was more important to destroy Japan's will to fight as expeditiously and as directly as possible. And to the Navy and the AAF, that meant attention to the Japanese home islands, to blockade and bombing. British requests for a share of operational control were politely set aside.[42]

Spruance said what many Navy officers thought, that operations for the final defeat of Japan should be a logical extension of the success already achieved in the central-Pacific campaign and that there should be no need for a final invasion. In June 1945 a U.S. submarine task group penetrated the Sea of Japan, putting under attack the remaining sea-lanes that connected Japan to the mainland. The enemy was surrounded by sea and by air. Said Spruance:

> The question of what operations should be undertaken after Okinawa, whether to the coast of China or to the main islands of Japan was a most important one. It was my opinion at the time, and I have never had any reason to change it, that landings in Japan proper, such as the planned Kyushu landings on 1 November 1945, were not necessary and would have been extremely costly. From our island positions around Japan, we had enough airfields for bombing objectives in Japan itself if further bombing attacks were needed. We controlled the sea approaches to Japan. Japan was cut off from the outside world, except to Korea and North China, and our submarines had been able to enter the Sea of Japan and operate there. . . . In the case of World War II, towards the end, time was decidedly on our side. Japan was cut off and could well have been permitted to "die on the vine" as we had done with the by-passed islands in the Pacific.[43]

Army Air Forces B-29s had been bombing Japan from bases on Saipan, Guam, and Tinian since November 1944. These missions, high-altitude, precision, high-explosive bombardments of war-industrial targets, disappointed the proponents of strategic bombing. U.S. losses were heavy, accuracy was poor, and the effects of the bombing uncertain. Navy pilots took this as confirmation of their suspicions that horizontal bombing was inaccurate. Thoughtful Japanese, however, were greatly alarmed. Prince Higashikuni Naruhiko, commander of Home Defense, said: "We had nothing in Japan that we could use against such a weapon. From the point of view of the Home Defense Command, we felt that the war was lost and said so. If the B-29s could come over Japan, there was nothing that could be done."[44] That was not the view of the Japanese cabinet, and so the war went on.

The AAF was disappointed. Strategic-bombing practice had not followed concept. The command decided to change targets and tactics, from factories to cities and from the use of high-explosive bombs to the use of incendiary ones. The changes were made in March 1945 by the new commander of XXI Bomber Command, Major General Curtis LeMay. The target became urban areas at large, to undermine civilian morale. Tactics became maximum-effort incendiary strikes from low altitudes. Japan's cities would be set ablaze.

The great fire raids beginning in March 1945 devastated Japan's main industrial cities. By July the six most important had been hit, as had hundreds of secondary cities. A fire raid destroyed over half of Tokyo. Radio Tokyo called it "slaughter bombing." Tailgunners in returning B-29s could see the fire from 150 miles away. U.S. losses in the fire raids were minimal. In a campaign of seventeen maximum-effort incendiary attacks conducted by B-29s flying 6,960 sorties, only 136 planes were lost.[45] Also during these months, LeMay renewed the precision bombing attacks, notably against Japan's petroleum industry. He also began using B-29s for the very important operation of mining Japanese waters, an operation for which the Navy did not have suitable aircraft. It was the B-29s of the Army Air Forces that in March 1945, before the Okinawa invasion, sealed the Shimonoseki Strait to large warships. Thereafter the mines they dropped closed port after port, a contribution to sea control that yielded what Nimitz described as "phenomenal results."[46]

Still, a JCS decision for invasion was formalized in May 1945, with King's approval. This invasion was to follow blockade and siege "at the earliest practicable date," but it would be an invasion nonetheless, first of the southern island of Kyushu (Operation Olympic) and then, in a critical follow-on attack, of Hokkaido (Operation Coronet).

The JCS plan of May 1945 recommended:

a. Apply full and unremitting pressure against Japan by strategic bombing and carrier raids in order to reduce war-making capacity and to demoralize the country, in preparation for invasion.

b. Tighten blockade by means of air and sea patrols, and of air striking force and light naval forces to include blocking passages between Korea and Kyushu and routes through the Yellow Sea.

c. Conduct only such contributory operations as are essential to establish the conditions prerequisite to invasion.

d. Invade Japan at the earliest practicable date.

e. Occupy such areas in the industrial complex of Japan as are necessary to bring about unconditional surrender and to establish absolute military control.[47]

The bombing-and-blockade alternative to invasion had been fiercely attacked by the Army staff, which argued that it would take at least as many men as an invasion of Kyushu, perhaps twice that number, and might assure no decisive result. With the war in Europe over, it was important to be done with Japan. The encirclement strategy, Army critics maintained, would not force unconditional surrender until mid- or late 1946. Spruance said that "time was decidedly on our side." Was it? Blockades took time; no one doubted that. Time was part of the Navy's attrition strategy, which was expected to reduce the costs of combat. But according to the counterargument, a blockade would take more time than a war-weary American public opinion—and perhaps war-weary soldiers—would accept. What to Spruance seemed good strategy would be perceived at home as unnecessary delay. Marshall remembered the lesson he had learned in 1942—that to a public expecting a rapid victory, delay could bring a devastating letdown in fighting spirit. Invasion was the alternative to indefinite blockade.[48]

It was perhaps these arguments that convinced King to support invasion. They were not unreasonable. The goal was a speedy and unconditional surrender. Sieges do commit men and take time, and the United States was tired of war. We do not know King's reasoning on this critical decision, or his influence on it. Charles Brower suggests that King's acceptance was tactical, that he thought Japan would fall to the double pressures of air bombardment and naval blockade before an invasion was necessary.[49] The Navy would still control the amphibious part of the invasion and maintain a blockade. Jointness, moreover, could not be denied. King was accustomed to running a joint war. JCS decisions were unanimous. And there were other considerations at the moment, such as the prospect of Soviet entry into the Pacific war. A Soviet entry would be full of uncertain consequences. Thus although an invasion went against the thrust of Navy—and Air Force—doctrines, perhaps to King it made political sense.

It also may have made military sense. We have the record of the meeting of June 18, 1945, of the Joint Chiefs with President Harry S. Truman, in which the new commander in chief approved the Kyushu invasion. There King said that the U.S. casualties (dead and wounded) expected in capturing the island would be between the 31,000 Luzon losses and the (then approximated) 41,700 casualties of the Okinawa campaign. The sense of the meeting was that Japan would surrender when southern Kyushu was taken. One can interpolate from this an expectation of fewer than 20,000 American deaths, and it may have been the tolerable cost that the invasion plan presented that led King to give it his support.[50]

The logistical preparations for a one-front war were under way before Okinawa fell. Germany had surrendered on May 8, and at once an immense redeployment of Army troops and supplies from Europe to the Pacific began. A total of 155,354 soldiers were redeployed directly to the Pacific between May 12 and August 25, 1945, and of the 886,000 sent from Europe to the United States, between one-half and two-thirds were designated to go to the Pacific from there.[51]

The Navy was ready for the invasion. By mid-August, 90 percent of its forces of submarine size or larger were in the Pacific. The numbers are staggering: 1,137 combatant ships, 14,847 combat aircraft, 2,783 large landing craft, and thousands and thousands of smaller landing craft, all supported by over 400 advance bases and hundreds of ships for the Pacific Fleet Service Squadrons. Here was deployed "the greatest naval force and the most extensive system of logistic support in the history of warfare."[52]

This force was not used, and there was no invasion of Kyushu, because on August 14 the government of Japan declared its intention to surrender. The determining events were the entry of the Soviet Union into the war and the dropping of the second atomic bomb, on Nagasaki. Japan faced insurmountable disaster. America's unremitting pressure had destroyed popular morale and the country's defensive capability. An advance across the continent by the Soviet Union, the state that throughout the 1930s had been the primary threat to Japan's security, was about to destroy Japan's mainland holdings and reach the islands themselves. The United States showed it could deliver weapons of unimagined power, and its forces at sea were preparing an invasion. Japan had nothing left. The emperor decided that his direct intervention was necessary to prevent Japan's cultural suicide, its material destruction, and its social and religious collapse.

On September 2, 1945, the Japanese government formally surrendered on the U.S. battleship *Missouri* in Tokyo Bay. Victorious men-of-war spread across the water to the horizon. At the moment of surrender, 400 B-29s and 450 planes from the fleet carriers swept above the *Mis-*

souri's deck. It was the apotheosis of American military power. The war was over.

In World War II, 57,595 Navy men were either killed or missing. Another 94,165 were wounded. The Marine Corps lost 26,267 men, and 67,207 were wounded. The Coast Guard lost 1,917 men, with 955 wounded. Of the merchant marine, 881 died, and 4,780 were counted missing. A total of 502 Navy ships were sunk, of which 156 were combatants. For a country that treasured its men and used its resources with great care, these figures are a measure of its commitment to sea power—and of the sacrifice of its maritime services—in the great victory.

PART TWO

FROM THE SEA

12

Why Do We Need a Navy? 1945-1949

THE NEED TO REBLUE

In September 1945, at the moment of the Navy's apotheosis, Navy Secretary James Forrestal appeared before the House Committee on Naval Affairs and asked, "Why should we maintain any Navy after this war?"[1]

Forrestal was facing up to the question asked with increasing acerbity by the Army Air Forces and by cost-conscious members of Congress who said that the offensive Navy had worked itself out of a job. The only foreseeable enemy lay deep within a distant continental landmass and had no offensive fleet. Absent a maritime enemy, and with air-atomic warfare the apparent mode of the future, the Navy did not have a mission. The Navy's offensive sea-control doctrine had become irrelevant. The force supporting that doctrine could be demobilized or transferred. History had passed the offensive Navy by. The service should return to its pre-Mahanian task of patrol.

When the Navy replied that it was now a modern triphibious force, centered around the projection potential of attack aircraft carriers and amphibious assault, critics responded that the era demanded functional specialization and command centralization. The AAF should take over carrier air and the Army should take over the Marine Corps. What could the Navy do that the AAF could not? Why did the Navy need the

Fleet Marines? There were no islands to invade in a war against the Soviet Union. The model of the next war was the European campaign of World War II, not the war in the Pacific; and in Europe at the great amphibious invasions, there were neither aircraft carriers nor marines. In a war of the future, the Navy would be a support service.

AAF officers confidently proclaimed a new military destiny. Their long battle for autonomy was confirmed in 1947 when the Army Air Forces became the United States Air Force, an independent branch of the military, coequal with the Army and the Navy. Air Force proponents resembled the battle-fleet admirals of 50 years before: both promoted the doctrine of the knockout blow. Like the admirals, advocates of strategic bombing mixed logic and wishful thinking in a doctrine attractive for its simplicity. Like the admirals, their enthusiasm was based on a premise only partially tested by experience. Air-power enthusiasts spoke to a public tired of war, to people entranced with the imagery of the airplane, eager to endorse the aesthetics and economy of a quick, remote victory delivered by a few pilots. The Air Force took over the most popular Navy positions—and turned them against the Navy.

Command of the air replaced command of the sea as the main determinant of national destiny. The air was now, or would soon be, the world's new wide common, its great highway. Indirect sea wars, based on blockade and attrition, took time. Air power acted immediately on the enemy's capacity and will, attacking directly the heart of the enemy's homeland without having to engage a fleet, assault the land, or confront an army in battle. Air bombardment was the cheapest, most efficient way to project power.

A. P. De Seversky wrote during the war:

> Clearly the time is approaching when even the phrase "sea power" will lose all real meaning. All military issues will be settled by relative strength in the skies. At that time, I dare to foresee, by the inexorable logic of military progress, the Navy as a separate entity will cease to exist. The weapons it represents will have atrophied to the point where it is, at best, a minor auxiliary of air power.[2]

The Navy could not deny that technology had changed the relative strategic importance of nature's elements. Weapons systems in the air did move faster and were more maneuverable than those upon the sea. The Navy recognized that fact when it made the air wing of the attack carrier its postwar centerpiece, and opened half a century of debate on naval purpose. The Navy as well as the Air Force started developing guided missiles. Naval officers no longer looked at the world through a gun barrel.

But if the Navy had started looking at the world exclusively through a bomb bay, it would have ceased to be the Navy. The Navy was ships, or it was nothing. On the other hand, to maintain the carriers at the center of its offensive functions, to lay claim to what was generally conceded to be the central military weapon of the day, it had to hold on to naval air.

The Navy's diversity had been its strength. At the end of 1945 it was its vulnerability. Diversity was not consistent with the idea that the armed services should be organized not on the basis of tradition or function, but on the basis of weapons systems and the physical environment in which they moved. What flies belonged to the Air Force. What went on land belonged to the Army. What sailed belonged to the Navy. There was at the same time an increasingly strong congressional call, based on the experiences of joint commands during the war, for a merger of all the services into a single national defense establishment under a unitary command.

The need to justify itself came upon the Navy with unnerving suddenness and left the service confused. The Navy was hard put to counter the Air Force's appropriation of its most popular concepts. The Navy did not know what to do about its ships, its aircraft, or the atomic bomb, that wonder weapon that was gaining strategic primacy and budgetary advantage. And it did not know how to respond to the political pressure for unification of the services.

The postwar Navy was not prepared for peacetime politics. In part, that was a consequence of Roosevelt's vague postwar policy. Roosevelt's wartime goals of unconditional surrender and alliance solidarity had taken the urgency out of postwar strategic planning. His hazy internationalism suggested order and cooperation, not a reversion to competition in a hostile, fragmented world in which the Navy would defend, as it had for 50 years, the interests of an insular America. From the political perspective, preparedness was called for if America was to be one of the policemen of the world, but no one knew how the beats would be divided around the globe. Would the United States look after the western hemisphere and the Pacific and Britain and the Soviet Union look after Eurasia? Navy planners blithely assumed that the nation would want a peacekeeping force of at least 5 task forces, each consisting of 2 large carriers, 1 fast battleship, 6 cruisers, and 27 destroyers.[3]

Navy leaders had assumed that sea power was a notion sufficiently appreciated to enable the service to be kept at a high level of preparedness without much discussion. The Navy is by nature highly mobilized, and preparedness is a service principle. M-Day (mobilization day) is every day for ships at sea. At the end of 1945, preparedness was in effect a substitute for strategy. Officers assumed that the Navy's wartime service had earned it comfortable sea room in Washington. As a consequence, the Navy had deferred long-range planning and neglected its public relations. The service enjoyed a force cushion of hundreds of ships remaining from the war, which it planned to modernize as needed. It thought it could postpone for a decade costly and politically contentious force-building decisions. Preparedness did not even have to be directed at an enemy. In 1945 Navy preparedness reflected a continued insecurity. The memory of Pearl Harbor, the experience of the war, and the yet undigested impact of the atomic bomb each contributed to a belief in the importance of continued mobilization, even before the Soviet Union was declared the national foe.[4]

Preparedness fell victim to the economizers. In 1946 Congress turned aside Secretary Forrestal's request to limit demobilization and keep an active and reserve fleet of over 6,000 ships. As far as Congress was concerned, the United States had command of the sea and was in no danger of losing it. Congress did not consider other uses of the Navy—power projection ashore, for instance, or intervention in limited wars. Predictable postwar retrenchment whittled the Navy down. The Bureau of Ships canceled construction of almost 10,000 ships; over 2,000 were put into moth balls; and about 7,000 were declared surplus. On June 30, 1945, the number of naval personnel on active duty stood at 3,380,817. Five years later, at the end of June 1950, as the United States entered the Korean War, the number of men and officers on active duty was only 381,538.[5]

Insufficient planning and poor articulation of needs was also the result of the secretiveness of the Navy's high command. During the war Admiral King had not talked to his staff about general policies. "As a result," recalled Admiral Arleigh Burke,

> people in the navy did not know very much about strategy. . . . That's why we did not have any organization to lay out the navy's case or defend ourselves. . . . We suffered from a lack of knowledge within the navy of what the navy was all about and how the navy was going to be run. . . . [Accepting that ignorance] was an ingrained attitude, and it had terrible consequences. . . . Not that [naval officers] didn't believe in [support for a pro-Navy position], but they didn't believe they should do anything about it.[6]

Strategic thinking was shrouded in secrecy. Few naval officers wanted to get involved in forecasting or in public relations, and fewer still wished to take part in interservice squabbles. In the Naval War College's copy of Vincent Davis's *The Admirals Lobby*, at the place where the author argues the need for an effective public relations office in the Navy, a reader wrote, "A sailor's place is on his ship, a ship's place is at sea."

For another reason as well, the Navy was reluctant to plan too far ahead. Diversity had to be protected, for it was what gave the Navy its strategic, and hence its political, latitude. If Navy planners got too specific, they would not only draw the attention of rivals from without, but they would also create competition among the Navy's own communities—pilots, surface-warfare officers, submariners, and the Marines. So the CNOs focused on balance and cohesion. Keeping the service intact meant continual adjustment within the Navy. That discouraged long-range planning.[7]

Above all, Navy leaders wanted to avoid institutional fracture. Their nightmare was a breakaway of one of the Navy's specialties or its absorption by another service. That had happened when the Army lost its air force, and with it control of tactical air. If the Air Force took over naval aviation, the Navy would be left simply to sail floating airfields, unable even to guarantee their safety, for closely held tactical air was part of the defense of the carriers. But how should the Navy make its case for diversity, in the face of increasingly ferocious competition between the services and the related pressure for service unification? What, for instance, could the Navy say to the Army's claim that the Army should take over the Marine Corps so the corps could be absorbed into a more appropriate land-force context?

Navy ineffectiveness in reacting to calls for unification angered the Marine Corps. Its commandant, General Alexander Vandegrift, said: "I feel that our Navy friends have rested too long on their laurels and the belief that no harm could come to them. . . . This is not the day when knighthood was in flower and it's more like a street brawl than a tilting joust."[8] At the end of 1945, the Navy undertook a modest effort to stem the tide, by forming a temporary organization, called Scoror, to argue against weapons specialization and operational unification. But Scoror's small 69-member staff, even with Vice Admiral Arthur Radford as point man, made no headway against the well-oiled juggernaut of the Air Force.

The threat to Navy independence and structure remained. Operational unification would mean the end of naval air. In the name of weapons specialization, air forces in Great Britain and in Germany had taken control of the land-based air of those countries' navies. Centralization of the control of aircraft meant Navy subordination to the Air Force. That, the Navy claimed, would destroy its ability to fight at sea. A swiftly moving naval campaign required operational flexibility and command autonomy.

Sea control was behind the postwar testimony of Navy Secretary Forrestal and CNO King in 1945. Their appeal for support, however, was heavily constrained. Neither could say in public hearings that they thought Soviet submarines were capable of threatening Western use of the seas. The Soviet navy was using captured U-boats and modeling new designs on them. These gave its hitherto defensive submarine force an offensive ocean reach. New models would be equipped with the snorkel, making them less susceptible than the old boats to radar discovery. That meant that aerial surveillance by planes from escort carriers that had been perfected during the war for convoy protection would be unreliable. The most urgent sea-control need of the United States was a new form of antisubmarine warfare.

The imputation that the Soviet Union was the future enemy stayed an official secret in 1945. So did the Navy's assessment of Soviet offensive strength. As a result, the Navy could not express in public the nature of its sea-control problem. Thus it could not appeal frankly for public support. Nor could Navy leaders talk about atomic weapons, which were at the center of strategic speculation. The best they could do in public was call for a slowdown in demobilization. The value of the September 1945 congressional hearing at which Forrestal responded to the question of why the Navy was needed was, he said, "largely psychological."[9] He wanted to put the Navy's point of view before Congress, although in generalities. Forrestal answered the question by saying, "The means to wage war must be in the hands of those who hate war." An aphorism, however, is not a doctrine.

Forrestal, who remained secretary of the Navy until September 1947, when he became the first secretary of defense, had to do more. His tasks were to protect the Navy's independence and reconstitute its strategy. "It is no exaggeration to say," said Vincent Davis, "that Forrestal at this time was beginning a period of leadership that was to have a more profound and lasting influence on the thinking and political behavior of the senior naval officers than any man since Captain Mahan."[10]

Forrestal was not in a major position to influence national policy, but he had a vision of America's global position and a definite view of the Soviet Union. These ideas directed his thinking about the use of naval strength, and the Navy's role in national policy. Security for Forrestal meant armed readiness, not international cooperation. As he noted in April 1945, "Both the Army and the Navy are aware that they are not makers of policy, but they have a responsibility to define to the makers of policy what they believe are the military necessities of the United States, both for its own defense and for the implementation of its responsibility for the maintenance of world peace."[11]

The Cold War was not necessarily a direct confrontation. The Soviets might seek incremental gains on their periphery, aiming at targets of opportunity in China, central Europe, and the oil-rich Middle East. The Soviet Union was always pushing, looking for an opening to advance. Forrestal anxiously watched the movement of Soviet troops in northern Iran and southeastern Europe; the Soviet pressure for a pro-Communist settlement of the status of Trieste; and the Soviet Union's effort to induce Turkey to renegotiate the Montreux Convention, which governed sea access to the Black Sea, and so gain for itself a role in the control of the Dardanelles.[12]

Concerned that Western weakness would lead to appeasement and that appeasement would encourage aggression, Forrestal was a fervent early proponent of containment. In February 1946 the U.S. naval attaché in Moscow forwarded a copy of a long telegram written by George Kennan, and Forrestal inserted it into his private diary. In the telegram, Kennan concluded that Soviet conduct was determined but malleable. The contest with the Soviet Union would be long and demanding, Kennan said. The response of the United States should be rational counterpressure—in short, containment. It was to Forrestal that Kennan amplified his views in a private paper that Kennan then published anonymously in *Foreign Affairs* in July 1947 as the enormously influential "X" article. This article was destined to be the foundation text of the containment consensus that directed U.S. foreign policy for the next 45 years.[13]

For Forrestal, containment meant a military buildup. In general, however, containment was popular because it seemed to be a way to defeat Communism and defend the West without war. Containment, at least in its original version, was defensive, calling for a specified and limited effort, a response designed to preserve the status quo. The defense would work because it would force Soviet imperialism back upon itself, leading to the internal transformation of a flawed and frustrated system that could not relieve its internal contradictions by aggression abroad. Containment was not a form of limited war. Limited-war doctrine was hardly thought of in the late 1940s and early 1950s. A hot war with the Soviet Union, if it should happen, might be short, as the Air Force envisioned, or it might be long, as Navy planners imagined, but it would be total, a struggle between systems.

For the West, containment was a defensive and reactive strategy. It was understood, however, that there might be occasions when the West would initiate the use of force as part of containment. In those cases, especially where the United States lacked air bases and garrisons, the Navy's capabilities counted. The Navy's advantages were those of ships: mobility, readiness, versatility, and a seaborne force with land-projection capability that was easily inserted and just as easily withdrawn. The Navy offered policymakers flexibility of response and the options of quick and precise air strikes and cannon shots—in short, instruments more discriminating and more available than the unwieldy club of Air Force bombers and atomic war.

For example, in 1946 Forrestal sent the battleship *Missouri* to Turkey to take home the body of the Turkish ambassador, who had died in Washington during the war. The anchoring of the *Missouri* in the Bosporus was meant to show that the United States recognized the strategic importance of the eastern Mediterranean, upon whose waters warships, including aircraft carriers (which were, in effect, floating air bases), could move 2,500 miles along the southern edge of Europe. Forrestal originally wanted to send more than just a symbol to the Mediterranean. He wanted the Eighth Fleet, the Atlantic Fleet's striking arm, to accompany the *Missouri* and to stay in the Mediterranean for maneuvers, as the first step toward establishing a permanent naval presence there.

The administration did not approve sending the Eighth Fleet. In 1946 the government was in the last stage of its hope of settling issues with the Soviet Union by diplomatic agreement. Still, President Truman was happy to signal some encouragement to Turkey and Greece, and in February 1946 he agreed to let the *Missouri* sail to Istanbul and to stop at Athens on its way home.[14]

The *Missouri*'s trip that spring showed what the Navy could do that the Army and Air Force could not. The Navy could deploy enormous power to troubled areas without making any regional commitments. Air Force bombers and Army divisions needed bases on land, and hence local arrangements. Ships did not. They had no foreign commitments and set their own timetables. Mobile force could be sent, kept, and withdrawn as desired. Ships could be held continuously on station, supplied from the United States by long-range under-way replenishment. The independent presence of naval power could be put to political use, and such use could be converted instantly to active force. A warship was at all times, as it is today, both an offensive and a defensive weapon.

The battleship's visit did not cause the Soviets to reduce their diplomatic pressure on Istanbul or to stop assisting the Greek rebels. Yet an observer could imagine that the visit showed U.S. support for the Montreux Convention and showed an American interest in Balkan stability. It may have been a deterrent to aggression.[15] Deterrence, however, is an uncertain business. We do not know the reasons for Soviet restraint. But where inaction may be viewed as invitation, it is wiser to act. The *Missouri*'s visit showed the United States was not deserting Europe.

Official Washington was at the same time hardening toward the expansion of Soviet influence in southeastern Europe and in the Near East. Gloomy logistical studies foretold the importance of Persian Gulf oil and its vulnerability to a Soviet advance.[16] The *Missouri*'s visit to the Mediterranean encouraged the Navy to undertake other missions of presence and to begin the introduction of carriers into that sea. In the summer of 1946, Admiral Nimitz, King's successor as CNO (December 1945–December 1947), sent Vice Admiral Bernhard Bieri in the cruiser *Fargo* to the contested city of Trieste. As in the case of the *Missouri*, the *Fargo*'s deployment was more a nineteenth-century-style showing-of-the-flag than a specific move in foreign policy. Bieri asked whether the State Department had approved his visit. Forrestal said no. Policy and strategy kept only presumptive company. Forrestal told Bieri: "For your own information, it is my hope that the American policy will be to have units of the American Navy sail in any waters in any part of the globe. I am anxious to get this established as a common practice so that the movements of our ships *anywhere* will not be a matter for excitement or speculation."[17]

In August 1946 the world's largest carrier, the *Franklin D. Roosevelt*, was sent to the eastern Mediterranean in direct response to a Soviet troop buildup on the Turkish border. The ship's presence introduced the possibility of deep penetration inland by carrier aviation. Potentially, the carrier could carry atomic bombs. The month before, Forrestal had asked President Truman for authorization to prepare naval air to deliver atomic weapons. In the opening stage of a general war, while the Army and the Air Force mobilized, and until *naval forces* seized and secured advance land bases for use by the Air Force's long-range bombers, carrier air would be the West's main offensive strike force.[18]

The British welcomed the transfer of power to the United States. The London *Sunday Observer* wrote: "For the first time in 250 years the active assertion of sea power in the Mediterranean rests with a country other than Britain. . . . The United States assuming the historic role of British diplomacy had undertaken the lead in opposing Russian demands for the control of the Straits."[19]

British naval officers told their American counterparts that the defense of the Mediterranean was part of the defense of Britain.[20] For certain Navy planners the Mediterranean was the critical theater. There, as Vice Admiral Forrest Sherman told President Truman in a briefing in January 1947, the U.S. counteroffensive would begin. The Mediterranean was where the United States could best use its "sea, air and amphibious strength in which [it could] be vastly superior."[21] The full meaning of the signals emanating from Britain came later that year when the British handed responsibility for maintaining stability in the eastern Mediterranean to the United States, which accepted it through the Truman Doctrine of 1947.

At the end of 1946 Forrestal received permission to establish in the Mediterranean a peacetime force of cruisers, destroyers, and an aircraft carrier. The Navy promptly established a Mediterranean task force that in 1950 was designated the Sixth Fleet. This was a complete departure from the prewar practice of concentrating the Navy in the western hemisphere and a return to nineteenth-century practices of stationing ships in friendly ports. And, if necessary, the Sixth Fleet could stand alone from these ports, which meant that it was an entirely independent instrument. The creation of the Sixth Fleet ended the priority of the Pacific, which had governed the Navy's thinking for a quarter of a century. At the same time, containment was a global policy and required that force be deployed in forward positions. If the United States was to be kept from the horrors of war, Forrestal had written during World War II, "we must hit our enemies at great distances from our shores."[22] All postwar strategy of the Army, Navy, and Air Force reflected that thought. The Navy's claim during these years was that it was the best service for the purpose.

ATTACK AT THE SOURCE

In the summer of 1946 Washington gave up hope of cooperating with the Soviet Union. While demobilization in both countries showed a profound war weariness and wish for recovery, U.S. military officers anticipated some form of Soviet aggression. The most valuable prize was Europe. Few doubted that Soviet aggression there would mean general war.

For this eventuality, but without political guidance on such a war's purpose, the Joint Chiefs in 1946 and 1947 drew up joint war plans. Independent of this planning, and entirely within the Navy, Vice Admiral Sherman was working up a new naval strategy.

Only a month after V-J Day, Joint Staff planners "on their own initiative" submitted to the Joint Chiefs a study for an offensive strategy in response to a possible Soviet aggression. Devising such a strategy was "the most difficult problem to resolve from a military point of view."[23]

Not surprisingly, the first joint plans extrapolated from World War II. The war with the Soviet Union was expected to be global and total—nothing less. Plans were made to "enlarge our strategic frontier," keep "a prospective enemy at the maximum possible distance," and establish advance bases in "areas well removed from the United States." Admirals King and Leahy on the Joint Chiefs argued for a defense in depth in the Pacific, a zone under American control running from Alaska through the Aleutians to the Philippines and back to Hawaii, one element of which would be forward bases in the Marshall, Mariana, and Caroline island groups.[24] For the next decade, and despite Korea, the services gave no doctrinal consideration to anything less than a general war. They did not plan for a limited war with the Soviets or with anyone else.

It was that unlimited cast of mind, combined with the restrictive military budgets, that fostered the decisive-strategic-bombing doctrine and gave air-atomic war its pride of place in American strategy. "Strategy wears a dollar sign," Bernard Brodie said, and bombs were cheaper than men. Because bombs fell from the air, and because only very large land-based bombers of the Air Force could carry very large weapons, the Air Force argued that it should have a monopoly on atomic bombs. That would exclude Navy air from an atomic role. The Navy refused to be cut out of a share in what was becoming the predominant postwar weapons system, or to be denied a share of the dollars associated with that system. To justify its participation, it had to find an alternative to decisive-bombing doctrine. For a different use of atomic weapons, it had to posit a different form of war.

In doing this the Navy had to accommodate a certain level of contradiction. The Navy could never cut its line to sea control, which was its reason for being. Sea control was the basis of a maritime strategy that assumed a protracted war of attrition. Air-atomic war, on the other hand, meant deep strikes onto land. If the service was going to find a place for naval air in the atomic era, it had to make such strikes a Navy mission. That would save the offensive, forward-deployed carrier fleets, and save naval air. At the same time, the Navy had to deny the Air Force's contention, on which its claim to atomic privilege was based, that strategic atomic bombing would be decisive.

The leaders of the postwar Navy rejected out of hand the idea that naval strategy should be essentially defensive, that it should concentrate on support and supply, following the Atlantic model of World War II and not the Pacific one. That would have turned the Navy into a transport service and antisubmarine force that concerned itself exclusively with sea control and thus needed no attack carriers or Fleet Marines.[25] In the anxious, confused 1940s, it is no surprise that the Navy, increasingly dominated by its aviators and its memories of the war, protected its offensive, carrier-fleet position. That was what brought it into conflict with the Air Force.[26]

Admiral King prepared the ground for a post-Mahanian naval doctrine in his final report to the secretary of the Navy in December 1945:

> Our fleet in World War II was not solely engaged in fighting enemy fleets. On numerous occasions a large part of the fleet effort was devoted to operations against land objectives. A striking example is the capture of Okinawa. During the three months that this operation was in progress our Pacific Fleet—the greatest naval force ever assembled in the history of the world—was engaged in a continuous battle which for sustained intensity has never been equaled in naval history; yet at this time the Japanese Navy had virtually ceased to exist—we were fighting an island, not an enemy fleet.[27]

As CNO, Admiral Nimitz had connected sea control to power projection to discount the popular contention that air power alone could win a war. His testimony at Senate hearings in 1946 expressed ancient maritime principles by which navies for millennia had acted in support of actions on land. If these principles sounded unusual, it was only because 50 years of Mahanian theory had accustomed people to thinking of naval strategy as autonomous, as if warfare at sea were a thing-by-itself and decisive in its own right. Of course, for Mahan a great battle-fleet engagement merely opened the way to the follow-on operations of blockade and support for armies ashore. Naval strategy envisions a long war. Maritime strategy, a better and broader term, supports action on land. It was the latter notion onto which Navy leaders hoped to graft naval aviation.

Nimitz began by arguing against the Air Force's appropriation of the notions of autonomous operations and swift decision:

> Fleets do not exist only to fight other fleets and to contest with them the command of the sea. Actually, command of the sea is only the means to an end. Wars cannot be concluded by naval action alone or by air action alone. Wars are conducted and concluded by the combined action of sea, land, air, diplomatic, and economic effort. . . . Upon our sea power hinges our ability to seize, hold, and cover strategic positions, to build them into adequate bases, and to transport to them the personnel, services, equipment, food, and fuel vital to carry the war to successful conclusion.[28]

The Navy thus envisioned a war that was different from a short atomic spasm. It said that strategy was more than targeting. There were, as we shall see, influential naval-air enthusiasts who in the late 1940s thought the Navy should take advantage of an Air Force shortage of long-range planes, overseas bases, and atomic bombs to beat the competition at its own game. The more fervent Navy officers, detaching naval-air projection from the sea-control function, claimed that the Navy was an autonomous strategic air force in its own right. So great was the anxiety that the Navy might be left behind in the rapid development of air-atomic strategy that these naval officers forgot that the Navy must be about sea power, and they declared that outdoing the Air Force was the only way to save the Navy. But most naval officers held to the belief that a war against the Soviet Union would be more than bombings over a mere span of days. It would be a war of sequential campaigns in which control of the oceans would be the essential element of U.S. strategy. In this scenario, atomic weapons would play a part, but only a part, in an overall general war strategy.

The atomic bomb, therefore, did not end the need to think about war. A booklet on the Pacific war issued by the CNO's office in 1947 expressed this point:

> The fact is that there exists no single science of war. There are many sciences with which war is concerned, but war itself is a practical art and skill. It is impossible ever wholly to anticipate war's requirements. . . . Any exclusive adoption of a single weapon or type of weapon immediately limits freedom of action and greatly simplifies the enemy's problem of defense. War is a phenomenon of immense complexity whose problems are solved pragmatically by hard experience and clear thinking. There is danger that investigation of a single aspect of one war may give rise to an unbalanced interpretation. Limitations are as significant as accomplishments.[29]

Atomic bombs were part of operations, not a substitute for them. In a lengthy war, all arms would contribute. In a lengthy war, advantage would lie with the side that had world access. Such a war could be shaped into one of attrition, in which sea control would be all-important.

In this period, in 1946 and 1947, the Navy made a fundamental doctrinal commitment. It declared that regardless of whether atomic weapons were used, sea control was not something a surface fleet alone could provide. A new naval strategy was created by Vice Admiral Forrest Sherman, deputy chief of naval operations for operations. Sherman held the Navy to the tradition of forward deployment and offensive operations. He preserved the Navy's diversity of functions and forces. He kept carriers at the core of his planning and proposed that they be given the option of delivering conventional or atomic weapons. All this he presented in the name of sea control and as an alternative to the big-bang plans of air enthusiasts. Deep air strikes, with or without atomic capability, thus became part of a sea-control strategy for a forward-deployed, offensive, fleet Navy, a strategy that preserved the centrality of the aircraft carrier.[30]

Sherman assumed the next war would resemble the last one in the need to hold on in Europe until the United States could mount a sustained counteroffensive. The United States could not conduct an immediately decisive air-atomic blitz. The country had only nine atomic bombs in July 1946 and only thirteen a year later, with only two dozen B-29s modified to deliver them. These planes had a range of no more than 1,700 miles. Until advance bases were found, any attack on the main targets in the Soviet Union would be a one-way, suicide flight.[31]

Sherman told President Truman in January 1947:

> In any event we must not devote so much of our resources to development of any new weapons and techniques that as a result we are unprepared to fight an unexpected war. We must recognize the vital importance to our security of maintaining adequate forces in being to fight such a war. . . . Equally important, we must not allow ourselves or the public to think that the era of "push button" or "Buck Rogers" warfare has arrived or that it is likely to have arrived by 1956.[32]

In 1947 the expectation was that the Soviet army would be able to roll forward in Europe virtually unopposed, putting the United States on the strategic defensive. The West's response would be a war of sequential phases. The Navy's role would be to extract American troops from the continent, then to gain and hold advance bases for a counteroffensive, and then to move reinforcements across the ocean to invade Western Europe once the United States had mobilized. This, of course, had been the offensive pattern of the recent war.

These essential tasks required sea control. The threat to sea control did not come from the Soviet surface force. That force had only fifteen heavy ships, and none of them could stand up to an American counterpart. In addition, the Soviet force had no carrier. Soviet ships stayed close to home, dispersed in widely separated fleets that were based in the White and Barents seas, the Baltic Sea, the Black Sea, and the Sea of Japan. The United States could cover the exits of those waters and control the water routes between them. Stalin was a big-navy advocate and envisioned a monster fleet of battleships and carriers, but his program was unrealized. In the late 1940s, the Soviet surface navy had no depth or strategic mobility.

The sea-control threat would come from the Soviet submarine force, which amounted to some 250 boats in 1948. These boats were meant to protect the seaward flanks of the Red Army and, if called upon, to cut sea communications to Britain and across the Atlantic. Soviet submarines, together with a strong Soviet mining capability and the 2,400 to 3,000 land-based bombers directed by Soviet Naval Air, had the ability to put forward naval operations at risk. If a U.S. carrier task force was going to support the withdrawal of U.S. troops from Europe, or try to outflank the Red Army by moving up the coast of the North Sea or into the eastern Mediterranean, it would be in narrow waters and thus particularly susceptible to attacks from submarines and stand-off bombers.

At the same time, part of the Soviet submarine force would be trying to sever the Allied sea-lanes. More than half the Soviet submarines were of long or medium endurance, five were equipped with snorkel breathing-and-venting tubes, and perhaps a dozen or more were based on the new, fully submersible, German Type XXI.[33] The Red Army had captured the major German submarine bases in its sweep along the Baltic, taking back to the Soviet Union boats, construction plans, and designers as well. Stalin rehabilitated Soviet shipyards, and in 1947 the first keels of the postwar submarine fleet were laid. These activities led Americans to think that the Soviets might surpass Germany's wartime building strength within a decade.[34] The fear of German miracle boats was being realized, under Soviet command.

The Navy concluded that against these submarines, an open-ocean defensive strategy would not work. Customary antisubmarine-warfare techniques of aerial spotting, radar, and surface patrol were not enough to find true submersibles or boats fitted with snorkels. Tests with captured German Type XXIs showed that aerial observation was only 5 percent effective. The new boats could outrun World War II destroyer escorts. An effective defensive convoy strategy would be enormously costly. Thus Navy leaders opted to plan for an offensive campaign.[35]

Sherman proposed to "attack at the sources of the trouble," to deploy naval air to hit the submarines in their still-unhardened pens, and to destroy their maintenance and replenishment bases as well, cutting off support to boats out on patrol. In port, enemy submarines were easy to locate. The hornets would be killed in their nests, as President Wilson had recommended in World War I, not chased around the farm or held off by point defense at sea. Officers remembered their frustration when

German submarine pens in Atlantic ports were not bombed early and effectively in World War II. Above all, Sherman's plan was politically astute at a time when the Navy desperately needed wise and creative thinking. It pulled together many loose ends. It was a sea-control plan, giving the Navy an undeniable antisubmarine rationale for using its carrier air against coastal land targets.

Deep air strikes would be launched to protect the forward deployment of the expensive carriers. Sailing carriers close to shore to launch their short-legged 250-mile-range bombers exposed them to the extensive Soviet naval-air defense force. It is easier to hit planes on the ground, taking them by surprise and coming at them from unexpected directions, than to shoot them out of the sky, as the Navy learned in its attacks against kamikaze aircraft. Carrier air thus took on the task of striking inland airfields. Only the Navy could protect its own. The Air Force's level-flying, land-based, area bombers did not have the necessary precision. They were ineffective for reconnaissance and ship defense and for covering the amphibious landings of the Fleet Marine Force. Anyway, in the first stage of the conflict, the Air Force lacked forward operating bases. Forward operating bases, of course, are exactly what aircraft carriers are.

The doctrine of "attack at the source" expressed a practice as old as naval warfare. Nonetheless, it reconceptualized naval strategy just when the Navy needed a contemporary categorization of its position. In its justification of existing offensive force, the doctrine was as brilliant as Mahan's had been 50 years before. Power projection in the name of sea control gave the Navy a role in the late 1940s, as it would also in the 1980s. The genius of the doctrine, Norman Friedman noted, was in its equating freedom of action at sea with freedom to strike at targets on land.[36] Even the Air Force could not rebut the argument that deep land strikes served a sea-control function. While the offensive-defensive argument looked suspiciously circular and self-fulfilling, as carrier doctrine always does to critics, the Navy, in the absence of a surface threat, had found a way to tie carrier strike projection to sea control. It all fit together.

The proposed strikes by naval air were not strategic in the Air Force sense; that is, they were not will-breaking blows against the enemy's urban-industrial centers.[37] Those targets, in the Soviet Union, were beyond the reach of naval air, and, the Navy noted, beyond Air Force reach as well. That fact muted for the moment Air Force criticism. It was not until the early 1950s that the Air Force had the numbers and the reach to realize its doctrine of strategic bombardment. For the moment, all planning had to concede that a war might not be over in 72 hours. In the case of a long war, then, attack at the source was surely a strategic mission. And in these terms, the National Security Act of 1947 was a Navy victory. It denied the Air Force the control of naval aviation. The Navy could keep direct control of its carrier-based and land-based aircraft that pertained to the sea-control function.

The Navy thus found a naval reason for, and a naval method of, participating offensively in a war against a continental power. The Navy's strategy satisfied all of its own communities, fit the war plans of the JCS, and preserved the force structure the Navy had employed so successfully in the Pacific war. That this line of planning foreclosed thinking about contrary maritime strategies, virtually eliminating consideration of defensive alternatives and of limited war, bothered no Navy leader.

Indeed, taking offensive land-strike thinking a step further, the precision bombing of carrier air could be used also to support a land campaign, independent of the naval sea-control mission. Sherman wanted to establish a heavy naval strike force in the Mediterranean to cover the southern flank of Europe and penetrate to the valuable, and vulnerable, oil fields of the Middle East.

Here was a comprehensive sea-power package that made use of all the Navy's arms. With sea control, the Navy could support allies in and along maritime lands that surrounded the Soviet Union—Turkey, southern Europe, the Suez-Cairo area, Spain, the Azores, the British Isles, Iceland, the Aleutians, Japan, the Ryukyus, and the Philippines. With sea control, Marine Corps amphibious troops could secure bases on European land, the footholds that would permit the Air Force's long-range bombers to move up and begin the counteroffensive. With sea control, an Army invasion force could be put ashore and the land war supplied.

Thus Sherman's maritime strategy was based on service interdependence. He incorporated the Navy's actions into a larger, cooperative interservice campaign to retake Western Europe, the Navy being in a position and having the assets to play a crucial offensive role at the beginning. In the first phase, the Navy could, as Edward Rhodes described it, "hold the ring and prepare the way, so that the Air Force and the Army could administer a one-two knockout blow." The strategy put the Navy at the center of a transoceanic campaign in which it would be used first alone, and then for support, in a war against a distant continent. A further and immensely important dimension of Sherman's strategy was that, as Rhodes notes, it reestablished the Navy's sense of mission, gave the Navy a way to cooperate with the other services, and restored harmony among the communities within the Navy itself. It was a joint strategy in more ways than one.[38]

Finding popular support for the big Navy that Sherman's strategy required was not easy. First, the strategy was based on political assumptions—such as the likelihood of the fall of Europe, the perilous state of Britain, and the weak atomic arsenal—that were official secrets. The limitations of operating behind a security curtain constrained the Navy's search for a public endorsement. Second, Sherman's strategy was put aside in 1949 when, as we will see, a bitter interservice rivalry reemerged over control of the atomic bomb. At that time, a powerful lobby of naval aviators imagined that the Navy was threatened by Air Force advocacy of a strategic monopoly for itself, an advocacy that was based on the growing capacity of the Air Force's long-range bomber fleet. The naval aviators sought to steal the Air Force's thunder by advocating a naval strategic mission of air-atomic strikes against urban-industrial targets that lay beyond sea-control targets and beyond the areas in which, under Sherman's mandate, tactical support would be rendered to ground troops.

WAYS OF WAR

The projection of carrier air against land targets was not, originally, an atomic strategy. In 1947 the Navy made sure that its attack-at-the-source doctrine stood on its own, regardless of the weapon involved. It rejected the Air Force distinction between the so-called strategic atomic bomb and conventional ordnance. Weapons were weapons. In any case, there were precious few atomic bombs at hand, certainly not enough on which to base a strategy for war. That fact alone caused the Joint Chiefs' war plans to reflect the Navy's view of a phased and protracted war, in which sea control would give the United States one of war's most precious commodities, time—time to hold onto or to regain forward position, time to mobilize, time to launch a counteroffensive onto a distant continent.

Meanwhile, however, knowing technology never sleeps, in January 1947 the Navy got the go-ahead to develop a heavy attack carrier able to launch long-range strike aircraft that could carry an atomic bomb. That exacerbated the yet unresolved question of the proper roles and missions of the U.S. military services. Sherman's intra-Navy war planning of 1946–47 was one thing; the rough and tumble competition between the Navy and the Air Force for service functions and forces, and above all for the atomic role, was another.

Both Sherman's maritime strategy and the parallel Joint Chiefs' war planning had been generated entirely within the services. As essentially hermetic intellectual exercises, they were vulnerable to external criticism. Most notably, they were criticized for being contrived when the force needed for execution did not exist and for lacking political content.[39] Military planners had only the most rudimentary civil direction on the use of the atomic bomb. The national purpose in a general war was not much more clearly specified than a National Security Council statement to reduce or eliminate Soviet or "bolshevik" control inside and outside the Soviet Union. There was no other definition of victory and certainly no guidance on how the atomic bomb should be used. At the same time, from the military perspective, the atomic bomb became all the more important, in the face of the presumed giant Red Army, to compensate for the relatively small size of the American conventional force, which was being radically reduced by presidential insistence on budgetary restraints. On the other hand, what was one to do with the bomb? Here too planning was removed from political guidance. The first fact was that the president retained the authority to decide when and where the bomb would be used. That led to confusion about who might use the atomic weapon. It also led to unfocused planning. The tendency was simply to envision using all available weapons in a massive nuclear offensive against urban, industrial, and military targets without taking political considerations into account. That was not good war planning.[40]

The Joint Chiefs' paramount concern was the Red Army's superiority on land. The Soviet army could overrun Europe, Korea, North China, Manchuria, and the Middle East as well. It could drive British and American troops off the European continent. The first need, therefore, as Sherman realized, was to secure the British Isles and hold onto—or be prepared swiftly to regain—land bases on the periphery of Europe. From these bases, the United States would mount a counteroffensive, first by air and then by a land invasion of the continent, drawing on the American advantages of sea control, long-range air power, and the nuclear monopoly.[41]

That monopoly might in itself restrain aggression. If not, the Joint Chiefs, including CNOs Nimitz and his successor Admiral Louis Denfeld (December 1947–November 1949), agreed that atomic bombs would be used in the land war that would ensue. The Joint Chiefs, however, did not assume that atomic bombing alone would compel the Soviet government to surrender.

By 1949 the atomic arsenal had grown to around 150 bombs, each weighing 10,300 pounds. Their delivery was in the hands of the Air Force, but only a few dozen 1,700-mile-range B-29s and their assembly teams were ready for action. Final readiness involved a five- or six-day delay while the bombers were sent to advance bases in Britain or Okinawa, where specially fitted storage and loading facilities and long-range escorts and refueling aircraft were likewise virtually ready to go.[42]

More important, there was disagreement, or at best confusion, about what the country's atomic force was for. Were the bombs to be used against industrial plants, transportation systems, and people in cities (later called *countervalue targets*), or against armies, equipment, and military installations (*counterforce targets*)? Was the intent to destroy the will, or the means, to make war? Was it to destroy a nation or to win political terms in a negotiated settlement? As Navy officers suggested, might not countervalue bombing only increase the resolve of the enemy to continue the war?

One feature of the uncertainty was whether the president would permit the employment of atomic weapons at all. Atomic weapons were viewed from two perspectives, from that of the military on the one hand, and from that of political authorities on the other. Each group was divided within itself as well. In 1948, the first National Security Council study on atomic control decided there should be no advance decision "either to use or not to use atomic weapons in any possible future conflict," and none "as to the time and circumstances under which atomic weapons might or might not be employed."[43] Bomb manufacturing continued, and in large numbers, but any military planning for their use had to be undertaken without political guidance.

Nor was the basic political question answered: What kind of postwar world did the United States expect to find, or want to shape? These questions, left politically open, meant that military planning operated in something of a vacuum. The absence of guidelines, the specter of unification of the services and thus the fear of a crippling institutional loss, and the sense that there was an urgent need to position the Navy for any eventuality made all the more intense the Navy's dispute with the Air Force. The subject of that dispute came down to what each service's role would be in a war.

One Navy officer, Rear Admiral Daniel Gallery, in charge of the Navy's guided-missile program, early in 1947 proposed taking over the

Air Force's strategy, lock, stock, and barrel. Gallery argued that carrier aircraft could do what the limited-range B-29 and vulnerable B-36 bombers could not—that is, get close enough to deliver a knockout blow to the central Soviet Union. Service roles should be reversed, said Gallery. The Air Force should defend the United States and undertake secondary, follow-on missions. The Navy should be given responsibility for the initial strategic delivery of the atomic bomb. This was not only a matter of sound national strategy. It was the only way to save the Navy. No doubt Gallery was thinking too of the missiles on which he was working, which might become the dominant air-atomic weapons of the future. Who controlled air might control space. A 1947 memo by Gallery, as presented in an article by Paul Hammond, contains Gallery's proposal:

"I believe," wrote Gallery to CNO Nimitz, that the Navy has an "excellent opportunity to present its case as being the branch of the National Defense destined to deliver the Atom Bomb. Ever since the end of the war, the Navy has been on the defensive and has been answering arguments of those who say that Navies are obsolete and useless. We have been protecting ourselves against attempts to abolish the Navy—the original merger proposal. For the past two years our defense of the Navy has been based mainly on old familiar arguments about exercising control of the seas. Much has been said about anti-submarine warfare, naval reconnaissance, protection of shipping, and amphibious operations. It has been assumed, at least implicitly, that the next war will not be much different from the last one. This assumption is basically wrong, and if we stick to it the Navy will soon be obsolete. The next war will be a lot different from any previous one. It seems obvious that the next time our Sunday Punch will be an Atom Bomb aimed at the enemy capitals or industrial centers and that the outcome of the war will be determined by strategic bombing. The war will be won by whichever side is able to deliver the Atom Bomb to the enemy, and at the same time protect its own territory against similar delivery. I think 'the time is right now for the Navy to start an aggressive campaign aimed at proving that the Navy can deliver the Atom Bomb more efficiently than the Air Forces [sic] can.' "[44]

When this inflammatory memo was leaked to the press, the secretary of the Navy, John L. Sullivan (September 1947 to May 1949), and the CNO, Admiral Denfeld, immediately disavowed it. Still, it is obvious that many officers bought the Air Force line and concluded that the Navy must stake out an atomic mission or naval air would become only a limited tactical force, one adjunctive and peripheral to the air-atomic age.

Intimations of this concern could be discerned in Admiral Nimitz's farewell address as CNO in December 1947, in which he proposed that naval *land-based* air could be used for strategic bombing "on vital enemy installations," above and beyond naval-related sea-control missions. A few months later, Rear Admiral Edwin Cruise suggested that the United States might simply do away with the Air Force's land-based bomber fleet. Naval air could support sea control and fleet defense, strike naval-related targets such as submarine pens, and also take on the mission of strategic bombing. His argument was that the Navy's precision bombing of military targets was likely to be more effective in bringing the Soviet government to terms than the inaccurate area bombing of cities by the high-altitude planes of the Air Force. Cruise wrote:

> Carrier attacks can potentially be made not only on enemy urban and industrial targets [the countervalue targets of Air Force strategists], using mass destruction weapons, but with all types of weapons against the enemy's air forces and air bases. . . . Such attacks [on counterforce targets] can halt enemy bombing more quickly than can the destruction of industrial targets. They can be carried out promptly by mobile carrier forces not dependent on the prior acquisition of overseas bases.[45]

In 1947 and 1948, before the Air Force had the planes, weapons, and advance bases to launch the decisive retaliatory bombing campaign of its dreams, the Navy's association with strategic air power gave it a leg up in the scramble for appropriations. In 1948 the vice CNO, Vice Admiral Arthur Radford, the highest-ranking Navy aviator, called for supplemental appropriations for a full naval-air program that would include strategic missions—that is, missions beyond those related to sea control and direct support of an invasion. For all the talk of a rounded naval strategy, for all of Sherman's insistence on joint operations and sea control as the rationale for projecting naval air power over the beach, the aviators in 1948 started to lead the Navy up the Air Force's garden path. They were convinced that if there was going to be any expansion of Navy responsibility it was going to be in strike aviation. And that was the direction in which they headed the Navy to the fullest extent possible, which meant claiming that the Navy should be given use of the atomic bomb.[46]

This tilt toward the deep strike and strategic bombing reflected changes in Navy leadership. In 1947 Nimitz retired as CNO and Forrestal left the Navy Department to become secretary of defense. Sherman left Washington in January 1948 to head the task fleet in the Mediterranean. Those men had by and large cooperated with the other services, planned joint strategies, and kept the Navy tied to its sea-control birthright, while maintaining the carrier at the Navy's core. In their place came the full-air-program proponents Admiral Louis Denfeld, who became CNO in December 1947, and his vice chief, Vice Admiral Radford.

Denfeld and Radford held the view that an air-atomic war would be short and that in a short war sea control would be less necessary. So it made sense to shift Navy emphasis toward air-power projection and an atomic mission. Others in the naval establishment thought the carrier aviators were becoming too much like the Air Force and that they misjudged the Navy's role in the next war and perhaps the nature of that war itself. According to these critics, the business of the Navy, and the Navy's top priority, was sea control. To concede that was to give up the Navy.

To bring the service back to basics, to an independent position less exposed to a certain Air Force counterattack, the General Board in 1948, through the pen of then Captain Arleigh Burke, drew up a report entitled "National Security and Navy Contributions Thereto Over the Next Ten Years." The report called for the Navy to return to "established concepts and techniques of war." It did not reject atomic bombing but noted that bombing alone could not win a war. Prudence called for preparing broadly. "We must be wary of our national predilection for panaceas [i.e., atomic bombs], which tempts us to act as though future possibilities were today's facts. Concentration of available resources upon a single concept of war, method, or tool is an almost irretrievable act." Atomic bombing might suggest decisive battle; but such bombing would not in fact be decisive. A meaningful political victory was not to be won by turning cities into radioactive ash heaps. A war with a great power like the Soviet Union would be a long war. The Navy's job was to keep the war overseas and help mount the counteroffensive, not to fight the whole war. The sea was the primary line of communication between America and the rest of the world. Accordingly, the first job of the Navy, and of the fast-carrier task forces, was sea control.[47]

Sea control meant antisubmarine warfare. Since Sherman, that meant bombing naval targets ashore. The General Board did not deny the air arm. "The greatest single threat to United States military effectiveness overseas," it said,

> is the possibility of an efficient enemy submarine force using submarines equal to or better than the German type 21. . . . [It is] imperative that every effort be made to deny enemy submarines access to the open seas immediately upon the outbreak of war. . . . The submarine danger may become so great that the carrier task force initial effort may have to be devoted to destroying submarine bases or sealing submarine exits by atomic bombing or mining.[48]

To meet this submarine threat, British and American submarines were in the first instance to be deployed in the Barents Sea off the Kola Inlet, in the approaches to the White Sea, in the Kattegat, and in the western approaches to the Baltic.[49]

The problem was, the General Board warned, that the Navy at current funding might be promising more than it could deliver.

> The Navy's initial tasks of control of the seas, occupation or seizure of advanced bases, attacks on Russian bases and denial of advanced bases to Russia, combined with the enormous logistic supporting effort for the other services and our allies, will place so many demands upon the Navy for immediate operations in widely separated parts of the world that fulfillment of all demands may well be beyond the capacity of the Navy in being. Accordingly, it is imperative that a priority list of operations be prepared so that no time will be lost by indecision or rearrangement of forces when war starts.[50]

Naval aviation should thus stick to sea-control basics.

This debate on naval strategy stayed hidden from public and congressional view. Sherman refused to issue a declassified version of his strategic thinking.[51] Burke regarded his General Board report as solely for internal use. It was true that some issues required secrecy or were best left for professional judgment. They included such questions as, How far should the Navy penetrate into Soviet maritime zones? Did submarines or land-based air pose the greater danger to that penetration? What was the optimal mix of attack bombers and surface ships? Other matters, however, would have benefited from wider discussion: What was the carrier's role going to be in a war? Should the Navy be assigned strategic bombing? Was the United States prepared to fight a long war? Were there strategic alternatives to general war? Until the Navy issued an official position and overcame its disinclination to engage in public instruction, it seemed to outsiders that it was more concerned with Potomac battles for status and funding than with explaining how it intended to fight a war at sea.

WHO WILL DO WHAT WITH WHAT?

In the skeptical and parsimonious postwar environment, Navy reticence was costly. Captain Walter Karig, an officer experienced in Navy publicity, wrote to CNO Denfeld in 1948 that the Navy would necessarily be what the people wanted it to be, and so the Navy's public-relations task was to educate the public in what the Navy should be. Karig later that year unbuttoned his exasperation to a committee inspecting public relations for the Navy secretary:

The Navy prides itself on precision in gunnery, precision in bombing, precision in courts martial and real estate procurement, but in public relations it still uses the technique of the manure spreader (But it isn't spreading awfully good fertilizer). The output as a whole is dull, uninspired, tardy. The element of zeal, esprit de corps, all the devotion to a cause that the Air Force exhibits, is lacking. (I don't know how it can be acquired, either.)[52]

"You can't peddle prestige from a push-cart," Karig warned. The Navy had kept public relations "on a par with garbage collecting." He claimed that "the be-all of Navy Public Relations is appropriations."[53]

The problem was more than how to make a pitch. The administration told no service what was expected of it, beyond saving money, because nothing much was. Straitened budgets were not met with creative thinking. From reduced forces came limited options. The services had to choose between weapons systems (between carriers and submarines, for instance), decide whether to modernize or maintain out-of-date equipment, and choose how much, and where, to reduce research and development. But there was no external guidance on how to make these decisions, and that bred interservice competition.[54]

Forrestal had cast preparedness in broad Mahanian terms, according to which the country at large—producers, the public, and the military—would unite in a common concern for national security and act in self-adjusting cooperation.[55] That view disappeared in the uncontrolled interservice rivalry that resulted from the draconian cuts made under Louis Johnson, Forrestal's successor as secretary of defense. Johnson served in the post from March 1949 to September 1950. The services' first priority became just staying intact. Under a mercantilist defense budget, in which Johnson sent up a single request for appropriations over which each service then fought, zero-sum thinking prevailed. Increases for one service could be gained only at the expense of another. Johnson made the decisions. If he did not, or delayed, the anxious and self-conscious services turned on one another.

At the same time, the Navy's flexibility was getting a bad name. Here is a representative view of a later observer, political scientist Edward Kolodziej, on the Navy's budget requests for fiscal year 1947, written evidently without an understanding of the effort by Forrestal and Sherman to establish Navy missions and functions:

The flexibility of naval planning was precisely the issue of concern. It was too flexible. The changing conditions to which it was readjusted were determined more by budgetary constraints than by strategic imperatives. . . . There was no precise linkage between navy planning and probable military conflicts abroad. . . . Still, the justification of a navy plan had to rest on a projection of its political consequences abroad and, relatedly, of its impact on shifting international power positions that affected American interests. The navy did not present its estimates in this more complicated, yet more relevant, framework. . . . Governed principally by budgetary, not foreign policy, considerations, the services filled the political vacuum in which they operated with elaborately developed plans and detailed requests for equipment and trained personnel, guided largely by their own inflated conceptions of their particular roles in a future war.[56]

In reality, the Navy's view was that only through a flexible strategy could the United States shape a protracted war to take advantage of "shifting international power positions." This view made excellent sense. But it was by nature indefinite and little known, and hence unable to hook the public. Decisive-bombing doctrine, on the other hand, captured imaginations and suggested economy (as well as inspiring horror). The prospect of protracted war did neither. Outsiders did not recognize the practical limits of bases, bombers, and bombs. What the public did know was that conventional forces were expensive. So were long wars. For 50 years U.S. strategic culture was unwilling to stand the political and social costs of extensive and protracted mobilization when cheaper and socially unobtrusive high-tech air- and nuclear-weapons systems promised a quick decision.

Captain Arleigh Burke told President Truman: "The navy is very much in the same position with regard to public relations as a virtuous woman. Virtue is seldom spectacular . . . and naval philosophy and maritime strategy are not spectacular either. . . . Success depends upon long, dull hours of hard work and there's no action that's clearly decisive by itself. Final success is dependent upon a series of previous small actions."[57] That was true enough. But virtue does not always prevail.

The Navy might have improved matters by some systematic long-range planning. It did not. After the few studies of 1947 and 1948, the Navy Department reassigned the most imaginative members of the General Board to current operations. Burke, for instance, was sent to sea, although in less than six months he was brought back to advise on the great public squabble of 1949, the supercarrier vs. B-36 debate, to which we shall shortly turn.

A try at planning was made in 1949 by the Organizational Research and Policy Division (OP-23). Inspired by Burke, this effort came late, when the interservice storm was at its height, and focused too narrowly on tactics of debate. As Burke said, "We finally came to the conclusion that what we were trying to do was to give a one-lesson course on sea power, and nobody learns anything in one hour."[58] Secretary of the Navy Francis P. Matthews (1949–51) in fact was so incensed at OP-23 for setting up congressional testimony that contradicted the administration's position that he impounded its office and put Burke, for some hours, under house arrest. To control public relations, Matthews in 1949 created the two-star position of chief of information, to serve both the CNO and the secretary. But there was no Mahan to win broad popular support for the Navy. His spirit had been captured by the Air Force.

In 1951 Matthews abolished the General Board, claiming it had outlived its usefulness in an era when the Defense Department was looking toward the creation of unified commands. This was a loss to the service. After 1951, strategic estimates were made by the Strategic Studies Branch (OP-303) of then Rear Admiral Arleigh Burke's new Strategic Plans Division (OP-30) or handed down by war planners in the form of annual five-year Joint Strategic Objective Plans and fifteen-year Joint Long Range Strategic Estimates. These plans gave some guidance for force levels. But they were not the same as long-term naval or maritime strategies. A systematic long-range strategic planning process was not reconstituted in the Navy Department until 1954, when the department's Strategic Plans Division moved to the Office of the Deputy CNO for Plans and Policy (OP-60). A year later, with the creation of the Long Range Objectives Group (OP-93), long-range planning was moved to a more central location, the Office of the CNO.[59]

WAR PLANS

Joint war planning did not help. Tough decisions were deferred. In the spring of 1948, for instance, the Joint Staff working up the long-range plan called Bushwacker was not able to resolve the central operational dispute over whether the Air Force or the Navy would conduct the strategic air campaign, although with the force at hand neither could claim an ability to do so.[60] The matter remained moot because, as a JCS staffer, Rear Admiral Cato D. Glover, noted, Bushwacker "employs the forces in being as of 1 July 1948 and that there are therefore no questions [that is to say, rationales] concerning justification [strategic or organizational] for the forces. It is for this reason and this reason only that we are able to submit this Plan without a solution."[61] In response, the JCS simply ordered short-range emergency plans to fit the budget, not the perceived threat.[62]

The Navy was still in the atomic game. The National Security Act of 1947 had denied the Air Force control of naval aviation and stated that the Navy could control its own carrier-based aviation as well as its land-based planes that pertained to its sea-control mission, or that were, in the words of the act, "organic therein." The law saved naval air. But it did not settle the air-atomic controversy. To decide "who will do what with what," Forrestal, recently installed as secretary of defense, in March 1948 called a meeting of the service chiefs in Key West. From that meeting came a service-functions paper that conceded to the Navy several further crucial points. One was the continuation of the Marine Corps, which was limited to four divisions, with the stipulation that the Navy not create "a second land army." The next point was the Air Force's acknowledgment that the Navy had a right to atomic weapons, or, more precisely, that each service could "carry through the development stage any . . . new weapons development program." This came with the proviso that the Navy would not develop a strategic air force, that function being reserved to the Air Force. The Navy, however, was given the right to attack targets "inland or otherwise" to accomplish its mission, which was left vague enough to include the contribution naval air might make to "strategic air warfare." By this agreement, the Air Force accepted Navy participation, in Forrestal's words, in an "all-out air campaign," including support of land operations that went beyond the Navy's sea-control function. Thus the Navy could develop carrier air and an air-atomic arm and attack land targets, as long as the service did not try to create a "strategic air force," whatever that was. Many in the Navy thought the term had no meaning.[63]

These agreements could not be relied on. A few days after Key West, even Forrestal backed away from Navy access to nuclear weapons. At a later meeting of the JCS, however, at Newport, Rhode Island, in August 1948, Forrestal's irresolution and a sense that a growing abundance of atomic bombs would permit overlapping missions, led to a renewed acceptance of the Navy's role in the country's air-atomic strategy. Compromise dealing between the service chiefs saved the supercarriers, but the Newport decision was, as Forrestal's biographers wrote, "perhaps the first major example of the political logrolling which later became the principal means of doing business in the Joint Chiefs of Staff." Ambiguity and feuding continued, and Forrestal was either not able or not willing to resolve the structural defects of the Defense Department that gave rise to often bitter disputes.[64]

The Air Force continued to disagree in principle with the idea of two air forces. Some kind of air-atomic war dominated strategic thinking, and all the more so with the continued slashing of nonatomic forces. The Joint Chiefs gave no attention to any strategic alternatives. For instance, they never took up a State Department view in 1948 and 1949 that the United States should have highly mobile divisions to fight limited wars of containment, not atomic wars of annihilation or conquest.[65] Strategy was not guided by policy and hardly by force realities. Budgeteers defined the strategic direction, acting without a policy for atomic use and without a concept of what they wanted a postwar world to look like. What was important was that bombs were cheaper than men. The result was catchall war planning.

The budget process exacerbated the disarray. Before 1947 each service had submitted its own appropriation request to Congress. The reform of 1947 put appropriation requests under the control of the secretary of defense. President Truman set a limit on what the secretary could recommend but gave no guidance on how the military forces should spend the lump sum received. Division of this single figure could come only from agreement between the services, which did not exist, or executive decision, which under Secretary Johnson was fitful and contested. Possessed of a deep fear of deficits and inflation and foreseeing little use for armed force, Truman and Congress adopted as their main aim the reduction of spending.

In mid-1948 Truman capped the military budget for fiscal year 1950 at $14.4 billion, $9.2 billion beneath the lowest combined-service estimate. The issue thereupon became how, and where, to make the cuts. The "leaderless" process, this "blind policy," led to near total confusion.[66] The General Board report of 1948 stated, "For the security of the United States we urgently need a national plan of action."[67]

The North Atlantic Treaty was signed in 1949. From then on, defense of Western Europe was the top military priority. The Joint Chiefs put their reliance on atomic weapons. In 1949 they wrote a war plan, Offtackle, to counter a Soviet invasion of Europe. Offtackle envisioned, in line with the military pessimism of the time, that the Red Army could not be held and that U.S. forces would most likely have to withdraw from the continent. For retaliation, the plan aimed at overthrowing the Soviet government and breaking up the Communist system by atomic assault. Offtackle proposed that the Strategic Air Command attack 104 Soviet cities with 220 atomic bombs, causing around 7 million casualties and dislocating some 28 million more civilians. No one could say what would be left. Europe was to be liberated by bombing the Soviet Union into political incoherence.[68] This was a far cry from the restrained and cautious policy of containment, which relied on firm resolve working over time.

The problem with Offtackle was that the Air Force in 1949 could not deliver the bombs. Nor, because of the deep penetration required, could carrier-based air. "Offtackle," the Joint Logistics Plans Committee reported, "is logistically infeasible with respect to aircraft."[69] And it was so not just with respect to aircraft. The JCS thought that the Navy would not be able to force a reentry into Western Europe until two years after the start of a Soviet invasion.

Finally, Offtackle left unresolved strong disagreement over the effectiveness of an atomic blitz and the rightness of choosing cities as targets—questions both of military feasibility and of political morality, and part of an increasingly hot Navy vs. Air Force debate. That dispute was of long standing, going back to the question of how to beat Japan.

A war should not be defined by atomic bombing, Navy officers said. High-altitude horizontal bombers could not make precision strikes, and area and terror bombing was wasteful and, some insisted, immoral. The officers recalled the Pacific campaign, in which carrier fighters, dive-bombers, and torpedo planes had hit only military targets. One could, through precise counterforce attacks and joint operations over an extended period, bring an enemy government to terms by destroying its capacity to wage war. In this way, one would avoid permanently alienating, through terror bombing, the enemy's civilian population, whose cooperation would be required for establishing peace.[70] There was much debate over how to interpret studies of the World War II strategic bombing of Germany and Japan. The Air Force claimed the studies vindicated air power. The Navy said they showed that such bombing had only limited effect and in any case had been made possible only by the establishment of advance bases such as the Navy had created in the Pacific and planned to create in a future war in Europe.[71]

"By summer 1948," David Rosenberg wrote, "it had become apparent that not only the navy's role, but its entire understanding of strategy and warfare, was being threatened: war between armed forces was being replaced by war against supporting civilian populations."[72] There is no "push-button war," Vice Admiral Radford said, "*there can be no shortcut to victory*," which meant there could be no atomic war.[73]

Perhaps most important, it was not certain that the president would authorize the use of atomic bombs. Quite the contrary. Despite all the plans for atomic war, President Truman and, after him, President Dwight Eisenhower practiced what John Gaddis has described as "self-deterrence."[74] No matter, then, what one said about an atomic offensive, it might be forbidden by the commander in chief. With that uncertainty it was impossible for the military to make realistic plans for a nuclear war. That fact increasingly made the Air Force's plans look dangerously inflexible as the Strategic Air Command targeted without political supervision.

CNO Denfeld, though a strong supporter of developing atomic bombs, said war planning could not rely on their use. What if the president refused to authorize release? What if the bombing did not work? What if the Soviets absorbed the atomic attack—there would be only one—and through their control of Europe denied the United States use of North Africa and England, thereby preventing the return to Europe of American troops? The territorial losses both in and outside Europe might be irredeemable. Europe, Turkey, the Mediterranean, the oil-rich Middle East—these were areas that the United States might never recover. Denfeld's alternative was to do everything to hold the Red Army in Europe, deploy deeply in the Mediterranean to secure lines at Cairo-Suez and Basra, hold to the maritime alliance with Great Britain, and conduct the war with conventional weapons, using atomic bombs only tactically.[75]

The Navy's argument was that atomic bombers might destroy interior Soviet cities and industrial sites but fail to bring about a political victory, fail to end the war, because deep bombing might not keep the Red Army from advancing to conquer Western Europe and the Middle East. The political need was to get the Soviet political authorities to stop the war, and the way to do that was to stop the Soviet invasion east of the Rhine. That required not huge deep-penetrating bombers, but "a tactical air force of fighters and dive-bombers suitable for strafing railroads and highways, and for blowing up bridges and munitions dumps," suitable, that is, for use against military lines of communication and supplies. "When the Russian armies are stopped short of the Rhine, their leaders and people may see that they had better negotiate a peace or else they will be in for a large-scale atomic blitz."[76]

That was the war Navy planners proposed. Such a war required a flexible doctrine and a diversified war machine capable of executing widely varied missions, such as the Navy, which, moving close to shore, would exercise its air power decisively against land forces. A strategy that relied on a single weapon system, on a single concept of operations, or any management practice that, like unification, would put services under central control, was dangerously restrictive.

A JCS document written late in World War II had put it this way:

The Navy concept [of organization] maintains that the *function* should be the basis of organization, i.e., the Army, Navy, and Air Force should be assigned basic functions and given the weapons and equipment to fulfill the functions regardless of whether the weapons operate on land, sea, or in the air. The Navy concept maintains further that the fundamental objective of all military services is essentially the same; to strike the enemy whenever and wherever he can be reached; and that no service should be artificially restricted in the employment of its weapons as opportunity offers, provided of course that the basic function is also fulfilled.

The Army–Air Force concept maintains that the *weapon* should be the basis of organization, i.e., that the Air Force, for instance, should control and operate all aircraft and perform all functions of which the aircraft is capable; the Navy should control and operate all ships, etc.[77]

These differences were reflected in a mid-1949 JCS report on the potential effects of strategic bombing. That report, named after its drafter, Air Force Lieutenant General H. R. Harmon, responded to the fact that the defense budget for fiscal year 1951, at about $13.3 billion, was even lower than that of fiscal year 1950. The report concluded that, in that circumstance, the most efficient, expeditious, and economical way to respond to a Soviet invasion of Europe was to use the atomic bomb against military targets to inflict immediate "shock and serious damage to vital elements of the Soviet war-making capacity."

The Harmon Report thus approved counterforce targeting, the kind of tactical air-atomic war against precise military targets that the Navy preferred. It downplayed the countervalue targeting of cities and the indiscriminate bombing that the Air Force had planned to use to demoralize the enemy population. An urban strategy, the report said, would backfire. "For the majority of Soviet people, atomic bombing would validate Soviet propaganda against the foreign powers, stimulate resentment against the United States, unify these people, and increase their will to fight." Earlier, the report had estimated that under current countervalue strategy, "the initial atomic offensive could produce as many as 2,700,000 mortalities, and 4,000,000 additional casualties. . . . The problems of living for the remainder of the 28,000,000 people in the 70 target cities would be vastly complicated." And complications would result not just for the people of the Soviet Union. "Atomic bombing would open the field and set the pattern for all adversaries to use any weapons of mass destruction and result in maximum retaliatory measures within Soviet capabilities."[78]

There the report ended. While its qualifications were so numerous that the chairman of the Joint Chiefs, General Bradley, called it "maddeningly ambiguous," still it challenged the Air Force's support of a strategic atomic offensive. The report's conclusion, however, was kept from the highest policy levels. The Air Force strenuously opposed the conclusion, and that service's champion, Secretary of Defense Johnson, withheld the report from President Truman. Although the report supported the contention of Navy officers, for security reasons they did not introduce it in their argument against the Air Force's way of war in their testimony in 1949 before the House Armed Services Committee.[79]

So the conflict over the use of the atom bomb festered on. The JCS was not a venue of resolution. It had no formal chairman until August 1949. The secretary of defense did not sit with it. Nor was he more successful at resolving the dispute.

Secretary of Defense Forrestal had sought to end the contentiousness in the summer of 1948. He told Air Force Chief of Staff General Hoyt Vandenberg that he supported the Air Force claim to "predominance in the field of strategic air warfare" but "would not extend that to denial of another Service of the development of a weapon which it thought it needed in its particular field." Vandenberg replied that "the whole matter, of course, came down to a question of money and that the nation could not afford to continue spending money for two duplicating programs, particularly when one involved the use of obsolescing weapons."[80]

Those "obsolescing weapons" were the Navy's heavy bombers and the new supercarrier designed to carry them. The Air Force wanted to sink at once the new Navy interest in using atomic bombs to strike at targets beyond the sea-control pale. According to the Air Force, that thinking was out of date. The Navy was no longer needed to carry planes close to the enemy homeland or to establish advance bases. The Air Force now had the B-36 intercontinental bomber, which could carry a 10,000-pound payload (the weight of each of the large bombs of the atomic arsenal) 8,000 miles. Here was the single weapon for contemporary war. The Air Force could now carry out attacks without waiting for the Navy.

Yet the Navy was trying to enlarge its missions, to extend them beyond the function of sea control. New Navy leaders had dropped the Navy's cooperative stance toward the Air Force after Sherman left for the Mediterranean. In the anxious confusion of the time, when every service was concerned that it would be hurt by budget cuts, the Navy's claims for naval air expanded.

The argument came to a head in 1949, at the point when more bombers and bigger planes both improved the Air Force's delivery system and at last put atomic delivery within the Navy's grasp as well. In April 1949 the Navy laid the keel of a huge flush-deck supercarrier CVA-58, the USS *United States*, with a standard displacement (when unfueled) of 65,000 tons. The purpose of that ship was to launch and retrieve naval attack aircraft capable of delivering atomic bombs. The plane was the AJ-1 Savage, on order for delivery in September 1949, a plane designed to take the 5-ton atomic bomb, or 10,000 pounds of conventional ordnance, to a target a thousand miles away. The range of the AJ-1 and the mobility of the supercarrier, which could deploy close to Eurasia, gave the Navy a range and operational ability comparable to those the Air Force had acquired with the B-36. That gave a new lease on life to the weakening claim of Navy aviators to an air-atomic strategy that would be both part of and independent of the sea-control function.[81]

In 1949 Navy aviators thought the moment of truth was at hand. Congress, in its enthusiasm for the B-36 and for service unification, threatened to restrict the Navy's capacity and authority to deliver the atomic bomb. If Navy deep strikes were denied, it would be, the aviators thought, the end of carrier air. Without tactical atomic delivery at the source of enemy strength, the Navy could not enforce sea control. Nor would it be able to carry out other types of atomic bombing, such as attacks on the installations of Soviet long-range bombers or, said Navy apostates, on strategic countervalue targets.

That was why the supercarrier was so important to Navy airmen. The "obsolescing weapon" was the heart of their strategy. Bigger carriers were needed for bigger aircraft. The North Atlantic Treaty was turning primary Navy attention away from the Mediterranean and toward the harsh seas of Europe's northwestern flank. There the Soviet navy was most vulnerable. There the crucial attack would be made on the source of the Soviet threat to sea control. The north was also the best direction from which to strike at some of the most important Soviet cities and bomber bases. Northern waters were rough, but the bigger the carrier, the more stable it was. Huge size enabled a ship to approach close to its Soviet targets, in the most favorable zone of attack.

Some of those very targets of course were what the Air Force had in view, and in April 1949, the same month the keel of the *United States* was laid, President Truman ordered the purchase of three dozen B-36 bombers, to bring the total up to around 135. A few days later the new secretary of defense, Louis Johnson, wishing to economize, accepting the Air Force position, and perhaps feeling a need to display his official authority, peremptorily canceled construction of the supercarrier.

Johnson was backed by the president, the Air Force and Army chiefs of staff, and public opinion. It was a disaster for naval aviation. Johnson's action seemed proof that unification would scuttle the Navy's offensive capability. Captain Arleigh Burke, at this time presiding over OP-23 as assistant chief of naval operations for organizational research and policy, thought the existence of the service as an effective combat force was on the line. To the CNO, Admiral Denfeld, he wrote, "It appears that one of the Air Force objectives is to take over the Navy's roles and missions of control of the sea." There were rumors, Burke continued, that naval units such as Marine aviation, attack carriers, naval shore-based aviation, and amphibious units would be reduced in numbers or disbanded. Of exceptional danger to the Navy's necessary autonomy was the possibility of a single general staff, a sure recipe for a management disaster. "If these rumors are based on fact," Burke concluded, "the Navy will be unable to perform its primary role of control of the seas."[82]

UNIFICATION AND STRATEGY

The great fear was that unification meant a loss of the Navy's operational autonomy and the amputation of its air and amphibious arms. Secretary of Defense Johnson was anti-Navy and pro–Air Force. In 1949 he abolished Navy Day, which had been celebrated on Theodore Roosevelt's birthday. Secretary of the Navy John L. Sullivan resigned in May 1949 over the supercarrier cancellation. Vice Admiral Radford, a firebrand among the aviators, was sent to cool his heels in the Pacific. The new secretary of the Navy, Francis Matthews who served from May 1949 to July 1951, was in league with the administration.

Matthews stood behind Johnson's economizing and his efforts to categorize the services along the environmental lines of land, sea, and air. That type of categorization would confine the Navy to a sea-control function. Naval aviators thought Matthews was taking far too narrow a view and putting Navy air at risk. They complained and sounded alarms publicly, furthering institutional disarray.

In October 1949 the House Armed Services Committee, holding "unification and strategy" hearings, summoned a team of naval officers headed by Vice Admiral Radford and joined by CNO Denfeld. The team felt it was then or never for naval aviation and for a proper, flexible bombing strategy in the national interest. Their views ran directly contrary to the administration's, to those of the Navy secretary and the secretary of defense. The team members, all dissidents, put their careers on the line. When the smoke cleared President Truman ordered Secretary Matthews to fire CNO Denfeld for insubordination to civil authority.[83]

Denfeld and Radford appealed to Congress to save offensive carrier air. Because the finite defense budget made one service's gain another's loss, the Navy officers brought in Navy experts to discredit the B-36. They denounced the Air Force's expectation of a short war. What they did not do was explain the Navy's strategic alternative.

The Navy had an uphill fight. Not all of its officers shared the aviators' panic or Radford's view that the Navy should press to the limit demands for a deep-strike atomic-bombing capability. And what were the essential issues? Was Air Force countervalue bombing immoral, or was it just that the Air Force could not hit its targets? Or would countervalue bombing stand in the way of a rational ending of the war? Did the Air Force position make it harder to end the war? Was strategic bombing really the Navy's job?[84] It was hard for the Navy, hard for anyone during this period, to make judgments on conflicting claims in the absence of a declared national purpose.

There was a strong disposition in Congress to go with the Air Force, for reasons of economy and simplicity. A dramatic illustration of what the Navy was up against was the conversion to the Air Force position of the great Navy champion, and the chairman of the hearings, Representative Carl Vinson. Some months before the hearings, the columnist Stewart Alsop had written of Vinson: "His long love affair with the Navy is now definitely at an end. . . . His line is—and it seems to me a sensible line—that our only potential enemy is Russia, that we can't touch Russia with a navy, that we can't hope to equal Russia in ground forces, and that the only way we can really and immediately bring our superiority to bear is by air."[85]

The Navy case was hurt too by the first Soviet atomic explosion in September 1949, on the eve of the hearings. That ended the atomic monopoly under which the Navy had formed its offensive air-projection strategy. Only the month before, a report issued by the CNO's Air Warfare Division had concluded that future employment of heavy-attack, nuclear-capable naval air would be used against tactical, not strategic, targets. For this a flush-deck supercarrier was "*necessary* and logical." It was logical, the report concluded, because the Soviet submarine danger was not as great as the General Board had forecast a year earlier. The Soviet submarines could be contained. The main threat to the Navy was from stand-off, land-based Soviet naval aircraft, whose bases the carrier strikers would have to destroy.[86] After September, however, it was possible that forward-deployed carriers and amphibious operations would be under atomic threat. Did that mean the end of forward deployment?

It seemed the United States itself was now under the gun. A joint study concluded: "The Continental United States will be for the first time vulnerable to serious damage from air and guided missile attack. . . . The loss of the United States atomic monopoly reduces the effectiveness both militarily and psychologically of the Atlantic pact."[87]

The Navy was not prepared to respond to the Soviet bomb. The Air Force was. The Soviet bomb thus strengthened the hand of the Air Force. Long-range, high-altitude bombers were the answer for the United States, not vulnerable ships that would have to sail into the range of atomic weapons. "Against such a background," David Rosenberg and Floyd Kennedy wrote, "the Navy's presentation seemed to belong to the era of the battleship fleets of the 1920s and 1930s."[88]

At the 1949 hearings, the chief of staff of the Air Force, General Hoyt S. Vandenberg, dismissed the whole idea that the Navy needed to bomb inland targets to advance its sea-control mission. The next war, he said, would be like the war against Germany, not like the one against Japan. The Air Force, not the carriers, had faced the land-based Luftwaffe. The chairman of the Joint Chiefs, General Omar Bradley, testified that he had participated in "the two largest amphibious assaults ever made in history [Sicily and Normandy]. In neither case were any marines present. And in neither case were any Navy carriers used."[89]

The testifying Navy officers, expecting to deliver a military brief, were not ready to be put in the dock. Arleigh Burke's OP-23 worked up the lines of testimony, but OP-23 was understaffed, inexperienced, working without guidance or coordination, and possessed of views contrary to those of the Navy secretary. Its recommendations ended up either bland, inflammatory, or wide of the mark. The officers scattered their fire. Their attack on the B-36 was weak in that much of the criticism (the short range of fighter protection, the lack of advance bases, the size of nuclear weapons) was subject to rapid political or technological change, or could be turned against the Navy. If Air Force bombers could not get through, could naval air?

Above all, the officers failed to give a public defense of the Navy's sea-control function and of the service's joint operations, on which any Navy case had to rest. That would have been the tack of Sherman and the General Board, as sketched out during the two previous years. Such a defense would have explained the contemporary relevance of sea power, suggested a true maritime strategy, and stated the importance of naval air. It would have stated what the Navy was for, not what it was against. There were important differences between the Navy and the Air Force in their definitions of strategy and in their ideas about the conduct of modern war. Naval officers should have put the value of the Navy's "established concepts and techniques of war" to Congress, to illuminate the radical and, in the eyes of many Navy officers, inappropriate overreaction of the Air Force. It was in the Air Force that the real "revolt" was taking place. The Navy did not make such a presentation because of the secret nature of the material and, even more, because of its ignorance of the importance of, and its reluctance to engage in, public debate. So the Navy's interests suffered.

Navy Secretary Matthews supported a narrow sea-control mission, pure and simple. Fleet aviation should support that mission only, not take off and seek to win the war. The existing Essex-class carriers were adequate for protecting ships at sea. The Navy did not need an attack supercarrier or a heavy bomber. Insubordinate aviators, in Matthews's view, were illegitimately redefining the Navy's purpose and thus sowing confusion and lowering morale.

It was true that the testifying aviators did not speak for all the uniformed Navy. Admiral Sherman distanced himself from the narrow focus of the "admirals' revolt." Sherman tried to move the discussion away from the feud with the Air Force and back toward a positive expression of Navy versatility and the advantages of a balanced fleet. Let the Air Force have its bombers if they could do the job, said Sherman. Radford dismissed this as "wishy-washy" and "compromising" and refused to submit Sherman's views as testimony. Admiral Richard Conolly, in command of the naval forces in the eastern Atlantic and in the Mediterranean, declared that Radford spoke for naval aviation, not for the Navy as a whole. Conolly needed carriers for sea control, shipping defense, and assault support. He made the point that carriers served many purposes beyond functioning as a strategic-weapons platform.[90]

After the hearings, the Navy learned how to speak more effectively to Congress. Certainly the hearings helped clear the air.[91] The House Committee's report satisfied all sides. Navy and Marine aviation would not be integrated into the Air Force, and the report declared there were air missions other than those of the Air Force. Strategic bombing "is just one phase" of American air power. The B-36 purchases would go forward, pending an independent study of Soviet air defenses.[92]

Radford thought the fight for naval aviation helped bring the Navy "out of a deep pit" and later, looking back, said he would not change a word he uttered.[93] But in the end, the costly futility of continued controversy over roles and missions was obvious. Within the service the debate exhausted the effort to match the Air Force in atomic warfare. David Rosenberg and Floyd Kennedy wrote, "The Navy never again chose to attempt to shift the basic direction of American military strategy."[94]

At the close of 1949 the Joint Staff drew up Dropshot, a long-term procurement plan for a hypothetical war in 1957. It planned for a phased war and gave an ample role to the Navy's sea-control function. At the same time, Dropshot proposed ending the war as soon as possible, and that meant a massive atomic campaign. It proposed up to 435 atomic bombs for use in the first month against industrial and military targets in the Soviet Union and its satellites.[95] Some of these might be delivered "from aircraft carriers when available from other tasks." Those tasks were defined as protecting communications to the United Kingdom, destroying Soviet naval power, and securing overseas bases, an enormous menu demanding a huge Navy, far larger than the one that was likely to be on hand. Essentially, though, Dropshot was an atomic air offensive dominated by the Air Force.

After the unification-and-strategy controversy, the Navy needed to rethink its sea-power basics. The hearings did not sway Secretary of Defense Johnson to rethink his veto of the supercarrier. Shortly after the hearings Johnson said to Admiral Conolly, "Admiral, the Navy is on its way out. Now, take amphibious operations. There's no reason for having a Navy and a Marine Corps. General Bradley [chairman of the Joint Chiefs] . . . tells me that amphibious operations are a thing of the past. We'll never have any more amphibious operations. That does away with the Marine Corps. And the Air Force can do anything that the Navy can do nowadays, so that does away with the Navy."[96]

Navy Secretary Matthews was of course furious at the officers who testified before the House Armed Services Committee. They paid the price.[97] President Truman sacked CNO Denfeld to restore discipline, and Radford was kept out in the distant Pacific command, which was a backwater in the late 1940s. Matthews harassed Burke and OP-23, and tried (unsuccessfully) to prevent Burke's promotion to rear admiral. Conolly found he was considered too political by Washington authorities and did not get the job he had expected, that of CNO in relief of Denfeld. Truman instead appointed Admiral Forrest Sherman. Sherman had stayed aloof from the hearings. He had showed himself amenable to the service limits that Johnson sought. He was a willing interservice negotiator. And he was a naval aviator besides. It would be up to Sherman to pick up the pieces and put naval strategy and sea-power doctrine together again. Until that was done, the Navy as a whole still could not give a consistent answer to Forrestal's question of four years before: What, exactly, did the United States need a Navy for?

13

Naval Strategy 1950-1954

SHERMAN

Admiral Forrest Sherman took office as chief of naval operations in November 1949 to put the Navy on a steady course and to prevent the service from being swamped in the movement toward centralization. In the recent debates the Navy had isolated itself by stiff-neckedness. It had made claims that went beyond its accepted sea-control function and had not even tried to make a case for the Navy's versatility. Sherman had to reknit a cooperative relationship with the other services.

He was in a good position to do that. Two years before he had worked out the fundamentals of a maritime strategy in which the Navy would support the other services. In 1946 Sherman, with Major General Lauris Norstad of the Army Air Forces, had broken a Joint Chiefs' stalemate over roles and missions. Out of this breakthrough had come the National Security Act of 1947, under which the Navy retained its air force and control of the Marine Corps. Sherman was therefore well positioned to move beyond the acrimony displayed in the congressional hearings of 1949. As for the Navy's atomic role, Sherman conceded to the now independent Air Force its self-proclaimed strategic function, while retaining for the Navy a tactical atomic capability. It had been Sherman who, as deputy CNO in 1946 and 1947 when Forrestal was

Navy secretary, began the modification of Navy aircraft for atomic payloads. Sherman was "the one man in the Navy" who could "smooth the way for the Navy to undertake the deployment of an operational nuclear strike force."[1] What that meant, however, in the absence of the supercarrier was not clear in 1949.

Sherman had enemies. Navy pilots knew Sherman did not share their gung ho view that aviation should dominate the service. Critics tagged him a compromiser, a puppet of Navy Secretary Matthews and Defense Secretary Johnson. They said his focus on the Navy's joint role sold out the service's potential for an independent air offensive, a potential represented by the supercarrier. Marine Corps critics resented Sherman's insistence that the CNO could decide Marine missions and Marine force composition without consulting the commandant. They feared Sherman might, to save carrier air, concede to proponents of service specialization the Marines' spearhead role in amphibious projection, by which concession the corps would run the risk of being absorbed into either the Army or the Navy.[2] Critics said that Sherman's conciliatory stance might be appropriate to peacetime politics but that it did not meet the needs of military strategy.[3]

The critics were wrong. The 1946 Sherman-Norstad agreement had kept the Navy together, saved Navy air and the Fleet Marine Force, and at the same time blunted attacks on the idea of a Navy of varied missions. Cooperation did not have to restrict the Navy's fighting effectiveness or diminish its corporate identity. After the bruising interservice competition, it was time for cooperation. On that point, moreover, the administration insisted.

Sherman did work well with Secretaries Matthews and Johnson, officials by and large deplored within the fleet, but he did not take office as CNO to disempower the general-purpose Navy. Under Sherman the Navy survived the attempts to unify the services without loss of autonomy or amputation of its parts. Then, unexpectedly, the vast military buildup associated with the Korean War and the transformation of the North Atlantic alliance into a military organization enabled Sherman to give the Navy the force it wanted. These developments confirmed the Navy's value as a versatile, global force divided into widely separated forward-deployed fleets that were centered on the carrier task forces. The forces were capable of many offensive missions: sea control, antisubmarine warfare, amphibious operations, and conventional or nuclear air strikes against targets ashore. In the Korean War naval air and the Marine Corps played such conspicuous and valuable roles that their future as part of the Navy was never again challenged, and the conceptual and operational value of sea power in a limited, protracted war was confirmed. All this of course greatly improved morale and Navy and Marine Corps faith in themselves.[4]

Sherman's thinking had been, when he left Washington back in 1946, that the Navy had more strategic latitude than any other service. In case of a general war with the Soviet Union, it alone could take an immediate strategic initiative. It could do this in the Mediterranean, where U.S. ships could sail 2,500 miles behind the Atlantic shore to launch an immediate counteroffensive at the center of Europe or against a Soviet advance toward Middle Eastern oil, on which America's European allies depended.

When Sherman returned from the Mediterranean at the end of 1949, however, he found Navy options much reduced. A new defensive North Atlantic peripheral strategy was in place, and it took precedence over his plan of a Mediterranean offensive. The eastern Mediterranean had been demoted to a minor theater. Greece and Turkey were not members of the North Atlantic alliance and were to be abandoned in a war for northwestern Europe. Strategic attention had turned from Europe's southeastern flank to the danger of Soviet expansion in central Europe. The Prague coup and Berlin blockade of 1948, and the division of Germany the following year, exemplified the reasons for the reorientation. The Army always had been reluctant to commit to the Mediterranean and the Middle East anyway, because of the difficulty of assuring communication across the inland sea, a problem of maneuver room and security from attack that the Navy, in its enchantment with forward deployment deep into the heart of Europe, had underplayed.[5] Sea control was still the bridge between the United States and Europe, but in 1949 the Navy was no longer at the center of the country's offensive strategy. In the Pacific, refusal to get involved on mainland Asia and weak U.S. forces in the region limited the Navy's mission to the defense of a few insular strongpoints: Japan, the Philippines, and Okinawa.[6]

As we have seen, Offtackle, the Joint Chiefs' 1949 war plan, gave up protection of Greece and Turkey and the oil reserves of the Middle East in favor of an atomic air offensive. Yet the Strategic Air Command did not then have the aircraft it needed to carry out the plan, which called for the destruction of the Soviet regime by an attack on 104 Soviet cities with 220 atomic bombs. Offtackle presented no fallback, no other option. This all-or-nothing thinking, with no consideration of how the war might end or what the postwar order might look like, seemed to many Navy officers to prove Air Force rigidity. "In the struggle within the JCS over Offtackle during 1949 and 1950," Michael Palmer has written, "one can see the origins of the strategic debate of the 1980s in which the merits of a continental or a maritime focus were argued."[7]

Offtackle, a member of the Navy's strategic plans division warned, was all in all a bad plan:

It lacks flexibility, in that no provision is made for alternate courses of action which might be preferable under certain circumstances. It inferentially places undue reliance on the results expected of the atomic phase of the strategic air offensive. And last, but not least, it provides for no diversionary action along the "soft underbelly" of Europe. From the aspect of the successful accomplishment of Task I (the security and the utility of the U.K.) this is a serious and possible fatal defect, since the principal Soviet air effort both offensive and defensive can then be channeled against the U.K. and against the strategic bombing effort emanating from the U.K.[8]

The naval dimension of Offtackle was mainly defensive, a sea-control campaign of running convoys for the coalition. Forward submarine deployment was expected to keep Soviet submarines away from sea-lanes, doing away with the need for an air attack at the source. Offtackle defined the threats to sea control as mines, aircraft, submarines, and surface raiders. Protection of shipping could therefore be by escort of convoys. The U.S. commander in chief in the Atlantic, Rear Admiral Lynde McCormick, intent on hunting and killing, had still been thinking in late 1948 that merchantmen should avoid convoys and sail independently until a stronger escort force was available. It took British persuasion to convince him that the British wartime doctrine of convoy even with a weak escort was preferable in assuring the safe and timely arrival of cargo and troops to the defense of shipping by independent hunter-killer operations against elusive submarines. Under Offtackle a powerful U.S. fast-carrier strike capacity was to be retained in the Mediterranean, but it was pulled west to defend the American base area in French North Africa.[9]

Offtackle, then, at the end of 1949, confirmed the pessimism and anxiety of offensive-minded naval pilots and broad-thinking Navy strategists. At the same time, cuts to the fleet, above all a slash in carriers, reduced Navy force. Defense Secretary Johnson executed President Truman's insistence on rigid economy. Budgets—not national policy, external threats, or service programs—set force levels. Strategy was designed to take advantage of the apparent economy of air power. For fiscal year 1950 the Navy asked for sixteen active-duty attack carriers. It got eight. In requests in late 1949 for fiscal year 1951, the Air Force proposed eliminating the attack carriers altogether, the Army proposed cutting them to four, and the Navy asked for funds to operate ten. It got funds to run six, with a seventh for temporary use in the unstable Far East.

Budget cuts hit the Navy hardest in the Pacific. In his briefing of President Truman in January 1947, Sherman had asked for a 24-carrier fleet, 8 of which would be stationed in the Pacific. As we have just seen, however, the 1950 budget, called for reducing the Navy as a whole to 8 carriers. When the Korean War broke out in June 1950, only one carrier, the *Valley Forge*, was deployed in the western Pacific.

The United States had hoped it could just sit tight in Asia. The problem was that by 1949 much of Asia was coming unhinged. In 1949 the Chinese Communists threw Chiang Kai-shek and the Kuomintang (Chinese Nationalist Party) off the mainland, and within months, in February 1950, the Soviet Union signed a treaty of alliance with "Red" China. The U.S. administration did not know what to do about its old ally, Chiang, who was now a refugee on Taiwan (Formosa).

A National Security Council (NSC) report of December 1949 postulated a domino effect from the Communist takeover of China. It read, "If southeast Asia also is swept by communism we shall have suffered a major political rout the repercussions of which will be felt throughout the rest of the world, especially in the Middle East and in a then critically exposed Australia."[10] At the end of the month, the NSC proposed extending the containment policy to the Far East.[11]

In April 1950, practicing a hands-off policy with regard to the Chinese civil war, the United States pulled its officials out of China. There was no decision on what to do next, on where to draw the defensive line against Communism, or on what to draw the line with.[12] Sherman warned of the consequences of cutting Taiwan adrift. Within a year, he said, the United States might be faced with a stark choice. When the end of the autumn typhoon season came, Chiang's forces might not be able to protect themselves. Sherman warned the other Joint Chiefs that Soviet influence and Communist Chinese strength were growing and that the JCS should consider alternative strategies should Taiwan, Japan, or the Philippines fall to the Communists.[13] What was needed was a very flexible military force.

It was hard to imagine where such a force would come from, given Truman's pared-back budgets. The Navy was shrinking. For fiscal year 1950 Congress had appropriated funds for operating only 288 major combatant ships. For fiscal year 1951, the Navy Department proposed an allocation for 40,000 personnel and only 239 major combatant ships—with a cut, as we have seen, of heavy carriers from 8 to 7, and possibly 6—as part of a Defense Department budget of $13.3 billion.

The Navy proposed several ways to defend the Chinese Nationalist redoubt, but the JCS rejected them. Even though Taiwan had an obvious value for America's position in the western Pacific, the United States had too little military strength to cover the entire globe.[14] Rather than defend Taiwan, the United States would take it by force if necessary in a general war, to secure the air bases on Okinawa from which the Air Force would launch a nuclear strike against the Soviet Union.

Europe had priority. So strategy in the Pacific became passive defense along a specified perimeter, an island chain defined in January 1950 by Secretary of State Dean Acheson (1949–53) as running from the Aleutians to Japan, and then through the Ryukyus to the Philippines. Taiwan was excluded. So was South Korea.[15] This Pacific policy was the misshapened result of uncoordinated planning and erratic definitions of national interests.[16] Behind it all was the fact of America's limited military strength. Limited options had led to compromises, which turned into shortsighted policy.

At the same time, in early 1950, America's reduced military condition led officials to declare a window of vulnerability. The Cold War was heating up, reflecting, it seemed, new Soviet confidence and opportunism. The explosion in 1949 of a Soviet atomic bomb revealed that the United States had lost its monopoly. That meant the United States would be at risk when guided-missile systems were deployed on Soviet submarines. It also meant that the whole Atlantic alliance system might unravel if allies of the United States drew pessimistic conclusions from America's vulnerability. The "fall" of China, the division of Germany, the revelation that Soviet spies had penetrated Western war and state departments all convinced officials that the West was entering a danger zone in which the balance of power could turn against the United States.[17]

In April 1950 a State Department–Defense Department group issued a review of security policy known as NSC-68, which bluntly called for an assertive anti-Communist strategy.[18] "The cold war is in fact a real war," the review said, "in which the survival of the free world is at stake. . . . A continuation of present trends would result in a serious decline in the strength of the free world relative to the Soviet Union and its satellites." The document warned, "It is imperative that this trend be reversed by a much more rapid and concerted build-up of the actual strength of both the United States and the other nations of the free world." The United States would have to reverse its economizing, its unilateral force reduction, and its de facto isolationism. NSC-68 called for rapid rearmament to meet Soviet aggression throughout the world. There was no time, or space, to lose.[19]

The answer to the question of whether the American public would accept a costly militarization of the containment policy came with the Korean War. The North Korean offensive was a strategic surprise. It confirmed the aggressiveness predicted in NSC-68. It revealed America's military weakness. All officials would have agreed with Stuart Symington, former secretary of the Air Force and then the chairman of the National Security Resources Board, who said that the North Korean invasion showed (1) "the now unmasked great and growing combined military strength of the Soviet Union, and such of its willing and ambitious satellites as China and North Korea"; (2) "the serious current inadequacy of our own military forces"; and (3) the fact that the United States had "no long-range strategic defense plan."[20]

KOREA

Korea confirmed the opinion that American interests were threatened everywhere. The reaction to this global threat militarized U.S. foreign policy.[21] Naval force and Navy confidence rose on the tide. The war in Korea strengthened support for an interventionist maritime policy. It showed the importance of sea control, flexibility, and a balanced force. The experience in Korea did not, however, lead to a strategy befitting the limited war fought there. Planning remained preoccupied with an all-out, air-atomic, central-front war in Europe. Korea led to no major changes in Navy, Air Force, or Army thinking. In James Lacy's words, the circumstance that "virtually nothing in pre-Korea U.S. political military strategy had anticipated the kinds of military challenges Korea posed became a quickly lost fact."[22]

The decision to limit the war in Korea was political. Limited war was not part of an American war plan. Nor was a protracted conflict. General Matthew Ridgway, who was Army deputy chief of staff for operations and administration when the war broke out, and who later commanded the Eighth Army and then relieved General Douglas MacArthur as head of U.S. and other United Nations (UN) troops in Korea, said of prewar planning: "The concept of 'limited warfare' never entered our councils."[23] Korea had been declared outside the Pacific defense perimeter. Limiting a war there depended on the restraint of states. Had the Soviets openly intervened in Korea or made a move in Europe, had the Chinese Communists attacked Taiwan, or had the United States used its heavy bombers against mainland China, there might have been, so was the fear, World War III.[24] For this reason every great power, and all the 22 states engaged in the war, chose to limit fighting to the Korean Peninsula.[25]

With one exception, the navies under the UN flag had uncontested mobility at sea. That made intervention possible in the first place. Thereafter, free UN naval movement up and down the three sides of the coast shaped the war. Sea access enabled the United States to undertake three major amphibious operations: Inchon, which broke North Korea's drive southward by an attack on its flank; Wonsan, which spurred the counteroffensive into North Korea; and Hungnam, which rescued and redeployed troops in retreat from the Chinese invasion. Sea control, however, was not enough to win the war.

President Truman did not hesitate to oppose the North Korean invasion of June 1950.[26] It was assumed that any Communist aggression must be Soviet-sponsored. Thus there was a double reason for stopping it. The line from North Korea's capital, Pyongyang, ran to Moscow and perhaps through Beijing. In February 1950 the Chinese and Soviet governments had signed a 30-year treaty of friendship, alliance, and mutual assistance that confirmed the American opinion that the Chinese were the Asian "junior partners of Soviet Communism."[27]

At stake in Korea, in Washington's eyes, was the postwar system of collective security. Unprepared as U.S. forces were, Truman wanted to support the United Nations and its principles. At stake too was containment. Never before, a State Department intelligence estimate said in June 1950, had the Soviet government risked engagement with U.S. armed forces and hence risked general war.[28] Concession was out of the question. The lesson of the 1930s, one in which every American official was steeped, was that appeasement encouraged aggression. Containing aggression in Asia would prevent it in Europe. When officers in the Pentagon thought of Korea, they thought of Berlin and Taiwan.[29] They wondered if there was a hidden connection. Was Korea the first step in a coordinated global advance? Was the North Korean action a feint meant to draw American resources away from the big prize of Europe? From beginning to end, the JCS saw the war in Korea in terms of a larger, growing, and global security threat.[30]

U.S. officials knew that scarce American forces were insufficient to defend Europe. In case of a Soviet advance, war plans prescribed successive planned withdrawals. When news of the Korean invasion arrived in Washington, the Navy ordered the Sixth Fleet in the Mediterranean to put to sea. In a naval exercise in the Atlantic in 1952, the carrier *Wasp* rammed a U.S. minesweeper, which sank with 176 men. That was the greatest single Navy loss during the Korean War.[31] The incident indicates how preoccupied with Europe the United States and its allies were. The exercise was a NATO drill of around 200 ships in rough weather off Norway.

In the western Pacific, the main naval concern was that the Soviets might attack by air or by submarine from Vladivostok (where there were 70 submarines only a few miles from the North Korean border) or from southern Sakhalin. That Soviet threat never materialized. Navy planes did shoot down a Soviet bomber on the premise of hostile intent, and Navy ships chased what they thought were Soviet submarines. A few dogfights took place with Soviet fighters. But that was all. During the course of the Korean War, the Soviet navy remained coastal and defensive. It attacked no ships and made no effort to cut the lines of communication at sea, without which the UN forces could not continue the fight.

There were only 45 vessels in the North Korean navy. Most of them were torpedo boats or gunboats, and both types were easily destroyed or diverted by the Americans. China, which entered the war at the end of November 1950, posed no naval threat.

Mines did. The only opposition the Navy faced from the sea was the mining campaign at Wonsan harbor, where the Soviets helped the North Koreans lay 3,000 mines. Until the harbor was swept, gunfire support ships could not get close enough to shore to lay a barrage. The need to clear the water delayed an amphibious strike at Wonsan in October 1950. The strike was part of a drive on Pyongyang. The situation facing the Navy in clearing the mines, namely its loss of local sea control for the six days of clearing and its lack of minesweeping equipment (which was "the outstanding naval deficiency of the conflict"), was the low point of naval operations in the Korean War.[32]

With sea control, the Navy moved troops up and down the peninsula and put ships in a position to support ground forces by air strikes and gunfire. Sea control was vital to supply. It is true that American forces in Japan were nearby. Sasebo was only 165 nautical miles from Pusan, roughly the distance from Key West to naval operations in the Spanish-American War. Korea, like the campaign in Cuba, was a "suburban" war. As the North Koreans found to their sorrow, of all the Cold War battlefields, Korea was "the area where the United States could best extemporize a reply."[33]

On the other hand, whether or not they went first to Japan, men and supplies came from the United States, and Pusan was 4,914 nautical miles from San Francisco. Air transport carried part of the men and supplies, but it was expensive and of limited capacity. Ships did the main hauling. Six of every seven men who landed in Korea came by sea. For every ton of freight that crossed the Pacific in an airplane, 270 tons went by water. Fifty-four million tons of dry cargo and 22 million tons of gasoline and oil were sent by ship to the western Pacific.[34] Of supplies sent to the war zone, the U.S. merchant marine carried over 85 percent. In 1950, the merchant marine comprised 1,248 privately held ships. In addition, 2,277 vessels of World War II vintage, such as the Liberty ships, were held in a National Defense Reserve Fleet. Of these, 778 were drawn for Korean transport duty to supplement the other U.S.-flag vessels.[35] From whatever distance, and for whatever purpose, use of the sea was essential, and that use the Navy guaranteed.

Sea control also means sea denial. The president ordered a close naval blockade of North Korea within a week after the invasion. The blockade cut the enemy's seaborne maneuvers and closed its seaborne supply lines. The ships on blockade also secured the flanks of the battle line, shooting at coastal roadways. Naval units from seven other UN countries, and from South Korea, joined the Americans. The British contributed 32 warships, making Korea "a major British naval war."[36]

China was not blockaded. A naval blockade would have crippled China's war-making potential. China imported most of its industrial products and 90 percent of its petroleum.[37] A UN naval blockade, under the UN Charter, is not an act of war. A unilateral U.S. blockade would have been and might have provoked a Soviet response. Sherman thought the Soviets might respect a UN blockade of China (if it got past a Soviet veto in the Security Council) as they did the UN blockade of Korea. But the major U.S. allies refused to join a blockade of China. And because the U.S. goal was to keep the war limited and localized, the Americans accepted the military cost of leaving the China coast open.

That is not to say the United States did not seal off the Nationalist Chinese on Taiwan. Two days after North Korea invaded South Korea, President Truman ordered the Navy to isolate Taiwan. Neutralization was meant to protect Chiang in exile on the island. It was also to keep Chiang from attacking the regime that had just chased him off the mainland. Holding back the Nationalists was a change of U.S. policy, a means of limiting the hostility of the United States's enemies at a time of military and political overstretch. President Truman told Chiang to "cease all air and sea operations against the mainland." The Seventh Fleet, Truman said, "will see that this is done."[38] Throughout most of the Korean War, this mission of the Seventh Fleet in the Formosa Strait limited its capacity to commit its carrier-based aircraft to ground support in Korea.

Sea control made possible the brilliant amphibious operations of the first six months of the war. These operations, at Inchon, Wonsan, and Hungnam, "halted one invasion, defeated one enemy, and saved the day when a second intervened."[39] For years, Army and Air Force leaders had been questioning the continued utility of amphibious-assault doctrine. The Navy itself had reduced the number of its amphibious ships from 610 in 1945 to 81 in 1950. What revived the doctrine was the landing at Inchon in September 1950.

Inchon was a deep-envelopment operation of great brilliance. It was inspired by General MacArthur and carried out with great dexterity mainly by the Navy and the Marines. On the 31-foot tide of D-Day, through narrow channel approaches and over high seawalls, the Navy with split-second timing landed 13,000 marines and about 70,000 troops. Inchon and its follow-on operation, the recapture of the South Korean capital of Seoul, high against the enemy flank, dislocated the supply system that supported the North Korean offensive through the southern half of the peninsula. The Inchon invasion thus loosened the North Korean hold on the Allied troops that had retreated into the Pusan pocket. The U.S. Eighth Army, which had been trapped with its back to the sea, broke out and began a march northward.[40]

"History records," wrote Malcolm Cagle and Frank Manson, "no more striking example of the effectiveness of an amphibious operation."[41] The operation vindicated the Fleet Marine Force. Marine and Navy close air support was flawless.[42] Inchon showed that amphibious operations—and the combat Marine Corps—were relevant in the atomic age.[43]

Adm. S. G. Gorshkov, commander in chief of the Soviet navy in the 1970s, wrote: "Without wide, active use of the fleet, the interventionists could hardly have escaped military defeat in Korea. . . . Thanks to the use of the fleet, the Americans were able to create in a narrow portion of the front a powerful strike grouping of forces enabling them to avoid total defeat in Korea."[44]

The Inchon-Seoul operation and the march north by the Eighth Army expelled North Korean troops from South Korea and fulfilled the United Nations' initial war aim, the defense of the sovereignty of South Korea. Three months later, when South Korean and UN forces were in retreat from the Chinese invasion of Korea, the same amphibious expertise of the Navy and the Marine Corps was used to evacuate 196,000 servicemen and refugees from Hungnam.

The Chinese invasion at the end of November and first of December 1950 stunned Washington. MacArthur had told President Truman that he could take the Eighth Army to the Yalu River without disturbing the Chinese—or the Soviets, whose territory fronted a few dozen miles of North Korea's border. "If successful," MacArthur declared of his march to the Yalu, "this should for all practical purposes end the war."[45] Such a military victory would permit accomplishment of the by then revised UN war aim, political unification of the peninsula. Sherman noted to the other Joint Chiefs, "He [MacArthur] seems very disdainful of our concern over the major conflict with the Chinese."[46] But neither his political nor his military superiors sent MacArthur orders to stop. The responsibility for the debacle of the Allies' November offensive is shared by many.[47]

With all troops reeling back under the intense Chinese advance, military logic called either for evacuation or for expanding the war into China itself.[48] Admiral Sherman urged that the JCS order MacArthur to get American troops into beachheads at once. No one on the JCS wanted to go to war with China.

First it was necessary to save the 118,000 American and Korean troops recoiling from the Yalu. The disaster that befell the Eighth Army's Seventh Infantry Division, which lost 1,000 men, and the heroic withdrawal of the First Marine Division from Chosin Reservoir to an orderly evacuation (or, as the Marine Corps correctly called it, redeployment) of 22,215 of their men at Hungnam are part of American military legend.[49] After Inchon and the heroic retreat from the reservoir, Congress rewarded the Marine Corps. In 1952—over the opposition of President Truman, the Department of Defense, the JCS, and Admiral Sherman (who wanted command of the corps to be put in the hands of the CNO)—Congress mandated a minimum Marine force level of three combat divisions and three air wings and gave the Marine commandant a seat with the Joint Chiefs in matters relating to the corps.[50]

The Hungnam evacuation of December 1950 was another amphibious success. Navy ships laid a wall of gunfire in front of an Army-held barrier and, behind the barrier, took off the troops. Navy and Marine air squadrons flew some 1,700 protective sorties. At one point, 4 attack carriers, 1 battleship, 2 cruisers, and 22 destroyers were pounding the shore. Under the amphibious-operations expert Rear Admiral James Doyle, 193 ships removed 196,000 people, 350,000 tons of cargo, and 17,500 vehicles. All American and Allied military personnel were safely evacuated from Hungnam, as, just before, several thousand others had been removed from Inchon and Wonsan.

Control of the sea gives the freedom to depart as well as the freedom to arrive. If the First Marine Division had been caught and destroyed in northeastern Korea, the U.S. government might not have kept the war limited. That a tragedy was avoided, and limitation maintained, is thus at least in part due to the capacity of the naval forces that made the Hungnam evacuation possible.[51]

At Hungnam, however, the embarking troops did not face hostile air power or a determined enemy driving at the beaches with armor and artillery.[52] That would not be the case in an evacuation of Europe. The Soviets would not permit a Dunkerque. All planning assumed that an evacuation from Europe would take place in the teeth of a Soviet air and armored attack against waiting ships and retreating troops. It was unlikely that a Soviet advance could be halted by carrier air or naval gunfire.

Keeping the war limited was the great issue of Korea. In December 1950, anxiety about an imminent war with the Soviet Union reached its height. Maybe the Chinese invasion was part of a concerted plan of global pressure. A State Department document entitled "Moscow-Peiping Time-Table for War," written in the dark days of mid-December 1950, concluded that a war with the Soviet Union was "probable" and "in the near rather than distant future" and that "by the present estimate, for our defense moves we have left to us only days and hours, not months and years."[53]

The West's window of vulnerability would remain open until rearmament restored the superiority of Western power, sometime around 1954. There was one cold comfort. The U.S. ambassador to the Soviet Union, Alan G. Kirk, told President Truman that the Soviets were "gaining so much by bleeding the United States, in particular, and the Western world in general, through the war in Korea, that it would not be in their immediate advantage to move against us."[54] That was just as well. A month before, the chairman of the Joint Chiefs, General Bradley, had told the National Security Council that if a global war broke out the United States might lose.[55]

That is why the United States wanted to prevent enlarging the Korean War. Already too many scarce resources were tied up in that remote arena, whose political importance diminished as it became evident that the North Korean invasion was an isolated event and not part of a global conspiracy. Europe remained the strategic theater, the Soviets remained the primary enemy, and both were quiet. Truman's administration and then Eisenhower's, which took office in early 1953, were eager to be done with the Korean War. Chinese intervention did not change this fact. It just made the endgame more complicated. Bernard Brodie characterized the Korean War as "one long story of earnest desire to disengage from China."[56]

In 1951 General Bradley told Congress that a war with China that year would be "the wrong war in the wrong place at the wrong time."[57] His comment referred to the fact that the United States was working to acquire by around 1954, when the United States would have regained a position of military and technological superiority in Europe, the capacity to launch an air-atomic offensive, and that a war with China should not be allowed to detract from that effort. The United States, Bradley said, should not rush into a "showdown" with the Soviet Union "before we are ready."[58]

One alternative to a war with China was a voluntary withdrawal of American forces from Korea. Admiral Sherman spoke in favor of voluntary withdrawal on December 19, 1950, when it appeared that UN forces would be overwhelmed by the Chinese onslaught. He said that withdrawal would improve America's "capacity to deal with the overall situation" and that "Western Europe would be delighted to see us withdraw." But as the UN command recovered from the rout and held its ground, a preferred third alternative arose—that of a negotiated settlement.[59]

Negotiation had to be from a position of strength. This did not mean expanding the war, although the heads of the Air Force and the Navy were confident that the United States would win a war with China. The problem was that fighting in China might entail the use of nuclear weapons, and there were too many arguments against that. The British were vehemently opposed to such use. And more than alliance solidarity was at stake. Administration officials thought world public opinion might so strongly condemn U.S. use of nuclear weapons that the United Nations itself could be destroyed. Asians would view any use as proof that the atomic bomb was a racist "Asian weapon." And always, there was the worry of Soviet intervention out of fear, an intervention that might not be restrained by some of the inhibitions experienced by the United States.[60]

Further, an expansion of the Korean War into China would reopen the Chinese civil war, for an obvious step in such an expansion would be to move Chiang's troops from Taiwan onto the mainland. Japan and Taiwan would be vulnerable to the Soviet-supplied Chinese air force. An expanded land war in Asia would demand moving huge American reinforcements to the Far East at a time when scarce resources were committed to Korea and NATO was so underarmed that the Allied forces in Europe would have to withdraw to the Rhine if not to the sea.

That was the strategic dilemma. The Air Force chief of staff, General Hoyt Vandenberg, declared that action against China "would not affect our capacity in Europe. All we would need would be the naval blockade and the use of one or two air groups. It would be a long-range job."[61] But most officials thought that a war with China would completely destroy the premise of Offtackle, which was to wage a strategic offensive in western Eurasia while holding the strategic defensive in the Far East.[62]

If China was not going to be coerced by direct attack, the United Nations had to pursue goals that could be met by military action on the ground in Korea and use any resulting gains as the basis of a negotiated peace. That was the mission of the reconstituted Eighth Army under General Matthew Ridgway. After having been pushed south of the 38th parallel in January 1951, Ridgway counterattacked northward in Operation Killer, and in March 1951 American forces crossed that famous parallel for the third time, moving again into North Korea and driving the Chinese troops before them. And then they stopped. The JCS was unwilling to go farther without political guidance as to the purpose of the American action.[63] That ended, after one year, the mobile period of the Korean War.

Then came the fourth and final phase, which lasted two years. Ridgway's successor, General James Van Fleet, was told to hold the line, not to push it forward. With a return to the goal of status quo ante bellum, the United States was ready for truce talks, which began in July 1951.[64]

In the final phase, the two years of negotiations before an armistice was signed in July 1953, the battlefront resembled the western front of World War I. For those two years, the UN forces held the defensive in a war of dug-in emplacements and barbed wire. Battles seesawed, and so did the talks. In the end, after holding off two major Chinese offensives, the United States got what it wanted at the negotiating table. But this period of static, positional warfare was frustrating, dangerous, and costly. The United States sustained fully 45 percent of its casualties during the period of the truce talks. Having suffered 78,000 casualties in the first year of the war, it suffered 63,200 in the next two years. And there was always the danger that the Chinese might break through.

To prevent an enemy buildup able to break through and sustain a forward advance, Navy air from Task Force 77 and the Air Force from land bases in South Korea and Japan continued their interdiction campaign. Of all combat sorties flown in the war, Navy and Marine Corps aviators flew 41 percent, some 275,000 in all, about half of which were interdiction missions. The other half were close air support and counterair sorties. A total of 7,571 sorties were flown in two weeks in July 1953 to stop what appeared to be a Chinese attempt to break through.

The interdiction campaign in the Chinese phase, however, was only partially successful. It destroyed North Korea's logistical infrastructure, but that did not stop the war. Assessing the results of a sustained attack on North Korea's transport system, Robert Futrell, the Air Force's historian, concluded, "Ten months of comprehensive railway interdiction [from August 1951] so badly shattered the North Korean railway system that it would not be able to support a sustained Communist ground offensive, but the railway-interdiction attacks—which delayed and disrupted enemy logistical support—did not place enough military pressure upon the Reds to force them to accept United Nations armistice terms."[65] Political exigencies limited pressure from the air. Important targets were proscribed, such as Rashin (Najin), a North Korean port city near the Soviet border. At first, Rashin had been attacked with the sole stipulation that it be bombed from the air—Navy ships were ordered to keep their distance. Two B-29 raids, however, failed to hit the target, and so the JCS put the city off-limits for air attacks.[66]

Above all, the Chinese had their sanctuary beyond the Yalu River. That gave them secure staging grounds for reinforcements and supply trains, places from which to pour men and supplies down into North Korea, and safe fields for their Soviet-supplied MIG fighters. Nor did the American political position make it easy for the Army to wear the Chinese down on the ground. The static war gave the foe a great advantage. In a period of stalemate, he could accumulate stockpiles of supplies just outside the range of UN artillery, supplies necessary for any sustained offensive. Navy, Marine, and Air Force fighters and fighter-bombers attacked these stockpiles and enemy strongpoints close to the front line with considerable success. But without continual forward action, American ground forces could not take advantage of their mobility and superior firepower to prevent more supplies from arriving and to keep the enemy off balance. Said the aggressive General James Van Fleet of this stalemate phase, "If we had ever put on some pressure and made him fight, we would have given him an insoluble supply problem."[67] Van Fleet wanted to launch his Eighth Army and the rest of the UN command into an all-out attack to roll back the Chinese line. That, with his mobility and superior firepower, he might have been able to do. The JCS denied him the opportunity. The United States was trying to get out of the war. The government did not want to sustain further casualties. Nor were its allies, save perhaps South Korea, ready to advance again toward the Yalu. The State Department vetoed a JCS recommendation for a joint Navy–Air Force sweep along the coast of China.[68]

Could the A-bomb have hastened the end? We cannot say. Cagle and Manson, historians of the Navy's war, wrote, "Interdiction failed owing to our inability to use the one weapon—the atomic bomb—in our arsenal which might have severed Communist supply lines in Korea."[69] But those lines after 1951 were dispersed and concealed, and the iron bombs of the B-29s were hitting them as effectively as tactical air power could. Because Cagle and Manson's subject is a limited war, it does not seem that they are referring to bombing China. Washington did consider using atomic bombs to halt the advancing North Koreans in mid-1950 and to halt the Chinese advance in late 1950 and early 1951. But in the early phase of the war, the U.S. forces on the ground did not know where enemy concentrations were forming, and hence could not have called the target. The Air Force, accustomed to considering European sources of war production as its A-bomb targets, was not prepared to use atomic bombs in a very different interdiction campaign in mountainous Korea or China.[70] The two main controllers of the bombs, President Truman and Gordon Dean, chairman of the Atomic Energy Commission, agreed that on the North Korean terrain atomic explosions would be "completely ineffective and psychological 'duds.' "[71] Thus the tide was held by conventional means. With their eyes on the Soviet Union, officers and officials did not want to use the limited number of U.S. atomic bombs in out-of-the-way action—which Korea really was—however intense.

The Soviets had built up their naval presence in Vladivostok. The U.S. Navy, worried about submarines, took heed. In 1951, for the first time since 1945, President Truman ordered that complete atomic weapons be deployed abroad. They were sent, with an atomic-capable Air Force wing, to Guam. The weapons were then to be taken to Okinawa, within range of Soviet targets. That did not stop the Chinese, who opened a great offensive in April 1951. Moscow meanwhile took no action. The Chinese offensive was met by the Eighth Army on the field, and the nuclear weapons never left Guam. They were returned to the United States in June 1951. Whether their deployment had anything to do with the Soviet (and then the Chinese and North Korean) agreement to begin armistice negotiations in July 1951 we cannot say, although that was the conclusion drawn by the Truman administration.[72]

Negotiations dragged on for two years. We do not know why the Chinese and the North Koreans decided to end hostilities and sign the armistice in July 1953, just as we do not know why the North Koreans had invaded three years before or why the Chinese intervened.[73] Neither side had won a military victory or suffered a political defeat. All kinds of reasons have been offered for the decision to end the fighting: local Allied pressure in the form of a solid military line of defense; widened conventional bombing, notably the destruction of the Toksan irrigation dam in May 1953; a new Sino-Soviet policy of peaceful coexistence with the West, a policy attendant upon a feeling of vulnerability after Stalin's death; the threat of the atomic bomb; and internal considerations of various sorts. It was certainly clear that the Communist forces were not going to prevail in their object of destroying the South Korean regime and throwing the Americans off the peninsula. Nor, it should be noted, would a return to the status quo ante bellum along the existing battle line represent a loss of territory or regime. But as to why Korea and China gave up, one must share Robert Futrell's lament: "In view of the importance of the Korean conflict to American military thought, it would have been helpful if the communists had seen fit to disclose the factors which led to their capitulation."[74] The answer probably is: All of the above.[75]

14

Containment and the Navy 1952-1960

COLD WAR MISSIONS

Containment was the basic policy of the United States during the Cold War. It took advantage of Western strengths and Soviet weaknesses. It surrounded a continental enemy with an alliance connected by the sea. Containment was designed to turn the Soviet Union inward, to put an insupportable strain on the Communist regime, and to turn the surrounding states of the resource-rich Eurasian rimland outward, away from the continental Soviet core and toward the oceanic world, toward the United States. Sea control was what tied the non-Communist world together.

It was with good reason that the main Western military alliance, the North Atlantic Treaty Organization, was named for a connecting ocean. The sea bound other agreements as well. To the Rio Treaty of 1947 were added in 1951 the Philippine Defense Pact, the ANZUS Treaty, and a security treaty with Japan. The Navy, as the Strategic Plans Division put it dryly, was to assist allies "in the execution of their responsibilities."[1] To its defensive obligations in Europe, Japan, and Korea, each of which by treaty demanded a continued U.S. presence supported directly by sea, the United States in 1954 added an agreement with the Nationalist regime on Taiwan and also signed the SEATO Treaty. Each was a maritime connection. The Navy's role was obvious, at least to the Navy: to keep open the sea-lanes to the allies that hemmed the Soviet empire. The question was, Did the Navy have an offensive mission as well? Or to put it bluntly, What was the role of naval air and was there a role for amphibious force?

The answer depended on how one envisioned the next war. Most analysts expected that it would be with the Soviet Union and that it would be total, short, and atomic. That meant, for the Navy, that it would not be a protracted conflict open to classic maritime strategies of blockade and peripheral action, and so the Navy would not be able to take advantage of the existing maritime network. Military attention returned ever more anxiously to the central front in Europe and to the advantages of the atomic bomb. The dominant Air Force–driven expectation of a short, atomic war virtually ignored the strategic significance of the maritime alliance system. This led to a contradiction between alliance maintenance and atomic war plans that was to bedevil maritime strategists for decades.

Nor would the next war be a limited and isolated conflict like Korea. Korea was treated as a special case not to be repeated, a land war in Asia fought under regrettable political limitations under which America, for all its technological superiority, could not win. Admiral Arthur Radford called Korea an aberration. Korea, said Army Chief of Staff General Omar Bradley in 1951, was "a reversion to old-style fighting—more comparable to that of our own Indian frontier days than to modern war."[2] His successor, General Matthew Ridgway, said in 1954 that wars of the future would not be limited, or stalemated, like Korea. "If we must fight, we must win. There can be no other goal."[3] All commanders shared the opinion expressed by the commander of the Seventh Fleet, Vice Admiral J. J. Clark, in the war's bitter last year: "You shouldn't be in a war if you don't want to win it."[4]

The Air Force disparaged the Navy's offensive action in Korea and by extension minimized the value of Navy air in the next war. Everyone agreed that the Navy had served a maritime support function. It held sea control, permitting U.S. shipping to support the war, and its joint amphibious operations were a notable success in a dismal time. Its air power, however, was deemed of limited effectiveness. So the question returned, Was there a place for over-the-shore air projection in a short atomic war against a foe deep in the Eurasian continent? Air Force officers, contending that only their land-based heavy bombers could deliver the decisive weapon, moved Navy air to the margin.

Carrier aircraft, they said, could move about the periphery but not penetrate to core targets. Air Force critics noted that Korea was not proof of projection value because the carriers had never been under challenge. Against the Soviet Union, however, carriers would have to expose themselves to sea-denial defenses. In the Norwegian and Mediterranean seas, when approaching land to launch and recover their aircraft, the carriers would not have the maneuvering room and distance that gave them a degree of safety on the open ocean.[5]

Still, for all its operational limitations and close-in vulnerability, Navy air was armed with doctrinal authority for tactical over-the-shore missions. In 1951 the Joint Chiefs had declared that Navy air was to strike naval targets ashore and give battlefield support:

> "These forces [carrier air] represent the major striking power of the Navy and are primarily responsible for neutralizing at the source the enemy's offensive capabilities to threaten control of the seas. . . . In addition to the above, these forces will provide naval support essential to the conduct of operations by the Supreme Allied Commander, Europe (SACEUR), the Commander in Chief, Far East (CINCFE) and other area commanders. For example, the 6th Fleet, now in the Mediterranean, will provide naval support to SACEUR in the accomplishment of his missions."[6]

That statement endorsed both the attack-at-the-source doctrine and the forward-flank strategy of Sherman and Forrestal. In case of a Soviet advance in the central front, the first SACEUR, General Dwight Eisenhower, told President Truman in 1951, he wanted a "great combination of sea and air strength" in the Mediterranean and the North Sea, to "hit them awfully hard from both flanks."[7] Navy planners recommended naval air-atomic operations against the Soviet fleet and against naval-related support targets located up to 600 miles from Navy ships in the western Pacific and in the Mediterranean, Norwegian, Barents, and Bering seas, and against airfields used by Soviet land-based naval air.[8] These were ambitious plans. Soviet naval targets on land came to 98 naval bases and 287 airfields, each accessible to Navy air if the carriers were in position. The immediate problem for the Navy was that until atomic weapons could be carried by standard Navy aircraft, the service had neither a serious air-atomic capability nor sufficient reach of arms, except in its forces off the southern coast of Europe and, at the very end of the Korean War, off Japan.[9]

The Navy went atomic in the early 1950s. First, patrol planes were fitted to carry atomic bombs from a carrier launch. These planes could land only at a recovery base ashore. Later, carrier AJ-1 Savage strike planes, to be launched and recovered at sea, on the *Coral Sea* in the Mediterranean were fitted for atomic bombs. These limited preparations were intended only for tactical operations. They were not part of an integrated atomic strategy. But they broke the Air Force's atomic monopoly.

The carrier attack force rested on the ships of the new general-purpose *Forrestal*-class. The *Forrestal,* successor to the ill-fated *United States,* was a product of the Korean War, which had changed many minds about many things. Within weeks of the North Korean invasion, Defense Secretary Johnson, who had scrubbed the *United States,* told Admiral Sherman, "I will give you another carrier when you want it," and the *Forrestal* went into the budget for fiscal year 1952.[10] Scientists meanwhile were reducing the weight of the atomic bomb. By 1952 the bomb had been reduced from 10,000 to 3,600 pounds. The Navy no longer had to have heavy attack bombers to deliver the weapon. So the *Forrestal* was planned to carry fighters and light attack planes that could provide limited tactical air support as well as deliver the atomic bomb.[11]

Thus the focus of attention for attack carriers, the great World War II legacy still at the core of the fleet, remained targets on land. The continuation of this focus renewed the over-the-shore strike doctrine that had been established at the 1929 Panama Canal raid of Fleet Problem IX and had been at the center of carrier use since the battle for Leyte Gulf. Carrier strikes on land targets were suitable for the support of sea control, for limited war and intervention, and now for a general war with the Soviet Union as well. The Air Force might deride the carrier as an offensive land-attack force, but Congress and the Truman and Eisenhower administrations approved, and the 1950s turned out to be good years for the fists of the fleet. The Navy kept up its carrier strength. Six supercarriers of the *Forrestal* class were built, and they were prepared for all missions. By 1962 the Navy had 26 carriers in service: the half-dozen puissant *Forrestals;* recommissioned ships of the *Kitty Hawk* and *Midway* classes, either dedicated to antisubmarine warfare or modernized with angled decks and strengthened to carry atomic-capable bombers; and a large number of the *Essex* class acting as support carriers, as amphibious assault ships, or as auxiliary aircraft transports. In 1961 the Navy brought into service the *Enterprise,* its first nuclear-powered attack carrier.

The Navy thereby supported the containment policy by surrounding the Soviet Union with offensive forces and covering the seas between. The U.S. Sixth Task Fleet, which had been created for permanent peacetime duty in the Mediterranean in June 1948, was reorganized as the Sixth Fleet in February 1950, anchoring Europe's southern flank. A

NATO Atlantic Command was created in 1952 with a separate British-U.S. Atlantic Striking Fleet of two carrier groups. The British First Lord of the Admiralty described the Striking Fleet in these words:

> Its role is analogous to the Grand Fleet of World War I and the British Home Fleet of World War II, namely the offensive force for Atlantic and Northern waters and the essential cover under which defensive forces, protecting our shipping from attack by aircraft, submarine and mine can do their work. . . . Attacks by aircraft from the Carrier Striking Fleet on the sources of the various threats to our sea communications can materially reduce these threats. In this they are complementary to attacks by shore-based air forces.[12]

It is true that the allied nature of NATO operations took some getting used to. NATO's Southern Command was beset by differences of operational concepts and distracted by the call of British units to colonial emergencies. Admiral Robert Carney, commander in chief of Allied Forces Southern Europe, said in 1951 that the only forces he commanded on Europe's southern flank were American.[13] In northern waters, cooperation was smoother. There the British contribution was well understood, and larger, and by 1953 the problems of operating combined forces at sea were worked out.[14]

Large British-American NATO naval exercises in 1952 and 1953 were not great displays of power projection, however. In the first exercise, rough weather reduced air action by 80 percent and forced changes in amphibious targets. In the second, weather was so bad that carrier air could not fly in the original deployment area, and the carriers were declared vulnerable to Soviet land-based air.[15] These exercises renewed the argument in favor of a supercarrier because of the large ship's stability in rough northern seas. They also renewed the opposite argument, of its vulnerability. The price of exposing such an expensive asset was likely to be greater than any benefit gained.

It would be dangerous to approach the Soviets' sea-denial force. That force was a logical counter to the West's maritime system and to the offensive movement of carriers against European coasts. The Soviets did not have a surface navy, but they had submarines, many submarines (261 in 1950, 353 in 1955, and 437 in 1960), mainly for home-water control—that is, for defense against attackers. Also in the 1950s, the Soviets added advanced land-based bombers to their sea-denial strategy. Increasingly, too, new classes of submarines permitted the Soviets to push out into open sea. With a longer reach and an offensive capacity, Soviet submarines menaced Allied sea-lanes. Even more threatening, in mid-1950 around 70 of their submarines were fitted with a deck hangar and launching equipment for two V-1–type guided missiles. By the 1960s these boats, with missiles on board, had both shores of the United States within target range.

So the Navy faced two challenges. Soviet stand-off defenses made it more difficult to execute both attack at the source and air projection in general, and Soviet submarines compelled the Navy into an urgent reassertion of sea control.

Conceptually, sea control had to underlie all Navy missions. Sea control was the Navy's main reason for existence. Sea control validated the service to the public. It gave the service coherence. Officers forgot sea control at their peril.

Captain Arleigh Burke of the General Board had insisted on that point back in 1948 when he sought to pull the service away from a numbing rivalry with the Army and the Air Force. There was an independent Navy mission at sea, Burke said, that had nothing to do with decisive bombing. That mission was to counter Soviet submarines. America's security depended on its use of the seas. Suppression of submarines was the Navy's responsibility. That was what had made attack at the source a sea-control function. Navy air could stand alone. It did not have to be part of the Air Force's pursuit of the will-o'-the-wisp of so-called strategic bombing. The Navy was not likely to win the nervous and defensive debate of 1948 and 1949 over who was to fight a strategic war. The Navy should not continue the debate on Air Force terms.

Sea control was the key to naval air. Sea control was part of the alternative strategy, according to which the country must prepare for a phased, protracted war. That kind of war took advantage of America's maritime position and served its political interests better than did the Air Force concept of a short, sharp war based on countervalue targeting. The long-war strategy gave the Navy its claim to carriers and atomic weapons because in such a war counterforce attack-at-the-source would be a necessary Navy job, the means of preventing the large Soviet submarine fleet from getting into the open ocean.[16]

The Soviet submarine force in 1948 stood at about 250 boats. Construction of new classes was under way. These classes were based on the German models and plans and on the work of the German engineers that the Red Army had captured when it swarmed across the U-boat installations of the Baltic Sea. By 1950 the U.S. Navy was confident that its vigorous antisubmarine program had taken submarine danger in hand. Five years later, in the fear of surprise attack and the first submarine-launched ballistic missiles, the Navy sounded the submarine alert again. In 1955 intelligence estimated that the Soviets were building about 100 boats a year and had about 350 submarines operational. These included 93 of a new medium-range Whiskey class, and the first Zulus. The Zulu was a diesel-powered, long-range attack submarine capable of carrying atomic-tipped ballistic missiles. At the end of the decade, 437 boats sailed in the Soviet submarine fleet.

Against these the Navy set a three-track strategy. One was an attrition campaign by hunter-killer groups to destroy submarines at sea. To that job it dedicated half the carrier force. Ships of the recalled *Essex* class were to protect the attack carriers and, even more important, Allied shipping lanes. The units on carrier-protection duty were joined by an increasingly sophisticated screen of antiaircraft destroyers, which mounted surface-to-air missiles. That allowed the large carriers to concentrate entirely on attack. All units on hunter-killer patrol relied on ever-improving detection methods and devices, products from the technological cornucopia of the world war, which were still pouring forth and being assimilated into the fleet. These means of detection included advanced codebreaking methods; helicopter searches; very long range sonar; and acoustic hydrophones dropped, in buoys, by carrier aircraft. Antisubmarine warfare from the air became feasible again.[17]

The second approach was the barrier strategy, by which American submarines waited off Soviet bases and at the entrances to the Barents, Baltic, and Black seas, and to the Seas of Japan and Okhotsk, at the straits through which any Soviet vessel had to sortie to reach the ocean. The strategy relied on forward employment of very long range sonar and on a passive system of hydrophones fastened permanently to the ocean bottom. In this way, the Navy took its antisubmarine force right to the entrances of the hornets' nests.

Third was the carrier-air strike at the nests themselves, the sea-control rationale for an air-atomic force. "The most effective and economical means of destroying threats to our control of the Seas is to destroy those threats at the source," ran a typical expression, in this case from a Navy planning document of 1951 that promoted the whole array of missions. "Our carrier task forces will destroy enemy Naval forces and shipping, attack naval bases, attack airfields threatening control of the seas, support amphibious assault forces and support the mining offensive."[18]

JCS approval in the early 1950s of an over-the-shore mission secured the carriers and gave the Navy time to catch its breath. The recommissioning of World War II ships gave an additional cushion, permitting a fast buildup without expensive new construction and attendant political controversy. The Navy had something of a second honeymoon, during which the fleet consolidated its postwar technical and operational innovations.

Amid all the attention given carriers and submarines, a few officers continued to remind the fleet of its supporting role, of the fact that transport and escort remained the backbone of a maritime strategy. Emphasizing that the West's strength was its maritime alliance and that a general war might be protracted, Captain George Miller, in the Strategic Plans Division (OP-30) under then Rear Admiral Arleigh Burke, reiterated in 1952 the importance of sea control in Allied strategy. The Navy's jobs, Miller said, were these:

1. Supply and support U.S. forces deployed overseas.
2. Supply and support U.S. allies, in support of treaty commitments.
3. Deny use of the Seas by the Soviet Union to further its objectives or interfere with ours.
4. Import the raw materials and commodities necessary to sustain U.S. armed forces and the U.S. war effort.[19]

This list won few adherents. Miller's sea-control conclusion was correct, however, as the experience of two world wars had shown. Protection of shipping had to be the U.S. Navy's prime concern. Contemporary British naval opinion understood that full well. The "safe and timely arrival" of convoys served Allied defensive and offensive strategies better than did the "hunting to death of U-boats." For that the escorted convoy was the answer, and for such escort NATO and the U.S. Navy should be prepared.[20]

In light of the importance the Navy was to assign in the next decades to limited war and to the idea that war might be limited in objective and theater but not limited in time, it is well to keep in mind that regional limited war was not a concern of the mid-1950s. Although Korea had confirmed, at least to some Navy officers, the fallacy of the short-war theory based on strategic bombing, almost all Navy strategists in the 1950s, Burke and Miller included, prepared almost exclusively for a general war with the Soviet Union and embraced a central role for atomic weapons in that war. The Navy's disagreement with the Air Force was over time, over the prospective war's duration, and over the extent of reliance on atomic weapons. Vice Admiral C. Turner Joy was the naval theater commander in the first two years of the Korean War and later head of the UN Command Truce Delegation. He summed up the lesson of the war as he left the Far East: "We know now that there is no quick, easy, cheap way to win a war. Sole reliance for our security cannot be placed in any one weapon or in any one branch of the Services."[21] In principle, that lesson opened the possibility of developing a complete theory of protracted war, of a maritime strategy that took into account advantages of using force over a longer period of time. But doctrinally this possibility remained undeveloped in Navy circles.

EISENHOWER'S NEW LOOK

Navy planning was not helped by the ambiguity of the new look that President Eisenhower gave the containment policy. Eisenhower's expression of the policy left military officers wondering whether massive retaliation was a ruse or a plan of war.

There was great concern in the 1950s that the United States was exposed to grave danger. In August 1953, less than a month after the Korean armistice was signed and less than a year after the first U.S. thermonuclear explosion, the Soviet Union set off a nuclear blast widely thought to be from a hydrogen bomb.[22] It was only a matter of time—the following year, experts predicted—before the Soviet Union could deploy a delivery system capable of reaching the United States. Many officers feared a first strike by a long-range bomber fleet on a one-way mission. Memories of Pearl Harbor, compounded by the unclear terrors of world revolution and the atomic bomb, haunted officials. What many today think of as the quiet 1950s was a decade of insecurity.

At issue was a counterstrategy. The burden of NSC-68 of 1950 had been that the United States must react globally, proportionally, and symmetrically to any Soviet aggression.[23] Containment had come to mean meeting the enemy when and where he chose and on his terms, a practice that, as Korea showed, could lead to prolonged wars of uncertain value far from the great power centers.

The Eisenhower administration took office in January 1953. Its leaders—the president, Secretary of State John Foster Dulles, and Secretary of the Treasury George Humphrey—took a "new look" at force and containment. They were determined to avoid the costs of military overextension. A way had to be found to deter Soviet aggression without bankrupting the country. A wounded economy would be a Communist victory.[24]

At the same time, Eisenhower's administration was politically assertive. Its leaders were determined to regain the initiative, to shape events. The United States would decide for itself how it would respond to aggression. It would set the terms, the level of intensity, and the locale. Retaliation did not have to be proportional to the provocation, of the same kind, or even in the same theater. Uncertainty of response, the administration hoped, would deter aggression because an aggressor would never be able to foresee where he would be hit, how strongly, or with what. The new strategy rested on America's nuclear arsenal. Atomic bombs were the country's most cost-efficient weapon, and to the A-bombs were added, during Eisenhower's administration, the H-bombs, thermonuclear weapons first detonated in tests at Eniwetok Atoll in October and November 1952. The generic term "nuclear" was used henceforth to cover both types of weapons and a war employing them.

NSC-162/2 of October 1953 declared that in case of war "nuclear weapons" were "to be as available for use as other munitions."[25] Because the enemy must know fear to be deterred, President Eisenhower in his State of the Union message in January 1954 and then later that month Secretary Dulles publicly connected containment to nuclear weapons. There was, Dulles said, "no local defense which alone will contain the mighty landpower of the Communist world. Local defenses must be reinforced by the further deterrent of massive retaliatory power. A potential aggressor must know that he cannot always prescribe battle conditions that suit him." The "free community," Dulles continued, must "be willing and able to respond vigorously at places and with means of its own choosing" and to do so "with old weapons and with new weapons."

With massive retaliation Dulles sought to increase his options, not limit them. He wanted to avoid what he saw as costly and "superficial" reactions that would largely be subject to terms set by the enemy. At the same time he wanted to set in place a "long time" foreign policy that did not necessitate vast, standing military expenditures that would lead, he feared, to "practical bankruptcy." Atomic weapons, which at that time numbered around 1,000 in the U.S. arsenal, gave "more basic security at less cost."[26]

The problem for military planners was that it is hard to make a strategy to fit a bluff. Would the United States actually back up its threat? Strategists could never be sure.

Take the problem of responding to the Soviet threat. Over 1,300 Soviet aircraft could reach the United States. Planes on one-way missions could hit the 53 major urban areas that encompassed 63 percent of America's industrial capacity. Few had confidence in direct defense measures such as antiaircraft missiles or bomb shelters. Until the U-2 overflights began in July 1956, intelligence could not locate Soviet nuclear weapon facilities, and so could not target them, and thus SAC could not guarantee they could be destroyed. In January 1955 the Basic National Security Policy paper superseding NSC-162/2 stated that during the next five years the Soviet Union would "almost certainly" gain the ability to cripple the United States. Bombs could be hidden in ships sailed into harbors or delivered from submarines hugging the shore. Against intercontinental ballistic missiles (ICBMs), expected in a few years, "there is no known defense . . . at this time."[27] Brinksmanship might be the deterrent, but it meant looking down the barrel of national suicide. Was that an acceptable strategy?

The magnitude of concern may be inferred from the United States's own experience with its hydrogen bomb test at Eniwetok Atoll in 1954. The bomb's crater was over a mile wide, and by the end of the test the area where traffic was forbidden was two times the size of Texas. After a blast big enough to take the heart out of any U.S. city, a pattern of fallout resulted that, superimposed on a map of the eastern United States—with Washington, D.C., as ground zero—extended north through Baltimore, Philadelphia, New York City, and Albany, all the way to the Canadian border.[28]

Another unresolved question of the new look was what the mix of U.S. forces was to be. Here cost was paramount. The Eisenhower administration based the planning of the nation's forces not on a threat assessment but on what would strain the economy least. The greatest deterrence at the lowest cost was the refrain. That did not answer major strategic questions. Was it wise to place such a reliance on nuclear weapons? Should the country not instead maintain conventional strength sufficient to have an alternative to massive retaliation? Was there such a thing, anyway, as a strategic nuclear war that would be over in days thanks to strategic bombing? And if the value of the bombs was reduced, would the value of the Navy's protracted-war strategy be enhanced, or its air-atomic role reduced, or both?

Mixed judgments in the mid-1950s on the purpose of the atomic bomb made it difficult to determine its employment. The administration did not answer the key question of whether atomic bombs were to be fully integrated into military planning or were to be reserved as a deterrent held for discretionary retaliation, a card the president might or might not play.[29] Eisenhower early on loosened the tight civilian control that had been imposed by President Truman and immediately made atomic weapons available to the military. It seems that in Eisenhower's mind there was no doubt that the weapons could be used in a general war.[30] There now were also more types of bombs. Eisenhower's attention to small atomic weapons for tactical use was "a major innovation in the evolution of American nuclear strategy," the basis of a new generation of weapons stemming from the reduction of the size of implosion fission bombs from 10,000 pounds to 1,000 pounds by 1954, making them easier to carry on the Navy's attack planes and missiles and in its depth charges.[31] At the same time, the president never ordered the use of nuclear weapons. Eisenhower, like Truman and all his successors, practiced "self-deterrence."[32] In practice, the bomb was not just another bullet.

There was no serious public debate about whether to use nuclear weapons. Within the services, the Air Force and its Strategic Air Command supported the general nuclear emphasis. The Navy, at least CNO Admiral Robert Carney (August 1953 to August 1955) and his top planner, Rear Admiral Arleigh Burke, accepted their use, but only in a particular context. In October 1953 Carney responded to NSC-162/2 with the argument that nuclear dependency confined foreign policy. A Soviet counterbuildup, already well advanced, would result in a strategic stalemate. There had to be, Carney said, a conventional force capable of action below the level of general war, a force that would not provoke escalation. That force, of course, was the Navy.

Yet the Navy wanted more—a semistrategic air-atomic role as well. In December 1953 and January 1954, Carney sent to the JCS studies drafted by Arleigh Burke and his Strategic Plans Division that argued that the United States must have a highly mobile, combat-ready strategic reserve "to continue over the long term to be ready to cope with limited aggression and at the same time be prepared for general war." With the reference to general war, the Navy leaders wanted to move naval aviation beyond the tactical support of land forces to the support of massive retaliation, a semistrategic role. Navy air, Carney said, was able to inflict "massive damage," deliver tactical support, and of course provide sea control.[33]

This versatility was meant to be seen in favorable contrast to the narrow, only hypothetically decisive role of the Strategic Air Command. Carney and Burke thus reordered the Navy to accommodate the new look and the administration's emphasis on atomic weapons. In February 1954 the JCS broadened its endorsement of Navy air to include a semistrategic role in a general war with the Soviet Union. This role would be independent of and in addition to over-the-shore strikes to assure sea control and air strikes in support of land operations.

That culminated the Navy's naval-air doctrine with regard to the atomic bomb. "In 1954," David Rosenberg has written, the Navy "demonstrated an ability to adapt to a changing environment without losing sight of its own goals and identity," by finding a place even in the massive-retaliation policy it opposed.[34]

INTERVENTION

The Eisenhower administration had not ignored limited military engagements. The president, however, wanted to hold intervention as much as possible to the level of covert operations, aid, or the shaking of a big stick. He did not want another Korea. If the United States did not have an Army garrison in place, and if it wanted to contain an action by a foreign power, it could send ships. Warships did not need local bases and airfields. They arrived, stayed on station, and departed at will. They permitted controlled U.S. action. In the 1950s, gunboat diplomacy was reborn within the containment policy as peacetime presence and crisis intervention.[35]

The prospect of Chinese engagement in Indochina was one of the first concerns of Admiral Carney when he became CNO in August 1953. With the war in Korea winding down, the Navy had planned a major reduction in the western Pacific. The prospect that the Beijing regime might move against Indochina and Taiwan changed that, and Carney canceled the cutbacks. A U.S. naval force was to be the main local deterrent to Chinese aggression.[36] The CNO readied attack carriers and destroyers in the Pacific in case Washington should decide to use them. President Eisenhower had warned in December 1953, and Secretary Dulles repeated in his speech in January on the "deterrent of massive retaliatory power," that U.S. forces in the Far East would be composed of "highly mobile naval, air, and amphibious units" and that these would have a capacity to oppose aggression "with even greater effect than heretofore."[37] This was an unmistakable reference to the use of atomic weapons.

The crisis in Indochina came to a head in March 1954 when 13,000 French troops found themselves besieged in a valley at Dien Bien Phu. The chairman of the Joint Chiefs, Admiral Arthur Radford, the most determined advocate of a massive U.S. air strike to relieve the French garrison, informed Eisenhower that the Attack Carrier Striking Group in the Gulf of Tonkin was ready. Radford thought Dien Bien Phu was a test of American resolve. If the French position was lost, he told the president, "the consequences can well lead to the loss of all of S.E. Asia to Communist domination. If this is to be avoided, I consider that the U.S. must be prepared to act promptly and in force possibly to a frantic and belated request by the French for U.S. intervention."[38]

That French request "to save the situation" came in April 1954. The fact of Chinese intervention, the French government said, was "fully established." Washington refused to approve an air strike, atomic or otherwise. Carney thought that air strikes in the highland jungles around Dien Bien Phu, though no doubt tactically helpful to the French, would not be enough to win.[39] As for the future, the JCS concluded after the fall of Dien Bien Phu that "*Indochina is devoid of decisive military objectives and the allocation of more than token* U.S. armed forces *in Indochina would be a serious diversion of limited U.S. capabilities.*" At the same time, with an eye on China, they continued to base their planning on the assumption that "atomic weapons will be used whenever it is to our military advantage."[40]

The political cost of using an A-bomb in a conflict peripheral to the Soviet threat was very high. It was the doomsday weapon, held in reserve for a truly great national security crisis. If, as in Korea and possibly Indochina, its use would not be decisive because of mountainous terrain and a dispersed enemy, or if a bomb did not explode, its deterrent impact would be much reduced.[41] The atomic bomb was a specialty weapon. That meant that at the very time Navy air and, a fortiori, the Air Force were becoming nuclear-dependent, they were limiting themselves strategically. For with a growing Soviet counterforce, the paradox of nuclear weapons was that as they increasingly served deterrence of a big-power nuclear war, their effectiveness depended more and more on their nonuse, and so they became a less useful instrument for peripheral containment.

The crisis in the Formosa Strait the next year, 1955, rehearsed these matters, again without resolution. Admiral Radford saw the mainland government's shelling of offshore islands as an opportunity to reestablish American prestige in Asia, which had been weakened, he thought, by submitting to stalemates in Korea and Indochina. Naval forces were in place. President Eisenhower was equivocal about the use of atomic weapons to defend Quemoy (Jinmen)—an island on the approach to the mainland port of Amoy (Hsia-men)—and the Matsu (Mazu) group. Both Quemoy and Matsu were about a dozen miles offshore and held by the Taiwan-based Nationalist government. A war would set back the Beijing regime, end its threat to Taiwan, and refurbish America's containment policy, but an atomic bomb was a last resort.[42]

For Radford the crisis was a fundamental test of United States resolve. Was the new look for real or just an excuse for cutting the armed forces? In March 1955 Radford told President Eisenhower that the country's "whole military structure" was built on the assumption that in a war with Communists, America would use nuclear weapons, and he called for fulfillment—for preemptive strikes against mainland airfields and an atomic warning issued directly to Beijing and Moscow. Dulles conceded the dilemma. He said the administration had to "face up to the question whether its military program was or was not in fact designed to permit use of atomic weapons." If it was not, then "our entire military program would have to be revised." Were atomic bombs for use, or not? Eisenhower did not answer.[43]

The Seventh Fleet established a defense zone between Taiwan and the mainland. The fleet operated close to mainland airfields. To retain air superiority if Communist Chinese forces interfered with any movements within the defense zone, Admiral Carney supported strikes against the mainland. That called for Air Force assistance and, all assumed, the possible use of atomic weapons.[44] The Air Force ordered the Strategic Air Command to select targets for an "enlarged atomic offensive."

The Formosa Strait crisis ceased when the mainland government stopped the shelling. The crisis left a residue of doubt. Had the new look become counterproductive? What if Chinese attacks had been countered by atomic bombs? Had self-deterrence led to paralysis? If so, what could the United States put in its place? There was no doctrine of limited war.

In January 1955 the National Security Council recognized for the first time the bipolar nuclear standoff and the need for the United States to be able to meet limited aggression without escalation. It stated, "The ability to apply force selectively and flexibly will become increasingly important in maintaining the morale and will of the free world to resist aggression."[45] The government would have an alternative to the immobility born of the nuclear stalemate, an alternative to general war. This was by no means the end of the new look, but thereafter doubt about its utility forced consideration of other strategies.

BURKE'S COLD WAR NAVY

The officer who fit the Navy to the new look and who then led it to flexible response was Admiral Arleigh A. Burke, who served as chief of naval operations during most of the Eisenhower administration. Burke was the first rear admiral promoted to the top job, having been selected over 92 officers his senior. He held the post for an unprecedented three successive terms, from August 1955 to August 1961.

Burke was a staunch anti-Communist, a cold warrior, and a strong supporter of Eisenhower's nuclear-arms buildup. He understood that atomic weapons were the means by which the Navy would substantially share Eisenhower's military budgets. He preserved the air-atomic missions that the Navy had won in previous years. He moved the Navy to the strategic center with the offensive / deterrence capability of the atomic submarine-launched Polaris fleet ballistic missile. Burke, a skillful politician, never went beyond the national position on defense, and he kept the support of Congress.

At the same time, Burke was a critic of any single strategy in war. Atomic weapons were useful, but the country should not rely on them exclusively. More and more in the last half of the 1950s, Burke pushed for alternatives to the increasingly moribund "new look."

A heavy-fleet man, Burke tended the Navy's air-atomic capability. The *Forrestal* class of carriers, with angled decks and steam catapults, carried a dozen heavy-attack, nuclear-capable aircraft and stored six times as many bombs as the previous *Midway* class did. The *Forrestal* was commissioned in 1955, followed by the *Saratoga* and the *Ranger* in 1956 and 1957, the *Independence* in 1959, and the *Kitty Hawk* and the *Constellation* in 1961. Also in 1961, the immense 35-knot *Enterprise* was commissioned. The first of the nuclear-powered strike carriers, it had 4,660 men aboard.

And the carriers launched better planes. In 1956 the Douglas A3D Skywarrior twin-jet, all-weather, heavy-attack bomber began replacing the AJ-1s and AJ-2s in the carrier force. The A3D had a high-altitude range of over 3,000 miles and could accelerate to speeds of close to 600 miles per hour. That meant a U.S. carrier in the eastern Mediterranean was within striking distance of semistrategic targets in the southern European part of the Soviet Union—the oil refineries at Baku, the military-industrial targets of Stalingrad (Volgograd) and Kharkov, and all the naval facilities on the Black Sea. In 1960 the first Grumman A-6A Intruder was flown, an atomic-bomb-capable attack plane that flew low, day or night, in all weather.[46]

Strike carriers bore some fighter protection, but because most of their planes were for attack missions, more defense was required. Antiaircraft guns afloat could not shoot down the new classes of standoff, nuclear-capable, missile-carrying, land-based bombers that Soviet naval air deployed in the second half of the 1950s. These planes were known in Western military terminology as Bison, comparable to the B-52; Beagle, a light tactical bomber; Badger, comparable to the B-47; Blinder, a medium bomber; and the large, turboprop Bear. Navy defense shifted to reliance on surface-to-air missiles launched from a protective screen of cruisers, destroyers, and frigates. Burke had been trained as an ordnance officer, and he led in retraining sailors, reconfiguring combat operations, and rethinking the design of ships to better adapt them for use as missile platforms. In the 1950s the Navy entered the missile age.[47]

Strategists were most exercised by the increase in Soviet submarines. There were some 353 in operation in the mid-1950s, including the first of the Zulu class, a diesel-powered long-range attack boat that had test-fired a submarine-launched ballistic missile. The intelligence estimate was that the Soviets were producing 100 new boats a year.

Submarines posed a triple threat. First, the Soviets were beefing up their submarine forces for defense against strike carriers. Second, Soviet submarines carrying guided missiles were able to approach the coast of the United States and put the homeland at risk. The brunt of the Killian Committee's report to Eisenhower in 1955 was a warning that an attack from the sea "with conventional high-explosive weapons, with BW [biological] and CW [chemical] agents, and with nuclear weapons: sea-launched missiles, mines, and truly massive off-shore explosions" would take the United States by surprise and deliver a devastating blow.[48] Third, the submarines put at risk the Navy's control of the sea insofar as they could attack warships and interdict transport, both of which were critical in a protracted war.

A prospective offensive against shipping and Navy vessels by Soviet attack submarines led Burke in 1955 to reemphasize sea control. Updated *Essex*-class carriers continued to form the core of surface hunter-killer groups, which were the basic antisubmarine units. Improved passive and active underwater sensor systems, antisubmarine mines, and torpedoes were put in use. The new Regulus I surface-to-surface cruise bombardment missile was introduced in 1954 for use against naval targets ashore such as bases, shipyards, and airfields. Carried by a submarine, Regulus I and its supersonic successor, Regulus II, provided a missile version of attack at the source, and of semistrategic deep-penetration missions as well. Most dramatically, the U.S. submarine fleet was reconstituted. Already in January 1955 the *Nautilus*, the world's first true submersible, had flashed her historic message, "Underway on nuclear power."[49] In September 1955 the Navy announced that all future attack submarines would be propelled by nuclear power.[50] Six nuclear attack submarines of the *Skipjack* class were commissioned between 1959 and 1961.

Burke was supported by a sympathetic Congress. Following NSC-68 and Korea, the Navy's share of Defense Department appropriations held steady through the 1950s, averaging around 27 percent of the military total. It varied only 4.4 percent, compared to an 18.1 percent variation for the Army and a 15.3 percent variation for the Air Force.[51] Force levels of aircraft carriers and attack submarines were remarkably stable. The Navy operated between 13 and 15 attack carriers and around 90 attack submarines. While the Navy was notably disinterested in amphibious warfare, the Marine Corps insisted on attention to amphibious lift, on which it based its modern force. The Marines wanted lift for two divisions, split evenly between the two oceans. The Navy and the administration after Korea decided on one and one-third, the number met.[52] And from Korea through Lebanon, amphibious operations were the main feature of many of the most notable Navy and Marine Corps operations of the decade.

Burke had been an early critic of massive retaliation, on several grounds. One was the need for strategic flexibility. An all-out atomic war would not be worth fighting, for no political goals could match the cost. Second, he predicted that arms competition would end in an atomic stalemate. To regain the ability to take the strategic initiative, and to capitalize on America's geographic position, the country had to prepare for a protracted, conventional general war. To meet peripheral aggression—perhaps with tactical atomic weapons—a flexible maritime strategy was needed, one based on a mobile sea force. Finally, in a nuclear stalemate the purpose of the swiftly growing stockpile of nuclear weapons would become less that of containment of aggression (which a more flexible strategy could provide) than that of deterrence of a general nuclear war, with deterrence itself perpetuating the stalemate.

For deterrence fewer nuclear weapons were needed. What was important was that those weapons be secure. In 1955 Burke reinstated a long-range planning group (OP-93) in the immediate office of the CNO. Its job was to look at force levels and other needs of naval strategy a decade ahead. The next year Burke got the Joint Chiefs to agree that a nuclear exchange with the Soviets might not be decisive and that in a protracted war a complex sea-control strategy would be essential.[53]

Almost immediately, however, debate over the defense budget for fiscal year 1958 threatened Burke's moves toward a broader national, and naval, strategy.

The budget debate in 1957 was intense because, as Army Chief of Staff General Maxwell Taylor bitterly expressed it, "*All the services were given money ceilings in terms of expenditures rather than in obligations*, as had formerly been the case." Those ceilings benefited the services that spent the most, not those that had the most men, most equipment, or, they would say, the most to do. In a high-tech strategy, that meant benefiting the Air Force, which asked for almost 50 percent of the defense budget, mostly for its Strategic Air Command. For Taylor and Burke this spread represented a resurgence of the doctrine of massive retaliation just when its value was most in question. The Joint Chiefs' chairman, Admiral Radford, was, according to Taylor, "determined to eliminate from military planning any consideration of the possibility of a conventional war with the Soviet Union." That meant cutting the Army to the bone and retreating to Fortress America instead of forward-deploying deterrent ground and sea forces in cooperation with allies.[54]

Burke wrote to Secretary of Defense Charles Wilson (January 1953 to October 1957) that building more bombers would not assure national survival, improve the chances of avoiding a nuclear holocaust, or win a war worth winning. More bombers would only support a misguided philosophy of war and drain scarce money from more useful weapons systems that were more likely to be used in a more probable conflict for more realizable national goals. A budget that put money in the vulnerable planes of the Strategic Air Command at the expense of research and development, that slowed the installation of missiles, and that proposed to reduce the Navy within a decade to two-thirds of the strength it needed to operate effectively was misconceived and counterproductive.[55]

In the JCS, Burke and Taylor attacked the Air Force's domination of nuclear strategy. SAC's hyperbolic targeting plans assigned such excessive bomb loads that execution would create so great a radiation field that fallout might impede other military operations and certainly destroy the possibility of a political conclusion to the war. SAC's manned bombers, furthermore, were vulnerable to a first strike, and their destruction would eliminate the United States' capacity for strategic retaliation. The Air Force, in short, had no strategy below the level of all-out war, and that was politically and militarily self-defeating.[56]

General Taylor wrote a manifesto for a "New National Military Program of Flexible Response." The "Great Fallacy" of massive retaliation, he wrote, was the assumption that it was "an all-weather, all purpose strategy which is adequate to cope with any military challenge." It was not. There were many circumstances in which lesser force would serve, he said, in which the situation was not all or nothing, circumstances in which conventional ground combat, integrated sea-land warfare, and mobility and flexibility were in order.[57]

The Air Force won the day, taking over 48 percent of the budget for fiscal year 1958. The Navy got what it wanted, almost 29 percent. The

Army was the big loser. It got 21 percent of the defense dollar; for fiscal year 1951 it had taken 39 percent.[58]

How did the Navy do so well? Taylor watched Burke at work and summed up the adaptability that was the hallmark of Navy planning, an adaptability derived from the sea-power claim, according to which the Navy gave the country strengths of all kinds:

> The Navy–Marine Corps representatives in the JCS have rather belatedly joined with the Army in supporting the concept of Flexible Response against the advocates of Massive Retaliation. However, they have shown little enthusiasm for the budgeting by operational functions rather than by service, maintaining that naval forces cannot be broken down into functional categories. They point out that a ship may concurrently contribute to strategic bombing, antisubmarine warfare, and air defense. . . .
>
> The Navy, like the Army, opposes the concept of "Fortress America." Although recognizing the need to cope quickly with limited war, the Navy resists planning for any limited war situation large enough to justify substantial Army forces. Every effort is made to depict the Navy–Marine Corps combination as the answer to the limited war problem. Consequently, the Navy shows no interest in the strategic air and sea lift requirements of the Army.
>
> The Navy fights hard for the preservation of its present large carrier force, attempting to justify the numbers by the requirements of both general and limited war. While the other services would like to see the Navy concentrate its attention more upon antisubmarine warfare, the Navy prefers to advance along three parallel lines, seeking to expand its role in strategic bombardment and limited ground warfare while retaining its responsibility for antisubmarine warfare.
>
> The Navy agrees with the Army that the short-war concept is dangerous and that responsible provisions must be made for post-M-Day mobilization.
>
> In general, the Navy–Marine Corps are satisfied with the *status quo* and opposed to any significant changes in the present roles and missions of the services.[59]

Behind the defense budget for fiscal year 1958 had been the idea that a containment force based on unchallenged nuclear supremacy could be built cheaply. It was a hope shattered at once. In August 1957 the Soviets announced the successful test of an intercontinental ballistic missile, and two months later, in October, they lofted *Sputnik*, the earth's first artificial satellite. Public opinion throughout the world took these events as evidence that the Soviets had overtaken the Americans in the race for space. Eisenhower's economizing had not kept up with the challenges of national defense.

A shift in thinking was represented by the Gaither Report of November 1957, which denied that there would be a stable strategic balance. According to the report, the Soviets had "probably surpassed us in

ICBM development." It said, "The USSR will probably achieve a significant ICBM delivery capability with megaton warheads by 1959" and the "U.S. will probably have not achieved such a capability." By 1960 "SAC could be completely vulnerable to an ICBM attack directly against its bases and weapons stockpile." By 1960 the United States would be entering "a very critical period." Here was a warning of a missile gap. Already "the submarine-launched missile threat is a formidable one for which there is presently no known adequate countermeasure." For the future, everything must be done to develop an invulnerable second-strike force. ICBM bases must be hardened. "The Polaris submarine-based weapon system, with its great mobility and security from attack," should be speeded up. The report recommended across-the-board increases in military spending.[60]

President Eisenhower, intent on minimum cost, did not endorse the Gaither Report, and it had little direct impact on U.S. strategy or on the distribution of the defense budget. Still, the Soviet ICBM test, *Sputnik*, and the report's conclusions provoked much thinking. The immediate beneficiary was the heavy-missile program, of which Polaris was a central feature. Polaris broke the Air Force monopoly of strategic deterrence. Polaris gave the Navy a strategic role, and Burke, in a bold conceptualization, defined it as just what the Navy wanted.

POLARIS

Deterrence depended upon credibility. Opinion in the late 1950s was that the United States had to have a secure retaliatory capability able to destroy half the Soviet Union's industrial capacity and 20 to 25 percent of its population. The better that force was protected from a Soviet first strike, the greater its deterrent effect. There were three parts to the strategic strike force: the Strategic Air Command's manned bombers; SAC's siloed missiles, the Titan and Atlas first-generation liquid-fuel intercontinental ballistic missiles; and the Navy's submarine-launched intermediate-range ballistic missile (IRBM), Polaris. Polaris was the most difficult for an enemy to find, and hence the most secure.

The development of Polaris had been controversial and slow. The Navy was the last service to embrace ballistic missiles. Until the mid-1950s long-range missiles were seen as distracting the service from ongoing air and sea-control preparedness. A solid-fuel, sea-based IRBM force, and the ships to carry it, would have had to come out of the existing construction budget. There were technical difficulties many thought would take years to overcome. Missiles aboard a ship were different from missiles siloed in the ground. Navigation devices and fire-control systems had to direct a missile launched from an ever-moving seaborne platform. Seagoing strategic missiles had to be smaller, and the Navy required solid-propellant motors to prevent leaks of enormously flammable liquid. Strategic missiles on Soviet submarines were (and those on Russian submarines still are) liquid fueled, and carrying them can be hazardous. A 10,000-ton Soviet Yankee-class submarine was lost in 1986 after a fire and explosion in its missile compartment.

The Navy had been working on several ram-jet, low-level, air-breathing cruise missiles, the Regulus and Triton series, to be launched from a cruiser or a surfaced submarine. Those missiles fit the attack-at-the-source doctrine of the early 1950s. In October 1955 the Navy's leading missileers informed the new CNO Admiral Burke that giving high priority to a fleet ballistic missile would jeopardize the development of the Reguluses and Tritons—as indeed it did. A sea-based IRBM program, they said, was distracting and impractical. Let the other services develop the missile designs and prototypes, and the Navy could draw on the results.[61]

Burke, CNO from August 1955 to August 1961, rejected that advice and turned the Navy decisively toward Polaris. His decision reflected the Killian Report of February 1955, which had warned against strategic surprise and stated the need of a secure retaliatory capability. The report specifically argued that the United States should develop a medium-range, 1,500-mile missile, that speed was vital, and that the medium-range system could be deployed in a shorter time than its intercontinental, 5,500-mile counterpart. The report concluded that "ship basing probably would allow better coverage of Soviet Bloc targets [than would land basing] and be free of political restraints [i.e., there would be no need to base them on foreign soil]."[62]

The Killian recommendations, as Vincent Davis said, "broke the logjam of confusion and controversy in the development of ballistic missiles not only within the Navy but within the armed forces as a whole."[63] The report helped fleet ballistic missile proponents persuade the Bureau of Aeronautics to get behind a program. Also, a breakthrough in inertial-guidance development permitted the application of inertial guidance to sea-based ballistic missiles. In light of these considerations, Burke decided that the Navy should press on as fast as possible. In December 1955 he established a Special Projects Office that reported directly to the CNO and the secretary of the Navy. Burke gave the head job to the masterful Rear Admiral William F. Raborn and gave Raborn a "hunting license" to get the 50 best people he could find.

Reservations remained. Burke thought that "many naval officers (perhaps most naval officers) [had] serious and valid doubts about the desirability of making the effort at all." He listed their questions:

> How can we raise the money? Is it possible to get the funds in addition to our present budget? How can we provide enough men to man the new ships? What will happen to other important projects? Since this new weapon system will be good only for general nuclear war, how can we maintain our conventional and limited war capacity at the necessary level? How can this program be organized so as not to disrupt everything else we must do?[64]

It would not be easy. Burke knew a sea-based IRBM system would be costly. He decided in favor of it because he thought it was technically feasible, strategically plausible, and institutionally valuable. An intermediate-range missile, able to reach any part of the Soviet Union or China from an ocean submarine, would support a deterrence policy better than SAC's massive-retaliation strategy would. And he knew that if the Navy did not take an independent and aggressive interest in ballistic-missile development, the Air Force and the Army would never come up with a model suitable for shipboard deployment. The Navy would have lost its chance. This decision, Burke's biographer wrote, "was probably the single most significant action of his six years as chief of naval operations."[65]

Burke's decision raised a sensitive issue. In the preceding decade, as we have seen, notably in the B-36 debate in 1949, some Navy officers had objected to the Air Force's version of national strategy, part of it based on countervalue bombing of population centers. This was a quarrel that went back to World War II and Navy–Air Force differences about what should be considered the least destructive and most efficient way to beat Japan. It was an argument about blockade versus urban bombing, about timing and effectiveness, and, more broadly, about the nature of war.

In a sense, the Navy had lost this argument, as shown by the triumph of the vision of strategic bombing and massive retaliation, the belief in swift victory, and the integrated targeting program controlled by the Air Force. Naval officers who opposed the development of Polaris did not want to support an effort that they felt would reopen an air-space competition the Navy would lose. It was better to stay with sea-control missions than to arm the Navy with what in 1955 was likely to be a low-yield and inaccurate weapon directed against civilian and industrial targets in the expectation of a short war—exactly what Navy officers had opposed in Air Force doctrine in 1945 and 1949 and thereafter. To embrace Polaris, which in its early stage had an unreliable propulsion system and might land as much as four miles off target—as opposed to such accurate, measured, and controlled counterforce missiles as Regulus and the very accurate, pilot-controlled flights of carrier-launched tactical naval air—would be to reverse the Navy's position and accept the Air Force's target selection and its definition of nuclear war.[66]

To mute those concerns, to pacify carrier proponents, and to avoid overt competition with the Air Force, the Navy's leadership declared that Polaris was to be used only for sea control, mainly in attack-at-the-source operations. Polaris was for "striking targets of naval opportunity," such as submarine pens and ports. Raborn wrote, "Its tactical mission would be to beat down fixed base air and missile defenses to pave the way for carrier strikes aimed at destroying mobile or concealed primary targets." But no one could hide Polaris's real purpose. The Naval Warfare Analysis Group in early 1957 said that Polaris's mission was national deterrence and that Polaris was thus different and separate from the Navy's offensive systems, such as strike aircraft carriers. Raborn's earlier statements had been misleading. The fleet ballistic missile should be programmed to hit "population or industrial targets." The Navy's other forces were for military targets, for sea control. One reason for this was practical: the continued inaccuracy of Polaris compared to land-based missiles, which made it less effective than those missiles were against hardened military targets.[67]

Burke redirected the strategic discussion by introducing a concept he called *finite deterrence*. "All-out war," he wrote, "is obsolete as an instrument of national policy." A mobile, concealed, second-strike retaliatory missile force, of which sea-based Polaris was the exemplar, would be sized not to hit every target imaginable, nor to win a war—a false goal in the nuclear age—but to have deterrence value alone. This force could be small if it were hidden and invulnerable. It would permit controlled retaliation and eliminate the need for a first strike. Finite deterrence was the Navy's answer to the Strategic Air Command. In 1959, when SAC had some 3,261 points on its target list, when there were 3,000 SAC bombers and 1,000 SAC tankers, the Navy proposed 232 targets to be covered by 29 deployed Polaris submarines loaded with 16 missiles each, a force "sufficient to destroy all of Russia." The Navy could deter nuclear war cheaper, and more safely, than the Air Force could. The proposal also meant that the Navy had embraced what it earlier condemned: countervalue targeting, or the bombing of cities. So went the nuclear age.[68]

The worry that Polaris would bite into the Navy's other programs proved true. Hopes that the Defense Department would carry Polaris as a national program and fund it outside the Navy budget came to nothing. At first the cost to the Navy was concealed. Development began as a joint Army-Navy venture. At the end of 1956, however, the Navy separated its research and development from that joint program. That was the real beginning of the Polaris program, which was more exactly called the fleet ballistic missile system program because it included the development of the nuclear submarine as the missile's carrying and launching platform. The price of autonomy was not reduced by supplements from the Defense Department. Of the Navy budget, Polaris took 0.19 percent in fiscal year 1956, 4.87 percent in fiscal year 1958, 8.96 percent in fiscal year 1960, and 14.06, 13.41, and 11.51 percent in the big buildup under Defense Secretary Robert McNamara during fiscal year 1961–63.[69]

So Polaris did grow at the expense of other programs and consequently reduced other naval systems and hence strategic options. Canceled were development and production of Triton, then Regulus II, and then the Seamaster, a jet-powered bomber that could land on the sea. The money went to Polaris. The idea of a nuclear-powered airplane was scuttled. Top technical personnel were siphoned off to Polaris from the rest of the Navy. The shift of resources cut into ship maintenance, already a serious problem in the fleet. Balanced development of other weapons, such as naval guns, was stopped, and so was growth in the number of cruisers, attack submarines, lighter-than-air craft, fast-deployment logistics ships, and transport aircraft.

Admiral Elmo R. Zumwalt, Jr., who as CNO from 1970 to 1974 moved the Navy in a new direction toward sea control, regarded the killing of the Regulus program, a move that stopped development of the cruise missile, as "the single worst decision about weapons [the Navy] made during my years of service." The decision, Zumwalt said, was rationalized by the proposition that the effectiveness of carrier air had made cruise missiles superfluous. The result, said Zumwalt, was that "without cruise missiles practically all our long-range offensive capability was crowded onto the decks of a few carriers. . . . It was another case of numbers being more to the point than quality."[70] Not until the early 1970s, under Zumwalt, did the Navy return to cruise missiles with the 60-mile-range antiship Harpoon. Then at the end of that decade came the Tomahawk, which had a range of over 1,000 miles and became the means of unmanned attacks from surface ships and submarines against land targets of many kinds.

In the 1960s, then, the non-fleet-ballistic-missile portion of the Navy suffered a decline, in part because of the diversion of funds, talent, and intellectual focus to Polaris. "The choice among weapons projects is the choice among defense strategies."[71]

Burke would have agreed. The national strategy was a war of nuclear retaliation. The Polaris system supported that. Limited war was not the issue. The issue was the Navy's role in retaliation—or finite deterrence.

From early on, Burke and Raborn and the Special Projects Office staff envisioned a solid-fuel missile being launched from a submarine. The Navy's Bureau of Ships began designing such a vessel, which would have to be of unprecedented size. Because the submarines were likely to be nuclear powered, a problem of jurisdiction arose. While ship design was the province of the Bureau of Ships, nuclear propulsion was the province of a semiautonomous realm presided over by Rear Admiral Hyman G. Rickover. Rickover wore two hats. As head of the Navy's nuclear propulsion program, he answered, titularly, to the Bureau of Ships and through it to the CNO. As the Navy representative to the Division of Reactor Development of the Atomic Energy Commission, however, he operated outside the Navy network, in close alliance with the civilian world of Congress. That gave Rickover a power base beyond Navy control, from which he preached his crusade for a vast nuclear Navy.[72]

Rickover's control of nuclear propulsion involved him in other Navy programs. A vessel's shape and safety—and for a submarine, its silence—were affected by the size, weight, and power of the ship's nuclear reactor, all factors that Rickover controlled. On that basis, Rickover claimed a role in design, construction, and overhaul. That in turn gave him a handle on weapons development, and through that, influence on the Navy's strategic mission itself. He insisted on choosing a nuclear ship's key personnel. The commanding officer of a nuclear submarine had to be a trained "nuc," a Rickover man.[73]

Few could argue with Rickover's success. The Navy embraced nuclear propulsion.[74] As the Navy's ballistic-missile program was just getting under way, Rickover, and the service at large, basked in the well-deserved triumph of the USS *Nautilus*, which in January 1955 went to sea on nuclear power. The *Nautilus* was the first of the Navy's nuclear submarine fleet, the first nuclear-powered warship, the first truly underwater vessel, built to travel faster below the water's surface than upon it. It was the world's fastest combat submarine, able to remain submerged for months. The *Nautilus* was the first ship of Rickover's nuclear "second Navy."

The first successful underwater launch of the Polaris missile was from the *George Washington*, a converted attack submarine, in July 1960.

That December the *George Washington* went to sea with a full load of Polaris A-1s. The following class of submarine after the *George Washington* class, the *Ethan Allen* class, was designed from keel up to hold any of the three types of Polaris missiles. The five boats of this class were the first true fleet ballistic missile submarines (SSBNs). The *Ethan Allen* itself was begun in September 1959, launched in November 1960, and commissioned in August 1961. The building pace was fast. By 1980, 25 years after the *Nautilus* was launched, the Navy operated, Rickover's men commanded, and Rickover's reactors propelled a nuclear fleet of 126 warships—74 attack submarines, 41 strategic-missile submarines, 3 aircraft carriers, and 8 missile cruisers. These vessels represented a third of the Navy's warships and the bulk of its offensive force.[75]

Rickover was so possessive, so difficult to keep within the Navy's terms of planning and control, so intent on following his own agenda for achieving an almost unlimited expansion of the nuclear Navy, an agenda for which he wanted to use the Navy's limited funds, that the developers of Polaris had at first sought to keep him out of ship design. That proved impossible. Burke could keep Rickover from decisions about the missile program, which was Raborn's bailiwick, but he could not detach him from ship construction or, consequently, from the selection of ship personnel. The submarine had to be nuclear powered, and that meant that, wearing one hat or another, Rickover must have a say. In late 1956, the secretary of the Navy, Charles Thomas (May 1954 to April 1957), gave the Special Projects Office responsibility for the entire fleet ballistic missile system, both the submarine and the weapon—that meant the missile itself, a solid-fuel A-1 that was 28 feet tall and 5 feet around, weighed 15 tons, and had a range of 1,200 miles, long enough to hit Moscow from the sea. That missile was retired in 1965. The second generation, Polaris A-2, which became operational at the end of 1962, had a 1,500-mile range and much greater reliability. Model A-3, in the fleet in 1964, had a range of 2,500 miles and carried a revolutionary payload of three warheads in a multiple reentry vehicle system, each warhead having a force of 200 kilotons. The A-3, a counter-city weapon whose warheads hit in a triangular pattern, was meant to destroy an area with the effect of a single 1-megaton bomb.[76]

Awkward as the process of managing this development was, given the very different styles of leadership and research in Raborn's shop compared with Rickover's, work went forward. In 1957, after several years of slow movement, *Sputnik* galvanized the program, and the Navy gave the missiles and their submarines the highest priority. The result was "possibly the most revolutionary development in weapons technology in the twentieth century."[77] One year after *Sputnik*, six submarines were being built to house, transport, and launch the Navy's strategic ballistic missile force. The Polaris system worked, and the program was one of the great managerial and technical successes of Navy history.

FINITE DETERRENCE AND LIMITED WARS

The concept of finite deterrence gained adherents in the final years of the Eisenhower administration as an alternative to massive retaliation and as a way to limit nuclear force levels. As a strategy it grew naturally from the concern of the Army, the Navy, and increasingly the political leadership that the swollen bomber and weapons requests of the Strategic Air Command were far above what was needed to deter war.

With deterrence at less cost, the armed forces could prepare for limited wars. A Navy Long Range Objectives Group (OP-93) report at the end of 1957 stated: "Preparedness to fight and win a general war must subordinate itself to [deterrence and maintenance of U.S. global interests by, if necessary, limited war]. Where the implementation of the Air Force [air power] concept makes general war more likely to occur and endangers U.S. security by alienating allies and diverting resources from conventional preparedness it is subject to challenge."[78]

At the same time, the Army, thinking along parallel lines, was proposing its own strategic alternative—flexible response—which involved, like the Navy's concept, limiting the nuclear retaliatory force and preparing conventional, as well as nuclear, means for stopping aggression that did not call for general war.[79]

In January 1958, OP-93's long-range planning study, "The Navy of the 1970 Era," recognized a relationship between finite deterrence and controlled retaliation. It argued for a force of 40 Polaris submarines. That would be the Navy's contribution to the retaliatory system on which deterrence was based. But the Navy was more than submarines, and war was more than strategic retaliation. In a stalemate, expansionary Communism was free to turn to other avenues. To meet an indirect attack, to fight a limited war, Americans must think in new strategic categories.

Americans, said Burke in a statement based on OP-93's report, did not need to burrow underground in expectation of imminent incineration. "If human life is to be human," Burke wrote, warning against defeatism, "we have to stay on top, rather than become cave dwellers." The most likely challenge to U.S. interests was aggression on the great-power periphery, which the United States could meet with a calibrated response. "One reason why we resist inflating our retaliatory forces," he said, arguing in favor of finite deterrence, "is the urgency and magnitude of the limited war problem." The less the country spent for general-war deterrence, the more it could dedicate to meeting other crises at an early stage and to doing so by more controlled means.[80]

Urgency and magnitude were not merely theoretical issues. The Suez crisis in 1956, the persistent unrest in the Near East, the need for U.S. intervention in Lebanon in 1958, the unresolved civil war in Indochina, the ever-open conflict in the Formosa Strait, the perpetual problem of Berlin, Castro's seizure of Cuba in 1959, and the turmoil in the Congo all were proof to Burke and to the administration of global Communist aggressiveness. The Soviet goal, Burke said, was to turn the world upside down and then rebuild it in its image. For the Soviets, "the fulcrum of the struggle will be in the underdeveloped areas of the Free World—from the Asian periphery, through the Middle East and Africa to Latin America." In any of these places limited intervention might be required.[81]

For that, there was the Navy, powerful and mobile, ready to carry out a strategy and (in Burke's words) "to control and limit war to magnitudes we can tolerate." Naval activism had a moral dimension for Burke as it had for Mahan. "Our Navy of the future, then," Burke wrote, connecting value and force, "expresses our conviction that we can remain human, and not become moles."[82]

For the combined tasks of providing finite deterrence and graduated response with Polaris, of maintaining sea control against the Soviet submarine force, and of intervening in limited wars away from the central front the Navy needed, Burke said, a fleet of 933 ships and 7,000 aircraft by 1970. That went far beyond the funding the Navy could expect, beyond, indeed, U.S. building capacity. The future looked bleak. The large fleet of World War II ships in service in the 1950s would soon disappear as the old ships were retired. The Polaris program, ship modernization, and rehabilitation cut into construction and development funds. Little remained for new designs and new construction.[83]

Burke gave the strike carriers a new mission. He did not of course give up their nuclear role in a general war with the Soviet Union. On the other hand, it was obvious that long-range missiles had taken over the strategic role of carrier air and had decreased the need to expose carriers to Soviet stand-off defenses. Missiles could sail from bases out of reach of enemy defenses and could penetrate farther inland than any carrier aircraft, with almost no risk to weapon or platform.

The Navy's leaders conceded a disappearing carrier function and grasped a waxing reality to give the carrier fleet another lease on life. They relegated strike carriers to the role of auxiliary backups with regard to strategic retaliation, a role in which they could provide "a continuing, flexible, alternate capability," as Burke phrased it, and serve as a filler of a missile gap. But, he continued,

> I want to make it very clear, so I repeat—that for 1970 we are optimizing the carrier force for limited war, to be the nation's primary cutting tool for this purpose. The deterrence of all-out war will not then be the carriers' number one job. The carrier force need not measure up to the defensive requirements of that role in 1970, however useful it may be in that context in the next few years.

Burke's deputy CNO for fleet operations, Vice Admiral Wallace Beakley, told Congress that the carrier's "contribution to the [strategic retaliatory] mission is strictly a bonus and no way detracts from its essentiality for naval purposes."[84] The strike carrier would again become an interventionist weapon.

Carriers could move swiftly and easily into and out of crisis areas. Their aircraft could deliver weapons with a precision and proportionality that no missile system could match. Because the long-range land- and sea-based missiles and the SAC's manned-bomber force were neither configured for nor appropriate to fighting limited wars, Burke could declare that the Navy's strike carriers and its Marine assault force were now the country's "point of the spear."[85] And of course any intervention required control of the seas.

In the Suez crisis of October 1956, Burke positioned the Sixth Fleet in the eastern Mediterranean and told its commander to be ready to defend U.S. interests. The question of who might disturb these interests had been so unclearly defined that since June the administration had prepositioned in the eastern Mediterranean ships carrying arms to be given to any country that became the victim of aggression, whether it be Israel or an Arab state. On receiving Burke's message, the Sixth Fleet commander, Vice Admiral Charles R. Brown, signaled back, "Am prepared for imminent hostilities; but which side are we on?" Burke replied, "If U.S. citizens are in danger, protect them: take no guff from anyone." The combatants were not Soviets, but this was at the height of the Cold War, and there was a fear that the Soviets, despite their preoccupation with the Hungarian revolution, might take advantage of the revolution's distraction of NATO by acting in Western Europe or involving themselves in the Middle East.[86]

Burke increased antisubmarine patrols along the Atlantic Barrier from Newfoundland to the Azores and along the line from Greenland through Iceland to the United Kingdom. The new underwater sound surveillance system was used with positive results. Burke put amphibious troops in the Indian Ocean and placed the entire Pacific Fleet on alert. He said of the Suez crisis, "As usual, only naval forces could take the military action that was required when the situation broke." That was true. The Navy supervised the overland evacuation of over 1,500 Americans from Cairo because the Anglo-French attacks on the airport made it too dangerous to lift them out by plane.[87]

Mobility and modulation were demonstrated again in two containment moves in 1958—in Lebanon, and in the Formosa Strait in the second Quemoy and Matsu crisis.

A rebellion against the government in Beirut broke out in the summer of 1958. The conflict cut across Cold War lines, however, and could not be seen as the van of the march of international Communism. The CIA told Eisenhower that the Soviets "have not entered the Lebanese situation at all except by radio." But Eisenhower associated the revolutionary turmoil with Egyptian President Gamal Abdel Nasser's Pan-Arabism and pro-Soviet stance; with the pattern of Communist takeovers in Czechoslovakia, China, North Korea, and Indochina; and with the failed takeover in Greece. There was, Eisenhower said, a pattern of "internal aggression."[88]

There was also an enormous concern that U.S. credibility had been put at risk by the weakness of Britain and France in the Suez fiasco. If the Soviet Union, or Middle Eastern states motivated by militant Pan-Arabism, thought the United States was a paper tiger, an attack on its interests would surely follow. Eisenhower was determined to counter the perception that, as he said, "Americans were capable only of words, that we were afraid of Soviet reaction if we attempted military action." He wanted action "to demonstrate in a timely and practical way that the United States was capable of supporting its friends."[89] Lebanon's government had specifically accepted the Eisenhower doctrine of military support and had incurred the hostility of Syria and Egypt in consequence. So Eisenhower swiftly accepted its request for military assistance, "to stop the trend toward chaos."[90]

The operation in Lebanon in the summer of 1958 was "the first United States airborne-amphibious operation to occur in peacetime" and the "largest American troop deployment between the Korean and Vietnam wars."[91] At one time there were 14,357 U.S. combat troops on the ground—5,842 from the Marines and 8,515 from the Army. The Navy was rightly proud that the Sixth Fleet needed only thirteen hours to put marines ashore. It was also proud of how easily, with the formation of a coalition government in Beirut a few weeks later, it pulled them out. The operation vindicated Navy and Marine Corps capacities, their forward deployment, their ability to come and go, and the effectiveness with which they operated far below the nuclear threshold. Neither the Army nor the Air Force was positioned for such limited operations.[92]

The Lebanon operation was poorly integrated; there had been no interservice planning for limited operations. The specified joint commander had been dubbed on the spot. Even then, each service went largely its own way and according to its own devices. The Army and Air Force units sent to reinforce the Marine assault became embroiled in logistical chaos. The fast-reaction Air Force composite strike force took five days to get ready at its advance base in Turkey (compared to the thirteen hours spent by the Navy from order to assault). Army troops airlifted from Germany had to be rerouted because Austria complained about overflights.[93] Many noted that it was fortunate the marines and then the follow-on Army troops did not face serious opposition. "Virtually every official report opens with the caveat that had Operation Bluebat been opposed, disasters would have occurred, and argues that problems encountered during the operation's course could have been solved well before the order to execute was given."[94] It remained to be seen if legislation under consideration at that moment to reorganize the Defense Department would force more effective joint planning.

The importance of naval readiness and mobility was demonstrated again in August 1958 when the government of mainland China began a bombardment of the little islands of Quemoy and Matsu. The United States was committed to defending Taiwan, not Quemoy and Matsu, and no one in Washington would argue that the islands in themselves held strategic value. On the other hand, as in the case of Lebanon, the U.S. government took the attack as a test of American resolve. Eisenhower's advisers held that defense of the offshore islands was necessary to protect the American position in no less than Japan, Korea, Taiwan, the Philippines, and Indochina and to keep neutral Asian dominoes from tumbling all the way to Indonesia and Burma.[95] Naval leaders interpreted this as a reason to press for clarification on the use of atomic ordnance. The commander of the Pacific Fleet, Admiral Felix Stump, had told Burke the previous year that it was time "to stop pussy footing about the use of atomic weapons. . . . In personal conversations with 2 Presidents, Diem and Chiang, they have insisted that we must use our atomic weapons capability, but they have both expressed disturbing doubts about our willingness to do so."[96] Burke and the Joint

Chiefs of Staff recommended stopping any invasion of Taiwan by using atomic bombs.

Burke said in an interview in September 1958:

> President Chiang can't give up those islands—and we can't ask him to give them up—without giving up one of the most important things in the world to him and to us—prestige, standing up under fire for principles, little things, intangible things. . . . If we retreat under fire and retreat under pressure, where does that leave us in the eyes of the rest of the world—and our own eyes?[97]

This was military containment at the height of the Cold War. It was a test of resolve.

Holding fast was the job given the Seventh Fleet, whose activities during these months constituted the last major naval operation conducted by a CNO before the Defense Reorganization Act of 1958 removed the office of CNO from command. Before the shelling began, Burke had ordered an attack-carrier group to the area, following his practice of building up forces in potential trouble spots. Ships and aircraft reconnoitered the mainland, assisted convoy supply of Quemoy and Matsu from Taiwan, and prepared to deliver carrier-launched atomic attacks.

In this instance as in others, Eisenhower's and Dulles's atomic practice was restrained. They were as worried as ever about a likely popular revulsion in Asia and Europe and, in Eisenhower's opinion, among half the people of the United States itself if the third atomic bomb were to be dropped on Asians. Restraint was mandated further by an implicit warning from Nikita Khrushchev, the premier of the Soviet Union, that his country too had the atomic bomb: "To touch off a war against People's China means to doom to certain death sons of the American people and to spark off the conflagration of a world war." In this instance as in others where national security was not at stake, there were more compelling reasons for nonuse than for employment.[98] Reserving the increasing and varied inventory of atomic and nuclear weapons for a last resort, however, left many military men thinking that the atomic threat had virtually lost its force.

After two months, the crisis ended. The Communist Chinese stopped their shelling, and the threat of invasion went away. What prompted this change by the Beijing leaders we do not know. We can say, however, that naval force helped the Eisenhower administration keep the level of U.S. involvement within a politically and militarily acceptable limit. The crisis showed how the Navy could increase pressure if needed, localize it, and also hold it down.[99]

Economy had remained the Eisenhower administration's watchword. There was neither central control of force planning nor integration of the various service budgets. Each service judged its own needs, and then they all competed for a finite congressional appropriation. None got what it wanted. The Navy's proportion remained fairly constant, but Polaris's development and antisubmarine operations were taken from the hide of other elements of the fleet. Manning levels dropped. It was well the operations off Lebanon and Taiwan ended quickly, for there were not enough sailors on hand to sustain them. Cuts seriously undermined the combat effectiveness of each Marine Corps division and air wing.

The fleet was shrinking. Between 1957 and 1960 the Navy gave up 33 warships, bringing the total down to 376. The president had "lost faith" in the huge, expensive, nuclear-powered attack carriers on which Burke based the Navy and his force for limited war. Eisenhower did not accept the argument that the carriers were justified by their versatility. Because they no longer supported massive retaliation, critics said they unbalanced the fleet. The administration refused to approve a carrier that would be a follow-on to the *Enterprise*. Attack carriers no longer had much of a sea-control function. There were no Soviet carriers to oppose, and attack at the source was too risky. If the main job of the platform was intervention, why should the Navy not build smaller, less expensive ships? It was a fair question, and when Burke heard it, he must have felt that the rationale of the great offensive carrier-centered fleet was slipping. He told Congress in his last posture statement, in 1961, that the service had been "squeezed down to the bare minimum which will do the jobs the Navy must do."[100] That was fine with Congress and the administration, but a far cry from the interventionist, sea-control, deterrent Navy that Burke had envisioned.

Finite deterrence based on Polaris was not yet a national strategy. The first underwater launching of the missile did not take place until mid-1960. At the end of Eisenhower's term only two Polaris-loaded submarines were on deterrent patrol, though six fleet ballistic missile submarines had been launched, another launch was imminent, and additional submarines, under construction, were fully funded. Only 32 Polaris missiles were deployed.[101]

As a result, in 1961 Eisenhower ended his presidency and John F. Kennedy began his with the costly, enormous, and almost indigestible Strategic Air Command–driven Single Integrated Operational Plan (SIOP) of massive nuclear attack still firmly in place, a plan based almost exclusively on the manned bomber force. At that time, SAC's total ICBM force consisted of only sixteen Atlas-D missiles.

It was this SIOP that Burke opposed. He thought it embodied a rigid orthodoxy that was intellectually bankrupt and operationally vulnerable, that it prepared for a war unlikely to occur, and that it was a strategy unlikely to give victory. In 1959, the Air Force had asked for operational control of all Polaris submarines. Its purpose was to put all so-called strategic forces under SAC's control. Burke fought the air command off, on the argument that Polaris was a special system that, by its seaborne invulnerability, offered the nation the strategic option of delayed response, while SAC's strategy was based on immediate—and even first-strike—operations. Having won that battle, Burke lost the next. With the creation in 1960 of the Joint Strategic Target Planning Staff, the Navy lost control of Polaris targeting. Polaris had a place in the SIOP, of course, but under air-command principles its role was not to support finite deterrence and graduated escalation.[102]

At the end of the 1950s, then, after a decade of successful adaptation and innovation, the Navy still was not where its leaders wanted it to be. The surface force was shrinking, Burke's forward thinking was far from institutionalized, and the force's command structure had been substantially changed. The Defense Reorganization Act of 1958 took direct control of the fleet away from the CNO and gave it to the secretary of defense. This, as it turned out, was a prelude to a further centralization of control by the secretary of defense that took place in the 1960s during the administration of President Kennedy.

15

The McNamara Years 1961-1970

SECDEF TAKES CHARGE

Although in the 1950s the Navy maintained a balanced force and, with Polaris, recovered a paramount position in the national strategy of deterrence, the Defense Reorganization Act of 1958 took operational command of naval combat forces and control of the Navy's force structure away from the chief of naval operations and gave them to the secretary of defense. The secretary of defense, or SecDef, now had the authority to combine the services' combat forces into unified commands under his control and to make the final decisions on the research and development of new weapons. Giving the secretary the first of these powers meant taking combat control away from the service chiefs; giving him the second ended the practice by which a service that developed a new weapons system, such as a missile or aircraft, laid claim to controlling its use and thus to defining its military function. The secretary of defense could now control a unified military strategy.

Before 1958, modifications of the original National Security Act of 1947 had steadily increased the authority of the secretary of defense, but none had taken the radical step of removing operational authority from the chiefs of the service departments. Legislation in 1949, for example, had created the Department of Defense and ended the status of the Navy as a separate executive department, removing the secretary of the Navy from the cabinet. Changes in 1953 created a system of parallel civilian and military administration by which nine assistant secretaries in the Office of the Secretary of Defense were given responsibilities that were the functional counterparts of those already held by uniformed officers within the service departments.[1] Still, before 1958, each service retained responsibility for its combat force. Each service department continued to set its strategy and define its force structure and to make budget requests accordingly.

As we have seen, these conditions led to much interservice competition for exclusive control of particular weapons, such as nuclear bombs and missiles, and for functions, such as strategic bombing. This competition remained between the services, with the secretary of defense serving as referee, until 1958.

Eisenhower saw that these interservice controversies confused the American public. Duplication of missions and weapon systems and conflicting claims among services for their control seemed to trivialize civilian control, which was supposed to achieve a common defense effort, to give the country "the most bang for the buck." Eisenhower's solution was to move further toward unification. "Separate ground, sea, and air warfare is going forever," Eisenhower said, introducing the legislation in 1958. "If ever again we should be involved in war, we will fight it in all elements, with all services, as one single concentrated effort. Peacetime preparatory and organizational activity must conform to this fact. Strategic and tactical planning must be completely unified, combat forces organized into unified commands . . . singly led and prepared to fight as one, regardless of service."[2]

The 1958 law invested the secretary of defense with full control over strategy, operations, and force planning. The Army, the Navy, and the Air Force remained as individual departments but were shorn of operational responsibilities. Control of operations went to new commands, their commanders in chief (CinCs) reporting to the president through the secretary of defense, not to the officer at the head of the commander's service or to that service's secretary. These commands were organized according to function and mission, not according to service interests or tradition.[3] In principle, a CinC could come from any service, and he could command the assets of any according to the needs of his command. There would no longer be a strictly naval strategy or even strictly Navy weapons.

In 1958 the secretary of defense also gained direct authority over all military research and development. New weapons would be built only with the approval of his Directorate of Defense Research and Engineering. The purpose of this arrangement was to eliminate the preemptive competition that had beset research and development. By that process the first service to develop a new weapons system had acquired the mission that went with it. After 1958 the directorate controlled research and development regardless of service jurisdictions or claims.[4]

Centralization thus controlled the teeth of the Navy. On the combat line, fighting was the responsibility of unified or specified commanders who were responsible to the secretary of defense, usually through the secretary's advisory body, the Joint Chiefs of Staff. These commanders, regardless of which service they came from, ordered naval and other forces as they saw fit in pursuit of a national defense strategy. This was a great loss for the chief of naval operations, from whom was taken command of the fleet, and for the secretary of the Navy, to whom the CNO had reported. The secretary of the Navy had been the responsible political authority under the 1947 act and consistently had been granted considerable latitude. To the CNO and the Navy Department was left maintenance of the combat Navy. The Navy Department, the CNO, and the commandant of the Marine Corps trained sailors and marines and prepared them and their equipment for war. The department could no longer order them to battle.

Centralization had been favored by Air Force officers as a chance to capture the lead in an era they saw as dominated by air power. Navy leadership since 1947 had opposed it, worried that centralization would give rise to a single general staff and a complete merger of the services. The amorphous position of the Joint Chiefs of Staff, as both adviser to the secretary of defense and transmitter of his orders, did not dispel the Navy's concern.

No senior Navy leader thought a central non-Navy authority—whether that person came from the Air Force or the Army or was a civilian secretary of defense with however large a staff of assistant secretaries—could understand or run the Navy, whose esprit de corps depended on a long tradition of decentralization and a very considerable delegation of individual responsibility. Arleigh Burke wrote:

> Decentralization means we offer officers the opportunity to rise to positions of responsibility, of decision, of identity and stature—if they want it, and as soon as they can take it. We believe in *command*, not *staff*. We believe we have "real" things to do. . . . We decentralize and capitalize on the capabilities of our individual people rather than centralize and make automatons of them. This builds that essential pride of service and sense of accomplishment. If it results in a certain amount of cockiness, I am for it. But this is the direction in which we should move.[5]

Burke went directly to President Eisenhower to state that the 1958 law would undercut Navy morale. Eisenhower replied that the Navy would have to adjust.[6] Burke, seeing no victory to be won by taking to Congress a fight against a popular reform and knowing that the president would brook no insubordination, brought the Navy around. The Navy, after all, remained intact, the 1958 legislation declaring the continued separate existence of each service.[7]

ACTIVE MANAGEMENT

When Robert McNamara became secretary of defense in 1961, the Navy thought it was well positioned if underforced. At sea it supported the policy of containment with a force that was ready to project men and ordnance against, over, and around any coastline in the world.

The Kennedy administration pursued two strategic concepts: deterrence of nuclear war by the threat of assured destruction, and a containment variant called flexible response. Both reflected the prospect of imminent Soviet nuclear strategic parity. Deterrence was meant to prevent a Soviet first strike. Flexible response was meant to find a way around massive retaliation. It called for a level of fighting that was proportional to the strength of the opposing force, permitting limited, peripheral, and primarily conventional warfare.

To size the U.S. military accordingly, McNamara pushed to the limit the authority granted him under the reorganization act of 1958. He was going to run the Defense Department by "active management." A manager, he said,

> can either act as a judge or a leader. In the former case, he sits and waits until subordinates bring to him problems for solution, or alternatives for choice. In the latter case, he immerses himself in the operations of the business or the governmental activity, examines the problems, the objectives, the alternative courses of action, chooses among them, and leads the organization to their accomplishment. In the one case, it's a passive role; in the other case, an active role. . . . I have always believed in and endeavored to follow the active leadership role as opposed to the passive judicial role.[8]

Two of McNamara's civilian lieutenants, Alain Enthoven and K. Wayne Smith, explained it further:

> "The principal task of the Secretary of Defense is *personally* to grasp the strategic issues and provide *active leadership* to develop a defense program that sensibly relates all these factors [foreign policy, military strategy, defense budgets, and the choice of major weapons and forces]. In short, his main job is to shape the defense program in the national interest. *In particular*, it is his job to decide what forces are needed."[9]

That expressed the 1958 act with a vengeance. The services already could not command their troops, and now they would not be able to choose their weapons. McNamara's predecessors had divided the total available money among the services and then left it up to the Joint Chiefs and the individual services to determine how it would be spent. That strengthened the sense of the separation of the services. Critics said that it encouraged duplication, a parochial view of entitlement, and a failure of service special interests to relate their forces to a common defense program.

Indeed, Samuel Huntington has made the point that from a strictly institutional perspective, the Defense Reorganization Act released the services—especially the Army and the Air Force—from what had become a burden, namely the practice of establishing and then protecting the strategic and tactical significance of new weapons. Services were claiming exclusive employment rights based on development and identifying exclusive functions on the basis of certain force structures. Such practices had already become unsustainable. Strategic bombing could not be kept an Air Force preserve, for instance, when the Navy deployed the Polaris missile. Whatever flew did not necessarily belong to the Air Force.[10] The Navy could benefit from this broadening of perspective. It sailed, it flew, and it marched.

Lack of unprejudiced central oversight had led to fears concerning institutional survival, to strategic rigidity, and to panicky claims to the limited budget dollar, as we saw in the bitter Navy–Air Force debates of the late 1940s. Eisenhower was determined to end that zero-sum military mercantilism. That was why the reorganization act of 1958, and then McNamara, forbade the service departments to self-define combat functions and make independent strategic claims. Weapons development went to a neutral umbrella agency. And at the same time, the act and McNamara assured the services that they would remain individual institutions.

To weapons procurement McNamara applied the criterion of cost-effectiveness. McNamara asked not what a service wanted, but what it could do for his policy. He asked not what a weapons system was, but how it compared with others. If the service chiefs would not think in terms of an integrated program, the secretary would do the thinking for them.[11] Economy and efficiency seemed possible only through central control of decisions from start to finish.

McNamara combined most of the services' service-and-supply functions into Defense Department–wide agencies for manpower, research and development, logistics, intelligence, and communications. He established an independent analytic capability called PPBS—the Planning, Programming, and Budgeting System—run by legions of his own analysts. They were to evaluate force plans and service programs from beginning to end. Analysts would determine needs and costs simultaneously and envision alternatives and decide among them, and the secretary would enforce the decision. Systems analysis gave the secretary a way to intervene at every level in every service, from planning through management to control of operations.

To make independent decisions, to avoid service biases, to explicitly relate force to policy, McNamara created the Office of the Secretary of Defense (OSD), "the fourth service department."[12] "We believe," wrote his aides Enthoven and Smith,

> that the only satisfactory answer to the problem is for the Secretary of Defense personally to shape the defense program in the national interest—to study the problems of strategy, force requirements, and budgets in detail, to explain and defend his conclusions to the Congress and the public, and to supervise the execution of his decisions. . . . To do this job effectively, the Secretary needs both management tools and independent staff assistance.[13]

The instrument for integrating strategy, forces, and costs was of course the defense budget, every major item of which was brought under the control of the Office of the Secretary of Defense. Strategy and force requirements were to be made compatible and computable. The following two statements by Enthoven and Smith sum up this OSD thinking: (1) "The problems of military strategy and force requirements, though complex, can be grasped, analyzed, and understood. They can be importantly, even if not wholly, quantified. Satisfactory answers can and should be found through a combination of judgment and analysis. Defense issues can and should be decided on their merits." (2) "As for the formulation of military needs, at the strategic level there is no such thing as a 'pure' military requirement, only alternatives with varying risks and costs attached. Choosing among these alternatives is the main job of the Secretary of Defense."[14]

Making such choices was also the job of his civilian staff. In 1960, at the end of Eisenhower's administration, there was a total of 1,865 civilian employees in the Office of the Secretary of Defense, the Joint Chiefs of Staff, and other Defense Department agencies. By mid-1962, after a year and a half of McNamara's leadership, the number of civilian employees had risen to 21,457.[15]

Although from a management perspective there were obvious advantages to a centralized planning process under civilian control and to an independent evaluation program run by experts who looked at forms and functions from outside the services, to the Navy this seemed as the unwarranted interference of the uninformed. The service tried preemptive accommodation. It created its own cost-efficiency planning staff; and OPNAV, the Office of the Chief of Naval Operations, came to resemble the Office of the Secretary of Defense. OPNAV became a hybrid: "part platform-oriented, part OSD-oriented (especially Program Planning), and part JCS-oriented (Plans and Policy)," as Thomas Hone put it.[16] In 1966 Navy Secretary Paul Nitze (November 1963 to June 1967) and CNO Admiral David McDonald (August 1963 to August 1967) set up a Division of Systems Analysis and appointed Rear Admiral Elmo Zumwalt, Jr., to head it. Programs were directly linked to the budget process, rather than stated in terms of force structure.

It was not enough. Critics from OSD said the Navy did bad planning, that it had not established a reliable process to its own check performance.[17] In 1966, McNamara did away with the material bureaus and replaced them with systems commands. Out went the Bureaus of Naval Weapons, Ships, and Yards and Docks. The new organizations, subcommands under a central and coordinating Naval Material Command, were defined by function: Air Systems Command, Ship Systems Command, Facilities Engineering Command, and so on. These subcommands reported to the CNO and through him to the secretary of defense. No longer would the Navy have a decisive voice in its own administration.[18]

McNamara's problem was that he could not reform the service bureaucracies without alienating them. Although he made many sound decisions, such as halting development of the B-70 manned bomber, the Skybolt missile, a nuclear-propelled aircraft, and the Nike X missile, these edicts were unpopular with the services and lost him considerable support. Officers felt their advice was being discounted, their opinions ignored. It does not take much imagination to envision the annoyance with which an officer seasoned in a combat service would have read these blunt words by two whiz kids: "There is little in the typical officer's early career experience that qualifies him to be a better *strategic* planner than, say, a graduate of the Harvard Business School" (such as their boss, Robert McNamara, Harvard MBA 1939).[19]

The services found themselves united against the overbearing secretary. "The unintended organizational effect was to shift the axis of conflict from interservice to a civil-military debate."[20] When all was totted up, active management turned out to have an "impact on outputs [that] was substantially indistinguishable from that of its predecessors."[21] The system turned out to be overcentralized. Decisions of the center were inadequately linked to responsibility at the fighting edge. Despite the declared unification of strategic and operational authority in the person of the secretary of defense, there were too few lateral connections to integrate service programs except those that existed in the highly controversial person of the secretary himself. And the systems analysts, who were "subject only to management criteria such as costs . . . lost the very 'national view' that was used to justify their creation."[22] While a great deal changed in the organization and style of management, in the end it was policy shifts, technology, service adaptability, and, in particular, definitions of what kinds of wars were to be fought that determined the services' force profiles and drove performances.[23]

The Navy was adaptable. It had already defeated the idea of defining a service by natural element. It had avoided being tied to a single strategic concept. It had sited itself for easy movement into many kinds of missions. This diversification enabled it to adjust more easily than the other services to the changes of the 1960s. General Maxwell Taylor, Burke's Army colleague on the JCS, noted how easily the Navy justified itself by functional value. The fleet could contribute simultaneously to strategic bombing, antisubmarine warfare, air defense, and limited ground war.[24] On the other hand, that flexibility and force spread was difficult for analysts to program and for the Navy to express in the terms of McNamara's standards.

Certainly central direction restricted the Navy's doctrine of operational independence. As we have seen, Arleigh Burke stated that Navy officers "believe in *command*, not *staff*." Decentralized command was the nature of their profession. Such command was founded on individual responsibility and permitted wide operational latitude. Naval command, validated by centuries of ship handling and ocean combat, was arbitrary.[25] It was that operational independence that bureaucratic centralization seemed intent on thwarting. The vice chief of naval operations warned in 1962: "Historically, the Navy has tried to provide for flexibility in organization and operations. The very nature of the oceans and sea-power demand it. I recommend that we not move toward organizations that pyramid administrative echelons, especially when evidence of a commensurate increase in effectiveness is inconclusive."[26]

For McNamara the guide to the Navy of the future was centralization and the rational calculation of cost-effectiveness. For officers hardened in the experiences of sea duty, McNamara's reforms might be satisfactory for a peacetime structuring of forces, but they were neither designed for nor capable of managing an armed service in the uncertainties of war itself.

FLEXIBLE RESPONSE

The Kennedy administration modified the strategy of massive retaliation by stressing, on the one hand, a deterrence of general nuclear war by assured destruction, and, on the other, a combat alternative called flexible response.

Kennedy and McNamara were shocked at the indiscriminate nature of the Single Integrated Operational Plan they found in 1961. This plan, SIOP-62, the apotheosis of Strategic Air Command planning for massive retaliation (or for a crushing first strike), called for launching 3,500 nuclear weapons within 24 hours against 1,050 Communist-bloc targets, including all the major urban centers in the Soviet Union and China and hundreds of military targets.[27] The SIOP stated no rationale for the targets chosen and made no distinction between civilian and military hits. It paid no attention to secondary effects such as radioactive fallout. And—as Navy critics had pointed out when the first SIOP was introduced in November 1960—contrary to principles of strategic thinking, it expressed capabilities, not objectives.

It planned for massive use of the country's nuclear weapons delivered by the Strategic Air Command's 1,849 bombers, 1,094 tankers, and 12 ICBMs. What it did not do was designate targets by war aims. Critics such as Arleigh Burke, himself no foe of the use of nuclear weapons in another kind of war-fighting, declared that the targeting served neither a retaliatory nor a preemptive mission, that it aimed at more military targets than were needed for retaliation and at less than were needed for preemption. And a single targeting plan took control of the initial stages of the war away from the military and political authorities in Washington. The SIOP was a recipe for overkill. President Eisenhower said, "[It] frighten[ed] the devil out of me."[28]

That was also the reaction of Kennedy and McNamara when they were briefed on the completed SIOP in September 1961. They rejected its inflexible targeting, in which 1,000 target areas were to be hit in a blanket retaliation. The SIOP was all or nothing. There was no place in it for a proposal approved by McNamara for "controlled response and negotiated pauses" in a nuclear war, or for a second-strike counterforce and a "partial withholding" strategy that were called for by McNamara's strategy of flexible response.[29]

McNamara tried to break up the components of the SIOP by giving commanders more targeting options and by controlling the timing of attacks. He wanted to be able to use tactical nuclear weapons should conventional defenses collapse in Europe. He wanted an invulnerable second-strike nuclear force. But he was unable to change the SIOP's rigid configuration. In the high days of the Cold War, the military's independence in targeting had profound and troubling strategic consequences. Still, McNamara could, up to a point, redefine the purpose of the nuclear arsenal. That purpose was to be deterrence, and counterforce (military) targets were to be stressed. He called his second-strike doctrine *assured destruction*.[30] Whether this doctrine (which was sometimes called, for a different political twist, *mutual assured destruction*) was a deterrent strategy, a war-fighting strategy, or both was never made clear. It bore that troubling ambiguity for the next 30 years. But it had to be a deterrent because it is impossible to imagine any policy benefit from the full use of both sides' nuclear arsenals. By any rational view of warfare, mutual assured destruction had to be a strategy of nonuse.

Yet deterrence rested on crediting the incredible. For assured destruction the United States had to have a secure retaliatory force able to threaten half of the Soviet Union's industry and 20 to 25 percent of its population. The better protected from a Soviet first strike the U.S. force was, the greater its deterrent effect. There were three parts to the U.S. strategic strike force: SAC's manned bombers; its siloed missiles (authorization existed for 650 Titan and Atlas liquid-fuel ICBMs and for the second generation of ICBMs, the solid-fuel, hard-siloed Minuteman); and the Navy's submarine-launched IRBM, Polaris. Of these three parts, Polaris was the most secure, and it was also further advanced than the Minuteman, which in 1961 was not fully tested. When President Kennedy took office, there were six fleet ballistic missile submarines in operation. The Polaris program, therefore, seemed "the easiest to get hold of." As a result, one of Kennedy's first decisions was to accelerate it.[31]

In 1961 Navy leaders received that decision as a mixed blessing. Who was going to pay for this enormously expensive leap in the Navy's strategic missile force?

The Navy had floated the argument that the program should be funded not from the limited Navy budget, at the cost of other Navy programs, but from somewhere else in the defense budget. This was a double-edged and potentially self-defeating position, and it was soon dropped. For if the Navy argued that Polaris was something new, a national missile outside the traditional Navy mission, the Air Force would agree and attack Polaris by asserting the superiority of its own missile programs. Indeed, the Air Force was developing the air-launched Skybolt to compete directly with Polaris. McNamara had warned that technology had destroyed many traditional service boundaries. "The Navy has absolutely unique capabilities in certain areas," he said. "In other areas it is in competition with other forms of power. The best illustration is the Polaris. The Polaris is not unique. The Polaris is a substitute for other forms of strategic power."[32]

Logically, there was a further problem with the claim that Polaris was a national rather than a Navy responsibility. If it was a national responsibility, then whose responsibility was a carrier or a submarine or any other Navy asset? Were they, and the Navy too, national, and if not, how could one explain the discrepancy?[33] The argument was a can of worms.

If the Navy favored national responsibility for Polaris development, the Air Force could say that Polaris submarines should be assigned to SAC on the presumption that missiles were an already authorized part of the Air Force mission. The head of SAC had in fact submitted a proposal to the JCS in 1959 that SAC take operational control of all Polaris submarines, and Admiral Burke had to expend much effort to keep Polaris in the Navy. Burke's argument was that control by SAC, with its doctrine of immediate and massive retaliation, would take away the option of delayed response, which was precisely the Navy's strongest strategic suit.[34]

Polaris was too important to the Navy to give up or to dilute. Whatever it cost to keep it, Burke was willing to pay. Polaris put the Navy back into the forefront of the central national strategy, and this position brought great benefits. "It was the popularity of the Polaris and not the Navy that accounts for the Navy department's steady claim on the defense budget in the years between Korea and Vietnam."[35]

McNamara and Kennedy accelerated Polaris by increasing to ten the number of SSBNs in the budget for fiscal year 1962 and by allowing for six in each of the fiscal years 1963 and 1964. They supported the next class of SSBNs, the *Lafayette* class, the construction of which would help the Navy reach its goal of 41 nuclear, ballistic-missile submarines. At the same time, the administration accelerated construction of the still-unproven Minuteman, eventually raising to 1,000 the number it planned to have deployed. These decisions fundamentally changed the character of the U.S. strategic-missile posture. Secure, small-payload weapons began to replace such vulnerable, large-payload missiles as Atlas and Titan. That permitted flexible response—and assured destruction.[36]

Two consequences of the development of Polaris (and Minuteman) were the downplaying of the counterforce targeting that the Navy had upheld and the removal of the attack carrier from a strategic role. Regarding the first consequence, missiles were less accurate than attack bombers. As a result, missile-backed, assured-destruction targeting went after cities, which meant countervalue targeting against civilians. The second consequence of missile development involved the replacement of carriers by missiles in the SIOP. Because of this replacement, the Navy might well have gone through the great drawdown of its forces that Burke feared. That it did not was due to a change in the role of naval air and to the expansion of the carrier force that came with the escalation of the war in Vietnam.

The Navy accepted McNamara's removal of the attack carrier from the SIOP in 1962 as a blessing in disguise. Carrier-air doctrine had reached a dead end. Soviet stand-off defenses would have put the expensive carriers at great risk as the carriers approached for launch. The deterrent role of carrier air had been outpaced by missile technology, which now allowed missiles to be shot more safely and from longer distances. As part of the strategy of flexible response, however, the carrier could be shifted to a more suitable role in a limited war.[37] The attack carrier's future was in support missions. The ease with which the Navy accepted that reality showed that it was pragmatic, that it was governed more by opportunity than by orthodoxy. In fact, its experience with multiple missions had made it a practitioner of limited war *avant la lettre*.

Furthermore, planes from attack carriers could still carry nuclear bombs. The sea-control targets the Navy had with such care established in the 1950s remained within its province, as well as other important littoral and near-coastal targets along the Mediterranean and in the Far East. The vice chief of naval operations said that McNamara's decision to remove the attack carrier from the SIOP "removed a restraint on CVA [i.e., attack] carrier operations and restored flexibility for conventional missions while retaining a nuclear capability against non-time-sensitive targets and tactical targets."[38] These two kinds of targets included traditional naval targets such as submarine pens and naval air bases, and, especially in the Mediterranean and Far East, nonnaval targets within range of the low-flying, all-weather A-6 attack bomber, the Intruder.

McNamara appreciated the ability of carriers and their aircraft to approach (at possible risk to be sure) any sea-rimmed piece of land, to advance, appear, assault, and withdraw over the ocean vastness. Their value was in their mobility, speed, and (in the case of the nuclear-powered *Enterprise*) endurance in entering, staying within, and exiting a crisis area. All these were exceptionally attractive features to an administration that thought in terms of limited war, discrete influence, and crisis management, in terms, that is, of flexible response.

Thus the Navy reconstituted its attack-carrier doctrine within the national defense program and by so doing revived Navy air. At the same time, however, McNamara refused to build new carriers. No one anticipated Vietnam. The best the Navy could do was take its case to the public. In 1964 CNO McDonald published an article titled "Carrier Employment Since 1950," in which he cited cases in which attack carriers had provided air cover for amphibious landings and evacuations, close air support for ground forces, military presence (seven cases), blockade, interdiction, transport, and contributions to overall strategic deterrence.[39] Vietnam, in the second half of the 1960s, confirmed the trend toward intervention and support missions. In 1966 McNamara reversed himself and recommended the construction of three *Nimitz*-class nuclear attack carriers.[40]

In the 1960s the greater part of military spending went to improve conventional and tactical capabilities. Beyond Europe, the U.S. nuclear threat seemed increasingly inadequate to contain armed conflict. Anticolonial struggles often took on a Communist hue. The United States was committed to 9 treaties and more than 40 formal allies and was tied to informal connections around the globe. In most situations, readiness of conventional forces was called for.

Kennedy and McNamara realized this in the Berlin crisis of 1961. The president found he had no conventional options that would be decisive against Soviet Premier Nikita Khrushchev's pressure. Kennedy discovered he could not deploy strong forces on the ground without resorting to atomic artillery. The surprising unreadiness of some transport commands prevented an immediate move of two regular Army divisions to Germany. A reinforcement airlift furnished by the Air Force and the sealift furnished by the Navy brought too little too late. The Army was counting on close air support in a nonnuclear war, but the Tactical Air Command of the Air Force was concentrating almost exclusively on preparation for a theater nuclear war. Conventional-force weakness exposed the United States to the danger of escalation to nuclear war.[41]

Flexible response was the idea of having a force ready to show resolve locally, to meet a challenge proportionally, and if at all possible, and certainly at first, to meet the challenge conventionally. The planning in McNamara's office in 1962 concentrated on preparing the Army and the Air Force for action in eleven separate theaters. The Navy was not included in these studies because it was already a service of global reach and flexible response, placed and prepared for missions in support of limited and conventional combat and for multiple actions of whatever duration.[42] Proof of its flexibility was the speed with which it adapted its carrier force to changes in strategy, and the success with which it executed the Cuban naval blockade of 1962.

THE CUBAN MISSILE CRISIS

With regard to the Cuban crisis we must consider two elements of strategy: the importance of local control and the importance of general superiority. Each played a part in the disposition of the crisis. The Soviet government removed the medium- and intermediate-range ballistic missiles and the IL-28 twin-jet light bombers it had placed 90 miles off the coast of Florida because the United States commanded the sea and the air around Cuba and because the United States held overall nuclear strategic superiority on a global scale. If the United States had decided to destroy the missile sites or invade Cuba, there was no way the Soviets could have protected their rash investment on the island without escalating the conflict into a nuclear war. Resisting U.S. operations in theater, or taking proportionally threatening action elsewhere, would have put the Soviet homeland at risk. Khrushchev had played a hand beyond both his local and his intercontinental capabilities.[43]

SAC generals had little doubt that their strategic arsenal made the difference in the settlement of the crisis. They resented that the advantage conferred by the biggest airborne alert in SAC history and by SAC's maximum readiness to fire its ICBM arsenal was missing from the accounts of the crisis, which stressed instead the administration's management of the affair. "The Russians had no alternative but to step down and do what they were asked to do," recalled one Air Force general, General Jack J. Catton. "During that very critical time," said General Curtis LeMay, "in my mind there wasn't a chance that we would have gone to war with Russia because we had overwhelming strategic capability and the Russians knew it." They knew it because the United States told them so—if, as it appears, the SAC commander, General Thomas Power, sent an uncoded and easily intercepted message to the Pentagon stating the full strength and readiness of his command. "We could have written our own book at the time," said another Air Force general, General David A. Burchinal, because "the Russians were so thoroughly stood down, and we knew it. They didn't make any move. They did not increase their alert; they did not increase any flights, or their air defense posture. They didn't do a thing, they froze in place. We were never further from nuclear war than at the time of Cuba, never further."[44]

This was apparent only from the broadest perspective. Most of the civilian leaders of the U.S. government thought Cuba was a global test in which America's strategic superiority kept the peace. It is likely that the Soviet backdown came in large measure from Moscow's fear that perpetuating the missile presence would bring disaster to the Soviet Union, perhaps a preemptive U.S. strike.[45] Whether the SAC alert deterred Soviet countermoves elsewhere in the world, against Berlin for example, we can only guess.[46] The U.S. military believed that the Soviet government rationally evaluated its position and, in recognition of America's nuclear strength, backed down. General Maxwell Taylor, chairman of the Joint Chiefs and a proponent of an air strike against the Cuban missile installations, recalled, "I was so sure we had 'em over a barrel, I never worried much about the final outcome, but what things might happen in between."[47]

The final outcome, however, was exactly what concerned political leaders. Although considerable uncertainty existed among U.S. leaders about whether there was an immediate danger of war, Raymond Garthoff asserts that "the common nuclear danger was a far more potent force in constraining the crisis than all the calculated criteria of the military balance and deterrence. The common nuclear danger indeed proved far more significant than the massive American nuclear superiority."[48] Uncertainties or missteps might take the crisis out of control.

The U.S. government acted on the CIA assumption that nuclear warheads would be available to the missiles in Cuba as soon as they were operational. It is possible that the local danger was potentially greater than assumed, because the Soviet field commander had been given permission to fire a tactical nuclear attack in the event of a U.S. invasion and if his communications with Moscow were cut. Kennedy understood that the missiles were not worth a nuclear war. Still, they had to be removed. The Cuban missiles, when readied and tipped with nuclear warheads, could, as part of a Soviet surprise first strike, hit targets throughout practically all of the continental United States. They would also, SAC said, improve by 39 percent the Soviets' ability to destroy SAC's retaliatory capacity. On Cuba, Raymond Garthoff, then a State Department expert, wrote, the Soviets could "literally multiply the number of launchers to a force large enough to threaten the entire strategic balance of power."[49]

So U.S. political leaders sought to minimize risk, not to take advantage of strategic strength. Here the problem was to find a way to get

Khrushchev to reverse his decision. President Kennedy decided to move slowly and deliberately, and both governments felt their way through the crisis. Hence it is important to consider local force, the force on the scene. That was where the immediate focus was on both sides.

Kennedy decided that his best first step was to take direct action in the Caribbean. Either the Soviets would withdraw the missiles, or the United States would destroy them on the ground and, as a probable corollary, seek to overthrow Castro. But the missiles would be destroyed only if the Soviets could not be made to remove them, because an attack and an invasion would destroy an important Soviet client and harm large numbers of the 43,000 Soviet soldiers and technicians on duty in Cuba, provoking, perhaps, a Soviet counterstrike against the United States.

What was needed was graduated pressure, controlled from the center, in which the discriminating use of force—its final extent being left unstated—would convince Khrushchev that he would have to either withdraw the missiles or face more severe action. Proportionality in the practice of crisis management became a Kennedy and McNamara hallmark and a part of the strategy of flexible response. The United States built up a large conventional force in the Caribbean theater. Over 100,000 Army ground troops were assembled in Florida and the Canal Zone in preparation for a possible invasion of the island. As SAC bombers moved out of Florida to safer locations, a third of the Air Force's tactical fighters moved in. Before the crisis, Navy and Marine Corps units had been preparing for an exercise in Puerto Rico. The government reconstituted those units as a striking force against Cuba. The Navy collected in the area the largest concentration of amphibious forces since World War II and put them through exercises in mid-November 1962.[50]

For its first action the administration chose a selective naval blockade. This local sea control prohibited the shipment of offensive weapons to Cuba, including warheads for the missiles already on the ground, further surface-to-surface missiles, bombers, and their support and accessories. The blockade did not bar food or petroleum or other goods. Selective blockade was Kennedy's Cuban razor, the most easily enforceable and least provocative action. It gave Khrushchev time to recognize the seriousness of his problem and begin withdrawal. The weakness of the try-and-see blockade was that it in itself could not remove the missiles.[51] Blockades are agents of influence only. The blockade of Cuba was conducted hand in hand with diplomacy, behind which stood clear American strategic superiority.[52]

In enforcing the blockade, the United States created a situation that reversed the roles played in the Berlin crisis the year before. In Cuba the U.S. Navy, not the Red Army, isolated the crisis zone. Task Force 136, under the JCS's specified commander Admiral Robert L. Dennison, conducted the operation with great effectiveness. Ninety warships established the blockade and steamed 780,000 miles in covering the blockade zones. A total of 183 warships participated in the operation overall. Naval aircraft from 68 squadrons flew 9,000 sorties. All Soviet-flag vessels approaching Cuba were put under the closest surveillance.[53]

The blockade worked. The Soviets respected the line drawn on the sea. There was no confrontation, no incident. The Soviet planes and missiles in Cuba did not move. No Soviet-flag ship ran the blockade, as it appears Khrushchev at first had threatened. The Kremlin turned away the freighters the Navy thought were most likely to be carrying missiles before they reached the U.S. destroyer patrol line. There was no belligerent activity from the five Soviet Foxtrot diesel attack submarines that arrived in the blockade zone. None reacted forcefully when they were ridden and surfaced by the ships and aircraft of the Navy's pervasive antisubmarine net. The Navy's blanket surveillance, which extended to the establishment of a barrier of attack submarines southeast of Newfoundland to intercept possible southbound Soviet missile-launching submarines, was part of the success of Kennedy's strategy of applying increasing pressure.[54] These were the naval elements of sea control.

Within days, on October 28, 1962, Khrushchev announced he would withdraw Soviet offensive weapons from Cuba. U.S. Navy observers confirmed that 42 missiles were sent out on 9 freighters. Six weeks later the 42 light bombers were shipped out as well. The Cuban missile crisis, an example of flexible response with naval force at its center, was over.

Much attention has been given the fact that President Kennedy directed American actions through a small ad hoc group of advisers known as the Executive Committee. This form of crisis management was of a piece with the highly centralized control of the services Secretary McNamara had established in the Defense Department. Distrust of military judgment was a reason both for reliance on the Executive Committee and for McNamara's active management of the department. Flexible response, after all, was an alternative to massive retaliation, and McNamara was no fan of the Strategic Air Command and its major mission. In the Cuban crisis, moreover, central direction was intensified as a result of Kennedy's and McNamara's feeling that they had been let down by the Joint Chiefs in the abortive Bay of Pigs invasion the previous year, a feeling the Joint Chiefs reciprocated.

One casualty of the tension was CNO Admiral George Anderson, McNamara's most consistent opponent on the Joint Chiefs of Staff. Anderson (CNO from August 1961 to August 1963) shared many a senior officer's opinion that McNamara's staff was treating uniformed chiefs like second-class citizens. Anderson thought that McNamara, no expert in military affairs, endangered national security because he directed rather than advised the Joint Chiefs.[55] Anderson strongly objected to McNamara's direct involvement in operational details in the Cuban missile crisis. In their most notorious run-in, Anderson told McNamara to go back to his office and leave the blockade to the Navy, which had had experience with blockades since the days of John Paul Jones.[56] Years later Anderson said, "McNamara wanted options for the President. The hell with options—the President needs good advice administratively, economically, politically, as well as military. I think when you have dominant people like McNamara playing, they throw the whole thing off balance."[57]

It is hard to fault either the Navy or the administration in its handling of the Cuban missile crisis. Crisis management worked, and the Navy did its job. Anderson's real complaint was centered elsewhere. His biographer supports the CNO for objecting to McNamara's reforms in command as violations of the spirit of the Constitution and of the National Security Act of 1947 and its amendments. On the other hand, he faults Anderson for not making a public protest against the secretary's reforms when he, Anderson, was relieved in 1963. "The two men had diametrically opposed views on the roles that the secretary of defense and the service chiefs should play in the process of making military policy."[58] A public debate would have been useful to everyone on the eve of Vietnam.

VIETNAM

The war in Vietnam was fought to enforce containment. Arleigh Burke, when he was CNO, had been an early proponent of stopping national Communist revolutionary movements in Southeast Asia, to halt the "erosion" of the "free world" by Communist guerrillas. He saw early on that concentration on a general nuclear war limited the country's ability to fight small and localized conflicts, by constraining the military's doctrine and its force structure. The United States, Burke said, was in danger of going "too far on the megaton road." What the country needed was fast-moving forces configured for limited war, and "a *forward strategy*, so as to present our allies and the Communists with tangible evidence of our capacity to resist aggression." In this, the Navy's role was clear. "In these situations we must take advantage of the ocean highways to project the force necessary to eliminate the menace where it occurs. The Navy is more than a 'first line' of defense. It frequently is and must be the spearhead of our military actions overseas. It is a 'first line of impact' on many occasions."[59]

Planning with this in mind began in the Pacific Command in 1959, where the Navy's chief component was the Seventh Fleet, the main U.S. defense force for covering 30 million square miles of the western Pacific and its islands and littoral, including Japan, South Korea, Taiwan, the Philippines, and countries of Southeast Asia. The Seventh Fleet was an aging force. About 80 percent of its ships had been built during World War II and would soon become obsolete, almost all of them simultaneously. In 1959, the Navy's Board of Inspection and Survey found that 72 percent of the ships they looked at were in unsatisfactory condition. A Fleet Rehabilitation and Modernization Program was begun to recondition and modernize this deteriorating force, but action was slow, and not surprisingly so in an era when Polaris was taking a large slice of the Navy's already limited portion of the defense budget. Amphibious forces were particularly hard hit, bringing into question just how the Navy would be the nation's "first line of impact." The result was that the Pacific commander declared the "United States has no sustaining power in the Pacific for conventional war."[60]

Burke looked around for alternatives. In September 1960 he said that it was "necessary that the Navy take the lead if our nation is to develop the new concepts and techniques which will be necessary to exploit our maritime advantage in the cold war." He supported Navy roles in counterinsurgency and clandestine warfare. The Navy began planning for counterguerrilla operations: the use of riverine and coastal patrol boats, the insertion of Seabee technical assistance teams, and beginning in 1962, the employment of units for special operations.[61]

All this, however, was on a small scale. The government did not intervene in Laos in 1961, despite the urgings of Burke and CinCPac Admiral Harry D. Felt. Elements of the Seventh Fleet were sent to the South China Sea, including three carrier task groups and an embarked Marine Amphibious Readiness Group. "If we lose Laos," warned Burke, "we will probably lose Thailand and the rest of SE Asia. We will have demonstrated to the world that we cannot or will not stand when challenged. The effect will quickly show up in Asia, Africa, and Latin America." Despite this advice, the United States in April 1961, under the new Kennedy administration, decided against military intervention in Laos. Airlift to Laos was limited. The main point to note, of course, is that Laos is not on the sea.[62]

South Vietnam was. Since 1950, a small group of U.S. Navy personnel (amounting to two dozen men at the end of the decade) had been operating as the Navy Section of the U.S. Military Assistance Advisory Group, advising the new South Vietnamese navy. That navy in 1959 was a modest force of about 3,600 sailors and 1,500 marines, whose 119 craft, divided between a sea force and a river force, were well below U.S. standards.[63] Nor was it likely that the small and inexperienced South Vietnamese navy could absorb much in the way of modern ships, boats, or doctrine—or, experts reluctantly concluded, even defend the rivers and coast of its own country. In May 1961 Burke said that the United States was "going to have to take over such operations as river patrol in the Saigon Delta, in the Mekong River, and other areas." A week later he told CinCPac Admiral Felt, "We don't need a lot of troops in there but I feel strongly we do need [a] few organized units. . . . We have missed the boat in Laos by not having a foot in the door."[64]

From 1962 to 1964 the United States increased its assistance to South Vietnam. The Navy conducted counterinsurgency operations with in-country special-operation units and Seabee technical assistance teams. It supported the South Vietnamese navy in coastal patrols. The internal confusion that followed the coup d'état of November 1963, which removed Prime Minister Ngo Dinh Diem, resulted in a loss of Saigon's naval combat readiness, and advances of the Viet Cong made it clear that the government was on the verge of losing control of the Mekong Delta. South Vietnam would require more from the United States than advisers and covert operations. In April 1964, following a coup in Laos, a carrier task group was ordered to position itself at a point off South Vietnam that came to be known as Yankee Station.

In August 1964 the destroyer *Maddox*, sailing off North Vietnam on surveillance patrol (and perhaps also in support of small-unit sabotage missions) in the Gulf of Tonkin, was pursued by three North Vietnamese torpedo boats. About to be overtaken, the *Maddox* opened fire, avoided three torpedoes, and called in air support from a conveniently positioned carrier. A day or two later, now accompanied by the destroyer *C. Turner Joy*, the *Maddox* returned to the Gulf of Tonkin. On a very dark night, the *Turner Joy* opened fire on radar contacts that were suspected to be approaching hostile torpedo boats.[65]

That was the Gulf of Tonkin incident, an attack—perhaps two attacks—against a U.S. ship on the high seas. On the basis of the incident, President Lyndon Johnson ordered a one-time retaliatory action against

North Vietnam (an action that was conducted by Navy air), and then received from Congress on August 7, 1964, the Tonkin Gulf Resolution. This resolution permitted the president to "take all necessary steps, including the use of armed force," to assist South Vietnam.

For some months Johnson hesitated to commit the United States to further direct combat operations. He restrained coastal patrols and ruled out more action against the North. But after a Viet Cong attack on an American installation near Saigon in November 1964, the argument grew for stronger action to cut North Vietnam's support to the southern insurgents. Proposed actions included mining North Vietnamese ports and conducting a coastal blockade against the North. Nothing was done, in part because of concern that sea-power pressure might provoke a Chinese reaction. Nonetheless, increased Viet Cong aggressiveness caused naval leaders to think in terms of commitment to war. The director of naval intelligence, Vice Admiral Rufus L. Taylor, reported in early 1965, "We should be prepared at an early date to either commit U.S. forces in sufficient strength to insure victory of our side or get out before it is too late."[66]

In March 1965 the Seventh Fleet landed some 1,500 Marines at Da Nang to secure the air base there.[67] With that force on the ground, the United States committed itself to unilateral ground combat. America was taking over the struggle for the independence of South Vietnam, and in the fighting on the ground through 1973, where 88 percent of the 47,205 American combat deaths took place, 30,864 men from the Army were killed, 13,034 from the Marine Corps, 1,708 from the Air Force and 1,599 from the Navy.[68]

Sending marines to a strategically static land war in the northern part of South Vietnam meant breaking the amphibious-assault connection between the Navy and the Marine Corps. The Navy, however, kept the marines supplied in the north by sea and kept the northern river routes open. Most probably, it would have been better to join the two forces in the southern part of South Vietnam, to secure the rivers and canals of the Mekong Delta, a more suitable use of Navy–Marine Corps maritime mobility.[69]

In the rest of the war the Navy conducted three distinct campaigns. One was in the air over Vietnam, another was on the South China Sea, and a third was in the brown water of South Vietnam's rivers. These operations were not under a single command. Forces in South Vietnam were under the commander of the U.S. Military Assistance Command in Vietnam. The commander of the Seventh Fleet operated under the commander in chief of the Pacific Fleet, who was subordinate to

CinCPac, who headed a unified command and answered, through the JCS, to the secretary of defense and the president. Navy aircraft attacking targets ashore in support of the land war being fought by the Army and the Marine Corps, and in support of the air war being fought by the Air Force, were under yet other commands. Coastal patrol and interdiction, and the river war, were put under operational control of the naval component of the U.S. Military Assistance Command in Vietnam, which was based in Saigon and was itself subordinate to the operational command of CinCPac. In April 1966 an umbrella command for all U.S. naval forces operating in Vietnamese waters was established under the name Naval Forces Vietnam.

The Navy's tactical air war was conducted by A-4 and later A-7 light attack aircraft flying off carriers of the Seventh Fleet. These carriers were operating from Yankee Station as Task Force 77. Yankee Station had been moved north to a point off the coast of the Demilitarized Zone to reduce the flight time of the carrier planes attacking military targets in North Vietnam. In the rainy and cloudy monsoon weather, tactical bombing was made possible by electronics aboard the newly introduced all-weather day-and-night A-6A Intruder. E-2A Hawkeyes gave the A-6As essential early-warning surveillance. The air war required joint coordination because all services were involved in all kinds of air missions. Task Force 77 insisted on its operational autonomy. It would support the theater commander's needs on land, but because naval air's primary mission was sea control for fleet defense, the aircraft had to be under fleet control. Jurisdictional disputes and operational diversities had to be ironed out, though some were ignored, only to become sources of bitter contention after the war. At one point the Marines refused to use their aircraft for close support of Army troops, which was such a serious problem of command that General William Westmoreland, then in charge of all U.S. forces in Vietnam, considered resigning.[70] To minimize the confusion, but without resolving the problem of the lack of an integrated functional air command, CinCPac Admiral U. S. Grant Sharp assigned to each service its own operating area, wherein each could fight its own air war.[71] In the employment of combat air power, the Army incurred 2,508 deaths, the Air Force 851, the Marine Corps 575, and the Navy 244.

The Navy's first call for patrol duty was along the coast of South Vietnam. In 1965 the United States authorized ships from the Seventh Fleet to search and seize enemy supply vessels along the 1,200 miles of South Vietnam's coast. For sea-lane infiltration the Navy did suggest a simpler solution, that of mining or blockading the North Vietnamese ports through which ammunition was shipped south. That, however, was politically unacceptable before 1972. So the United States decided to blockade the entire South Vietnamese coast and catch infiltrators whenever possible in the rivers and canals and along the mountain trails. "The United States would do it the hard way by stopping up the broad end of the funnel."[72]

The operation was called Market Time. A separate operation, called Sea Dragon, was initiated two years later and conducted along enemy supply routes north of the Demilitarized Zone. In both Market Time and Sea Dragon, the navy of South Vietnam played little part. In Market Time, the U.S. Navy mounted a three-tiered barrier operation. The three tiers were (1) air patrol, beyond the patrol range of ships; (2) an outer surface barrier of combat ships, including seagoing Coast Guard cutters; and (3) an inshore patrol of 82-foot Coast Guard patrol boats and 50-foot, well-armed aluminum Swift patrol boats. The effectiveness of these forces was, and still is, probably impossible to determine. But Market Time was successful within limits, in spite of the busy and confusing local shipping and trawler traffic, the lack of intelligence, the often halfhearted coordination with South Vietnamese intelligence sources, and the uncertain though critical air surveillance. Interdiction patrols did not recover much in the way of supplies or ammunition, but they forced the North Vietnamese to move their seaborne supply lines to a terminal at the port of Sihanoukville in supposedly neutral Cambodia. Few naval officers would have agreed with General Westmoreland's estimate that before 1965 the Viet Cong were receiving about 70 percent of their infiltrated supplies by sea and that by the end of 1966 this had been reduced to below 10 percent.[73] Yet the level of interdiction at sea was very high. In 1967 and 1968, Market Time ships inspected about half a million junks a year.

The problem was that the U.S. ships did not stop the movement of supplies. The North Vietnamese increased the amount of ammunition transported south on overland trails, along routes the U.S. Army could not cut. In addition, North Vietnam's seaborne supply lines stayed open to Cambodia and thence to hiding places inland, and from those supposedly neutral sanctuaries out through rivers and canals to active Viet Cong units in the Mekong Delta, where 40 percent of the population of South Vietnam lived. Every Market Time success against the trawlers increased the use of these alternate routes. The river system became for the Navy what the Ho Chi Minh Trail was for the Army and the Air Force: an artery that had to be cut. The sources of supply—the Soviet Union and other Communist states—could not be touched without breaking the self-imposed rules under which the United States fought the limited war in Vietnam.

The Navy was criticized for assigning too many of its assets to carrier air and too few to the inland-waters interdiction campaign. Part of the reason is that patrols in the Mekong River system and surveillance of the Cambodian connection were not part of an overall national strategy. The Navy found it easier to act where it had a free hand—in Market Time and Sea Dragon, in open waters off the Vietnam coast, and in the air strikes against the land from the carriers of Task Force 77 on Yankee Station—not in the narrow, turgid rivers and canals of the delta, where brown-water sailors were under fire from jungle cover along the banks. Whatever the value of the air and the coastal campaigns, U.S. leaders made a strategic mistake in leaving the river campaign undervalued and undersupported for so long.[74]

Looking back, Admiral Elmo Zumwalt, Jr., contended that the tilt toward carrier air and away from the riverine force was a functional dislocation of the Navy itself, the result of the domination within the service of aviators who based strategic decisions not on threat assessment but on their deep-rooted prejudices in favor of carrier air. Aviators, he said, saw the chance to validate the carriers' role in strike support and sacrificed other Navy functions so they could pursue that validation. Their emphasis on "high end" air strikes, Zumwalt wrote, degraded the two "low end" campaigns of coastal control and river patrol. The Navy was thus deprived of its claim to many-missioned balance. Zumwalt blamed Admiral Thomas Moorer, the CNO from August 1967 to July 1970. "I think the second-rate Navy effort at that point grew out of decisions deliberately made by Admiral Moorer. Air strikes meant glory for the Navy. He did not want to waste the Navy's resources fighting the war inside Vietnam."[75]

Perhaps. But the United States did not entirely ignore riverine warfare. A River Patrol Force, Task Force 116, aggressively conducted an operation called Game Warden. The force's problems were that it followed a wide-river philosophy, staying on the major waterways, and that its tasks included not only interdiction, but protection missions as well, however useful those missions might have been. Game Warden patrols did force the enemy onto secondary rivers, disrupt Viet Cong troop movements, and open some areas to commercial traffic, but they did not capture any important shipments of war matériel.[76] A joint Army-Navy command was established and called the Mobile Riverine Force (MRF). It included 3,717 naval officers and men in 1968 and was under the control of the U.S. Military Assistance Command in Vietnam.

The MRF used Navy personnel to transport Army troops on search-and-destroy missions against the Viet Cong. Until 1968, however, this was too little too late, and Army-Navy cooperation in Vietnam was anything but smooth. Despite instances of solid cooperation in the Mobile Riverine Force, the Army accused the Navy of not supporting its combat needs. The Army supreme commander in Vietnam refused to speak to the commander of Navy forces.[77]

In early 1968 the shock of the Tet offensive revealed the extent to which the Viet Cong had conserved their forces. A want of offensive spirit among supporting units of the South Vietnamese military meant that waterways, when cleared and handed over to Vietnamese troops, were not kept secure. Given the specialized nature of riverine warfare, it has been plausibly argued that the Marines, with their amphibious experience and long history of cooperation with the Navy, should have been deployed instead of the Army as the assault troops in the Mobile Riverine Force. They were not, because they were committed to operations in the northern part of South Vietnam, in I Corps, and because General Westmoreland decided that the heavy equipment of the Marine battalions was not suitable for use in the Mekong Delta.[78] Reliance on surface craft in the absence of both sufficient numbers of helicopters and an air-mobile doctrine led the Marine Corps officer who commanded the Fleet Marine Force in the Pacific, Lieutenant General Victor H. Krulak, to conclude that the Navy and the Army "really blew it in the Delta." There seems no reason why the Army and the Navy could not have cooperated better. They had done so on American rivers in the Civil War and overseas in World War II. Still, during Tet, in the vast Mekong Delta, which was called the V Corps Tactical Zone, the Mobile Riverine Force retained its counteroffensive capability, and General Westmoreland said it "saved the Delta."[79]

In the aftermath of Tet, Zumwalt was given a third star (becoming the youngest vice admiral in Navy history) and sent out to the naval command in Vietnam. Zumwalt put life into the inland-waters campaign. Following the conclusion of Captain Robert C. Salzer, commander of the River Assault Force, that search-and-destroy operations were futile, Zumwalt integrated the coastal and inland elements of naval strategy. He combined the assets of Market Time, Game Warden, the River Patrol Force, and the Mobile Riverine Force into a comprehensive delta-wide interdiction program known as Sea Lords. Through this program, Zumwalt sought to establish an integrated and multilayered pattern of interdiction in the small rivers and to back up this activity with a ready-reaction force. Zumwalt recaptured control of the Rung Sat Special

Zone that secured the vital 45-mile-long Long Tau shipping canal to Saigon.

While Market Time pressed against the coast, an operation called Garden Time forced the enemy off the main rivers. Zumwalt ordered river patrols to spread out, to be more aggressive, to go where the enemy had gone. Patrols penetrated the lesser rivers and canals, and narrow-water operations were extended right across Vietnam to the Cambodian border. Troops were brought in to close every waterway they could, forcing the enemy to move supplies overland. Within a year the Navy had blockaded the river and canal system along the Cambodian frontier. Combined with the devastation that the Army and the Marine Corps had wreaked against the Viet Cong in the Tet fighting, this denial of enemy resupply improved the military situation in the southern part of South Vietnam and showed the importance of selecting a strategy appropriate to the need at hand.[80]

As in Korea, in Vietnam U.S. forces received about 95 percent of their supplies by sea from the United States. Vietnam is 7,000 miles from America. To supply its troops the United States had to maintain one of the longest logistical lines in history. "That vast fighting force in Vietnam depended utterly on a few thousand seamen, mostly middle-aged, sailing a few hundred ships, mostly old."[81] The introduction of one-stop-replenishment fleet-auxiliary ships meant the fighting capabilities of the Seventh Fleet could be continually renewed at sea. In fiscal year 1967, "a typical year," over 70 percent of the fleet's ship fuel, 95 percent of its jet fuel, virtually all of its aviation gasoline, more than 95 percent of its ammunition, 97 percent of its provisions, and over 70 percent of its other stores were transported by sea.[82]

The Vietnam War, however, threw the Navy off balance. Off the coast of Vietnam and along the logistical line from the United States, the Navy's ships operated unopposed. The Seventh Fleet faced no air threat, no surface threat, no submarine threat, no threat to its control of the sea. It could concentrate entirely on power projection—that is, on carrier air strikes. Vietnam was the limited war the Navy had talked about, involving a coastal country against which it could bring its major tactical firepower to bear, a place where it could use its attack carriers and attack bombers in a support role against targets on land. What the Navy was much less prepared for was the other dimensions of limited war: small-unit actions in coastal control and riverine patrol. As the junior partner in Vietnam, it lost out in budgets for readiness replenishment to the Army, Air Force, and Marine Corps, which bore the brunt of the fighting, the losses, and the drawdowns. The main renewal the

Navy did experience, the restarting of its nuclear-carrier program, reflected its most dearly held doctrine and most conspicuous battle function, that of big-time air strikes from enormously expensive mainline capital ships. This would not necessarily have been the result had the less dramatic but certainly at least as important naval and maritime lessons of interdiction, protection, and littoral action been drawn from the experience in Vietnam and had been taken more into account.

Overall, Vietnam unbalanced the Navy by emphasizing strike warfare at the expense of an array of sea-control functions. It reinforced carrier-air doctrine instead of encouraging naval officers to think of carrier air strikes as only one of several Navy missions in an age of flexible response. The air wing prospered; but in readiness for sea control and in broad adaptability to low-intensity warfare, the Navy did not keep up. When Admiral Zumwalt as CNO took over the aging and shrinking fleet in July 1970, therefore, he determined to right the balance and give the Navy a full-service doctrine and a full-service force.

16

Disarray 1970-1980

THE SOVIET NAVY

The Soviet navy had never had a global sea-control mission. It stayed close to home, deployed for homeland defense, for holding off approaching attackers.[1] Its attack submarines ventured out to the Atlantic sea-lanes, it is true, but by and large U.S. and NATO forces thought they could contain any damage the submarines might do there.

In the 1950s the job of the Soviet navy was to prevent any amphibious assault on the Soviet Union's flanks. Its coastal submarines, destroyers, and cruisers were under the cover of supportive land-based naval air. In 1954, after Joseph Stalin's death, the Soviets' fear of invasion subsided. The United States and NATO dropped amphibious attacks from their strategies. The Soviet government thereupon curtailed construction of surface vessels. The result was that in the 1960s the Soviet navy could not contest sea control in any area vital to the Western Allies, nor did it want to.

On the other hand, while the threat of amphibious invasion disappeared, the danger of attack by U.S. carrier air increased. To meet it, the Soviets established a defensive anticarrier fleet that mounted stand-off guided missiles on ships, submarines, and land-based naval aircraft.[2]

In 1957–58, when longer-range supersonic attack aircraft enabled

U.S. carriers to stand farther out to sea, the Soviet navy moved its barrier force farther outward to meet them, into the South Norwegian Sea and the eastern Mediterranean. That put the Soviet force beyond land-based air cover. U.S. carriers threatening Soviet territory were to be struck at once with surface-to-surface missiles launched from their ocean-patrolling surface and submarine fleets. New attention was given to attacking advancing NATO submarines. The Soviets called their sea-denial layering the "blue belt of defense."[3]

The tactics of this strategy of destroying American ships with missiles occasioned an enormous debate in the Soviet Union during the 1960s. The strategy entailed a defense based on salvos from only a few weapons platforms, and that meant the end of the traditional Soviet naval doctrine of massed action. A Soviet consensus on the tactical-strike doctrine emerged in the late 1960s, and correspondingly in the United States, the thought of what that first salvo might do to vulnerable U.S. aircraft carriers contributed to Washington's increasing concern about the carriers' utility in forward operations.[4]

During the 1950s the Soviets also developed a sea-based strategic nuclear weapons system. This was not part of a sea-control challenge. Its purpose was to create secure platforms from which land targets could be hit. In 1955 the Soviets launched a ballistic missile from a surfaced submarine. In 1958 they began construction of the Golf and Hotel submarine classes, each carrying three sea-launched ballistic missiles. These first-generation missile submarines and their missiles were short-range. The early missiles had a range of less than 400 miles. Their targets would be carriers and Polaris submarines in port, at the opening of hostilities.[5] To reach a close-in station, however, the submarines had to pass through strong NATO defenses and go deep into dangerous seas. The next missile class, the Serb, installed in Golf II–class submarines in 1964, had a range of 1,000 miles. That was better, but it meant the Golfs, which themselves had only limited endurance, and the Hotels, which were extremely noisy, still had to run the gauntlet through the breakout gaps into the Atlantic. Both classes risked detection while they were outbound, on station, and returning. These disadvantages were so great that the submarines and their missiles were not serious strategic weapons and, in the event, were largely withheld from forward deployment.[6] By the end of the 1950s, the U.S. Navy thought it had contained this offensive threat. Throughout the decade Soviet strategic priority remained with its land-based ICBMs, and Soviet naval missions remained defensively focused on anticarrier and antisubmarine warfare.

In the 1960s, responding to the American buildup, Premier Khrushchev sought strategic parity. He made the Strategic Missile Forces, created in 1959, the primary armed service and gave it control of the land-based nuclear ICBM program, which was designed for a deep initial strike against the continental United States. To match the invulnerable second-strike Polaris, Soviet missilers improved their own submarine-based ballistic-missile system. This improvement emerged at the end of the decade in the form of the nuclear-powered Yankee-class submarine armed with sixteen ballistic missiles.

Yankees gave the Soviet Union many movable platforms from which to threaten the American homeland. However, throughout the 1960s the Yankees and their successors shot only missiles of restricted range—around 1,500 miles—which limited the submarines to coastal targets. The range of the Yankees themselves, and the use of an under-way supply system gave the submarines more sea in which to hide, but their missiles' limited range meant the boats had to take up positions far beyond the reach of Soviet land-based naval-air protection and deep inside U.S. and NATO antisubmarine barriers. Yankees turned up in the mid-Atlantic and off the east coast of the United States in 1968 and off the nation's Pacific coast in 1971. The head of the Soviet navy, Fleet Admiral Sergei G. Gorshkov, argued consistently and passionately that his SSBNs should be part of the initial-strike strategy. The Soviet authorities just as consistently refused to grant the mission, which, one should note, they also withheld from the Soviet long-range air force. Neither the navy nor the air force was able to break the initial offensive monopoly of the Strategic Missile Forces. In a nuclear war the SSBNs would be only a backup.[7]

Technology soon gave submarine-launched ballistic missiles more distance. In 1974 SS-N-8 ICBMs, with a range of 4,300 miles, were deployed aboard Delta I-class submarines, giving the Soviets an intercontinental strategic force that had the whole ocean in which to hide from American hunters. These new Soviet weapons closed the strategic gap that had been mercilessly revealed in the Cuban crisis. General Secretary Leonid Brezhnev declared that the Soviet Union had an assured-destruction capability against the United States. With this capability, the Soviet navy's main mission became destruction of the enemy's military forces on the ground. In a decision of utmost importance to Cold War strategy, the Soviet navy deployed this insurance force close to home. Instead of venturing out into the open ocean, toward the target, it was possible to keep the SSBNs near Soviet waters, behind defensive screens, withholding their power in order to have decisive force on hand to influence a postwar settlement. For influence, for deterrence, the Soviet SSBNs did not have to expose themselves to enemy hunters at all.[8]

Also during these years the Soviets solved their inability to assert distant-area sea control, an inability that had bedeviled them around Cuba in 1962. In response to President Kennedy's 1961 announcement of a U.S. military buildup, the Soviet Union had begun a crash rearmament program. The Soviet naval high command concluded from the Cuban crisis, as it had from Suez in 1956 and Lebanon in 1958, that the government needed a maritime force able to exert influence off any shore, to open possibilities for, and to provide support of, Soviet interventionist policy around the world. The purpose, as Gorshkov put it, was to withstand "the ocean strategy of imperialism."[9] The Soviet navy, like its American counterpart, was calling for a more flexible and useful strategy that included an independent sea-control force as an alternative to an overreliance on the blunt political strategy of nuclear parity. The navy was to include an advanced attack-submarine force—the Victor class—which would ultimately number 48 units, and a 'bluewater,' long-distance, surface-combat force. This force would give the Soviet Union worldwide offensive capability.

In the 1970s, then, the Soviet navy was in a position to play a more active role in Soviet foreign policy. In 1971 it possessed a strategic offensive capacity of over 50 ballistic-missile submarines (only a small fraction of which, however, were ever deployed simultaneously). Its sea-denial force of attack submarines had grown to over 300. In 1971 the Soviet Union overtook the United States in total number of nuclear-propelled submarines built and under construction.[10] Its surface force took on global missions, presenting the United States for the first time since World War II with a competitor on the seas.

Foreign observers were of mixed minds on how to interpret these developments. Was Soviet naval doctrine fundamentally offensive or defensive, strategic or interventionary? Were Soviet naval pronouncements about the acquisition of a sea-control force advocating an as yet unrealized ambition or announcing an achievement? Should one look at ships or speeches, capabilities or intentions? Was there a naval policy at all, or did the seemingly endless debate within the Soviet Union on naval purpose indicate a shifting of doctrinal positions that had ended in an unstable compromise? Soviet surface ships armed with antiship missiles and the large Soviet attack-submarine fleet could represent an offensive, oceanic sea-control force, the beginning of a naval arms race and a two-ocean sea-control challenge. On the other hand, the Soviets were not building attack aircraft carriers, on which the United States had established its command of the sea, nor were their general-purpose ships configured for hunting submarines. But then again, they would not need carriers if their concentrated missiles could sink approaching U.S. and NATO surface fleets, and if antisubmarine ships were present to protect their strategic-missile fleet from intruders. Maybe the new force was just part of the blue-belt defense, moving the zone farther out into the oceans. Or was it the forerunner of an offensive sea-control strategy meant to cut the sea-lanes used for Allied communication?

The U.S. Navy looked at Soviet capabilities and decided that no matter what was said in the USSR, the Soviet force threatened the Western arteries. U.S. naval officers had since World War II argued that their own weapons could be used in many ways and for many purposes. If the Soviets had a sea-control capability, that meant that defending sea-lanes had to be the primary U.S. response. So war at sea returned to center stage.

Academics argued that this overreacted to Soviet notions of sea control. "From the earliest days," Michael MccGwire contended, "the Soviet theoretical debate has been concerned with the problem of how to conduct naval operations *without* command of the sea." That distinction was not easy for U.S. Navy planners in the 1970s to grasp. " 'Command' is no longer a realistic concept," MccGwire continued, "outside certain geographical areas that are amenable to area defense." What the Soviets wanted was to create and exploit areas of "no command," to use their surface force to open up political opportunities and their submarine force to inhibit the ability of the United States to use its naval superiority for strategic advantage.[11]

Most security officials in the West saw the situation as more problematic and would have agreed with Laurence W. Martin, who wrote:

> We should recognize that the significance of maritime capability varies greatly according to the political context. To say that the Soviet Union seeks "dominance" in particular sea areas, for instance, has very different implications according to whether we have in mind a state of peace or war. For the moment the Soviet Navy is a very effective instrument for a forward diplomatic policy in the Mediterranean but would be very much on the defensive in open hostilities with the west.
>
> Nevertheless, there is an intimate connection between the potential balance in war and the actual relationship in peace. If the Soviet Navy must at present seek to avoid a military confrontation with the west, it is still the servant of an activist foreign policy, controlled by an unstable regime. It is consequently a vital western interest to see that the overall naval balance never shifts in Russian favor to an extent that would encourage Soviet leaders to reassess and minimize the dangers of military action.[12]

To this, Carl Amme added, "The key to understanding Soviet Naval strategy is in separating legitimate naval roles in peacetime in the Cold War environment and those roles the Russian fleets might be required to carry out in time of war."[13]

Beginning in 1963 Soviet surface warships routinely pushed out beyond their coastal seas. A Soviet squadron in the eastern Mediterranean tailed the American Sixth Fleet and, within ten years, numbered more ships than its quarry. In 1964 Gorshkov's cruisers and destroyers began making port calls along the East African coast, athwart the southern routes to the Suez Canal. Units trailed NATO maneuvers in the North Atlantic. Extensive submarine operations took place under the Arctic ice, as the Arctic Ocean became a theater of operations increasingly important to Soviet strategists. In 1962, four years after the *Nautilus* sailed under the North Pole, the feat was duplicated by a boat of the Soviet November class. Under-way replenishment gave the Soviet strategic submarines the potential to operate from stations and missile positions where they were hard to find. All this constituted, for CNO Moorer, "proof of the expansionist nature of Soviet naval operations" and of the need for the United States to return to a mission of sea control.[14]

The Soviet exercise in 1970, known in the West as Okean 70, was a display of an oceanic navy. Central command in Moscow coordinated the movement of the four Soviet fleets (Northern, Baltic, Black Sea, and Pacific), a squadron in the Indian Ocean, and a virtual fleet the Mediterranean. More than 200 ships and submarines took part, including guided-missile ships and helicopter carriers. Most of the vessels were concentrated in NATO waters of the North Atlantic and the Norwegian Sea.[15]

This exercise impressed the U.S. Navy. More than 99 percent of Soviet surface combatants and submarines were less than twenty years old. By contrast, much of the U.S. force was ready for retirement. Over half the U.S. surface fleet had been in service for more than twenty years. The exorbitant cost of the war in Vietnam and the very expensive conversion of 30 Polaris submarines to carry the Poseidon missile were eating up the Navy's shipbuilding budget.

Consider Lawrence Korb's figures:

> In 1964, the last pre-Vietnam year, the navy budget contained funds for the procurement of 74 ships. Four years later that number had dropped to 26, and in fiscal year 1972 it was down to 23. Between 1966 and 1970 the navy constructed only 88 ships. During the same period the Soviet navy built 209, 237 percent more than the American effort, or a difference of 121 ships. In 1964 the U.S. Navy received $2 billion for shipbuilding. Throughout the duration of the war

in Southeast Asia the navy received an annual average of only $1.1 billion for construction of new ships. In constant dollars, the funds for shipbuilding stayed below their fiscal 1964 levels for the following eleven years. This hiatus in the U.S. Navy's shipbuilding program could not have come at a more critical time for the American fleet.[16]

The United States could not count on the unquestioned sea mastery that characterized the naval actions in Korea, Cuba, and Vietnam. The Soviet missile fleet at first appeared to have neutralized U.S. carriers. Soviet attack submarines and surface missile-shooters appeared able to go to hitherto American corners of the sea and interfere with U.S. naval missions. This threat was compounded by the Navy's opinion that the Soviets did not separate nonnuclear and nuclear war at sea. The United States was not practiced in close-quarters combat in the nuclear and missile age. A sobering observation was that a preemptive first strike by one naval force against the other might decide the battle. Or the American strategy of keeping an engagement nonnuclear and restricted might fail, overcome by Soviet escalation. In short, in the early 1970s the Navy did not think it would be able to force a fight at sea that would remain conventional. Admiral Elmo R. Zumwalt, Jr., who had been CNO since July 1970, stated clearly that the U.S. government should not assume the Navy would prevail in battle if it had to fight without responding in kind to a Soviet nuclear attack. Zumwalt warned President Richard Nixon against exerting strong diplomatic pressure where the U.S. Navy could not, without nuclear support, stand up to the local Soviet force.[17] Admiral Moorer (who had become chairman of the Joint Chiefs when Zumult relieved him as CNO) repeated the Navy's worry that the Soviets might escalate a local naval conflict to a world war. The Navy's overall weakness impaired the service's confidence further. In lift, in ability to move the fleets, in preparedness, none of the Joint Chiefs thought the United States had the capability to wage a "one-and-a-half" conventional war—that is, a general war in Europe plus a limited embroilment anywhere else.[18] This loss of strategic initiative constrained U.S. foreign policy.

Particularly, Zumwalt thought the Navy's capacity to maintain sea control was at risk in the eastern Mediterranean, which had been the geographic focus of the resurgence of the Navy's doctrine of forward deployment 25 years before. If there was a confrontation on the order of the Cuban missile crisis there, arising, say, from an Arab-Israeli conflict, the power relation of the Cuban crisis would be reversed. The Soviet threat of nuclear war might force the United States to back down. As Zumwalt said: "The Soviet Union could place the President of the

United States in a position similar to that experienced by Khrushchev in 1962."[19] Operationally, the danger came from Soviet ships concentrated in the eastern Mediterranean, with port facilities in Egypt, and backed up by Soviet land-based air cover from airfields around the Black Sea and in Egypt.

The Soviet force was displayed during the Jordan crisis in 1970. At that time some 20 Soviet ships and submarines shadowed the Sixth Fleet, with 50 additional Soviet warships within a day's steaming distance. The eastern Mediterranean, said Sixth Fleet commander Admiral Issac Kidd, looked like "an international boat show." In high-threat environments, carriers need room to maneuver. Dispersal is their protection from submarines and missiles. In the eastern Mediterranean they were boxed in and hence vulnerable. These close operations with a prospective foe, Kidd said, opened a new chapter in naval tactics in the missile age. No longer, he wrote, "may naval task forces expect to group in classical manner, search out the enemy, and engage."[20]

The Soviets recognized the danger of escalation if aggressive tactics led to an exchange of fire. They proposed reopening negotiations on an agreement that would provide for the peaceful resolution of incidents at sea. Such an agreement was concluded in 1972. The Soviets took this as a prestige victory in which their diplomats won U.S. recognition of a kind of parity between the Soviet navy and that of the United States.[21]

The need for mutual self-restraint was evident when American support to Israel in 1973 was followed by a further buildup of the Soviet forces in the eastern Mediterranean. Admiral Moorer said that victory would go to the side that struck first. The strong Soviet position was bolstered by the Soviet Union's access to five Egyptian port facilities and by its use of seven Egyptian airfields for land-based air. The Soviet navy brought in four anticarrier groups to cover each of the Sixth Fleet's three attack carriers and its amphibious group. By the end of October 1973, the Soviet Mediterranean Fleet was up to 95 warships, "with a first-launch capability of 88 SSMs [surface-to-surface cruise missiles for antiship use], 348 torpedoes, [and] 46 SAMs [surface-to-air missiles]." For the first time in a crisis area, the Soviet naval force was larger than the American, in this case by a third. The Soviet Union also had the ability to attack Sixth Fleet units with land-based air flying from four directions: from Yugoslavia, Egypt, Syria, and the Crimea (in the latter case, violating the airspace of NATO allies). Power counts. In consideration of the Soviet force, the United States accepted a Soviet ultimatum that the Israelis allow the entrapped Egyptian Third Army to escape.[22]

Zumwalt said, "I doubt that major units of the U.S. Navy were ever in a tenser situation since World War II ended than the Sixth Fleet in the Mediterranean." In the event, naval forces did not engage. The Soviets took care to avoid a provocative incident.[23]

To regain the edge, the Navy needed numbers as well as modern ships. How many, and at what cost were the questions of the 1970s. Moorer had wanted 16 nuclear carriers at the center of an 850-warship fleet. That was unrealistic, representing thinking that was, as then Vice Admiral Stansfield Turner put it later, too much input (ships, aircraft, and manpower) and too little output (national objectives and missions).[24] In the period of reduction toward the end of the Vietnam War, terms of input were not the best ones to use in arguing the Navy's case. Nor was it obvious that deploying a concentrated carrier strike force was still the most appropriate naval strategy because neither U.S. nor NATO doctrine continued to envision a carrier offensive against the Soviet Union. The risks of putting a carrier against Soviet stand-off, antiship barriers outweighed the likely benefits.

The colossal expense of each heavy nuclear-powered attack carrier, $1.44 billion in 1977, and the many years it would take to replace one if it was sunk, had become reasons for being more cautious about using such carriers on the offense. To be sure, carriers retained a much-debated value as politically unencumbered strike bases, but their use increasingly depended on existing sea control and on the ability to defend them. The Air Force never let the Navy forget that in Korea, Cuba, and Vietnam the carriers had gone into action without opposition. But if carriers were not going to be used on the offensive, if their venue of action were to be so limited, then their value as a means of attrition in a general war would be reduced. Congress was not likely to give the Navy the sixteen modern carriers that Moorer had wanted. On appropriations grounds as well as on the basis of mission analysis, the Navy in the 1970s found it hard to justify asking for more of the fabulously expensive showcases of the 1960s.

REFORMS AND DECLINE

To meet modernization and procurement needs at a time when the Navy was retiring hundreds of overaged ships, Admiral Zumwalt, CNO from July 1970 to July 1974, tried to reconfigure the fleet in mission and ship design. Emphasis on the attack carriers, he thought, had narrowed strategic planning. Twenty-five years of power-projection doctrine, of reliance on attrition air strikes from the sea against the land, had tied the Navy to a strategy that was unlikely to be executed. And the Navy had adhered to this doctrine at the cost of neglecting a mission that was becoming more important—sea control.

Furthermore, Zumwalt's thinking went, the technologically complicated carrier (and the similarly sophisticated and expensive nuclear submarine) required Navy personnel to go early into intensive specialization. Officers and sailors were thus forced to adopt a narrow, operational focus, to form "unions," particularist and exclusive communities within the Navy that closed minds and limited vision. Officers looked at procurement in terms of the attributes of their specialty, of surface, or subsurface, or aviation warfare, or of nuclear propulsion, instead of taking a broader, Navy-wide, mission-oriented perspective, the view of unrestricted general line officers. Absence of a comprehensive mission outlook diminished awareness of campaign or strategic alternatives. Loss of mission focus led, simply put, to concentration on the delivery platform, not on the mission. In practice, that favored power projection, not sea control.[25] Admiral Zumwalt wrote:

> In the war in Southeast Asia, as in the Korean War, the enemy could not dispute U.S. control of the seas and so the Navy's main business became projection: amphibious landings, air strikes, and occasional episodes of naval shore bombardment. Not only did the Navy's share of the budget shrink during those wars because the Army and the Air Force underwent greater attrition of equipment, but under the circumstances the Navy had to put a disproportionate share of the money it did receive into maintaining its capability for projection—its carriers and attack planes, its amphibious vessels, its ships with the weapons for bombardment. Sea-control forces—antisubmarine planes and their carriers and ships suitable for patrol and escort duty—were allowed to obsolesce, and, finally, retire without replacement. More damaging yet, work on future sea-control requirements—new types of ships from which planes or helicopters could operate, new techniques for combatting submarines, new vessels to escort convoys, new kinds of weapons with which to fight on the surface was postponed for many years. The one exception was nuclear-powered attack submarines, which through Admiral Hyman Rickover's special influence on Capitol Hill got built in ample numbers.[26]

Within tight budgetary restraints, Zumwalt, like Moorer before him, decided the Navy could risk scrapping old ships in that period of relative international calm, and take a drop in current numbers in order to build new ships for a more dangerous future, a future in which the Navy would face a larger and more modern Soviet fleet.[27] The Navy could not have everything. To get a sea-control fleet within a limited budget, Zumwalt proposed what he called a "high-low mix," which was to be achieved by adding a new high-value carrier and some submarines while procuring newly designed, low-value combatants for a broad-based sea-control mission.

It was later noted that in reordering priorities Zumwalt did not integrate into a naval strategy the various Navy missions he had to consider—strategic deterrence, sea control, projection of power ashore, and naval presence. He left them unconnected to national political considerations, which was to be a troublesome conceptual weakness in Navy thinking throughout the 1970s. Nonetheless, framing discussion in terms of missions at least put the focus on objectives, not community specialization. Establishing sea control at the center of a campaign, for instance, reminded operators that their task was not to kill submarines but to make maritime operations safe, to get ships through. That perspective, Zumwalt hoped, would break union traditions and encourage a more flexible use of ships. The focus would be the campaign, not its parts.

Zumwalt preferred the term *sea control* to Mahan's *control of the sea,* the latter implying total use or total denial. Such extreme measures were neither possible nor necessary in the 1970s. *Sea control* connoted all the Navy need realistically aim for: use of a limited area for a limited time. *Sea control,* Zumwalt's collaborator Captain (later Admiral) Stansfield Turner said, was an ability to sail at one's choosing and for one's purposes at any time and in any place. Tactics would involve sortie control, choke-point control, open-area operations, and local engagement.[28] This was hardly extraordinary thinking, although it was meant to shift Navy attention. Critics in the service said that the sea-control approach came down to nothing more than a list of tactical objectives, that it was not a naval or maritime strategy or a definition of sea power, and that it inhibited strategic thinking as much as did the "union" and operational perspective that Zumwalt attacked.[29]

It is true that both Zumwalt's approach and the one he opposed were deductive and intra-Navy. Neither sea control nor power projection was expressed in terms of a national strategy in the early 1970s. Like the Army and the Air Force, the Navy continued to think about itself in isolation.

At this level of planning Zumwalt reflected the planning process of his time. His 1970 statement of what ships the Navy needed, titled "Project 60," was not drawn up by the Navy's long-range planning group. That group no longer existed, having been disestablished earlier that year, when conceptual planning in terms of national strategy was replaced by the form of functional procurement developed in the 1960s along PPBS lines. Long-range planning in the CNO's Systems Analysis

Division was limited to considering force levels and weapons innovations. Reports such as Project 60, and Zumwalt's subsequent Project 2000, were considered the CNO's ad hoc brainchildren and not given institutional life. Without the input of a broadly constituted long-range planning group, these studies were limited to mission statements and plans for weapons development. They turned out to be efforts that did not last beyond their sponsor's term of office.[30]

Project 60, then, was an internal Navy document that listed the forces Zumwalt wanted. It did not prioritize them because the report did not reflect a national strategy. President Nixon's foreign policy was based on nuclear deterrence, disarmament, and détente. How naval force might help was not stated. Nixon's policy was the consequence of a public unwillingness to undertake further military involvement or to increase military expenditure. On this barren field, Zumwalt and his planning assistants Vice Admiral Worth Bagley and Vice Admiral Stansfield Turner deduced the Navy's proper role from their own evaluation of growing Soviet capabilities.

The less expensive ships called for by Project 60 were meant to meet the Soviets at sea. The report proposed construction of four classes of these ships. One was a patrol frigate, half the size and cost of a destroyer escort. This frigate was not particularly fast or sophisticated, but it was cheap and designed for easy maintenance. It carried antisubmarine helicopters and the Harpoon guided missile. The patrol frigate was an archetypal low-value ship, and the only ones constructed were the *Oliver Hazard Perry*–class FFG-7s.

A second low-end design was more ambitious, a 17,000-ton, 25-knot vessel called the Sea Control Ship. Its cost would be less than 15 percent that of a new nuclear carrier. It would carry fourteen helicopters and three vertical / short-takeoff-and-landing (V / STOL) airplanes. The Sea Control Ships would be relatively cheap surrogates of the heavy carriers, and there were to be eight times as many of them as there were carriers. The theory went that the Sea Control Ship could be inserted in waters that were dangerous to the heavy attack carrier, particularly in the Mediterranean and western Pacific. The carriers could then withdraw from high-threat areas, put themselves out of reach of a missile first strike, and prepare to use their great offensive power to fight their way back to the combat theater. At that point, with the enemy threat overcome, the Sea Control Ships would retire to provide mid-ocean protection to under-way-replenishment groups, amphibious forces, convoys, or task groups, leaving the carriers free for forward offensive operations.[31]

That was the theory. It was rejected by officers who could not see how a less powerful force could go where an aircraft carrier could not and still withdraw intact. The Sea Control Ship did not have the armament to intercept a hostile bomber before it launched its missile, nor did it have the capacity to protect a convoy against a Soviet attack submarine. Weapons technology had not yet invested a light-hulled ship with enough firepower both to defend itself and to carry out an offensive mission. Rickover opposed the Sea Control Ship because he thought its construction would limit the rate of increase of nuclear propulsion systems. To his critics, Zumwalt was intent not so much on a balanced force as on sacrificing punch for numbers.

The main argument against the less-sophisticated, low-end ships and weapons, then, was that they could not compete in war. Limited in size, endurance, and force, they could not carry out the long-range, global sea-control or power-projection missions that were demanded by America's geopolitical position. More hulls did not make up for light arms. The proposed high-low mix was essentially defensive, critics said, and America needed an offensive Navy to overcome the essentially defensive Soviets. Carrier aviators declared that V/STOL aircraft were too slow and too lightly armed for strikes against land targets or Soviet defenses. Retired Vice Admiral Gerald E. Miller, a former commander of the Sixth Fleet, wrote that Zumwalt envisioned a Navy better suited to the Greeks or Turks in the Aegean Sea, or to the Soviet homeland defense force, than to a great oceanic state with worldwide interests. Current policy and the Soviet threat, Miller argued, demanded forward deployment, sustainability, and offensive strength, and that meant reliance on the great carriers and their attack aircraft and on other clearly offensive and superior combat vessels. Low-value vessels might exercise sea control, but they could not win it. Only a modernized fleet of the very highest technology and firepower could defeat the Soviet navy. Perhaps, Miller speculated derisively, Zumwalt's lack of big-ship sea command had kept him out of reach of "the realities of modern command at sea."[32] The critics' views prevailed. To general relief in the Navy, the Sea Control Ship never got past Congress. Congress also rejected the other two low-end ships Zumwalt proposed—a 60-knot hydrofoil patrol boat that would be armed with Harpoon cruise missiles and could shadow Soviet warships and an air-cushion skimmer. Surface speed was less important in an age of fast missiles and long-range sensors.[33]

Debate on force and mission of course continued. One can gauge its intensity by the reappearance of an old argument at the end of the decade. In the May 1979 issue of the United States Naval Institute's journal, *Proceedings*, for instance, the then Chief of Naval Operations Admiral Thomas B. Hayward, who was CNO from July 1978 to June 1982, revived the argument for an offensive strategy of launching attacks at the source by aircraft from the large attack carriers:

> The familiar concepts of Sea Control and Power Projection, which have some utility in the analytical world, do not serve as well in understanding the real world. Indeed, they have the potential to confuse the issue by suggesting that Sea Control and Power Projection are discrete categories when, in fact, they are closely intertwined. Projecting power against the sources of Soviet naval strength may well be the most rapid and efficient way to gain control of the seas (as contrasted with the simplistic concept held by many that Sea Control simply means escorting convoys to Europe and little else).[34]

Admiral Zumwalt, then retired, countered with a warning against letting the aviators' union, of which Hayward was a charter member, expand naval missions to such risky deep-strike actions in the name of sea control. "The modern naval officer must find ways to win over the traditionalists who cling to old large carrier platforms and their associated strategies." He called again for an essentially defensive force based on the very model that Hayward derided—increased reliance on low-end equipment and weapons, small V/STOL carriers and targeting sensors. Warships, said Zumwalt, instead of concentrating, should disperse, because a close formation would be a rich target for long-range missiles and torpedoes. He rejected the offensive doctrine of attack at the source. The big ships were simply too vulnerable to Soviet missiles. The point of many low-value vessels doing sea-control work was that "the large carriers [could then] be used in the less threatened areas until an acceptable degree of sea control [was] attained." Carriers, in short, were to stay out of harm's way.[35]

Norman Friedman asked "whether the usual distinction between sea control and power projection is really useful, or whether it does not amount to an implicit strategic choice."[36] It did in fact amount to such a choice, and because a national strategy was not brought forward to settle this issue, the differences between the two concepts kept the debate alive and fueled strategic uncertainty within Navy circles for a decade.

Related to Zumwalt's effort to reduce the influence of the carrier admirals when he was CNO was his enthusiasm for cruise missiles. Cruise missiles were to compensate for the Soviet buildup that had occurred during the interruption of Navy force modernization. The offensive capability of these missiles would free the Navy from its dependence on the strike aircraft that were "crowded on the decks of a few carriers."[37]

The Harpoon cruise missile seemed as if it would be the all-purpose weapon against Soviet surface ships, just as Soviet missileers expected their weapons to prevail against the American surface fleet. Harpoon could be launched from any platform. From an airplane it had a range of about 100 miles; from a ship or submarine, about 35. It skimmed the surface of the sea and was hard to detect and hard to hit. According to Norman Friedman, "The Harpoon program symbolized the shift from an American navy so powerful it could ignore Soviet surface-ship interference and concentrate on carrier-strike warfare against land targets, to a force that might have to face the Russian fleet in sea battles and might not always be able to supply carrier aircraft to protect its surface ships against those of the enemy."[38]

So as CNO, Zumwalt scrapped ships without getting the replacements he wanted for the sea-control mission he had declared. Lawrence Korb drew this pessimistic picture of fleet preparedness, a picture suggestive of the extent to which many observers thought the Navy had declined:

> Between FY 68 and FY 74 . . . the number of commissioned ships in the fleet dropped from 976 to 495, a decline of 481 ships, or 49%, in just six years. This was the lowest level the American fleet had reached since before World War II. The only types of vessels that did not experience a reduction during this period were the strategic and attack nuclear submarines. The number of fleet ballistic missile submarines remained level at 41, while the number of nuclear attack submarines nearly doubled, increasing from 33 to 61.[39]

These figures stretch back over a time before Zumwalt's time in office, but his tenure was not popular with many of the Navy's higher officers for reasons other than a drawdown of the fleet. He lacked the personal authority and the major command background of CNOs Burke and Moorer before him and Admirals James L. Holloway III and Hayward after him. His unorthodox methods, above all his reforms that bypassed traditional lines of command, disaffected men whose support he needed. Aviators charged him with anticarrier prejudice.[40] He never overcame the "union" structure against which he famously complained, nor did he overcome the antagonisms he created. His high-low force mix benefited some and angered others. For instance, attack carriers declined by only one or two from fifteen to the lowest number since the Korean War, but tonnage actually increased, and two more carriers of the nuclear-powered *Nimitz* class were added. What did decline was the number of antisubmarine carriers of the *Essex* class, from nine to two. The cut resulted from a decision to sacrifice these antisubmarine ships to preserve the attack-carrier force. Zumwalt could not square every circle.

Notable resentment, as well as strong support, was stirred by Zumwalt's effort to restore morale among the sailors. Services draw from society, and discipline and professionalism in the Navy of the early 1970s were buffeted by the social upheavals of the time. Long deployments off Vietnam, the strong antiwar sentiment at home, and the demobilization after the war encouraged sailors to leave the service. The Navy seemed out of touch with changing social norms in its treatment of women and minorities. Discipline began to break down, jeopardizing fighting effectiveness. There were racial riots aboard ships. The reenlistment rate for sailors plunged to an all-time low. For an increasingly high-tech service dependent on sophisticated skills, experience, and long-term commitments, problems in fleet manpower created what Zumwalt called "a catastrophic situation."[41]

Zumwalt took radical action that was supported by Secretary of the Navy John Chafee (January 1969 to April 1972) and Secretary of Defense Melvin R. Laird (January 1969 to January 1973). Indeed, it was to liberalize personnel administration as well as to modernize ships and weapons that Laird had chosen Zumwalt to be CNO over 33 of his seniors. Zumwalt deserves much credit for taking the lead in ending racial strife and improving race relations in the service. To speed reform Zumwalt bypassed the chain of command and dictated personnel changes on his own authority. He established committees aboard ship, called human relations councils, through which sailors could jump command lines to appeal to higher authority. That allowed for direct intervention that took disciplinary authority away from the chief petty officers. There was a strong sentiment that Zumwalt had degraded his captains and encouraged violation of a principle of naval leadership—that of "loyalty down." Resentful senior enlisted men left the Navy in droves. "We lost it in the chiefs' quarters," a later CNO stated, and Zumwalt's successors were left the task of restoring professional pride to discouraged petty officers.[42]

Younger officers generally supported Zumwalt's reforms. They correctly saw them as changes overdue. But his failure to satisfy proponents of other customary professional values cost him respect among traditionalists. His task was not smoothed by the fact that his tenure was a period of political stress, fiscal retrenchment, the winding down of Vietnam, and Watergate. One does not choose one's watch.[43]

When considered in the light of administration policy, the decline in naval force need not have been discouraging. The number of ships mattered, but numbers were not everything. National policies mattered more, for a war at sea would be a war between states at large. Despite the disquieting signs of Soviet global maritime movements, neither side was headed toward a collision at sea. Even strictly in terms of naval warfare, each side held certain advantages, and no one could say for sure how the respective navies would fare in combat. Certainly in any war great or small, much would depend on the effectiveness of the total force, on the wisdom of the national strategy, and on diplomacy and the international context, elements that were beyond the Navy's control. In these areas overall, the United States still stood strong. Zumwalt never received due credit for his successful campaign for the fourth U.S. nuclear strike carrier, the *Carl Vinson*, or for his support of the huge Trident missile-and-submarine system to replace Polaris and Poseidon. Strategic deterrence held, in large measure thanks to invulnerable SSBNs. Strategic deterrence was the Navy's first mission.

Zumwalt said he gambled on a force gap to pursue a modernization program, scrapping old ships in expectation of the new, and that this gap would be at its greatest in 1974, the year of his relief by Admiral Holloway. The United States, he said, "has lost the control of the sea lanes to the Soviet Union."[44] "We stand now at our point of greatest weakness, and, in my estimate, in our greatest jeopardy," Zumwalt told Congress. If the building program he had laid out continued as planned, the gap would close in the second half of the 1970s, when the country would realize the payback for the program of modernization "for which we have sacrificed current capabilities."[45] That was Zumwalt's assessment. It took nerve to hold to it. And it turned out to be wrong.

The turnaround did not take place. Unexpectedly high rates of inflation in the shipbuilding industry, between 15 and 20 percent in the mid-1970s, drove up unit costs to four times what Navy planners had predicted.[46] The Navy lost the purchasing power it had counted on. High costs made it impossible to replace an old ship with a new one. The six *Forrestal* carriers built before Vietnam cost around $250 million each. *Nimitz*-class supercarriers were edging toward $2 billion apiece. F-14 Tomcat fighters, used for carrier defense, cost about $25 million each. They replaced F-4 Phantoms, which had been built for $3 million apiece. Destroyers had been built for under $50 million, but now, with the DD-963 *Spruance* class, they cost over $350 million. There simply was not enough money to go around.[47] In 1975, the Navy's 200th anniversary, the active fleet dropped below 500 ships, the smallest number since 1939. In 1977 it was down to 464. The year before, Admiral Rickover, with reckless hyperbole, told Congress that in a submarine war he would prefer to be in command of the Soviet submarine force.[48]

In 1975 the Soviets held their second global exercise, which in the West was called Okean 75. It revealed the extent to which the Red Navy had grown in the five years since the eye-opening Okean 70. A total of 220 warships and submarines acted out an offensive strategy. They were supported by Soviet naval air, which included the long-range strike bomber called the Backfire. Backfires bore two antiship missiles and had an unrefueled range of around 3,000 miles. Many Soviet ships operated well beyond the Soviet Union's 1,500-mile defense perimeter. Okean 75, clearly a sea-control exercise, was performed in areas where the Soviets would try to cut Atlantic lines of resupply.[49]

The year 1976 marked the high point of Fleet Admiral Gorshkov's doctrine of forward deployment, of the Soviet navy's aspiration to gunboat diplomacy. Political events were making it too risky to pursue independent global interventionism. The departure of the United States from Vietnam in 1973, the U.S. rapprochement with China, and the opening of Tokyo's connections with Beijing caused the Soviets to focus their attention on great-power issues and to give new importance to the Pacific. For the rest of the 1970s, the Soviet navy restricted its "presence" visits to Third World states and sent nuclear ballistic-missile submarines and amphibious and antisubmarine forces to the Soviet east coast. By the end of the decade, there were more men in the Soviet Union's Pacific Fleet than in its Northern Fleet.

SLACK TIDE

The confusion of the 1970s got worse as the decade came to an end. Presidents Nixon, Gerald Ford, and Jimmy Carter reduced the Navy's role in national war plans to a minor one and downsized its force accordingly. The fleet of nuclear ballistic-missile submarines, which remained steady at 41, was for deterrence, not war fighting, and may be separated from this discussion. Strategic decisions were driven by a determination to control costs, a wish to deal with the Soviets through diplomacy, a hope for arms-control agreements, and a rejection of limited wars like Vietnam. The U.S. shift away from land commitments in Asia diminished the value of force in the Pacific. Containment would be pursued by balance-of-power diplomacy, notably through improved relations with China, and by a strong stand on the NATO central front.

As in the late 1940s, if a war broke out in Europe, it was expected to begin with a lightning thrust in the center of the continent, a thrust contained, however, by a defense that was designed to keep the war conventional and in-theater. Flexible response permitted the use of tactical nuclear weapons if conventional forces did not hold. Even if tactical nuclear weapons were used, the theory behind the planning went, the war would be short, restrained by the vast strategic arsenal and ultimate deterrence policy of each superpower. With the idea that a central-front invasion would be stopped in weeks, less and less attention was paid to action in the Mediterranean, the North Atlantic, or the Pacific—the customary venues of the Navy—or to the possibilities inherent in a maritime strategy. This was bad planning, foreclosing strategic options that might have been open to a vast maritime coalition.[50]

If the national strategy could contain the conflict to a "1.0" war, or perhaps more accurately a "0.5" war, a short one fought with troops on the ground in Europe and with the Pacific remaining calm, then "you really didn't need naval forces."[51] Antisubmarine warfare and convoy were the Navy's charge, but in a war of days there would be no time for sealift, no reason to sweep the seas of enemy submarines, no demand for reinforcement. Estimates were that in the face of Soviet submarines it might take a month to clear the Atlantic sea-lanes and additional time to move men and material, too long for the central-front campaign. So sea control would not materially affect the course of a war in Europe. Troops on the ground either would hold against a Soviet attack, or they would not. In either case, it was assumed the war would soon be over.

The Navy's sea-control mission was thus rendered meaningless by the strategy it was supposed to support. Few took seriously Navy talk of a U.S. fleet being swung from the Pacific through the Panama Canal to the Atlantic. Although the swing strategy remained part of the NATO plan through the 1980s, it was generally thought to take much too long, and in NATO planning there was no role for attrition-war carriers anyway. Proposing a swing strategy did not help the Navy's case either, because the proposal denied the argument of keeping a force in place in the Pacific to cover that theater should the war in Europe expand.

No alarm followed the statement of Secretary of Defense Donald Rumsfeld in 1976 that because of a shortage of surface combatants the Navy might not be able to protect the sea-lanes to the western Pacific.[52] President Carter and his defense secretary Harold Brown (January 1977 to January 1981) continued to divert resources from a strategy of flexible, global preparedness to the specialized function of meeting the Soviet army on the ground; from a maritime strategy to a continental commitment; from the Pacific to Europe; and from the maintenance of a two-ocean Navy to the development of a one-ocean Navy. The Navy, Brown declared, was for antisubmarine warfare, convoy in the Atlantic, and "localized contingencies outside Europe and peacetime presence."[53] During the 1970s the Navy and Marine Corps were called upon 33 times to respond to international crises. Attack carriers were deployed on over 70 percent of those occasions.[54] But there was no place for offensive sea power in a general war. The United States reduced its general-purpose forces, inflation ate away at building programs, the Army built up in Europe, and the Navy thought it was paying the bill.

There was widespread disillusionment on all sides. The administration and critics in Congress thought the Navy mismanaged shipbuilding contracts. Navy officers, unable to set clear priorities, got into disputes among themselves over which ship types should be preferred. The Navy was told to "get its act together."[55] President Carter in 1978 cut the Navy's shipbuilding program by half and stopped construction plans for another large *Nimitz*-class attack carrier, rejecting the recommendation of the CNO, Admiral Thomas B. Hayward.[56] The large carriers, Carter and Brown thought, had had their day. They were enormously expensive, of limited military value, and vulnerable to cruise-missile attack. In war they would be forced to strike first or withdraw. Carrier battle groups could be reduced to eleven or twelve. Carter and Brown took a page from Zumwalt's book and favored building a smaller, oil-burning, medium-sized V/STOL carrier, one that would pack much less firepower than a *Nimitz*-class carrier but would be more appropriate, they and their budget analysts deemed, for a sea-control strategy and for crisis intervention in the Third World.

The administration's orientation did not add up to a two-ocean force or, in the opinion of Navy leaders, to the necessary offensive clout. CNO Admiral Thomas B. Hayward, speaking to an association of naval aviators, contemptuously ridiculed the idea that sea control could be established by small, cheap ships and that the powerful carriers should move to the periphery. "It's a Third World strategy. It's what I call the 'convoy syndrome.'" That was "their" Navy, said Hayward, naming Zumwalt and his collaborator Vice Admiral Worth Bagley, not the Navy of Hayward himself and of his audience of aviators.[57] It was only with the power of the attack carrier that the United States would have the margin of victory at sea. Said Hayward, "If we design a Navy through intent that does not have the ability to take the initiative, we have designed a losing Navy."[58] But in the administration's war plan there was no combat role for strike carriers.

That the Navy was given no offensive role in a Europe-first policy was, Navy Secretary W. Graham Claytor (February 1977 to August 1979) charged, nothing less than a "fundamental change in national strategy."[59] Certainly the rejection of an offensive maritime strategy, as James Lacy said, amounted to "one of the sternest assaults on the Navy's traditional roles and missions in decades."[60] It called into question the position the service had built up for over 30 years as a versatile, multipurpose offensive force that could participate in every level of war fighting. Apart from the problematic antisubmarine and convoy missions in the Atlantic, the Carter administration consigned the Navy to gunboat diplomacy. The budgeted outlays for the Navy for fiscal year 1980 were smaller in proportion to GNP than for any year since 1950.[61]

The creation of what Secretary Claytor ridiculed as "the naval equivalent of the Maginot Line," coupled with the deep cuts in the active force and in replacement shipbuilding, caused many in the Navy to feel as if the fears of the 1940s had come to pass.[62] No one listened to the old version of sea power. Critics said that because of the risk to its carriers the Navy would not take the fight to the enemy for fear of loss.[63] Antisubmarine missions, lesser ships, and Air Force planes were enough to handle sea control. The administration thought the Navy had greatly exaggerated the significance of the Soviets' global reach. Of the world beyond Europe, Secretary of Defense Brown declared in 1979: "The military capabilities of the Soviet Union and its satellites are far from unlimited. The Soviets cannot be powerful everywhere at once, any more than we can."[64] In fiscal year 1980 the Defense Department accorded only about 10 percent of its budget to Navy general-purpose forces (excluding naval aviation), which consisted of an active and reserve fleet of 457 warships. This fleet was being reduced, specialized, and moved to the margin in accordance with a foreign policy assessment with which Navy leaders disagreed. For a year or two at the end of the decade the Navy lost its course.

To be sure, naval officers had criticized almost every element of U.S. foreign policy in the post-Vietnam 1970s. They had challenged the contentions that a war in Europe would be short; that it could be confined to that theater; that the use of tactical nuclear weapons would stay limited; that the carrier was vulnerable; that a massive, offensive, carrier-centered fleet had no place in war; and that naval force could be reduced and still execute sea control. Their arguments carried little weight with the national security community because the arguments failed to connect with the politics of the time.

Mahan would have seen the problem in a moment. As in the mid-

1940s, the Navy thought its interests would be taken for granted. In fact they had to be established, both within and outside the service. That indeed is the central thesis of this book, that the Navy, as any other agent of government, is the instrument of national policy, its junior partner in every regard, and to disassociate itself from the broad national position is to disassociate itself from the source of its purpose and its strength. In the 1970s the Navy's coercive and expensive sea-power doctrine, its interest in a war of attrition, fit less and less the policies of post-Vietnam America. The Navy's close adherence to heavy-carrier doctrine, and the resulting definition of sea power, put the service in a double bind. It could not detach its central doctrine from a weapons system that had lost its credibility, a system that the Navy's political masters had declared irrelevant. The divergence of dominant Navy thinking from national policy was a recipe for disaster.

The Navy looked to Soviet capabilities, saw a challenge, and stressed preparation for an imminent conflict. The administrations, Nixon's as well as Carter's, looked to Soviet intentions, saw stability, and envisioned peace. The Navy saw a threat, prospective if not existing, that was naval in nature, that would give rise to more, not fewer, small wars anywhere in the world. That threat could be met, global allies could be reassured, and Japan, Korea, and Western Europe could be secured, only with countervailing naval power, centered of course on the great, globally deployable capital ships and their air-delivery systems, which had to be ready for a war of attrition. The administrations, matching the public's desire for retrenchment and economy, stressed diplomacy under the reliable umbrella of deterrence. If it came to war, the conflict would be short, localized, and on the ground, a war for which only a small Navy was needed.[65]

The Navy made a mistake in stating its case largely in terms of competition with Soviet capabilities—that is, in terms of force structure, the same terms in which it justified its own doctrine. The mistake was that impassioned arguments about force structure, about the size of hulls and the speed of airplanes, passed by most listeners outside the service. Such arguments failed to convey their implicit political and hence strategic content. And as we have seen, listeners became confused when the Navy did not speak with a single voice. In the debates on the high-low–mix program, for instance, and in those on carrier size, nuclear propulsion, and aircraft types—as well as in the confusion about setting priorities between power-projection and sea-control missions—there were always officers who represented the interests of contending warfare communities and who were willing to put forward contrary views. Exaggeration, contradictory predictions, and a failure to relate hardware discussions to national interests all made the Navy seem unsure of itself, as indeed it was.

Thomas Etzold wrote:

> Unfortunately . . . the 1970s divergence on national security assumptions rendered the Navy's intimations of coming calamity useless, or worse, self-defeating. There was no agreement on the exact extent of American national interests and what they might require in the way of defense; there was no general understanding of what maritime superiority might be and what benefits it could confer on the United States; there was no common concept of the political and strategic implications of having either the first or second navy in the world, nor even any common standard for measuring one navy against another. In this situation, suggestions of imminent or ultimate doom robbed the navy of credibility; they did not win fundamental or budgetary arguments.[66]

The service, in sum, lost touch with its sustaining political base. Mahan had known above all that the Navy depended on having a public and political leaders who shared its sea-power assumptions, and that the Navy was the secondary partner in its relationship with the nation and its leaders. The tendency to put means (force structures) before ends (political purpose) worked against the Navy.

As Etzold wrote: "This is a classic error, one perhaps possible in the Navy in that time only because of shortcomings mentioned earlier: the overconfidence in an enfeebled theory, and relative inattention to people in the national security community holding the power over assumptions. . . . The Navy attempted to use force structure and systems analysis to prevail in arguments about essentially political assumptions."[67]

In the 1970s that approach failed. There was less and less agreement that sea power was somehow autonomous, that it was separate from land power in political and military calculations, that America could define its security and its strategy as insular. Technology reduced distance and time and created weapons with which the small could destroy the large. That changed the value of geography, the environment of naval strategy. Again, to quote Etzold:

> The idea of insularity always applied to the United States less than assumed in classical naval theory. In the 1970s, it became manifestly inappropriate. . . . For in classical naval theory, insular and coastal states of certain characteristics went to sea to augment meager power bases. Overseas connections were to become sources of strength and to increase national power, not to become strategic vulnerabilities or long-term liabilities on the national power and resources of the home country. In the 1970s, it was a near thing to judge whether American reliance on the sea constituted a strength or a weakness.[68]

That was the Navy's problem, and Navy leaders took it in hand at the end of the decade. Service and political views were reknit in the form of an offensive maritime strategy that argued that overseas connections and reliance on the sea were in fact among the country's foremost strengths. On that proposition was based the Navy's sea-power answer to the question of how it proposed to counter the growing Soviet naval power and to the question of why America needed a big, expensive Navy whose fleet was centered on the attack carrier.

17

High Tide
1980-1990

REASSESSING THE SOVIET NAVY

In the 1980s, Admirals Thomas B. Hayward (CNO, July 1978 to June 1982) and James D. Watkins (CNO, June 1982 to June 1986), together with Secretary of the Navy John F. Lehman, Jr. (February 1981 to May 1987), overcame the dispute about the use of naval force that had beset the 1970s by tying together, into a comprehensive, easily understood doctrine, the main offensive elements of Navy thinking. That synthesis established a basis for professional and public discussion of the importance of sea power. With its maritime strategy of the 1980s the Navy laid claim to global offensive action in a general war with the Soviet Union. Hayward, Watkins, and Lehman moved the Navy's missions away from NATO-centered, reactive sea control and limited Third-World interventionism toward a worldwide offensive in a general war. The Navy hoped that in such a war it would be able to achieve a related shift—that of national strategy away from a sharp, nuclear conflict on the European central front, toward a long, conventional, maritime war of global scope. Such a maritime strategy would recommit the Navy to power-projection missions of direct air-and-amphibious support in a European land war, as well as to offensive sea control through aggressive antisubmarine warfare. To bring about these changes, Admiral Zumwalt's unpopular insistence on dispersible, low-end ships designed for point-specific sea control, his plan for a "geopolitical cavalry" that would be used in low- to middle-level peripheral conflicts, was succeeded by Admiral Hayward's concentration both on deep onshore air strikes from large attack carriers and on offensive antisubmarine warfare.

On this forward maritime strategy the Navy rode the national rearmament wave of the 1980s. However, because this particular strategy and the force it called for were designed to meet the Soviet threat, the rationale on which they were based disappeared with the end of the Cold War. In 1990, one hundred years after Mahan produced his influential writings, the United States found itself again without a doctrine of sea power or agreement on what constituted the proper use and composition of its Navy.

The maritime strategy of the 1980s, however, did end the disputes that had existed within the Navy during the previous decade over the nature of American naval power. The first step to ending these arguments had been to agree on the character and purpose of the Soviet navy.

The difference of opinion that existed during the 1970s can be seen in two papers presented in Washington in 1977. The first was delivered by the then deputy chief of naval operations for plans, policy, and operations, Vice Admiral William J. Crowe. It expressed an ocean sea-control strategy that focused on attacking enemy ships at sea, not at their bases. For protecting both merchant ships on NATO surface sea-lanes and American ballistic-missile submarines, Crowe said, "sea control is the [U.S.] navy's preeminent function."[1] Crowe and his boss, CNO Admiral James L. Holloway III (June 1974–July 1978), were working in the context of Nixon's and Carter's downgrading of over-the-shore attack. Restrained from arguing for attack at the source, that is, the enemy's home ports and support bases, and aware that convoy protection in the narrow sense was increasingly problematic in the age of satellite surveillance, over-the-horizon weapons, and the ability of an enemy to patrol vast sea spaces, Crowe set out a protection strategy that was based on aggressive attacks against Soviet submarines at sea. That was the Navy's maritime strategy at the time, and it aimed at sea control.[2]

The second paper, by James McConnell, asserted that those Soviet submarines Crowe was sending the Navy after were in fact on the least important of the Soviet navy's missions. Soviet resources dedicated to interference with NATO sea-lanes, McConnell said, accounted for less than 5 percent of Soviet naval investment. That statement suggested a need to redirect the attention Crowe had placed on direct sea control, because Soviet naval forces would be committed elsewhere in a general war. The first Soviet naval mission, McConnell said, was to hold a force of ballistic-missile submarines in reserve for a secondary strike. That strategic reserve was meant to deter America's use of nuclear weapons against the Soviet homeland, even if NATO was losing the battle for Europe. The Soviet navy's second mission was purely defensive: to protect that insurance reserve in waters near home, where it was kept. That called for local, not blue-water, sea control by the Soviets. The Soviets' third and considerably less important naval mission was to protect the homeland against enemy seaborne air strikes. This mission was based on a strategy that called for a blue-belt zone of torpedo and cruise-missile defense against U.S. submarines and carriers. The fourth and least important mission, said McConnell, was interdiction of NATO sea-lanes.[3]

Fleet Admiral Gorshkov, it appeared on this analysis, had failed to win approval for an initial, deep-strike role for his SSBNs, for a true strategic reach in the first moments of a general war. According to this interpretation, the first long-range nuclear salvo remained the preserve of the land-based Strategic Missile Forces (SMF). By the end of the 1970s, then, the mission of the Soviet submarine-launched ballistic missiles was a strategic second strike. Gorshkov and offensive-minded admirals might protest, but they could not break "the SMF's bureaucratic stranglehold on the deep strike mission," nor could the Soviet navy "otherwise relieve itself of the withholding role."[4] According to this argument, there was little point to Crowe's sea-control strategy because the Soviet attack submarines would be pulled back for bastion defense.[5]

Frank Uhlig, a seasoned and acute naval thinker, said of the two outlooks:

> Let us assume that these people's views [those of Crowe and Holloway favoring a sea-control strategy with an offensive twist, a strategy that assumes the primacy of sea logistics and the importance of transit] carry some weight, and that the U.S. Navy and the navies of our allies hasten, when war comes, to protect shipping. Let us also assume that Mr. McConnell's views are accurate and that the Soviets intend to do very little in the way of attacking U.S. and allied shipping at sea, and very little more about NATO's naval forces except when they threaten the Soviet Union's ballistic missile submarines. Does this mean that, in war, a large part of the U.S. fleet will be busy protecting ships which are not in danger? Does it mean that a large part of the U.S. fleet will be operating in one part of the ocean while most of the Soviet fleet will be in another? Does it mean that those ships which we so employ will have no useful

role to play? . . . Is it conceivable, then, that the opposing fleets would seldom be in contact with each other? Yes. It is conceivable.[6]

The two papers, Herschel Kanter commented, showed that "the naval missions of the two countries . . . have little to do with each other." He continued:

> This is true despite the fact that the U.S. and Soviet naval leaders have developed their navies as instruments to control and oppose each other's navy, or at least have sold much of their naval forces to their respective political leaders on that basis. . . . Admiral Crowe goes on to describe a Soviet navy designed to challenge Western supremacy, not as reported by McConnell in the strategic warfare area, but against our sea lines of communication in a conventional war. The U.S. Navy exists to oppose the Soviet naval mission that, according to McConnell, is barely mentioned by the Soviet strategists and then only in the broken-back phase of a general nuclear war.[7]

Here was the confusion that Navy leaders had to resolve.

Progress toward resolution began with a growing awareness that in the 1970s Soviet military doctrine had changed. That doctrine no longer considered all-out nuclear war inevitable. While maintaining the importance of controlling Europe, the Soviet government had evidently given up the objective of destroying American capitalism and thus would not attack the American military-industrial base directly. That would allow the United States to continue to fight, but the Soviets would hold Europe. Control of Europe would be secured by deterring an American nuclear attack with the threat of the Soviet submarine ballistic-missile reserve. To protect that essential deterrent force, Soviet naval strategy remained primarily defensive, with its main forces held close to home.[8]

It was on these assumptions that Navy planners revived their offensive thinking. If the navies of the United States and its allies could overcome the Soviet defenses, they could put at risk the Soviets' strategic reserve. If they destroyed submarines before the submarines sailed into the open ocean, they would assure the safety of NATO shipping. If they conducted amphibious campaigns on Europe's flanks in support of a ground war to hold or regain Europe, they would bring to a general war a great maritime asset. In short, in a return to the forward naval role that had lain buried for decades under the doctrines of air power and massive retaliation, short-war theory, fear of nuclear war, simple interventionism, and a sharply limited definition of sea control, the Navy could remarry power projection to sea control.[9] The United States, from its central maritime position, could seize the strategic initiative.

Deployment intelligence supported the interpretation that Soviet naval strategy had become deterrent and defensive. During the 1970s the Soviets deployed longer-range missiles aboard nuclear submarines of the Delta class: the twelve 4,300-mile SS-N-8s carried on each of the eighteen Delta I boats and the sixteen SS-N-8 missiles on each of the four Delta IIs, followed by the sixteen 3,500-mile-range SS-N-18s, equipped with multiple independently targeted warheads, on each of the fourteen Delta IIIs. These were breakthrough combinations of range and offensive power. Missile-launching submarines no longer had to go out into the Atlantic or the eastern Pacific. They could shoot at U.S. and allied targets from the Norwegian Sea or from the western Pacific. When these boats were surged to the open ocean they showed an "excellent" capacity for rapid movement.[10] For the most part, however, they were kept close to home. Once a bastion patrol was established, the strategic reserve could be kept within protected zones of the Barents Sea and Arctic Ocean, and in the Sea of Okhotsk, operating over the top of the world on interior lines, virtually without interference. That was the new Soviet blue belt of defense.[11]

The bastion defense resolved the "paradox" that U.S. Naval Intelligence had noted: the concentration of Soviet antisubmarine forces near the Soviet coasts "which are not likely submarine operating areas."[12] The benefit to U.S. and allied shipping was immediately obvious. The more that attack submarines were kept back in barrier duty instead of being sent out on ocean patrols, the closer the United States and its allies would come to their sea-control goal of safe use of the seas.

Furthermore, if only a small percentage of Soviet naval assets were forward deployed, U.S. and allied maritime strategists had a Soviet weakness to exploit. Soviet thinness in the outer ocean permitted U.S. and allied forces to operate farther forward and encouraged them to take the fight to the enemy. Admiral Thomas Hayward, then U.S. fleet commander in the Pacific, concluded that an offensive strategy would be practicable if it could be executed with great swiftness at the beginning of hostilities. That meant the Navy would have to use its carrier battle groups and attack submarines, the forces that were best able to destroy all targets afloat and on land. The counterforce offensive nature of the ensuing forward maritime strategy, its risky—and intensely criticized—theory of attacking the Soviet underwater strategic reserve, and its plans for air and amphibious assault on the European flanks, rested on the conclusions that Soviet forces were close-held, could be attacked, and could be overcome.

THE PACIFIC MODEL

The Soviets in the 1970s rapidly and steadily built up their Pacific Fleet and their support bases for that fleet. This buildup appears to have been the consequence of a judgment that it was too expensive to maintain the SSBNs in the Arctic Ocean and that commanding the Norwegian Sea was too difficult. That theater was accordingly downgraded, and priority was given to securing the Sea of Okhotsk, improving the defenses of the Kuril Islands, and reinforcing the Soviet Pacific Fleet. By 1984, 23 SSBNs and 125 attack submarines, over 30 percent of all active Soviet submarines, were in the Pacific. Also in the Pacific were 90 major surface combatants, around 30 percent of the Soviet total, ships that included the *Minsk* and the *Novorossiysk*, which were V/STOL aircraft carriers of the *Kiev* class; heavy cruisers, notably the nuclear-propelled battle cruiser *Frunze*, second ship of the *Kirov* class; guided-missile cruisers; and one of the two largest amphibious ships in the Soviet Navy, the versatile *Nikolayev*, carrying 550 troops and four helicopters. The *Nikolayev*'s sister ship, the *Rogov*, had been withdrawn from the Pacific in 1981 for modification and was expected back as the flagship of a powerful amphibious force. By the mid-1980s the Soviet Union's Pacific Fleet deployed more ships than did the Soviet Northern Fleet. The Pacific Fleet was protected by the largest of the fleet air arms, a force comprising about 30 percent of Soviet naval air. Around 440 aircraft were assigned to this force, 150 of which were tactical-strike and fighter bombers.[13] The fleet also was backed by the great bases of Vladivostok and Petropavlovsk-Kamchatski, the latter being for submarines. After 1979 the Soviets had a support base at Cam Ranh Bay in Vietnam for patrol in the South China Sea.

This expanded Pacific Fleet, known as the Red Banner Pacific Fleet, was established for several missions. One was to maintain a Pacific bastion for the submarine missile force. Also, from Pacific bases the Soviets could shadow American naval movements. Obvious too, at least to U.S. Navy leaders, was the potential for intervention, for threats or actions against U.S. interests and allies, from Japan through the Indian Ocean to the Persian Gulf, and for establishing an out-of-area naval presence. Navies do many things, and while Gorshkov's ideas of a naval strategic offensive had been reined in, his appreciation of the value of global coercive naval diplomacy remained intact. A book published in 1979 for the Center for Naval Analyses, *Soviet Naval Diplomacy*, detailed Soviet out-of-area deployments and the spread of Soviet naval-

and air-support facilities in the Mediterranean and the Indian Ocean and concluded that to maintain its global interests the United States would have to "keep up its capabilities, its commitment to the *status quo*, and its resolve to demonstrate that commitment."[14] All evidence suggested that the Soviets were preparing for action of one kind or another in the Pacific.

Few U.S. Navy officers thought that a European war would be contained. They rejected the opinion of Carter's defense secretary, Harold Brown, that "the Soviets cannot be powerful everywhere at once, any more than we can."[15] Brown's assessment dismissed the global buildup too lightly. The Soviet Union would move war to the Pacific whether it was winning or losing in Europe. It was a Pacific power, like the United States. Unless its buildup was countered, America's maritime alliances in Asia would be under challenge. The Soviets were in fact a strategic threat in the Pacific. Brown's predecessor as secretary of defense, Donald Rumsfeld, had told Congress in 1976 that the Navy could protect the sea-lanes to Hawaii and Alaska but without more surface ships "would have difficulty" defending those to the western Pacific, and that the problem would get worse when the number of Soviet attack submarines increased.[16]

The 1.5-war assumption surmised a swing of ships from the Pacific to the Atlantic, implying an insupportable desertion of American interests in the Pacific. To remove the fleet would expose the Aleutians, discredit the confidence that the Japanese had in America's commitment to their defense, call into question the politically important cooperation with China, leave the Indian Ocean unprotected (an area of acute concern after the Iranian hostage crisis and the Soviet invasion of Afghanistan), and in short, undermine the U.S. containment policy on the Soviet Union's eastern and southwestern flanks. It was bad enough to neglect the Pacific in the late 1970s; to abandon it would be disastrous. The Pacific part of a global war with the Soviet Union would not be a half war but part of a two-ocean war for which the Navy was not ready. Through the mid-1970s the Navy received no clear guidance from the Defense Department on how to deal with a possible crisis in the western Pacific, an eventuality to which national strategy had given too little attention.

The first response from the Navy was the offensive Sea Strike campaign model put together by Admiral Thomas Hayward in his tenures as Seventh Fleet commander from 1975 to 1976 and as CinCPacFlt from 1976 to 1978, and by CinCPac Admiral Robert L. J. Long (1979–83).[17] In the Pacific theater the Navy had a wide range of possible strategies.

There, assuming a general but nonnuclear war, the Navy could get away from what most of its officers thought was a diminishing interventionist mode to which it had been too long confined and free itself from the scenario that possessed the Atlantic strategists, that of a continental war in which the Navy either did nothing or at the utmost engaged in purely supportive convoy and invasion tasks. For the vast Pacific, Hayward created a campaign plan for existing ships of the Seventh Fleet and a major offensive role for Navy forces in the first stage of a war.

Hayward started from the proposition that the Soviet strategy presented an opportunity for attack. The Soviet Union's ships and bases were vulnerable to "prompt offensive action" by the great attack carriers, by attack submarines, by proposed battleship-centered surface-action groups, and by Marine amphibious units. The Soviet force in the Pacific was the most exposed of Soviet fleets. Vladivostok was at the end of a 5,778-mile railroad line that was susceptible to air strikes. The line's final 450 miles ran within 30 miles of the Chinese border. To sail from Leningrad to Vladivostok was a voyage of over 19,000 miles via the Cape of Good Hope and 15,800 by way of the Suez Canal. Those long sea routes could easily be put under surveillance. Supplies to Petropavlovsk-Kamchatski had to be shipped by sea or air. Soviet ships, to get to the ocean from their bases on the Sea of Japan, had to pass through narrow straits, passages controlled by Japan and South Korea. Prompt offensive action by forward-deployed U.S. forces, led by the Seventh Fleet's attack carriers, could devastate forces so constrained.[18]

Hayward, who became CNO in 1978, was blunt about the importance of having the Navy ready for an immediate strike and about the global implications of the Pacific model. There was a direct link, he said, between success in a war in central Europe and control of the foe elsewhere. A Pacific offensive would tie down Soviet forces that might otherwise be used against NATO flanks, used in the Persian Gulf or Asia, or used to cut sea-lanes. An offensive would capitalize on U.S. advantages of force and geography and on the Soviets' strategically weak geographic position. An offensive, led by carrier battle groups, would rob the enemy of the ability to act. It would be a campaign in which "there [would] be no sanctuaries."[19]

A parallel force-planning study at the Naval War College, adopted in 1977 by CNO Holloway and published as *Sea Plan 2000*, reinforced this offensive thinking.[20] *Sea Plan 2000* challenged the Carter administration's focus on Europe. It also challenged the swing strategy, the highly tailored North Atlantic barrier sea-control approach by which submarines patrolled the "gaps" opening from the North Sea to the Atlantic, the relegation of the carriers to occasional peripheral interventions, and the contention that the country needed only a minimal Navy. These ideas, in the eyes of Navy critics, had impoverished the service, doomed the big-fleet, high-value ships to obsolescence, and endangered the country by deliberately reducing its global influence through a decrease in its capacity to respond to the unexpected. Readiness meant the ability to move in any direction immediately and effectively. A force designed to deter a general war also had to be a force that could win one.

Sea Plan 2000 listed the things a large Navy could do and thereby recognized an enlarged range of strategic options. Rejecting the North Atlantic barrier strategy by which NATO naval forces had in effect given up the Norwegian Sea, it argued for a forward, offensive Navy, and for an offensive strategy that would reexpress support for the NATO northern flank. The plan envisioned the expansion of the war to the Pacific. And it said that the United States should use large-carrier battle groups. Holloway and Hayward were major proponents of carrier air. Each believed America's advantage lay with an offensive punch deliverable by the high-value sea force—that is, by carrier battle groups and battleship-led, surface-action groups. *Sea Plan 2000* revived the carrier and the battleship by denying the assumption that they had become vulnerable to Soviet missile attack. In fact, new sensors were giving surface platforms a new lease on life. By the 1980s the carrier would be able to defend itself through a phased-array radar system associated with improvements in antiaircraft and antimissile defense. *Sea Plan 2000*'s first priority was deploying carrier-protecting cruisers equipped with the Aegis Air Defense System.

Sea Plan 2000, then, was a force-planning study that suggested strategic options by stating the operational versatility of ship capabilities. It became "by far the main vehicle in the 1970s for responding to navy critics and advancing navy arguments."[21]

At the end of 1979 and in early 1980, the United States was jolted by a series of crises: the failure of American policy in Iran, reflected in the seizure of the American embassy in Teheran in November 1979 and the humiliation of seeing the embassy staff held hostage; the introduction of Soviet ships and planes to the recently forsaken American naval facilities at Cam Ranh Bay and Da Nang, which lay along Japanese oil routes and were only an hour or so by air from the Navy's base at Subic Bay; the Soviet Union's December 1979 invasion of Afghanistan, a country from which the Soviets could threaten the gulf oil supply as well as exert direct pressure on the Indian subcontinent; the war between Iran and Iraq; and the rediscovery of a Soviet combat brigade in Cuba. Each of these developments was seen as a blow to American foreign policy. Before they occurred, President Carter, following a human-rights policy, had turned away from great-power politics and defined the Soviet menace as more or less isolated to Europe. Now Soviet offensive moves appeared on a global scale, and turbulence in critical regions of the world shocked both the complacent and those who, in the aftermath of Vietnam, wanted to turn away from the costs and responsibilities of intervention. Strategy needs a threat, and these crises confirmed the Navy's contention that the country might face multiple threats simultaneously in different parts of the world and that, both conceptually and materially, the Navy, and the country, were not ready.

After the onset of these crises, however, the Carter administration did not fundamentally change its maritime position. War planning remained centered on Europe. President Carter identified other crisis areas, notably Southwest Asia, but the kind of force that would be used remained in question. He created a crisis intervention command drawn from the services, but this was not a force in place, nor was it yet able to act in several places at once, as Navy leaders thought it should be able to do. In practice, to respond immediately to crises outside Europe, that left whatever assets the Navy and the Marine Corps could deploy beforehand. The Navy beefed up its presence in the South China Sea and the Indian Ocean, and U.S. aircraft carriers and seaborne Marine Corps units became fixtures in waters leading to the Persian Gulf.

President Carter had preferred reducing the number of large attack carriers in favor of the V/STOL alternative, a position resisted by Navy leaders. The Navy leaders' arguments, however, had little effect until 1980. Big-deckers, they said, were safer, faster, and hardier. Such ships were versatile, stayed on station longer, permitted 30 percent more flight operations, and carried more weapons. Above all, they were already afloat. Light carriers, on the other hand, still only conceptual, were expected to be more like fleet escorts than like capital ships that could perform a variety of missions against the worst the enemy could offer. V/STOL aircraft, said big-deck aviators, were too slow, underpowered, and underarmed.[22] But so long as the United States had a naval strategy that declared it was better to react in defense than to destroy by attack, and so long as policy focused on a continental strategy that rejected the use of carriers where they were vulnerable to Soviet air-to-ship missiles, political leaders favored cheaper alternatives that were suitable only for escort duty and low-threat intervention.

That state of mind changed at the turn of the decade, following the crises mentioned above. Big carriers already existed, whereas V/STOL light carriers and Sea Control Ships did not. That was the carriers' first advantage. It was the big ships that the government called upon to deploy immediately to distant regions to handle crises of uncertain magnitude and to stand in high-threat environments for long periods of time. And technology, in the form of the Aegis Air Defense System, had at last given the Navy, or so it said, the means of defending the platform.

Vulnerability to missiles was the carriers' weakness, and it was seen as becoming more acute as Soviet naval air deployed larger planes with longer ranges and better weapons. Defense had to keep attack planes and missiles—and of course submarines, a separate operational problem—far away or destroy them on approach. At the end of the 1970s, the Navy claimed it was on the verge of doing that. Its carriers, covered by their own fighters, would be screened additionally by destroyers and frigates equipped with the Aegis system. Aegis employed a computer capable of tracking hundreds of air targets simultaneously, including sea-skimming cruise missiles, and could shoot anti-air missiles at multiple targets at the same time. If Aegis worked as promised, carrier battle groups could be deployed as a credible power-projection force against the Soviet stand-off air defenses or any missile-bearing enemy.[23]

It was President Carter who began the arms buildup that would last through the administration of his successor, Ronald Reagan.[24] The Navy began to make up for its post-Vietnam lack of maintenance, avoided the replacement gap that had been about to appear with the retirement of many ships, and began to fill empty munitions lockers. The deployment of attack carriers, and an appropriation in 1980 to build another *Nimitz*-class heavy attack carrier—the *Theodore Roosevelt*, at a cost of well over $2 billion—ended the high-low debate of the 1970s.

Regional responsiveness, however, and high-end rearmament, were not combined in a global offensive maritime strategy. For that, there had to be a statement of doctrine that tied together national purpose, naval policy, and force structure. Neither Carter, following a strategy of regional focus, nor the Navy, thinking yet in terms of force planning and campaign operations, had made a full connection.[25]

AN OFFENSIVE FRAMEWORK

The maritime strategy that Navy planners wrote, and publicly argued, in the period from 1978 to 1986 was meant to give coherence to existing intellectual and material positions. Its purpose was to establish an internal consensus on the offensive value of the forward-deployed, big-fleet, triphibious Navy and, with Mahan's admonitions ever present, to engage public as well as professional support. On this maritime strategy, the service defined its missions and based its acquisition program. Hayward, when he became CNO in July 1978, said he wanted to shift congressional debate from dispute over the value of specific budget items to a discussion of the Navy's purpose. For that, he had to show that the Navy had "its act together." The key to success was professional agreement on fundamentals.

Blue-suited commanders were consulted and study groups established at the Naval War College. Drafts circulated among the top officers. War games at Newport tested hypotheses. The Office of the Chief of Naval Operations undertook many reviews. Testimony before Congress sharpened arguments. The process irritated some officers, who thought the result was the lowest common denominator, a committee effort whose polishing glossed over tough realities. That criticism contains some truth. But the goal was consensus on a basic rationale; and simplification, inclusion, and vagueness were better than the division and restriction that had been the Navy's bane in the 1970s. In 1984 the CNO's Strategic Concepts Branch pulled the surviving ideas together in a classified booklet called *The Maritime Strategy*. That booklet was briefed for Congress in 1985, and in 1986 its themes were published under the signature of Hayward's successor as CNO, Admiral James D. Watkins.[26]

The central point of the maritime strategy of the 1980s was that the Navy would begin direct offensive action against the Soviet Union from the first moment of a general war in order to shape that war and to turn it into a protracted, global, nonnuclear conflict that would take advantage of the geographic, political, military, and economic positions of the United States. That view of the war (an alternative to expecting it to be confined to Europe with the use, very probably, of tactical nuclear weapons), and the offensive nature of immediate Navy action, were the plan's strategic innovations.

Offensive action over the beach against the Soviet Union was not a new concept, but that dimension of naval power projection had been dormant since the late 1940s, having been rejected as either unnecessary or infeasible. Protraction of a general war, keeping it nonnuclear, and fighting it globally were sea-power concepts long present in Navy circles. Secretary of Defense James R. Schlesinger in 1975 had suggested that "fast mobilization and deployment scenarios are not the only cases that we should consider." The country, Schlesinger said, should have a "long-war hedge." That certainly fit Navy thinking, which held that the United States would be better off, have more options, and be able to take advantage of its position more fully in a war of attrition and maneuver.[27] The maritime strategy contended that the United States should win, not just contain, a general conflict, and that if the United States was prepared to win, that fact in itself would be the best deterrent.

For those two related (but not identical) missions—victory and deterrence—the Navy designed its force. That force was to be able to do more of everything in the way of power projection and offensive sea control that its most aggressive officers had since 1945 wanted it to be able to do. With maritime superiority, all other missions, on Mahanian principles, would follow as consequences of command of the sea.[28]

The Navy stated its goal of a 600-ship fleet. With the maritime strategy, its composition moved toward a high-value force for offensive missions: 4 combat fleets deploying 15 heavy-carrier battle groups (each composed notionally of 1 carrier, 2 cruisers, 4 guided-missile destroyers, and 4 frigates); 4 battleship surface-action groups, beginning with the recommissioning of the *New Jersey* in 1982 (each consisting notionally of 1 battleship, 1 cruiser, 4 destroyers, and 4 frigates); 100 attack submarines; lift for the assault echelons of a Marine amphibious force and a Marine amphibious brigade; several under-way-replenishment groups; and many support craft. Every existing combat activity in the service would have a fighting mission and each, if Congress went along, would have a full force. Six hundred ships would give the Navy an increase of 120 active combatants above the force level of 1980 and 60 above the level of 1985. Beyond that total, the Navy proposed to control 25 maritime prepositioning ships, vessels with troops and supplies positioned in waters near areas of possible action, and 116 Ready Reserve ships.[29]

Neither Hayward nor Watkins nor Navy Secretary John Lehman would accept the point escort and gunboat diplomacy of Zumwalt, Nixon, and Carter, or a doctrine based on an unbuilt ship. Local sea control and Third World intervention had their place, but they were not central to prevailing in the main bout, in which the country must gain immediate control of the nature of the war. The maritime strategy returned offensive carrier air, attack submarines, and assault marines to the center of Navy planning. As for V/STOL carriers and diesel-electric submarines and minesweepers, NATO partners had them. The United States had, and must stay with, the high-performance, big-ticket platforms. Those were present assets, and they alone could execute an immediate offensive.

The attack carriers existed in the 1980s in spite of strategic downgrading. The decade saw the Navy deploying fourteen carriers, to provide global coverage as part of the containment called for by NSC-68 of 1950.[30] The proposed 600-ship Navy was to have fifteen carriers, each at the center of a battle group.

Force levels of attack submarines also had remained high, and stable, in the decades since the 1950s. During those decades, the submarine force had averaged 92 boats. Ninety-five were deployed in 1985. The importance of U.S. submarines in surveillance and intelligence gathering, and of their silent service during the Cold War, remains an untold story. Astonishing advances in marine technology were applied to submarines. The nuclear boats, though expensive, had great capability, as did new diesel-electric submarines. A program of building and upgrading the nuclear, attack *Los Angeles* class gave the United States a one-on-one advantage over Soviet submarines.

That edge was blunted by the mysteriously improved stealth and competence of the latest classes of Soviet submarines, whose technology leapfrogged to meet American advances. Not until the mid-1980s was it learned that the Soviets had been drawing for eighteen years on secrets of immeasurable importance passed to them by a spy ring operating within the U.S. Navy. This ring detailed capabilities and weapons systems and gave the Soviets access to years of American naval communications.

The Marines' amphibious-assault troops stood at around 48,000 men in the 1980s, part of a proven, balanced maritime force. The Navy's amphibious warships provided transport for those marines, their equipment, and their command. The Navy could carry one and one-third divisions in enough assault ships to keep task-directed Marine Expeditionary Brigades at sea for long periods, ready for intervention, close to (but not upon) a foreign territory. For offensive action by 50,000 marines under the maritime strategy, somewhat greater transport capacity was needed, as were adequate assault ships and craft, including more than one of the multipurpose helicopter / dock landing amphibious assault ships with V / STOL carrier capability. Construction of the first of these, the *Wasp*, began in 1985.

In the integrative maritime strategy Navy and Marine Corps missions were connected, not considered discretely as sea control, say, or intervention. Instead they were placed under the broad, synthetic categories of peaceful presence, crisis response, and global conventional war. The American maritime force would act in any of its modes in any part of the world according to the requirements of loosely defined phases of combat, which were tagged as deterrence, transition to war, seizing the initiative, carrying the fight to the enemy, or ending a war on favorable terms. At any time, in any circumstance, the Navy was to be prepared to act more or less at any point along a continuum of violence whose levels ranged from display to Armageddon. There was no timetable, no distinct division between levels of force. This was a resounding reassertion of the flexibility and versatility of the fleet, with offensive combat returned front-and-center—a strong restatement of the complex, unpredictable, and overlapping ways in which wars have always been fought.

Irritating as this inclusiveness was to critics who saw it as a catch-all net thrown to conceal an attempt to justify the acquisition of expensive carriers and submarines, Navy planners were in truth trying at least as much to broaden national strategic planning. Inclusiveness, untimetabled phased-war thinking, diversification of force, a broad description of maritime purpose: all these were elements of doctrinal strength. More than any other service, and to the envy and exasperation of the others, the capaciousness of naval warfare enabled the Navy to sustain in the 1980s a concept of war that gave it internal cohesion, public position, and initiative in U.S. strategic thinking.[31]

Not since Mahan had the Navy presented in peacetime such a comprehensive doctrine. The maritime strategy developed under the steady evolutionary guidance of CNOs Hayward and Watkins and was energetically espoused by Navy Secretary Lehman. Meanwhile, President Reagan and Defense Secretary Caspar Weinberger (January 1981 to November 1987) let the Navy promulgate the strategy and thus revive the relevance of sea power for the last, reheated decade of the Cold War.

The Navy's leaders had learned that in moments of institutional uncertainty, an effort to define a doctrine was the first measure of self-support. The maritime strategy imparted coherence and a sense of purposeful leadership. It thus improved professional morale and provided guidance in program planning. As Admiral Watkins said, the Navy was seen "singing from the same sheet of music."

EVALUATING THE MARITIME STRATEGY

What the strategy's employment potential was, we will never know. Its sponsors never tired of pointing out that it was not a war plan; yet if it was anything, it was a war-fighting strategy. The maritime strategy remained a largely Navy plan that never received a final political imprimatur. By the end of the decade some of its features had been merged into U.S. defense planning. But the Reagan administration never reformulated national policy and strategy to match the maritime strategy's innovations. Such an embodiment in national policy was what the maritime strategy's proponents had hoped for and what Mahan had taught was necessary in order for a national doctrine of sea power to be fully successful.

Still, the Navy could draw campaign scenarios from the maritime strategy. One was for a direct naval impact on the flanks of a Soviet offensive in Europe. This naval campaign would include U.S. Marine amphibious landings, and the employment of Tomahawk cruise missiles and carrier air, to protect and reassure maritime allies in the North Sea and Mediterranean regions and in the Far East. It would also include diversionary actions in support of U.S. and allied forces fighting on the European central front.[32] Related to that campaign was the concept of horizontal escalation, by which the Navy would open new fronts, notably in the Pacific, to split the enemy's forces.[33] The idea of asymmetrical response, of widening the war geographically and temporally, had long been present in the Navy's global thinking. All maritime strategies stress the utility of peripheral or "indirect" approaches, actions particularly fitting to naval powers able to move freely about the seas, hitting a foe in unexpected places to divert the enemy's attention away from his central theater of operation. During the Carter years, *Sea Plan 2000* posited opening a second front. In the 1980s amphibious exercises were conducted in Norway to draw Soviet attention away from Germany. Although the Reagan administration never accepted a bluntly declared policy of horizontal escalation, and war games in Newport called such escalation into question, the ability to strike at the land from an unexpected and advantageous direction was central to the Navy's power-projection capability, giving it the flexibility that Basil Liddell Hart called the greatest strategic asset a maritime nation can possess.[34]

Offensive sea control also included attacks at the source to keep submarines from penetrating the Atlantic and Pacific. This was a rejection of the reactive barrier strategy, which left a NATO ally, Norway, on the wrong side of the barrier, and which limited maritime operations against Europe's northern flank. Offensive sea control meant not only closing the portals of access to the oceans, but also challenging the Soviet fleet and Soviet naval air in the high-risk areas of the Barents Sea and Soviet defense zones in Asia. It meant hitting the enemy ships at home and thus opening up the sea for the final and most dramatic and controversial of the maritime strategy's offensives: an attack on the

Soviet strategic reserve, the country's missile submarines in their bastions. As Admiral Watkins liked to put it, the Navy had to hit the archer before he shot the arrow.[35]

No one disagreed about the Navy's role in crisis intervention in non-Soviet areas, or about its sea-control mission, although whether the latter should be offensive or defensive, attack at the source or point defense, remained in dispute.[36] Wise people saw the value of having a strategy that was phased to prevent or to slow escalation, and of not relying on the virtually automatic, massive second-strike nuclear response that was the staple of the SIOP. There was no dispute that the Navy's ballistic-missile submarines were key to the U.S. policy of nuclear deterrence, which rested more and more on the security and accuracy of the wet leg of the deterrent triad.

Underwater-launched ballistic missiles had improved steadily. One such missile, Poseidon, carrying usually ten warheads, had a range of roughly 3,000 miles. Another, a type called Trident I (C-4), carried eight Mark 4 warheads about 5,000 miles. With these missiles the United States could be confident of its threat of assured destruction. Each missile was housed in a submarine that carried either 16 or 24 missiles of the same type. In the mid-1980s, the U.S. deployed 36 SSBNs, which were loaded with a total of 640 Poseidons and Tridents. Altogether, these missiles held over 5,000 warheads. The SSBNs were the core of the U.S. strategic forces, and they were as safe from Soviet attack as the Navy could make them.[37]

Critics attacked four main features of the maritime strategy: its assumption about the nature of a general war, its assessment of the likely Soviet actions in such a war, its lack of connection to national political objectives, and its proposed offensive operations. One cannot yet answer whether the Navy was wise to assume that the Soviets would refrain from using nuclear weapons against the United States in the opening, European phase of the war. The Navy's argument was that the Soviets thought they did not need to. They could prevent an American nuclear response to an invasion in Europe (a response on which the protection of NATO allies was based and which lay at the center of NATO deterrence policy) by holding America hostage to the counterthreat of the Soviet submarine-launched ballistic missiles that lay secure in their heavily defended bastions. In a still nonnuclear war, the United States might then regroup around what was left of its maritime alliance, and the alliance might attempt to regain a hold on northwestern Eurasia. But because an American response could not be nuclear against the Soviet Union for fear of retaliation, the Soviets would win the endgame—without, that is, U.S. reliance on the Navy's maritime strategy.

According to the maritime strategy, the United States did not need to accept the single-theater war the Soviets wanted, the nuclear war the Air Force wanted, a short war, a reactive war, or a war of sequential operations. Although the United States might at first give up Europe and might refrain from launching a nuclear counterattack, it would not give up the war. On the contrary, with control of the oceans it could determine when the war was over because it would turn the Soviet blitzkrieg into a global war of attrition. The Navy, the other U.S. services, and the nation's maritime allies would continue the war from the sea. The United States would control the outcome if it could destroy the Soviet hole cards themselves, the submarines in their bastions. That, hopefully in simultaneous conjunction with Air Force strikes against land-based missiles, would change the nuclear balance and open the Soviet Union again to the leverage of a nuclear threat from the West.

The Navy was reasonably confident that it could conduct such close, forward operations, thanks to the superiority of its submarines and the ability of its missiles and carriers to penetrate Soviet defense zones.

The creators of the Aegis Air Defense System hoped it would bring about an operational revolution. Aegis was developed under the leadership of Rear Admiral Wayne E. Meyer, who envisioned it as an impenetrable screen of radar and weapons fire that would govern a high-tech concept of surface warfare called Battle Group System Engineering. This never came to pass. Aegis was very expensive. Its effectiveness was called into question in Congress after initial test failures. The Navy almost lost the system's funding, as well as that of the new *Ticonderoga* class of cruisers, which were meant to be the Navy's main Aegis platform. Meyer ran afoul of Secretary Lehman's traditionalism with regard to the operation of carrier battle groups and battleship-centered surface-action groups. Still, Aegis worked well enough to give confidence to advancing carriers and battleships that planned to move against stand-off Soviet naval air defenses in such critical areas as the Norwegian Sea and around the North Cape.[38] At the end of the decade, with the 27th and final cruiser of the Aegis-equipped *Ticonderoga* class to be delivered in 1994, the missile-bearing *Arleigh Burke* destroyer, also Aegis directed, was the only other remaining main surface combatant class under construction in the U.S. Navy.[39]

The Tomahawk cruise missile came in two versions—antiship and land-attack, the latter having the longer range. The Tomahawk could carry conventional or nuclear warheads. It hugged the surface, evading radar, and was able to penetrate beyond the range of the Navy's manned aircraft, without risking American lives. It could be launched by any platform and was distributed throughout the fleet to submarines and to more than a hundred surface ships. Here was strength for hammering the Soviets on land and at sea. The Tomahawk's partner, the antiship missile Harpoon, was placed aboard 300 U.S. ships. The introduction of these two sea missiles consolidated a new era of sea control and power projection.[40]

Vice Admiral Henry Mustin, deputy CNO for plans, policy, and operations, said in 1988:

> Long-range, highly accurate cruise missiles launched from mobile, survivable naval platforms represent a fundamental change in the nature of naval matters on the order of the advance from sail to steam. . . . The power projection capability represented by U.S. SLCMs [sea-launched cruise missiles] is as important to our naval strength as were earlier developments of the aircraft carrier and nuclear submarines. . . . The synergistic effect of combining carrier or land based air with cruise missiles has . . . revolutionized the very nature of naval war.[41]

Mustin was referring to a concept called the *distributive offensive*, in which carriers exchanged over-the-shore assault duty for that of providing a defensive umbrella for Tomahawk shooters, the latter ranging in size from battleships to frigates. The shooting fleet would no longer concentrate but scatter, to avoid presenting an easy target to the enemy. Units then would fire at the Soviets' air-defense system, destroy the bomber force of land-based, stand-off Soviet naval air, wear down Soviet defensive networks on shore and inland, and take out missile sites, preparing the way for landings, assault on Soviet nuclear forces, and victory. Here was the culmination of the Navy's concept of employing surface and airborne offensive power in the 1980s.[42]

All this thinking followed from the premise that in the 1980s the Soviets had raised their nuclear threshold, that they would withhold their long-range nuclear reserve, accept a general conventional war or, at worst, limit nuclear exchanges to theater and short-range ones in Europe. That would give the United States a maritime opportunity to launch peripheral campaigns, work at alliance development, and reap the benefits of time.[43]

What worried critics most was that the assumption of Soviet restraint might be wrong, above all that an attack on their submarine missile reserve might cause the very vertical escalation the Navy thought it could avoid. The same criticism held for horizontal escalation—who could tell if an elegant concept of peripheral influence might not get out of hand? Soviet military doctrine had a high nuclear threshold at the moment, but it might drop immediately when faced with attack in the home regions. If the Soviets were faced with a use-or-lose alternative regarding their missile reserve, might they not launch against the United States to draw the attackers off or to destroy the enemy's homeland? Was this a risk American political authorities were willing to take? The Navy never convinced them that there was a strategic advantage in attacking the Soviet SSBN's that was worth the risk of escalation.[44]

Further, what if the assumption of Soviet naval defensiveness was inaccurate? If that were so, the Soviet navy might surge attack submarines against American forces, installations, and Atlantic sea routes, willing to reduce its bastion defenses for a measure of sea control, to blunt a U.S. attack.[45] That possibility bothered many U.S. and allied officers, especially when they faced the improved Soviet submarines of the late 1970s and early 1980s. Their concern led, as the decade progressed and the danger of war in Europe receded, to a renewed emphasis on sea control.

Because the presumptive maritime strategy did not answer political questions, and because its volatile offensive scenarios had so many sides, the fear remained that it could jeopardize the high-stakes national policy of deterrence that, for all the mania of the arms race, had apparently kept a stable framework for rational judgment on both sides. The Navy's attention to war fighting appeared out of step with the strategy of caution and deterrence.

The Navy responded to this fear by arguing that evidence supported its assessment that Soviet doctrine was defensive, just as it supported the Navy's confidence in U.S. antisubmarine technology and in its own ability to conduct a well-orchestrated antisubmarine program. Attrition at sea, the argument went, would not invalidate rational deterrence judgments by the Soviet government. Soviet doctrine led the U.S. Navy to the conclusion that the Soviet government would keep its submarine reserve intact as long as possible. That is why the Soviets had withdrawn the SSBNs to bastions in the first place and surrounded them with the attack submarines. Destruction of that strategic reserve would give the United States its leverage for demanding an end to the war.[46]

This position, as we saw, contained an element of contradiction, one which the Navy never removed and which became a central part of the public debate. It was hard to maintain both that the Soviets were likely to forgo nuclear war while U.S. submarines destroyed much of their strategic reserve, and at the same time maintain that those Soviet SSBNs hidden in the bastions were of such value—precisely for the retaliatory value of their nuclear missiles—that their loss would give the strategic advantage to the United States. If the Soviets thought they had nothing to gain by shooting their missiles, would they also be likely to decide that they had nothing to gain by making peace despite losing them? It so, the claim that the United States would gain strategic advantage by destroying them would be much diminished.[47] Planning on information that remains classified and, ultimately, on assumptions that could never be tested short of war, the Navy could never overcome public doubt about the main premise of its offensive strategy against the Soviet SSBN fleet, namely, that its strategy had at least the possibility of keeping the war conventional.

When all was said and done, the Navy failed to achieve national standing for its maritime strategy, failed to make it a central part of a new national strategy. What to the Navy seemed a virtue and the best way to fight a war seemed to political authorities, and to the other services, unnecessary and dangerous in the nuclear age. Few were willing to forsake the grotesque stability of deterrence to approve the Navy's offensive strategy, or to value an actual war with the Soviet Union as an instrument of policy. The social cost of a prolonged, global conflict involving such elements as blockade and escalation was too much to bear, as opposed to reliance on the socially marginal but familiar and ostensibly quick and decisive nuclear weapons of air and space. Those weapons for 40 years, it seemed, had prevented war and protected the West. Why disturb a stalemate? Why risk movement at all? Air Force and Army planning for an offensive air-land battle in Europe received similar criticism during this decade. But the Army and Air Force, with their own main interests still essentially served by the reigning tradition of deterrence and containment, saw no reason to associate themselves with the Navy's offensive sea-power demarche.

The Navy's presumption thus took it only so far: the Navy kept its force, but national strategy was not changed. Aaron Friedberg has written of the "interior dimension" of American strategy in the Cold War, of how the policies of deterrence and containment were shaped and bolstered by the American people's preference for capital-intensive rather than labor-intensive solutions, by their wish for the minimum of state intrusion into their lives.[48] Deterrence of nuclear war and defensive political containment remained the essential American positions. The maritime strategy stayed exclusively a Navy and Marine Corps concept.

So the maritime strategy was not put in the service of specified political goals. It did not relate naval fighting to national war aims. Nor could it, for the country had none. The Navy had to evade discussion of war aims by using the vague phrase "war termination on favorable terms." This was a serious practical and conceptual drawback. The Navy, like the Air Force with its air-power doctrine two decades earlier, in the absence of political guidance had deduced its role in order to plan its force, hoping that national strategy would catch up. To this risky extension of doctrine beyond its base, the political authorities in the Reagan administration turned an only half-opened eye.

The Navy, therefore, for want of anything more favorable, argued that the maritime strategy was useful as an instrument of deterrence. The deterrence policy was meant to create doubt in the Soviet mind. There is an element of deception in all war, but never more than in deterrence planning.[49] Deterrence did not aim at fighting a war, but at preventing one. As such, it was not an employment strategy, in which fighting is for a political goal. On the other hand, its credibility lay in its capacity to do harm. Nuclear deterrence assumed mutual assured destruction. Nuclear use assumed escalation. The maritime strategy proposed conventional deterrence and assumed that the war would be one the Soviet Union, unwilling to use nuclear weapons, did not have the staying power to win. This doctrine of conventional deterrence was weakened because the Navy could not announce its plans for combat operations or reveal the technological and intelligence foundations of the proposed operations. The fact that the maritime strategy was not embraced as national strategy appears to explain why the Soviet response to it was remarkably tepid. So perhaps it was not a strong deterrent after all. While the Soviets certainly took the quality and possible actions of the U.S. Navy seriously, the Soviet leaders do not appear to have paid much attention to the maritime strategy as a naval doctrine.[50]

Allies were also concerned by the Navy's reassertion that the United States was a Pacific as well as an Atlantic power, that it had important political and military interests beyond NATO, that "the European campaign [was] not the same as the war," and that multiple simultaneous crises would disprove the Europeanists' idea that the West must rely on sequential operations.[51] On this reasoning, a Soviet victory in Europe, a throwback of NATO forces to the English Channel, need not be the end of the war. Even if Europe were conquered, even if the Soviets sat on the Bay of Biscay, the war would continue. Did such a unilateralist position imply a desertion of America's main allies?

Continentalist opponents, which included much Army opinion, claimed it did so, or that it would be so perceived. It was, they said, a form of neo-isolationism likely to devastate the postwar coalition, which was based on the idea of protecting NATO's central front.[52] That criticism was not just. Exactly the opposite position can be taken, that a maritime strategy was meant to uphold, in the worst case, America's global strength. And it served the interests of America's allies to plan to defeat the Soviets by using the most important geopolitical advantage of the strongest power in the maritime alliance, thereby keeping the war alive to show that the Soviets could not win, and ultimately bringing the immense industrial strength of the alliance to bear on the foe. For what was the alternative if the Soviets breached the defense line in Europe, and NATO was unwilling to resort to nuclear war? And what more, despite all the carping, could any planner ask of the Navy? The Navy's most vociferous opponents, and the maritime strategy itself, conceded that the Navy's combat role in a great central European war would be at best supplemental.

Navy officials emphatically denied the charge of desertion and of an anti-European, pro-Pacific bias, and most allies, while anxious about any sign of weakened American resolve, accepted the Navy's, and the government's, assurances that coalitions were central to American policy and to the maritime strategy. Those with memories noted that the maritime strategy, full of classical resonance, was also very similar to the cooperative coalition strategy developed in Europe in the late 1940s and early 1950s by officers such as then Vice Admiral Forrest Sherman and then Commander Richard G. Colbert.[53] Cooperation had a force-planning value. NATO assigned antisubmarine and mining roles to the United States's NATO allies, enabling the offense-oriented leaders of the U.S. Navy to answer in the negative the question of whether it should pay much more attention to low-value warships and defensive sea control.

Anyway, Navy officers noted, the real problem of NATO was not the alliance's maritime posture, but the fact that the Soviets might prove superior after a Soviet land-and-air attack in an area where NATO forces had little room to maneuver and little time for resupply.[54] The Navy asserted that its global reach deterred such a war by forcing the Soviets to consider more than one theater. It said that its peripheral strategy supported the allies on the lightly defended perimeter of Europe, an area that included Norway, Iceland, Denmark, Italy, Greece, and Turkey. Secretary Lehman put his finger on a key point of the maritime strategy when he called it "a NATO strategy that was never taken seriously, a formula for holding Norway and the Eastern Mediterranean, two high-threat areas."[55]

For America's allies and its other associates worldwide, the problem was that the political implications of almost every part of the maritime strategy were never spelled out by the United States's national leadership. The strategy certainly sounded as if it could lead to unilateral U.S. action that might draw the country's allies into a broad conflict, or as if the United States, lacking sufficient force to cover all regions, might reposition its naval force in such a way as to leave some allies to fend for themselves. Norway had only a vague promise that U.S. forces would arrive in time. In Japan, there were unresolved concerns over the use of Japanese territory. There was also no agreement among U.S. allies and associates on the validity of the American estimate of Soviet strategy. For most of the decade foreign governments and military leaders avoided the issue by declaring that the maritime strategy was a domestic doctrine directed at the budget and at the Navy's standing within the Reagan administration and that it was not part of a genuine national strategy at all.[56]

Here we return to a final evaluation of Navy planning in the 1980s. Its central failure lay in the fact that the maritime strategy was not fully accepted as the basis for a national policy of sea power. This did not mean that all was lost. The Navy had hoped it could justify major acquisitions for an offensive carrier-and-submarine fleet, and that it did. It had also hoped that, after debate, a new national strategy for a global maritime war would emerge, a strategy in which this offensive force would be the main naval component. That did not happen.

To make its point the Navy undertook an intense public relations campaign. Its entry into popular and scholarly debate, and its reemphasis on sea power and traditional Navy functions, were each meant to establish the wisdom and the good faith of its proposal. This campaign enabled the Navy to take advantage of the arms buildup. The campaign was easily associated with, and indeed part of, the shift in national policy back toward putting pressure on the Soviet Union. In this shift President Reagan broke from the self-imposed limits of the Carter administration and returned to a policy of global military preparedness. Part of the renewed containment policy was to meet and prevail over the Soviets at sea, although choosing the mode was left more to operations than to maritime strategy.[57] A high degree of offensive sea-control readiness was nonetheless required, and obtained.

The declarative dimension of the maritime strategy reflected the urgency and confidence that characterized President Reagan's administration. Congress or the president did not have to formally approve, or disapprove, the Navy's independently created doctrine. The political authorities found that they did not have to declare an opinion on the likelihood or feasibility of a conventional, protracted general war, or bring such a war into national strategy, for the maritime strategy to be seen, and used, as part of a concentrated effort to build up the military, or for the Navy to recover its self-confidence. So they let the Navy alone.

For an administration that sought to open every military option, for a JCS that permitted each service to take its own guidance, for officials looking for an alternative to an inadequate nuclear strategy, the diversity and amplitude of the Navy's position were compelling and comforting. The Navy's confident scenario considered all uses of maritime force and expressed arguments for versatility in traditional maritime themes. The deliberate vagueness of the nation's military planning helped the Navy make its case. That did not mean, however, in an operationally pluralistic administration, that the maritime strategy need be adopted. It was left to coexist with the war plan of the Strategic Air Command, a plan that envisioned a different kind of war. The JCS kept open a choice between the plan for the early use of nuclear weapons, in which case much of the maritime strategy would be irrelevant, and that for a protracted conventional war, in which case the Navy doctrine would centrally contribute to an integrated national strategy. A thousand opportunities bloomed in the military of the 1980s.[58] But the failure to impose integration from the top made any particular presentation appear self-serving and fed fiery debate.

Although Congress did not fund the 600-ship Navy, the service had no reason for complaint about its force. The Navy in 1990 had around 574 ships, including 15 attack carriers. It had reached its goal of 100 attack submarines, an increase of 20 since 1980. The old dispute over small-deck versus large-deck carriers, and over smaller versus larger submarines, was settled for the moment in favor of the larger in both cases. Four recommissioned battleships were added to the blue-water capital fleet to cushion the demands that were stretching the deployed carrier force. Amphibious-assault capability stayed steady. Ship modernization took place at all levels, ammunition lockers were filled, and pay and morale improved in all grades. The 1980s were a period of Navy readiness, although to critics in and outside the service, the emphasis on the anti-Soviet offensive had moved the Navy too far from the limited sea control and interventionist duties it was still called upon to perform.

The Navy had waxed. And remarkably, it had not done so at the expense of the other services. The maritime strategy naturally drew the skepticism of the Army and the Air Force, which, with their own visions of the war to come, dismissed it as a set of dangerous axioms meant to satisfy the nervous carrier warriors represented by Secretary Lehman and the submariners represented by Admiral Watkins. The other services predicted the artful creation would not outlast its sponsors' tenure. Substantive disagreement arose among the services over the relevance of the maritime strategy's assumptions and over the issues of short versus long wars, maritime versus continental emphasis, and global versus theater strategies. But because battles over budget were muted during these well-funded years, the arguments lacked the bitter, panicky edge of previous interservice rivalries.

The Army and the Air Force did envy the way the Navy used its vaunted flexibility to present a contemporary case that left the other services looking parochial, outmoded, or tongue-tied. Whether the Navy was right or wrong, it seemed to be looking ahead, in a broadly adaptable way, and stealing the thunder, if not the budgets, of the other services. The value of the Air Force's air-power doctrine was increasingly called into question by big-power stability and the horrendous nature of a general nuclear war. The Army asked analyst Carl Builder: "Why don't you find out why the Army does so poorly in strategic planning? We do a terrible job as compared to the Navy or Air Force." Builder compared the Navy's confident position, which he dismissed as solipsistic, to the Army's identity crisis, which he asserted was unnecessary inasmuch as there was a clear land strategy waiting to be expressed.[59] The joint Army–Air Force AirLand Battle doctrine was a step forward, a plan for an immediate Army offensive with deep air penetration against second-echelon Soviet troops, but it was a European battle plan, wise and useful but without broad public expression or resonance. The Navy's maritime strategy was far more general and problematic, but it presented war-fighting situations in overlapping substrategic categories that suggested familiar naval traditions suitably adapted to contemporary needs.

Administratively during the 1980s the Navy lost a battle against greater Defense Department centralization. The Goldwater-Nichols Department of Defense Reorganization Act of 1986 marked the triumph of vertical reorganization. It gave the chairman of the Joint Chiefs power to communicate his own opinion to the president via the secretary of defense. Previously, the chairman had to report differing views held by the service chiefs. Now, he could cut out dissent. At the same time, the new law increased the authority for joint operations over the various CinCs, the military heads of the unified and specified commands around the world. Formerly, and more appropriately to Navy thinking, joint operations were the result of a compromise between the services, each cooperating according to its particular practices and service requirements. Now, in a reaffirmation of the long trend toward centralization, the authority to conduct naval operations such as reconnaissance and antisubmarine warfare and to protect shipping was specifically taken from the Navy and put under whomever might be the appropriate commander in chief. From the Navy perspective, that was a victory for the rigid organization desired by the Army and Air Force for a war on the central front, and a defeat for the mobile, opportunistic use of naval force as expressed in the maritime strategy. Few Navy officers thought that an Air Force or Army general would use naval assets or strategy to best advantage. How much of that view would prove false would depend on the expertise and wisdom of the CinC. At the least, separating naval operations according to needs of various CinCs could discourage the lateral, global flexibility coordinated by the vision of a clearly naval command on which a protracted, global, maritime war was to be based.[60]

We can say in conclusion that articulation of the maritime strategy served a peacetime Navy well in the favorable winds of the decade. It helped reopen a moribund debate about national strategy, although it did not carry its influence as far as its authors had hoped. It gave the service a sea-power doctrine to which most of the Navy rallied. But as with Mahan's concentrated and offensive force, its insistence on a large fleet required a proportionally large threat—or opportunity—to sustain it. How great the threat or opportunity was during the high years of the maritime strategy is open to dispute, but declaring it, believing it existed, and declaring a maritime strategy to deal with it gave Navy planning and Navy cohesion a powerful boost.

The threat disappeared in the last years of the decade, and with it the need for the global, Soviet-oriented maritime strategy. Economically weakened, the Soviet government under Mikhail Gorbachev called for peaceful coexistence. To the astonishment of all, between 1989 and 1991 the states of central Europe made themselves independent, and the Soviet Union itself dissolved. Those political changes ended the danger that a general war would begin in Europe. They also ended what was left of Admiral Gorshkov's blue-water doctrine for a global Soviet maritime strategy. The Soviet navy began to scrap many of its ships, declined in readiness, and stayed close to home in an indisputably defensive posture.[61] With the disappearing danger of general war, the value of a massive U.S. offensive naval response disappeared also. In 1989 the U.S. Navy put its ambitious testament to sea power "on the shelf."[62]

Conclusion

WHAT was left was a certainty that the Navy would be reduced in force and that there would be a return to the old question, What do we need a Navy for?

Navy leaders in 1990 knew they would have to restate the value of the service. Their first call was for slow change. Opposition to Western interests could reemerge in, for instance, Russian nationalism. The Soviet submarine force still existed. Third World states operated many attack submarines. The Navy's preference was to keep all sea-power options open. Flexibility had served it well, and flexibility was what American policy called for at the beginning of the 1990s.

Navy leaders in 1990 hoped at best to hold on to 451 ships until 1995, a decrease of almost 100 from the 1990 level. The decrease would take place as retirements outpaced replacements. Requirements drive force levels, and the country's uncertain access to overseas bases, the proliferation of high-technology weapons, and uncertain political events affecting U.S. interests worldwide demanded at least that size. Below that number, said Navy leaders, they could not assure maritime superiority.[1]

Critics of perpetuating a capital-ship fleet argued that the decade-long emphasis of the 1980s on a high-end offensive combat force and the costly forward deployment of carrier battle groups and attack submarines had led the Navy to neglect "traditional, real-world, everyday maritime missions." With the specter of general war removed, without a major sea-control challenge, the responsibilities that the service would most likely be charged with—participation in coalition naval diplomacy, point protection of U.S. ships, support of forces ashore, and sea-control measures such as minesweeping—were particular missions that could be executed by smaller warships and a smaller Navy.[2]

The argument that crisis response was best handled by the low end of the force structure was not prima facie conclusive. Carriers had been used in 140 (68 percent) of the 207 documented cases of U.S. naval-force response actions since World War II.[3]

The Navy's general-purpose force had enjoyed some highly visible successes during the decade of the 1980s, both within and beyond the Cold War context. There was a counterterrorist air strike on Libya, an amphibious invasion of Grenada, and support for the invasion of Panama, each executed in conjunction with other services and each an example of a swift, limited use of force unconnected to the main thrust of the maritime strategy. There were valuable missions about which little was said, such as surveillance in many coastal waters and the diplomatically influential preparation to interdict embargoed shipping bound for Nicaragua from Cuba. The Navy executed a politically awkward and potentially dangerous escort of reflagged oil tankers in the Persian Gulf in the face of possible Iranian interference. All in all, the Navy and Marine Corps responded to 47 crises during the 1980s, a level of involvement far higher than that of the other two services.[4]

The Marine Corps also suffered a highly visible disaster in Lebanon. In 1982 marines were sent ashore when the expected Army deployment was too slow. This was an uncertain mission that was compromised by command confusion. Faulty security permitted the terror bombing of a Marine barracks there in 1983, causing the death of 241 servicemen, a national tragedy. President Reagan then ordered the Navy to evacuate the remaining force from Lebanon and withdraw, which it immediately did.

Win or lose, these were all in line with traditional Navy and Marine Corps missions, and it was through its capabilities in crisis response that the Navy reasserted its utility as American policy moved beyond the Cold War. President George Bush, in a speech delivered at Aspen, Colorado, on August 2, 1990, spoke of localized action in "a world less driven by the immediate threat to Europe and the danger of global war . . . a world where the size of our forces will increasingly be shaped by the need of regional contingencies and peacetime presence." The secretary of the Navy, H. Lawrence Garrett III (May 1989 to June 1992), said that meant formulating a "new naval policy," that the "new strategy should be one of stability, focussing on peacetime presence and regional conflict."[5] While the strategic SSBNs remained at their Cold War stations, the general-purpose Navy turned to meet the demands of the inherent variability of an interventionist maritime strategy.[6]

The Gulf War against Iraq in 1991 was a transitional conflict in this respect. It was confined to a limited theater of operations while making use of the full range of existing Cold War weapons and allies. Every conventional weapon in the American arsenal was available to ensure a quick victory. There was no need to withhold force for another major action or to extend the conflict. The Gulf War took place because the United States could readily bring overwhelming force to bear without political distraction. The Soviet Union was a tacit American ally. The United States could fight the Gulf War because the Cold War was over.

With that freedom of action, the country pulled out all stops. The war was "the most complex, fast-moving, successful, major joint power projection operation in history," at one time employing over half a million U.S. military personnel in-theater.[7] In an essentially air-and-land war, the Navy played a supporting role. The Gulf War was fitted to the scenarios the Air Force and Army had drawn up for the European central front, a war short and limited, not a protracted maritime campaign.

On the other hand, maritime superiority was an essential element of the international coalition. The United Nations established a naval blockade, a tangible manifestation of coalition resolve during the period of military buildup. Naval interdiction by ships and airplanes from fourteen allied states intercepted and challenged more than 7,500 merchant ships, and sailors boarded 1,200 of them for inspection. This blockade closed down Iraq's oil exports, reduced the country's gross national product by 50 percent, and cut off supplies. It thus reduced the fighting effectiveness of Iraqi soldiers and forced Saddam Hussein to limit the movements of his armed forces to prevent deterioration of their equipment.[8] U.S. Navy and Coast Guard teams conducted 582 of the boardings and took part with coalition partners in another 25.

The United States had two war aims: the destruction of Iraq's offensive capability and the expulsion of the Iraqi army from Kuwait. Officials decided early that these goals could not be achieved by blockade alone, by air strikes from carriers or distant bases, or by aid to adjacent Saudi Arabia. Direct military action on the ground was required. That meant forces had to be based in neighboring countries. Saudi participation was a requirement of U.S. strategy. The Navy's stand-off mobile forces were used for particular purposes, but offshore platforms and amphibious operations were not enough to cripple a land-based force the size of Iraq's—or the size of the Soviet Union's, as the maritime strategy had recognized. Saudi Arabia had to be brought in as the base for air and land operations and, for political reasons, as an Arab state committed to an anti-Iraq coalition.

So first Saudi Arabia had to be defended. The initial American forces in the region were Navy and Marine. Five days after August 2, 1990, the day on which Iraq invaded Kuwait for oil, sea access, and prestige, a U.S. carrier battle group was in the Gulf of Oman ready to launch long-range strikes. On August 7, 1990, when President Bush committed the United States to the protection of Saudi Arabia, there were in or about to arrive in the Persian Gulf two carrier battle groups, a surface-action group with a powerfully armed, missile-carrying battleship, and a command ship. The ships were joined in the gulf one week later by the first of the marines who had been at a prepositioning station in the Indian Ocean, ready to support the airlifted advance elements of the Marine expeditionary force. That force, arriving in Saudi Arabia first by air and then by sea, came to constitute, with 92,900 officers and men, the largest Marine Corps operation in history.[9] The mission of the carriers and fast-reaction marines was to draw the line against any further advance by the Iraqi army. This impressive display of readiness was made possible by the forward deployment of Navy and Marine Corps units.

For the United States, combat operations known as Desert Storm began, as had World War I and World War II, with a naval action, in this case the shooting of a Tomahawk cruise missile on January 17, 1991, from a Navy ship in the Red Sea, followed on that day by the firing of over 116 Tomahawks by nine Navy ships in the Persian Gulf and the Red Sea. So dense was the damage from overall air bombardment, as manned aircraft followed the Tomahawks in, and another 172 Tomahawks subsequently were shot, that the Pentagon study of the war was unable to determine precisely how well the Navy's land-attack missiles performed. The evidence indicated at least "moderate" success.[10] The initial goal of the United States was to control the air and destroy command sites. Over 1,000 combat sorties were flown on the first day of combat, the Navy launching 228 of them from six aircraft carriers in the Red Sea and the gulf, and a similar tempo was sustained throughout the war. The battleship *Wisconsin* fired her 16-inch guns 324 times in support missions, using for the first time an unmanned drone aircraft as a spotter for naval gunfire.

In the Gulf War the Navy assembled the largest force of warships in a single theater since World War II, a force that at one time numbered over 165 combat vessels. Command of the sea by the enormous American and coalition naval force (the United States's coalition partners provided an additional 65 warships) enabled the Military Sealift Command freely to transport 95 percent of the supplies required by U.S. forces. The supplies transported by the command amounted to well over 9 million tons of fuel and equipment. Sealift Command controlled up to 247 ships, each covering on an average voyage more than 8,700 miles, the largest and longest sealift since World War II. Still, Sealift Command found itself with too few ships to meet the surge requirements of warfighting commanders in the postulated two-month buildup schedule, and delays in getting important forces to the theater highlighted the need to have maritime assets available to move highly mobile forces into crisis areas on very short notice.[11]

Shipborne marines were part a major strategic deception, threatening the land from the sea in classic maritime fashion to divert the enemy from the primary inland campaign. Held off the coast of Kuwait was "the largest combined amphibious assault force since the Inchon landing in Korea": 17,000 Marines backed by 10,000 sailors ready to go over the beach at the order of the local commander in chief, Army General H. Norman Schwarzkopf. The commander decided their value as a threat was enough. The Iraqis had responded by committing 50,000 troops to coastal defense. Those troops remained tied to the coast while coalition air and land forces, following a variant of NATO AirLand Battle doctrine, with an army in support of an air campaign for the first time in history, pinned, bombed, outflanked, and then defeated the remainder of the Iraqi army that was deployed in Kuwait and southern Iraq.[12]

To summarize the course of the war, after a long military and political buildup, during which the blockade tightened its noose, a massive air pounding was launched on January 16, 1991, followed in February by a ground war that lasted less than four days. The overwhelming coalition force brought the Iraqi army to its knees. A cease-fire was declared on February 28 and the Iraqis evacuated Kuwait. It was an astounding victory. American servicemen killed in action numbered 146; around 120 more died of noncombat causes.

Studies of the Gulf War routinely begin by proclaiming the war's uniqueness. Certainly U.S. political and military leaders derived remarkable advantages from the isolation and military incompetence of Iraq; the formation of a coalition that included Arabs who had rejected Arab solidarity; the extent of domestic and international support for the coalition's policy; the speed of the military victory, which kept the coalition from fracturing; the adept organization of military cooperation that made combined operations possible (an adeptness that on the naval side owed much to decades of NATO experience); and the United States's locally centralized command of joint forces (a successful implementation of the recent Pentagon reform under the Goldwater-Nichols Act).

Among the U.S. services, the Navy most readily accepted the interpretation that the war should not be viewed as a model for the future. The more the Gulf War was viewed as a unique conflict, the more one realized that the next war might not break out in a place where there were friendly states next door from which to fly or to march, or where there was a barren desert in which to fight. And the more the Gulf War was viewed as unique, the less the Air Force or the Army could claim that air power or massed armor was key to future victory, however stupendously effective each had been in Kuwait. The Navy did experience serious operational shortfalls—very inadequate mine and standoff missile countermeasures, too few sealift and prepositioning ships for early armor deployment, and poor realization of naval gunfire support. But the Navy's roles in the Gulf War—sea control, tactical air strikes, amphibious operations, transport, and supply—fell easily into its redefinition of sea power as *intervention from the sea*. These roles answered the question What's the Navy for?

The Navy therefore could claim that although the Gulf War was mainly an Air Force and Army victory, those services had not established the military pattern of the future. At the war's outbreak, the Air Force and the Army stood in need of foreign basing; the Navy did not. The Navy remained a unilateral agent of American policy, independent of foreign opinion. Hence the importance of the Navy's mobility and its sustainability. The Air Force and the Army could not assure sea control; the Navy could, and with it maritime pressure and maritime access. What was unique, said Navy leaders, was that the Navy and Marine Corps "have the capability to act swiftly and decisively anywhere in the world—through unilateral action, joint U.S. forces operations, or as part of a coalition of allies."[13] The Navy, they said, could deliver more of the most likely needed forms of support and power than the other services could. It also had the ability to force entry and seize ports and littoral targets while continuing to assure the free passage, protection, and interdiction that national strategy would require under diverse and unpredictable circumstances. The Navy could give political authorities the widest array of military options.

So the Navy made the Gulf War part of its adjustment, conceding what no longer pertained—the escalatory, offensive features of the high end of an anti-Soviet maritime strategy—and stressing the Navy's practical value in low-end support. There was no point in continuing to express sea power in terms of the Mahanian dicta of autonomy and decisive fleet engagement, no point in refusing to let go of the doctrine that navies existed to fight navies.

The test of a navy in the last analysis is not its ideology, but its practical value, its ability to fight successfully on the sea or to support a fight from the sea. Its declarations, however, do serve a purpose, for a people and their leaders should know what their navy thinks. And as Mahan showed, a serious maritime policy must have popular support.

In 1990 everyone agreed that the United States was a maritime state with innumerable global interests. Once again, there was no threat on the high seas, and none could be easily presumed. The tradition of seeing the Navy as essentially autonomous, of defining sea power as fleet force and naval engagement, no longer fit national needs. To defend and advance the country's global interests in the diffused international environment, the Navy and Marine Corps had to restate what maritime force meant to the United States. That restatement, which accorded with national insistence both on a shift in strategic direction and on joint and combined operations, was expressed in a Navy White Paper published in 1992 called *. . . From the Sea: Preparing the Naval Service for the 21st Century*. This paper recognized the need for a Navy and Marine Corps able simultaneously to assure free communication over the seas and to mount and support expeditionary forces on any shore in campaigns of limited territorial objectives.[14] It was, the declaration said, "a fundamental shift away from open-ocean warfighting *on* the sea toward joint operations conducted *from* the sea."[15] In 1992 the U.S. Navy, after one hundred years, closed its book on sea power doctrine in the image of Mahan. For how long remained to be seen.

Notes

Notes

INTRODUCTION

1. Alfred T. Mahan, *The Influence of Sea Power upon History, 1660–1783* (Boston: Little, Brown, 1890).

2. B. F. Tracy, *Annual Report of the Secretary of the Navy for the Year 1889* (Washington, D.C.: U.S. Government Printing Office, 1890).

3. See, for instance, Bradley S. Klein, "Hegemony and Strategic Culture: American Power Projection and Alliance Defence Politics," *Review of International Studies* 14: 2 (Apr. 1988): 138–41, who traces "power projection" back to Mahan.

4. Julian S. Corbett, *Some Principles of Maritime Strategy* (London: Longmans, Green, 1911), pp. 38–48.

5. Aaron L. Friedberg, "Why Didn't the United States Become a Garrison State?" *International Security* 16: 4 (Spring 1992): 109–42.

6. Secretary of the Navy Sean O'Keefe, CNO Admiral Frank B. Kelso II, and commandant of the Marine Corps General C. E. Mundy, Jr., . . . *From the Sea: Preparing the Naval Service for the 21st Century* (Washington, D.C.: Department of the Navy, 1992), pp. 2, 10.

CHAPTER 1

1. Kenneth J. Hagan, *American Gunboat Diplomacy and the Old Navy, 1877–1889* (Westport: Greenwood, 1973), pp. 5–8, 45–56, 188, quotation on p. 20.

2. C. I. Hamilton, "Naval Power and Diplomacy in the Nineteenth Century," *Journal of Strategic Studies* 3: 1 (Apr. 1980): 77–88.

3. Today the percentage of overseas trade carried on U.S.-flag ships is 3

percent and falling. In 1990 the U.S. merchant fleet was 28th in the world, with 141 ships in the U.S.-flag general cargo fleet, and in 1988, 1989, and early 1990, not one commercial vessel was on order in the United States to be built for carrying international trade under the U.S. flag. The U.S. Maritime Administration estimated that the fleet could shrink to 30 ships by the year 2005. For data and discussion, see H. David Bess and Martin T. Farris, *U.S. Maritime Policy: History and Prospects* (New York: Praeger, 1981), p. 27; John P. Clancy and J. George Hayashi, "The State of Orderly Liquidation," U.S. Naval Institute *Proceedings* 118: 4 (Apr. 1992): 13 (hereafter *Proceedings*); Richard T. Ackley, "Sealift and National Security," *Proceedings* 118: 7 (July 1992): 45–46.

4. Hagan, *American Gunboat Diplomacy*, pp. 8–9, 190.

5. Alfred T. Mahan, *The Influence of Sea Power upon History, 1660–1783* (Boston: Little, Brown, 1890), p. 1.

6. Ibid., pp. 26–27.

7. Alfred T. Mahan, "The United States Looking Outward," first published in 1890 and later reprinted in Alfred T. Mahan, *The Interest of America in Sea Power, Present and Future* (Boston: Little, Brown, 1898). The quotation is on p. 13. This book also contains an article by Mahan entitled "The Isthmus and Sea Power," which was originally published in 1893 and in which Mahan repeats the argument with great emphasis.

8. Alfred T. Mahan, *Sea Power and Its Relations to the War of 1812* (Boston: Little, Brown, 1905), pp. 295–313.

9. Donald M. Schurman, "Mahan Revisited," in John B. Hattendorf and Robert S. Jordan, eds., *Maritime Strategy and the Balance of Power: Britain and America in the Twentieth Century* (New York: St. Martin's, 1988), pp. 103–6.

10. Alfred T. Mahan, "Blockade in Relation to Naval Strategy," *Proceedings* 21: 4 (1895): 866, and Philip A. Crowl, "Alfred Thayer Mahan: The Naval Historian," in Peter Paret, ed., *Makers of Modern Strategy from Machiavelli to the Nuclear Age* (Princeton: Princeton University Press, 1986), p. 455.

11. Jomini is presented by John Shy in "Jomini," in Paret, ed., *Makers of Modern Strategy*, p. 146.

12. Alfred T. Mahan, "The Panama Canal and the Distribution of the Fleet," *North American Review*, Sept. 1914, p. 406.

13. Alfred T. Mahan, "Considerations Governing the Disposition of Navies," *National Review*, July 1902, p. 706.

14. Alfred T. Mahan, "Preparedness for Naval War," first published in 1896 and later reprinted in Mahan, *The Interest of America in Sea Power*. The quotation is on p. 214.

15. Mahan, *The Influence of Sea Power*, p. 26.

16. B. F. Tracy, *Annual Report of the Secretary of the Navy for 1889* (Washington, D.C.: GPO, 1890), p. 4. On Tracy see Benjamin Franklin Cooling, *Benjamin Franklin Tracy: Father of the American Fighting Navy* (Hamden: Archon, 1973), pp. 72–78. On Tracy's connection to Mahan and the new navalists, see Walter R. Herrick, Jr., *The American Naval Revolution* (Baton Rouge: Louisiana State University Press, 1966), pp. 43–54.

17. Mahan, "The Panama Canal," p. 412. See also William E. Livezey, *Mahan on Sea Power*, rev. ed. (Norman: University of Oklahoma Press, 1980), pp. 334–44.

18. Peter Karsten, *The Naval Aristocracy: The Golden Age of Annapolis and the Emergence of Modern American Navalism* (New York: Free Press, 1972), p. 326. See also Robert Seager II, *Alfred Thayer Mahan: The Man and His Letters* (Annapolis: Naval Institute Press, 1977), pp. 160–90, 197–210.

19. Stephen B. Luce, "On the Study of Naval Warfare as a Science," *Proceedings* 12: 4 (1886), p. 546.

20. An encomium, published in England in 1893 in *Fortnightly Review* and reinforced by its reprinting in the Naval Institute's *Proceedings*, reads: "Sea power, of course, has influenced the world in all ages. So has oxygen. Yet, just as oxygen, but for Priestly, might have remained until this day an indefinite and undetected factor, so also might sea power but for Mahan. . . . Not until a factor has been defined and separated can it be intelligently and fully utilized. Here lies the merit of Mahan as of Priestly. The discovery of oxygen went far towards placing the science of chemistry on a sound basis. The discovery—for it is a genuine discovery—of the nature, limitations, and importance of sea power does as much, and perhaps even more, for naval strategy." "Sea Power: Its Past and Its Future," *Proceedings* 19: 4 (1893): 465.

21. Samuel P. Huntington, *The Soldier and the State: The Theory and Practice of Civil-Military Relations* (Cambridge: Harvard University Press, 1957), pp. 276–77.

22. Paul Y. Hammond, *Organizing for Peace: The American Military Establishment in the Twentieth Century* (Princeton: Princeton University Press, 1961), p. 83.

23. The quote comes from John D. Hayes, "The Influence of Modern Sea Power, 1945–1970," *Proceedings* 97: 1 (May 1971): 279–80. See also John D. Hayes and John B. Hattendorf, eds., *The Writings of Stephen B. Luce* (Newport: Naval War College, 1975), pp. 216–17. For bibliographic information on Mahan's book, see note 7 above.

24. Benjamin Franklin Cooling, *Gray Steel and Blue Water Navy: The Formative Years of America's Military-Industrial Complex, 1881–1917* (Hamden: Archon Books, 1979), p. 88.

25. Elting E. Morison, *The War of Ideas: The United States Navy, 1870–1890* (Colorado Springs: U.S. Air Force Academy, 1969), p. 8.

26. Bradley A. Fiske, *From Midshipman to Rear-Admiral* (New York: Century, 1919), p. 362.

27. Henry C. Taylor, "Battle Tactics: The Value of Concentration," *Proceedings* 12: 2 (1886), pp. 141–55.

28. Lawrence C. Allin, "An Antediluvian Monstrosity: The Battleship Revisited," in William B. Cogar, ed., *Naval History: The Seventh Symposium of the United States Military Academy* (Wilmington: Scholarly Resources, 1988), pp. 284–92.

29. Richard Wainwright, "Fleet Tactics," *Proceedings* 16: 1 (1890): 69.

30. *Autobiography of George Dewey* (New York: Scribner's, 1913), pp. 162–63.

31. Norman Friedman, *U.S. Battleships: An Illustrated Design History* (Annapolis: Naval Institute Press, 1985), pp. 1–6, quotation on p. 1. John D. Reilly, Jr., and Robert L. Scheina, *American Battleships, 1886–1923: Predreadnought Design and Construction* (Annapolis: Naval Institute Press, 1980), p. 21. Wayne Hughes wrote: "It is widely thought now that gunnery usurped the ram, or that the ram was never an effective weapon at all. A better conclusion is that the torpedo

superseded the ram. The Whitehead torpedo was a ram with reach: if it hit, it was almost as lethal and a lot safer to use. The study of gunnery became as obsessed with countering torpedo boats as with penetrating armor." Wayne P. Hughes, Jr., *Fleet Tactics: Theory and Practice* (Annapolis: Naval Institute Press, 1986), p. 62.

32. Quotation on concentration from B. F. Tracy, *Annual Report of the Secretary of the Navy for the Year 1890* (Washington, D.C.: GPO, 1890), p. 40. For Tracy's support of a balanced fleet, see ibid., pp. 37–41, and his *Annual Report for the Year 1889*, pp. 10–17. In addition, see Cooling, *Benjamin Franklin Tracy*, pp. 72–78.

33. Harold Sprout and Margaret Sprout, *The Rise of American Naval Power, 1776–1918* (Princeton: Princeton University Press, 1939), pp. 207–12; Friedman, *U.S. Battleships*, pp. 23–25.

34. Graham A. Cosmas, *An Army for Empire: The United States Army in the Spanish-American War* (Columbia: University of Missouri Press, 1971), p. 38.

35. Russell F. Weigley, *The American Way of War: A History of United States Military Strategy and Policy* (Bloomington: Indiana University Press, 1973), p. 192.

36. Mahan, *The Influence of Sea Power*, p. 87.

37. Ibid., p. 86. See also Alfred T. Mahan, *Naval Strategy Compared and Contrasted with the Principles and Practice of Military Operations on Land* (Boston: Little, Brown, 1911), p. 249.

38. Friedman, *U.S. Battleships*, p. 25, and Reilly and Scheina, *American Battleships*, pp. 11–12, 52–54, 71–74. For a clear description of the ships, see William Hovgaard, *Modern History of Warships* (1920; reprint, Annapolis: United States Naval Institute, 1971), pp. 100–107.

39. Robert Seager II, "Ten Years Before Mahan: The Unofficial Case for the New Navy, 1880–1890," *Mississippi Valley Historical Review* 40: 3 (Dec. 1953): 511.

40. Crowl, "Alfred Thayer Mahan," p. 477. For the quote from Mahan, Crowl cites Alfred T. Mahan, *Naval Administration and Warfare* (Boston: Little, Brown, 1908), p. 229.

41. See the discussion of the process in Karl Lautenschläger, "The Dreadnought Revolution Reconsidered," in Daniel M. Masterson, ed., *Naval History: The Sixth Symposium of the U.S. Naval Academy* (Wilmington: Scholarly Resources, 1987), p. 142.

42. Elting E. Morison, "Inventing a Modern Navy," *American Heritage* 37: 4 (June–July 1986): 94. See also Morison's superb biography *Admiral Sims and the Modern American Navy* (Boston: Houghton Mifflin, 1942), pp. 156–75.

43. Mahan, *Naval Strategy*, p. 5.

44. Charles H. Fairbank, Jr., "The Origins of the *Dreadnought* Revolution: A Historiographic Essay," *International History Review* 13: 2 (May 1991): 246–48.

45. Friedman, *U.S. Battleships*, p. 41.

46. William S. Sims, "The Inherent Tactical Qualities of All-Big-Gun, One-Caliber Battleships of High Speed, Large Displacement and Gunpower," *Proceedings* 32: 4 (Dec. 1906): 1337–66. See also the chapter "Sims vs. Mahan" in Morison, *Admiral Sims*; Ronald Spector, *Admiral of the New Empire: The Life and Career of George Dewey* (Baton Rouge: Louisiana State University Press, 1974), pp. 171–77; D. R. Morris, "Homer Clark Poundstone and the All-Big-Gun Ship,"

Proceedings 74: 6 (June 1948): 707–21; Damon E. Cummings, *Admiral Richard Wainwright and the United States Fleet* (Washington, D.C.: GPO, 1962), pp. 155–61; and Richard W. Turk, *The Ambiguous Relationship: Theodore Roosevelt and Alfred Thayer Mahan* (New York: Greenwood, 1987), pp. 57–61.

47. Mahan's phrase quoted by his biographer Robert Seager, cited in Paolo E. Coletta, *Admiral Bradley A. Fiske and the American Navy* (Lawrence: Regents Press of Kansas, 1979), p. 235.

48. Wayne P. Hughes, Jr., "Mahan, Tactics and Principles of Strategy," in John B. Hattendorf, ed., *The Influence of History on Mahan* (Newport: Naval War College Press, 1991), pp. 25–27.

49. Friedman, *U.S. Battleships*, p. 63, which also quotes the congressional authorization.

50. Morison, *Admiral Sims*, p. 171.

51. John H. Maurer, "American Naval Concentration and the German Battle Fleet, 1900–1918," *Journal of Strategic Studies* 6: 2 (June 1983): 147–49.

52. Vincent Davis, *The Admirals Lobby* (Chapel Hill: University of North Carolina Press, 1967), p. 113.

53. Mahan, *Naval Strategy*, p. 382.

54. Ibid., p. 381.

CHAPTER 2

1. Alfred T. Mahan, *Lessons of the War with Spain* (Boston: Little, Brown, 1899), pp. 231–32.

2. The best book on the war with Spain, which gives a fine account of naval plans and operations, is David F. Trask, *The War with Spain in 1898* (New York: Macmillan, 1981). A contemporary detailed study of the Mahanian persuasion is H. W. Wilson, *The Downfall of Spain: Naval History of the Spanish-American War* (London: Sampson Low, Marston, 1900).

3. Trask, *War with Spain*, pp. 109–13.

4. Ibid., p. 113.

5. Julian S. Corbett, *Some Principles of Maritime Strategy* (London: Longmans, Green, 1911), pp. 171–72. Mahan's mea culpa is found in his *Lessons of the War with Spain*, pp. 167–70.

6. Trask, *War with Spain*, pp. 257–60; Walter R. Herrick, *The American Naval Revolution* (Baton Rouge: Louisiana State University Press, 1967), pp. 238–47; Joseph G. Dawson III, "William T. Sampson: Progressive Technologist as Naval Commander," in James C. Bradford, ed., *Admirals of the New Steel Navy: Makers of the American Naval Tradition, 1880–1930* (Annapolis: Naval Institute Press, 1990), pp. 149–79, at p. 162.

7. Trask, *War with Spain*, pp. 375–77; Robert Seager II and Doris Maguire, eds., *Letters and Papers of Alfred Thayer Mahan*: vol. 3, *1902–1904* (Annapolis: Naval Institute Press, 1975), pp. 445–47. Mahan claimed that Dewey could have returned and destroyed the Spanish reinforcements when the two monitors sent to reinforce him arrived. Mahan, *Lessons of the War with Spain*, pp. 34–35. But it was more likely that the Spaniards would have destroyed these unseaworthy vessels before they joined up with Dewey.

8. Wayne P. Hayes, Jr., *Fleet Tactics: Theory and Practice* (Annapolis: Naval Institute Press, 1986), p. 277.

9. Harold Sprout and Margaret Sprout, *The Rise of American Naval Power, 1776–1918* (Princeton: Princeton University Press, 1939), pp. 208–9.

10. Alfred T. Mahan, *The Influence of Sea Power upon History, 1660–1783* (Boston: Little, Brown, 1890), p. 87.

11. John Hattendorf has some useful observations on this connection of fortress and fleet in his "Alfred Thayer Mahan and His Strategic Thought," in Hattendorf and Robert S. Jordan, eds., *Maritime Strategy and the Balance of Power: Britain and America in the Twentieth Century* (New York: St. Martin's Press, 1989), pp. 88–92.

12. Quoted by Emanuel Raymond Lewis, *Seacoast Fortifications of the United States* (Washington, D.C.: Smithsonian Institution Press, 1970), p. 99. See also Gordon C. O'Gara, *Theodore Roosevelt and the Rise of the Modern Navy* (Princeton: Princeton University Press, 1943), p. 71.

13. Samuel A. Lawrence, *United States Merchant Shipping Policies and Politics* (Washington, D.C.: Brookings Institution, 1966), p. 33; Mahan, *Lessons of the War with Spain*, pp. 191–92.

14. "Report of the Secretary of the Navy," in *Annual Report of the Navy Department for the Year 1905* (Washington, D.C.: GPO, 1906), p. 24.

15. Alfred T. Mahan, *Naval Strategy Compared and Contrasted with the Principles and Practice of Military Operations on Land* (Boston: Little, Brown, 1911), pp. 446–47.

16. Vincent Davis, *The Admirals Lobby* (Chapel Hill: University of North Carolina Press, 1967), pp. 114–15.

17. Ronald Spector, *Admiral of the New Empire: The Life and Career of George Dewey* (Baton Rouge: Louisiana State University Press, 1974), p. 149.

18. Ibid., pp. 150–52, 159.

19. H. J. Mackinder, *Democratic Ideals and Reality: A Study in the Politics of Reconstruction* (New York: Holt, 1919), p. 76. The British commander at Manila Bay, like the British government, had been sympathetic but neutral. During an American bombardment, the commander had positioned his ships between the U.S. and German fleets, apparently out of purely technical interest, to get a better view of the operation. The story grew, however, that he had done this to deter a German attack on the U.S. force. See Thomas A. Bailey, "Dewey and the Germans at Manila Bay," *American Historical Review* 45: 1 (Oct. 1939): 74–78; and Trask, *War with Spain*, p. 419. On the importance of growing British-American sympathy more generally during this period, see A. E. Campbell, *Great Britain and the United States, 1895–1903* (London: Longmans, 1960).

20. David Healy, *Drive to Hegemony: The United States in the Caribbean, 1898–1917* (Madison: University of Wisconsin Press, 1988), p. 35. Cleveland's assertion cited on p. 34.

21. Elting E. Morison, *The Letters of Theodore Roosevelt*, vol. 2 (Cambridge: Harvard University Press, 1951), p. 1192.

22. For a reliable overview, see Healy, *Drive to Hegemony*, pp. 80–81, 97–99.

23. Samuel Wells, Jr., "British Strategic Withdrawal from the Western Hemisphere, 1904–1906," *Canadian Historical Review* 49: 4 (Dec. 1968): 335–36.

24. On this and the broader diplomatic background, see Charles S. Campbell, Jr., *Anglo-American Understanding, 1898–1903* (1957; reprint, Westport: Greenwood Press, 1980), pp. 269–300.

25. William R. Braisted, *The United States Navy in the Pacific, 1897–1909* (Austin: University of Texas Press, 1958), p. 63; Paul M. Kennedy, *The Samoan Tangle: A Study in Anglo-German-American Relations, 1878–1900* (New York: Harper & Row, 1974), pp. 221, 280, 290–93.

26. Richard D. Challener, *Admirals, Generals, and American Foreign Policy, 1898–1914* (Princeton: Princeton University Press, 1973), p. 32; Russell F. Weigley, *The American Way of War: A History of United States Military Strategy and Policy* (Bloomington: Indiana University Press, 1973), pp. 189–90.

27. John H. Maurer, "Fuel and the Battle Fleet: Coal, Oil, and American Naval Strategy, 1898–1925," *Naval War College Review* 34: 6 (Nov.–Dec. 1981): 66–67.

28. Holger H. Herwig, *Politics of Frustration: The United States in German Naval Planning, 1889–1941* (Boston: Little, Brown, 1976), pp. 72–76, 86.

29. Ibid., pp. 68, 83.

30. Spector, *Admiral of the New Empire*, p. 141.

31. Edward Parsons, cited in Herwig, *Politics of Frustration*, p. 81.

32. Challener shows that the initiative in assembling the force was taken by Roosevelt, who wished to make political use of the occasion, and not by the Navy, despite its concern that Germany might establish a base in the Caribbean. Challener, *Admirals, Generals, and American Foreign Policy*, pp. 111–17.

33. Ronald Spector, "Roosevelt, the Navy, and the Venezuela Controversy: 1902–1903," *American Neptune* 32: 4 (Oct. 1972): 259–63.

34. The absence of evidence leads some authors to dismiss Roosevelt's claim. See Holger H. Herwig, *Germany's Vision of Empire in Venezuela, 1871–1914* (Princeton: Princeton University Press, 1986), pp. 201–208; John M. Maurer, "American Naval Concentration and the German Battle Fleet, 1900–1918," *Journal of Strategic Studies* 6: 2 (June 1983): 153. Frederick Marks, on the other hand, argues that there were reasons to suppress such an ultimatum, that there are unexplained gaps in the files, and that the circumstantial evidence supports Roosevelt's contention that he threatened the Germans with naval war in the Caribbean. Frederick W. Marks III, *Velvet on Iron: The Diplomacy of Theodore Roosevelt* (Lincoln: University of Nebraska Press, 1979), pp. 37–54. An evenhanded evaluation of the German danger is made by Healy in his *Drive to Hegemony*, pp. 71–76.

35. Albert C. Stillson, "Military Policy Without Political Guidance: Theodore Roosevelt's Navy," *Military Affairs* 26: 1 (Spring 1961): 23.

36. Spector, *Admiral of the New Empire*, p. 151.

37. The discussion above follows Stillson, "Military Policy Without Political Guidance," pp. 18–31. The quote is on p. 25.

38. George T. Davis, *A Navy Second to None: The Development of Modern American Naval Policy* (New York: Harcourt, Brace, 1940), p. 169.

39. "Annual Report of the Secretary of the Navy," in *Annual Report of the Navy Department for the Fiscal Year 1907* (Washington, D.C.: GPO, 1908), p. 6.

40. See Sprout and Sprout, *Rise of American Naval Power*, pp. 282–84.
41. Elting E. Morison, ed., *The Letters of Theodore Roosevelt*: vol. 6 (Cambridge: Harvard University Press, 1952), p. 1543.
42. Seward W. Livermore, "The American Navy as a Factor in World Politics, 1903–1913," *American Historical Review* 63: 4 (July 1958): 879. See also William N. Still, Jr., *American Sea Power in the Old World: The United States Navy in European and Near Eastern Waters, 1865–1917* (Westport: Greenwood, 1980), pp. 139–52; William J. Hourihan, "The Best Ambassador: Rear Admiral Cotton and the Cruise of the European Squadron, 1903," *Naval War College Review* 32: 4 (July–Aug. 1979): 63–71; and Hourihan, "Marlin Spike Diplomacy: The Navy in the Mediterranean, 1904," *Proceedings* 105: 1 (Jan. 1979): 42–51.
43. Spector, *Admiral of the New Empire*, p. 164.
44. Hermann Hagedorn, *Leonard Wood: A Biography* (New York: Harper and Brothers, 1931), 2: 71.
45. Spector, *Admiral of the New Empire*, p. 167.
46. Ibid., pp. 168–69; Hagedorn, *Leonard Wood*, 2: 81.
47. Challener, *Admirals, Generals, and American Foreign Policy*, p. 237.
48. Ibid., p. 762.
49. Mahan, *Naval Strategy*, p. 8.
50. Challener, *Admirals, Generals, and American Foreign Policy*, p. 251.
51. Ibid., p. 253; Livermore, "The American Navy as a Factor in World Politics," p. 864.
52. Morison, ed., *Letters of Theodore Roosevelt*, 6: 717.
53. Braisted, *United States Navy in the Pacific, 1897–1909*, pp. 214–15; Akira Iriye, *Pacific Estrangement: Japanese and American Expansion, 1897–1911* (Cambridge: Harvard University Press, 1972), pp. 147–50. Quote in Marks, *Velvet on Iron*, p. 57. For the story of how Roosevelt used the cruise to quiet anti-Japanese sentiments in California, see Thomas A. Bailey, *Theodore Roosevelt and the Japanese-American Crisis* (Stanford: Stanford University Press, 1934).
54. Maurer, "American Naval Concentration and the German Battle Fleet," pp. 159–60.
55. Maurer, "Fuel and the Battle Fleet," pp. 68–69.
56. James R. Reckner, *Teddy Roosevelt's Great White Fleet* (Annapolis: Naval Institute Press, 1988), p. 161.
57. William R. Braisted, *The United States Navy in the Pacific, 1909–1922* (Austin: University of Texas, 1971), p. 118. Taft's "suitable Navy" quotation on p. 21.
58. Akira Iriye discusses these events under the indicative chapter heading "The Genesis of American-Japanese Antagonism." Akira Iriye, *Across the Pacific: An Inner History of American–East Asian Relations* (New York: Harcourt, Brace and World, 1967), chap. 5.
59. George Davis, *A Navy Second to None*, pp. 170–73.

CHAPTER 3

1. Warner R. Schilling, "Admirals and Foreign Policy, 1913–1919" (Ph.D. diss., Yale University, 1953), p. 1.
2. James W. Moore, "National Security in the American Army's Definition of Mission, 1865–1914," *Military Affairs* 46: 3 (Oct. 1982): 127–131.

3. Holger H. Herwig and David F. Trask, "Naval Operations Plans Between Germany and the USA, 1898–1913: A Study of Strategic Planning in the Age of Imperialism," in P. M. Kennedy, ed., *The War Plans of the Great Powers, 1880–1914* (London: Allen & Unwin, 1979), p. 62.

4. See Paul Y. Hammond, *Organizing for Defense: The American Military Establishment in the Twentieth Century* (Princeton: Princeton University Press, 1961), p. 83.

5. E. David Cronon, ed., *The Cabinet Diaries of Josephus Daniels, 1913–1921* (Lincoln: University of Nebraska Press, 1963), p. 68.

6. Josephus Daniels, *The Wilson Era: Years of Peace, 1910–1917* (Chapel Hill: University of North Carolina Press, 1944), pp. 166–67.

7. Schilling, "Admirals and Foreign Policy," pp. 49–56; John H. Maurer, "American Naval Concentration and the German Battle Fleet, 1900–1918," *Journal of Strategic Studies* 6: 2 (June 1983): 176–77.

8. William I. Puleston, *Mahan* (New Haven: Yale University Press, 1939), pp. 340–45; Arthur S. Link, *Wilson: The Struggle for Neutrality, 1914–1915* (Princeton: Princeton University Press, 1960), p. 66.

9. Paolo E. Coletta, *Admiral Bradley A. Fiske and the American Navy* (Lawrence: Regents Press of Kansas, 1979), p. 132.

10. Bradley A. Fiske, *From Midshipman to Rear-Admiral* (New York: Century, 1919), p. 550.

11. Hammond, *Organizing for Defense*, pp. 49–84. Daniels's views are given in *Naval Investigation. Hearings Before the Subcommittee of the Committee on Naval Affairs, United States Senate, Sixty-Sixth Congress, Second Session* (Washington, D.C.: GPO, 1921), pp. 2279–2313, 2972–93.

12. These testimonies are collected in Office of Chief of Naval Operations, *Naval Administration: Selected Documents on Navy Department Organization, 1915–1940* (Washington, D.C.: Department of the Navy, 1945), pp. II-7 to II-46.

13. David F. Trask, "William Shepherd Benson, 11 May 1915–25 September 1919," in Robert William Love, Jr., ed., *The Chiefs of Naval Operations* (Annapolis: Naval Institute Press, 1980), p. 9, shows Benson's reasoning. Benson's testimony quoted here is from *Naval Investigation*, p. 1836. See also Mary Klachko with David Trask, *Admiral William Shepherd Benson: First Chief of Naval Operations* (Annapolis: Naval Institute Press, 1987), pp. 41–51.

14. Elting E. Morison, *Admiral Sims and the Modern American Navy* (Boston: Houghton Mifflin, 1942), pp. 451–52.

15. As a rule Wilson was not concerned with military strategy at the operational level. He never asked the advice of a naval officer before the United States entered the war. In a comparable circumstance, President Franklin Roosevelt, with a keener interest in the details of naval affairs, met privately with key admirals at least five times in April 1941 to prepare action in support of Great Britain in the Atlantic. Waldo Heinrichs, "President Franklin D. Roosevelt's Intervention in the Battle of the Atlantic, 1941," *Diplomatic History* 10: 4 (Fall 1986): 316. Wilson held one short interview with General John J. Pershing before he left to command the American Expeditionary Forces in Europe. In this interview the president discussed neither the war nor America's part in it and gave Pershing no instructions as to the course he should pursue. Donald Smythe,

Pershing's biographer, states, "Perhaps no field commander in history was ever given a freer hand to conduct operations than was Pershing by Wilson." Smythe, *Pershing: General of the Armies* (Bloomington: Indiana University Press, 1986), p. 11.

16. William R. Braisted, *The United States Navy in the Pacific, 1909–1922* (Austin: University of Texas Press, 1971), p. 182.

17. Schilling, "Admirals and Foreign Policy," pp. 82–84.

18. According to Arthur Link, "This was easily the most important decision on domestic policy Wilson made during the year 1915." Link, *Wilson: The Struggle for Neutrality*, p. 591.

19. Daniels, *Wilson Era*, p. 327.

20. Arthur S. Link, *Woodrow Wilson and the Progressive Era, 1910–1917* (New York: Harper, 1954), p. 190.

21. "Report of the General Board to the Secretary of the Navy: November 9, 1915," in *Annual Reports of the Navy Department for the Fiscal Year 1915* (Washington, D.C.: GPO, 1916), pp. 73–74.

22. George T. Davis, *A Navy Second to None: The Development of Modern American Naval Policy* (New York: Harcourt, Brace, 1940), p. 231.

23. J. A. S. Grenville, "Diplomacy and War Plans in the United States, 1890–1917," in Kennedy, ed., *War Plans of the Great Powers*, p. 36.

24. Braisted, *United States Navy in the Pacific, 1909–1922*, pp. 201–2. Of discussions of the 1916 naval bill, Braisted's is the most illuminating. There are also pertinent comments in Ronald Spector, *Admiral of the New Empire: The Life and Career of George Dewey* (Baton Rouge: Louisiana State University Press, 1974), pp. 200–202.

25. For the "importance and ubiquity of *small* ships, the sheer variety of tasks they were required to carry out . . . , and the absence of any significant reference to them in the maritime strategy of both the British and American navies," see Paul M. Kennedy, "The Relevance of the Prewar British and American Maritime Strategies to the First World War and its Aftermath, 1898–1920," in John B. Hattendorf and Robert S. Jordan, eds., *Maritime Strategy and the Balance of Power: Britain and America in the Twentieth Century* (New York: St. Martin's Press, 1989), pp. 179–84. The point is vividly illustrated in Paul G. Halpern, *The Naval War in the Mediterranean, 1914–1918* (Annapolis: Naval Institute Press, 1987).

26. David F. Trask, *Captains and Cabinets: Anglo-American Naval Relations, 1917–1918* (Columbia: University of Missouri Press, 1972), p. 60. Trask's book contains a profound analysis of the prewar naval position.

27. "Report of the General Board to the Secretary of the Navy, October 16, 1915," in *Annual Reports of the Navy Department for the Fiscal Year 1916* (Washington, D.C.: GPO, 1917), p. 81.

28. Schilling, "Admirals and Foreign Policy," p. 68.

29. "Report of the General Board to the Secretary of the Navy, November 9, 1915," in *Annual Reports of the Navy Department for the Fiscal Year 1915*, pp. 74–75.

30. Trask, *Captains and Cabinets*, p. 49.

31. The qualification when they were ready is a substantial one. The destroyers funded in 1916 were not built until after 1919.

CHAPTER 4

1. Arthur S. Link, *Wilson the Diplomatist: A Look at His Major Foreign Policies* (Chicago: Quadrangle Books, 1965), p. 89.

2. Arthur S. Link, *Wilson: Campaigns for Progressivism and Peace, 1916–1917* (Princeton: Princeton University Press, 1965), p. 414.

3. For a profound analysis of the prewar naval position, see David F. Trask, *Captains and Cabinets: Anglo-American Naval Relations, 1917–1918* (Columbia: University of Missouri Press, 1972), pp. 44–52, which gives these quotations from Benson.

4. Ibid., p. 48.

5. *Naval Investigation. Hearings Before the Subcommittee of the Committee on Naval Affairs, United States Senate, Sixty-Sixth Congress, Second Session* (Washington, D.C.: GPO, 1921), p. 600.

6. David F. Trask, "William Shepherd Benson, 11 May 1915–25 September 1919," in Robert William Love, Jr., ed., *The Chiefs of Naval Operations* (Annapolis: Naval Institute Press, 1980), p. 10.

7. Gerald W. Wheeler, *Admiral William Veazie Pratt, U.S. Navy: A Sailor's Life* (Washington, D.C.: Department of the Navy, 1974), pp. 92–93.

8. *Naval Investigation*, p. 1825.

9. William Sowden Sims, *The Victory at Sea* (Garden City: Doubleday, Page, 1920), p. 9.

10. J. Winton, *Convoy: The Defence of Sea Trade, 1890–1990* (London: Michael Joseph, 1983), p. 40, cited in Paul M. Kennedy, "The Relevance of the Prewar British and American Maritime Strategies to the First World War and its Aftermath, 1898–1920," in John B. Hattendorf and Robert S. Jordan, eds., *Maritime Strategy and the Balance of Power: Britain and America in the Twentieth Century* (New York: St. Martin's Press, 1989), p. 176.

11. Martin Doughty, *Merchant Shipping and War: A Study of Defence Planning in Twentieth-Century Britain* (London: Royal Historical Society, 1982), pp. 5–8, 37.

12. Holger H. Herwig, *Politics of Frustration: The United States in German Naval Planning, 1889–1941* (Boston: Little, Brown, 1976), p. 127; Elting E. Morison, *Admiral Sims and the Modern American Navy* (Boston: Houghton Mifflin, 1942), p. 353.

13. *Naval Investigation*, p. 120.

14. For the change in naval and strategic thought behind this decision to convoy, see the very astute study in Robert W. H. M. McKillip, "Undermining Technology by Strategy: Resolving the Trade Protection Dilemma of 1917," *Naval War College Review* 44: 3 (Summer 1991): 18–37.

15. Arthur J. Marder, *From the Dreadnought to Scapa Flow: The Royal Navy in the Fisher Era, 1904–1919*: vol. 4, *1917: Year of Crisis* (London: Oxford University Press, 1969), pp. 145–46; Henry Newbolt, *Naval Operations*, vol. 5 (London: Longmans, Green, 1931), pp. 17, 19, 32.

16. Peter Gretton, "The U-Boat Campaign in Two World Wars," in Gerald Jordan, ed., *Naval Warfare in the Twentieth Century, 1900–1945: Essays in Honour of Arthur Marder* (London: Croom Helm, 1977), p. 134.

17. U.S. Department of State, *Papers Relating to the Foreign Relations of the United States, 1917*: supp. 2, *The World War*, vol. 1 (Washington, D.C.: GPO, 1932), p. 115.

18. These are Dean Allard's words. See Allard, "Anglo-American Naval Differences During World War I," *Military Affairs* 40: 2 (Apr. 1980): 75–80.

19. See Pratt's message to Sims on July 2, 1917, in which he said that Britain should coöperate in giving the United States more detailed information about the way it saw the war. Mary Klachko with David F. Trask, *Admiral William Shepherd Benson, First Chief of Naval Operations* (Annapolis: Naval Institute Press, 1987), p. 75.

20. Emphases added. U.S. Department of State, *Papers Relating to the Foreign Relations of the United States, 1917*: supp. 2, vol. 1, p. 116; *Naval Investigation*, pp. 592–93; Michael Simpson, ed., *Anglo-American Naval Relations, 1917–1919* (London: Scolar Press for the Navy Records Society, 1991), pp. 78–79, 88.

21. Klachko with Trask, *Benson*, p. 69.

22. Holger H. Herwig and David F. Trask, "The Failure of Imperial Germany's Undersea Offensive Against World Shipping, February 1917–October 1918," *The Historian* 33: 4 (Aug. 1971): 626–28.

23. U.S. Department of State, *Papers Relating to the Foreign Relations of the United States, 1917*: supp. 2, vol. 1, p. 117.

24. Klachko with Trask, *Benson*, pp. 76–77.

25. For Wilson's criticisms see Trask, *Captains and Cabinets*, pp. 131–34; and E. David Cronon, ed., *The Cabinet Diaries of Josephus Daniels, 1913–1921* (Lincoln: University of Nebraska Press, 1963), pp. 109, 191. On the hornets, here is a quotation from Mahan: "When the enemy confines himself to commerce destroying by crowds of small privateers, then the true military policy is to stamp out the nests where they swarm." A. T. Mahan, *The Influence of Sea Power upon the French Revolution and Empire, 1793–1812*, vol. 2 (Boston: Little, Brown, 1893), p. 252.

26. Simpson, ed., *Anglo-American Naval Relations*, p. 80.

27. Wilson to Col. E. M. House, quoted in Trask, *Captains and Cabinets*, p. 126.

28. Cronon, *Cabinet Diaries of Josephus Daniels*, p. 133.

29. Wheeler, *Pratt*, pp. 97–109.

30. For Wilson's interests in maritime expansion, leading to the Jones Act of 1920, see Jeffrey J. Safford, "The American Merchant Marine as an Expression of Foreign Policy: Woodrow Wilson and the Genesis of Modern Maritime Diplomacy," in B. W. Larabee, ed., *The Atlantic World of Robert G. Albion* (Middletown: Wesleyan University Press, 1975), pp. 144–68.

31. Warner R. Schilling, "Admirals and Foreign Policy, 1913–1919" (Ph.D. diss., Yale University, 1953), pp. 94–105; George T. Davis, *A Navy Second to None: The Development of Modern American Naval Policy* (New York: Harcourt, Brace, 1940), pp. 236–37.

32. Trask, *Captains and Cabinets*, p. 139. See further on this matter in Klachko with Trask, *Benson*, p. 72.

33. Josephus Daniels, *The Wilson Era: Years of War and After, 1917–1923* (Chapel Hill: University of North Carolina Press, 1946), p. 91. Daniels had

overcome his initial reservations. In October 1917, when the General Board approved the barrier project, Daniels wrote in his diary that it was "of doubtful practicability. North Sea too rough & will necessitate withdrawing all our ships for other work and then can we destroy the hornets nest or keep the hornets in?" At this point, Wilson and Sims shared his reservations. Trask, *Captains and Cabinets*, p. 154.

34. Arthur J. Marder, *From the Dreadnought to Scapa Flow: The Royal Navy in the Fisher Era, 1904–1919*: vol. 5, *Victory and Aftermath (January 1918–June 1919)* (London: Oxford University Press, 1970), pp. 68–69.

35. Josephus Daniels, *Our Navy at War* (New York: Doran, 1922), p. 130.

36. Arthur J. Marder, *From the Dardanelles to Oran: Studies of the Royal Navy in War and Peace, 1915–1940* (London: Oxford University Press, 1974), p. 50.

37. "Annual Report of the Secretary of the Navy," in *Annual Reports of the Navy Department for the Fiscal Year 1919* (Washington, D.C.: GPO, 1920), p. 45; Marder, *Victory and Aftermath*, pp. 66–75; Gregory K. Hartmann, *Weapons That Wait: Mine Warfare in the U.S. Navy* (Annapolis: Naval Institute Press, 1979), p. 53; and the documents in Simpson, ed., *Anglo-American Naval Relations*, pp. 365–94. The Otranto barrier, "a theatre of war on its own," supported by some 300 warships, sank two U-boats but did not appear to hamper U-boat operations. Winton, *Convoy*, p. 100.

38. Allard, "Anglo-American Naval Differences," p. 77.

39. Ibid., pp. 85–87.

40. Marder, *Victory and Aftermath*, p. 103.

41. Richard Hough, *The Great War at Sea, 1914–1918* (Oxford: Oxford University Press, 1983), p. 310.

42. Marder, *Victory and Aftermath*, p. 111.

43. Arthur Hezlet, *The Submarine and Seapower* (New York: Stein and Day, 1967), p. 106.

44. No strategic alternative made sense. See Ronald Spector, "'You're Not Going to Send Soldiers over There Are You?': The American Search for an Alternative to the Western Front 1916–1917," *Military Affairs* 36: 1 (Feb. 1972): 1–4.

45. John J. Pershing, *Final Report* (Washington, D.C.: GPO, 1919), p. 11.

46. Thomas G. Frothingham, *The Naval History of the World War: The United States in the War, 1917–1918* (Cambridge: Harvard University Press, 1926), p. 128.

47. Ibid., p. 129.

48. Albert Gleaves, *A History of the Transport Service: Adventures and Experiences of United States Transports and Cruisers in the World War* (New York: Doran, 1921), p. 29. Vice-Admiral Gleaves was commander of convoy operations.

49. Benedict Crowell and Robert Forrest Wilson, *The Road to France: The Transportation of Troops and Military Supplies, 1917–1918*, 2 vols. (New Haven: Yale University Press, 1921). Crowell was assistant secretary for war and director of munitions during the war.

50. Ibid., 1: 14.

51. William J. Wilgus, *Transporting the A.E.F. in Western Europe, 1917–1919* (New York: Columbia University Press, 1931), pp. 344, 501–2. Wilgus was deputy director general of transportation for the American Expeditionary Forces.

52. Ibid., pp. 149, 243.

53. Pershing, *Final Report*, p. 11. For plans to ship additional millions of troops to Europe in 1919, see Crowell and Wilson, *Road to France*, 2: 368–70.

54. Robert H. Ferrell, *Woodrow Wilson and World War I, 1917–1921* (New York: Harper & Row, 1985), p. 42; Wheeler, *Pratt*, p. 117.

55. Message from Daniels to Sims, July 28, 1917. Daniels, *Wilson Era*, p. 95.

56. Sims, *Victory at Sea*, pp. 355–64; Morison, *Admiral Sims*, pp. 418–23. Daniels and Sims aired their differences before Congress. *Naval Investigation*, pp. 2136–43 and 3348–54.

57. John L. Leighton, *SIMSADUS: LONDON, The American Navy in Europe* (New York: Holt, 1920), pp. 139–40.

58. Allard, "Anglo-American Naval Differences," p. 77.

59. Trask, *Captains and Cabinets*, p. 360.

CHAPTER 5

1. David F. Trask, *Captains and Cabinets: Anglo-American Naval Relations, 1917–1918* (Columbia: University of Missouri Press, 1972), p. 290.

2. From Planning Section Memorandum No. 21, "U.S. Naval Building Policy," issued May 1918, cited in Trask, *Captains and Cabinets*, p. 290.

3. Norman Friedman, *U.S. Cruisers: An Illustrated Design History* (Annapolis: Naval Institute Press, 1984), p. 109.

4. Trask, *Captains and Cabinets*, p. 314.

5. Christopher Hall, *Britain, America and Arms Control, 1921–37* (New York: St. Martin's Press, 1987), p. 202.

6. For the first quote, see Warner R. Schilling, "Admirals and Foreign Policy, 1913–1919" (Ph.D. diss., Yale University, 1953), p. 252; for the second quotation, see Jeffrey J. Safford, "Anglo-American Maritime Relations During the Two World Wars: A Comparative Analysis," *American Neptune* 41: 4 (Oct. 1981): 268.

7. Mary Klachko with David F. Trask, *Admiral William Shepherd Benson, First Chief of Naval Operations* (Annapolis: Naval Institute Press, 1987), p. 183.

8. U.S. Naval Advisory Staff, Paris, Memorandum No. 25, April 7, 1919, in Ray Stannard Baker, *Woodrow Wilson and World Settlement*, vol. 3 (Garden City: Doubleday, Page, 1922), pp. 211 and 213.

9. Memorandum by Comdr. W. S. Pye, "Building Program for U.S. Navy," to Commander in Chief, U.S. Atlantic Fleet, January 20, 1919, p. 13. Pye's memorandum was immediately forwarded by Admiral H. T. Mayo to the secretary of the Navy and then by him to the General Board's General Board Study No. 420-6, Serial No. 894, U.S. Naval War College Archives.

10. Josephus Daniels, *The Wilson Era: Years of War and After, 1917–1923* (Chapel Hill: University of North Carolina Press, 1946), pp. 370–71; Elting E. Morison, *Admiral Sims and the Modern American Navy* (Boston: Houghton Mifflin, 1942), p. 431. For Sims's support of a superior Navy if Britain were a declared foe, see Harold Sprout and Margaret Sprout, *Toward a New Order of Sea Power: American Naval Policy and the World Scene, 1918–1922* (Princeton: Princeton University Press, 1940), p. 80.

11. Naval Advisory Staff, Paris, Memorandum No. 25, April 7, 1919, in Baker,

Woodrow Wilson and World Settlement, 3: 214; Michael Simpson, ed., *Anglo-American Naval Relations, 1917–1919* (London: Scolar Press for the Navy Records Society, 1991), pp. 604–5.

12. Daniels, *Wilson Era*, pp. 378–79. In his memoirs of the peace conference, Lloyd George makes no mention of this performance.

13. Inga Floto, *Colonel House in Paris: A Study of American Policy at the Paris Peace Conference, 1919* (Princeton: Princeton University Press, 1980), p. 210.

14. Seth P. Tillman, *Anglo-American Relations at the Paris Peace Conference of 1919* (Princeton: Princeton University Press, 1961), pp. 293–94.

15. Yarnell is quoted in William R. Braisted, *The United States Navy in the Pacific, 1909–1922* (Austin: University of Texas Press, 1971), p. 457.

16. Friedman, *U.S. Cruisers*, p. 10; Michael Vlahos, *The Blue Sword: The Naval War College and the American Mission, 1919–1941* (Newport: Naval War College Press, 1980), pp. 99–112; William R. Braisted, "On the American Red and Red-Orange Plans, 1919–1939," in Gerald Jordan, ed., *Naval Warfare in the Twentieth Century, 1900–1945: Essays in Honour of Arthur Marder* (London: Croom Helm, 1977), pp. 167–85. As late as 1938, there was a Blue (U.S.)–Red (U.K.) war game, with Crimson (Canada) coming to the aid of Red, Blue planning to capture Halifax, and the game culminating in the final decisive fleet "Battle of Sable Island." John B. Hattendorf, B. Mitchell Simpson III, and John R. Wadleigh, *Sailors and Scholars: The Centennial History of the U.S. Naval War College* (Newport: Naval War College Press, 1984), p. 164.

17. Braisted, *United States Navy in the Pacific, 1909–1922*, pp. 545–48. Daniels defended his decision in "Annual Report of the Secretary of the Navy," in *Annual Reports of the Navy Department for the Fiscal Year 1919* (Washington, D.C.: GPO, 1920), pp. 7–14, and "Annual Report of the Secretary of the Navy," in *Annual Reports of the Navy Department for the Fiscal Year 1920* (Washington, D.C.: GPO, 1921), p. 24.

18. See Braisted, *United States Navy in the Pacific, 1909–1922*, pp. 462–75. The Navy's position regarding the Pacific was stated clearly at the end of 1919 in the Joint Board's "Strategy of the Pacific," which is reprinted in Steven T. Ross, ed., *American War Plans, 1919–1941*: vol. 1, *Peacetime War Plans, 1919–1935* (New York: Garland, 1992), pp. 15–21.

19. Louis Morton, "War Plan ORANGE: Evolution of a Strategy," *World Politics* 11: 2 (Jan. 1959): 224.

20. Roger Dingman, *Power in the Pacific: The Origins of Naval Arms Limitation, 1914–1922* (Chicago: University of Chicago Press, 1976), p. 99.

21. Braisted, *United States Navy in the Pacific, 1909–1922*, pp. 526–27. Coontz suggested in April 1921 that the State Department be represented on the Joint Army-Navy Board, but nothing came of it. Lawrence H. Douglas, "Robert Edward Coontz, 1 November 1919–21 July 1923," in Robert William Love, Jr., ed., *The Chiefs of Naval Operations* (Annapolis: Naval Institute Press, 1980), p. 29.

22. David J. Danelski and Joseph S. Tulchin, eds., *The Autobiographical Notes of Charles Evans Hughes* (Cambridge: Harvard University Press, 1973), p. 242.

23. Sprout and Sprout, *Toward a New Order of Sea Power*, pp. 100–117.

24. Response of General Board to Hughes, September 12, 1921. The Board

added, "It is not practicable to commute the combatant value of one class of ships into combatant value of another class for purposes of comparative measurement, even in the case of our own navy." Both of the board's statements can be found in Raymond G. O'Connor, "The 'Yardstick' and Naval Disarmament in the 1920's," in O'Connor, *War, Diplomacy, and History: Papers and Review* (N.p.: University Press of America, 1979), p. 104.

25. Braisted, *United States Navy in the Pacific, 1909–1922*, pp. 582–88.

26. Gerald E. Wheeler, *Prelude to Pearl Harbor: The United States Navy and the Far East, 1921–1931* (Columbia: University of Missouri Press, 1963), p. 56.

27. Robert Albion reported what he called "one of the most amazing incidents in the history of the Navy Department," when civilian pressure in the person of Assistant Secretary Theodore Roosevelt, Jr., appeared before the General Board and told it either to cut down its figures *"or we will tear the heart out of your Navy."* Robert G. Albion, *Makers of Naval Policy, 1798–1947*, ed. Rowena Reed (Annapolis: Naval Institute Press, 1980), p. 230, emphasis in original.

28. The observer was the British correspondent Charles Repington, *After the War* (Boston: Houghton Mifflin, 1922), p. 432, cited in Thomas H. Buckley, *The United States and the Washington Conference, 1921–1922* (Knoxville: University of Tennessee Press, 1970), p. 73. Hughes's conclusion is in Merlo J. Pusey, *Charles Evans Hughes*, vol. 2 (New York: Columbia University Press, 1963), p. 471. Additional details on the formulation of the American position may be found in J. Kenneth McDonald, "The Washington Conference and the Naval Balance of Power," in John B. Hattendorf and Robert S. Jordan, eds., *Maritime Strategy and the Balance of Power: Britain and America in the Twentieth Century* (New York: St. Martin's Press, 1989), pp. 199–213.

29. Root is quoted in Braisted, *United States Navy in the Pacific, 1909–1922*, p. 595.

30. Comment made in March 1921, cited in Dingman, *Power in the Pacific*, p. 121.

31. Braisted, *United States Navy in the Pacific, 1909–1922*, p. 569.

32. Wm. Roger Louis, *British Strategy in the Far East, 1919–1939* (Oxford: Clarendon Press, 1971), pp. 49, 105, 108.

33. Kimitada Miwa, "Japanese Images of War with the United States," in Akira Iriye, ed., *Mutual Images: Essays in American-Japanese Relations* (Cambridge: Harvard University Press, 1975), pp. 117–18.

34. This was known as the Five Power Treaty because France and Italy also agreed to limit their capital ships. Harlow Hyde observed in 1988: "This treaty was, and still is, the only multilateral arms limitation and disarmament agreement which was ever signed, ratified, and implemented in all of human history." Hyde, *Scraps of Paper: The Disarmament Treaties Between the World Wars* (Lincoln, Neb.: Media, 1988), p. 98.

35. Asada Sadao, "The Japanese Navy and the United States," in Dorothy Borg and Shumpei Okamoto, eds., *Pearl Harbor as History: Japanese-American Relations, 1931–1941* (New York: Columbia University Press, 1973), p. 237.

36. Daniels, *Wilson Era*, p. 587.

37. Braisted, *United States Navy in the Pacific, 1909–1922*, p. 670.

38. Dudley W. Knox, *The Eclipse of American Sea Power* (New York: American Army and Navy Journal, 1922), pp. vii, 136–37.

39. Brian McKercher, "Wealth, Power, and the New International Order: Britain and the American Challenge in the 1920s," *Diplomatic History* 12: 4 (Fall 1988): 425–27.

40. Hall, *Britain, America and Arms Control*, pp. 201, 218. Economically and politically, the British could not have sustained a capital-ship race. Stephen Roskill, *Naval Policy Between the Wars*: vol. 1, *The Period of Anglo-American Antagonism, 1919–1929* (London: Collins, 1968), p. 330.

41. Knox, *Eclipse of American Sea Power*, p. 137.

42. Edwin Denby, "Annual Report of the Secretary of the Navy," in *Annual Reports of the Navy Department for the Fiscal Year 1922* (Washington, D.C.: GPO, 1923), p. 1.

43. Gerald W. Wheeler, *Admiral William Veazie Pratt, U.S. Navy* (Washington, D.C.: Department of the Navy, 1974), pp. 185–86.

44. Denby, "Annual Report," pp. 1–2.

CHAPTER 6

1. Edwin Denby, "Annual Report of the Secretary of the Navy," in *Annual Reports of the Navy Department for the Fiscal Year 1922* (Washington, D.C.: GPO, 1923), pp. 1–2.

2. William V. Pratt, "Naval Policy and Its Relation to World Politics," United States Naval Institute *Proceedings* (hereafter *Proceedings*) 49: 7 (July 1923): 1083.

3. Jeffery M. Dorwart, *Conflict of Duty: The U.S. Navy's Intelligence Dilemma, 1919–1945* (Annapolis: Naval Institute Press, 1983), p. 22.

4. Lecture given by Captain Frank H. Schofield, October 14, 1922, at the Postgraduate School of the United States Naval Academy, entitled "The General Board and the Building Programs." Record Group 8, Naval War College Archives.

5. See Robert Gordon Kaufman, *Arms Control During the Pre-Nuclear Era: The United States and Naval Limitation Between the Two World Wars* (New York: Columbia University Press, 1990), pp. 83–88, 197–98.

6. A. P. Niblack, "By-products of the Washington Conference," in Sir Alexander Richardson and Archibald Hurd, eds., *Brassey's Naval and Shipping Annual, 1926* (London: Clowes, n.d.), p. 108.

7. Gerald E. Wheeler, *Prelude to Pearl Harbor: The United States Navy and the Far East, 1921–1931* (Columbia: University of Missouri Press, 1963), p. 116.

8. Norman Friedman, *U.S. Cruisers: An Illustrated Design History* (Annapolis: Naval Institute Press, 1984), p. 111.

9. Wheeler, *Prelude to Pearl Harbor*, p. 141. Jones's political myopia is confirmed in William F. Trimble, "Admiral Hilary P. Jones and the 1927 Geneva Naval Conference," *Military Affairs* 43: 1 (Feb. 1979): 1–4.

10. Ernest Andrade, Jr., "The Cruiser Controversy in Naval Limitations Negotiations, 1922–1936," *Military Affairs* 48: 3 (July 1984): 115.

11. Stephen Roskill, *Naval Policy Between the Wars*: vol. 1, *The Period of Anglo-American Antagonism, 1919–1929* (London: Collins, 1968), p. 516. See also Brian

McKercher, "Wealth, Power, and the New International Order: Britain and the American Challenge in the 1920s," *Diplomatic History* 12: 4 (Fall 1988): 436–38; Richard W. Fanning, "The Coolidge Conference of 1927: Disarmament in Disarray," in B. J. C. McKercher, ed., *Arms Limitation and Disarmament: Restraints on War, 1899–1939* (Westport: Praeger, 1992), pp. 105–27. And, for some other areas of contention, Kaufman, *Arms Control During the Pre-Nuclear Era*, p. 111.

12. David Carlton stressed the American concern that British merchantmen could be fitted with the 6-inch guns. Carlton, "Great Britain and the Coolidge Naval Disarmament Conference of 1927," *Political Science Quarterly* 83: 4 (Dec. 1968): 582, 597.

13. Gerald Wheeler makes this assessment in *Prelude to Pearl Harbor*, pp. 123–29, 150.

14. William R. Braisted, "Charles Frederick Hughes, 14 November 1927–17 September 1930," in Robert William Love, Jr., ed., *The Chiefs of Naval Operations* (Annapolis: Naval Institute Press, 1980), p. 54.

15. Cited in Melvyn P. Leffler, "1921–1932: Expansionist Impulses and Domestic Constraints," in William H. Becker and Samuel F. Wells, Jr., eds., *Economics and World Power: An Assessment of American Diplomacy Since 1789* (New York: Columbia University Press, 1984), p. 237. See also William R. Braisted, "On the American Red and Red-Orange Plans, 1919–1939," in Gerald Jordan, ed., *Naval Warfare in the Twentieth Century, 1900–1945: Essays in Honour of Arthur Marder* (London: Croom Helm, 1977), pp. 167–85.

16. Michael Vlahos offers an imaginative essay on the Navy's corporate psychology which maintains that Mahan gave the Navy a "subliminal sensation of maritime inferiority" toward the Royal Navy, a sensation that it worked out through rhetoric and war games (as well as ship modernization) in the 1920s. Vlahos, *The Blue Sword: The Naval War College and the American Mission, 1919–1941* (Newport: Naval War College Press, 1980), pp. 99–112, quotation on p. 107.

17. Kaufman, *Arms Control During the Pre-Nuclear Era*, pp. 99–106; Stephen Roskill, *Naval Policy Between the Wars*: vol. 2, *The Period of Reluctant Rearmament, 1930–1939* (Annapolis: Naval Institute Press, 1976), p. 27.

18. George T. Davis, *A Navy Second to None: The Development of Modern American Naval Policy* (New York: Harcourt, Brace, 1940), p. 329.

19. Herbert Hoover, *The Memoirs of Herbert Hoover: The Cabinet and the Presidency, 1920–1933* (New York: Macmillan, 1952), p. 338.

20. Henry L. Stimson and McGeorge Bundy, *On Active Service in Peace and War* (New York: Harper & Brothers, 1948), p. 506. At the same time, Stimson recognized, as most Navy officers averred, that the "doctrine of parity between the American and British fleets which was adopted by the Washington Conference in 1922 was not a military doctrine but a doctrine of statesmanship." Quoted by Gregory C. Kennedy, "The 1930 London Naval Conference and Anglo-American Maritime Strength, 1927–1930," in McKercher, ed., *Arms Limitation and Disarmament*, p. 163.

21. Rear Admiral W. V. Pratt, "Naval Policy and Its Relation to World Politics," *Proceedings* 49: 7 (July 1923): 1084.

22. Gerald E. Wheeler, "Naval Diplomacy in the Interwar Years," in Richard

A. von Doenhoff, ed., *Versatile Guardian: Research in Naval History* (Washington, D.C.: Howard University Press, 1979), pp. 45–46; Craig Symonds, "William Veazie Pratt," in Love, ed., *Chiefs of Naval Operations*, pp. 76–77.

23. For arguments developed later in favor of light cruisers with the 6-inch guns, see Friedman, *U.S. Cruisers*, pp. 165–67, in the chapter "The London Treaty of 1930: Admiral Pratt's Navy."

24. Kennedy, "1930 London Naval Conference," p. 157; McKercher, "Wealth, Power, and the New International Order," p. 440; B. J. C. McKercher, "'Our Most Dangerous Enemy': Great Britain Preeminent in the 1930s," *International History Review* 13: 4 (Nov. 1991): 765.

25. Gerald E. Wheeler, *Admiral William Veazie Pratt: A Sailor's Life* (Washington, D.C.: Department of the Navy, 1974), p. 308.

26. Stimson and Bundy, *On Active Service in Peace and War*, p. 174. See also Elting E. Morison, *Turmoil and Tradition: A Study of the Life and Times of Henry L. Stimson* (Boston: Houghton Mifflin, 1960), p. 336.

27. Raymond O'Connor suggests that Hoover may also have seen Japan as a bulwark against Soviet aggression in China, thanks to Japan's acknowledgment of the territorial integrity of China. O'Connor, *Perilous Equilibrium: The United States and the London Naval Conference of 1930* (Lawrence: University of Kansas Press, 1962), p. 83.

28. Michael A. Barnhart, "Japanese Intelligence Before the Second World War: 'Best Case' Analysis," in Ernest R. May, ed., *Knowing One's Enemies: Intelligence Assessment Before the Two World Wars* (Princeton: Princeton University Press, 1984), p. 451.

29. For a review of the opposition see Sadao Asada, "The Revolt Against the Washington Treaty: The Imperial Japanese Navy and Naval Limitation, 1921–1927," *Naval War College Review* 46: 3 (Summer 1993): 82–97.

30. Sterling Tatsuji Takeuchi, "Japan and the London Naval Treaty," *Institute of Oriental Students*, vol. 4 (N.p., 1930). The political quarrel is detailed in Tatsuo Kobayashi, "The London Naval Treaty, 1930," trans. Arthur E. Tiedman, in James William Morley, ed., *Japan's Road to the Pacific War. Japan Erupts: The London Naval Conference and the Manchurian Incident, 1928–1932* (New York: Columbia University Press, 1984), pp. 3–118 and in the introduction by Tiedman. For the views of the moderate, protreaty, and internationalist last *genro* in Japan, see Thomas F. Mayer-Oakes, trans., *Fragile Victory: Prince Saionji and the 1930 London Treaty Issue from the Memoirs of Baron Harada Kumao* (Detroit: Wayne State University Press, 1968); and Sadao Asada, "The Japanese Navy and the United States," in Dorothy Borg and Shumpei Okamoto, eds., *Pearl Harbor as History: Japanese-American Relations, 1931–1941* (New York: Columbia University Press, 1973), pp. 225–33.

CHAPTER 7

1. Waldo H. Heinrichs, Jr., "The Role of the United States Navy," in Dorothy Borg and Shumpei Okamoto, eds., *Pearl Harbor as History: Japanese-American Relations, 1931–1941* (New York: Columbia University Press, 1973), p. 205.

2. For a critical assessment at the theater level, see James O. Richardson, *On*

the Treadmill to Pearl Harbor: The Memoirs of Admiral James O. Richardson, ed. George C. Dyer (Washington, D.C.: Department of the Navy, 1973), pp. 254–95.

3. Louis Morton, "War Plane ORANGE: Evolution of a Strategy," *World Politics* 11: 2 (Jan. 1959): 241–42. The full story of War Plan Orange is told in Edward S. Miller, *War Plan Orange: The U.S. Strategy to Defeat Japan, 1897–1945* (Annapolis: Naval Institute Press, 1991).

4. James S. Thomson, Jr., "The Role of the Department of State," in Borg and Okamoto, eds., *Pearl Harbor as History*, pp. 81–106; Michael A. Barnhart, *Japan Prepares for Total War: The Search for Economic Security, 1919–1941* (Ithaca: Cornell University Press, 1987), pp. 52–55, 59–62, 216–17.

5. Cited in Christopher Throne, *The Limits of Foreign Policy: The West, the League, and the Far Eastern Crisis of 1931–1933* (London: Hamish Hamilton, 1972), p. 61. For a revealing discussion of Japan's intervention in China in the 1920s, an account that notes the intervention was impelled more by the emergence of perceived threats to Japanese interests than by the failure of other powers to coordinate their policies of opposition, see Arthur Waldron's introduction and John MacMurray's memorandum in Arthur Waldron, ed., *How the Peace Was Lost: The 1935 Memorandum "Developments Affecting American Policy in the Far East" Prepared for the State Department by John Van Antwerp MacMurray* (Stanford: Hoover Institution Press, 1992), pp. 53–54, 64.

6. Herbert Hoover, *The Memoirs of Herbert Hoover: The Cabinet and the Presidency, 1920–1933* (New York: Macmillan, 1952), pp. 367–68.

7. Russell F. Weigley, "The Role of the War Department and the Army," in Borg and Okamoto, eds., *Pearl Harbor as History*, p. 171.

8. Ray Lyman Wilbur and Arthur Mastick Hyde, *The Hoover Policies* (New York: Scribner's, 1937), p. 617.

9. See John F. Shiner, "The Air Corps, the Navy, and Coast Defense, 1919–1941," *Military Affairs* 45: 3 (Oct. 1981): 113–21.

10. On the positions of Pratt and Adams, see Gerald E. Wheeler, "Charles Francis Adams, 5 March 1929–4 March 1933," in Paolo E. Coletta, ed., *American Secretaries of the Navy*: vol. 2, *1913–1972* (Annapolis: Naval Institute Press, 1980), pp. 633–50; Gerald E. Wheeler, *Admiral William Veazie Pratt, U.S. Navy: A Sailor's Life* (Washington, D.C.: Department of the Navy, 1974), pp. 327–62; Craig L. Symonds, "William Veazie Pratt, 17 September 1930–30 June 1933," in Robert William Love, Jr., ed., *The Chiefs of Naval Operations* (Annapolis: Naval Institute Press, 1980), pp. 69–86.

11. Symonds, "William Veazie Pratt," p. 81.

12. Thomas C. Hone and Mark David Mandeles, "Managerial Style in the Interwar Navy: An Appraisal," *Naval War College Review* 33: 5 (Sept.–Oct. 1980): 91.

13. Michael Vlahos, *The Blue Sword: The Naval War College and the American Mission, 1919–1941* (Newport: Naval War College Press, 1980), p. 118.

14. Stephen E. Pelz, *Race to Pearl Harbor: The Failure of the Second London Naval Conference and the Onset of World War II* (Cambridge: Harvard University Press, 1974), pp. 25–40; Asada Sadao, "The Japanese Navy and the United States," in Borg and Okamoto, eds., *Pearl Harbor as History*, pp. 225–59.

15. My discussion of the Army follows the superb chapter by Russell F. Weigley, "The Role of the War Department and the Army," pp. 165–95. A well-documented account of the Army's "Strategical Plan Orange" is in Dana George Mede, "United States Peacetime Strategic Planning, 1920–1941: The Color Plans to the Victory Program" (Ph.D. diss., Massachusetts Institute of Technology, 1967). Specimen Joint Board documents are reproduced in Steven T. Ross, ed., *American War Plans, 1919–1941*, vol. 2, *Plans for War Against the British Empire and Japan: The Red, Orange, and Red-Orange Plans, 1923–1938* (New York: Garland, 1992).

16. Japan's naval intelligence monitored the exercise from a disguised tanker, collecting signals from which analysts broke the Navy code. Edward J. Drea, "Reading Each Other's Mail: Japanese Communication Intelligence, 1920–1941," *Journal of Military History* 55: 2 (Apr. 1991): 188–90.

17. Louis Morton, "War Plan ORANGE," p. 237. Morton's pioneering study is based on the planning of the Joint Board and on Army records. Both the Navy and the Army worked from the Joint Board's basic document. See also Charles M. Melhorn, *Two-Block Fox: The Rise of the Aircraft Carrier, 1911–1929* (Annapolis: Naval Institute Press, 1974), p. 103.

18. This is an example of a situation in which the Navy could "veto" or offset Army reservations on the Joint Board. Heinrichs, "Role of the United States Navy," p. 209.

19. Michael Vlahos, "Wargaming, an Enforcer of Strategic Realism: 1919–1942," *Naval War College Review* 39: 2 (Mar.–Apr. 1986): 7–22; Michael Vlahos, "The Naval War College and the Origins of War-Planning Against Japan," *Naval War College Review* 33: 4 (July–Aug. 1980): 23–37; Pelz, *Race to Pearl Harbor*, p. 198.

20. Robert Gordon Kaufman, *Arms Control During the Pre-Nuclear Era: The United States and Naval Limitation Between the Two World Wars* (New York: Columbia University Press, 1990), pp. 102–8. An emphatic claim that Japan did not establish shore installations on those islands before 1941 is made in Masatake Okumiya, "For Sugar Boats or Submarines?" *United States Naval Institute Proceedings* (hereafter *Proceedings*) 94: 8 (Aug. 1968): 63–73.

21. Jeter A. Isely and Philip A. Crowl, *The U.S. Marines and Amphibious War: Its Theory, and Its Practice in the Pacific* (Princeton: Princeton University Press, 1951), pp. 14–71.

22. Morton, "War Plan ORANGE," pp. 241–43.

23. Louis Morton, *Strategy and Command: The First Two Years* (Washington, D.C.: Department of the Army, 1962), p. 39; John Major, "William Daniel Leahy, 2 January 1937–1 August 1939," in Love, ed., *Chiefs of Naval Operations*, p. 105.

24. Morton, "War Plan ORANGE," p. 241.

25. Ronald Spector, *Eagle Against the Sun: The American War with Japan* (New York: Free Press, 1984), p. 57.

26. Hone and Mandeles, "Managerial Style in the Interwar Navy," pp. 88–90, 98. It has been suggested that the Navy too was lukewarm to Orange because of the plan's unresolved problems but held on to it during the second half of the 1930s largely to keep open other strategic possibilities in the Pacific, such as linking up with the British navy in a war against Japan.

27. Michael Vlahos looked at 136 war games and chart maneuvers played during this period at the Naval War College. Of these, 127 simulated a war with Japan. Vlahos, *Blue Sword*, p. 143. Heinrichs quotes a graduate who claimed that in the 1930s the War College substituted a Red game every now and then "just to be able to say we weren't always fighting the Orange Fleet." Heinrichs, "Role of the United States Navy," p. 203. See also Vlahos, "Wargaming, an Enforcer of Strategic Realism."

28. Edward S. Miller, "War Plan Orange, 1897–1941: The Blue Thrust Through the Pacific," in William B. Cogar, ed., *Naval History: The Seventh Symposium of the U.S. Naval Academy* (Wilmington: Scholarly Resources, 1988), p. 246.

29. Morton, "War Plan ORANGE," pp. 247–48.

30. Allison Saville, "Claude Augustus Swanson, 4 March 1933–7 July 1939," in Coletta, ed., *American Secretaries of the Navy*: vol. 2, *1913–1972*, p. 658.

31. Claude A. Swanson, *Annual Report of the Secretary of the Navy for the Fiscal Year 1933* (Washington, D.C.: GPO, 1933), p. 2.

32. For the political context of these shipbuilding decisions, and a good study of the Navy Department's own varied interests, see Robert H. Levine, "The Politics of American Naval Rearmament, 1930–1938" (Ph.D. diss., Harvard University, 1972).

33. Congress's role in these events is discussed in John C. Walter, "The Navy Department and the Campaign for Expanded Appropriations, 1933–1938" (Ph.D. diss., University of Maine at Orono, 1972).

34. Thomas C. Hone, "The Navy, Industrial Recovery, and Mobilization Preparedness, 1933–1940," paper prepared for the 1990 meeting of the American Military Institute, Washington, D.C., pp. 1–31.

35. So Roosevelt told his arms control negotiator, delegate Norman Davis, who is quoted in Dorothy Borg, *The United States and the Far Eastern Crisis of 1933–1938* (Cambridge: Harvard University Press, 1964), p. 103.

36. Akira Iriye, *The Origins of the Second World War in Asia and the Pacific* (London: Longman, 1987), pp. 27–28.

37. Pelz, *Race to Pearl Harbor*, pp. 32–40; Yôichi Hirama, "Japanese Naval Preparations for World War II," *Naval War College Review* 44: 2 (Spring 1991): 63–75; Asada Sadao, "The Japanese Navy and the United States," pp. 235–42; Asada Sadao, "Japanese Admirals and the Politics of Naval Limitation: Katō Tomosaburō vs. Katō Kanji," in Gerald Jordan, ed., *Naval Warfare in the Twentieth Century, 1900–1945: Essays in Honour of Arthur Marder* (London: Croom Helm, 1977), pp. 141–66.

38. Pelz, *Race to Pearl Harbor*, pp. 172–77. Concise, reliable interpretations of the change in 1936 are found in Iriye, *Origins of the Second World War*, pp. 34–35; and Waldo H. Heinrichs, Jr., "1931–1937," in Ernest R. May and James C. Thomson, Jr., eds., *American–East Asian Relations: A Survey* (Cambridge: Harvard University Press, 1972), p. 245.

39. Manny T. Koginos, *The Panay Incident: Prelude to War* (Lafayette: Purdue University Studies, 1967), p. 57; W. D. Leahy, *I Was There* (New York: McGraw-Hill, 1950), pp. 64, 128. The idea of a U.S.-British naval quarantine of Japan, in part to watch for any southward movement of Japanese forces, foundered on

British refusal to participate. John McVickar Haight, Jr., "Franklin D. Roosevelt and a Naval Quarantine of Japan," *Pacific Historical Review* 40: 2 (May 1971): 203–26.

40. Calvin W. Enders, "The Vinson Navy" (Ph.D. diss., Michigan State University, 1970), pp. 106–9.

41. Roosevelt's quotations are cited in Walter, "The Navy Department," pp. 306–7. See also Levine, "Politics of American Naval Rearmament," pp. 484–87.

42. All depended on the sense of threat and urgency. Robert Albion noted that in the late 1930s the country could have paid all of its national defense bills with the taxes it was drawing from the sales of tobacco and liquor. When war came, of course, there was plenty of money. In the last year of the war, the Navy budget was twice the entire cost of the U.S. Navy from 1798 to 1939. Robert Greenhaigh Albion, *Makers of Naval Policy, 1798–1947* (Annapolis: Naval Institute Press, 1980), pp. 113–14.

43. Hone and Mandeles, "Managerial Style in the Interwar Navy"; Hone, "The Navy, Industrial Recovery, and Mobilization Preparedness"; Thomas C. Hone, "Fighting on Our Own Ground: The War of Production, 1920–1942," *Naval War College Review* 45: 2 (Spring 1992): 93–107.

44. Malcolm Muir, Jr., "The United States Navy in World War II: An Assessment," in James J. Sadkovich, ed., *Reevaluating Major Naval Combatants of World War II* (New York: Greenwood, 1990), p. 2.

45. Ronald Spector, "The Military Effectiveness of the U.S. Armed Forces, 1919–1939," in Allan R. Millett and Williamson Murray, eds., *Military Effectiveness*: vol. 2, *The Interwar Period* (Boston: Allen & Unwin, 1988), p. 84.

46. John H. Maurer, "Fuel and the Battle Fleet: Coal, Oil, and American Naval Strategy, 1898–1925," *Naval War College Review* 34: 6 (Nov.–Dec. 1981): 73–74; Philip T. Rosen, "The Treaty Navy, 1919–1937," in Kenneth J. Hagen, ed., *In Peace and War: Interpretations of American Naval History, 1775–1984*, 2d ed. (Westport: Greenwood Press, 1984), pp. 223–24.

47. Design issues and their operational implications are covered best in Norman Friedman, *U.S. Battleships: An Illustrated Design History* (Annapolis: Naval Institute Press, 1985), chaps. 10–14. An assessment of these issues is given in Thomas C. Hone, "The Destruction of the Battle Line at Pearl Harbor," *Proceedings* 103: 12 (Dec. 1977): 49–59.

48. Laurence F. Safford, "A Brief History of Communications Intelligence in the United States," in Ronald H. Spector, ed., *Listening to the Enemy: Key Documents on the Role of Communications Intelligence in the War with Japan* (Wilmington: Scholarly Resources, 1988), p. 9.

49. John C. Reilly, Jr., *United States Navy Destroyers of World War II* (Poole: Blandford Press, 1983), p. 7.

50. For the argument of good management, see Thomas C. Hone, "Spending Patterns of the United States Navy, 1921–1941," *Armed Forces and Society* 8: 3 (Spring 1982): 443–62; Hone and Mandeles, "Managerial Style in the Interwar Navy"; Thomas C. Hone, "The Effectiveness of the 'Washington Treaty' Navy," *Naval War College Review* 32: 6 (Nov.–Dec. 1979): 35–59.

51. Isely and Crowl, *The U.S. Marines and Amphibious War*, pp. 14–71.

52. *U.S. Naval Administration in World War II: BUORD. Naval Torpedo Station, Newport, Rhode Island*: vol. 3 (Washington, D.C.: Department of the Navy, n.d.), pp. i–vii; Luther G. Ingram, Jr., "Deficiencies of the United States Submarine Torpedo in the Pacific Theatre: World War II" (M.A. thesis, San Diego State University, 1978); Department of the Navy, Office of Naval Research, *History of United States Research and Development in World War II* (Washington, D.C.: Department of the Navy, n.d.), pp. 921–37; Muir, "United States Navy in World War II," p. 3.

53. That development was not all-purpose proves the Pacific focus. At least one design type, the top-heavy *Sims*-class destroyer, was ill-suited to the stormy North Atlantic.

54. Hone, "Effectiveness of the 'Washington Treaty' Navy," p. 56.

55. Figures and analysis are given in Thomas C. Hone, "Battleships vs. Aircraft Carriers: The Patterns of U.S. Navy Operating Expenditures, 1932–1941," *Military Affairs* 41: 3 (Oct. 1977): 133–41.

56. Gerald H. Wheeler, "Comments," in Arnold R. Shapack, ed., *The Navy in an Age of Change and Crisis: Some Challenges and Responses of the Twentieth Century* (Annapolis: United States Naval Academy, 1973), p. 15.

57. W. J. Jurens, "The Evolution of Battleship Gunnery in the U.S. Navy, 1920–1945," *Warship International* 28: 3 (Sept. 1991): 264–65.

58. Admiral William H. Standley, "Naval Aviation, an Evolution of Naval Gunfire," *Proceedings* 73: 3 (Mar. 1952): 251–55. See also Edward L. Beach, *The United States Navy: 200 Years* (New York: Holt, 1986), pp. 430–36.

59. Wheeler, "Comments," p. 16; Richard K. Smith, *The Airships* Akron & Macon: *Flying Aircraft Carriers of the United States Navy* (Annapolis: Naval Institute Press, 1965).

60. Ernest Andrade, Jr., "Operational Innovators: Admirals Reeves and Moffett," in Shapack, ed., *Navy in an Age of Change*, pp. 7–13; Stephen Peter Rosen, "New Ways of War: Understanding Military Innovation," *International Security* 13: 1 (Summer 1988): 154. For a good study of one of the pioneer carrier aviation strategists, see Clark G. Reynolds, *Admiral John H. Towers: The Struggle for Naval Air Supremacy* (Annapolis: Naval Institute Press, 1991).

61. Thomas C. Hone, "Seapower: From Ideology to Technology," paper delivered at the annual meeting of the American Historical Association in San Francisco, 1989, p. 11.

62. Thomas C. Hone and Mark D. Mandeles, "Interwar Innovation in Three Navies: U.S. Navy, Royal Navy, Imperial Japanese Navy," *Naval War College Review* 40: 2 (Spring 1987): 72.

63. Edward Arpee, *From Frigates to Flat-Tops* (n.p. 1953), p. 121.

64. Eugene E. Wilson, *Slipstream: The Autobiography of an Air Craftsman* (New York: McGraw-Hill, 1950), p. 148. See also pp. 377–411 of "The Gift of Foresight," the 1962 interview of Wilson for the Columbia University Oral History Research Office's Naval History Project.

65. Recent commentaries on this exercise are found in Melhorn, *Two-Block Fox*, pp. 113–15; Norman Polmar, *Aircraft Carriers* (Garden City: Doubleday,

1969), pp. 54–60; and Scot MacDonald, *Evolution of Aircraft Carriers* (Washington, D.C.: GPO, for the Department of the Navy, 1964), p. 33.

66. See Norman Friedman, *U.S. Aircraft Carriers: An Illustrated Design History* (Annapolis: Naval Institute Press, 1983), pp. 116–18, for the 1938 comments of Admiral Robert Ghormley, who was looking at the situation from the perspective of the War Plans Division, not from that of the Bureau of Aeronautics.

67. Gary E. Weir, *Building American Submarines, 1914–1940* (Washington, D.C.: Naval Historical Center, 1991), pp. 23–46.

68. Cited in Samuel E. Morison, *Coral Sea, Midway and Submarine Actions, May 1942–August 1942* (Boston: Little, Brown, 1950), pp. 189–90.

69. For details see John D. Alden, *The Fleet Submarine of the U.S. Navy: A Design and Construction History* (Annapolis: Naval Institute Press, 1979), pp. 58–75, 101–9. For a size comparison, the current *Los Angeles* class nuclear attack boat displaces almost 7,000 tons submerged; the ballistic-missile-carrying *Trident* displaces 18,700 tons. The former-Soviet Typhoon class displaces 25,000 tons.

CHAPTER 8

1. Waldo Heinrichs, *Threshold of War: Franklin D. Roosevelt and American Entry into World War II* (New York: Oxford University Press, 1988), p. 11.

2. Leahy's comment from Adm. William D. Leahy, "Annual Report of the Chief of Naval Operations for the Fiscal Year 1939" (Washington, D.C., 1939), p. 1. Typescript, Navy Department Library, Naval Historical Center, Washington, D.C. Pratt's prediction is from Fletcher Pratt, *Sea Power and Today's War* (New York: Harrison-Hilton, 1939), p. 237.

3. Stetson Conn and Byron Fairchild, *The Framework of Hemisphere Defense* (Washington, D.C.: Department of the Army, 1960), pp. 14–16, 410–13. Francis MacDonnell, "The Search for a Second Zimmermann Telegram: FDR, BSC, and the Latin American Front," *International Journal of Intelligence and Counterintelligence* 4: 4 (Winter 1990): 487–505, shows the hand of British intelligence in exaggerating the sense of imminent threat and its role in concocting the "secret map" used by Roosevelt in his Navy Day message of October 1941, in which he declared that the United States had a direct security stake in the war in Europe.

4. See David G. Haglund, "George C. Marshall and the Question of Military Aid to England, May–June 1940," *Journal of Contemporary History* 15: 4 (Oct. 1980): 745–60. The broader question of "Aid to Britain Versus Rearming of America" is discussed in the chapter of that title in Mark Skinner Watson, *Chief of Staff: Prewar Plans and Preparations* (Washington, D.C.: Department of the Army, 1950).

5. Conn and Fairchild, *The Framework of Hemisphere Defense*, p. 67.

6. William L. Langer and S. Everett Gleason, *The Challenge to Isolation, 1937–1940* (New York: Harper, 1952), p. 756.

7. Robert Dallek, *Franklin D. Roosevelt and American Foreign Poli*
(New York: Oxford University Press, 1979), p. 530.

8. Chairman of the General Board to Secretary of the Navy, "A
II," July 1, 1940, G.B. No. 425 (Serial No. 1959), Microfilm Record

Board, U.S. Naval War College Archives. The first "Are We Ready," of September 9, 1939, to which mention is made below, is filed as G.B. No. 425 (Serial No. 1868) and found in the same microfilm collection.

9. These quotations are from correspondence printed in *Pearl Harbor Attack: Hearings Before the Joint Committee on the Investigation of the Pearl Harbor Attack*, Congress of the United States, *Seventy-Ninth Congress*, First Sess. (Washington, D.C.: GPO, 1946), pt. 14, pp. 940, 968 (hereafter cited as *Pearl Harbor Attack Hearings*). Richardson's position, backed by his testimony at Congress's Pearl Harbor investigation, is found in his memoirs, James O. Richardson, *On the Treadmill to Pearl Harbor* (Washington, D.C.: Department of the Navy, 1973), pp. 307–33. The decision to keep the fleet at Hawaii is discussed in Robert J. Quinlan, "The United States Fleet: Diplomacy, Strategy, and the Allocation of Ships (1940–1941)," in Harold Stein, ed., *American Civil-Military Decisions* (University, Ala.: University of Alabama Press, 1963), pp. 153–201.

10. *Pearl Harbor Attack Hearings*, pt. 14, p. 943.

11. Quotations from Richardson's correspondence to Stark and Knox from ibid., pp. 957–58, 968–69, and Richardson, *On the Treadmill to Pearl Harbor*, p. 318.

12. Quoted in Jonathan G. Utley, *Going to War with Japan, 1937–1941* (Knoxville: University of Tennessee Press, 1985), p. 112.

13. Richardson's report of his conversation with Roosevelt is in his *On the Treadmill to Pearl Harbor*, pp. 434–35, and in his testimony to Congress, which is printed in *Pearl Harbor Attack Hearings*, pt. 1, pp. 265–66.

14. Hosoya Chihiro, "The Tripartite Pact, 1939–1940," trans. James William Morley, in Morley, ed., *Deterrent Diplomacy: Japan, Germany, and the USSR, 1935–1940* (New York: Columbia University Press, 1976), p. 257.

15. The ambiguities of this pact are noted in Herbert Feis, *The Road to Pearl Harbor: The Coming of the War Between the United States and Japan* (Princeton: Princeton University Press, 1950), pp. 112–21.

16. Cited in Akira Iriye, *The Origins of the Second World War in Asia and the Pacific* (London: Longman, 1987), p. 116.

17. Maurice Matloff and Edwin M. Snell, *Strategic Planning for Coalition Warfare, 1941–1942* (Washington, D.C.: Department of the Army, 1953), p. 8. The Joint Board's May 1939 directive, "Basic War Plans, Rainbows Nos. 1, 2, 3 and 4," is reproduced in Steven T. Ross, ed., *American War Plans, 1919–1941*: vol. 3, *Plans to Meet the Axis Threat, 1939–1940* (New York: Garland, 1992), pp. 69–72.

18. Utley, *Going to War with Japan*, p. 102.

19. In October Roosevelt told the hawks, particularly Secretary of War Henry Stimson and Secretary of the Treasury Henry Morgenthau, that he and the secretary of state, not they, set the foreign policy of the United States. Feis, *Road to Pearl Harbor*, p. 124. Soon Roosevelt bypassed the State Department too.

20. Stark's memorandum is reproduced in the microfilm collection *Strategic Planning in the United States Navy: Its Evolution and Its Execution, 1891–1945* (Wilmington: Scholarly Resources, 1977), reel 5; and in Ross, ed., *Plans to Meet the Axis Threat*, pp. 225–50. See also Mark M. Lowenthal, "The Stark Memorandum and the American Security Process, 1940," in Robert William Love, Jr., ed., *Changing Interpretations and New Sources in Naval History* (New York: Garland,

1980), p. 356; and James R. Leutze, *Bargaining for Supremacy: Anglo-American Naval Collaboration, 1937–1941* (Chapel Hill: University of North Carolina Press, 1977), pp. 183–95.

21. Louis Morton, "Germany First: The Basic Concept of Allied Strategy in World War II," in Kent R. Greenfield, ed., *Command Decisions* (New York: Harcourt, Brace, 1959), p. 26.

22. Stark's memorandum is well discussed in Morton, "Germany First," pp. 24–29; and in Matloff and Snell, *Strategic Planning*, pp. 25–28.

23. So notes Iriye, *Origins of the Second World War*, pp. 122–23.

24. Adm. Thomas C. Hart, USN (Ret.), "The Reminiscences of Thomas C. Hart," p. 92, Columbia University Oral History Research Office, 1972), Archives, U.S. Naval War College.

25. Leutze, *Bargaining for Supremacy*, p. 241. A year before, when France was being invaded, Randolph Churchill visited his father's bedroom. The prime minister said, "Sit down, dear boy, and read the papers while I finish shaving." Randolph recorded: "After two or three minutes of hacking away, he [the Prime Minister] half turned and said: 'I think I see my way through.' He resumed his shaving. I was astounded, and said: 'Do you mean that we can avoid defeat? (which seemed credible) or beat the bastards' (which seemed incredible). He flung his Valet razor in to the basin, swung around and said:—'Of course I mean we can beat them.' " Randolph replied: " 'Well, I'm all for it, but I don't see how you can do it.' By this time he [the prime minister] had dried and sponged his face and turning round to me, said with great intensity:—'I shall drag the United States in.' " Martin Gilbert, *Winston S. Churchill*: vol. 4, *Finest Hour, 1939–1941* (Boston: Houghton Mifflin, 1983), p. 358.

26. Watson, *Chief of Staff*, p. 124; Matloff and Snell, *Strategic Planning*, pp. 45–46. ABC-1 is reproduced in Steven T. Ross, ed., *American War Plans, 1919–1941*: vol. 4, *Coalition War Plans and Hemisphere Defense Plans, 1940–1941* (New York: Garland, 1992), pp. 3–58.

27. Harold L. Ickes, *The Secret Diary of Harold L. Ickes*: vol. 3, *The Lowering Clouds* (New York: Simon & Schuster, 1954), p. 521.

28. Robert E. Sherwood, *Roosevelt and Hopkins, An Intimate History* (New York: Harper, 1948), p. 272.

29. Thomas B. Buell, *Master of Sea Power: A Biography of Fleet Admiral Ernest J. King* (Boston: Little, Brown, 1980), p. 125.

30. Chairman, General Board, to Secretary of the Navy, "Are We Ready—III," June 14, 1941, G.B. No. 425 (Serial No. 144), Microfilm Records of the General Board, Archives, U.S. Naval War College.

31. Waldo Heinrichs, "President Franklin D. Roosevelt's Intervention in the Battle of the Atlantic, 1941," *Diplomatic History* 10: 4 (Fall 1986): 314.

32. King's memorandum is printed in Samuel Eliot Morison, *The B[illegible] the Atlantic, September 1939–May 1943* (Boston: Little, Brown, 1950), pp.[illegible]

33. Ernest J. King and Walter Muir Whitehill, *Fleet Admiral Ki[illegible] Record* (New York: Norton, 1952), pp. 324–26, 339–40.

34. MacDonnell, "The Search for a Second Zimmermann Tele[illegible] 505, shows the fine hand of British intelligence in exaggerat[illegible]

South America and Roosevelt's use of its "secret map" in his Navy Day speech of October 1941 to signal to Americans that they had a direct security stake in the outcome of the war in Europe.

35. The complexity of coordinating convoy movement was considerable, and added to the strain on the Royal Navy. Between the gathering points on the American or Canadian seaboard on one side of the Atlantic and the Port of London on the other, four different escort groups might have responsibility for a convoy. S. W. Roskill, *The War at Sea, 1939–1945*: vol. 1, *The Defensive* (London: HMSO, 1954), p. 456.

36. Buell, *Master of Sea Power*, p. 127. See also Henry H. Adams, "The Neutrality Patrol and Other Belligerencies," in Richard A. von Doenhoff, ed., *Versatile Guardian: Research in Naval History* (Washington, D.C.: Howard University Press, 1979), pp. 211–25.

37. Heinrichs, *Threshold of War*, p. 90.

38. The quote is from Maurice Matloff, *President Roosevelt's Three Wars: FDR as War Leader* (Boulder: Air Force Academy, 1964), p. 2.

39. Heinrichs, *Threshold of War*, pp. 159, 179.

40. Gilbert, *Finest Hour*, p. 1168.

41. Warren F. Kimball, ed., *Churchill and Roosevelt: The Complete Correspondence*: vol. 1, *Alliance Emerging, October 1933–November 1942* (Princeton: Princeton University Press, 1984), pp. 229–30.

42. Thomas A. Bailey and Paul B. Ryan, *Hitler vs. Roosevelt: The Undeclared Naval War* (New York: Free Press, 1979), pp. 166, 209–10. In his memoirs, Churchill quotes the president: "I may never declare war; I may never make war. If I were to ask Congress to declare war, they might argue about it for three months." Winston S. Churchill, *The Grand Alliance* (Boston: Houghton Mifflin, 1950), p. 593.

43. Arthur J. Marder, *Old Friends, New Enemies: The Royal Navy and the Imperial Japanese Navy, Strategic Illusions, 1936–1941* (Oxford: Clarendon Press, 1981), p. 200.

44. William L. Langer and S. Everett Gleason, *The Undeclared War, 1940–1941* (New York: Harper, 1953), p. 666. See also Watson, *Chief of Staff*, pp. 386–410.

45. Patrick Abbazia, *Mr. Roosevelt's Navy: The Private War of the U.S. Atlantic Fleet, 1939–1942* (Annapolis: Naval Institute Press, 1975), pp. 305–7.

46. Langer and Gleason, *Undeclared War*, p. 748.

47. Dallek, *Franklin D. Roosevelt and American Foreign Policy*, pp. 291–92; MacDonnell, "The Search for a Second Zimmermann Telegram," p. 497.

48. Holger H. Herwig, *Politics of Frustration: The United States in German Naval Planning, 1889–1941* (Boston: Little, Brown, 1976), pp. 228–34; Roskill, *Defensive*, pp. 481–82; F. H. Hinsley et al., *British Intelligence in the Second World War: Its Influence on Strategy and Operations*, vol. 2 (London: HMSO, 1981), pp. 163, 178; Gilbert, *Finest Hour*, pp. 1146–47.

49. Roosevelt to Grew, January 21, 1941, quoted in Arnold A. Offner, *The Origins of the Second World War: American Foreign Policy and World Politics, 1917–1941* (New York: Holt, Rinehart and Winston, 1975), p. 193.

50. Heinrichs, *Threshold of War*, p. 131.

51. On Hornbeck and the State Department, see James C. Thomson, Jr., "The Role of the Department of State," in Dorothy Borg and Shumpei Okamoto, eds., *Pearl Harbor as History: Japanese-American Relations, 1931–1941* (New York: Columbia University Press, 1973), pp. 81–106; Michael Barnhart, "Hornbeck Was Right: A Realist Approach to American Policy Toward Japan," in Hilary Conroy and Harry Wray, eds., *Pearl Harbor Reexamined: Prologue to the Pacific War* (Honolulu: University of Hawaii Press, 1990), pp. 65–72.

52. Iriye, *Origins of the Second World War*, pp. 126–27.

53. The urgency of Japan's situation is shown in Stephen E. Pelz, *Race to Pearl Harbor: The Failure of the Second London Naval Conference and the Onset of World War II* (Cambridge: Harvard University Press, 1974), pp. 220–23.

54. Iriye suggests the Imperial Japanese Navy supported the occupation of southern Indochina to keep its influence alive. The proposed war with the Soviet Union was the army's affair and would clearly become the dominant strategic undertaking. An occupation of Indochina was, at the moment, the extent to which the navy's southern strategy could aspire. Akira Iriye, *Power and Culture: The Japanese-American War, 1941–1945* (Cambridge: Harvard University Press, 1981), p. 273.

55. Heinrichs, *Threshold of War*, p. 179; Waldo Heinrichs, "The Russian Factor in Japanese-American Relations, 1941," in Conroy and Wray, eds., *Pearl Harbor Reexamined*, pp. 163–77.

56. Ickes, *Lowering Clouds*, p. 567.

57. James H. Herzog, "Influence of the United States Navy in the Embargo of Oil to Japan, 1940–1941," *Pacific Historical Review* 35: 3 (Aug. 1966): 317–28.

58. Ickes, *Lowering Clouds*, p. 58.

59. Dallek, *Franklin D. Roosevelt and American Foreign Policy*, p. 275.

60. Iriye, *Origins of the Second World War*, p. 150. Michael Barnhart shows some of the effects of the prospect of a depleted oil supply and, even more, of the prospect of a lack of steel, on the deliberations of the Japanese military. Barnhart, *Japan Prepares for Total War: The Search for Economic Security, 1919–1941* (Ithaca: Cornell University Press, 1987), pp. 239–73.

61. Tsunoda Jun, "The Navy's Role in the Southern Strategy," trans. Robert A. Scalapino, in James William Morley, ed., *The Fateful Choice: Japan's Advance into Southeast Asia, 1939–1941* (New York: Columbia University Press, 1980), p. 242.

62. Kimitada Miwa, "Japanese Images of War with the United States," in Akira Iriye, ed., *Mutual Images: Essays in American-Japanese Relations* (Cambridge: Harvard University Press, 1975), pp. 119–20.

63. Pelz, *Race to Pearl Harbor*, p. 224, gives the Japanese study's conclusions. See also Michael Vlahos and Dale K. Pace, "War Experience and Force Requirements," *Naval War College Review* 41: 4 (Autumn 1988): 30–33.

64. Tsunoda Jun, "The Navy's Role in the Southern Strategy," p. 274.

65. Kimitada Miwa, "Japanese Images of War," p. 118. An alternative translation, by Gordon Prange, is "If I am told to fight regardless of the consequences, I shall run wild for the first six months or a year, but I have utterly no confidence for the second or third year." Gordon W. Prange, *At Dawn We Slept: The Untold Story of Pearl Harbor* (New York: McGraw-Hill, 1981), p. 10.

66. Asada Sadao, "The Japanese Navy and the United States," in Borg and Okamoto, eds., *Pearl Harbor as History*, p. 256.

67. Samuel Eliot Morison, *The Rising Sun in the Pacific, 1931–April 1942* (Boston: Little, Brown, 1948), pp. 51–52.

68. Kimmel's plan is treated most fully in Edward S. Miller, *War Plan Orange: The U.S. Strategy to Defeat Japan, 1897–1945* (Annapolis: Naval Institute Press, 1991), pp. 287–312. See also Miller, "War Plan Orange, 1897–1941: The Blue Thrust Through the Pacific," in William B. Cogar, ed., *Naval History: The Seventh Symposium at the U.S. Naval Academy* (Wilmington: Scholarly Resources, 1988), pp. 244–45; Miller, "Kimmel's Hidden Agenda," *Military History Quarterly* 4: 1 (Autumn 1991): 36–43; and Michael Slackman, *Target: Pearl Harbor* (Honolulu: University of Hawaii Press, 1990), pp. 154–55.

69. These words were used on November 1, 1941, to explain the Combined Fleet's Secret Operations Order No. 1, cited in Watson, *Chief of Staff*, p. 501.

70. Prange, *At Dawn We Slept*, pp. 9–29. The first blow had better succeed, Yamamoto knew, for the Japanese navy, long committed to the strategy of gradual attrition and surface warfare, would find it hard, and had almost no time, to adjust its planning and practices to the rapid shift in objectives and strategy. Yoji Koda, "A Commander's Dilemma: Admiral Yamamoto and the 'Gradual Attrition' Strategy," *Naval War College Review* 46: 4 (Autumn 1993): 63–74.

71. Dallek, *Franklin D. Roosevelt and American Foreign Policy*, p. 305.

72. Cordell Hull, *The Memoirs of Cordell Hull* (New York: Macmillan, 1948), p. 1015.

73. Report and reply in Langer and Gleason, *Undeclared War*, pp. 845–46.

74. Louis Morton, *The Fall of the Philippines* (Washington, D.C.: Department of the Army, 1953), pp. 45–50. As Clay Blair wrote, "Little by little most of the available fleet submarines were being siphoned off to carry out a mission for which they were not designed, coast defense of the Philippines." Clay Blair, Jr., *Silent Victory: The U.S. Submarine War Against Japan* (New York: Lippincott, 1975), p. 78.

75. Quotations of Stimson in Russell F. Weigley, "The Role of the War Department and the Army," in Borg and Okamoto, eds., *Pearl Harbor as History*, p. 183, and Prange, *At Dawn We Slept*, p. 292.

76. Heinrichs, *Threshold of War*, p. 130.

77. Morton, *Fall of the Philippines*, pp. 37–45.

78. Langer and Gleason, *Undeclared War*, p. 900. See also Feis, *Road to Pearl Harbor*, p. 321.

79. Utley, *Going to War with Japan*, pp. 165–82.

80. Hull's position is discussed in Lester H. Brune, "Considerations of Force in Cordell Hull's Diplomacy, July 26 to November 26, 1941," *Diplomatic History* 2: 4 (Fall 1978): 389–405; and Alvin D. Coox, "Repulsing the Pearl Harbor Revisionists: The State of Present Literature on the Debacle," *Military Affairs* 51: 1 (Jan. 1986): 30. The Stimson quote is from Feis, *Road to Pearl Harbor*, p. 321.

81. Weigley, "The Role of the War Department and the Army," pp. 185–86.

82. Ibid., p. 188.

83. Louis Morton, *Strategy and Command: The First Two Years* (Washington, D.C.: Department of the Army, 1962), p. 125.

84. Hart, "Reminiscences," p. 188. The question of whether war might have been avoided is the main theme of the eighteen papers by American and Japanese scholars collected in Conroy and Wray, eds., *Pearl Harbor Reexamined.*

85. Stimson preferred a preemptive strike against the Japanese convoys but was overruled. Japanese intelligence knew the weakness of Singapore, but we do not know how this information affected Japan's offensive plans, or if it did at all. Edward J. Drea, "Reading Each Other's Mail: Japanese Communication Intelligence, 1920–1941," *Journal of Military History* 55: 2 (Apr. 1991): 202–5.

86. Prange, *At Dawn We Slept,* p. 730. For a sense of how the threat was degraded by a denigration of Japanese fighting ability, by "the widespread view that the Japanese Navy was a standing joke," see Howard Young, "Racial Attitudes of the U.S. Navy's Unpreparedness for War with Japan," in Department of History, U.S. Naval Academy, ed., *New Aspects of Naval History* (Baltimore: Nautical and Aviation, 1985), pp. 177–81.

87. This, at any rate, is the burden of Rear Admiral Edwin T. Layton's defense of the Navy commands under Admiral Kimmel and Rear Admiral Claude Bloch. Edwin T. Layton with Roger Pineau and John Costello, *"And I Was There": Pearl Harbor and Midway—Breaking the Secrets* (New York: Morrow, 1985), pp. 161–68, 244–45.

88. David Kahn, "The United States Views Germany and Japan in 1941," in Ernest R. May, ed., *Knowing One's Enemies: Intelligence Assessment Before the Two World Wars* (Princeton: Princeton University Press, 1984), pp. 500–501. See also David Kahn, "Why Weren't We Warned?" *Military History Quarterly* 4: 1 (Autumn 1991): 59; and a responding letter by Richard Lehman in *Military History Quarterly* 4: 4 (Summer 1992): 6.

89. Admiral J. O. Richardson noted this point in *On the Treadmill to Pearl Harbor,* pp. 337–39.

90. This is Prange's conclusion, and it is indisputable. Prange, *At Dawn We Slept,* p. 731. A review of the many reasons behind the Army's unpreparedness is found in Watson, *Chief of Staff,* pp. 496–519; and in Leatrice R. Arakaki and John R. Kuborn, *7 December 1941: The Air Force Story* (Hickman Air Force Base: Pacific Air Forces, 1991).

91. John F. Shiner, "The Air Corps, the Navy, and Coast Defense, 1919–1941," *Military Affairs* 45: 3 (Oct. 1981): 119. For the argument that the intelligence failure was also the result of an almost complete lack of cooperation between the services, see Henry C. Clausen and Bruce Lee, *Pearl Harbor: Final Judgement* (New York: Crown, 1992).

CHAPTER 9

1. Dwight D. Eisenhower, *Crusade in Europe* (Garden City: Doubleday, 1951); Douglas MacArthur, *A Soldier Speaks* (New York: Praeger, 1965), p. 150.

2. Maurice Matloff and Edwin M. Snell, *Strategic Planning for Coalition Warfare, 1941–1942* (Washington, D.C.: Department of the Army, 1953), p. 380.

3. Edward L. Beach, *The United States Navy: 200 Years* (New York: Holt, 1986), p. 451.

4. The central importance of the interaction of prewar planning with civilian control of war emergency production is established in Thomas C. Hone, "Fighting on Our Own Ground: The War of Production, 1920–1942," *Naval War College Review* 45: 2 (Spring 1992): 93–107.

5. Data from James Forrestal, Secretary of the Navy to the President of the United States, *Annual Report, Fiscal Year 1945*, pt. 3, "Statistical Record of the Navy's War Program" (Washington, D.C.: Department of the Navy, 1946). See also Julius A. Furer, *Administration of the Navy Department in World War II* (Washington, D.C.: Department of the Navy, 1959), pp. 35, 261, 334.

6. Robert Greenhalgh Albion and Robert Howe Connery, *Forrestal and the Navy* (New York: Columbia University Press, 1962), p. 39.

7. Thomas B. Buell, *Master of Sea Power: A Biography of Fleet Admiral Ernest J. King* (Boston: Little, Brown, 1980), p. 140.

8. Paul Y. Hammond, *Organizing for Defense: The American Military Establishment in the Twentieth Century* (Princeton: Princeton University Press, 1961), p. 140.

9. Buell, *Master of Sea Power*, pp. 161–62. Stark's resignation was voluntary. He was not forced out by Roosevelt, although his resignation permitted the president to simplify the Navy's structure of command. See B. Mitchell Simpson III, "Harold Raynsford Stark, 1 August 1939–26 March 1942," in Robert William Love, Jr., ed., *The Chiefs of Naval Operations* (Annapolis: Naval Institute Press, 1980), pp. 130–31; and Simpson, *Admiral Harold R. Stark: Architect of Victory, 1939–1945* (Columbia: University of South Carolina Press, 1989), pp. 126, 128. Roosevelt sent Stark to London as commander of the United States Naval Forces in Europe.

10. Buell, *Master of Sea Power*, p. 219, and, for Roosevelt's order, pp. 500–502.

11. Hammond, *Organizing for Defense*, p. 142.

12. Albion and Connery, *Forrestal and the Navy*, p. 92.

13. Robert Greenhalgh Albion, *Makers of Naval Policy, 1798–1947*, ed. Rowena Reed (Annapolis: Naval Institute Press, 1980), pp. 384–85, 529–40.

14. Hammond, *Organizing for Defense*, pp. 144–45, 156–58, 180–84.

15. Albion and Connery, *Forrestal and the Navy*, p. 90.

16. Buell, *Master of Sea Power*, p. 172.

17. See Clark G. Reynolds, "The Continental Strategy of Imperial Japan," United States Naval Institute *Proceedings* (hereafter cited as *Proceedings*) 109: 8 (Aug. 1983): 65–70.

18. It must be remembered that a two-front war was already under way in Europe. Britain was an open western front for Germany, even if Hitler failed to understand this danger. Soviet complaints about the lack of a second front were invalid. Such a front existed from the beginning. Indeed, looking back on the two years the Soviets were in alliance with Germany, the British could have asked the Russians, Where was the second front then?

19. A reminder of these maritime dimensions is found in Clark G. Reynolds, "The Maritime Strategy of 1943–1945: Implications?" *Naval War College Review* 39: 3 (May–June 1986): 43–50.

20. The logistical advantages of Europe are discussed in Robert W. Coakley and Richard M. Leighton, *Global Logistics and Strategy, 1943–1945* (Washington, D.C.: GPO, 1968), p. 800.

21. Matloff and Snell, *Strategic Planning*, p. 269.

22. Holger H. Herwig, *The Politics of Frustration: The United States in German Naval Planning, 1889–1941* (Boston: Little, Brown, 1976), pp. 237–38.

23. Karl Doenitz, *Memoirs: Ten Years and Twenty Days*, trans. R. H. Stevens (Cleveland: World, 1959), pp. 13–16; Jak P. Mallmann Showell, *The German Navy in World War Two* (Annapolis: Naval Institute Press, 1979), pp. 32–33.

24. Doenitz, *Memoirs*, pp. 150, 228.

25. Robert E. Kuenne, *The Attack Submarine: A Study in Strategy* (New Haven: Yale University Press, 1965), pp. 126–55.

26. F. H. Hinsley et al., *British Intelligence in the Second World War: Its Influence on Strategy and Operations*, vol. 2 (London: HMSO, 1981), pp. 176–79, 681–82.

27. Andrew J. Withers, ed., for the U.K. Ministry of Defence (Navy), *German Naval History: The U-Boat War in the Atlantic, 1939–1945* (London: HMSO, 1989), sec. 191. This semiofficial history was written right after the war, at the Admiralty's request, by former Fregattenkapitän Günter Hessler, Dönitz's son-in-law. Withers has added the intelligence data that was operationally relevant.

28. See, for instance, Samuel Eliot Morison, *The Battle of the Atlantic, September 1939–May 1943* (Boston: Little, Brown, 1950), p. 200.

29. Michael Gannon, *Operation Drumbeat: The Dramatic True Story of Germany's First U-Boat Attacks Along the American Coast in World War II* (New York: Harper & Row, 1990), p. 240.

30. The figures are cited in Marc Milner, "The Battle of the Atlantic," in John Gooch, ed., *Decisive Campaigns of the Second World War* (London: Cass, 1990), p. 52.

31. Montgomery C. Meigs, *Slide Rules and Submarines: American Scientists and Subsurface Warfare in World War II* (Washington, D.C.: National Defense University Press, 1989), pp. 46–49, 91. Robert McKillip's study of the British experience of World War I concludes with cautionary words: "It would be a mistake to conclude that a lesson learned from the First World War is that convoying is an inherently good general strategy. First, convoying is not a strategy. It is a tactical formation within a system of naval control of shipping, a formation with qualities that can be either good or bad, depending on the situation . . . Convoying should not, therefore, be adopted relexively as *the* method of controlling and protecting commerce without a critical examination of potential costs and benefits at all levels, from the tactical to the grand-strategic." McKillip, "Undermining Technology by Strategy: Resolving the Trade Protecting Dilemma of 1917," *Naval War College Review* 44: 3 (Summer 1991): 34.

32. Marc Milner, "Anglo-American Naval Co-operation in the Second World War, 1939–45," in John B. Hattendorf and Robert S. Jordan, *Maritime Strategy and the Balance of Power: Britain and America in the Twentieth Century* (New York: St. Martin's Press, 1989), p. 250.

33. This analysis is developed by Eliot A. Cohen in his chapter "Failure to Learn: American Antisubmarine Warfare in 1942," in Eliot A. Cohen and John

Gooch, *Military Misfortunes: The Anatomy of Failure in War* (New York: Free Press, 1990), pp. 59–94.

34. This fact should be kept in mind when considering the accusation by Michael Gannon that King failed to use those destroyers available on Atlantic duty to stop the approach of the first U-boats. "On Ernest King's desk as commander in chief must lie the final responsibility for this defeat, this embarrassment, this awful loss of blood and treasure, this failed chance to staunch a wound before it hemorrhaged." Gannon, *Operation Drumbeat*, p. 240.

35. Ibid., p. 385.

36. Cohen, "Failure to Learn," pp. 73–84. See also John Winton, *Convoy: The Defence of Sea Trade, 1890–1990* (London: Michael Joseph, 1983), pp. 229–32.

37. Robert William Love, Jr., "Ernest Joseph King," in Love, ed., *Chiefs of Naval Operations*, p. 154, gives this reasoning for King's delay in starting up the convoy system. A discussion by the Operations Evaluation Group of the costs and benefits of independents vs. those of convoys is in Charles M. Sternhell and Alan M. Thorndike, *Antisubmarine Warfare in World War II* (Washington, D.C.: Department of the Navy, 1946), pp. 93–112.

38. Milner, "Battle of the Atlantic," p. 54.

39. Ibid. See also Marc Milner, "RCN-USN, 1939–1945: Some Reflections on the Origins of a New Alliance," in William B. Cogar, ed., *Naval History: The Seventh Symposium of the U.S. Naval Academy* (Wilmington: Scholarly Resources, 1988), pp. 276–83.

40. Milner, "Anglo-American Naval Co-operation," p. 253; Marc Milner, "Inshore ASW: The Canadian Experience in Home Waters," in W. A. B. Douglas, ed., *The RCN in Transition, 1910–1985* (Vancouver: University of British Columbia Press, 1988), 144–45.

41. This point is emphatically made by a German participant, Klaus Friedland, in his "Raiding Merchant Shipping: U-Boats on the North American Coast, 1942," *American Neptune* 51: 2 (Spring 1991): 112–14.

42. Meigs, *Slide Rules and Submarines*, pp. 47, 225.

43. Ibid., pp. 64–65; Elting E. Morison, *Turmoil and Tradition: A Study in the Life and Times of Henry L. Stimson* (Boston: Houghton Mifflin, 1960), pp. 561–80.

44. Ernest J. King and Walter Muir Whitehill, *Fleet Admiral King: A Naval Record* (New York: Norton, 1952), pp. 451–59. For Stimson's perspective, see E. Morison, *Turmoil and Tradition*, p. 574–80.

45. Jürgen Rohwer, "The U-Boat War Against the Allied Supply Lines," in H. A. Jacobsen and Jürgen Rohwer, eds., *Decisive Battles of World War II: The German View*, trans. Edward Fitzgerald (New York: Putnam's, 1965), pp. 271–75; Doenitz, *Memoirs*, p. 250. Dönitz has been criticized, based on his own theory, for leaving a fertile field while a good harvest was still in it (his decision to leave was not due to his losses: an average of only about 1.3 U-boats had been sunk monthly in the United States Strategic Zone in the first half of 1942).

46. The story is told in Frederic C. Lane, *Ships for Victory: A History of Shipbuilding Under the U.S. Maritime Commission in World War II* (Baltimore: Johns Hopkins University Press, 1951). See also Terry Hughes and John Costello, *The Battle of the Atlantic* (New York: Dial, 1977), chap. 14.

47. Richard M. Leighton and Robert W. Coakley, *Global Logistics and Strategy, 1940–1943* (Washington, D.C.: Department of the Army, 1955), p. 712.

48. Ibid., pp. 208, 712.

49. Buell, *Master of Sea Power*, pp. 293–94.

50. Hinsley et al., *British Intelligence in the Second World War*, 2: 554; Ralph Erskine, "Naval Enigma: The Breaking of Heimisch and Triton," *Intelligence and National Security* 3: 1 (Jan. 1988): 162–83.

51. Quotation in Stephen Roskill, *The War at Sea, 1939–1945*, vol. 2 (London: HMSO, 1956), p. 317. See also Hinsley et al., *British Intelligence in the Second World War*, 2: 465–78 and Jürgen Rohwer, *The Critical Convoy Battles of 1943*, cited in Patrick Beesly, *Very Special Intelligence: The Story of the Admiralty's Operational Intelligence Centre, 1939–1945* (Garden City: Doubleday, 1978), p. 192.

52. The War Cabinet quote is in Hughes and John Costello, *Battle of the Atlantic*, p. 259. See also S. E. Morison, *Battle of the Atlantic*, p. 344; and Samuel Eliot Morison, *The Atlantic Battle Won: May 1943, May 1945* (Boston: Little, Brown, 1956), p. 20.

53. Doenitz, *Memoirs*, p. 341.

54. Ibid.

55. S. E. Morison, *Atlantic Battle Won*, pp. 21–31; Buell, *Master of Sea Power*, pp. 275–77.

56. For the ideological basis of Dönitz's leadership, his blind emphasis on heroics regardless of cost or strategic value, see Charles S. Thomas, *The German Navy in the Nazi Era* (Annapolis: Naval Institute Press, 1990), pp. 230–64.

57. For the problems of attacking the nests, see Josef W. Konvitz, "Bombs, Cities, and Submarines: Allied Bombing of the French Ports, 1942–1943," *International History Review* 14: 1 (Feb. 1992): 23–44.

58. F. H. Hinsley et al., *British Intelligence in the Second World War*, vol. 3, pt. 1 (New York: Cambridge University Press, 1984), pp. 223–24; Beesly, *Very Special Intelligence*, p. 210.

59. Buell, *Master of Sea Power*, pp. 280–81.

60. Rohwer, "The U-Boat War Against the Allied Supply Lines," pp. 307–12.

61. Withers, *German Naval History*, sec. 481.

62. Hughes and Costello, *Battle of the Atlantic*, pp. 300–303. See also Sternhell and Thorndike, *Antisubmarine Warfare in World War II*, pp. 64–65, 72.

63. Louis Morton, *The Fall of the Philippines* (Washington, D.C.: Department of the Army, 1953), p. 90.

64. Cited in James O. Richardson, *On the Treadmill to Pearl Harbor* (Washington, D.C.: Department of the Navy, 1973), p. 271.

65. Alvin D. Coox, "Japanese Military Education and Planning Before Pearl Harbor," in H. R. Borowski, ed., *Military Planning in the Twentieth Century* (Washington, D.C.: Department of the Air Force, 1986), p. 75; Michael A. Barnhart, *Japan Prepares for Total War: The Search for Economic Security, 1919–1941* (Ithaca: Cornell University Press, 1987), pp. 1–63.

66. Asada Sadao, "The Japanese Navy and the United States," in Dorothy Borg and Shumpei Okamoto, eds., *Pearl Harbor as History: Japanese-American Relations, 1931–1941* (New York: Columbia University Press, 1973), p. 235.

67. James E. Auer, *The Postwar Rearmament of Japanese Maritime Forces, 1945–1971* (New York: Praeger, 1973), pp. 13–14; Barnhart, *Japan Prepares for Total War*, p. 145.

68. E. G. Thursfield, "Fifteen Years of Naval Treaty-Making," in *Brassey's Naval Annual* (London: Clowes, 1937), p. 83.

69. Admiral George Day to the Senate Naval Committee in 1930, quoted in Richard Dean Burns, "Regulating Submarine Warfare, 1921–1941: A Case Study in Arms Control and Limited War," *Military Affairs* 35: 2 (Apr. 1971): 59.

70. J. E. Talbott, "Weapons Development, War Planning and Policy: The U.S. Navy and the Submarine, 1917–1941," *Naval War College Review* 37: 3 (May–June 1984): 59.

71. Kuenne, *Attack Submarine*, p. 156; Gary E. Weir, *Building American Submarines, 1914–1940* (Washington, D.C.: Naval Historical Center, 1991), pp. 115–16.

72. Theodore Roscoe, *United States Submarine Operations in World War II* (Annapolis: United States Naval Institute, 1949), p. 19.

73. Arthur J. Marder, *Old Friends, New Enemies: The Royal Navy and the Imperial Japanese Navy, Strategic Illusions, 1936–1941* (Oxford: Clarendon Press, 1981), pp. 512–13; S. Woodburn Kirby et al., *The War Against Japan*: vol. 1, *The Loss of Singapore* (London: HMSO, 1957), pp. 193–99.

74. J. C. Wylie, Jr., "Reflections on the War in the Pacific," *Proceedings* 78: 4 (Apr. 1952): 354–55; Jeffrey G. Barlow, "World War II: U.S. and Japanese Naval Strategies," in Colin S. Gray and Roger W. Barnett, eds., *Seapower and Strategy* (Annapolis: Naval Institute Press, 1989), pp. 258–59.

75. For an interpretation of the failure to follow up the surprise attack, see Saburo Toyama, "Japanese Use and Misuse of History in the Pacific War," in Department of History, U.S. Naval Academy, ed., *New Aspects of Naval History* (Baltimore: Nautical and Aviation, 1985), pp. 183–84.

76. Quoted in Ronald Spector, *Eagle Against the Sun: The American War with Japan* (New York: Vintage Books, 1985), p. 483.

77. Louis Morton, "The Decision to Withdraw to Bataan (1941)," in Kent Roberts Greenfield, ed., *Command Decisions* (New York: Harcourt, Brace, 1959), p. 126.

78. Spector, *Eagle Against the Sun*, p. 114.

79. Memorandum from King to Roosevelt, March 5, 1942, in Buell, *Master of Sea Power*, pp. 503–5.

80. Samuel Eliot Morison, *Coral Sea, Midway and Submarine Actions, May 1942–August 1942* (Boston: Little, Brown, 1950), p. 246.

81. Love, "Ernest Joseph King," p. 178.

82. Spector, *Eagle Against the Sun*, pp. 147–48, 167–68; S. E. Morison, *Coral Sea, Midway and Submarine Actions*, pp. 15, 82.

83. John B. Lundstrom, *The First South Pacific Campaign: Pacific Fleet Strategy, December 1941–June 1942* (Annapolis: Naval Institute Press, 1976), p. 176.

84. E. B. Potter, *Nimitz* (Annapolis: Naval Institute Press, 1976), p. 41.

85. Ronald H. Spector, ed., *Listening to the Enemy: Key Documents on the Role of*

Communications Intelligence in the War with Japan (Wilmington: Scholarly Resources, 1988), p. 9n.

86. Potter, *Nimitz*, p. 41.

87. Louis Morton, *Strategy and Command: The First Two Years* (Washington, D.C.: Department of the Army, 1962), p. 218.

88. Quotations from Matloff and Snell, *Strategic Planning*, pp. 154–56; Morton, *Strategy and Command*, p. 218; and Robert H. Ferrell, ed., *The Eisenhower Diaries* (New York: Norton, 1981), p. 48. The words *in time* at the end of the second quote refer to the Army's wish to be able to achieve at any time a quick buildup in Britain for "Sledgehammer," a cross-channel invasion that would be launched to encourage the Soviet Union to remain in the war if Soviet will started to falter.

89. Grace P. Hayes, *The History of the Joint Chiefs of Staff in World War II: The War Against Japan* (Annapolis: Naval Institute Press, 1982), pp. 113–14; Matloff and Snell, *Strategic Planning*, pp. 155–56.

90. Matloff and Snell, *Strategic Planning*, p. 118.

91. King and Whitehill, *Fleet Admiral King*, p. 373.

92. Matloff and Snell, *Strategic Planning*, p. 212.

93. Ibid., pp. 218–24; Hayes, *Joint Chiefs of Staff*, pp. 102–3, 139–40; Morton, *Strategy and Command*, pp. 292–93.

94. The effect of the carrier raids was studied by Rear Admiral Edwin Layton, who was first Kimmel's and then Nimitz's head of fleet intelligence. See Layton, "Early Carrier Raids During World War II," in Daniel M. Masterson, ed., *Naval History: The Sixth Symposium of the U.S. Naval Academy* (Wilmington: Scholarly Resources, 1987), pp. 263–67; and Layton with Roger Pineau and John Costello, *"And I Was There": Pearl Harbor and Midway—Breaking the Secrets* (New York: Morrow, 1985), p. 392.

95. The shortness of the carrier decks relative to the size of the bombers meant that the airplanes could not be recovered at sea, so they flew on to China, where most of the pilots were recovered. The Army got full credit for the raid because it was kept secret that Doolittle's planes were ferried up to Japan by a Navy carrier and launched at sea.

96. These points are developed with great insight in H. P. Willmott, *The Barrier and the Javelin: Japanese and Allied Pacific Strategies, February to June 1942* (Annapolis: Naval Institute Press, 1983), esp. pp. 518–29.

97. Willmott, *Barrier and the Javelin*, pp. 514–18.

98. Lundstrom, *First South Pacific Campaign*, p. 202.

99. Ibid., p. 203; Potter, *Nimitz*, p. 67.

100. Ernest J. King, *U.S. Navy at War, 1941–1945* (Washington, D.C.: Department of the Navy, 1946), p. 47; Love, "Ernest Joseph King," p. 150; Spector, *Eagle Against the Sun*, p. 163; Layton, *"And I Was There,"* pp. 383–405.

101. Willmott, *Barrier and the Javelin*, p. 518.

102. Admiral Layton gives an insider's view of the Hypo radio intelligence operation for Midway (and for Coral Sea and Guadalcanal) and a passionate defense of the remarkable work of Hypo's chief, Commander Joseph Rochefort, in Layton, *"And I Was There,"* pp. 405–48.

103. Mitsuo Fuchida and Masatake Okumiya, *Midway: The Battle That Doomed Japan* (Annapolis: Naval Institute Press, 1955), pp. 242–43.
104. Lundstrom, *First South Pacific Campaign*, pp. 174, 185, 204.

CHAPTER 10

1. It is probably more accurate to say that King shared the qualified view of his assistant chief of staff and key strategist, Rear Admiral Charles M. Cooke, who said in a memo to King of December 28, 1942, on the contention that Germany was the primary enemy: "This statement is frequently made. In my opinion, it is a misstatement as far as the United States is concerned. It would be more proper to state that Germany on the whole is a more powerful enemy—more properly in land and air power, and in submarine power. In general naval power she is less powerful than Japan. . . . The damage inflicted upon our naval power by Japan far exceeds the damage inflicted on us by Germany. Japan has occupied our territory and placed vital strategic points like Midway under attack. It is true that the defeat of Germany will release more military power for attack on Japan than would be the reverse. However the defeat of Germany will not release more United States power to be turned against Japan than would the defeat of Japan release for attack on Germany." The way to phrase the matter, said Cooke, was this: "Germany is such a powerful adversary it is necessary that all forces now directed at Germany should be maintained in full strength." Charles M. Cooke Papers, Hoover Institution Archives, Stanford University, "Strategic Policy for the Conduct of the War, 1942–1945," Box 24.
2. Maurice Matloff and Edwin M. Snell, *Strategic Planning for Coalition Warfare, 1941–1942* (Washington, D.C.: Department of the Army, 1953), pp. 267–73; Mark A. Stoler, "The 'Pacific-First' Alternative in American World War II Strategy," *International History Review* 2: 3 (July 1980): 432–52. The Pacific First idea stayed alive in the Navy for a while. In July 1943 Navy officers on the Joint Wars Plans Committee proposed shifting U.S. strategy away from the enormous commitment of the cross-channel attack, citing changed world conditions. It had been Marshall's worry about the Soviet Union's defeat that prompted him originally to push all out for the bridgehead cross-channel invasion called Sledgehammer and the larger follow-on, then known as Roundup. Now it appeared that Germany was about to be decisively defeated in the east, and so the naval officers suggested continuing the European war mainly from Italy, freeing forces for the Pacific. That of course would have completely reversed strategic principles that had been accepted by the Joint Chiefs and appears to be, as Gordon Harrison said, "the Navy's only open challenge of General Marshall's European strategy." Admiral King did not act on the planners' memo. Harrison, *Cross-Channel Attack* (Washington, D.C.: Department of the Army, 1951), pp. 93–94.
3. Samuel Eliot Morison, *Strategy and Compromise* (Boston: Little, Brown, 1958), p. 38.
4. This "ship to shore" form of amphibious invasion was risky. Loading men and equipment from ships to small boats was hard to do by day, and even more difficult at night. What was needed was an oceangoing landing craft, able to

move "shore to shore," either from advance bases or across the ocean itself, carrying men and matériel directly into battle. The first landing ship tank (LST) hit the water in October 1942. It was diesel-powered and oceanworthy, had two propellers, measured 328 feet in length, and was able to carry 2,100 tons. It could transport a loaded landing craft tank (LCT), the next smaller version of these seagoing landing vessels. With these vessels came the capacity of assault troops to land their own tanks and antitank guns at the same time the infantry went ashore. The landing craft infantry (LCI) was 158 feet long and carried 205 troops and 32 tons of cargo in addition to its crew and could cruise at 12 knots in a radius of 8,000 miles. All these classes of ships and assorted lesser landing craft, began crossing the oceans in 1943 and were used in the invasions of Sicily and in the Trobriand Islands in the Pacific that summer.

5. The British convoys, which the First Sea Lord called "the most valuable convoys ever to leave these shores," were heavily protected by land-based air throughout their voyage. F. H. Hinsley et al., *British Intelligence in the Second World War*, vol. 2 (New York: Cambridge University Press, 1981), p. 477. After the invasion, two U-boats did infiltrate American ships anchored offshore at Morocco and sank four transports and badly damaged several others, including a destroyer.

6. Robert W. Coakley and Richard M. Leighton, *Global Logistics and Strategy, 1943–1945* (Washington, D.C.: GPO, 1968), pp. 10–17, 797–99.

7. Robert Greenhalgh Albion and Robert Howe Connery, *Forrestal and the Navy* (New York: Columbia University Press, 1962), pp. 116–18. For the significance of the destroyer escort construction program and its cancellation in September 1943, see Norman Friedman, *U.S. Destroyers* (Annapolis: Naval Institute Press, 1982), pp. 149–53, 162–63.

8. Albion and Connery, *Forrestal and the Navy*, p. 119.

9. Coakley and Leighton, *Global Logistics and Strategy*, p. 18; Richard M. Leighton, "Overlord Versus the Mediterranean at the Cairo-Tehran Conferences (1943)," in Kent Roberts Greenfield, ed., *Command Decisions* (New York: Harcourt, Brace, 1959), p. 186.

10. William F. Halsey and J. Bryan III, *Admiral Halsey's Story* (New York: McGraw-Hill, 1947), p. 132.

11. Hinsley et al., *British Intelligence in the Second World War* vol. 2, pp. 110–16; and vol. 3, pt. 1 (New York: Cambridge University Press, 1984), pp. 67–77. For some other views of Ultra's significance, see Peter Calvocoressi, *Top Secret Ultra* (New York: Pantheon, 1980), p. 111; and Ronald Lewin, *Ultra Goes to War* (New York: McGraw-Hill, 1978), p. 244.

12. Maurice Matloff, *Strategic Planning for Coalition Warfare, 1943–1944* (Washington, D.C.: Department of the Army, 1959), p. 525; Louis Morton, *Strategy and Command: The First Two Years* (Washington, D.C.: Department of the Army, 1962), p. 382.

13. Kenneth A. Knowles, "Ultra and the Battle of the Atlantic: The American View," in Robert William Love, Jr., ed., *Changing Interpretations and New Sources in Naval History* (New York: Garland, 1980), pp. 446–48.

14. Samuel Eliot Morison, *The Battle of the Atlantic, September 1939–May 1943*

(Boston: Little, Brown, 1951), p. 201; Charles M. Sternhell and Alan M. Thorndike, *Antisubmarine Warfare in World War II* (Washington, D.C.: Department of the Navy, 1946), pp. 64–72; Holger H. Herwig, *The Politics of Frustration: The United States in German Naval Planning, 1889–1941* (Boston: Little, Brown, 1976), pp. 246–47.

15. Samuel Eliot Morison, *The Two-Ocean War* (Boston: Little, Brown, 1963), pp. 380–81.

16. Coakley and Leighton, *Global Logistics and Strategy*, p. 795. See also Chester Wardlow, *The Transportation Corps: Movements, Training, and Supply* (Washington, D.C.: Department of the Army, 1956), pp. 100–101.

17. Robert E. Sherwood, *Roosevelt and Hopkins: An Intimate History* (New York: Harper, 1948), pp. 783–84.

18. Cited in Malcolm Muir, Jr., "The United States Navy in World War II: An Assessment," in James J. Sadkovich, *Reevaluating Major Naval Combatants of World War II* (New York: Greenwood Press, 1990), p. 11; Robin Higham, "Weapons Old and Weapons New: Technology at D-Day," in Deutches Marine Institut, *Seemacht und Geschichte: Festschrift zum 80 Geburtstag von Friedrich Ruge* (Bonn: MOV, 1975), p. 127.

19. H. P. Willmott, *The Great Crusade: A New Complete History of the Second World War* (New York: Macmillan, 1989), p. 315. See also Rear Admiral Toshiyuki Yokoi, "Thoughts on Japan's Naval Defeat," *United States Naval Institute Proceedings* 86: 10 (Oct. 1960): 68–75.

20. D. Clayton James, "American and Japanese Strategies in the Pacific War," in Peter Paret, ed., *Makers of Modern Strategy: From Machiavelli to the Nuclear Age* (Princeton: Princeton University Press, 1986), p. 717.

21. H. P. Willmott, *The Barrier and the Javelin: Japanese and Allied Pacific Strategies, February to June 1942* (Annapolis: Naval Institute Press, 1983), p. 517.

22. Besides the 201 Japanese naval vessels sunk by U.S. submarines, an additional 112 were sunk by U.S. surface vessels, 161 by Navy-Marine carrier air, 70 by Army aircraft, and 19 by mines. In addition to the 1,113 Japanese merchant vessels sunk by U.S. submarines, 11 such vessels were sunk by the Navy's surface craft, 447 by Navy-Marine aircraft (mostly from carriers), and 247 by mines. Almost all the mines that sank Japanese merchant ships were laid by the Army Air Forces. Joint Army-Navy Assessment Committee, *Japanese Naval and Merchant Shipping Losses During World War II by All Causes* (Washington, D.C.: GPO, 1947), p. vii.

23. Clay Blair, Jr., *Silent Victory: The U.S. Submarine War Against Japan* (New York: Lippincott, 1963), pp. 20, 361–62.

24. Ibid., pp. 18–20, 361, 553.

25. Ibid., p. 470.

26. Ibid., pp. 818–19; Edward L. Beach, *The United States Navy: 200 Years* (New York: Holt, 1986), pp. 436–41.

27. Edward J. Drea, *MacArthur's ULTRA: Codebreaking and the War Against Japan, 1942–1945* (Lawrence: University of Kansas Press, 1992), pp. 62, 74–76.

28. This discussion follows Theodore Roscoe, *United States Submarine Operations in World War II* (Annapolis: United States Naval Institute, 1949), pp. 209–

17; and the chapter "The Campaign to Destroy Japanese Shipping" in United States Strategic Bombing Survey (Pacific), Naval Analysis Division, *The Campaigns of the Pacific War* (Washington, D.C.: GPO, 1946), pp. 378–82.

29. Norman Polmar, *The American Submarine* (Annapolis: Nautical and Aviation, 1983), pp. 61–63; Roscoe, *Submarine Operations*, p. 491.

30. This argument is emphatically made, and statistically supported, in John Ellis, *Brute Force: Allied Strategy and Tactics in the Second World War* (New York: Viking, 1990), pp. 467–80.

31. This discussion follows the revealing article by Michael Vlahos and Dale K. Pace, "War Experience and Force Requirements," in *Naval War College Review* 41: 4 (Autumn 1988): 26–36. John Ellis collects comparative wartime shipbuilding figures in *Brute Force*, pp. 478–96 and tables 57–60.

32. Morison, *Two-Ocean War*, p. 282.

33. Roscoe, *Submarine Operations*, p. 491.

34. Willmott, *Great Crusade*, p. 335.

35. Grace P. Hayes, *The History of the Joint Chiefs of Staff in World War II: The War Against Japan* (Annapolis: Naval Institute Press, 1982), p. 725–26.

36. Morton, *Strategy and Command*, p. 250.

37. Roosevelt ordered MacArthur to go to Australia to get him off Corregidor as the Japanese advanced. This was a rescue, not a banishment. On the other hand, Roosevelt left MacArthur in the antipodes. See D. Clayton James, *The Years of MacArthur, 1941–1945* (Boston: Houghton Mifflin, 1975), pp. 125–41.

38. Hayes, *Joint Chiefs of Staff*, p. 727.

39. The Solomons campaign eventually chewed up more men and ships than King expected. Ronald Spector, *Eagle Against the Sun: The American War with Japan* (New York: Vintage Books, 1985), p. 252.

40. Hayes, *Joint Chiefs of Staff*, p. 407.

41. Ibid., p. 547.

42. Jeter A. Isely and Philip A. Crowl, *The U.S. Marines and Amphibious War* (Princeton: Princeton University Press, 1951), pp. 192, 251–52.

43. Quoted in E. B. Potter, *Nimitz* (Annapolis: Naval Institute Press, 1976), p. 280.

44. Quoted in Isely and Crowl, *The U.S. Marines and Amphibious War*, p. 254.

45. This position was taken at a conference between Nimitz and MacArthur's representatives at Pearl Harbor in January 1944. Potter, *Nimitz*, pp. 279–82.

46. Quoted ibid., p. 283.

47. Ibid.

48. Robert William Love, Jr., "Ernest Joseph King," in Love, ed., *The Chiefs of Naval Operations* (Annapolis: Naval Institute Press, 1980), pp. 171–72.

49. Spector, *Eagle Against the Sun*, p. 268.

50. Morison, *Two-Ocean War*, p. 312. For the role of intelligence in selecting and preparing the Kwajalein operation, see Edwin T. Layton with Roger Pineau and John Costello, *"And I Was There": Pearl Harbor and Midway—Breaking the Secrets* (New York: Morrow, 1985), pp. 480–83.

51. Morison, *Two-Ocean War*, p. 314.

52. The story is best told in Worral Reed Carter, *Beans, Bullets, and Black Oil:*

The Story of Fleet Logistics Afloat in the Pacific During World War II (Washington, D.C.: GPO, 1953). Carter commanded Service Squadron Ten, the largest of the mobile squadrons and the main "distributor" in the battle zones. It should not be concluded that shore bases were irrelevant. Quite the contrary. It was just that they could be more distant than ever before from naval combat. Admiral Spruance noted the importance of shore bases in the south and southwest Pacific. These "continued to be close enough to the fighting front to retain practically their full usefulness." Ibid., p. viii.

53. The advantage of proximate land bases remains, however. See Barry M. Blechman and Robert G. Weinland, "Why Coaling Stations Are Necessary in the Nuclear Age," *International Security* 2: 1 (Summer 1977): 88–99.

54. An Army Intelligence assessment cited by Layton, *"And I Was There,"* p. 484. See also Edward J. Drea, "Ultra Intelligence and General MacArthur's Leap to Hollandia, January–April 1944," *Intelligence and National Security* 5: 2 (Apr. 1990): 323–49. Drea further details "Ultra's great victory" in *MacArthur's ULTRA*, pp. 94–122.

55. Spector, *Eagle Against the Sun*, pp. 246, 278; E. B. Potter, *Bull Halsey* (Annapolis: Naval Institute Press, 1985), p. 257. Sherman's quotes and his account are in Frederick C. Sherman, *Combat Command: The American Aircraft Carriers in the Pacific War* (New York: Dutton, 1950), p. 211.

CHAPTER 11

1. Paul S. Dull, *A Battle History of the Imperial Japanese Navy, 1941–1945* (Annapolis: Naval Institute Press, 1978), p. 303.

2. Of the many discussions of Spruance's decision, the reader should begin with Thomas B. Buell, *The Quiet Warrior: A Biography of Admiral Raymond A. Spruance* (Boston: Little, Brown, 1974), pp. 257–80. Russell F. Weigley, in *The American Way of War: A History of United States Military Strategy and Policy* (Bloomington: Indiana University Press, 1977), pp. 296–300, typifies criticism of Spruance's decision by favorably comparing Trafalgar (the bold engagement favored by the carrier aviators) with Jutland (the type of battle supposedly preferred by the conservative Spruance). This seems unfair. Spruance's intent was to use his fast battleships to destroy the enemy fleet. Deploying them to protect the carriers slowed this plan, and the prospect of a fleet engagement was thereafter scuttled when the battleship commander warned of great risks in any night action stemming from a lack of nighttime exercises. Malcolm Muir, Jr., "Misuse of the Fast Battleships in World War II," United States Naval Institute *Proceedings* (hereafter cited as *Proceedings* 105: 2 (Feb. 1979): 60–61. From another perspective, the debate is between Spruance's decision to protect the landing forces by tying the carriers to a beachhead and close support, and the preference shared by Admiral Halsey and Admiral John Towers, an airman and deputy CinCPac, for optimizing carrier mobility—their sole advantage over airfields—by striking at an enemy fleet or bases as the chief sources of a threatening counterattack. E. B. Potter, *Bull Halsey* (Annapolis: Naval Institute Press, 1985), p. 272. Eric Larrabee, reviewing postwar analyses, concluded that the disposition of the Japanese fleet (unknown at the time to Spruance) would have made

closure for the decisive engagement very dangerous and the chance of success unfavorable. Larrabee, *Commander in Chief: Franklin Delano Roosevelt, His Lieutenants, and Their War* (New York: Simon & Schuster, 1987), p. 392.

3. D. Clayton James, "American and Japanese Strategies in the Pacific War," in Peter Paret, ed., *Makers of Modern Strategy from Machiavelli to the Nuclear Age* (Princeton: Princeton University Press, 1986), p. 728.

4. Malcolm Muir, *The Iowa Class Battleships* (Poole: Blandford, 1987), p. 50.

5. Philip A. Crowl, *Campaign in the Marianas* (Washington, D.C.: Department of the Army, 1960), pp. 446–47. See also Jeter A. Isely and Philip A. Crowl, *The U.S. Marines and Amphibious War* (Princeton: Princeton University Press, 1951), p. 390.

6. This discussion follows Akira Iriye, *Power and Culture: The Japanese-American War, 1941–1945* (Cambridge: Harvard University Press, 1981), pp. 174–83; and Leon V. Sigal, *Fighting to a Finish: The Politics of War Termination in the United States and Japan, 1945* (Ithaca: Cornell University Press, 1988), pp. 33–39. The hope that the United States might quit in the face of a defeat seems to have lasted in Japanese government circles until the end. Saburo Hayasi and Alvin D. Coox, *Ko-gun: The Japanese Army in the Pacific War* (Quantico: Marine Corps Association, 1959), p. 140.

7. Thomas B. Buell, *Master of Sea Power: A Biography of Fleet Admiral Ernest J. King* (Boston: Little, Brown, 1980), p. 438.

8. Robert Ross Smith, "Luzon Versus Formosa," in Kent Roberts Greenfield, ed., *Command Decisions* (New York: Harcourt, Brace, 1959), pp. 367–69, 373; Robert Ross Smith, *Triumph in the Philippines* (Washington, D.C.: Department of the Army, 1963), pp. 8–17. For the strategic debate, see Grace Person Hayes, *The History of the Joint Chiefs of Staff in World War II: The War Against Japan* (Annapolis: Naval Institute Press, 1982), pp. 603–4, 615, 623; M. Hamlin Cannon, *Leyte: The Return to the Philippines* (Washington, D.C.: Department of the Army, 1954), p. 4; and D. Clayton James, *The Years of MacArthur, 1941–1945* (Boston: Houghton Mifflin, 1975), pp. 552–53.

9. Robert W. Coakley and Richard M. Leighton, *Global Logistics and Strategy, 1943–1945* (Washington, D.C.: Department of the Army, 1960), pp. 462–70, 560–62.

10. Ronald H. Spector, *Eagle Against the Sun: The American War with Japan* (New York: Vintage Books, 1985), p. 420.

11. Robert William Love, Jr., "Ernest Joseph King," in Love, ed., *The Chiefs of Naval Operations* (Annapolis: Naval Institute Press, 1980), pp. 174–75.

12. E. B. Potter, *Nimitz* (Annapolis: Naval Institute Press, 1976), p. 325.

13. Hanson Baldwin, *Sea Fights and Shipwrecks* (Garden City: Hanover House, 1955), p. 160. The views of Kinkaid and Halsey are given on pp. 165–82.

14. Potter, *Bull Halsey*, p. 276; Spector, *Eagle Against the Sun*, pp. 422–23.

15. United States Strategic Bombing Survey (Pacific), Naval Analysis Division, *Interrogations of Japanese Officials*, vol. 2 (Washington, D.C.: GPO, 1946), p. 317.

16. Tomiji Koyanagi, "The Battle of Leyete Gulf," in Raymond O'Connor, ed., *The Japanese Navy in World War II* (Annapolis: Naval Institute Press, 1971), p. 109.

17. United States Strategic Bombing Survey (Pacific), Naval Analysis Division, *Interrogations of Japanese Officials*, vol. 1 (Washington, D.C.: GPO, 1946), p. 221. Admiral Halsey ten years later warned against taking this statement at face value. "I am still far from sure that Ozawa's force was intended solely as a lure. The Japanese had continuously lied during the war, even to each other. Why believe them implicitly as soon as the war ends? They had plenty of time, before reciting them, to make their stories fit their needs. . . . It is still difficult for me to believe that they would deliberately use their potentially most dangerous ships as deliberate sacrifices." Baldwin, *Sea Fights and Shipwrecks*, p. 179. Beyond calculated mendacity, there were other problems with ready acceptance of the postwar prison interviews. Translators were not always fluent in Japanese. One interviewer said: "Many times things got mixed up in the course of translations, particularly in those days right after the war. Then too, the Japanese at the time were so scared they were willing to say about anything." Walter Lord, "On Writing Naval History: Techniques and Experiences," in Arnold R. Shapak, ed., *The Navy in an Age of Change and Crisis: Some Challenges and Responses of the Twentieth Century* (Annapolis: U.S. Naval Academy, 1973), p. 58.

18. Samuel Eliot Morison, *Leyte* (Boston: Little, Brown, 1958), pp. 159–60.

19. H. P. Willmott, *The Great Crusade* (New York: Free Press, 1990), p. 409.

20. Morison, *Leyte*, p. 240.

21. United States Strategic Bombing Survey, *Interrogations of Japanese Officials*, 1: 221.

22. William F. Halsey and J. Bryan III, *Admiral Halsey's Story* (New York: McGraw-Hill, 1947), p. 216. See also Potter, *Bull Halsey*, p. 296.

23. Potter, *Nimitz*, pp. 325–26. For King's subsequent criticism of Halsey, see Ernest J. King and Walter Muir Whitehill, *Fleet Admiral King: A Naval Record* (New York: Norton, 1952), p. 580; and Buell, *Master of Sea Power*, pp. 450–52.

24. Bernard Brodie, "A Guide for Reading *On War*," in Carl von Clausewitz, *On War*, ed. Michael Howard and Peter Paret (Princeton University Press, 1970), p. 663; Bernard Brodie, *War and Politics* (New York: Macmillan, 1973), p. 450.

25. Cited in Morison, *Leyte*, p. 189.

26. This is suggested in Saburo Toyama, "Japanese Use and Misuse of History in the Pacific War," Department of History, U.S. Naval Academy, ed., *New Aspects of Naval History: Selected Papers from the 5th Naval History Symposium* (Baltimore: Nautical and Aviation, 1985), pp. 186–87.

27. Weigley, *American Way of War*, p. 304.

28. The quote is from James A. Field, Jr., "Leyte Gulf: The First Uncensored Japanese Account," *Proceedings* 77: 3 (Mar. 1951): 264. See also Willmott, *Great Crusade*, pp. 406–7; and Masanori Ito with Roger Pineau, *The End of the Imperial Japanese Navy*, trans. Andrew Y. Kuroda and Roger Pineau (New York: Norton, 1962), pp. 149–73, which includes comments by Kurita himself. Another source, to be used with caution, is Rear Admiral Tomiji Koyanagi, "With Kurita in the Battle for Leyte Gulf," *Proceedings* 79: 2 (Feb. 1953): 119–33.

29. Dull, *Imperial Japanese Navy*, p. 331.

30. Hayes, *Joint Chiefs of Staff*, p. 619. See also William D. Leahy, *I Was There* (New York: Whittlesey House, 1950), p. 259.

31. Buell, *Quiet Warrior*, pp. 303–10. For Spruance's doubts and second thoughts, see ibid., pp. 323–24 and 341–42. See also Buell, *Master of Sea Power*, pp. 446–48.

32. Samuel Eliot Morison, *The Liberation of the Philippines, Luzon, Mindanao, the Visayas, 1944–1945* (Boston: Little, Brown, 1959), p. 5.

33. Love, "Ernest Joseph King," p. 175.

34. Willmott, *Great Crusade*, p. 413.

35. Isely and Crowl, *U.S. Marines and Amphibious War*, pp. 432, 529–30.

36. Two judicious Marine Corps historians surveyed the arguments and concluded that "the controversy [over the amount of preparatory naval gunfire] simply becomes one of the vantage point occupied by each of the participants at the time of the operation. To a Marine . . . it becomes inconceivable that, regardless of time limits and restrictions on ammunition expenditure, more was not done. . . . From the Navy's vantage point . . . the Iwo Jima operation had been tightly wedged in a time frame between the invasion of Luzon and the coming assault on Okinawa. Under such pressure, perhaps the best that could be achieved was neutralization, not destruction of the enemy artillery as desired by the Marines. . . . Thus, for the purposes of this history, the controversy must remain unsolved." George W. Garand and Truman R. Strobridge, *Western Pacific Operations: History of U.S. Marine Corps Operations in World War II*, vol. 4 (Washington, D.C.: Headquarters, U.S. Marine Corps, 1971), pp. 713–17, 736–37. For other sensible comments on the controversy which opened up major questions about the nature of sea-air-land cooperation in amphibious warfare, see Isely and Crowl, *U.S. Marines and Amphibious Warfare*, pp. 433–51. For a defense of Spruance, see George Carroll Dyer, *The Amphibians Came to Conquer: The Story of Admiral Richmond Kelly Turner*, vol. 2 (Washington, D.C.: GPO, 1971), pp. 1046–51. Turner commanded the amphibious forces afloat. For criticism of Spruance, see Holland M. Smith and Percy Finch, *Coral and Brass* (New York: Scribner's, 1949), pp. 242–49. The operation, said General Smith, "was planned for the capture of Iwo Jima, but Spruance permitted the attack on Japan to overshadow the real objective."

37. Roy E. Appleman, James M. Burns, Russell A. Gugeler, and John Stevens, *Okinawa: The Last Battle* (Washington, D.C.: Department of the Army, 1948), pp. 473–74. The campaign for the liberation of Luzon was close in battle casualties. In that campaign, 47,000 soldiers and 2,000 sailors were killed or wounded.

38. This was the opinion shared by Vice Admiral Teraoka Kimpei and his relief Vice Admiral Ohnishi Takijiro. Rikihei Inoguchi and Tadashi Nakajima, "The Kamikaze Attack Corps," trans. Masataka Chihaya and Roger Pineau, *Proceedings* 79: 9 (Sept. 1953): 935. See also Toshiyuki Yokoi with Roger Pineau, "Kamikazes and the Okinawa Campaign," *Proceedings* 80: 5 (May 1954): 510; United States Strategic Bombing Survey (Pacific), Naval Analysis Division, *The Campaigns of the Pacific War* (Washington, D.C.: GPO, 1946), pp. 326–29; Appleman et al., *Okinawa*, pp. 362–64.

39. So intense was this and other kamikaze attacks that battleships, carriers, and destroyers were attacked more in the war by kamikazes than by gunfire, bombs, or torpedoes. The figures given in the text for the damage inflicted on

U.S. forces at Okinawa are cited in Arthur M. Smith, "Can We Effectively Control Human Costs During War at Sea?," *Naval War College Review* 45: 1 (Winter 1992): 15. D. Clayton James raised the idea that had the Japanese adopted integrated air-sea-land suicide operations earlier in the war—in 1942—they might have inflicted so much damage on allied forces that the Allies would have negotiated a peace. James, "American and Japanese Strategies in the Pacific War," p. 718.

40. Samuel Eliot Morison, *Victory in the Pacific, 1945* (Boston: Little, Brown, 1960), p. 250.

41. Ito with Pineau, *End of the Imperial Japanese Navy*, pp. 184–92.

42. On JCS rejection of the China alternative and of British overtures, see Hayes, *Joint Chiefs of Staff*, pp. 661–67, 678–79, 695–701, 711–12.

43. E. P. Forrestel, *Admiral Raymond A. Spruance, USN: A Study in Command* (Washington, D.C.: GPO, 1966), pp. 209–10.

44. Crowl, *Campaign in the Marianas*, p. 445.

45. Wesley Frank Craven and James Lea Cate, *The Army Air Forces in World War II*: vol. 5, *The Pacific: Matterhorn to Nagasaki, June 1944 to August 1945* (Chicago: University of Chicago Press, 1953), pp. 608–44.

46. Ibid., pp. 645–75, wherein the authors note (p. 664) that "in light of the spectacular results of B-29 mining operations later, it is ironical that the decision to cooperate with Nimitz came not from any great liking in the AAF for mining but rather from the sort of logic that often colored interservice comity during the war—the fear that otherwise the AAF might allow 'a possible major usage of long-range aircraft to develop, by default, into a matter of special interest to the Navy.' "

47. Hayes, *Joint Chiefs of Staff*, p. 703.

48. The Army position is set out in Charles F. Brower IV, "The Joint Chiefs of Staff and National Policy: American Strategy and the War with Japan, 1943–1945" (Ph.D. diss., University of Pennsylvania, 1987), pp. 260–99. See also the criticism of Spruance's position in Buell, *Quiet Warrior*, p. 365.

49. Charles F. Brower IV, "Sophisticated Strategist: General George A. Lincoln and the Defeat of Japan, 1944–45," *Diplomatic History* 15: 3 (Summer 1991): 317–37.

50. This view is presented in Rufus E. Miles, Jr., "Hiroshima: The Strange Myth of Half a Million American Lives Saved," *International Security* 10: 2 (Fall 1985): 133–35. For predictions of higher losses and a discussion of the planned invasion in light of what the U.S. Army knew from special intelligence about Japanese last-ditch homeland defenses, see Edward J. Drea, *MacArthur's ULTRA: Codebreaking and the War Against Japan, 1942–1945* (Lawrence: University of Kansas Press, 1992), pp. 202–25.

51. Coakley and Leighton, *Global Logistics and Strategy*, p. 614.

52. Duncan S. Ballantine, *U.S. Naval Logistics in the Second World War* (Princeton: Princeton University Press, 1947), p. 286.

CHAPTER 12

1. Forrestal asked the question in testimony of September 19, 1945, which can be found in House Committee on Naval Affairs, *Composition of the Postwar Navy:*

Hearings on House Concurrent Resolution 80, 79th Cong., 1st sess. The quote is on p. 1164.

2. Alexander P. De Seversky, *Victory Through Air Power* (New York: Simon & Schuster, 1942), pp. 182–83. Robert Frank Futrell, *Ideas, Concepts, Doctrine: A History of Basic Thinking in the United States Air Force, 1907–1964*, vol. 1 (Montgomery: Air University, 1971), shows that senior Air Force officers were not united on how "decisive" bombing might be, but all agreed that air power was the main element of future war. For an overview of the foundation of air-power doctrine, see Michael S. Sherry, *The Rise of American Air Power: The Creation of Armageddon* (New Haven: Yale University Press, 1987).

3. Norman Friedman, *The Postwar Naval Revolution* (Annapolis: Naval Institute Press, 1986), pp. 47–48.

4. Bradley F. Smith, "An Idiosyncratic View of Where We Stand on the History of American Intelligence in the Early Post-1945 Era," *Intelligence and National Security* 3: 4 (Oct. 1988): 117–19.

5. The other services were no better off. The Army Air Forces went from a high point of almost 2.5 million personnel in 1943 to a little over 300,000 in 1947. Air-combat strength fell from 243 fully operational groups to 11. In the six months after Japan surrendered, the AAF released 734,715 personnel.

6. Arleigh Burke, *Reminiscenses of Admiral Arleigh A. Burke, U.S. Navy (Ret.): Special Series on Selected Subjects*, 4 vols. (Annapolis: United States Naval Institute, 1979–83), 3: 146 and 4: 472–84. Quotations from Burke's *Reminiscenses* used with permission.

7. Naval Research Advisory Committee, *Historical Perspectives in Long-Range Planning in the Navy* (Washington, D.C.: Department of the Navy, 1980), pp. ii, 22, 67–71.

8. Gordon W. Keiser, *The U.S. Marine Corps and Defense Unification, 1944–47: The Politics of Survival* (Washington, D.C.: National Defense University Press, 1982), p. 45.

9. Walter Millis, ed., *The Forrestal Diaries* (New York: Viking, 1951), p. 97; Calvin W. Enders, "The Vinson Navy" (Ph.D. diss., Michigan State University, 1970), pp. 162–65.

10. Vincent Davis, *Postwar Defense Policy and the U.S. Navy, 1943–1946* (Chapel Hill: University of North Carolina Press, 1966), pp. 208–9.

11. Millis, *Forrestal Diaries*, p. 45. See also pp. 184–85.

12. For the deeper dimensions of Forrestal's concern see Townsend Hoopes and Douglas Brinkley, *Driven Patriot: The Life and Times of James Forrestal* (New York: Knopf, 1992), pp. 227–69. See also Robert Greenhalgh Albion and Robert Howe Connery, *Forrestal and the Navy* (New York: Columbia University Press, 1962), pp. 169–72; and James F. Schnabel, *The History of the Joint Chiefs of Staff: The Joint Chiefs of Staff and National Policy*: vol. 1, *1945–1947* (Wilmington: Glazier, 1979), pp. 321–41.

13. George F. Kennan, *Memoirs, 1925–1950* (Boston: Little, Brown, 1967), pp. 354–55; Hoopes and Brinkley, *Driven Patriot*, pp. 270–81.

14. Stephen George Xydis, "The American Naval Visits to Greece and the Eastern Mediterranean in 1946: Their Impact on American-Soviet Relations. A Case Study of the Functions of Modern Sea Power in Peacetime Foreign Policy"

(Ph.D. diss., Columbia University, 1956); M. P. Leffler, "Strategy, Diplomacy, and the Cold War: The United States, Turkey, and NATO, 1945–1952," *Journal of American History* 71: 4 (Mar. 1985): 807–25.

15. So speculates Edward Luttwak in *The Political Uses of Sea Power* (Baltimore: Johns Hopkins University Press, 1974), pp. 28–34.

16. David Alan Rosenberg, "The U.S. Navy and the Problem of Oil in a Future War: The Outline of a Strategic Dilemma, 1945–1950," *Naval War College Review* 29: 1 (Summer 1976): 54–55; Ian O. Lesser, *Resources and Strategy* (New York: St. Martin's, 1989), pp. 97–111.

17. Millis, *Forrestal Diaries*, p. 184; Dennis M. Pricolo, *Naval Presence and Cold War Foreign Policy: A Study of the Decision to Station the 6th Fleet in the Mediterranean, 1945–1958* (Annapolis: United States Naval Academy, Trident Scholar Project, 1978), p. 90. The extent of naval movements is detailed in Edward J. Sherry, *The U.S. Navy, the Mediterranean, and the Cold War, 1945–1947* (Westport: Greenwood, 1992).

18. Paolo E. Coletta, *The United States Navy and Defense Unification, 1947–1953* (Newark: University of Delaware Press, 1981), p. 31; Steven T. Ross, "Chester William Nimitz, 15 December 1945–15 December 1947," in Robert William Love, Jr., ed., *The Chiefs of Naval Operations* (Annapolis: Naval Institute Press, 1980), pp. 188–89.

19. Xydis, "American Naval Visits," p. 194.

20. On the British Chiefs of Staff's emphasis on continuing a strong British Mediterranean naval presence, and Prime Minister Clement Attlee's reluctant acceptance of it as a means of indirect defense of the bomber offensive on which British defense rested, see Eric Grove and Geoffrey Till, "Anglo-American Maritime Strategy in the Era of Massive Retaliation, 1945–1960," in John B. Hattendorf and Robert S. Jordan, eds., *Maritime Strategy and the Balance of Power: Britain and America in the Twentieth Century* (New York: St. Martin's, 1989), p. 275.

21. Michael A. Palmer, *Origins of the Maritime Strategy: American Naval Strategy in the First Postwar Decade* (Washington, D.C.: Naval Historical Center, 1988), p. 87.

22. Michael Sherry, *Preparing for the Next War: America Plans for Postwar Defense, 1941–1945* (New Haven: Yale University Press, 1977), p. 54.

23. Palmer, *Origins of the Maritime Strategy*, pp. 12–13, 99.

24. Lester J. Foltos, "The New Pacific Barrier: America's Search for Security in the Pacific, 1945–1947," *Diplomatic History* 13: 3 (Summer 1989): 317–42.

25. There was fear in Marine Corps circles that the Navy would sacrifice the Fleet Marine Force, with its supporting Marine air units, if it had to do so to keep naval aviation. Keiser, *U.S. Marine Corps and Defense Unification*, pp. 45–46.

26. There is a good summary discussion of this in Friedman, *Postwar Naval Revolution*, pp. 1–28.

27. Ernest J. King, *U.S. Navy at War, 1941–1945: Official Reports to the Secretary of the Navy* (Washington, D.C.: Department of the Navy, 1946), pp. 169–70. King's later testimony can be found in *The National Defense Program—Unification and Strategy: Hearings Before the Committee on Armed Services, House of Representatives*, 81st Cong., 1st sess., p. 251.

28. *Unification of the Armed Forces: Hearings before the Committee on Naval Affairs, United States Senate*, 79th Cong., 2d sess. The quote is on p. 79.

29. Vincent Davis, *The Admirals Lobby* (Chapel Hill: University of North Carolina Press, 1967), p. 206.

30. The following appreciation of Sherman draws on Palmer's excellent study *Origins of the Maritime Strategy*.

31. The available sources are cited in Russell D. Buhite and Wm. Christopher Hamel, "War for Peace: The Question of an American Preventive War Against the Soviet Union, 1945–1955," *Diplomatic History* 14: 3 (Summer 1990): 383.

32. David A. Rosenberg and Floyd D. Kennedy, Jr., *U.S. Aircraft Carriers in the Strategic Role*: pt. 1, *Naval Strategy in a Period of Change: Interservice Rivalry, Strategic Interaction, and the Development of Nuclear Attack Capabilities, 1945–1951* (Falls Church: Lulejian, 1975), pp. 31–32.

33. From an evaluation of December 16, 1948, "Soviet Intentions and Capabilities, 1949, 1956/57," pp. 24–27, printed in Steven T. Ross and David Alan Rosenberg, eds., *America's Plans for War Against the Soviet Union, 1945–1950*: vol. 10, *Assessing the Threat* (New York: Garland, 1990).

34. Norman Polmar and Jurrien Noot, *Submarines of the Russian and Soviet Navies, 1718–1990* (Annapolis: Naval Institute Press, 1991), pp. 136–48.

35. Palmer, *Origins of the Maritime Strategy*, pp. 25–28; Friedman, *Postwar Naval Revolution*, p. 25.

36. Friedman, *Postwar Naval Revolution*, p. 22.

37. Palmer, *Origins of the Maritime Strategy*, p. 28.

38. See Edward Rhodes's review of Palmer's *Origins of the Maritime Strategy*, in *Survival* 32: 4 (July–Aug. 1990): 375–77. A distinction between oceanic and transoceanic strategy was made in the early 1950s in a seminal article by Samuel P. Huntington, "National Policy and the Transoceanic Navy," United States Naval Institute *Proceedings* 80: 5 (May 1954): 483–93.

39. Some of the difficulties of war planning in this period are analyzed in Roger Dingman, "Strategic Planning and the Policy Process: American Plans for War in East Asia, 1945–1950," *Naval War College Review* 32: 6 (Nov.–Dec. 1979): 4–21.

40. David Alan Rosenberg, "The Origins of Overkill: Nuclear Weapons and American Strategy, 1945–1969," *International Security* 7: 4 (Spring 1983): 11–15; Rosenberg, "American Atomic Strategy and the Hydrogen Bomb Decision," *Journal of American History* 69: 1 (June 1979): 62–71; Rosenberg, "Reality and Responsibility: Power and Process in the Making of United States Nuclear Strategy, 1945–68," *Journal of Strategic Studies* 9: 1 (Mar. 1986): 38–41.

41. For a discussion of the war plans of this period, see the overview in Steven T. Ross, *American War Plans, 1945–1950* (New York: Garland, 1988), pp. 6–20. For the originals, consult Steven T. Ross and David Alan Rosenberg, eds., *America's Plans for War Against the Soviet Union, 1945–1950* (New York: Garland, 1989–90), a 15-volume set reproducing in facsimile 98 war plans and studies created by the JCS.

42. In 1948, when Lieutenant General Curtis LeMay took over the Air Force's preemptively named Strategic Air Command (SAC), SAC followed no war plan

and its crews were not prepared for combat operations. See the interview of LeMay and other SAC generals in Richard H. Kohn and Joseph P. Harahan, eds., *Strategic Air Warfare* (Washington, D.C.: United States Air Force, 1988), pp. 77–82. SAC's shortfalls in light of JCS war plans are brought out in detail in "Evaluation of the Effectiveness of Strategic Air Operations," also known as WSEG 1 Study, which was prepared by a Defense Department Weapons Systems Evaluation Group. It is printed in Ross and Rosenberg, *America's Plans for War*: vol. 13, *Evaluating the Air Offensive.* See also Rosenberg, "American Atomic Strategy and the Hydrogen Bomb Decision," pp. 64–66.

43. John Lewis Gaddis, "The Origins of Self-Deterrence: The United States and the Non-Use of Nuclear Weapons, 1945–1958," in Gaddis, *The Long Peace: Inquiries into the History of the Cold War* (New York: Oxford University Press, 1987), p. 108. Some naval officers, remembering Pearl Harbor, shared the view of some Air Force officers who were entranced by the short-war air-power theory. Both groups thought that when the Soviets got the atomic bomb, they might make a direct, one-way air attack against the United States from across the North Pole, or cache a bomb in a freighter or submarine and bring it up along the coast. The officers advocated a preemptive strike. That was rejected by the White House on political grounds, but atomic preemption was never formally vetoed by the president, and the JCS never gave up the first-strike option it had adopted three weeks after Hiroshima. If the direct defense of the United States appeared at stake, the government would not rule out "the first blow." Rosenberg, "Reality and Responsibility," p. 40; Sherry, *Preparing for the Next War*, pp. 201–2.

44. Paul Y. Hammond, "Super Carriers and B-36 Bombers: Appropriations, Strategy and Politics," in Harold Stein, ed., *American Civil-Military Decisions: A Book of Case Studies* (Birmingham: University of Alabama Press, 1963), p. 480.

45. Nimitz quote in Palmer, *Origins of the Maritime Strategy*, p. 37, and Rosenberg and Kennedy, *Naval Strategy in a Period of Change*, pp. 40–41. Cruise quote ibid., pp. 73–75. See also Coletta, *United States Navy and Defense Unification*, p. 90.

46. Palmer, *Origins of the Maritime Strategy*, pp. 43–44.

47. Quotations from Rosenberg and Kennedy, *Naval Strategy in a Period of Change*, pp. 46–54. See also David Alan Rosenberg, "American Postwar Air Doctrine and Organization: The Navy Experience," in A. F. Hurley and R. C. Ehrhart, eds., *Air Power and Warfare* (Washington, D.C.: Department of the Air Force, 1979), pp. 256–57; James L. Lacy, *Within Bounds: The Navy in Postwar American Security Policy* (Alexandria: Center for Naval Analyses, 1983), pp. 86–87.

48. Quoted in Lacy, *Within Bounds*, p. 109. See also Naval Research Advisory Committee, *Historical Perspectives*, pp. 20–21.

49. Grove and Till, "Anglo-American Maritime Strategy," p. 278.

50. Rosenberg and Kennedy, *Naval Strategy in a Period of Change*, p. 53.

51. Palmer, *Origins of the Maritime Strategy*, pp. 30, 78.

52. Quoted in Jeffrey G. Barlow, "'The Revolt of the Admirals' Reconsidered," in William B. Cogar, ed., *New Interpretations in Naval History* (Annapolis: Naval Institute Press, 1989), p. 228.

53. Coletta, *United States Navy and Defense Unification*, p. 161; Paolo E. Coletta, "Francis P. Matthews," in Paolo E. Coletta, ed., *American Secretaries of the Navy*, vol. 2 (Annapolis: Naval Institute Press, 1980), p. 787.

54. Harold Stein, "Editorial Comment," in Stein, *American Civil-Military Decisions*, pp. 566–67. The subject of Stein's comment is Paul Hammond's article "Super Carriers and B-36 Bombers: Appropriations, Strategy and Politics," which is printed in the same book.

55. Jeffrey M. Dorwart, "Forrestal and the Navy Plan of 1945: Mahanian Doctrine or Corporatist Blueprint?" in Cogar, *New Interpretations in Naval History*, pp. 209–23; Jeffrey M. Dorwart, *Eberstadt and Forrestal: A National Security Partnership, 1909–1949* (College Station: Texas A&M University Press, 1991), pp. 86–89.

56. Edward A. Kolodziej, *The Uncommon Defense and Congress, 1945–1963* (Columbus: Ohio State University Press, 1966), p. 48.

57. Burke, *Reminiscences*, 2: 241.

58. Burke, *Reminiscences*, 4: 656.

59. Naval Research Advisory Committee, *Historical Perspectives*, pp. 20–40. See also a useful summary by David Alan Rosenberg, who was in fact the author of *Historical Perspectives*, in his "History of Navy Long-Range Planning: An Overview," in James L. George et al., *Review of USN Long-Range Planning* (Alexandria: Center for Naval Analyses, 1985), p. B-5.

60. Ross, *American War Plans*, p. 84. Bushwacker is reproduced as *Plan Bushwacker*, vol. 8 of Ross and Rosenberg, *America's Plans for War*.

61. Kenneth W. Condit, *The History of the Joint Chiefs of Staff*, vol. 2, *The Joint Chiefs of Staff and National Policy 1947–1949* (Wilmington: Michael Glazier, 1979), p. 165.

62. Lacy, *Within Bounds*, p. 95. The short-range emergency plans are printed in Ross and Rosenberg, *America's Plans for War*: vol. 6, *Plan Frolic and American Resources*; and vol. 7, *From Crankshaft to Halfmoon*.

63. The texts are printed in Alice C. Cole et al., eds., *The Department of Defense: Documents on Establishment and Organization, 1944–1978* (Washington, D.C.: Office of the Secretary of Defense, 1978), pp. 35–50, 286–88. Forrestal's summary is in Millis, *Forrestal Diaries*, pp. 392–93.

64. Hoopes and Brinkley, *Driven Patriot*, p. 412; Cole et al., *Department of Defense*, p. 290; Steven L. Rearden, *History of the Office of the Secretary of Defense*: vol. 1, *The Formative Years, 1947–1950* (Washington, D.C.: Office of the Secretary of Defense, 1984), pp. 393–402; Hammond, "Super Carriers and B-36 Bombers," pp. 474–75. For an interesting critique of the contributions of the Key West structure to interservice disharmony, see Morton H. Halperin and David Halperin, "The Key West Key," *Foreign Policy* 53 (Winter 1983–84): 114–30.

65. Lacy, *Within Bounds*, pp. 101–2.

66. Warner R. Schilling, "The Politics of National Defense: Fiscal 1950," in Schilling, Paul Y. Hammond, and Glenn H. Snyder, *Strategy, Politics, and Defense Budgets* (New York: Columbia University Press, 1962).

67. Lacy, *Within Bounds*, p. 89.

68. This discussion draws on Rearden, *Formative Years*, pp. 349–50, for the

sense that the national goals the war plan proposed to meet by force had been established with a very different strategy in mind for their achievement. Offtackle is printed in Ross and Rosenberg, *America's Plans for War*: vol. 12, *Budgets and Strategy: The Road to Offtackle*.

69. "Logistic Implications of 'Offtackle,'" November 15, 1949, printed in Ross and Rosenberg, *Budgets and Strategy*.

70. Burke, *Reminiscences*, 4: 220–22, 638–40.

71. David MacIsaac, *Strategic Bombing in World War Two: The Story of the United States Strategic Bombing Survey* (New York: Garland, 1976), pp. 119–35, 144–50.

72. Rosenberg, "American Atomic Strategy and the Hydrogen Bomb Decision," p. 72.

73. Radford quoted in Rosenberg and Kennedy, *Naval Strategy in a Period of Change*, p. 84.

74. Gaddis, "Origins of Self-Deterrence," p. 108.

75. Ross, *American War Plans*, pp. 72–73; Gregg Herken, *The Winning Weapon: The Atomic Bomb in the Cold War, 1945–1950* (New York: Knopf, 1980), pp. 253–54; Harry R. Borowski, *A Hollow Threat: Strategic Air Power and Containment Before Korea* (Westport: Greenwood, 1982), pp. 96–107.

76. The quotations are the words of Admiral D. V. Gallery and can be found in Melvyn P. Leffler, *A Preponderance of Power: National Security, the Truman Administration, and the Cold War* (Stanford: Stanford University Press, 1992), p. 274.

77. Rosenberg and Kennedy, *Naval Strategy in a Period of Change*, pp. 67–68.

78. The Harmon Report, JCS 1953/1 of May 12, 1949, has been published in part in Ross and Rosenberg, *America's Plans for War*: vol. 11, *The Limits of Nuclear Strategy*.

79. Rearden, *Formative Years*, pp. 407–9; Rosenberg, "American Atomic Strategy and the Hydrogen Bomb Decision," pp. 72–79; Ross, *American War Plans*, pp. 106–7, 111–19, 128, 131; Herken, *Winning Weapon*, pp. 283–85, 296–97.

80. Millis, *Forrestal Diaries*, pp. 464–68.

81. See Davis, *Postwar Defense Policy and the U.S. Navy*, pp. 240–59; and Vincent Davis, "The Development of a Capability to Deliver Nuclear Weapons by Carrier-Based Aircraft," in Vincent Davis, *The Politics of Innovation: Patterns in Navy Cases* (Denver: University of Denver Press, 1967), pp. 7–22. These writings by Davis contain a good discussion of the design of the AJ-1, of the heroics of then Commanders F. L. Ashworth and J. T. Hayward in getting the plane, of the P2V heavy patrol bomber that was being modified for atomic use (one of which Hayward launched from a carrier in 1949 carrying the secretaries of defense, of the Air Force, and of the Navy, and the chairman of the JCS), and of the support the aircraft development got from Forrestal and Sherman. For details of the development of CVA-58, see Norman Friedman, *U.S. Aircraft Carriers: An Illustrated Design History* (Annapolis: Naval Institute Press, 1983), pp. 225–53. For a discussion of the rumor that the Air Force retarded the development of smaller and lighter nuclear weapons to make it harder for the Navy to deploy them, see Mark Bernard Schneider, "Nuclear Weapons and American Strategy, 1945–1953" (Ph.D. diss., University of Southern California, 1974), pp. 151–52.

82. Quoted in Coletta, *United States Navy and Defense Unification*, p. 139.

83. For a critique of the Navy's case (not that the Air Force's was much better), see Hammond, "Super Carriers and B-36 Bombers," esp. pp. 538–45. Barlow, in " 'The Revolt of the Admirals' Reconsidered," defends the testimony and considers it a success. The hearings themselves are published as *The National Defense Program—Unification and Strategy: Hearings Before the Committee on Armed Services, House of Representatives*, 81st Cong., 1st sess. (hereafter cited as *Unification and Strategy Hearings*).

84. Conflicting views are presented in Lacy, *Within Bounds*, pp. 112–14.

85. Barlow, " 'The Revolt of the Admirals' Reconsidered," pp. 19–21.

86. Rosenberg, "American Postwar Air Doctrine and Organization," pp. 261–63; Rosenberg and Kennedy, *Naval Strategy in a Period of Change*, p. 185.

87. JCS 2081 / 1 of February 13, 1950, published in Ross and Rosenberg, *Limits of Nuclear Strategy*.

88. Rosenberg and Kennedy, *Naval Strategy in a Period of Change*, p. 141.

89. *Unification and Strategy Hearings*, pp. 472, 525. Much on everyone's mind, of course, was the possibility that atomic weapons had made large-scale invasions impossible. After observing the atomic tests at Bikini Lagoon, a Marine Corps lieutenant general, Roy S. Geiger, said that "a small number of atomic bombs could destroy an expeditionary force as now organised, embarked and landed. . . . With the enemy in possession of atomic bombs, I cannot visualise another landing such as was executed at Normandy or Okinawa." Quoted in Geoffrey Till, *Maritime Strategy and the Nuclear Age*, 2d ed. (New York: St. Martin's, 1984), p. 199.

90. Palmer, *Origins of the Maritime Strategy*, pp. 50–52; Robert S. Jordan, "Introduction: The Balance of Power and the Anglo-American Maritime Relationship," in Hattendorf and Jordan, *Maritime Strategy and the Balance of Power*, p. 12.

91. Rearden, *Formative Years*, pp. 421–22.

92. See Stephen Peter Rosen, *Winning the Next War: Innovation and the Modern Military* (Ithaca: Cornell University Press, 1991), pp. 200–218, for the problems the Weapons Systems Evaluation Group had in getting accurate intelligence on Soviet air-defense systems and Soviet guided-missile programs and the lack of knowledge in general that war planners had of Soviet strategic weapons during this period. The planners' ignorance led them to base their evaluation of the Strategic Air Command not on enemy threat but SAC's ability to meet its own internal planning goals.

93. Barlow, " 'The Revolt of the Admirals' Reconsidered," p. 23.

94. Rosenberg and Kennedy, *Naval Strategy in a Period of Change*, p. 141. In a few years, the submarine-launched ballistic missile would complete the naval revolution of aerial power projection ashore, giving the Navy what the officers of 1949 had sought—a strategic nuclear weapon delivered by the Navy.

95. Ross, *American War Plans*, p. 128. Dropshot is published in part (some pages on target planning have been deleted) in Ross and Rosenberg, *America's Plans for War*: vol. 14, *Long Range Planning: Dropshot*.

96. Coletta, *United States Navy and Defense Unification*, p. 213. Johnson used General Bradley's testimony unfairly. At the hearings, Bradley referred to two

types of amphibious operations—*large-scale campaigns*, on the order of Sicily and Normandy, which he thought would be impossible against a Soviet territory defended by atomic bombs; and *island-hopping campaigns*, of which there would be no need in a war against the Soviet Union. Bradley did not address amphibious landings on a smaller scale—to secure air bases, for example. His assertions, nonetheless, stung the Navy. Officers remembered them bitterly when planning the carrier-assisted amphibious assault at Inchon less than a year later. See Omar N. Bradley and Clay Blair, *A General's Life* (New York: Simon & Schuster, 1983), pp. 54 and 715; and Clay Blair, *The Forgotten War: America in Korea, 1950–1953* (New York: Times Books, 1987), pp. 227, 288.

97. For the judgment that their testimony was unprofessional insubordination that could not, and should never again, be tolerated, see Phillip S. Meilinger, "The Admirals' Revolt of 1949: Lessons for Today," *Parameters* 19: 3 (Sept. 1989): 81–96.

CHAPTER 13

1. David A. Rosenberg and Floyd D. Kennedy, Jr., *U.S. Aircraft Carriers in the Strategic Role*: pt. 1, *Naval Strategy in a Period of Change: Interservice Rivalry, Strategic Interaction, and the Development of a Nuclear Attack Capability, 1945–1951* (Falls Church: Lulejian, 1975), p. 166. Also, Clark G. Reynolds, "Forrest Percival Sherman, 2 November 1949–22 July 1951," in Robert William Love, Jr., *The Chiefs of Naval Operations* (Annapolis: Naval Institute Press, 1980), p. 212.

2. For Marine criticism as an indication of the difficulty of satisfying the various Navy communities in the unification process, see Victor H. Krulak, *First to Fight: An Inside View of the U.S. Marine Corps* (Annapolis: Naval Institute Press, 1984), pp. 40–43, 57, 131; Gordon W. Keiser, *The U.S. Marine Corps and Defense Unification, 1944–1947* (Washington, D.C.: National Defense University Press, 1982), pp. 16, 45–46, 69; and Allan R. Millett, *Semper Fidelis: The History of the United States Marine Corps* (New York: Macmillan, 1980), p. 461.

3. Steven L. Rearden, *History of the Office of the Secretary of Defense*: vol. 1, *The Formative Years, 1947–1950* (Washington, D.C.: Office of the Secretary of Defense, 1984), pp. 391–92.

4. For convincing rehabilitations of Sherman, see Michael A. Palmer, *Origins of the Maritime Strategy: American Naval Strategy in the First Postwar Decade* (Washington, D.C.: Naval Historical Center, 1988), chap. 5; and Reynolds, "Sherman," pp. 229–32.

5. Eric Grove and Geoffrey Till, "Anglo-American Maritime Strategy in the Era of Massive Retaliation, 1945–1960," in John B. Hattendorf and Robert S. Jordan, eds., *Maritime Strategy and the Balance of Power: Britain and America in the Twentieth Century* (New York: St. Martin's, 1989), p. 276.

6. This discussion follows Palmer, *Origins of the Maritime Strategy*, pp. 66–68; and James F. Schnabel and Robert J. Watson, *The History of the Joint Chiefs of Staff: The Joint Chiefs and National Policy*: vol. 3, *The Korean War* (Wilmington: Michael Glazier, 1979), pp. 47–48.

7. Palmer, *Origins of the Maritime Strategy*, p. 67.

8. Ibid. The writer quoted was Captain Charles W. Lord.

9. For the British perspective, and the British estimate of the Soviet submarine threat from 1948 to 1950, see Grove and Till, "Anglo-American Maritime Strategy," pp. 277–79, 285–86.

10. Rearden, *Formative Years*, p. 270.

11. Schnabel and Watson, *Korean War*, p. 36.

12. John Lewis Gaddis, "Drawing Lines: The Defensive Perimeter Strategy in East Asia, 1947–1951," in his collection of essays, *The Long Peace: Inquiries into the History of the Cold War* (New York: Oxford University Press, 1987), pp. 72–103.

13. Reynolds, "Sherman," p. 221.

14. This point is emphasized in Paul Nitze, "The Development of NSC 68," *International Security* 4: 4 (Spring 1980): 175.

15. Kenneth W. Condit, *The History of the Joint Chiefs of Staff: The Joint Chiefs of Staff and National Policy*, vol. 2, *1947–1949* (Wilmington: Michael Glazier, 1979), pp. 302, 481–92, 520; Schnabel and Watson, *Korean War*, pp. 34–35. See Dean Acheson, *Present at the Creation: My Years in the State Department* (New York: New American Library, 1969), pp. 463–67, for Acheson's account of the meaning of the speech in which he defined the "defense perimeter," and his reply to critics who claimed the speech encouraged the aggression of the North Koreans by leaving South Korea outside the perimeter.

16. Roger Dingman, "Strategic Planning and the Policy Process: American Plans for War in East Asia, 1945–1950," *Naval War College Review* 32: 6 (Nov.–Dec. 1979): 4–21.

17. For two important discussions of this pre-Korea sense of danger, see Marc Trachtenberg, "A 'Wasting Asset': American Strategy and the Shifting Nuclear Balance, 1949–1954," *International Security* 13: 3 (Winter 1988–89): 5–49; and Nitze, "The Development of NSC 68," pp. 170–76. The February 1950 report by the Joint Intelligence Committee, "Implications of Soviet Possession of Atomic Weapons," JCS 1081 / 1, which declared that the United States was "for the first time vulnerable to serious danger from air and guided missile attack," is reprinted in Steven T. Ross and David Alan Rosenberg, eds., *America's Plans for War Against the Soviet Union, 1945–1950*: vol. 11, *The Limits of Nuclear Strategy* (New York: Garland, 1989).

18. See Samuel F. Wells's, "Sounding the Tocsin: NSC 68 and the Soviet Threat," *International Security*, 4: 2 (Fall 1979): 116–58.

19. There is a large interpretive literature on NSC-68. Most of it argues that the document stood for an essentially defensive and status quo policy. Trachtenberg, in his "A 'Wasting Asset,'" on the other hand, argues that NSC-68 was aggressive and was meant to coerce the Soviets and, as its text stated, to "check and to roll back the Kremlin's drive for world domination." NSC-68 is published in *Foreign Relations of the United States* hereafter cited as *FRUS, 1950*, 7 vols. (Washington, D.C.: GPO, 1976–78), 1: 234–92.

20. *FRUS 1950*, 1: 338–39.

21. See Robert Jervis, "The Impact of the Korean War on the Cold War," *Journal of Conflict Resolution* 24: 4 (Dec. 1980): 563–92; and Samuel F. Wells, Jr., "The First Cold War Buildup: Europe in United States Strategy and Policy, 1950–1953," in Olav Riste, ed., *Western Security: The Formative Years: European and

Atlantic Defence, 1947–1953 (Oslo: Universitetsforlaget; New York: Columbia University Press, 1985), pp. 181–97.

22. James L. Lacy, *Within Bounds: The Navy in Postwar American Security Policy* (Alexandria: Center for Naval Analyses, 1983), p. 145.

23. Matthew B. Ridgway, *The Korean War* (Garden City: Doubleday, 1967), p. 11.

24. For some observations on this point, see Trachtenberg, "A 'Wasting Asset,'" p. 18. The idea of expanding the war to China persisted in Washington circles. See Rosemary Foot, *The Wrong War: American Policy and the Dimensions of the Korean Conflict, 1950–1953* (Ithaca: Cornell University Press, 1985). Such an expansion greatly worried the British, for whom any intensification of an Asian war meant less American attention to Europe. And of course a nuclear war was of immediate concern to the British. See Rosemary J. Foot, "Anglo-American Relations in the Korean Crisis: The British Effort to Avert an Expanded War, December 1950–January 1951," *Diplomatic History* 10: 1 (Winter 1986): 43–57; and William Stueck, "The Limits of Influence: British Policy and American Expansion of the War in Korea," *Pacific Historical Review* 55: 1 (Feb. 1986): 68–74.

25. The ground forces of 19 states (20 if one counts 44 men from Luxembourg) and the ships of 10 served under the United Nations banner against forces of North Korea and China and against covertly participating forces of the Soviet Union. For figures and numbers of the UN Command, see Schnabel and Watson, *The Korean War*, pp. 1104–5.

26. Concerns about the decision are discussed in John Lewis Gaddis, "Drawing Lines," pp. 72–103.

27. *FRUS 1950*, 6: 349.

28. *FRUS 1950*, 7: 149.

29. It was Taiwan that jumped to the mind of the chairman of the Joint Chiefs, General Omar Bradley, when he learned of the North Korean invasion. Walter S. Poole, *The History of the Joint Chiefs of Staff: The Joint Chiefs of Staff and National Policy*: vol. 4, *1950–1952* (Wilmington: Michael Glazier, 1980), p. 387.

30. This is well examined in Doris M. Condit, *History of the Office of the Secretary of Defense*, vol. 2, *The Test of War, 1950–1953* (Washington, D.C.: Office of the Secretary of Defense, 1988).

31. James A. Field, Jr., *History of United States Naval Operations: Korea* (Washington, D.C.: Department of the Navy, 1962), pp. 398–401.

32. Navy leaders had not wanted to undertake the amphibious operation at Wonsan, considering, quite rightly, that it would have been easier to take Wonsan by marching overland toward it. See Clay Blair, *The Forgotten War: America in Korea, 1950–1953* (New York: Times Books, 1987), 341–46; Field, *United States Naval Operations: Korea*, p. 372; and Malcolm W. Cagle and Frank A. Manson, *The Sea War in Korea* (Annapolis: United States Naval Institute, 1957), pp. 107–51. For a study of the mines, the Navy's "humiliation" at Wonsan, and the effect of that experience on "the Wonsan generation" of mine countermeasure officers, see Tamara Moser Melia, *"Damn the Torpedoes": A Short History of U.S. Naval Mine Countermeasures, 1777–1991* (Washington, D.C.: Naval Historical Center, 1991), pp. 70–90. Melia quotes the reports of Rear Admiral Allan E.

Smith, the commander of the Amphibious Task Force: "We have lost control of the seas to a nation without a Navy, using pre–World War I weapons, laid by vessels that were utilized at the time of the birth of Christ." Later he commented, "The strongest Navy in the world had to remain in the Sea of Japan while a few minesweepers struggled to clear Wonsan."

33. Field, *United States Naval Operations: Korea*, p. 50.

34. Cagle and Manson, *Sea War in Korea*, pp. 491–92.

35. Gary W. Hampson, *Strategic Sealift Lessons Learned: A Historical Perspective* (Washington, D.C.: Industrial College of the Armed Forces, 1988), p. 9.

36. Eric J. Grove, *Vanguard to Trident: British Naval Policy Since World War II* (Annapolis: Naval Institute Press, 1987), pp. 138–50.

37. *Military Situation in the Far East: Hearings Before the Committee on Armed Services and the Committee on Foreign Relations, United States Senate*, 82d Cong., 1st sess., pp. 1512–25 (hereafter cited as *Far East Military Situation Hearings*).

38. Truman's statement was issued June 27, 1950. It is quoted in *FRUS 1950*, 6: 367.

39. Field, *United States Naval Operations: Korea*, p. 367.

40. This, of course, was the purpose of the invasion. James F. Schnabel, *The United States Army in the Korean War*, vol. 3, *Policy and Direction: The First Year* (Washington, D.C.: Department of the Army, 1972), p. 161. See also R. D. Heinle, Jr., *Victory at High Tide: The Inchon-Seoul Campaign* (New York: Lippincott, 1968).

41. Cagle and Manson, *Sea War in Korea*, p. 75. See also Lynn Montross and Nicholas A. Canzona, *U.S. Marine Operations in Korea, 1950–1953*: vol. 2, *The Inchon-Seoul Operation* (Washington, D.C.: United States Marine Corps, 1955), pp. 296–97.

42. In the early part of the war, Army forces on the ground lacked the means and doctrine to direct naval bombardments, and it proved hard to isolate a battlefield. Yet in the first six months, air strikes were vital in holding the North Koreans at bay around Pusan, and such strikes destroyed, it was estimated, twice as much equipment and personnel as did artillery. So successful, in fact, were combat air strikes and air interdiction that the services came to expect the same effects when air power was turned against the Chinese. That, as we shall see, turned out to be a different war. For commentary on the never resolved problem of coordinating close air support among all the services, see Robert F. Futrell, *The United States Air Force in Korea, 1950–1953*, rev. ed. (Washington, D.C.: United States Air Force, 1983), pp. 142–45; Cagle and Manson, *Sea War in Korea*, pp. 277–373; Allan R. Millett, "Korea, 1950–1953," in Benjamin Franklin Cooling, ed., *Case Studies in the Development of Close Air Support* (Washington, D.C.: Office of Air Force History, 1990), pp. 345–410; and Eliot A. Cohen and John Gooch, *Military Misfortunes: The Anatomy of Failure in War* (New York: Free Press, 1990), p. 179.

43. Cagle and Manson, *Sea War in Korea*, pp. 104–6.

44. S. G. Gorshkov, *The Sea Power of the State* (Oxford: Pergamon, 1979), p. 240.

45. Schnabel, *Policy and Direction: The First Year*, p. 273.

46. Schnabel and Watson, *Korean War*, p. 331. MacArthur's complacent opinion on the issue is printed in *FRUS 1950*, 7: 1231–33.

47. A point acknowledged by Secretary of State Dean Acheson in Acheson, *Present at the Creation*, pp. 602–5.

48. *FRUS 1950*, 7: 1330.

49. There is an important comparison of these operations in Roy E. Appleman, *East of Chosin: Entrapment and Breakout in Korea, 1950* (College Station: Texas A&M University Press, 1987), pp. 336–40. Appleman concludes: "I believe that the 1st Marine Division in the Chosin Reservoir Campaign was one of the most magnificent fighting organizations that ever served in the United States Armed Forces. It had to be to do what it did, to fight to a standstill the Chinese forces at every point and then carry out a fighting retreat southward against an enemy roadblock and fire block that extended . . . about 40 road miles. This was done in the midst of extremely adverse weather conditions. The Marines never had a brighter moment in their long history than in the Chosin Reservoir Campaign." Appleman, the author of the Army's official history *The United States Army in the Korean War*, vol. 1, *South to the Naktong, North to the Yalu* (Washington, D.C.: Department of the Army, 1961), shows that the success of the marines was based on their experience, their concentration of forces, their success at maintaining radio connections between units and the coast, and the magnificent close air support of the 1st Marine Air Wing. This verdict is fully supported by the detailed account in Lynn Montross and Nicholas A. Canzona with K. Jack Bauer, *U.S. Marine Operations in Korea, 1950–1953*: vol. 3, *The Chosin Reservoir Campaign* (Washington, D.C.: United States Marine Corps, 1957).

50. See among other good discussions Krulak, *First to Fight*, pp. 55–61. The issue of final command authority was decided two years later, in 1954, with the CNO losing to the commandant.

51. Field, *United States Naval Operations: Korea*, pp. 305, 367.

52. Cagle and Manson, *Sea War in Korea*, p. 190.

53. *FRUS 1950*, 1: 481.

54. Ibid., p. 482.

55. Trachtenberg, "A 'Wasting Asset,'" p. 21.

56. Bernard Brodie, *War and Politics* (New York: Macmillan, 1973), p. 115.

57. *Far East Military Situation Hearings*, p. 732.

58. Trachtenberg, "A 'Wasting Asset,'" p. 25.

59. *FRUS 1950*: vol. 7, pp. 1572, 1583.

60. John Lewis Gaddis, "The Origins of Self-Deterrence: The United States and the Non-Use of Nuclear Weapons, 1945–1948," in Gaddis, *Long Peace, 1950–1952*, pp. 115–28.

61. Ibid.

62. Poole, *The Joint Chiefs of Staff and National Policy*, vol. 4, *1950–1952*, pp. 161, 184–91.

63. The nature of the relationship between policy and military position is exemplified in an exchange of February 1951 between the JCS and the State Department. State said it preferred "not to express political objectives with respect to Korea until military capabilities there were established," and the JCS replied that "a political decision was required before there could be suitable determination of military courses of action." Martin Lichterman, "To the Yalu

and Back," in Harold Stein, ed., *American Civil-Military Decisions* (Birmingham: University of Alabama Press, 1963), pp. 625–26.

64. The United States, of course, did not declare that it had decided to halt the advance. That would have given up a potential military initiative and conceded an important bargaining point to the Chinese.

65. Futrell, *United States Air Force in Korea*, p. 703.

66. Schnabel and Watson, *Korean War*, pp. 609–10; Futrell, *United States Air Force in Korea*, p. 192. Navy fighters escorted the B-29s in the raids on Rashin.

67. Cagle and Manson, *Sea War in Korea*, p. 279.

68. Walter G. Hermes, *The United States Army in the Korean War: Truce Tent and Fighting Front* (Washington, D.C.: United States Army, 1966), pp. 73, 197.

69. Cagle and Manson, *Sea War in Korea*, p. 280.

70. Futrell, *United States Air Force in Korea*, pp. 701–2.

71. Ibid., Roger M. Anders, ed., *Forging the Atomic Shield: Excerpts from the Office Diary of Gordon E. Dean* (Chapel Hill: University of North Carolina Press, 1987), p. 137.

72. Roger Dingman, "Atomic Diplomacy During the Korean War," *International Security* 13: 3 (Winter 1988–89): 50–79.

73. See Allen S. Whiting, *China Crosses the Yalu: The Decision to Enter the Korean War* (Santa Monica: Rand Corporation, 1961).

74. Robert Frank Futrell, *Ideas, Concepts, Doctrine: A History of Basic Thinking in the United States Air Force, 1907–1964*, vol. 1 (Montgomery: Air University, 1971), p. 319.

75. For recent balanced judgments on the influence of the possible use of the atomic bomb, see Dingman, "Atomic Diplomacy"; Rosemary J. Foot, "Nuclear Coercion and the Ending of the Korean Conflict," *International Security* 13: 3 (Winter 1988–89): 92–112; Edward C. Keefer, "President Dwight D. Eisenhower and the End of the Korean War," *Diplomatic History* 10: 3 (Summer 1986): 267–89; Gaddis, "Origins of Self-Deterrence," pp. 124–29; and Richard K. Betts, *Nuclear Blackmail and Nuclear Balance* (Washington, D.C.: Brookings Institution, 1987), pp. 31–47. Each of these authors concludes that Eisenhower's consideration of the use of the bomb late in the war was tentative and one of several factors at the war's end whose actual effect on Moscow and Beijing we do not in fact know.

CHAPTER 14

1. Department of the Navy, Naval Research Advisory Committee, *Report on Historical Perspectives in Long-Range Planning in the Navy* (Washington, D.C.: Office of the Assistant Secretary of the Navy—Research, Engineering, and Systems, 1980), p. A-17.

2. Two years later Captain Arleigh Burke of the Strategic Plans Division of the Office of the CNO used the same expression about the war the French were fighting in Indochina, saying it was "much like the old Indian Wars in the United States." Edwin Bickford Hooper, Dean C. Allard, and Oscar P. Fitzgerald, *The United States Navy and the Vietnam Conflict*: vol. 1, *The Setting of the Stage to 1959* (Washington, D.C.: Department of the Navy, 1976), p. 204.

3. Quoted in Samuel P. Huntington, *The Common Defense: Strategic Programs in National Politics* (New York: Columbia University Press, 1961), pp. 344–45.

4. Malcolm W. Cagle and Frank A. Manson, *The Sea War in Korea* (Annapolis: United States Naval Institute, 1957), p. 491.

5. Some of the constraints are discussed in James L. Lacy, *Within Bounds: The Navy in Postwar American Security Policy* (Alexandria: Center for Naval Analyses, 1983), p. 316. Air Force officers further discounted the Navy's role in Korea, noting that after the initial naval air strikes delivered from the *Valley Forge* around Pusan in the first days of the war, the Air Force got its own land-based air swiftly into operation and thereafter flew the lion's share of the missions—720,980 sorties, compared to 167,552 for the Navy and 107,303 for the Marines.

6. This September 1951 statement is quoted in David Alan Rosenberg, "American Postwar Air Doctrine and Organization: The Navy Experience," in A. P. Hurley and R. C. Ehrhart, eds., *Air Power and Warfare* (Washington, D.C.: Office of Air Force History, 1979), p. 265.

7. Ibid.

8. David A. Rosenberg and Floyd D. Kennedy, Jr., *U.S. Aircraft Carriers in the Strategic Role*: pt. 1, *Naval Strategy in a Period of Change: Interservice Rivalry, Strategic Interaction, and the Development of a Nuclear Attack Capability, 1945–1951* (Falls Church: Lulejian, 1975), pp. 174–75; Rosenberg, "American Postwar Air Doctrine and Organization: The Navy Experience," pp. 264–65; Lacy, *Within Bounds*, p. 151.

9. Paolo E. Coletta, *The United States Navy and Defense Unification, 1947–1953* (Newark: University of Delaware Press, 1981), p. 283.

10. Rosenberg, "American Postwar Air Doctrine and Organization," p. 264.

11. Norman Friedman, *U.S. Aircraft Carriers: An Illustrated Design History* (Annapolis: Naval Institute Press, 1983), pp. 255–57; Norman Friedman, *The Postwar Naval Revolution* (Annapolis: Naval Institute Press, 1986), p. 19.

12. Eric Grove and Geoffrey Till, "Anglo-American Maritime Strategy in the Era of Massive Retaliation, 1945–1960," in John B. Hattendorf and Robert S. Jordan, eds., *Maritime Strategy and the Balance of Power: Britain and America in the Twentieth Century* (New York: St. Martin's, 1989), pp. 283–84. For British reservations about the use of strike carriers for attacks "at source," and for Royal Navy defense strategy at this point, see Eric J. Grove, *Vanguard to Trident: British Naval Policy Since World War II* (Annapolis: Naval Institute Press, 1987), pp. 101–18.

13. Stephen E. Ambrose with Morris Honick, "Eisenhower: Rekindling the Spirit of the West," in Robert S. Jordan, ed., *Generals in International Politics: NATO's Supreme Allied Commander, Europe* (Lexington: University Press of Kentucky, 1987), p. 20. The resolution of command problems in NATO's Southern Command in 1953 is noted in George Eugene Pelletier, "Ridgway: Trying to Make Good on the Promises," in Jordan, *Generals in International Politics*, pp. 44–48.

14. Robert Jordan discusses NATO organization in Robert S. Jordan, *Alliance Strategy and Navies: The Evolution and Scope of NATO's Maritime Dimension* (New York: St. Martin's, 1990), pp. 1–16, 35–62. On Britain see Grove, *Vanguard to Trident*, pp. 103–5, 164–70. On Norway see Rolf Tamnes, "Norway's Struggle for

the Northern Flank, 1950–1952," in Olav Riste, ed., *Western Security: The Formative Years: European and Atlantic Defence, 1947–1953* (Oslo: Universitetsforlaget; New York: Columbia University Press, 1985), pp. 215–43.

15. The projection problems experienced in the exercises Mainbrace, which involved over 200 NATO vessels, and Mariner, which involved 300 ships, 1,000 aircraft, and over 500,000 officers and men, are summarized in Grove and Till, "Anglo-American Maritime Strategy," p. 287. It should be noted that these were not "wartime" tests of carrier air, because the rules governing the flights were those of peacetime operations. NATO exercises were also held in the Mediterranean.

16. The General Board's study of 1948, "National Security and Navy Contributions Thereto Over the Next Ten Years," written by then Captain Arleigh Burke, is discussed in Naval Research Advisory Committee, *Historical Perspectives*, pp. 20–21.

17. Useful observations on these modes are made in Friedman, *U.S. Aircraft Carriers*, pp. 335–37.

18. Naval Research Advisory Committee, *Historical Perspectives*, pp. A-29 to A-31. A shift to the sea-control rationale is sketched in Friedman, *Postwar Naval Revolution*, pp. 22–26.

19. Naval Research Advisory Committee, *Historical Perspectives*, pp. 23–24.

20. Grove and Till, "Anglo-American Maritime Strategy," pp. 285–86.

21. Cagle and Manson, *Sea War in Korea*, p. 493.

22. The Soviet government years later revealed that the test was an atomic blast, not an explosion of a breakthrough thermonuclear weapon. William J. Broad, "Soviet H-Bomb Lag in 1950's Reported," *New York Times*, October 7, 1990.

23. John Lewis Gaddis's interpretation of NSC-68, an interpretation that develops the idea of "symmetrical" containment, was put forward in his *Strategies of Containment: A Critical Appraisal of Postwar American National Security Policy* (New York: Oxford, 1982), chap. 4. His elaboration of the idea in relation to the early 1950s is found in his article "Drawing Lines: The Defensive Perimeter Strategy in East Asia, 1947–1951," in John Lewis Gaddis, *The Long Peace: Inquiries into the History of the Cold War* (New York: Oxford University Press, 1987), pp. 72–103.

24. See NSC-153/1 of June 1953, printed in *Foreign Relations of the United States* (hereafter cited as *FRUS*) *1952–1954*, vol. 2, pt. 1 (Washington, D.C.: GPO, 1984), pp. 378–86. The document is reproduced in the useful collection edited by Marc Trachtenberg, *The Development of American Strategic Thought: Basic Documents from the Eisenhower and Kennedy Periods, Including the Basic National Security Papers from 1953 to 1959* (New York: Garland, 1988), hereafter cited as *Basic Documents*.

25. *FRUS 1952–1954*, vol. 2, pt. 1, p. 593.

26. Dulles's speech, "The Evolution of Foreign Policy," was delivered to the Council on Foreign Relations in New York City on January 12, 1954. It is published, as is Eisenhower's "State of the Union" address, in Peter V. Curl, ed., *Documents on American Foreign Relations, 1954* (New York: Harper, 1955), pp. 1–15.

27. The quote is from NSC-5501, reproduced in Trachtenberg, *Basic Documents*, p. 97.

28. Richard G. Hewlett and Jack M. Holl, *Atoms for Peace and War, 1953–1961: Eisenhower and the Atomic Energy Commission* (Berkeley: University of California Press, 1989), pp. 164–82.

29. For an incisive critique of this part of the confusion, see H. W. Brands, "The Age of Vulnerability: Eisenhower and the National Insecurity State," *American Historical Review* 94: 4 (Oct. 1989): 981–94.

30. David Alan Rosenberg, "The Origins of Overkill: Nuclear Weapons and American Strategy, 1945–1960," *International Security* 7: 4 (Spring 1983): 27–28.

31. David Alan Rosenberg, "Reality and Responsibility: Power and Process in the Making of United States Nuclear Strategy, 1945–68," *Journal of Strategic Studies* 9: 1 (Mar. 1986): 42; Rosenberg, "Origins of Overkill," p. 30.

32. The phrase is John Gaddis's, from his important article "The Origins of Self-Deterrence: The United States and the Non-Use of Nuclear Weapons, 1945–1958," in Gaddis, *Long Peace*, pp. 104–46. On a somewhat different subject, two recent articles on Eisenhower's position on preventive war show how scant evidence can lead different writers to different interpretations of intention and causality. The author of one of the articles concludes, "The notion of preventive war in the nuclear age violated [Eisenhower's] deepest beliefs. For this president, it was not an option, regardless of Solarium's logic—or that of the Cold War." Solarium was a 1953 study of strategic options. The authors of the second article concludes that two or three times "Eisenhower gave at least fleeting thought to preventive war." The first quotation is from Richard H. Immerman, "Confessions of an Eisenhower Revisionist: An Agonizing Reappraisal," *Diplomatic History* 14: 3 (Summer 1990): 337. The second is from Russell D. Buhite and Wm. Christopher Hamel, "War for Peace: The Question of an American Preventive War Against the Soviet Union, 1945–1955," ibid., p. 380. The best conclusion is David Rosenberg's: "The question of whether SAC would actually have been used for preemption remains open. . . . no high national policy decision in the gray area of preemption was ever made." David Alan Rosenberg, "A Smoking Radiating Ruin at the End of Two Hours: Documents on American Plans for Nuclear War with the Soviet Union, 1954–1955," *International Security* 6: 3 (Winter 1981–82): 13.

33. Rosenberg, "American Postwar Air Doctrine and Organization: The Navy Experience," pp. 267–68. Also, Edward J. Marolda, "The Influence of Burke's Boys on Limited War," United States Naval Institute *Proceedings* (hereafter cited as *Proceedings*) 107: 8 (Aug. 1981): 37.

34. Rosenberg, "American Postwar Air Doctrine and Organization: The Navy Experience," pp. 268–69.

35. Lacy, *Within Bounds*, pp. 206–12.

36. The first part of the following discussion of the Navy in the early phase of the Indochina war draws upon the official Navy history Hooper, Allard, and Fitzgerald, *Setting of the Stage to 1959*, pp. 232–55.

37. Curl, *Documents on American Foreign Relations, 1954*, p. 11.

38. Radford's insistence on a unilateral air strike and his unsuccessful at-

tempt to argue his case from the JCS platform against the advice of Army Chief of Staff General Matthew Ridgway and CNO Carney are discussed in Richard H. Immerman, "Between the Unattainable and the Unacceptable: Eisenhower and Dienbienphu," in Richard A. Melanson and David Mayers, eds., *Reevaluating Eisenhower: American Foreign Policy in the 1950s* (Urbana: University of Illinois Press, 1987), pp. 120, 138. Ridgway was sure that this was no place to "test the New Look." He thought that any air or naval action would not in itself suffice and would have to be followed by ground support, which he felt would be a grave commitment and bad allocation of U.S. forces. See Matthew B. Ridgway, *Soldier* (New York: Harper, 1976), pp. 275–77. The reluctance of the military leadership to commit to what it saw as a dangerous and pointless war in Indochina is detailed in Robert Buzzanco, "Prologue to Tragedy: U.S. Military Opposition to Intervention in Vietnam, 1950–1954," *Diplomatic History* 17: 2 (Spring 1993): 201–22.

39. For the argument that the basis of Dulles's opposition to using atomic weapons was both moral and diplomatic, the latter because his main concern was building up a defense community in Europe, see Frederick W. Marks III, "The Real Hawk at Dienbienphu: Dulles or Eisenhower?" *Pacific Historical Review* 59: 3 (Aug. 1990): 297–322. (The answer Marks gives to the question in the article's title is *the president*.) For the argument that Dulles's restraint came also from his opposition to unilateral action and his insistence on a collective response by colonial powers in, and the states of, Southeast Asia, see George C. Herring, "'A Good Stout Effort': John Foster Dulles and the Indochina Crisis, 1954–1955," in Richard H. Immerman, ed., *John Foster Dulles and the Diplomacy of the Cold War* (Princeton: Princeton University Press, 1990), pp. 213–33. In the opinion of V. Nguyen Giap, the Vietnamese commander besieging Dien Bien Phu, if the United States had intervened, "we would have had problems, but the outcome would have been the same. The battlefield was too big for effective bombing." Stanley Karnow, "Giap Remembers," *New York Times Magazine*, June 24, 1990, p. 59.

40. Department of Defense, *United States–Vietnam Relations, 1945–1967* (Washington, D.C.: GPO, 1971), 9: 478, 487.

41. General Taylor noted such reservations in the case of Korea. Maxwell D. Taylor, *Swords and Plowshares* (New York: Norton, 1972), p. 134.

42. H. W. Brands, Jr., "Testing Massive Retaliation: Credibility and Crisis Management in the Taiwan Strait," *International Security* 12: 4 (Spring 1988): 124–39; Gordon H. Chang, "To the Nuclear Brink: Eisenhower, Dulles, and the Quemoy-Matsu Crisis," ibid., pp. 96–123; Richard K. Betts, *Nuclear Blackmail and Nuclear Balance* (Washington, D.C.: Brookings Institution, 1987), pp. 48–67.

43. Brands, "Age of Vulnerability," pp. 983–84.

44. Carney to Radford, April 22, 1955, in *FRUS 1955–57*, vol. 2 (Washington, D.C.: GPO, 1986), p. 504.

45. NSC-5501 of January 1955, in Trachtenberg, *Basic Documents*, p. 106.

46. Richard K. Smith, *Cold War Navy* (Falls Church: Lulejian for the Department of the Navy, 1976), chap. 14; Lacy, *Within Bounds*, pp. 211–12.

47. Thomas C. Hone, *Power and Change: The Administrative History of the Office*

of the Chief of Naval Operations, 1946–1986 (Washington, D.C.: Department of the Navy, Naval Historical Center, 1989), pp. 34–39.

48. "Meeting the Threat of Surprise Attack," in Trachtenberg, *Basic Documents*, pp. 353, 451. The chairman of the committee was James R. Killian, Jr., of the Massachusetts Institute of Technology.

49. "And that submarine was the world's most revolutionary undersea craft to go to sea since the end of the previous century." Norman Polmar and Thomas B. Allen, *Rickover: Controversy and Genius* (New York: Simon & Schuster, 1982), p. 179.

50. David Alan Rosenberg, "Arleigh Albert Burke, 17 August 1955–1 August 1961," in Robert William Love, Jr., *The Chiefs of Naval Operations* (Annapolis: Naval Institute Press, 1980), pp. 276–77; "Estimate of Situation," annex to NSC-5602/1 of March 1956, in Trachtenberg, *Basic Documents*, p. 147.

51. Huntington, *Common Defense*, p. 424. These service proportions are reviewed in a sophisticated study by Arnold Kanter, *Defense Politics: A Budgetary Perspective* (Chicago: University of Chicago Press, 1979), pp. 30–37.

52. Michael M. McCrea et al., *The Offensive Navy Since World War II* (Alexandria: Center for Naval Analyses, 1989), pp. 6–26.

53. Rosenberg, "Arleigh Albert Burke," pp. 280–81; Naval Research Advisory Committee, *Historical Perspectives*, pp. 31–39; Friedman, *Postwar Naval Revolution*, pp. 49–55; Hone, *Power and Change*, pp. 52–55.

54. Maxwell D. Taylor, *The Uncertain Trumpet* (New York: Harper, 1959), pp. 38–41, 52.

55. Rosenberg, "Arleigh Albert Burke," pp. 281–84.

56. Rosenberg, "Origins of Overkill," pp. 37, 50–51.

57. Taylor, *Uncertain Trumpet*, pp. 115–80.

58. Huntington, *Common Defense*, p. 424; Edward A. Kolodziej, *The Uncommon Defense and Congress, 1945–1963* (Columbus: Ohio State University Press, 1966), pp. 238–52.

59. Taylor, *Uncertain Trumpet*, pp. 100–102.

60. For the Gaither Report (named for H. Rowan Gaither, Jr., the original leader of the reporting panel), the National Security Council's report "Deterrence and Survival in the Nuclear Age," and an accompanying editorial comment, see Trachtenberg, *Basic Documents*, pp. 511–99. The quotes are from pp. 529, 540–41, 551, and 554. For additional comments on the report, see Morton Halperin's "The Gaither Committee and the Policy Process," in Morton H. Halperin, *National Security Policy-Making: Analyses, Cases, and Proposals* (Lexington: Heath, 1975), pp. 47–109. Halperin's book also contains the text of the report.

61. Rosenberg, "Arleigh Albert Burke," p. 277–78; Michael H. Armacost, *The Politics of Weapons Innovation: The Thor-Jupiter Controversy* (New York: Columbia University Press, 1969), p. 68.

62. "Meeting the Threat of Surprise Attack," in Trachtenberg, *Basic Documents*, p. 405.

63. Vincent Davis, *The Politics of Innovation: Patterns in Navy Cases* (Denver: University of Denver Press, 1967), pp. 40–41.

64. Quoted in Desmond Ball, *Politics and Force Levels: The Strategic Missile Program of the Kennedy Administration* (Berkeley: University of California Press, 1980), pp. 60–61.

65. Rosenberg, "Arleigh Albert Burke," pp. 277–79.

66. Armacost, *Politics of Weapons Innovation*, p. 106n; Harvey M. Sapolsky, *The Polaris System Development: Bureaucratic and Programmatic Success in Government* (Cambridge: Harvard University Press, 1972), pp. 16–17; Graham Spinardi, "Why the U.S. Navy Went for Hard-Target Counterforce in Trident II (And Why It Didn't Get There Sooner)," *International Security* 15: 2 (Fall 1990): 153–54.

67. Spinardi, "Why the U.S. Navy Went for Hard-Target Counterforce," pp. 151–52, 157; Naval Research Advisory Committee, *Historical Perspectives*, pp. 48–49. See also Harvey Sapolsky, "Technological Innovators: Admirals Raborn and Rickover," in Arnold R. Shapack, *Naval History Symposium—The Navy in an Age of Change and Crisis: Some Challenges and Responses of the Twentieth Century* (Annapolis: United States Naval Academy, 1973), pp. 23–35, and the follow-up commentary by Eugene M. Emme, "Comments," pp. 36–40.

68. Rosenberg, "Origins of Overkill," pp. 50, 56–57.

69. Sapolsky, *Polaris System Development*, p. 169. The position that the development of Polaris should be a "national" program, a position that had anti–Air Force overtones, was subjected to the derision of McNamara's civilian planners in the Pentagon in the years ahead. Alain C. Enthoven and K. Wayne Smith, *How Much Is Enough? Shaping the Defense Program, 1961–1969* (New York: Harper & Row, 1971), p. 17.

70. Elmo R. Zumwalt, Jr., *On Watch: A Memoir* (New York: Quadrangle, 1976), p. 81. A rundown on Regulus's development is found in Floyd D. Kennedy, Jr., "The Creation of the Cold War Navy, 1953–1962," in Kenneth J. Hagan, ed., *In Peace and War: Interpretations of American Naval History, 1775–1984*, 2d ed. (Westport: Greenwood Press, 1984), p. 308.

71. Sapolsky, *Polaris System Development*, pp. 169–78. The quote is from p. 237.

72. On Rickover's strengths and limitations in his extra-Navy position, see the conclusions in Thomas C. Hone, "Seapower: From Ideology to Technology," paper delivered at the meeting of the American Historical Association in San Francisco in December 1989.

73. The technical story is told clearly in Francis Duncan, *Rickover and the Nuclear Navy: The Discipline of Technology* (Annapolis: Naval Institute Press, 1990), chap. 2, and, more generally, in Polmar and Allen, *Rickover*, pp. 547–50.

74. This is an important point because Rickover was prone to invent Navy opposition to gain sympathy in Congress and to secure his control. See the letter from Norman Polmar in *Proceedings* 116: 5 (May 1990): 37.

75. Polmar and Allen, *Rickover*, p. 353. For a critical look at Rickover's inflexibility in submarine design and the way he limited potentially valuable alternatives, see Harold C. Hemond, "The Flip Side of Rickover," *Proceedings* 115: 7 (July 1989): 42–47.

76. Spinardi, "Why the U.S. Navy Went for Hard-Target Counterforce," pp. 155–56.

77. James M. Roherty, *Decisions of Robert S. McNamara: A Study of the Role of the*

Secretary of Defense (Coral Gables: University of Miami Press, 1970), p. 122. For a study of Rickover's achievements that includes some trenchant comparisons of the accomplishments of Raborn and Rickover as managers of technological innovation, see the Atomic Energy Commission's official history of these years in Richard G. Hewlett and Francis Duncan, *Nuclear Navy, 1946–1962* (Chicago: University of Chicago Press, 1974), esp. pp. 306–17, 377–91.

78. Cited in Marolda, "The Influence of Burke's Boys on Limited War," p. 37.

79. See Rosenberg, "Arleigh Albert Burke," pp. 292–93, for the Navy's thinking on this issue. For the Army's thinking, see Taylor, *Uncertain Trumpet*, pp. 4–7, 47–63.

80. See the letters by Burke, discussing a posture statement and a building program based on the OP-93 report in Naval Research Advisory Committee, *Historical Perspectives*, pp. A-35 to A-50. The quotations are on pp. A-41, A-45, and A-46.

81. The quote can be found in Marolda, "The Influence of Burke's Boys on Limited War," p. 38.

82. Naval Research Advisory Committee, *Historical Perspectives*, p. A-46.

83. Ibid., p. 47.

84. Ibid., p. A-43; Marolda, "The Influence of Burke's Boys on Limited War," p. 40.

85. Naval Research Advisory Committee, *Historical Perspectives*, p. A-43; Rosenberg, "American Postwar Air Doctrine and Organization: The Navy Experience," p. 269; Rosenberg, "Arleigh Albert Burke," p. 293.

86. Messages found in Rosenberg, "Arleigh Albert Burke," p. 283. On general strategic situation in the area, see Michael A. Palmer, *On the Course to Desert Storm: The United States Navy and the Persian Gulf* (Washington, D.C.: Naval Historical Center, 1992), p. 64.

87. Rosenberg, "Arleigh Albert Burke," p. 283; Smith, *Cold War Navy*, p. 19 of chapter 11 and pp. 7–18 of chapter 13; William B. Garrett, "The U.S. Navy's Role in the 1956 Suez Crisis," *Naval War College Review* 22: 7 (Mar. 1970): 66–78.

88. William Stivers, "Eisenhower and the Middle East," in Melanson and Mayers, *Reevaluating Eisenhower*, p. 208.

89. So he told Robert Murphy, whom he sent to Lebanon as his personal representative to coordinate diplomatic and military operations. Robert Murphy, *Diplomat Among the Warriors* (Garden City: Doubleday, 1964), pp. 397–98.

90. Stivers, "Eisenhower and the Middle East," p. 208.

91. The quotes are from H. H. Lumpkin's "Operation Blue Bat," a contemporary command study cited in Gary H. Wade, *Rapid Deployment Logistics: Lebanon, 1958* (Fort Leavenworth: United States Army Command and General Staff College, 1984), p. ix; and from Roger J. Spiller, *"Not War but Like War": The American Intervention in Lebanon* (Fort Leavenworth: United States Army Command and General Staff College, 1981), p. 44. A commentary on Spiller's paper was written by David Gray, the commanding general of the 24th Airborne Brigade, in David W. Gray, *The U.S. Intervention in Lebanon, 1958: A Commander's Reminiscence* (Fort Leavenworth: United States Army Command and General Staff College, 1984).

92. See Arleigh Burke, "The Lebanon Crisis," in Shapack, *Naval History Symposium*, pp. 70–80; and Jack Shulimson, *Marines in Lebanon, 1958* (Washington, D.C.: Headquarters, United States Marine Corps, 1966).

93. Kennedy, "Creation of the Cold War Navy," pp. 321–22.

94. Spiller, *"Not War but Like War,"* p. 45.

95. For a discussion of how the "prediction of dire consequences" led to—or at least was given as the reason for—action, see the 1966 *Public Policy* article by Morton H. Halperin and Tang Tsou, "United States Policy Toward the Offshore Islands," which is reprinted in Halperin, *National Security Policy-Making*, pp. 38–40.

96. Cited in Betts, *Nuclear Blackmail and Nuclear Balance*, p. 70.

97. Quoted in Rosenberg, "Arleigh Albert Burke," p. 290.

98. Gaddis, "Origins of Self-Deterrence," pp. 144–45.

99. For Burke's fleet orders and the Navy's deployments, see Smith, *Cold War Navy*, chap. 16.

100. Lacy, *Within Bounds*, pp. 211–12, 269–70; Marolda, "The Influence of Burke's Boys on Limited War," p. 40; Rosenberg, "Arleigh Albert Burke," pp. 300–301.

101. Rosenberg, "Origins of Overkill," p. 69.

102. Rosenberg, "Arleigh Albert Burke," pp. 302–5.

CHAPTER 15

1. William A. Lucas and Raymond H. Dawson, *The Organizational Politics of Defense* (Pittsburgh: International Studies Association, 1974), p. 84.

2. The quotes are from Eisenhower's message to Congress of April 3, 1958, printed in Alice C. Cole et al., eds., *The Department of Defense: Documents on Establishment and Organization, 1944–1978* (Washington, D.C.: Office of the Secretary of Defense, 1978), pp. 175–76. This book also contains the text of the 1958 law, on pages 188–230.

3. There were eight: the Alaskan, Atlantic, Caribbean, Continental Air Defense, Eastern Atlantic and Mediterranean, European, Pacific, and Strategic Air commands.

4. John C. Ries, *The Management of Defense: Organization and Control of the U.S. Armed Services* (Baltimore: Johns Hopkins University Press, 1964), p. 130; Lucas and Dawson, *Organizational Politics of Defense*, pp. 84–85.

5. Burke to Rear Admiral Walter G. Schindler, May 14, 1958, quoted in David Alan Rosenberg, "Arleigh Albert Burke, 17 August 1955–1 August 1961," in Robert William Love, Jr., *The Chiefs of Naval Operations* (Annapolis: Naval Institute Press, 1980), p. 287.

6. Dwight D. Eisenhower, *Waging Peace: 1956–1961* (Garden City: Doubleday, 1965), p. 250.

7. Rosenberg, "Arleigh Albert Burke," pp. 286–88.

8. Quoted in Charles J. Hitch, *Decision-Making for Defense* (Berkeley: University of California Press, 1966), p. 27.

9. Alain C. Enthoven and K. Wayne Smith, *How Much Is Enough? Shaping the*

Defense Program, 1961–1969 (New York: Harper & Row, 1971), p. 3. Emphases added.

10. This discussion follows Samuel P. Huntington, *The Common Defense: Strategic Programs in National Politics* (New York: Columbia University Press, 1961), pp. 423–24.

11. See Robert J. Art, *The TFX Decision: McNamara and the Military* (Boston: Little, Brown, 1968), pp. 157–66.

12. Ries, *Management of Defense*, pp. 188–90; James L. Lacy, *Within Bounds: The Navy in Postwar American Security Policy* (Alexandria: Center for Naval Analyses, 1983), pp. 283–84.

13. Enthoven and Smith, *How Much Is Enough?* p. 6. The expansion of OSD is indicated by the growth in the number of its deputy assistant secretaries of defense, from 11 in 1960 to 29 in 1965 and 32 in 1967, and by a 50 percent increase in the number of its civilian employees during those same years. Figures cited in Lacy, *Within Bounds*, pp. 298–99.

14. Enthoven and Smith, *How Much Is Enough?* pp. 2, 7.

15. Five years later, in mid-1967, the total was up to 79,134. In 1990 the number was around 97,000.

16. Thomas C. Hone, *Power and Change: The Administrative History of the Office of the Chief of Naval Operations, 1946–1986* (Washington, D.C.: Naval Historical Center, Department of the Navy, 1989), p. 75. The mood within the Navy is conveyed by another historian of the Navy Department, Edwin Hooper: "By now [1966] the Navy Department bore little more than superficial resemblance to the highly effective, responsive, and efficient system of responsibility, authority, and relationships that had contributed so much to victory in World War II." Edwin B. Hooper, *The Navy Department: Evolution and Fragmentation* (Washington, D.C.: Navy Historical Foundation, 1970), p. 40.

17. Enthoven and Smith, *How Much Is Enough?* p. 232; Hone, *Power and Change*, p. 79.

18. Admiral David McDonald, CNO during the high McNamara years of 1963–67, noted of his time in office, "I often felt that I had no more authority than a Lieutenant Commander." No wonder McDonald had not wanted to take the job. For a study of his time in office, see Floyd D. Kennedy, Jr., "David Lamar McDonald, 1 August 1963–1 August 1967," in Love, *Chiefs of Naval Operations*, pp. 333–49. For McDonald's lament, see Hone, *Power and Change*, p. 129. During the same period, the secretary of the Navy was Paul Nitze, who "decided to make a virtue out of necessity." Paul H. Nitze, "Running the Navy: A Personal Memoir," United States Naval Institute *Proceedings* (hereafter cited as *Proceedings*) 115: 9 (Sept. 1989): 71–77.

19. Enthoven and Smith, *How Much Is Enough?* p. 91. On page 106, they add: "Freed from the frequent diversions to other tasks that the career military officer must face, the civilian has more time to concentrate on developing his analytical skills and more opportunities to use them. In any event, as the force planning process becomes more analytical, the argument for excluding civilians from this process on the grounds that they lack relevant operational experience becomes less and less convincing."

20. Lucas and Dawson, *Organizational Politics of Defense*, p. 118.

21. Arnold Kanter, *Defense Politics: A Budgetary Perspective* (Chicago: University of Chicago Press, 1979), p. 94.

22. Ries, *Management of Defense*, p. 191.

23. Kanter, *Defense Politics*, pp. 121–23.

24. Maxwell D. Taylor, *The Uncertain Trumpet* (New York: Harper, 1959), pp. 102, 166, 168.

25. Hone, *Power and Change*, pp. 64–66.

26. Admiral Claude V. Ricketts, quoted in Hooper, *Navy Department*, p. 39.

27. Desmond Ball, "The Development of the SIOP, 1960–1983," in Desmond Ball and Jeffrey Richelson, eds., *Strategic Nuclear Targeting* (Ithaca: Cornell University Press, 1986), p. 62.

28. David Alan Rosenberg, "The Origins of Overkill: Nuclear Weapons and American Strategy, 1945–1960," *International Security* 7: 4 (Spring 1983): 4–8.

29. Ibid., pp. 67–68. SIOP-62, as presented to President Kennedy in September 1961, is published in Scott D. Sagan, "SIOP-62: The Nuclear War Plan Briefing to President Kennedy," *International Security* 12: 1 (Summer 1987): 22–51.

30. David Alan Rosenberg, "Reality and Responsibility: Power and Process in the Making of United States Nuclear Strategy, 1945–1968," *Journal of Strategic Studies* 9: 1 (Mar. 1986): 43–50; Ball, "Development of the SIOP," 58–70.

31. Desmond Ball, *Politics and Force Levels: The Strategic Missile Program of the Kennedy Administration* (Berkeley: University of California Press, 1980), pp. 110–13.

32. Quoted in Lacy, *Within Bounds*, p. 327.

33. Enthoven and Smith, *How Much Is Enough?* pp. 16–17.

34. Rosenberg, "Arleigh Albert Burke," pp. 302–3.

35. Harvey M. Sapolsky, *The Polaris System Development: Bureaucratic and Programmatic Success in Government* (Cambridge: Harvard University Press, 1972), p. 172.

36. Ball, *Politics and Force Levels*, pp. 108, 205–11.

37. James M. Roherty, *Decisions of Robert S. McNamara: A Study of the Role of the Secretary of Defense* (Coral Gables: University of Miami Press, 1970), pp. 145, 150–51; Carl H. Amme, Jr., "Crisis of Confidence," *Proceedings* 90: 3 (Mar. 1964): 33.

38. Statement of Admiral Horacio Rivero, cited in Kennedy, "David Lamar McDonald," p. 344.

39. David L. McDonald, "Carrier Employment Since 1950," *Proceedings* 90: 11 (Nov. 1964): 26–33.

40. For McNamara's change of mind about carriers as U.S. commitment to Vietnam increased, see Roherty, *Decisions of Robert S. McNamara*, pp. 151–72.

41. Richard K. Betts, *Nuclear Blackmail and Nuclear Balance* (Washington, D.C.: Brookings Institution, 1987), pp. 92–109; Enthoven and Smith, *How Much Is Enough?* p. 167.

42. William W. Kaufmann, *Planning Conventional Forces, 1950–1980* (Washington, D.C.: Brookings Institution, 1982), pp. 4–14.

43. For a review of the three main possible Soviet motives (to deter an American invasion of Cuba, to redress the strategic missile imbalance, and to counter U.S. deployments of nuclear weapons on the Soviet periphery), see Bruce J. Allyn, James G. Blight, and David A. Welch, "Essence of Revision: Moscow, Havana, and the Cuban Missile Crisis," *International Security* 14: 3 (Winter 1989–90): 138–44. Andrey Gromyko, then Soviet foreign minister, said in 1989, "[The Soviet leaders'] action was intended to strengthen the defensive stability of Cuba. To avert threats against it. I repeat, to strengthen the defensive capability of Cuba. That is all." Robert S. McNamara, "One Minute to Doomsday," *New York Times*, October 14, 1992. The U.S. government followed the more likely CIA estimate: "A major Soviet objective in their military buildup in Cuba is to demonstrate that the world balance of forces has shifted so far in their favor that the US can no longer prevent the advance of Soviet offensive power even into its own hemisphere. . . . They expect their missile forces in Cuba to make an important contribution to their total strategic capability vis-à-vis the US." Mary S. McAuliffe, ed., *CIA Documents on the Cuban Missile Crisis, 1962* (Washington, D.C.: CIA, 1992), p. 214. There were also other interests. See Fedor Burlatsky, "Castro Wanted a Nuclear Strike," *New York Times*, October 23, 1992. Robert Weinland gives a lucid discussion of the crisis—and of its effect on the subsequent expansion of the Soviet ICBM and naval forces and consequently on strategic balance—in Robert G. Weinland, "The Evolution of Soviet Requirements for Naval Forces: Solving the Problems of the Early 1960s," *Survival* 26: 1 (Jan.–Feb. 1984): 16–25. See also Hannes Adomeit, "Bluff and Deception in the Khrushchev Era," in David A. Charters and Maurice A. J. Tugwell, eds., *Deception Operations: Studies in the East-West Conflict* (London: Brassey's, 1990), pp. 117–36.

44. The quotations are cited in Richard H. Kohn and Joseph P. Harahan, eds., "U.S. Strategic Air Power, 1948–1962: Excerpts from an interview with Generals Curtis E. LeMay, Leon W. Johnson, David A. Burchinal, and Jack J. Catton," *International Security* 12: 4 (Spring 1988): 78–95, with the quotes appearing on pp. 93–95. This interview has also been printed by the editors, Kohn and Harahan, in their book *Strategic Air Warfare* (Washington, D.C.: Office of Air Force History, 1988). The information about General Power is cited in Scott D. Sagan, "Nuclear Alerts and Crisis Management," *International Security* 9: 4 (Spring 1985): 108.

45. The overwhelming superiority of U.S. strategic forces is detailed in Weinland, "Evolution of Soviet Requirements for Naval Forces," p. 18. See also Marc Trachtenberg, "The Influence of Nuclear Weapons in the Cuban Missile Crisis," *International Security* 10: 1 (Summer 1985): 156–63. The ExComm transcripts suggest, as David Welch and James Blight note, "that the odds that the *Americans* would go to war were next to zero." This conclusion was borne out by later revelations. David A. Welch and James G. Blight, "The Eleventh Hour of the Cuban Missile Crisis: An Introduction to the ExComm Transcripts," *International Security* 12: 3 (Winter 1987–88): 27. "ExComm" stood for the Executive Committee of the National Security Council, a small group advising the president, with whom President Kennedy deliberated, and at whose meetings important decisions were made. The transcripts are printed in McGeorge Bundy,

transcriber, and James G. Blight, ed., "October 27, 1962: Transcripts of the Meetings of the ExComm," ibid., pp. 30–92; and in "White House Tapes and Minutes of the Cuban Missile Crisis: ExCom Meetings, October 1962," *International Security* 10: 1 (Summer 1985): 164–203.

46. See Sagan, "Nuclear Alerts and Crisis Management," pp. 109–11, 129–30.

47. James G. Blight, Joseph S. Nye, Jr., and David A. Welch, "The Cuban Missile Crisis Revisited," *Foreign Affairs* 66: 1 (Fall 1987): 174.

48. Raymond L. Garthoff, *Reflections on the Cuban Missile Crisis*, rev. ed. (Washington, D.C.: Brookings Institution, 1989), pp. 187–88. For a discussion of this uncertainty, see Betts, *Nuclear Blackmail and Nuclear Balance*, pp. 109–23. See also McGeorge Bundy, *Danger and Survival: Choices About the Bomb in the First Fifty Years* (New York: Random House, 1988), pp. 446–53.

49. Raymond L. Garthoff, *Intelligence Assessment and Policymaking: A Decision Point in the Kennedy Administration* (Washington, D.C.: Brookings Institution, 1984), p. 33, quoting from his memorandum of October 27, 1962, and, for further discussion, see pp. 24–34. The Soviets had 36 nuclear warheads on the island and 9 tactical missiles with nuclear warheads being readied for use against an invasion force. See McNamara, "One Minute to Doomsday." During the October crisis, the CIA could not directly confirm the warheads' presence, but it regularly stated that the United States should assume that nuclear—indeed, thermonuclear—warheads would be available. McAuliffe, *CIA Documents on the Cuban Missile Crisis*, pp. 212, 216, 223–24, 338. For a debate over whether the local commander had authority to use nuclear weapons in the event of a U.S. invasion, see Mark Kramer, "Tactical Nuclear Weapons, Soviet Command Authority, and the Cuban Missile Crisis," *Cold War International History Project Bulletin* 3 (Fall 1993): 40, 42–47, and, James G. Blight, Bruce J. Allyn, and David A. Welch, "Kramer vs. Kramer: Or, How Can You Have Revisionism in the Absence of Orthodoxy?" ibid., pp. 41, 47–50.

50. Richard K. Smith, *Cold War Navy* (Washington, D.C.: Information Planning Associates for the Department of the Navy, 1976), chap. 18.

51. This point, well understood at the time, is discussed in Alexander L. George, "The Cuban Missile Crisis, 1962," in Alexander L. George, David K. Hall, and William E. Simons, eds., *The Limits of Coercive Diplomacy: Laos, Cuba, Vietnam* (Boston: Little, Brown, 1971), pp. 86–143.

52. A clear statement of this is in W. W. Rostow, *View from the Seventh Floor* (New York: Harper & Row, 1964), pp. 38–39.

53. Smith, *Cold War Navy*, chap. 18; Dan Caldwell, ed., "Department of Defense Operations During the Cuban Crisis: A Report by Adam Yarmolinsky, Special Assistant to the Secretary of Defense, 13 February 1963," *Naval War College Review* 32: 4 (July–Aug. 1979): 83–99.

54. See Sagan, "Nuclear Alerts and Crisis Management," pp. 112–18; and, for antisubmarine operations, Norman Polmar and Jurrien Noot, *Submarines of the Russian and Soviet Navies, 1918–1990* (Annapolis: Naval Institute Press, 1991), pp. 171–74. On the other hand, illustrating further the civilian-military tension inherent in crisis management, the Navy's global antisubmarine surveillance was considered by some civilian policymakers as excessive. These officials

argued that under such close watch the Soviets might feel pushed to "use or lose" their submarine-launched missiles targeted on the United States.

55. Lawrence J. Korb, "*The Joint Chiefs of Staff: The First Twenty-Five Years* (Bloomington: Indiana University Press, 1976), pp. 118–20.

56. This information comes from Admiral Thomas Moorer, who was MacDonald's relief as CNO, and is cited in Victor H. Krulak, *Organization for National Security* (Washington, D.C.: United States Strategic Institute, 1983), pp. 86–87. See also Paul H. Nitze, *From Hiroshima to Glasnost: At the Center of Decision* (New York: Grove Weidenfeld, 1989), p. 231. Nitze was present at the incident.

57. George W. Anderson, "As I Recall . . . The Cuban Missile Crisis," *Proceedings* 113: 9 (Sept. 1987): 44–45.

58. Lawrence Korb, "George Whalen Anderson, Jr., 1 August 1961–1 August 1963," in Love, *Chiefs of Naval Operations*, pp. 323, 329–30.

59. Edward J. Marolda and Oscar P. Fitzgerald, *The United States Navy and the Vietnam Conflict*: vol. 2, *From Military Assistance to Combat, 1959–1965* (Washington, D.C.: Department of the Navy, 1986), pp. 3, 14, 20, 30.

60. Ibid., pp. 9–14.

61. Ibid., pp. 94–103. The limits and inadequacy of Navy and Marine advisory teams during this period are discussed in two articles in Robert William Love, Jr., ed., *Changing Interpretations and New Sources in Naval History: Papers from the Third United States Naval Academy History Symposium* (New York: Garland, 1980). The two articles are Oscar P. Fitzgerald, "U.S. Naval Forces in the Vietnam War: The Advisory Mission, 1961–1965," on pp. 450–58; and Lane Rodgers, "The U.S. Marine Corps in Vietnam: The Advisory Mission, 1961–1965," on pp. 459–71.

62. Marolda and Fitzgerald, *From Military Assistance to Combat*, pp. 55, 69–72.

63. Edwin Bickford Hooper, Dean C. Allard, and Oscar P. Fitzgerald, *The United States Navy and the Vietnam Conflict*: vol. 1, *The Setting of the Stage to 1959* (Washington, D.C.: Department of the Navy, 1976), pp. 337–38, 373–75; Marolda and Fitzgerald, *From Military Assistance to Combat*, pp. 134–37.

64. Marolda and Fitzgerald, *From Military Assistance to Combat*, pp. 108, 111, 162–63.

65. On this engagement, some of the operational wheat is sifted from the political chaff in ibid., pp. 393–443. The controversy about whether there was or was not a second attack is evaluated in the following three assessments, which are collected in William B. Cogar, ed., *New Interpretations in Naval History* (Annapolis: Naval Institute Press, 1989): Edward J. Marolda, "Tonkin Gulf: Fact and Fiction," pp. 281–303, which argues that the attack of August 4 occurred; Edwin E. Moise, "Tonkin Gulf: Reconsidered," pp. 304–22, which argues that it did not; and James A. Barber, Jr., "Tonkin Gulf: Comments," pp. 323–28, which reviews both sides of the argument and draws no conclusion. A serious charge that official Navy data is tainted was made by James Stockdale, the strike leader of the air cover that evening (and subsequently a vice admiral), who said he saw nothing on the night of August 4 and that the official evidence was cooked to satisfy a JCS request. See Jim and Sybil Stockdale, *In Love and War: The Story of a Family's Ordeal and Sacrifice During the Vietnam Years*, rev. ed. (Annapolis: Naval

Institute Press, 1990), pp. 3–27, 499–505; and James Stockdale, "Comment and Discussion," *Proceedings* 118: 4 (Apr. 1992): 20–21. Steve Edwards, "Stalking the Enemy's Coast," *Proceedings* 118: 2 (Feb. 1992): 56–62, shows the likelihood that the *Maddox* was supporting a covert operation.

66. Marolda and Fitzgerald, *From Military Assistance to Combat*, p. 486. See also U. S. Grant Sharp, *Strategy for Defeat: Vietnam in Retrospect* (San Rafael: Presidio Press, 1978), pp. 51–62.

67. On this landing, see the comments of the commanding general of the Fleet Marine Force in the Pacific, Lieutenant General Victor H. Krulak, in his *First to Fight: An Inside View of the U.S. Marine Corps* (Annapolis: Naval Institute Press, 1984), pp. 181–83.

68. Combat statistics from Thomas C. Thayer, *War Without Fronts: The American Experience in Vietnam* (Boulder: Westview, 1985), p. 110.

69. Frank Uhlig, Jr., "Half an Amphibious Force at War: The Marines in I Corps," in Frank Uhlig, Jr., ed., *Vietnam: The Naval Story* (Annapolis: Naval Institute Press, 1986), pp. 73–75. There were some exceptions to the break in the amphibious-assault connection, where seaborne assault provided support for ground attack. See the discussion of Operation Starlite in O. F. Peatross, "Application of Doctrine: Victory at Van Tuong Village," ibid., pp. 157–70. For a discussion of vital Navy logistical support, see, ibid., K. P. Huff, "Building the Advanced Base at Da Nang," pp. 175–201; and Frank C. Collins, Jr., "Maritime Support of the Campaign in I Corps," pp. 202–27. *Vietnam: The Naval Story* contains valuable articles written by on-the-scene officers, sometimes key commanders. The articles are reprinted from issues of the Naval Institute's *Naval Review*.

70. William C. Westmoreland, *A Soldier Reports* (Garden City: Doubleday, 1976), pp. 342–45. For a Marine account, see Keith B. McCutcheon, "Marine Aviation in Vietnam, 1962–1970," in Uhlig, *Vietnam*, pp. 76–117.

71. Sharp, *Strategy for Defeat*, pp. 58, 68.

72. Richard L. Schreadley, *From the Rivers to the Sea: The United States Navy in Vietnam* (Annapolis: Naval Institute Press, 1992), pp. 82, 373–74.

73. Westmoreland, *A Soldier Reports*, p. 184. For an explanation of the difficulty of measurement, and why such statistics must be used with care, see Clarence E. Wunderlin, Jr., "Paradox of Power: Infiltration, Coastal Surveillance, and the United States Navy in Vietnam, 1965–68," *Journal of Military History* 53 (July 1989): 280–86.

74. This criticism is strongly expressed in Wunderlin, "Paradox of Power," pp. 275–89. In the Indochina war of 1945–54, French naval officers, despite their fear that the French navy would be reduced to a coastal force, were led by the requirements of the war to create first a riverine and then an estuarine marine assault force not unlike the Americans'. These French forces became an essential part of the overall French strategy. Charles W. Koburger, Jr., *The French Navy in Indochina: Riverine and Coastal Forces, 1945–1954* (New York: Praeger, 1991).

75. Elmo Zumwalt, Jr., and Elmo Zumwalt III, with John Pekkanen, *My Father, My Son* (New York: Macmillan, 1986), p. 44.

76. Wunderlin, "Paradox of Power," pp. 287–88.

77. For problems of Army-Navy coordination, see Zumwalt and Zumwalt with Pekkanen, *My Father, My Son*, p. 42; and William B. Fulton, *Riverine Operations, 1966–1969* (Washington, D.C.: Department of the Army, 1973). For a discussion of early cooperation, see W. C. Wells, "The Riverine Force in Action, 1966–1967," in Uhlig, *Vietnam*, pp. 412–48.

78. Victor Croizat, *The Brown Water Navy: The River and Coastal War in Indo-China and Vietnam, 1948–1972* (Poole: Blandford, 1984), p. 157; Schreadley, *From the Rivers to the Sea*, p. 104.

79. BDM Corporation, *A Study of Strategic Lessons Learned in Vietnam*: vol. 6, *Conduct of the War*: bk. 1, *Operational Analyses* (McLean: BDM Corporation, 1980), pp. 1 to 62 of chapter 7, with quotations in this paragraph from pages 30 and 58.

80. Schreadley, *From the Rivers to the Sea*, pp. 143–61, 279–89; S. A. Swarztrauber, "River Patrol Relearned," *Proceedings* 96: 5 (May 1970): 120–57, reprinted in Uhlig, *Vietnam*, pp. 365–411; Robert E. Mumford, Jr., "Jackstay: New Dimensions in Amphibious Warfare," ibid., pp. 344–64; Elmo R. Zumwalt, Jr., *On Watch: A Memoir* (New York: Quadrangle, 1976), pp. 37–39. A good overall study is Thomas J. Cutler, *Brown Water, Black Berets: Coastal and Riverine Warfare in Vietnam* (Annapolis: Naval Institute Press, 1988), and an appreciation of Zumwalt's command in Vietnam in R. L. Schreadley, "The Naval War in Vietnam, 1950–1970," *Proceedings* 97: 5 (May 1971): 197–209, reprinted in Uhlig, *Vietnam*, pp. 275–307.

81. Frank Uhlig, Jr., "The Merchant Marine: The Last Satisfactory Solution?" in Uhlig, *Vietnam*, p. 479; Lane C. Kendall, "U.S. Merchant Shipping and Vietnam," ibid., pp. 481–500.

82. Edwin Bickford Hooper, *Mobility, Support, Endurance: A Story of Naval Operational Logistics in the Vietnam War, 1965–1968* (Washington, D.C.: Department of the Navy, 1972), p. 47; Willis C. Barnes, "Korea and Vietnam," in Randolph W. King, ed., *Naval Engineering and American Seapower* (Baltimore: Nautical and Aviation, 1989), pp. 299–300.

CHAPTER 16

1. See James McConnell, "The Gorshkov Articles, the New Gorshkov Book, and Their Relation to Policy," in Michael MccGwire and John McDonnell, eds., *Soviet Naval Influence: Domestic and Foreign Dimensions* (New York: Praeger, 1977), pp. 616–17. This article was published previously, in 1976, by the Center for Naval Analyses as Professional Paper No. 159.

2. For a useful categorization of Soviet fleet types and purposes, see Norman Friedman, "US vs. Soviet Style in Fleet Design," in Paul J. Murphy, ed., *Naval Power in Soviet Policy*, vol. 2 (Washington, D.C.: GPO for the United States Air Force, 1978), pp. 203–31. The best study of the submarine force is Jan Breemer, *Soviet Submarines: Design, Development and Tactics* (London: Jane's, 1979).

3. Robert Waring Herrick, "The USSR's 'Blue Belt of Defense' Concept: A Unified Military Plan for Defense Against Seaborne Nuclear Attack by Strike Carriers and Polaris / Poseidon SSBNs," in Murphy, *Naval Power in Soviet Policy*, pp. 169–78.

4. The Soviet debate is presented in Charles C. Petersen, *Soviet Tactics for Warfare at Sea: Two Decades of Upheaval* (Alexandria: Center for Naval Analyses, 1982), pp. 1–26.

5. Michael MccGwire, *Military Objectives in Soviet Foreign Policy* (Washington, D.C.: Brookings Institution, 1987), p. 413.

6. See Robert Waring Herrick, *Soviet Naval Mission Assignments*, pt. 3: *A Protracted Withholding Role for Soviet SSBNs?* (Arlington: Ketron, for the Assistant Director for Net Assessment, Navy Program Planning Office, 1980), pp. 1–14. For Soviet submarine classes, the best overview is Norman Polmar and Jurrien Noot, *Submarines of the Russian and Soviet Navies, 1718–1990* (Annapolis: Naval Institute Press, 1991).

7. Robert W. Herrick, *Soviet Naval Mission Assignments*, pt. 1: *Soviet SSBN Roles in Strategic Strike* (Arlington: Ketron, for the Assistant Director for Net Assessment, Navy Program Planning Office, 1979).

8. The seminal American work on the Soviet withholding strategy is James M. McConnell's. His thinking is summed up in McConnell, "The Gorshkov Articles, the New Gorshkov Book, and Their Relation to Policy," pp. 565–620. See also Robert G. Weinland, "The Evolution of Soviet Requirements for Naval Forces: Solving the Problems of the Early 1960s," *Survival* 26: 1 (Jan.–Feb. 1984): 23; MccGwire, *Military Objectives in Soviet Foreign Policy*, esp. pp. 28–29, 90; and V. Dotsenko, "Soviet Art of Naval Warfare in the Postwar Period," *Morskoy sbornik* 7 (1989): 27.

9. S. G. Gorshkov, *The Sea Power of the State* (Oxford: Pergamon, 1979), p. 284.

10. Polmar and Noot, *Submarines of the Russian and Soviet Navies*, pp. 198–99.

11. Michael MccGwire, "Command of the Sea in Soviet Naval Strategy," in Michael MccGwire, Ken Booth, and John McDonnell, eds., *Soviet Naval Policy: Objectives and Constraints* (New York: Praeger, 1975), pp. 632–34. Among the many overviews, recommended are Michael MccGwire, "The Evolution of Soviet Naval Policy: 1960–74," ibid., pp. 505–46; and three fine articles in the uniformly valuable and highly recommended collection edited by Philip S. Gillette and Willard C. Frank, Jr., *The Sources of Soviet Naval Conduct* (Lexington: Lexington Books, 1990). The three articles are Robert W. Herrick, "Soviet Naval Strategy and Missions, 1946–1960," on pp. 165–91; Michael MccGwire, "The Soviet Navy and World War," on pp. 195–235; and Jürgen Rohwer, "Alternating Russian and Soviet Naval Strategies," on pp. 95–120. See also Ken Booth, "Summary of Discussion," in MccGwire, Booth, and McDonnell, *Soviet Naval Policy*, pp. 363–71; Peter H. Vigor, "Soviet Understanding of 'Command of the Sea,'" ibid., pp. 601–22; and Michael MccGwire, "The Soviet Navy in the Seventies," in MccGwire and McDonnell, *Soviet Naval Influence*, pp. 621–52. For the Soviet navy's connection to the other Soviet armed forces, see Dale R. Herspring, *The Soviet High Command, 1967–1989: Personalities and Politics* (Princeton: Princeton University Press, 1990).

12. Center for Strategic and International Studies, Georgetown University, *Soviet Sea Power* (Washington, D.C.: Center for Strategic and International Studies, 1969), p. 115.

13. Ibid., pp. 126–27.

14. See J. Kenneth McDonald, "Thomas Hinman Moorer, 1 August 1967–1 July 1970," in Robert William Love, Jr., *The Chiefs of Naval Operations* (Annapolis: Naval Institute Press, 1980), p. 359; and Moorer's January 1969 testimony in *Status of Naval Ships: Hearings Before the Special Subcommittee on Sea Power of the Committee on Armed Services, House of Representatives*, 90th Cong., 2d sess., and 91st Cong., 1st sess., pp. 177–217.

15. For a discussion of Okean 70, see Bruce W. Watson, *Red Navy at Sea: Soviet Naval Operations on the High Seas, 1956–1980* (Boulder: Westview, 1982), pp. 28–30.

16. Lawrence J. Korb, "The Erosion of American Naval Preeminence, 1962–1978," in Kenneth J. Hagan, ed., *In Peace and War: Interpretations of American Naval History, 1775–1984*, 2d ed. (Westport: Greenwood, 1984), pp. 337–38.

17. Elmo R. Zumwalt, Jr., *On Watch: A Memoir* (New York: Quadrangle, 1976), pp. 295, 338.

18. Ibid., p. 279.

19. Ibid., pp. 444–45.

20. Ibid., pp. 292–301, 444–45; Admiral Issac C. Kidd, Jr., "View from the Bridge of the Sixth Fleet Flagship," United States Naval Institute *Proceedings* (hereafter cited as *Proceedings*) 98: 2 (Feb. 1972): 19, 27. See also Thomas A. Bryson, "The Projection of U.S. Naval Power in the 1970 Jordan Crisis," in Craig L. Symonds, ed., *New Aspects of Naval History* (Annapolis: Naval Institute Press, 1981), pp. 313–21. At this time, the purpose of the Soviets' close tailing of U.S. carriers was so that a Soviet ship might, should the call arise, destroy the carrier's aircraft or disable the vessel itself to prevent the launching of the aircraft. In later years, as command-and-control communications improved, the tailer's purpose was to give the precise location of the carrier to Soviet missile targeters over the horizon, in case Soviet aircraft surveillance was unable to penetrate the carrier's protective screen.

21. Ken Booth, "Naval Strategy and the Spread of Pyscho-Legal Boundaries at Sea," *International Journal* 38: 3 (Summer 1983): 387. On the subsequent success of U.S.-Soviet agreements and control of incidents at sea, see two articles in Barry M. Blechman et al., *Naval Arms Control: A Strategic Assessment* (New York: St. Martin's, 1991)—namely, Cathleen S. Fisher, "Controlling High-Risk U.S. and Soviet Naval Operations," pp. 29–92; and William J. Durch, "Things That Go Bump in the Bight: Assessing Maritime Incidents, 1972–1989," pp. 93–158.

22. Lawrence J. Korb, *The Fall and Rise of the Pentagon: American Defense Policies in the 1970s* (Westport: Greenwood, 1979), p. 149; Stephen S. Roberts, "The October 1973 Arab-Israeli War," in Bradford Dismukes and James M. McConnell, eds., *Soviet Naval Diplomacy* (New York: Pergamon, 1979), pp. 192–213. For a discussion of the Soviet-Egyptian connection, see Robert G. Weinland, "Egypt and Support for the Soviet Mediterranean Squadron: 1967–1976," in Murphy, *Naval Power in Soviet Policy*, 2: 259–73.

23. Zumwalt, *On Watch*, pp. 445–47; Sean M. Lynn-Jones, "A Quiet Success for Arms Control: Preventing Incidents at Sea," *International Security* 9: 4 (Spring 1985): 176–77.

24. McDonald, "Thomas Hinman Moorer," p. 359; VAdm Stansfield Turner, "Missions of the U.S. Navy," *Naval War College Review* 26: 5 (Mar.–Apr. 1974): 2.

25. Norman Friedman, "Elmo Russell Zumwalt, Jr., 1 July 1979–1 July 1974," in Love, *Chiefs of Naval Operations* pp. 368–69; Michael Krepon, "A Navy to Match National Purposes," *Foreign Affairs* (Jan. 1977): 355–67. Norman Friedman notes, however, that big-fleet exercises since the 1930s had forced officers and men to look beyond their "union" borders to overall strategic plans. As a result, surface officers such as Spruance had understood the potential of carrier operations. Norman Friedman, *The US Maritime Strategy* (London: Jane's, 1988), p. 19.

26. Zumwalt, *On Watch*, pp. 62–63.

27. "The only way I could see for the Navy to free funds for developing up to date ships and weapons systems that could cope with the new Russian armaments," Zumwalt wrote, "was to retire immediately large numbers of old ships and aircraft." Ibid., p. 59.

28. This discussion follows Turner, "Missions of the U.S. Navy," pp. 2–17.

29. Thomas H. Etzold, "The Navy and National Security Policy in the 1970s," in Harry R. Borowski, ed., *Military Planning in the Twentieth Century* (Washington, D.C.: Office of Air Force History, 1984), p. 288.

30. This discussion follows David A. Rosenberg, "History of Navy Long-Range Planning: An Overview," in James L. George et al., *Review of USN Long-Range Planning* (Alexandria: Center for Naval Analyses, 1985), pp. B-14 to B-21.

31. My discussion of force planning under Zumwalt follows Zumwalt, *On Watch*, pp. 65–84; Friedman, "Elmo Russell Zumwalt, Jr.," pp. 370–75; Korb, "Erosion of American Naval Preeminence," pp. 327–46; Joseph F. Yurso, "The Decline of the Seventies," in Randolph W. King, ed., *Naval Engineering and American Seapower* (Baltimore: Nautical and Aviation, 1989), pp. 325–58; and James L. Lacy, *Within Bounds: The Navy in Postwar American Security Policy* (Alexandria: Center for Naval Analyses, 1983), p. 436.

32. Vice Admiral Gerald E. Miller, "Comment and Discussion," *Proceedings* 102: 12 (Dec. 1976): 79–85. For a blistering attack on Zumwalt's competence see Vice Admiral John T. Hayward, "Comment and Discussion," *Proceedings* 102: 8 (Aug. 1976): 69–72. See also Paul B. Ryan, *First Line of Defense: The U.S. Navy Since 1945* (Stanford: Hoover Institution Press, 1981), pp. 67, 75–76.

33. The fortunes of the Sea Control Ship are discussed in Norman Friedman, *U.S. Aircraft Carriers* (Annapolis: Naval Institute Press, 1983), pp. 351–57. The tenets of the arguments about sea control and power projection are encapsulated in a study by the Congressional Budget Office, *Planning U.S. General Purpose Forces: The Navy* (Washington, D.C.: GPO, 1976).

34. Thomas B. Hayward, "The Future of U.S. Sea Power," *Proceedings* 105: 5 (May 1979): 68. This article is a reprint of Admiral Hayward's testimony of February 15, 1979, before the Subcommittee on Seapower and Strategic and Critical Materials of the House Armed Services Committee.

35. Elmo R. Zumwalt, "Total Force," *Proceedings* 105: 5 (May 1979): 105–6.

36. Friedman, *US Maritime Strategy*, pp. 115–16.

37. Zumwalt, *On Watch*, p. 81.

38. Friedman, "Elmo Russell Zumwalt, Jr.," p. 375.

39. Korb, *Fall and Rise of the Pentagon*, pp. 42–43.

40. Hayward, "Comment and Discussion," p. 70.

41. Quoted in Frederick H. Hartmann, *Naval Renaissance: The U.S. Navy in the 1980s* (Annapolis: Naval Institute Press, 1990), p. 18. See also Zumwalt's thorough treatment in "Men and Women," pt. 3 of *On Watch*.

42. The later CNO was Admiral James Watkins, who is quoted in Hartmann, *Naval Renaissance*, pp. 17, 19.

43. Thomas C. Hone, *Power and Change: The Administrative History of the Office of the Chief of Naval Operations, 1946–1986* (Washington, D.C.: Naval Historical Center, 1989), pp. 90–97.

44. Quoted in Yurso, "Decline of the Seventies," p. 356.

45. February 19, 1974, statement of Admiral Zumwalt, *Hearings Before the Committee on Armed Services, United States Senate*, 93d Cong., 2d sess., p. 455.

46. James K. Oliver, "Congress and the Future of American Seapower: An Analysis of US Navy Budget Requests in the 1970s," cited in Hone, *Power and Change*, p. 99. A new carrier built at the end of the 1970s cost almost four times what the *Enterprise* had cost twenty years earlier.

47. Korb, "Erosion of American Naval Preeminence," pp. 339–40.

48. Cited ibid., p. 342. See also the comparisons of aspects of U.S. naval forces with those of their Soviet counterparts in Congressional Budget Office, *The U.S. Sea Control Mission: Forces, Capabilities, and Requirements* (Washington, D.C.: GPO, 1976), pp. 1–7, 35–56; and in Norman Polmar, "Thinking About Soviet ASW," *Proceedings* 102: 5 (May 1976): 108–29.

49. Watson, *Red Navy at Sea*, pp. 30–35.

50. See Joel J. Sokolsky, "Anglo-American Maritime Strategy in the Era of Flexible Response, 1960–1980," in John B. Hattendorf and Robert S. Jordan, eds., *Maritime Strategy and the Balance of Power: Britain and America in the Twentieth Century* (New York: St. Martin's, 1989), pp. 304–29.

51. These are the no doubt sardonic words of Vice Admiral John Baldwin, quoted in Hartmann, *Naval Renaissance*, p. 26.

52. *Report of Secretary of Defense Donald H. Rumsfeld to the Congress on the FY 1977 Budget and Its Implications for the FY 1978 Authorization Request and the FY 1977–1981 Defense Programs, January 27, 1976* (Washington, D.C.: GPO, 1976), p. v. Rumsfeld served from November 1975 to January 1977.

53. Cited in Lacy, *Within Bounds*, p. 452.

54. Adam B. Siegel, *The Use of Naval Forces in the Post-War Era: U.S. Navy and U.S. Marine Corps Crisis Response Activity, 1946–1990* (Alexandria: Center for Naval Analyses, 1991), pp. 13–14.

55. So admonished Edward Jayne, an official of the Office of Management and Budget. See Ryan, *First Line of Defense*, pp. 122–23.

56. Navy supporters of the big carrier based their argument on the CNO's "CVNX Characteristics Study Group Report," issued in January 1976, which came down unequivocally on the side of an all-purpose, large-deck ship. For the report and related testimony to Congress favoring a *Nimitz*-sized follow-on, see record of the hearings of February 24, 1976, *Hearings on Military Posture and H.R.*

11500 *[H.R. 12438] Before the Committee on Armed Services, Subcommittee on Seapower and Strategic and Critical Materials, House of Representatives,* 94th Cong., 2d sess., pt. 4, pp. 225–347.

57. Thomas B. Hayward, "Remarks," *Wings of Gold* 7: 2 (Summer 1982): 59.
58. Lacy, *Within Bounds*, p. 459.
59. Cited in Ryan, *First Line of Defense*, p. 91.
60. Lacy, *Within Bounds*, pp. 449–53. The quote is on p. 452.
61. Ibid., p. 475.
62. "The naval equivalent of The Maginot Line has been constructed—betting that the future is so predictable that the Navy can be sized for a specific scenario without regard for a global strategy and the uncertainty of the real world." Quoted in Jan S. Breemer, *U.S. Naval Developments* (Annapolis: Nautical and Aviation, 1983), p. 29. See also Lacy, *Within Bounds*, p. 453.
63. Floyd D. Kennedy, Jr., "From SLOC Protection to a National Maritime Strategy: The U.S. Navy Under Carter and Reagan, 1977–1984," in Hagan, *In Peace and War*, p. 348.
64. Department of Defense, *Annual Report for Fiscal Year 1980. Harold Brown, Secretary of Defense* (Washington, D.C.: GPO, 1979), p. 12.
65. Etzold's "The Navy and National Security Policy" informs my discussion here.
66. Ibid., p. 290.
67. Ibid., p. 292.
68. Ibid., p. 287.

CHAPTER 17

1. William Crowe, "Western Strategy and Naval Missions Approaching the Twenty-First Century," in James L. George, ed., *Problems of Sea Power as We Approach the Twenty-First Century* (Washington, D.C.: American Enterprise Institute, 1978), pp. 21, 37.
2. This position was also taken in the paper by David Kassing, "Protecting the Fleet," in George, *Problems of Sea Power*, pp. 293–321. When he wrote this paper, Kassing was president of the Center for Naval Analyses.
3. James M. McConnell, "Strategy and Missions of the Soviet Navy in the Year 2000," in George, *Problems of Sea Power*, pp. 39–67. See also John B. Hattendorf, "The Evolution of the Maritime Strategy, 1977 to 1987," in *Naval War College Review* 41: 3 (Summer 1988): 12–13.
4. The quote is from Robert Waring Herrick, *Soviet Naval Mission Assignments*, pt. 3, *A Protracted Withholding Role for Soviet SSBNs?* (Arlington: Ketron, for the Assistant Director for Net Assessment, Navy Program Planning Office, 1980), p. vi. For Herrick's early thinking, which opened the way for a reconsideration of the Soviet navy in the 1970s, see Robert Waring Herrick, *Soviet Naval Strategy: Fifty Years of Theory and Practice* (Annapolis: United States Naval Institute, 1968). Herrick's *Soviet Naval Strategy* also contains a fascinating foreword by Admiral Arleigh Burke and a preface by the publisher indicating an uneasy awareness that Herrick's was a new way of looking at the Soviet navy.
5. There was Western speculation that the most that Soviet submarine mis-

sileers could hope for in the opening stage of a war would be to use their missiles to destroy NATO ports, terminals, and coastal military installations, as opposed to major political and economic targets in Europe and the United States. Robert Waring Herrick, *Soviet Naval Mission Assignments*, pt. 1, *Soviet SSBN Roles in Strategic Strike* (Arlington: Ketron, for the Assistant Director for Net Assessment, Navy Program Planning Office, 1979).

6. Frank Uhlig, Jr., "Commentaries," in George, *Problems of Sea Power*, pp. 70–72. Uhlig there said that this "is not a new kind of situation with which we are faced, nor is it necessarily bad."

7. Herschel Kanter, "Commentaries," in George, *Problems of Sea Power*, pp. 73–75.

8. A full development of this thinking is summed up in Michael McCGwire, *Military Objectives in Soviet Foreign Policy* (Washington, D.C.: Brookings Institution, 1987); and in James J. Tritten, *Soviet Naval Forces and Nuclear Warfare: Weapons, Employment, and Policy* (Boulder: Westview, 1986), pp. 98–101.

9. The reader will recall the forward offensive strategy of Admiral Forrest Sherman as described in Michael A. Palmer, *Origins of the Maritime Strategy: American Naval Strategy in the First Postwar Decade* (Washington, D.C.: Naval Historical Center, 1988), and be put in mind of the classical naval theories of Mahan and of Julian Corbett.

10. Tom Stefanick, *Strategic Antisubmarine Warfare and Naval Strategy* (Lexington: Lexington Books, for the Institute for Defense and Disarmament Studies, 1987), pp. 33–35. For reviews of the many and increasingly sophisticated classes of submarines built by the Soviets during the late 1970s and the 1980s, see Jan Breemer, *Soviet Submarines: Design, Development and Tactics* (London: Jane's, 1989), and Norman Polmar and Jurrien Noot, *Submarines of the Russian and Soviet Navies, 1718–1990* (Annapolis: Naval Institute Press, 1991), pp. 302–10.

11. Robert Waring Herrick, *The USSR's "Blue Belt of Defense" Concept: A Unified Military Plan for Defense Against Seaborne Attack by Strike Carriers and Polaris/Poseidon SSBNs* (Arlington: Center for Naval Analyses, 1973). For a look at the benefits the Soviets derived from Arctic operations, see Charles C. Petersen, *Soviet Military Objectives in the Arctic Theater and How They Might Be Attained* (Alexandria: Center for Naval Analyses, 1986), pp. 1–11.

12. Robert Waring Herrick, *Soviet Naval Mission Assignments*, pt. 2, *The SSBN-Protection Mission* (Arlington: Ketron, for the Assistant Director for Net Assessment, Navy Program Planning Office, 1979). The quotes are from pp. i, iv. Jan Breemer gives an excellent summary of the debate over whether Soviet submarines were operating in terms of bastion control and reserve or for breakout in his *Soviet Submarines*, pp. 131–37.

13. The Pacific Fleet Order of Battle in 1984 and its out-of-area deployments are given in Gerry S. Thomas, "The Pacific Fleet," in Bruce W. Watson and Susan M. Watson, eds., *The Soviet Navy: Strengths and Liabilities* (Boulder: Westview, 1986), pp. 232–35. For the decision to build up the Pacific Fleet in the late 1970s, see McCGwire, *Military Objectives in Soviet Foreign Policy*, pp. 162–82; and McCGwire, "The Changing Role of the Soviet Navy," *Bulletin of the Atomic Scientists* 43: 7 (Sept. 1987): 34–38.

14. James M. McConnell and Bradford Dismukes, "Conclusions," in Bradford Dismukes and James M. McConnell, eds., *Soviet Naval Diplomacy* (New York: Pergamon in cooperation with the Center for Naval Analyses, 1979), pp. 311–12.

15. *Department of Defense, Annual Report for Fiscal Year 1980, Harold Brown, Secretary of Defense* (Washington, D.C.: GPO, 1979), p. 12.

16. Cited in James L. Lacy, *Within Bounds: The Navy in Postwar American Security Policy* (Alexandria: Center for Naval Analyses, 1983), p. 446.

17. The following discussion of Hayward's planning is based on Frederick H. Hartmann, *Naval Renaissance: The U.S. Navy in the 1980s* (Annapolis: Naval Institute Press, 1990), pp. 27–30.

18. The operational plans are classified. Intimations are found in Hartmann, *Naval Renaissance*, pp. 28–30; and Kenneth R. McGruther, "Two Anchors in the Pacific: A Strategic Proposal for the U.S. Pacific Fleet," United States Naval Institute *Proceedings* (hereafter cited as *Proceedings*) 105: 5 (May 1979): 126–41. For Soviet vulnerabilities, see Michael A. Schoelwer, "Geographic Problems," in Watson and Watson, *Soviet Navy*, pp. 180–81; and Mark A. Carolla, "The Indian Ocean Squadron," ibid., pp. 245–46.

19. Admiral Thomas B. Hayward, "The Future of U.S. Sea Power," *Proceedings* 105: 5 (May 1979): 66–71. This article includes unclassified testimony of February 15, 1979, to the Subcommittee on Seapower and Strategic and Critical Materials of the House Armed Services Committee. See also Hattendorf, "Evolution of the Maritime Strategy," pp. 9, 13–14.

20. This discussion follows the unclassified "executive summary" contained in the document entitled *Sea Plan 2000: Naval Force Planning Study* (Washington, D.C.: Office of the Secretary of the Navy, 1978); Hartmann, *Naval Renaissance*, pp. 30–33, 201; and Paul B. Ryan, *First Line of Defense: The U.S. Navy Since 1945* (Stanford: Hoover Institution Press, 1981), pp. 128–34.

21. Hartmann, *Naval Renaissance*, p. 30. For a useful contemporary study that discusses Navy force planning in terms of replacement vs. growth, see Alva M. Bowen, Jr., *U.S. Naval Expansion Program: An Analysis of the Cost of Expanding the Navy from 500 to 600 Ships* (Washington, D.C.: Congressional Research Service, 1976).

22. A midsize alternative was advocated in 1978 by John Lehman, with Zumwalt's approval, in an effort to bridge the high-low gap. John Lehman, *Aircraft Carriers: The Real Choices* (Beverly Hills: Sage, for the Center for Strategic and International Studies, 1978), pp. 76–86. Zumwalt, who wrote the book's foreword, was concerned about keeping alive his concept of a high-low mix and his vision of a Sea Control Ship.

23. John R. Baylis, "The Six-Hundred Ship Navy and Merchant Marine Doldrums (1981–1988)," in Randolph W. King, ed., *Naval Engineering and American Seapower* (Baltimore: Nautical and Aviation, 1989), p. 368.

24. *Department of Defense, Annual Report for Fiscal Year 1981, Harold Brown, Secretary of Defense* (Washington, D.C.: GPO, 1980), pp. 2, 9; Lacy, *Within Bounds*, pp. 472–76, 501. What is striking is the conceptual and budgetary continuity between the Carter and Reagan administrations, with the image of change

being mainly declaratory. James K. Oliver and James A. Nathan, "The Reagan Defense Program: Concepts, Continuity, and Change," in Stephen J. Cimbala, ed., *The Reagan Defense Program: An Interim Assessment* (Wilmington: Scholarly Resources, 1986), pp. 1–21. Oliver and Nathan quote the following from Coral Bell: "Declaratory signals may sometimes look, at first glance, as if they were operational. . . . The almost popular impression is that President Reagan has achieved—not merely proposed—an unprecedented rate of increase in U.S. military muscle. But I would argue that since the image of U.S. military weakness was created chiefly by words (mostly from the Reagan camp from the Republican nomination fight of 1976 onwards) it is logical that more words from the same sources should have been effective in readjusting that somewhat distorted image to reflect the reality of effective (though asymmetrical) superpower parity." Coral Bell, "From Carter to Reagan," *Foreign Affairs* 63: 3 (1985): 492.

25. See Lacy, *Within Bounds*, pp. 537–611, for an analysis of the strategic "hodge-podge of hedges" on the national level that the maritime strategy both reflected and reacted against, and the absence of "anything approximating a grand strategy," as Admiral Thomas Moorer said in 1977.

26. James D. Watkins, "The Maritime Strategy," *Proceedings*, Special Supplement 112: 1 (Jan. 1986): 2–17; Hattendorf, "Evolution of the Maritime Strategy," pp. 7–25; Hartmann, *Naval Renaissance*, pp. 199–217. A fuller expression of the Navy's position at this time, including qualifications and dissent, is found in transcripts of the summer 1985 testimony of high Navy officials before the Seapower and Strategic and Critical Materials Subcommittee of the House Armed Services Committee. The committee published that testimony as *The 600-Ship Navy and the Maritime Strategy* (Washington, D.C.: GPO, 1986).

27. Lacy, *Within Bounds*, pp. 420, 430–31, 442–43; *Department of Defense, Annual Report for Fiscal Year 1976 and Fiscal Year 1977, James R. Schlesinger, Secretary of Defense* (Washington, D.C.: GPO, 1975), p. III-24.

28. The authors of the Navy's new maritime strategy deliberately drew on classic naval and maritime strategies as basic guides. Hattendorf, "Evolution of the Maritime Strategy," pp. 10–11.

29. The argument for this force and its relation to the maritime strategy was made in congressional testimony and was summarized by Navy Secretary Lehman in John F. Lehman, Jr., "The 600-Ship Navy," *Proceedings*, Special Supplement 112: 1 (Jan. 1986). This is the same supplement of *Proceedings* that contains Watkins's presentation of the maritime strategy. The supplement also contains a third article, by General P. X. Kelley, commandant of the Marine Corps, and Major Hugh K. O'Donnell, Jr., USMC, "The Amphibious Warfare Strategy," which covers the Marine Corps's offensive contribution. These three articles comprised the main public presentation of the new position, and 150,000 copies of the supplement were printed.

30. This discussion of force levels draws on Michael M. McCrea, Karen N. Domabyl, and Alexander F. Parker, *The Offensive Navy Since World War II: How Big and Why* (Alexandria: Center for Naval Analyses, 1989).

31. This is a point acknowledged by all fans and critics of, and commentators

on, service cohesion. See notably Carl H. Builder, *The Masks of War: American Military Styles in Strategy and Analysis* (Baltimore: Johns Hopkins University Press, for the RAND Corporation, 1989), pp. 74–85. Builder is concerned with comparing Air Force and Navy institutional inventiveness with "the Army's identity crisis."

32. John J. Mearsheimer, "A Strategic Misstep: The Maritime Strategy and Deterrence in Europe," *International Security* 11: 2 (Fall 1986): 5, 17–25, gives the most thorough academic critique of the maritime strategy. Students of naval thought in the 1980s will also want to consult the thorough and annotated bibliography by Peter M. Swartz and Jan S. Breemer with James J. Tritten, *The Maritime Strategy Debates: A Guide to the Renaissance of U.S. Naval Strategic Thinking in the 1980s*, rev. ed. (Monterey: Naval Postgraduate School, 1989).

33. For the value of supporting allies in this manner, see F. J. West, Jr., "The Maritime Strategy: The Next Step," *Proceedings* 113: 1 (Jan. 1987): 40–49. West was one of the creators of *Sea Plan 2000* and the concept of horizontal escalation.

34. Basil Liddell Hart is quoted in Geoffrey Till, *Maritime Strategy and the Nuclear Age* (New York: St. Martin's, 1982), p. 199. For criticism by Carter's defense secretary, Harold Brown, of horizontal escalation, see Harold Brown, *Thinking About National Security: Defense and Foreign Policy in a Dangerous World* (Boulder: Westview, 1983), p. 173. The connection of horizontal escalation to the Carter administration is noted in Oliver and Nathan, "Reagan Defense Program," pp. 12–19. For a discussion of the risks associated with escalation, see Joshua M. Epstein, "Horizontal Escalation: Sour Notes of a Recurrent Theme," *International Security* 8: 3 (Winter 1983–84): 19–31.

35. See Hartmann, *Naval Renaissance*, p. 204.

36. For an example of a different emphasis in Navy circles, see the paper "A Methodology for Developing Strategy and Relating Strategy to Resources," submitted by retired Admiral Stansfield Turner as part of his contribution to the 1985 congressional testimony that was published as *The 600-Ship Navy and the Maritime Strategy*. Turner's paper, which is printed on pp. 222–41, emphasizes amphibious forces and point-defense sea control. Turner was a candidate for CNO until appointed director of the Central Intelligence Agency in 1977.

37. For an evaluation of the condition of the SSBNs in the mid-1980s, see Donald C. Daniel, *Anti-Submarine Warfare and Superpower Strategic Stability* (Urbana: University of Illinois Press, 1986), pp. 161–97. Daniel concluded that U.S. security was adequate and that attention had to be paid mainly to countering a Soviet breakthrough in nonacoustic area-searching—that is, to countering the benefits the Soviets were reaping from information given them from within the U.S. Navy by the Walker spy ring. For a vivid technical assessment of the problems and opportunities faced by the hunters and the hunted, see Stefanick, *Strategic Antisubmarine Warfare*.

38. For a discussion of Meyer and the development of the Aegis program, compared with Rear Admiral William Moffett's vision of Navy air and Admiral Rickover's of a nuclear Navy, see Thomas C. Hone, "Bureaucratic Entrepreneurism and Understanding the Modern Navy," a paper delivered in Nashville at a meeting of the Southern Political Science Association, on November 9, 1985. On

testing Aegis and the problems of funding it, see Hartmann, *Naval Renaissance*, pp. 136–41. On Aegis in action, see Joseph L. McClane, Jr., and James L. McClane, "The *Ticonderoga* Story: Aegis Works," *Proceedings* 111: 5 (May 1985): 118–29.

39. Scott C. Truver, "Tomorrow's Fleet," *Proceedings* 118: 6 (June 1992): 43–51.

40. See Miles A. Libbey, "Tomahawk," *Proceedings* 111: 5 (May 1985): 150–63; and S. J. Froggett, "Tomahawk's Roles," *Proceedings* 113: 2 (Feb. 1987): 51–54.

41. Henry C. Mustin, "The Sea-Launched Cruise Missile: More Than a Bargaining Chip," *International Security* 13: 3 (Winter 1988–89): 184–85, 188.

42. At the same time, in the late 1980s, a new offensive dimension appeared in the form of counterforce targeting that was different from what had gone before. This happened when the Navy prepared to deploy the submarine-launched ballistic missile designated as Trident II (D-5), 24 missiles to a submarine, each missile carrying from 11 to 13 Mark 4, or 6 to 9 Mark 5, warheads. Trident II (D-5) was twice as accurate as the Trident I, matching in accuracy the Air Force's Mark 12A version of Minuteman III and MX land-based ballistic missiles, and able to cover all targets on the U.S. list with less cost and with virtually assured reserve security. It was its accuracy that would permit Trident II to go from assured destruction to hard-target counterforce targeting, which, as Graham Spinardi said, was "one of the most significant, and, to many, worrying trends in the history of nuclear weapons." Had the missile been deployed (it was not, in the 1980s), the Navy would have moved to a first-strike capability, the ultimate offensive position, with a missile capability that could substitute for that of the Air Force. This trend to hard targets had become a feature of fleet ballistic missile design in the late 1970s on the basis, critics asserted, of weapons policy decisions made by special technical and bureaucratic interests, without the administration's political approval. Was it a change made in the Navy's strategic mission without due political consideration of the events within the Soviet Union, an exchange of last-resort retaliatory deterrence for an immediate war-fighting role, made at the very moment when such offensive power became, so unexpectedly, superfluous? See Graham Spinardi, "Why the U.S. Navy Went for Hard-Target Counterforce in Trident II (And Why It Didn't Get There Sooner)," *International Security* 15: 2 (Fall 1990): 147–90; Congressional Budget Office, *Trident II Missiles: Capability, Costs, and Alternatives* (Washington, D.C.: GPO, 1986), pp. 31–32; and, for support of the new missile, which actually was deployed in the early 1990s, Owen Coté, "The Trident and the Triad: Collecting the D-5 Dividend," *International Security* 16: 2 (Fall 1991): 117–45.

43. That, at any rate, was the opinion in 1985 of some influential analysts. See Robert W. Herrick, "Roles and Missions of the Soviet Navy: Historical Evolution, Current Priorities, and Future Prospects," in James L. George, ed., *The Soviet and Other Communist Navies: The View from the Mid-1980s* (Annapolis: Naval Institute Press, 1986), p. 31; James M. McConnell, "The Soviet Naval Mission Structure: Past, Present, and Future," ibid., p. 53; and Michael MccGwire, "Contingency Plans for World War," ibid., pp. 75–78.

44. To some, the prospect of the United States taking such a risk had created "the worst of all possible worlds." Barry R. Posen, "Inadvertent Nuclear War?

Escalation and NATO's Northern Flank," *International Security* 7: 2 (Fall 1982): 28–54.

45. Thomas A. Fitzgerald, "Blitzkrieg at Sea," *Proceedings* 112: 1 (Jan. 1986): 12–16; Charles W. Mayer, Jr., "Looking Backwards into the Future of the Maritime Strategy, Are We Uncovering Our Center of Gravity in the Attempt to Strike our Opponent?" *Naval War College Review* 42: 1 (Winter 1989): 33–36.

46. See, among Navy authors of the maritime strategy, Linton F. Brooks, "Naval Power and National Security: The Case for the Maritime Strategy," *International Security* 11: 2 (Fall 1986): 73–74, 79–81; Roger W. Barnett, "U.S. Maritime Strategy: Sound and Safe," *Bulletin of the Atomic Scientists* 43: 7 (Sept. 1987): 30–33; William Pendley, "Comment and Discussion: The Maritime Strategy," *Proceedings* 112: 6 (June 1986): 84–89. See also Raymond L. Garthoff, *Deterrence and the Revolution in Soviet Military Doctrine* (Washington, D.C.: Brookings Institution, 1990), pp. 166–67. For a thorough survey of U.S. antisubmarine-warfare measures and their deployment as a unified system, see Daniel, *Anti-Submarine Warfare and Superpower Strategic Stability*.

47. James J. Wirtz, "Deterrence and the Maritime Strategy: Coupling MAD to the Defense of the Soviet SSBN Bastions," paper prepared for the 1990 meeting of the Northeastern Political Science Association in Providence, R.I.; Daniel, *Anti-Submarine Warfare and Superpower Strategic Stability*, pp. 151–56.

48. Aaron L. Friedberg, "Why Didn't the United States Become a Garrison State?" *International Security* 16: 4 (Spring 1992): 109–42.

49. Carlisle A. H. Trost, "Looking Beyond the Maritime Strategy," *Proceedings* 113: 1 (Jan. 1987): 16. Admiral Trost was CNO from 1986 to 1990.

50. David Alan Rosenberg, "'It Is Hardly Possible to Imagine Anything Worse': Soviet Thoughts on the Maritime Strategy," *Naval War College Review* 41: 3 (Summer 1988): 69–105; James T. Westwood, "Soviet Reaction to the Maritime Strategy," ibid., pp. 62–68.

51. For some of the assumptions of Navy leaders, which I draw on below, see Brooks, "Naval Power and National Security," pp. 67–69.

52. This is the line of criticism followed in Robert F. Komer, *Maritime Strategy or Coalition Defense?* (Cambridge, Mass.: Abt Books, 1984), pp. 68–70.

53. On Colbert, see Joel J. Sokolsky, *The Fraternity of the Blue Uniform: Admiral Richard G. Colbert, U.S. Navy, and Allied Naval Cooperation* (Newport: Naval War College Press, 1991).

54. Joel J. Sokolsky, "Anglo-American Maritime Strategy in the Era of Flexible Response, 1960–80," in John B. Hattendorf and Robert S. Jordan, eds., *Maritime Strategy and the Balance of Power: Britain and America in the Twentieth Century* (New York: St. Martin's, 1989), p. 325.

55. Interview in the June 15, 1987, issue of *U.S. News and World Report*, p. 28, quoted in Swartz and Breemer with Tritten, *Maritime Strategy Debates*, p. 45.

56. See Jan S. Breemer, "The Maritime Strategy: One Ally's View," *Naval War College Review* 41: 3 (Summer 1988): 41–47; Robert S. Wood, "Fleet Renewal and Maritime Strategy in the 1980s," in Hattendorf and Jordan, *Maritime Strategy and the Balance of Power*, pp. 330–47; and Swartz and Breemer with Tritten, *Maritime Strategy Debates*, pp. 61–82, for a review of articles, collected in that book, on the views of allies.

57. Lacy, *Within Bounds*, pp. 503–12.

58. Ibid., pp. 520–37. For a discussion of the JCS, see West, "Maritime Strategy," p. 49.

59. Builder, *Masks of War*. The quotation is on p. xi.

60. Navy concerns are described and defended in Norman Friedman, *Desert Victory: The War for Kuwait* (Annapolis: Naval Institute Press, 1991), pp. 74–84. The legislation is reviewed by James K. Gruetzner and William Caldwell, "DOD Reorganization," *Proceedings* 113: 5 (May 1987): 136–45.

61. This reconstitution of Soviet/Russian policy and strategy as part of the ending of the Cold War is described in Michael MccGwire, *Perestroika and Soviet National Security* (Washington, D.C.: Brookings Institution, 1991), pp. 174–344. See also the speech delivered by the commander in chief of the Soviet navy, Fleet Admiral V. N. Chernavin, at the U.S. Naval War College in November 1991, printed in the *Naval War College Review* 45: 4 (Autumn 1992): 9–19.

62. Secretary of the Navy H. Lawrence Garrett III, CNO Admiral Frank B. Kelso II, and General A. M. Gray, Commandant of the Marine Corps, "The Way Ahead," *Proceedings* 117: 4 (Apr. 1991): 38.

CONCLUSION

1. John F. Morton, "The U.S. Navy in 1988," United States Naval Institute *Proceedings* (hereafter cited as *Proceedings*) 115: 5 (May 1989): 154; Carlisle A. H. Trost, "Requirements Drive Navy Force Levels," ibid., pp. 34–38; Trost, "Maritime Strategy for the 1990s," *Proceedings* 116: 5 (May 1990): 92–100.

2. See, among many other articles, James L. George, "Maritime Mission or Strategy?" *Naval War College Review* 42: 1 (Winter 1989): 47–55; and Charles Morris, "Our Muscle-Bound Navy," *New York Times Magazine*, April 24, 1988, pp. 98–104. A judicious discussion of the future utility of U.S. naval forces is found in Adelphi Paper No. 261, by Donald C. F. Daniel, *Beyond the 600-Ship Navy* (London: International Institute for Strategic Studies, 1991). Kenneth Hagan has argued forcefully for the contemporary relevance of the nineteenth-century model of U.S. Navy "frigate diplomacy," of the pre-Mahanian Navy of squadrons on continuous patrol (often in coalition with ships of other navies), and of discrete, special-purpose expeditions. See Kenneth J. Hagan, *This People's Navy: The Making of American Sea Power* (New York: Free Press, 1991); and his article "What Goes Around . . ." *Proceedings* 118: 5 (May 1992): 88–91.

3. Adam B. Siegel, *The Use of Naval Forces in the Post-War Era: U.S. Navy and U.S. Marine Corps Crisis Response Activity, 1946–1990* (Alexandria: Center for Naval Analyses, 1991), p. 13. These numbers do not include humanitarian or law-enforcement operations, intelligence or special operations, or routine support of U.S. diplomacy, all of which were also valued naval functions.

4. Siegel, *Use of Naval Forces*, p. 10.

5. Secretary of the Navy H. Lawrence Garrett III, quoted in John F. Morton, "The U.S. Navy in 1990," *Proceedings* 117: 5 (May 1991): 124.

6. The variability of such a strategy was argued throughout the second half of the decade by several British authors, for instance James Cable in "More Crucial Now Than Ever," *Proceedings* 118: 5 (May 1992): 86–87.

7. Office of the Chief of Naval Operations, *The United States Navy in "Desert Shield"/"Desert Storm"* (Washington, D.C.: Department of the Navy, 1991), pp. v, 2. For a Pentagon overview, see Department of Defense, *Conduct of the Persian Gulf Conflict: Final Report to Congress* (Washington, D.C.: Department of Defense, 1992), in which the maritime campaign is discussed on pp. 61–82 and 249–309.

8. On this point, see James Blackwell, Michael J. Mazarr, and Don M. Snider, eds., *The Gulf War: Military Lessons Learned* (Washington, D.C.: Center for Strategic and International Studies, 1991), p. 19.

9. Edwin H. Simmons, "Getting Marines to the Gulf," *Proceedings* 117: 5 (May 1991): 50–64.

10. Department of Defense, *Conduct of the Persian Gulf Conflict*, pp. T-201 and T-202; Office of the Chief of Naval Operations, *The United States Navy in "Desert Shield"/"Desert Storm,"* p. 29; Douglas M. Norton, "Sealift: Keystone of Support," *Proceedings* 117: 5 (May 1991): 41–49.

11. Andrew E. Gibson and Jacob L. Shuford, "Desert Shield and Strategic Sealift," *Naval War College Review* 44: 2 (Spring 1991): 6–19; Richard T. Ackley, "Sealift and National Security," *Proceedings* 118: 7 (July 1992): 41–47.

12. Office of the Chief of Naval Operations, *The United States Navy in "Desert Shield"/"Desert Storm,"* pp. 44–45; John C. Sharfen, "The U.S. Marine Corps in 1990," *Proceedings* 117: 5 (May 1991): 134–40; Norman Friedman, *Desert Victory: The War for Kuwait* (Annapolis: Naval Institute Press, 1991), pp. 129–30, 208.

13. Secretary of the Navy H. Lawrence Garrett III, CNO Admiral Frank B. Kelso II, and Commandant of the Marine Corps General A. M. Gray, "The Way Ahead," *Proceedings* 117: 4 (Apr. 1991): 47. For discussion of Navy sealift capacity and that capacity's reliance on policy assumptions, see Center for Naval Analyses Research Memorandum 91–11, "A First Look at Sealift Options for the 1990s in Light of the Experience in Operation Desert Shield" (Alexandria: Center for Naval Analyses, 1991).

14. Readers will see here the revived utility of studying the maritime theory of Mahan's contemporary and critic Julian Corbett. Corbett had opened his counterblast with the declaration: "Naval strategy is but that part of it [maritime strategy] which determines the movements of the fleet when maritime strategy has determined what part the fleet must play in relation to the action of the land forces; for it scarcely needs saying that it is almost impossible that a war can be decided by naval action alone." Never ignoring the importance of securing command of the sea, which is "the object of naval warfare," Corbett theorized about the use of navies in limited war, in indirect and peripheral campaigns, in what he called wars of limited territorial objective and wars of intervention. Julian S. Corbett, *Some Principles of Maritime Strategy* (London: Longmans, Green, 1911), passim. The quotes are from pp. 13 and 87. For a valuable introduction to naval missions and operations, see Frank Uhlig, Jr., *How Navies Fight: The U.S. Navy and Its Allies* (Annapolis: Naval Institute Press, 1994).

15. Secretary of the Navy Sean O'Keefe, CNO Admiral Frank B. Kelso II, Commandant of the Marine Corps General C. E. Mundy, Jr., *. . . From the Sea: Preparing the Naval Service for the 21st Century* (Washington, D.C.: Department of the Navy, 1992), p. 2.

Index

In this index an "f" after a number indicates a separate reference on the next page, and an "ff" indicates separate references on the next two pages. A continuous discussion over two or more pages is indicated by a span of page numbers, e.g., "57–59." *Passim* is used for a cluster of references in close but not consecutive sequence.

Library of Congress Cataloguing-in-Publication Data

Baer, George W.

One hundred years of sea power : the U.S. Navy, 1890–1990 / George W. Baer

p. cm.

Includes bibliographical references and index.

ISBN 0-8047-2273-0 (alk. paper)

1. United States. Navy—History—19th century.
2. United States. Navy—History—20th century.
3. Sea-power—United States—History— 19th century.
4. Sea-power—United States—History—20th century.
5. United States—History, Naval. I. Title.

VA58.B283 1994

359'.00973—dc20 94-2595

CIP

∞ This book is printed on acid-free paper.